WOMEN'S HEALTH:
CONTEMPORARY INTERNATIONAL
PERSPECTIVES

WOMEN'S HEALTH:
CONTEMPORARY
INTERNATIONAL PERSPECTIVES

Edited by Jane M Ussher

Associate Professor
Centre for Critical Psychology
University of Western Sydney, Australia

BPS BOOKS THE BRITISH
PSYCHOLOGICAL
SOCIETY

First published in 2000 by BPS Books (The British Psychological Society), St Andrews House, 48 Princess Road East, Leicester, LE1 7DR, UK.

A catalogue record for this book is available from the British Library.

Library of Congress Cataloging-in-Publication Data on file.

ISBN 1 85433 308 9

Typeset by Book Production Services, London

Printed in Great Britain by Biddles Ltd, Guildford and King's Lynn

Distributed by Plymbridge Distributors, Estover, Plymouth, PL6 7PZ, UK

CONTENTS

Section Four: Physical Health and Illness

Section Seven: Mental Health

Section Eight: The Health of Older Women

LIST OF CONTRIBUTORS

Beth Alder is Professor and Director of Research in the Faculty of Health Studies, Napier University, Edinburgh, Scotland. She has a first degree in psychology and a doctorate in animal behaviour. Her research interests are in women's reproductive health, currently infant feeding, contraceptive needs, and post-natal depression. She has published a textbook for health professionals and numerous chapters and research papers on the psychology of women's health. She is a former Chair of the Psychobiology Section of The British Psychological Society.

Kate Allan is currently working as a full-time researcher at the Dementia Services Development Centre, University of Stirling, Scotland. Her project is exploring the process of staff undertaking service user consultation work with people with dementia. Her main areas of interest within the dementia field are communication and the subjective experience, especially awareness and insight in dementia. Her background is in clinical psychology where she worked with adults and older adults with mental health problems.

Tina Baker is a Chartered Clinical Psychologist based in Jersey since 1991. Previously she worked as a lecturer and clinician at the Institute of Psychiatry, London and for the past decade has devoted most of her clinical work to understanding and helping adult female survivors of sexual abuse. This experience progressively highlighted the fact that despite the surge of publications since the mid-1980s, there continue to exist misconceptions about what it means to have been sexually abused. This provided the impetus for her book entitled *Female Survivors of Sexual Abuse* (forthcoming in 2001).

Frances Baty is a Chartered Clinical Psychologist working in the National Health Service in Scotland. She has a particular interest in the development of Primary Care-based Services and in how clinical psychology can address the impact of social inequalities. She is a member of The British Psychological Society's Psychology of Women Section and the Psychologists' Special Interest Group, Working With Older People (PSIGE). She is active in local politics and community concerns.

Mary Boyle is Professor of Clinical Psychology at the University of East London and head of the Doctoral Program in Clinical Psychology. Her major interests are in the critical analysis of psychiatric theory and practice and in feminist approaches in clinical psychology. She has published widely in the area of women's health, particularly on contraception and abortion, HIV, and sexual problems and is currently working on projects on contraceptive use before abortion and psychological aspects of intersex conditions.

Eleanor Bradley is currently a research scholar at Staffordshire University, U.K. She is examining the follow-up needs of women who have been successfully treated for early stage gynaecological cancer. Previous research interests include the experience of chronic fatigue and counseling psychology.

Ailsa Burns recently retired from Macquarie University, Australia, where she was Associate Professor in Psychology. Her long-standing research interest in the changing nature of families in Australia has led to the publication of many articles and books, including *Mother-Headed Families and Why They Have Increased* (1994), *Australian Women: Contemporary Feminist Thought* (1994); *Children and Families in Australia: Contemporary Issues and Problems* (1985); *Australian Women: New Feminist Perspectives* (1986); and *Breaking Up: Separation and Divorce in Australia* (1980).

Jan Burns trained as a clinical psychologist after completing her Ph.D. at the University of Wales. After working as a clinician within the National Health Service she joined the University of Leeds as a Lecturer in Clinical Psychology. During this time she also worked as a researcher and manager in the NHS. In 1995 she moved to the Salomons Centre to work on the Clinical Training Scheme. She is now the Academic Director of the Centre for Social and Psychological Development, Canterbury Christ Church College. Throughout her career Jan has continued her clinical work with people with learning disabilities. Her research has also included gender and she was one of the founding members of the Psychology of Women section of The British Psychological Society.

Kerry Chamberlain is a health psychologist in the School of Psychology at Massey University, New Zealand. His research interests include psychological issues in chronic illness, the social context of health and illness, and socio-economic differentials in health and illness. He also has interests in research methodology, specifically in varieties of qualitative research. He is co-editor of *Qualitative Health Psychology: Theories and Methods* (with Michael Murray, 1999) and of *Exploring Existential Meaning: Optimizing Human Development Across the Life Span* (with Gary Reker, 2000)

David Clark-Carter is currently Senior Lecturer in Psychology at Staffordshire University, U.K. His research interests include the teaching, understanding, and use of research methods in psychology and the application of research methods

June Crawford works as a research consultant at the National Centre in HIV Social Research, University of New South Wales, Australia. She was formerly Associate Professor in the Department of Psychology at Macquarie University where her research interests included feminism and psychology and methodology, including memory-work.

Rosaleen Croghan is currently a Research Fellow in the Department of Psychology at the Open University, U.K. Before completing her Ph.D. she was a social worker. She has studied women's constructions of motherhood and heterosexual relationships, of abuse and professional identity and most recently women's experiences of counseling.

Precilla Choi is a Senior Lecturer in Health Psychology at Keele University, U.K. where she teaches psychobiology and runs the department's postgraduate research training programme. Her main research interests are women's reproductive health and exercise psychology. Current projects include a study of the relationship between post-natal depression and PMS and a book on femininity and the physically active woman.

Pippa Dell is a Principal Lecturer in the Psychology Department at the University of East London, where she teaches Critical Social Psychology and Media Theory, and co-ordinates the full-time psychology undergraduate program. Her recent publications focus on embodiment and women's health from a feminist post-structuralist perspective and current projects include women's experiences of hysterectomy, domestic violence, and disability. In conjunction with Robert Dighton from Whipps Cross Hospital she is also conducting research into childhood bereavement, funded by the charity Help the Hospices.

Jean Denious is a graduate student in the social psychology program at Arizona State University where she has also served as the technical editor for the *Psychology of Women Quarterly* for the past five years. Her research interests include attitudes toward abortion, sexual objectification, and other issues related to gender. She has collaborated with Nancy Felipe Russo on several projects examining the relationship of abortion to women's well-being.

Lorraine Dennerstein holds a Personal Chair at the University of Melbourne, Australia, where she is Foundation Director of the Office for Gender and Health. She previously established and directed the Key Centre for Women's Health at the University of Melbourne from 1988 to 1996. Professor Dennerstein's contribution to medical education and to research in women's health was recognized by the award of the Order of Australia in 1994. She is a member of the editorial committees of three international journals and is the author/editor of 20 books and over 200 journal articles and chapters in books. Professor Dennerstein is a consultant to the Commonwealth Secretariat (London), the World Health Organisation, the Global Commission on Women's Health (WHO), and the International Bioethics Committee of UNESCO.

Louise Dye is Lecturer in Biological Psychology in the School of Psychology, University of Leeds, U.K. Her main research interests are reproductive psychology, in particular the menstrual cycle and eating behavior. She has conducted research on food craving and appetite control in relation to the menstrual cycle and pregnancy, as well as examining effects of the menstrual cycle on cognitive performance. Her other interests include the psychobiology of infertility and the effects of drugs on performance. Before coming to Leeds, she held a Royal Society European Science Exchange Research Fellowship at the Ruhr University, Bochum, Germany and worked in the MRC Centre for Reproductive Biology in Edinburgh.

Maeve Ennis is a Lecturer in Psychology Applied to Medicine and Health Psychology at University College London. Her research interests are medical accidents, the culture of medical education, and involving patients in teaching of communications skills in the medical curriculum.

Julie Fish is conducting a (U.K.) national survey of lesbians and health care as part of her Ph.D. research. The study investigates lesbians' experiences of breast and cervical screening and their understanding of the risks of these cancers. The study uses focus groups which explore in more detail some of the themes raised in the survey. She is Senior Lecturer at De Montfort University, Leicester, U.K. and teaches social policy and research methods in the Department of Social and Community Studies.

Linda R. Gannon is a Professor in the Department of Psychology and the School of Medicine at Southern Illinois University. She completed her Ph.D. in clinical psychology and psychophysiology at the University of Wisconsin in 1975. She served as the Director of the Women's Studies program for six years. She has contributed numerous research articles and written several books in the areas of behavioral medicine, women's health, and the psychology of women. Her most recent publication is *Women and Aging: Transcending the Myths* (1999).

Anna Gibbs teaches in the School of Communication and Media at the University of Western Sydney, Australia. Her recent work in cultural studies crosses boundaries between classical and contemporary psychoanalysis, and between critical theory and clinical research and writing. She is currently working on a project dealing with affect in public life, paying particular attention to face and faciality.

Sheila Greene qualified as a clinical psychologist at the Institute of Psychiatry in London and worked for two years as the head of a research team at the Children's Hospital Medical Center in Boston. She is currently a Senior Lecturer in Psychology and Academic Co-Director of the Children's Research Centre at Trinity College Dublin. Her research and publications are primarily in the area of developmental psychology.

Christine Griffin is Senior Lecturer in Social Psychology at the University of Birmingham. Her research interests include representations of youth and adolescence, and young people's experiences; feminist approaches to sex and gender relations, including masculinities; and the use of qualitative methods in social psychology. She is one of the founding editors of the journal *Feminism and Psychology*; her publications include: *Typical Girls?* (1985) and *Representations of Youth* (1993).

Sarah Grogan is Senior Lecturer at Manchester Metropolitan University, U.K., where she teaches health psychology and research methods. Her main area of research interest is women's body image. She is currently involved in a longitudinal study of body image in children from 6 to 16 years, and in a study of women's motivations for body building and anabolic steroid use.

Harriet Gross is a Lecturer in Psychology at Loughborough University, U.K. Before doing her first degree and her Ph.D., Harriet ran a small bookshop in London. She joined Loughborough in 1988, where she teaches developmental and women's psychology. Her interests are in the psychosocial aspects of pregnancy and started with research into cognitive failure during pregnancy. Her research now covers a range of pregnancy-related issues, with a particular focus on pregnancy and employment and the impact of this experience on future work.

Helen Keane is currently a Lecturer in Women's Studies at the Australian National University where she completed her doctorate in 1998. She has published on foetal alcohol syndrome, medical models of addiction, recovery discourse and smoking. She is working on a book based on her doctoral thesis, *What's Wrong with Addiction?*

Susan Kippax is a social psychologist whose major research interest is the social aspects of HIV prevention, treatment and care. Professor Kippax is Director of the National Centre in HIV Social Research at the University of New South Wales. She has published extensively on HIV/AIDS, particularly in regard to sexual practice and sexuality. Her work with gay community members, public health practitioners, policy-makers and educators has convinced her of the benefits of reflexive and collaborative research.

Celia Kitzinger is Reader in Lesbian and Feminist Psychology at Loughborough University, U.K. She has published eight books, including *The Social Construction of Lesbianism* (1987), *Changing Our Minds: Lesbian Feminism and Psychology* (with Rachel Perkins, 1993) and *Heterosexuality* (with Sue Wilkinson, 1993). She is currently working on conversation analysis.

Annemarie Kolk is a clinical psychologist and senior lecturer in clinical psychology and health psychology at the University of Amsterdam. Her research interests are in the domain of women and health, in particular somatization, menstrual cycle and gender role stress.

Mary Koss is Professor of Public Health, Family and Community Medicine, Psychiatry, and Psychology in the Arizona Prevention Center of the University of Arizona College of Medicine. A member of the National Research Council Panel on Violence Against Women, she is the recipient of a Research Scientist Development Award from the National Institute of Mental Health. She is also the recipient of the Heritage Award from the APA Division of the Psychology of Women.

Hilary Lapsley and **Linda Waimarie Nikora** are the Principal Researchers and **Rose Black** has been Project Researcher on 'Success Stories: Narratives of Recovery from Disabling Mental Health Problems', a Health Research Council of New Zealand funded project based in Psychology and Women's and Gender Studies at the University of Waikato in Hamilton, New Zealand. Lapsley and Black are both Pakeha New Zealanders and Nikora's Kiwi affiliations are with Tuhoe and Te Aitanga-A-Hauiti; all three are psychologists interested in culture, identity, and mental health.

Rebecca Lawthom is a feminist and Senior Lecturer in Psychology at Manchester Metropolitan University, teaching social psychology, counseling, community psychology, and disability issues. She has worked with women both in community settings and organizations. Her research interests focus on the construction and performance of gender within work and community settings.

Christina Lee is Director of the Research Institute for Gender and Health and Project Manager for Women's Health Australia, a large-scale interdisciplinary longitudinal survey on the health of three large cohorts of Australian women, situated at the University of Newcastle, Australia. She is the author of *Women's Health: Psychological and Social Perspectives* (1998) and has a strong interest in the impact of gender on health and well-being. In her spare time she writes feminist crime fiction.

Sue Lees is Professor of Women's Studies at the University of North London, UK. Her publications include *Losing Out* (1986), *Sugar and Spice: Sexuality and Adolescent Girls* (1993), *Carnal Knowledge*(1997), *Policing Sexual Assault* (with J. Gregory, 1999). She has acted as consultant to five major TV documentaries: *Getting Away with Rape*, which won the Royal Television Award for the best home documentary of 1994, *Male Rape* (1995), *Till Death Do Us Part* (1996), and *Men Behaving Badly* (1998). She was a founder member of the Women's Studies Network Association of which she was joint Chair from 1988 to 1992 and is on the editorial board of the journal *Gender and Education*.

Rosemary Leonard is a Senior Lecturer and Deputy Chair of the School of Social, Community and Organisational Studies at the University of Western Sydney, Australia. She co-ordinates and teaches the major in Social Psychology and Social Research. She also has developed and taught Research Methods within the M.A. (Women's Studies) and other courses. Her current research and publications examine women's concerns in urban design, social capital and women's life-course, particularly the second half of women's lives.

Antonia Lyons is a Lecturer in the School of Psychology at the University of Birmingham. Her main research interests are in 'critical' approaches to health psychology and health research. She has written about the advantages of employing qualitative methods in health research, the social construction of the 'self' during language episodes and possible physiological correlates of this process, the effects of minor daily stress on physical health, and representations of men's health in the media. She is currently conducting research into women's understandings and experiences of the menopause and hormone replacement therapy.

Helen Malson is a Lecturer at the Centre for Critical Psychology, University of Western Sydney, Nepean, Australia where she is also deputy director of the M.A. in Critical Psychology. She has published a number of articles and chapters in the field of gender, health and health care, predominantly on feminist post-structuralist research into anorexia nervosa which is the focus of her book, *The Thin Woman: Feminism, Post-Structuralism and the Social Psychology of Anorexia Nervosa*, (1998).

Harriette Marshall is a Professor of Critical and Feminist Psychology at Staffordshire University, U.K. Her research interests include identities and identi-fications, issues around 'race', culture and gender and the role of psychology in relation to inequalities. Recent research projects include 'Transitions to adult-hood' (with Anne Woollett and Helen Malson) which is concerned with young people's accounts and visual representations, and 'Asian young women and self-harm' (with Anjum Yazdani).

Linda McGowan completed her Ph.D. on women's experiences of chronic pelvic pain in 1998 at Staffordshire University, U.K. She is currently a Senior Research Officer in the Department of Psychiatry, University of Manchester. Her current research work concerns coronary heart disease.

Dorothy Miell is a Senior Lecturer in the Psychology Department at the Open University in the U.K. Her research interests have for many years been in the field of personal relationships, covering a wide field of research from the effects of friendships on children's working relationships to studies of the processes of sense-making in women's adult relationships. She has worked with Rosaleen Croghan on a number of projects at the Open University, most recently on women's accounts of their experiences of doing identity work in counseling.

Julie Mooney-Somers has until recently been based at the Family and Child Psychology Research Centre at City University, London, researching child devel-opment in lesbian families, and the social and biological basis of gender develop-ment as part of a longitudinal study of pregnancy and childhood. She has recent-ly taken up an ARC Ph.D. scholarship in the Centre for Critical Psychology, University of Western Sydney, working on the subject of masculine sexuality.

Carol Morse, Dean of the Faculty of Human Development, Victoria University, Melbourne, Australia, is a health psychologist and cognitive behavioral therapist with a background in clinical nursing and midwifery. Her research interests focus on adult development across the lifespan and concerns psychological issues in women's reproductive disorders, pregnancy-related depression in women and men, psychological adaptation to becoming a parent, and issues arising from the menopause transition on women's cognitive abilities.

Michael Murray is Professor of Social and Health Psychology at Memorial University of Newfoundland, Canada. He recently co-authored (with David Marks, Brian Evans and Carla Willig) *Health Psychology: Theory, Research and Practice* (2000) and co-edited (with Kerry Chamberlain) *Qualitative Health Psychology: Theories and Methods* (1999). He is an associate editor of the *Journal of Health Psychology* and recently co-edited special issues on Qualitative Research (with Kerry Chamberlain) and Reconstructing Health Psychology.

Mervat Nasser is a Senior Lecturer at Leicester University, U.K. and consultant psychiatrist for the South Lincolnshire Mental Health Trust. She is a graduate of Cairo Medical School and a member of the Royal College of Psychiatrists London. Her academic research in the field of psychiatry focusses on the impact of the social environment and the role of cultural variables on mental health. This was particularly applied towards understanding the socio-cultural causation of eating disorders. Her research in this field is considered pioneering. She is the author of *Culture and Weight Consciousness* (1997).

Louise Newman is the Director of the New South Wales Institute of Psychiatry, Australia, and a Child and Adolescent Psychiatrist with expertise in the area of infancy and early childhood. She is undertaking research into the prevention of child maltreatment and was previously the Clinical Director of the Paediatric Mental Health Service at Liverpool, South West Sydney. Prior to studying medicine, Dr. Newman completed undergraduate degrees in psychology, philosophy and gender studies and she has a longstanding commitment to the promotion of women's mental health.

Paula Nicolson is Reader in Health Psychology at Sheffield University, U.K. in the School for Health and Related Research (ScHARR). Her research interests are women's reproductive and family health, particularly post-natal depression, chronic illness and the family and family violence. She is the main editor of *Psychology, Evolution and Gender* and Director of CHePAS (Consumer Health Psychology at ScHARR) which focusses upon the needs and expectations of health consumers through research-based consultancy in the health services and pharmaceutical industry.

Emmanuelle Peters is a Lecturer in the Department of Psychology, Institute of Psychiatry, U.K., and a Clinical Psychologist on the National Psychosis Unit, Bethlem Hospital, South London and Maudsley NHS Trust, which has a separate, specialist Women's Service. Her research interests are in psychological approaches to psychosis, namely cognitive processes involved in delusions, cognitive-behaviour therapy for psychosis, and on the continuum between 'normality' and 'mental illness'. She has published book chapters and scientific articles in a number of international peer-reviewed journals.

Maria Pini is currently a post-doctoral fellow at the University of Western Sydney, Australia where she is working on a project examining video diaries made by young women. Her Ph.D. research was on women's experiences of the British rave scene. This study is presented in her forthcoming book *From Home to House*. She is also author of numerous articles on femininity and dance cultures, social class, and post-structuralist feminisms.

Nancy Pistrang is currently a Senior Lecturer in Psychology at University College London. She obtained her clinical psychology doctorate from the University of California, Los Angeles, after which she worked for several years as a clinical psychologist in the British National Health Service. Her research focusses on psychological helping in everyday relationships, including communication in couples, non-professional helping, and doctor–patient communication.

Marian Pitts is Professor of Psychology at Staffordshire University, U.K. She has researched extensively in the area of women's health, focussing particularly on sexual health issues and on cancer. Her books include *The Psychology of Health* 1991 and 1998) and *The Psychology of Preventive Health* (1996). She previously worked in Southern Africa and retains close ties with the region. She will shortly be taking up a position as Director of the Australian Research Centre for Sex, Health and Society at LaTrobe University, Melbourne.

Luciana Ramos Lira is a senior researcher at the Division of Social and Epidemiological Research of the Mexican Institute of Psychiatry in Mexico City. She has a Ph.D. in social psychology from the National Autonomous University of Mexico (UNAM), and is a professor at the UNAM Department of Psychology and School of Medicine. She is a member of the Sexual and Family Violence Committee of the National Academy of Medicine in Mexico. Her contributions to research on violence against women have been disseminated in national and international forums.

Jacqueline Reilly is a Lecturer in the School of Psychology at the Queen's University of Belfast. Her research and teaching interests are in applied social psychology, with particular emphasis on gender issues and health. Recent research projects have included a qualitative study of women's perceptions of pre-menstrual syndrome and an examination of the influence of gender on career choice in nursing students.

John T.E. Richardson is Professor of Psychology in the Department of Human Sciences, Brunel University, U.K. He is a cognitive psychologist by background, but has carried out research in a variety of applied areas of psychology. He edited *Cognition and the Menstrual Cycle* (1992) and the *Handbook of Qualitative Research Methods for Psychology and the Social Sciences* (1996). Together with Paula Caplan, Mary Crawford and Janet Shibley Hyde he co-authored *Gender Differences in Human Cognition* (1997).

Celia Roberts has a Ph.D. in Women's Studies from the University of Sydney, Australia. Her thesis examined the theorization of biology within feminist thought through an analysis of sex hormones. She currently works at the National Breast Cancer Centre in Sydney.

Nancy Felipe Russo is Regents Professor of Psychology and Women's Studies at Arizona State University, editor of *Psychology of Women Quarterly*. Russo is author or editor of more than 160 publications related to the psychology of women and women's issues. A Fellow of the American Psychological Association and the American Psychological Society, she was the recipient of the American Psychological Association 1995 Award for Distinguished Contributions to Psychology in the Public Interest.

Janet Sayers teaches Psychoanalysis in the Sociology Department of the University of Kent at Canterbury, U.K. She also works part time as a psychotherapist both privately and for the NHS. Her books include *Biological Politics, Mothering Psychoanalysis, Freudian Tales,* and *Boy Crazy.* Her forthcoming book is *Kleinians: Psychoanalysis Inside Out* (2000)

Lynne Segal is Anniversary Professor of Psychology and Gender Studies at Birkbeck College, University of London. Her latest book is *Why Feminism? Gender, Psychology, Politics* (1999). Other books include *Is the Future Female?; Slow Motion: Changing Masculinities, Changing Men;* and *Straight Sex: The Politics of Pleasure.*

Sylvia Smith worked in Intensive Care Nursing for many years before starting her career in Health Psychology at the University of Central Lancashire, U.K. Her research interest is in health promotion, with specific reference to sexual health. Her work on the characteristics and needs of the student population, which identified key times for the delivery of interventions, led her to design an interactive CD ROM, *Direct Action For Sexual Health,* now available for students at her university.

Corinne Squire is based at the University of East London. She is the author of *Morality USA* (with Ellen Friedman, 1998) and editor of *Culture in Psychology* (2000) and *Lines of Narrative* (with Molly Andrews, Shelley Sclater and Amal Treacher, 2000). She is currently writing a book on HIV and citizenship.

Niamh Stephenson is a lecturer in the Centre for Critical Psychology at the University of Western Sydney, Nepean, Australia. Since working on the hetero-sexuality and HIV project at the National Centre in HIV Social Research, her research interests have extended to include social aspects of HIV treatments, as well as political lobbying and participation in New South Wales.

Janet Stoppard is Professor of Psychology at the University of New Brunswick, Canada. With a background in clinical psychology, her research focusses on women's mental health, particularly depression. She is the author of *Understanding Depression: Feminist Social Constructionist Approaches* (2000) and edi-tor (with Baukje Miedema and Vivienne Anderson) of *Women's Bodies /Women's Lives* (2000).

Alison Thomas is an Adjunct Associate Professor with the Sociology Department of the University of Victoria, Canada. After first becoming involved in research on sexual harassment ten years ago, in 1996 she undertook a comparative study of the impact of sexual harassment policies in universities in Canada and the U.K. She has published a number of articles and book chapters on her work in this field, and in 1997 was co-editor (with Celia Kitzinger) of *Sexual Harassment: Contemporary Feminist Perspectives*.

Leonore Tiefer is a feminist and psychologist who has specialized in sexuality for 30 years. She began with a Ph.D. on hormones and hamsters, but in response to the women's movement, she shifted into human sexual theories and problems, with an emphasis on how the politics of sexuality is reflected in and promoted by science and medicine. Her recent collection is a good introduction to her ideas: *Sex is Not a Natural Act, and Other Essays* (1995).

Deborah L. Tolman is Senior Research Scientist and Director of the Adolescent Sexuality Project at the Center for Research on Women at Wellesley College, U.S.A. She is currently completing a book on urban and suburban American ado-lescent girls' experiences of sexual desire, *Dilemma of Desire*, to be published by Harvard University Press. Her recent research activities include the development of the Femininity Ideology Scale and a longitudinal study of female and male adolescent sexual health, addressing both risks and resiliencies.

Jane Ussher is Associate Professor in the Centre for Critical Psychology at the University of Western Sydney, Australia. Her books include *The Psychology of the Female Body* (1989), *Women's Madness: Misogyny or Mental Illness?* (1991), *The Psychology of Women's Health and Health Care* (1992, with Paula Nicolson), *Body Talk: The Material and Discursive Regulation of Sexuality, Madness and Reproduction* (1997), and *Fantasies of Femininity: Reframing the Boundaries of Sex* (1997). Her research interests are women's sexuality, madness, and Premenstrual Syndrome. She is currently working on a project looking at narratives of depression and breakdown in women of different generations.

Wendy Vanselow is a general practitioner with a special interest in women's health and education. Based in Melbourne, Australia, she trained in obstetrics and gynaecology in England. Her research interest in pre-menstrual complaints arose from her work at the Key Centre for Women's Health in Society and formed the basis of her doctoral thesis. Recently appointed Associate Medical Editor of *Australian Family Physician*, she has an ambition to promote women's health physician training in Australia.

Jane Weaver trained as a nurse and midwife in England in the 1970s. More recent-ly she completed a B.Sc. in Psychology at University College London. This was followed by a Ph.D. exploring the issues of control around childbirth, again at

UCL, with the supervision and support of Jane Ussher and Lucy Yardley. She is now at the Centre for Family Research, Cambridge, U.K., researching choice and decision making in caesarean section.

Sue Wilkinson is Reader in Feminism and Social Psychology at Loughborough University, U.K. She is the founding and current editor of *Feminism and Psychology*, and the book series *Gender and Psychology: Feminist and Critical Perspectives*. Her books include: *Feminist Social Psychologies* and, with Celia Kitzinger, *Heterosexuality, Women and Health, Feminism and Discourse*, and *Representing the Other*. Her main research interests are in feminist and critical approaches to sexuality and health, especially breast cancer and lesbian health.

Anne Woollett is a Professor in the Department of Psychology, University of East London. She has a long-term interest in motherhood, mothering and women's reproductive health. In 1991 she edited, with Ann Phoenix and Eva Lloyd *Motherhood: Meanings, Practices and Ideologies*, and has contributed, with Harriette Marshall, to *Handbook on Psychology of Women and Gender*, edited by Rhoda Unger. She is now researching young people's ideas about families and family transitions.

Anjum Yazdani has several years of experience on qualitative research projects, particularly with black and ethnic minority participants. She was based at the Newham Innercity Multifund (a GP co-operative) from 1996 to 1998 where she worked as a researcher on a young Asian women and self-harm research project. She then worked as a Research Assistant with Anne Woollett and Harriette Marshall at the University of East London on a study exploring young people, identity and citizenship in the inner city. She is now working as an Assistant Psychologist for South Downs NHS Trust (U.K.).

Preface

Putting together this collection of papers on women's health has been a labour of love. At times it has felt as if the gestation period would never end – liaising with 71 contributors around the globe, each with their own idiosyncrasies, their own style of writing, their own concerns, has meant a stream of continuous dialogue across cyberspace for over a year. Now that it is coming to the point of birth (or at least publication), it feels both a relief (like all long-awaited progeny) and sadness. Letting go of any work of creation is never easy. There is never a point of perfect completion. There is always more to be said or done. Women who face labour after nine months of waiting may cry 'I'm not ready', but nature says otherwise, and come the baby does. In this case publication deadlines and promises to contributors push this book to the point of delivery. At least, as editor, I don't have birth pains to contend with, and won't afterwards be kept awake at night by the fruit of my labour. Indeed, as this book isn't my own creation, but the creation of a collection of inspired and inspiring others, it is perhaps inappropriate that I metaphorically claim the role of the one who gives birth at all. My role is much more one of midwife, gently encouraging each person to deliver to me. To be able to do this with so many different people, who are located in many different parts of the world, has been a pleasure and a privilege. It has brought home to me the power of new technologies to speed communication and collaboration across continents and across time zones. As I sleep in Sydney my emails are answered in North America and Europe. Those who wish to talk to each other about issues of concern to women's health do so regardless of time, distance or geographical boundary. It is a salutary experience.

ACKNOWLEDGEMENTS

I want to acknowledge the co-operation of each of the contributors and their generosity in donating the book's royalties to Marie Stopes International. I also want to acknowledge the important role played by Joyce Collins, Jon Reed and Rachel Gear at BPS who first conceived of the project and asked me to edit it. I didn't quite know what I was taking on when I said 'Yes', but I'm glad I did. I hope that everyone who has taken part is as happy as I am with the joint book we have produced. Finally, I would like to thank Sharon Mundy for helping with the layout of the final manuscript.

Jane M. Ussher, Sydney, May 2000

For Ann Game

WOMEN'S HEALTH: CONTEMPORARY CONCERNS

Jane M. Ussher

INTRODUCTION

The aim of this book *Women's Health: Contemporary International Perspectives* is to bring together, under a central focus, a collection of current thinking on the subject of women's health. Drawing on research and scholarship from a number of different disciplines, this book clearly demonstrates the importance of women's health as an area of research and professional practice. At the same time, it provides a forum for the cross-fertilization of ideas and approaches, aiming to further the progress of the discipline itself. This book intends to be the main authoritative guide to recent developments in the field of women's health for professionals and academics in the field of psychology, medicine, nursing, women's studies and feminist studies. It aims to be a source book for information, to provoke debate and, most important of all, to assert the importance of 'the woman question' in considerations of health.

The book consists of invited contributions from leading researchers and scholars, drawn from the international academic community, who have produced substantial assessments of major areas of research and theory, providing an authoritative guide to important issues in the field of women's health. These include both comprehensive and critical surveys of a chosen topic, as well as reports of innovative developments in the form of detailed descriptions of original research or theory that is of contemporary interest and relevance. Theorists from different disciplinary standpoints have been invited to contribute a definitive statement on their view of a subject, and the implications for assessment or intervention that arise from their approach. This type of analysis illustrates the plurality of theorizing in the field of women's health; the fact that there is no 'right' answer to a particular question, and no one correct approach.

THE LEGACY OF EARLY CRITIQUES OF WOMEN'S HEALTH

Thirty years ago women's health was a field fighting for recognition in a world dominated by androcentric research, theory and clinical intervention. Today it is a rich and vibrant body of work, spanning many diverse disciplines. The health of women is now firmly on the agenda of the World Health Organisation, government and research funding bodies, providers of health services, and educators. Researchers, theorists and social activists continue to move knowledge and practice forwards, improving service provision for women, at the same time as we reach a greater understanding of 'what women want' regarding their health.

Yet it hasn't always been this way. The last few decades of the twentieth century have seen the publication of a number of groundbreaking studies and critical polemics that highlighted the paucity of knowledge about the health and well-being of women. They documented how women's bodies, women's minds and, by extension, women's lives have historically been marginalized, ignored, or dealt with in a detrimental way by mainstream health professions. Whole disciplines such as medicine, psychology and psychiatry were subjected to critical scrutiny. It was argued that women's mental health was defined in relation to man as the norm, and inevitably found wanting as a result. Femininity was pathologized, with mental health treatments merely serving as vehicles of social control, pushing women back into patterns of behavior and social roles which were sources of distress and despair in the first place (Chelser, 1971; Penfold and Walker, 1984; Showalter, 1987; Ussher, 1991). It was argued that the reproductive body was positioned as a site of illness, irrationality and weakness, used as an excuse for excluding women from an equal place along side men (Ehrenreich and English, 1978; Sayers, 1983). Or it was positioned as a site of medical and psychological intervention, over which women had no choice or control (Scully, 1980; Oakley, 1984). It was also argued that there was a dearth of knowledge about the normal aspects of reproduction, as psychological and medical research focussed on and reinforced the notion of reproduction as site of deviancy or debilitation (Parlee, 1973; Ussher, 1989), framing the female body within a narrow scientific gaze (Fee, 1988; Harding, 1987).

It became clear that vast areas of health research excluded women altogether. For example, work on midlife concentrated on men, with Erikson's male model of midlife developmental changes being extrapolated unquestioningly to women, much as Kohlberg's theories of moral development had been (Gilligan, 1982). Both theories found women lacking. Their deviation from a male norm was deemed deficiency, not difference. Many major clinical trials on heart disease (e.g. Grobbee et al. 1990; Ockene et al. 1990) excluded women altogether, as did early research on AIDS (Squire, 1993). In research on cancer, there has been a focus on the breast and genitals, even though lung cancer surpasses breast cancer as a cause of death for women. Research on all other forms of cancer in women is rare, or gender differences are not analysed when women are included in clinical trials (Meyerowitz and Hart, 1995). Research on alcohol use (Sandmaier, 1980), or on drug use, has also focussed almost solely on men until recently – despite the fact that significant numbers of women experience substance abuse, as well as problems from prescribed psycho-active drugs. And even when women *are* included in health research, it is only a narrow and specific group, for in the main the focus has been on middle-class, able-bodied, heterosexual, white women.

These early critiques which focussed on the marginalization or exclusion of women's health issues have provided an important legacy for current research, theory and practice. They have highlighted the way in which 'woman' has been constructed in quite specific ways by powerful phallocentric health professions which did not always (or perhaps ever) have women's interests at heart. They have documented the way in which women have historically been excluded from shaping the agenda as researchers, clinicians and policy-makers, and how this has had a significant impact on the development of knowledge and professional practice in the arena of women's health (Ehrenreich and English, 1978; Albino *et al.*, 1990). These critiques provided the foundations for the current field of women's health, setting an example and an agenda, simultaneously. Today, in disciplines as disparate as psychology, sociology, cultural studies, women's studies, social work, nursing, psychoanalysis, anthropology, psychiatry and medicine, scholars and researchers have brought their considerable energies to bear on the question of women's health and a rapidly growing literature on the subject is the result. At the same time, at the grass roots level, developments such as the Boston Women's Health Collective have provided inspiration for women to work together to lobby, and to provide information and services about health. The Internet now is making this a global phenomenon that can reach women otherwise isolated from knowledge about their bodies and their health.

However, positive as this may appear, there is little room for complacency if we are not to lose hard won gains in a world where resources are increasingly scarce. There are also many voices clamouring for an end to women's health as a special concern. 'The health of all people should be our priority', we are told. '*Gender* and health should be our concern, not "*women* and health", otherwise we neglect the needs of men'. Project funds are now being targeted for *gender*, rather than *women* and health. After such a short life, it might appear that 'women's health' is in danger of becoming an extinct field. This must not happen. It would be a regressive step that would undo the hard work and the intellectual and political endeavors of the last 30 years (and all that came before which made the gains of second-wave feminism possible).

This book is unapologetically about women and health. Whilst studies of 'gender' (or 'feminism') are certainly of central interest to those working within the field of women's health, they are not identical areas of concern. A collection of work on 'gender and health' would be both too broad (not having a theoretical or critical focus, nor being focussed on women), and too generalized, not serving the function of pushing thinking on women's health to the forefront. It also implicitly focusses narrowly on the social construction of 'gender', a factor that results in important areas of research and practice being marginalized or ignored. For example, the biological aspects of female experience, the analysis of materiality, of the corporeal body, and the interactions between sex and gender are often left out of such a framework. This is not just an issue for women: similar arguments can be made about the health of men. Acknowledging this, a companion volume is planned to examine the specific health concerns of men.

WHAT CHARACTERIZES THE FIELD OF WOMEN'S HEALTH?

This raises one of the key questions, 'what characterizes the field of women's health?' Is it research on women's health, research by women in this field, or research which merely has implications for women? Are there health matters that are peculiar or particular to women, and if so, what are they? Is a specific perspective needed for addressing women's health which differs from that adopted in men's health? Does it have to be feminist, or carried out with a reflexive female gaze? And if so, what does it mean to carry out feminist work in women's health? Can theories of mainstream psychology or medicine, if they are objects of feminist criticism, be imported uncritically into the field of women's health? Is women's health a cohesive field, or merely a collection of disparate developments? Can it be part of the mainstream, or is it necessarily outside? Can it, or need it, include the analysis of men or masculinity?

This book sets out to address many of these questions, and to provide a coherent and identifiable framework for the publication and promotion of emerging research and professional practice. It is based on the premise that there are a number of qualities that characterize the field of women's health, and these form the basic philosophy behind the individual contributions.

In general, each of the contributors takes a woman-centered perspective on health. This starts from the assumption that women's perceptions and subjectivity are an important focus for research, theory and professional practice, as well as central to health. The wide range of issues covered in this volume are all arenas of health which have been related to the social construction of gender and women's subjectivity. Each of the contributors acknowledges the importance of women's social roles, the cultural context in which women live, and the way in which discursive representations and myths about femininity impact upon health.

There are a number of aspects of women's health which have not been covered in this book. Issues such as heart disease, cancer (other than gynaecological), diabetes, smoking, alcohol use, and health education and policy are covered in detail elsewhere (e.g. Niven and Carroll, 1994; Stanton and Gallant, 1995). The interested reader is referred there. In the main, the subjects that appear in this volume concern health issues that are particular or peculiar to women, for instance breast and gynaecological cancer, rather than cancer in general. They are all issues which have been associated with the gendered nature of health, or with women's social roles (see Lee 1998, for a similar approach to women's health).

In the majority of the contributions, the androcentric nature of traditional or mainstream psychology and medicine is asserted, and the role of traditional scientific theory and practice in maintaining woman's subordinate position in society is acknowledged (Ussher, 1999). However, it is also clear that psychology, medicine and related disciplines can play a role in both changing the misconceptions associated with women, and in providing a greater understanding of women's health. We must be wary about throwing the baby out with the bath water. It is better, in many ways, to work for change within these disciplines, as they exert such power over the materiality and discursive representations of women's health and women's lives. However, there are times when we have to step outside or become outsiders in order to find a space to work, to get our voices heard, or to be constructively critical. Many of the contributors to this volume have, at times, done just that.

In being critical, many of the taken-for-granted assumptions about the study of women's health are challenged; in particular the notion of the rational unitary subject who can be objectively analysed regardless of historical and cultural context. Consequently, research methods and philosophical assumptions underlying current orthodoxies are critically examined and evaluated, in an attempt to develop methods of working which are not phallocentric (Ussher, 2000a). Whilst many of the contributions are critical, questioning taken-for-granted assumptions in mainstream health psychology or medicine, at the same time they offer constructive ways of working and moving forward. The aim is to bridge the gap between abstract research and professional practice through integrating theory and practice, research and politics/policy. This book will thus be of key interest to practitioners in health psychology, clinical psychology, counseling, psychotherapy, medicine and nursing where a critical gendered analysis has to be integrated with the reality of daily work with women.

As an overarching principle, the notion of the researcher as objective observer, and research or clinical data as a unquestionable 'fact' is not accepted uncritically. The importance of reflexivity and of subjectivity as legitimate focus for academic attention is asserted. Due to limitations of space, the majority of the contributors have not commented specifically on themselves. However, they are always present in their work as their writing clearly demonstrates. Equally, the traditional divisions and hierarchies that separate 'theory/research' and 'practice' within psychology, medicine and the field of health are rejected. Being aware of the implications of theory and research for the materiality of women's lives is a central tenet of the field of women's health. Thus all the contributors share the view that the particular health issues that they write about must be seen in the context of women's lives. The perspective of those who are only interested in a disconnected part – such as hormones, the breast, the uterus, the vagina – have not been included here. However, they do appear as an object of critical attention in many of the chapters.

Whilst the focus of the contributions in this book is on women, the category 'woman' is seen neither as a biological given, an unquestionable pre-given fact, nor as solely a social construction. The materiality of biological sex and the social or discursive construction of gender are both acknowledged, but neither is privileged above the other. Equally, whilst the experience of the individual woman is a legitimate focus of inquiry, it is recognized that this cannot be carried out without reference to analyses of experiences of women as a group, and the socio-historical discourses which have positioned woman as Other. These have framed questions and practices around women's health and illness, many of which we would seek to overturn

There is a strong presence of qualitative work in this volume, alongside critical theoretical contributions on women's health. This stands in contrast to more mainstream texts which draw on the ubiquitous clinical trials, or large-scale epidemiological research, in making comments on women's health (e.g. Stanton and Gallant, 1995). These more traditional forms of analysis are valuable, and are certainly not to be dismissed. Indeed, a number of the contributors in this volume do draw significantly on mainstream scientific research and theory, including epidemiological and clinical trials. But there are other ways of looking at questions of women's health. Perhaps what most marks out this volume as different from others is the plurality of voices, the plurality of views. Whilst many of the contributing authors are situated within psychology, and their work has definite implications for research and practice within mainstream psychology, medicine, nursing, and related disciplines, much of the theoretical work in the individual contributions is heavily influenced by disciplines outside of psychology. Disciplines such as sociology, philosophy, psychoanalysis, linguistics, cultural studies, biology, philosophy of science, history, and anthropology have had a strong impact, and will have key relevance in future developments in the field of women's health. In this way the book differs from many collections on women's health, which are firmly within one discipline, or written from one theoretical position. Here, in contrast, there are contributions from a range of perspectives: including evolutionary, feminist, bio-psycho-social, material-discursive, systemic, cognitive, social-constructionist, post-structuralist, psychoanalytic, and self-psychological standpoints. The majority of the contributors are open and reflexive about their epistemological and ontological standpoint, acknowledging that this affects the focus of our academic or professional gaze. It affects the issues we consider to be of relevance, the questions we address, the methods we use in research, and the assumptions we make about the world – in particular about women.

This book also differs from others that focus on work from one particular geographical location (often North America or Britain), as there has been an attempt to include voices and views from a number of different countries. There are still many voices absent, and many perspectives that have not been included. We would like to have had more representations of the concerns of women in the developing world, in Eastern Europe, South America, Asia, Africa, and many Middle Eastern states. This is perhaps a future project. It is important that we acknowledge that women are not a homogenous group, and that it is a relatively privileged context within which most of us currently live and work. Basic human rights are a luxury for millions of women throughout the world today, and health concerns are concentrated on staying alive and maintaining basic human dignity. We should not forget this as we develop more sophisticated ways of understanding the health of women in Europe, the U.S., Canada and Australasia, the context of the work of the majority of contributors to this volume.

Primarily, the contributors are women, which is neither a coincidence nor a deliberate choice. The field of health, for centuries, has been dominated by men and by all matters masculine. The notion of male as norm, and the importance of attention being paid to matters specifically female, has long been challenged by outspoken thinkers and practitioners. However, it is only in recent decades, with the vast increase in women entering the professions of medicine, psychology, social work, and psychotherapy, as well as the increase in women graduating with degrees in social sciences, humanities, and related disciplines, that women have brought their own critical energies and attention to matters of women's health in such numbers. This book reflects the fruits of this thinking – a rich and eclectic selection of deliberations on matters that are close to the hearts of the authors, as they inevitably touch on our own lives. Men too have contributed much to the debates on women's health. A number have accepted invitations to contribute to this volume. But the gender imbalance reflects the fact that most of the cutting edge work in this field is by women researchers and practitioners.

There is every reason to suppose that this trend will continue. The sheer numbers of women in psychology, medicine, nursing, and women's studies, and the growing climate of 'consumer choice' in higher education suggest that critical attention to the experience of women, and in particular 'women's health', will grow over the next decade. For example, as in other disciplines, analyses of gender, feminism and female psychology are among the most popular options with psychology students. The growing number of postgraduate students working within the field (50 percent of postgraduates are female), as well as the increasing number of practitioners (75 percent of clinical psychologists are female; as are 60 percent of doctors; 94 percent of nurses) and academics carrying out research and practice in this area, will provide the foundations for the developing discipline. In the U.S.A., Britain, Australia, New Zealand, Canada, Israel, Italy and the Netherlands, there are active associations promoting the Psychology of Women, with women's health being a central concern. At the same time universities and professional training courses in clinical, organizational and educational psychology are beginning to recognize the salience of the 'Psychology of Women', and more specifically, 'Women's Health' for their programs. There are now a number of academic journals devoted specifically to women's health, or more broadly to the psychology of women, or feminist psychology. International conferences on women's health are held every year, with many receiving government support. This work both reflects this vibrant field, and will add to its continued growth.

THE ORGANIZATION OF THIS BOOK

The individual chapters are arranged in sections under broad themes, which are in many ways overlapping. The themes are: An Overview of

Critical Issues in Women's Health; Young Women's Health; Sexuality and Sexual Health; Physical Health and Illness; Reproductive Health; Bodies and Body Image; Mental Health; The Health of Older Women. The following overviews of each section, and of the individual chapters, serve as an introduction.

An overview of critical issues in women's health

The first three chapters introduce some of the critical issues in women's health research. Christina Lee argues that psychology has historically been problematic as a discipline in its dominant individual-focussed epistemology, which fails to position women's issues in their social and political context. She outlines an alternative feminist psychology of women's health, that focusses on the social construction of gender and the effects that this has on individual women's lives. Michael Murray and Kerry Chamberlain remind us that the past decade has seen a rapid growth of interest in qualitative research methods However, they argue that this can be confusing not least because the term 'qualitative methods' conceals a variety of theoretical and methodological assumptions. They review the assumptions and background of this turn to qualitative research, and discuss issues in the application of different qualitative methods to women's health research. Sheila Greene argues that life span developmental psychology provides a helpful knowledge base and conceptual orientation for those psychologists and allied practitioners who are attempting to effect change in women's health, whether it be physical or mental health. She provides a critique of a number of developmental models, and outlines one that she feels is satisfactory for the field of women's health. Together, these three chapters set the scene for those that follow, many of which are critical and qualitative, and organized in sections that cover the lifespan of women from puberty to old age.

Young women's health

The health of young women is an issue that is often overlooked by those concerned with women's health. There is perhaps a misconception that young women are intrinsically healthy, not yet afflicted by many of the chronic illnesses or reproductive problems which older women can experience. Or it may be because young women rarely form a strong lobbying group around health issues, and are less likely to present themselves to professionals with their health concerns. If young women are considered, the focus of attention tends to be on eating disorders and sexuality, with other health concerns often marginalized or neglected. Yet young women are a central part of the women's health agenda, as many of the contributors to this book acknowledge.

Harriette Marshall and Anjum Yazdani examine the issue of self-harm, focussing on the experiences of young Asian women living in Britain.

They highlight the complex meaning of self-harm, using interview data from their own research to illustrate their arguments. Whilst they make a plea for the importance of culturally sensitive care, they also argue that there is no simple cultural template that can be adopted in working with young women. Service providers need to attend to the needs and agenda of individual clients, locating self-harm in the particular circumstances which cause distress. This is an argument that can be extrapolated to all other areas of women's health. In her chapter on drug use and dance culture, again based on an interview study, Maria Pini argues that young women are not passive dupes, as they are often represented in health education literature. The majority negotiate drug use in the context of self-care, and are aware of risks and dangers, as well as pleasures, in drug taking. Seeing women as victims in relation to drugs ignores the complexity of the experience, and leaves little room for positive health education or care. Helen Keane takes up this argument, looking critically at the way in which women as substance users are discursively constructed in public health and therapeutic literature. This argument, which applies to women of all ages, powerfully demonstrates the way in which distorted 'truths' about women are produced by health professionals and researchers, as well as feminist critics.

In the chapter by Julie Mooney-Somers and Jane Ussher the issue of young women's mental health is addressed, with specific reference to young lesbians. A material-discursive-intrapsychic perspective is adopted in analysing narrative interviews with a group of lesbian avengers. This compliments the more general issues relating to depression which are considered by Janet Stoppard in her contribution (Chapter 46). The final chapter in this section deals with the sexuality of young women. Deborah Tolman examines the association between early adolescent girls' espousal of conventional beliefs about femininity and their diminished positive sexual health. To illustrate the ways in which a girl's femininity ideology interplays with her sexual health, she presents the example of a 13-year-old Latina girl, whose critique of and active resistance to complying with this conventional femininity ideology strengthens her sexual health.

Sexuality and sexual health

Continuing on from the previous section, the following 11 chapters focus on sexuality. The first group of papers presents a critical analysis of heterosexuality, the second an analysis of the impact of sexual abuse on women's health, and the third, an examination of women's sexual health.

Much has been written about the relationship between sexuality and women's health. Indeed, arguably sexuality is the one area that has received attention from mainstream health professionals. Perhaps this is because historically 'woman' has been defined and regulated through sexuality. Sex and femininity are synonymous, not always positively so in the experts eyes. In both first and second wave feminism, critical theorizing and campaigning practice has centered on the ways in which female sexuality is both denigrated and controlled, and how through this process so are women. Early feminist attention focussed on literal regulation of the physical body, on material practices that focus on the flesh – what Foucault termed control through the 'useful body'. More recently, critical attention has shifted to the institution of heterosexuality as a site of regulation – for both women and men. The way in which both femininity and masculinity are constructed and controlled through the imposition of the heterosexual matrix as the norm has resulted in a rethinking of both sexuality and gender roles (see Butler, 1990; Segal, 1994; Ussher, 1997a). In the first chapter in this section, in looking at issues of trust in heterosexual relationships, Niamh Stephenson, Susan Kippax and June Crawford examine the discursive practices and psychic fantasies through which young women's experiences are constituted and lived.

Largely due to the influence of post-structuralist theorizing, critical attention has also shifted to the power of symbolic representations of female sexuality and their role in the containment and control of women. This has led to critical analyses of how female sexuality is portrayed in science, the law, art, film, popular culture, literature and pornography (Ussher, 1997a). The focus here has been on the regulatory power of discourse – control through what Foucault termed the 'intelligible body'. These critiques focus on what semiotic theorists would term 'woman as sign', the analysis of what 'woman' signifies or symbolizes at a mythical level – the representation of woman as object, or as fetish, and the splitting of 'woman' into Madonna or whore. These representations are seen to maintain the position of woman as 'Other'. In a chapter on reclaiming women's sexual agency, Lynne Segal examines the way in which women's sexuality is conceptualized in this phallocentric context.

In the field of health, the regulation of sexuality through science, medicine and sexology has been subjected to particular scrutiny. It has been argued that sexual science defines 'normal' sexuality through regulating what is abnormal, through the clinical categorizations and treatments for dysfunction and perversion. This medical analysis of sex, which often reduces it to a biological instinct or response, is part of a wider process of secularized control of the body – and through controlling the body, controlling the person. It has been argued that sexual science is both gendered and phallocentric. The rhetorical objectivity which dominates in public discourse serves as a smokescreen for the acting out of ideologically motivated power and control. The model 'person' reflected in both science and medicine is the person of heterosexual man. He is the benchmark against which all else is measured; an active, powerful sexual man, in contrast to the passive, receptive, (or absent) sexuality of woman (Tiefer, 1991; Ussher, 1997a). Leonore Teifer develops her previous work on this subject, by presenting a strong critique of the role of the pharmaceutical industry in the construction and regulation of women's sexuality. She argues that commercial interests are shaping people's knowledge and experience of their own sexuality.

SEXUAL VIOLENCE AND ABUSE

Sexual violence is an emotive subject, but one which has significant implications for women's health. If we look at the statistics on sexual violence,
it is clear that it is a subject we cannot ignore. Official statistics lead to the
estimate that 1 to 2 percent of women have experienced rape at some time
in their lives (Stanko, 1985). Yet these official statistics only reflect reported crimes, or convicted offences. A National Women's Study which surveyed rape in the U.S. in 1990, found that 13 percent of American women
had been the victim of at least one forcible rape in their lifetime, but only
26 percent of them had ever reported the crime. This led to the estimate
that one in eight, or over 21 million adult women in the U.S. have been
raped – despite the fact that the study used a very conservative definition
of rape, excluding rapes which happened to women under the age of 18
(which consists of six out of 10 rapes). Other surveys suggest even higher
rates. In a random survey of women residents of San Francisco carried out
in the early eighties, Diana Russell (1982) reported that 44 percent had
experienced attempted or completed rape. In another study of over 3000
women, Mary Koss and her colleagues found that 54 percent of women
had experienced some form of sexual violence as adults, including
unwanted sexual contact (14.4 percent), sexual coercion (11.9 percent),
attempted rape (12.1 percent) and rape (15.4 percent). These different estimates reflect the sample of women studied, and the ways in which 'rape'
is defined by the researchers. However, regardless of disagreements as to
the actual percentage, the notion that only 1 percent of women are the victims of rape is clearly a serious underestimate.

Adult 'rape' is only one form of sexual crime. Of the 12 U.S. states
which report rape statistics in sufficient detail to distinguish juvenile from
adult rape, 51 percent of the rape victims were under the age of 18, and
one in six under the age of 12. Surveys of adult women suggest high rates
of child sexual abuse; ranging from 12 percent in a randomized community survey of 1049 women carried out in Britain, to 54 percent of women
in a community survey of 930 in San Francisco. Surveys of women attending clinics for psychological or sexual problems give even higher prevalence rates of childhood sexual abuse – between 30 percent and 60 percent.
Only a minority of children *ever* report childhood sexual abuse. For example, in a study of 767 women survivors in Britain (Ussher and Dewberry,
1994), in only 3 percent of cases had the abuse been reported to the authorities. Only 46 percent of women had ever disclosed the abuse to *anyone* –
the majority telling husbands or boyfriends later in life if they did talk of
it. So it 'officially' remains a hidden crime. As is the case with adult rape,
the official statistics are merely the tip of the iceberg. Women who experience domestic violence and sexual harassment are similarly silenced. In
one survey of 2000 homes of married couples, researchers reported that 28
percent had experienced at least one incident of physical assault, and 16
percent had experienced violence in the year prior to the study (Straus *et
al.* 1980). In North America, it is estimated that 3 to 4 million women each
year are battered by their male partners. In Britain, the figure is estimated

to be 530,000. This, again, is an invisible crime, as it has been estimated that only one out of 270 incidents of wife abuse are reported to the authorities (Steinmetz, 1977).

In this section, the impact of rape and sexual violence on women's health is considered by Nancy Felipe Russo, Mary P. Koss and Luciana Ramos. They outline a case for the increased appreciation of the diversity of forms and cultural definitions of rape, encourage increased understanding of how cultural definitions can affect rape consequences, and identify some of rape's physical and mental health outcomes.

Domestic violence, both sexual and physical, can have both direct and indirect effects on women's and children's physical and mental health. As Sue Lees argues, even the direct effects are not always recognized and it is only recently that the indirect effects of the witnessing of violence by children are beginning to be appreciated. She outlines some of the known effects of domestic violence and discusses how health workers can contribute to meeting this challenge.

Rosaleen Croghan and Dorothy Miell present a critique of traditional approaches to understanding child sexual abuse, and argue for the importance of narrative work. They argue that developments can only take place in therapy if a woman is in a position for change to take place, and thus the material context of women's lives is of vital importance. Finally, Alison Thomas considers the impact of sexual harassment on women's health, drawing on both feminist theory and clinical literature. She comments that while in an ideal world we would simply not have to deal with sexual harassment, as things stand we have to find ways of minimizing the stress it causes in women's lives. Understanding more about the process of how the effects of sexual harassment and women's responses to it are mediated by how they perceive and label it will help us to do so.

SEXUAL HEALTH

Women's sexuality is not merely a matter for feminist and post-structuralist critics, or those concerned with violence and abuse. Much work has been conducted on sexuality as an arena of physical and psychological health. This includes work on desire (see Tolman, Chapter 8), gender identity (see Newman and Kitzinger, Chapter 45), lesbian health (see Mooney-Somers and Ussher, Chapter 7) and sexual problems (see Tiefer, Chapter 11, Ussher and Baker, 1993).

In this section, Sylvia Smith provides an overview of a number of issues in the realm of women's sexual health, including sexually transmitted diseases, contraception, and gynaecological cancers. Beth Alder presents a biopsychosocial analysis of contraceptive choice, begging the question 'Why do women use contraception in some circumstances, and not others? Lorraine Dennerstein examines the relationship between sexual functioning and the menopause, drawing on large-scale epidemiological surveys. Finally, Jan Burns argues that one group of women who are normally left out of discussions of sexuality and sexual health are women with learning disabilities. She examines the ways in which this group of women are objectified, their sexual health needs ignored, and thus their position as sexual beings or mothers made invisible.

Physical Health and Illness

The physical body is at the center of women's health. However, this is not a body that can be conceptualized outside of the cultural context in which women live. The way in which women experience their bodies, as well as health care, in particular the diagnosis and treatment of illness, is always socially and culturally situated. Some forms of illness receive a great deal of attention from health professionals, others are marginalized. Some forms of illness are represented as unfortunate or innocuous, others are laden with blame on the part of the person who suffers. When illness is gendered – specific to women, or seen as different when experienced by women and men – these representations are rarely neutral. Equally, the physical body, and forms of illness clearly located in the body, cannot be seen as simply biological or physiological phenomena. The materiality of the corporeal body is irrevocably linked with social, discursive, and intra-psychic factors (Ussher, 1997b; Yardley, 1997), as the chapters in this section demonstrate. Women have very different subjective experience of illness, something which is often overlooked by health professionals and researchers, yet is central to prevention, treatment, as well as the understanding of the course of any particular health problem. The contributions in this section follow on from those in the previous section that looked at sexual health, examining a number of arenas of health problems and illness associated with gender and women's sexuality.

Corinne Squire takes the case of women living with HIV in Britain, and examines how this particular illness has been misrepresented as evidence of 'a specifically feminine threat'. She looks at how HIV positive women live with the epidemic, within a psychological, social and epidemiological matrix. She demonstrates that AIDS is an illness that is lived differently by men and women, regardless of their sexuality or where they live. The physiology of the disease is gendered. Marian Pitts and Eleanor Bradley look at the issue of gynaecological cancer, developing some of the issues touched on previously by Sylvia Smith (Chapter 16). They consider the psychological aspects of gynaecological cancer, and are critical of the fact that there is little research interest in this important area. Cancer is a stigmatized illness, gynaecological cancers particularly so, provoking shame and embarrassment for women who suffer from them. This can lead to psychological difficulties, which Pitts and Bradley examine.

Screening for gynaecological cancers currently focusses on cervical cancer. Julie Fish and Sue Wilkinson examine some of the problems in cervical screening, in particular the fact that a considerable proportion of women do not attend for screening. They look specifically at one group, lesbians, whose attendance for cervical screening has largely been ignored. Based on the results of a U.K. national survey of lesbian health care, they look at reasons why lesbians don't attend for cervical screening.

In a second chapter, Sue Wilkinson presents a feminist critique of breast cancer, one of the most common cancers among women. She examines women's subjective experience of breast cancer, and the political activism it has generated, based on her own research. Her argument is that feminism has acted to make breast cancer more visible, interrogated its social and cultural meanings, campaigned for and provided services for women, and acted to challenge the medical, scientific and political establishments. Continuing the theme of women's subjective experiences, Nancy Pistrang presents a process analysis approach to providing partner support for women with breast cancer. Some women adapt to serious illness better than others. Social support, in particular from a partner, is a key factor in this. Nancy Pistrang presents her own research on women with breast cancer to demonstrate how support is communicated (or fails to be communicated) within this relationship.

Chronic Pelvic Pain (CPP) is another example of a health problem which has been defined in gender specific terms, not always to the benefit of women. Marian Pitts, Linda McGowan and David Clark Carter examine the way in which CPP has been associated with psychiatric morbidity, despite the fact that research has not found any obvious pathology in women sufferers. They argue that medical practitioners invariably regard women with CPP negatively, and that what is often overlooked is the fact that many women with CPP have experienced childhood sexual abuse (CSA). CPP is not the only area where this could be argued. That CSA is a common factor in many somatic and psychological problems, has only recently been acknowledged by health professionals and researchers.

Somatic distress is highly prevalent in women, as Annemarie Kolk argues. Women experience more medically unexplained symptoms than men, and because of ill health, have a higher health care usage. Annemarie Kolk examines the validity of the differences in medically unexplained problems, and then develops a model for research into women's somatic distress. She argues that clinicians working with women's somatic distress should make an effort to eliminate gender bias, and look at the problem within a multi-dimensional framework, in order to provide good health care for women.

Reproductive Health

The majority of contributions in this section present a critical analysis of women's reproductive health, in particular the way it has historically been positioned by medical models and practices. The acceptance by health professionals of an association between reproduction and the psychological or physical state of women is centuries old, as is the medical management of the resultant 'symptoms'. Both Plato and Hippocrates documented the deleterious influence of the 'wandering womb', recommending 'passion and love' followed by pregnancy, as the cure for 'all manner of diseases' the womb 'provoked' (Veith, 1964: 7). In the nineteenth century, menstruation became the more specific focus of attention, being described by one commentator as 'the moral and physical barometer of the female constitution' (Burrows, 1828: 147), and by others as a cause of 'moral and physical derangement' (Maudsley, 1873: 88). This connection between menstruation and madness was first reified within the medical and psychological literature of 1931, with the early descriptions of 'premenstrual tension' (PMT): a condition manifested by a combination of physical and psychological symptoms occurring in the days immediately prior to menstruation, which ceased at the onset of menses. Robert Frank, the gynaecologist commonly credited with establishing the existence of PMT, attributed the symptomatology to accumulations of 'the female sex hormone', oestrogen (Frank, 1931), and, as a consequence, advocated medical intervention. Renamed Premenstrual Syndrome (PMS) by Greene and Dalton in 1953 as a means of acknowledging the wide array of symptoms, and more recently 'late luteal phase dysphoric disorder' (LLPDD) in the DSM-IV (American Psychiatric Association, 1994), pre-menstrual problems are now firmly established as a clinical condition. Yet the divisions between bio-medical and psycho-social positions which were evident in these first official descriptions of the problem are still in existence, and as a consequence, the disagreements over aetiology, over appropriate strategies for intervention or prevention, and the debate as to whether PMS is a pathological or normal condition continue as well (see Ussher, 1996; Walker, 1996). Jacqueline Reilly conducts a critical analysis of existing research on PMS, and argues that we need to develop a women-centered approach in order to reconcile the differences in this field. Taking a different tack, Wendy Vanselow presents a systems theory analysis of PMS, which provides both a way of understanding the multidisciplinary complexity of this problem, and a way forwards for treatment.

There has been a vast amount of research on the menstrual cycle outside of the pre-menstrual period (see Walker, 1996). Louise Dye examines one specific area, that of the relationship between menstrual cycle fluctuations and eating behavior. In contrast to many other contributors, she starts from the assumption that hormonal fluctuations are a key issue in menstrual cycle experience. However, she posits a bi-directional relationship, where the menstrual cycle affects food intake, but food intake also affects the menstrual cycle. This provides a good illustration of the importance of avoiding simplistic causal analysis where reproductive health is concerned. John Richardson also explores the relationship between hormones and behavior, in this case, cognition throughout the menstrual cycle and during menopause. Through an examination of existing empirical research in this area, and drawing on his own work, he concludes that there is no relationship between women's reproductive hormones and intellectual functioning. He thus disputes many of the commonly held beliefs and stereotypes about the effect of menstruation and menopause on women (Richardson, 1992; Sayers, 1982). Finally, Celia Roberts turns her attention to the question of how we understand hormones, from a cultural perspective. She proposes that hormones are 'bio-cultural actors', not neutral biological causes of women's behavior, as is often implicitly assumed in bio-medical analyses of health. This analysis turns on its head many existing theories and assumptions about reproductive health, and has wide implications for theory, research and practice. We can never simply accept, or dismiss, hormonal explanations again.

The discourse of reproductive lability and vulnerability is not confined to the menstrual cycle. Pregnancy, childbirth and the post-natal period have been pathologized in the same way, positioning women's experiences as an illness in need of intervention, and interpreting any distress or unhappiness as individual pathology. Since the male obstetricians wrested control of childbirth from the women midwives, as early as the sixteenth century childbirth has been construed as a technological accomplishment on the part of the expert – the woman herself positioned as a passive recipient. For a number of years now feminists have been challenging the medicalization of pregnancy and childbirth, attempting to reclaim from the male medics this arena of women's lives (e.g. Graham and Oakley 1981; Kitzinger 1983; Ussher, 1989). The concept of pregnancy as an illness, a state of abnormality, which is prevalent in the medical literature has been challenged, with the result that a growing number of women have attempted to gain more control in the antenatal period, asserting their rights to a voice in the birth of their child (although it is mostly white middle-class women who have succeeded in this). The same is now starting to be done in the post-natal period, and with other aspects of reproductive health.

Carol Morse presents a critical overview of issues in women's reproductive health. These include the social and psychological reasons for having children, for infertility, and for post-natal depression. The importance of being attentive to psycho-social issues when considering reproduction is emphasized. In a similar vein, in an analysis of pregnancy, Harriet Gross argues that pregnancy must always be understood in the context of women's lives. She presents a critique of the medicalization of pregnancy, looking at how women are discursively positioned in dominant medical models, where there is a focus on risk and an overemphasis on health problems. This serves to move attention away from the majority of women's normal experiences as mothers and carers. Maeve Ennis also presents a critique of the medicalization of pregnancy, in her scathing analysis of predictive testing and health screening. The benefits of screening are questioned, in the context of the psychological consequences for women. This raises serious questions about the increasing use of technology in pregnancy and childbirth, and begs the question 'Whose interests does it serve?' Jane Weaver presents a critique of the medical model of childbirth, and looks at the ways in which women's subjective experiences of control are potentially undermined by current practices. New policies in Britain are designed to give women more control; however, changing professional attitudes and behavior is a much slower process, as Jane Weaver found in her own research.

Looking specifically at motherhood, Anne Woollett and Harriette Marshall address the issues raised for women's health and well-being whether or not they become mothers. They look at the social construction of motherhood, at beliefs about who can and cannot become mothers, and the impact of mothering or childlessness on women's identity. Paula Nicolson contrasts medical and social science accounts of post-natal depression, looking critically at the benefits for women within each model. She concludes that women's subjective experiences of post-natal depression have been left out of most analyses to date. Pippa Dell presents a critical materio-discursive analysis of reproduction, focussing on hysterectomy. Drawing on her own research, she outlines how socio-cultural and medical discourses position the woman's body as diseased, and how this is used to regulate women's subjectivity. Finally, Mary Boyle takes the subject of abortion, and presents a critical analysis of the meaning of the legal and medical representations of abortion for women, complementing the analysis of abortion as a mental health issue presented by Jean Denious and Nancy Russo in Chapter 49.

Bodies and body image

One arena of women's health that has received a great deal of attention in recent years has been that of body image and bodily regulation. However, the desire to change shape and size is not a recent phenomenon, as women's bodies have been subjected to manipulation for centuries, often by women themselves. In order to achieve the wasp waist which was necessary to fit into the crinolines of the nineteenth century, women wore restrictive corsetry, or in some cases had their lower ribs removed. In the twenties, to achieve the flat chest of the flapper, the breasts had to be strapped down. Today, the ideal female body is both thin and sculpted. The slender toned body has come to represent the feminine ideal – stripped of fat, desire and all appetites that may be dangerously out of control. So body management for women has to go deep within, to the dangerous fat cells which threaten the very boundaries of what it is to be 'woman'.

Researchers have repeatedly shown that up to 80 percent of women wish to change their body shape or size. The majority want to be thinner and leaner. Dieting is now described by psychologists as 'the pathology of the norm'. Eating disorders such as anorexia nervosa and bulimia are rife, particularly in adolescent girls. Adult women regulate and restrain their food intake to an extreme which results in complete distortion of normal eating patterns. Women ban food, restrict intake below that which is needed to sustain energy, and then become obsessed with the very foods which are denied.

The emphasis today is not just on weight loss, but on achieving a tight taut boundary to the body. 'Even thin women can have cellulite' declare women's magazines. Starvation is no longer enough. So women are entreated to continuously monitor the intake to their bodies, though cutting out food and counting calories – but also to be fit and healthy and strong. What has been described as a 'tyranny of slenderness' (Chernin, 1981) has been transformed into a tyranny of fitness and firmness. Feminism has impacted upon the world of magazines, moving them away from notions of a frail or passive femininity, and starvation as a means of sexual success, to produce an ideal woman who is powerful, lean and strong. She is in control of her health, and her body – and, by implication, in control of her life. So women can 'eat healthily' (not diet), work out in the gym, and pay continuous attention to the boundaries of their flesh without feeling that they are giving up on the 'post-feminist' principles they are supposed to aspire to (Ussher, 1997a).

This obsession with food, with shape, with firm thighs is not just about health – it is about control of female sexuality and control of female sexual desire. Susan Bordo has argued that the images of unwanted bulges and fleshy round stomachs which pervade women's magazines and the talk of young girls are metaphors for anxiety about internal processes which are out of control: 'uncontained desire, unrestrained hunger, uncontrolled impulse' (Bordo, 1990). The emphasis on the need to control and regulate the boundaries is irrevocably connected to fears of the terrible consequences of unleashed sexuality. It is not *fat* that is frightening, but a body without clear firm boundaries. It is not weight that is disgusting, but the feminine form. The curves which signify femininity and sexuality are toned and trimmed to attain a muscular, masculine form. The ideal goal is to make them disappear altogether; as Susan Bordo has shown in her discussion of diet advertising, 'now [a typical ad runs] … Have a nice shape with no tummy' (Bordo, 1990: 89–90). Women who diet want to make the bodily signifiers of femininity disappear.

In this section, Sarah Grogan looks at the issue of body image, in particular why women desire to change their body shape or size. Taking a social constructionist perspective, she looks critically at the social pressure to be slim, the health implications of cosmetic surgery, dieting, eating disorders and exercise. Helen Malson delves more deeply into the subject of anorexia nervosa, and criticises those who would dismiss women's body concerns as natural or expected, because women are seen as vain or self-absorbed. She argues for a feminist perspective on anorexia nervosa, which allows us to see this particular health issue as expressive of a multiplicity of societal concerns and dilemmas that are constituted in contemporary Western culture. Mervat Nasser develops the theme of eating disorders as a cultural phenomenon, and the issue of the relationship between Westernization and anorexia. She argues that there are parallels between eating disorders and other forms of body regulation, such as the wearing (or not) of the veil in the Middle East, and is critical of feminist approaches which extrapolate from the experience of Western women to women in other cultural contexts.

The regulation of eating is not the only form of body management which has implications for women's health. Precilla Choi takes the subject of exercise, and asks why fewer women than men exercise. She also argues that whilst physical activity is potentially of great health benefit to women, reducing depression and increasing feelings of physical well-being, it has also become the latest commodity in a highly commercialized beauty culture.

Perhaps the most extreme form of manipulation or change of the body is found in the sphere of transgender transformation. Here the sexed body is swapped. Woman becomes man, or vice versa. Louise Newman provides an overview of transgender issues and their implications for women's health, looking at gender identity development and disorders in the context of current mental health practice. She also looks at the varying experience of the transgendered individual from a psychiatric perspective, focussing on issues of assessment and intervention. She argues that the meaning of the sexed body is culturally located, and the desire to change sex has a different meaning in different cultural contexts. The question of the relationship between gender and the body is also central to the experience of women with androgen insensitivity syndrome (AIS), a form of intersexuality where women are born with the usual male pattern of XY chromosomes. Celia Kitzinger provides a critical overview of the diagnosis and treatment of AIS, and the implications of misdiagnosis or misinformation on the subjective experience of women who are coming to terms with being different. She makes a number of suggestions for health care for this group of women, and suggests that AIS offers an important challenge to feminism and psychology.

Mental Health

The existence of gender differences in mental health problems is a well-established phenomenon. Prior to puberty, boys are represented in significantly greater numbers (by a factor of approximately 4:1) in the whole gamut of psychological or behavioral problems experienced by children. However, after puberty the situation is reversed. Estimates of the ratio of women to men suffering from disorders such as depression, anxiety and eating disorders range from 6:1 to 5:3. Community surveys, hospital admissions and statistics on outpatient treatment (both medical and psychological) all concur: women are represented in far greater numbers than men (Bebbington, 1996; Stoppard, 1999). The only exceptions are in the diagnosis of schizophrenia, where there are no clear gender differences, and alcoholism, where men dominate.

For decades, researchers have searched for the factors underlying this gender difference, claiming that if we can explain it, we will have the key to understanding mental health problems per se (e.g. Bebbington, 1996). Numerous competing biological, psychological and social etiological theories have been put forward as a result. The professions of psychiatry, clinical psychology, psychotherapy and social work dispense expert knowledge and care in the attempt to ameliorate or prevent such problems. Yet, as we know, these institutionalized investigations and interventions have not gone unquestioned. A range of critics, including anti-psychiatrists, post-modernists, and feminists from a number of different ideological camps, have subjected expert analyses of women and mental illness to critical deconstruction. Much of what has for decades (perhaps centuries) been taken for granted has been dissected and discarded as biased, misconceived, or misogynistic in the extreme (Ussher, 1991). However, in mainstream research and clinical practice, very little has changed. The categorization of women's mental health problems as pathology or illness remains unchallenged. Science categorizes symptoms into syndromes which are operationally defined and analysed in objective research. Individual women are offered reductionist explanations and invariably a bio-medical cure for symptomatology they experience. Psychological interventions may not blame the body, but they still focus, in the main, on the individual woman (or on her mind). The gap between critical analysis and the institutionalized regulation or treatment of mental health problems seems impossible to bridge (Ussher, 2000b).

The question is, why is this the case? And what can be done to effect change? In the following chapters these questions are addressed. Janet Stoppard briefly reviews both mainstream and critical approaches to the phenomenon of women and mental illness, as well as the relationship between the two. Drawing on her own research, she argues that a material-discursive perspective provides a workable alternative to many traditional approaches. Hilary Lapsley, Linda Waimarie Nikora and Rosanne Black examine women's narratives of recovery from disabling mental health problems, from a bio-cultural perspective. This analysis of individual women's stories demonstrates that whilst mental health problems are always culturally embedded, the experience is always embodied, and one of anguish, and sadness, as well as life-threatening depression.

Work has often been positioned as a protective factor in women's mental health (Ussher, 1991). However, it can also be a source of stress and mental health difficulties. Rebecca Lawthom examines the way in which women straddle the boundaries between home and work, experiencing stress and guilt within the family domain, at the same time as they suffer pressure (and often harassment) at work. She uses a feminist reading to understand women's subjective experiences in this sphere, illustrating it with a narrative of one particular woman. Jean Denious and Nancy Felipe Russo take the experience of abortion in a socio-political context and examine its relationship to women's mental health. Whilst this chapter has specific implications for the analysis and treatment of abortion, it also stands as an example of the relationship between a politically contentious health issue and women's subjective experiences. They argue that the meaning of abortion is socially constructed, and varies greatly across cultures and political contexts. Whilst some women may experience negative reactions to abortion, the majority see it as a solution to a stressful situation, and express positive emotions afterwards. They conclude that we must thus be wary of misrepresenting the health risks as a means to restrict access to safe abortion. This would be a threat to women's mental health.

Much has been written about sex differences in the epidemiology and aetiology of schizophrenia and other psychoses. However, as Emmanuelle

Peters argues, most of this work is biological in nature, concentrating on genetic, brain and diagnostic differences. Much less has been written on the social and environmental challenges faced by women with psychosis, and services appear to regard the chronically mentally ill as almost genderless. In her chapter, Emmanuelle Peters reviews the literature on sex differences and gender-specific needs of women with severe mental illness, and addresses the implications of these findings for service delivery issues. Kate Allan also looks at issues for health carers in the often overlooked subject of dementia. Women are at greater risk than men of experiencing dementia, largely because they live longer than men on average. Yet gender issues have been mostly ignored in this field. Kate Allan examines the meaning of dementia for women, in particular the need for empowerment, for communication, and for the use of creativity in working with women who experience dementia.

The treatment of mental health problems is a contentious issue – with many disagreements as to the most appropriate strategies or models. The final three chapters in this section present three very different approaches to working therapeutically with women. Christine Baker presents an account of her work with over 200 survivors of childhood sexual abuse, as a clinical psychologist using Schema-Focused Cognitive Behaviour Therapy (SFCBT). Janet Sayers examines how psycho-dynamic psychotherapy with women seeks to take into account social and more immediate interpersonal issues in seeking to alleviate the distress for which women seek therapy. Finally, Anna Gibbs argues that self-psychology provides a way of thinking and working clinically that may be especially helpful to women, both because of its particular emphasis on intersubjectivity in the therapeutic situation, and because of its willingness to engage critiques of gender and sexuality both at a theoretical level and as they impact directly on the therapy.

These are not the only therapeutic approaches used in the sphere of women's health – feminist therapy, humanistic therapy, group therapy, various forms of psychoanalysis, and somatic therapy are among many of the approaches available to women. What these three diverse approaches demonstrate is that there is no single way of working with mental health problems; there is no single ideal approach. Women need to be informed of the differences between therapeutic approaches, and the different assumptions about problems, as well as different ways of working, in order to make the most use of professional help. Finding a good match between a clinician and a client, as well as a therapeutic approach that meets the needs of the individual, at a particular time, is not a simple process. Open discussion and dialogue about psychotherapy, which includes women's subjective experiences, will only help to make this process more straightforward and transparent.

The Health of Older Women

Taking a lifecycle approach to women's health means that we start with adolescence, and end with the menopause and older women. Definitions of midlife and 'old age' change continuously as our life span lengthens, due to increased access to health care and good nutrition. Historically, women who lived past 40 were 'old', as the dangers of childbirth, combined with poor living conditions, resulted in early mortality. In the twentieth century, many women in the developed world lived into their eighties and beyond. Indeed, the health care needs of older women will become one of the most pressing issues facing governments, health care providers and social policy makers in the twenty-first century. For most of us, as we age, it will also become a pressing personal issue. We no longer expect older people to be dismissed as 'past it', or women to be considered redundant when they have left their reproductive years behind. There is life beyond fecundity, child-rearing, and retirement. Good health is an important part of this life.

In this final section, Antonia Lyons and Christine Griffin argue that linguistic and visual representations of women's health and menopause experience at midlife are revealing of social concerns regarding the control of health care, and the construction of women's aging. They also show the extent to which a consensus exists on the nature and character of menopausal women. Lyons and Griffin take their own analysis of self-help texts on menopause and HRT in order to examine representations of menopause and women at midlife in these texts, and compare these with representations across other textual sites, including medical textbooks, academic writing and advertisements.

In cultures where aging is despised and feared and women are valued for fertility and beauty, the aging woman is often the target of pity and ridicule – portrayed as lonely, sick, frail, and unhappy. While some scholars ascribe distress essentially to genetics and/or childhood trauma, Linda Gannon argues that psychological distress is due primarily to contextual causes such as poor working conditions, sexual and racial discrimination and oppression, poor health, hostile family environments, poverty, and inadequate social support. These potentially chronic stressors are likely to become increasingly destructive to an individual's well-being if they persist. A single incident of gender discrimination may be ignored, but 60 years of such discrimination may be devastating, rendering aging women vulnerable to both physical and psychological distress through the accumulated effects of chronic stress. In her chapter, Linda Gannon examines the factors which predict women's psychological and physical well-being as they age. She concludes that in spite of sexist and agist cultural imperatives, women seem to do well when progressing through middle and old age, as the traditional gender roles accorded to women have facilitated habits and skills of considerable value in maintaining psychological well-being.

Taking up this theme, Rosemary Leonard and Ailsa Burns comment that the paradox of older women's health is that, although statistics show that older women are prone to numerous health problems, most older women report to national surveys that their health is very good or at least satisfactory. They argue that this gap between illness statistics and women's lived experience reflects fundamental differences in assumptions. The illness statistics are part of a medical model which assumes a 'rise and fall' model of the life span. The women's reports are more consistent with a life course approach. They explore the differences between these two approaches using interviews with 60 midlife and older women and argue for the importance of keeping health concerns in perspective.

Not all women experience good health as they age. Many do experience psychological problems. In the final chapter Frances Baty examines what clinical psychologists can offer older women with mental health problems such as anxiety and depression. She examines how clinical psychology services are influenced by the health care system within which they are provided and how the interventions initiated by the clinician must take account not only of psychological factors, but also of the context within which the individual lives her life.

REFERENCES

Albino, J., Tedesco, L. and Shenkle, C. (1990) Images of women: Reflections from the medical care system. In M. Paludi and G. Steuernagel (Eds) *Foundations for a Feminist Restructuring of the Academic Disciplines*. New York: Haworth

American Psychiatric Association (1994) *Diagnostic And Statistical Manual of Mental Disorders* (4th edn). Washington: DC: APA

Baker, A.W. and Duncan, S.P. (1985) Child sexual abuse: A study of prevalence in great Britain. *Child Abuse and Neglect*, 9, 457–467

Bebbington, P. (1996) The origins of sex differences in depression: bridging the gap. *International Review of Psychiatry*, 8, 295–332

Bordo, S. (1990) Reading the Slender Body. In M. Jacobus, E. Fox Keller, and S. Shuttleworth (Eds) *Body Politics: Women and the Discourses of Science*. London: Routledge

Bureau of Justice. Statistics Survey of Rape (1992) Patrick A. Langan and Caroline W. Harlow; Crime Data brief June 1994 NCJ 147001; distributed on the Internet

Burrows, G.M. (1828) *Commentaries on Insanity*. London: Underwood

Chernin, K. (1981) *The Obsession: Reflections on the Tyranny of Slenderness*. New York: Harper and Row

Chesler, P. (1973) *Women and Madness*. New York: Doubleday

Ehrenreich, B. and English, D. (1978) *For Her Own Good: 150 Years of Expert's Advice to Women*. New York: Anchor Doubleday

Fee, E. (1988) Critique of modern science: The relationship of feminism to other radical epistemologies. In R. Blier, (Ed.) *Feminist Approaches to Science*. New York: Pergamon

Frank, R. (1931) The hormonal causes of premenstrual tension. *Archives of Neurological Psychiatry* 26, 1053

Gilligan, C. (1982) *In a Different Voice: Psychological Theory and Women's Development*. New Haven: Harvard University Press

Graham, H. and Oakley, A. (1981) Competing ideologies of reproduction: medical and psychological perspectives on pregnancy. In H. Roberts (Ed.) *Women, Health and Reproduction*. London: Routledge and Kegan Paul

Greene, R. and Dalton, K. (1953) The premenstrual syndrome. *British Medical Journal*, 1, 1007

Grobbee, D.E., Rimm, E.B., Giovannucci, E., Colditz, G., Stampfer, M. and Willett, W. (1990) Coffee, caffeine, and cardiovascular disease in men. *New England Journal of Medicine*, 323, 1026–1032

Harding, S. (Ed.) (1987) *Feminism and Methodology*. Indianapolis: Indiana University Press

Kitzinger, S. (1983) *The Woman's Experience Of Sex*. London: Dorling Kindersley

Koss, M.P., Gidycz, C.A. and Wisniewski, N. (1987) The scope of rape: Incidence and prevalence of sexual aggression and victimization in a national sample of higher education students. *Journal of Consulting and Clinical Psychology.* 55, 162–170

Lee, C. (1998) *Women's Health: Psychological and Social Perspectives.* London: Sage

Maudsley, H. (1873) *Body and Mind.* London: Macmillan

Meyerowitz, B.E. and Hart, S. (1995) Women and cancer: Have assumptions about women limited our research agenda? In A.L. Stanton. and S.J. Gallant (Eds.) *The Psychology of Women's Health: Progress and Challenges in Research and Application* (pp. 51–84). Washington, D.C.: American Psychological Association

Nivan, C.A. and Carroll, D. (1993) *The Health Psychology of Women.* Chur, Switzerland: Harwood

Oakley, A. (1984) *Taking It Like a Woman.* London: Flamingo

Ockene, J.K., Kuller, L.H., Svendsen, K.H. and Meilahn, E. (1990) The relationship of smoking cessation to coronary heart disease and lung cancer in the Multiple Risk Factor Intervention Trial (MRFIT). *American Journal of Public Health.* 80, 954–958

Parlee, M. (1973) The premenstrual syndrome. *Psychological Bulletin,* 80, 454–65

Penfold, S. and Walker, G. (1984) *Women and the Psychiatric Paradox.* Milton Keynes: Open University Press

Richardson, J.T.E. (Ed.) *Cognition and the Menstrual Cycle* (pp. 132–173). New York: Lawrence Erlbaum

Russell, D.E.H. (1986) *The Secret Trauma: Incest in the Lives of Girls and Women.* New York: Basic Books

Russell, D.E.H (1982) *Rape in Marriage.* New York: Macmillan

Sandmaier, M. (1980) *The Invisible Alcoholics: Women and Alcohol Abuse in America.* New York: McGraw Hill

Sayers, J. (1982) *Biological Politics.* London: Tavistock

Scully, D. (1980) *Men Who Control Women's Health: The Miseducation of Obsetrics-Gynaecologists.* Boston: Houghton Mifflin

Showalter, E. (1987) *The Female Malady: Women, Madness and English Culture 1830–1980.* London: Virago

Squire, C. (1993) *Women and AIDS.* London: Sage

Stanko, E.A. (1985) *Intimate Intrusions. Women's Experience of Sexual Violence.* London: Routledge and Kegan Paul

Stanton, A.L. and Gallant, S.J. (1995) *The Psychology of Women's Health: Progress and Challenges in Research and Application.* Washington: American Psychological Association

Steinmetz, S. (1977) *The Cycle of Violence.* New York: Praeger

Stoppard, J. (1999) *Women and Depression.* London: Routledge

Straus, M.A., Gelles, R.J. and Steinmetx, S. (1980) *Behind Closed Doors: Violence in the American Family.* New York: Doubleday

Teifer, L. (1991) Commentary on the status of sex research: Feminism, sexuality and sexology. *Journal of Psychology and Human Sexuality,* 43 (3), 5–42

Ussher, J.M. and Dewberry, C. (1994) The nature and long term effects of childhood sexual abuse: A survey of adult women survivors in Britain. *British Journal of Clinical Psychology,* 34, 177–192

Ussher, J.M. (1989) *The Psychology of the Female Body.* London: Routledge

Ussher, J.M. (1991) *Women's Madness: Misogyny or Mental Illness?* Hemel Hempstead: Harvester Wheatsheaf

Ussher, J.M. (1996) Premenstrual syndrome: Reconciling disciplinary divide through the adoption of a material-discursive epistemological standpoint. *Annual Review of Sex Research,* 7, 218–252

Ussher, J.M. (1997a) *Fantasies of Femininity: Reframing the Boundaries of 'Sex'.* London: Penguin

Ussher, J.M. (1997b) (Ed.) *Body Talk: The Material and Discursive Regulation of Sexuality, Madness and Reproduction.* London: Routledge

Ussher, J.M. (1999) Feminist approaches to qualitative health research. In M. Murray (Ed.) *Qualitative Health Psychology.* London: Sage

Ussher, J.M. (2000a) Women's madness: a material-discursive-intrapsychic approach. In D. Fee (Ed.) *Psychology and the Postmodern: Mental Illness as Discourse and Experience.* London: Sage

Ussher, J.M. (2000b) Women and mental illness. In Lorraine Sherr and Janet St Lawrence (Eds.) *Women, Health and The Mind.* London: John Wiley

Ussher, J. and Baker, C. (Eds.) (1993) *Psychological Perspectives on Sexual Problems: New Directions for Theory And Practice.* London, Routledge.

Veith, I. (1965) *Hysteria: The History of a Disease.* Chicago: University of Chicago Press

Walker, A. (1996) *The Menstrual Cycle.* London: Routledge

Wilson, G.D. (1988) The socio-biological basis of sexual dysfunction. In M. Cole and W. Dryden (Eds.) *Sex Therapy in Britain.* Milton Keynes: Open University Press

Yardley, L. (1997) *Material Discourses of Health and Illness.* London: Routledge

AN OVERVIEW OF CRITICAL ISSUES IN WOMEN'S HEALTH

CHAPTER 1

PSYCHOLOGY OF WOMEN'S HEALTH: A CRITIQUE

Christina Lee

INTRODUCTION

Psychology has been notably slow among the social sciences in recognizing the central role of gender in human behavior. Particularly problematic is its dominant individual-focussed epistemology which fails to position women's issues in their social and political context. A feminist psychology of women's health should focus on the social construction of gender and the effects that this has on individual women's lives. Such a psychology can most usefully focus on health and well-being in its broadest sense, rather than on specific illnesses; it should emphasize the contexts – social, cultural and political – which shape individual choices; it should explore diversity, use a range of quantitative and qualitative research methods, and must be openly political. This chapter argues that contemporary 'psychology of women's health' frequently supports, rather than challenges, cultural inequities, and outlines alternative approaches to a genuinely feminist psychology of women's health.

While disciplines such as sociology and history have well-developed specialities which deal with women's issues in general, and women's health more specifically, psychology has been notably slow to recognize the central role of gender in human behavior. Psychological theories, investigation strategies and research areas which focus on women or on gender remain marginalized. Perhaps more importantly, when women's issues are addressed, the dominant epistemology of psychology leads to an individualist and socially conservative approach which fails to position women's issues in their social and political context.

This chapter addresses the tension between mainstream psychological research and theorizing on the one hand, and a feminist approach to scholarship on the other. Psychology takes an individual-centered focus and concentrates, within the individual, on subjective cognitive processes. A feminist approach, by contrast, emphasizes and explores the sociocultural context of individuals' lives, and thus sits uneasily with the central principles of psychology.

Both historically and in the present day, psychology has emphasized the subjective and the individual in a way which turns its focus away from the physical world and from the social contexts in which people lead their lives (Lee, 1998a; Prilleltensky, 1989; Sarason, 1981). Although most psychologists would perceive such a perspective as apolitical and socially neutral, an examination of the political implications of this approach to the study of women's health suggests that it is highly conservative. If systemic social inequalities are to be addressed, there is a need for psychology to broaden its perspective of what constitutes women's health and what constitutes legitimate research.

The central issue for a socially and politically relevant psychology of women's health should be the social construction of gender. From a psychological point of view, critical aspects of women's health are not biological sex differences – breast cancer versus prostate cancer, menopause versus functional impotence – but gender-based social roles and expectations. The physical and emotional well-being of women is determined to a far greater extent by these expectations and limitations than by women's biology.

PSYCHOLOGICAL RESEARCH

In attempting to integrate a feminist perspective with mainstream psychology, there is an uncomfortable sense that the two start from incompatible epistemological standpoints. Psychology positions itself within an empiricist, positivist and experimental tradition (Bailey and Eastman, 1994; Howard, 1985). Empiricist science focusses on single problems in controlled conditions, artificially isolated from real-world contexts, and thus the psychology of women's health has tended to focus on specific problem behaviors: disordered eating, smoking, failure to participate in cancer screenings, and so forth.

Women's problems are seen as arising from individual deficiencies, from a dysfunctional world-view or a lack of appropriate skills. Psychological interventions aim to correct the woman's perspective or to teach her skills in coping with her circumstances. Thus, as Prilleltensky (1989) has argued, psychology promotes a world-view in which 'solutions for human predicaments are to be found within the self, leaving the social order unaffected' (p. 796). The individualism and subjectivism of psychology have limited both the questions which are asked and the answers which are obtained; in particular the nature of the social context of individual choices and specifically gender-based inequity are completely ignored.

For example, a large body of psychological research and theory deals with the effects of paid and unpaid work on individuals' health. Much of this work carries an implicit bias which reflects underlying social assumptions about gender and work. Psychological research with women is often predicated on the assumption that paid employment will necessarily be carried out in addition to a full-time load of childcare, family caregiving and unpaid domestic work, and will thus be inevitably accompanied by stress and poor health (Baruch and Barnett, 1986; Repetti *et al.*, 1989). Where high levels of overwork and stress are identified, the solutions which are offered tend to be attempts to correct assumed deficits in the individual women, such as stress management training (Koch *et al.*, 1991), rather than considering the possibility that a renegotiation of the division of labour might be more effective in reducing women's stress (see Lawthom, in this volume).

Research with men, by contrast, is more likely to start from the assumptions that a full-time, permanent job is necessary for self-esteem and general psychological well-being; lack of a full-time job is stressful (Price *et al.*, 1998), and unpaid domestic work is optional for men.

In these ways, paid work is implicitly positioned as normal for men but abnormal and potentially pathological for women, while unpaid domestic labor is positioned as unproblematically and naturally 'women's business'. Inequities in employment opportunities (e.g. Australian Bureau of Statistics, 1995), in income (e.g. Social Trends, 1995), in access to leisure time (Henderson, 1990), and in domestic labor (Bittman, 1992) are thus treated as neutral background phenomena, unquestioned and unquestionable.

Another example comes from the huge body of literature examining the impact of working mothers on their children's physical and emotional well-being. Most of this is based on the assumption that children must suffer if their mother is employed. The psychological literature overwhelmingly places the responsibility for child psychopathology and behavior problems on the shoulders of their mothers, excusing or completely ignoring fathers (see Caplan and Hall-McCorquodale, 1985; Phares, 1992). There is no parallel literature which examines the effects of men's paid employment on their children's well-being; psychological theories again assume that this state of affairs is 'normal'.

It has been demonstrated that maternal employment increases fathers' involvement in caring for their children (e.g. Bailey, 1994), suggesting that fathers may benefit from a richer involvement in family life, and that this involvement has positive effects on the parents' relationship (Hawkins *et al.*, 1993). But such research is marginalized while mainstream research and theory has ignored fathers, assuming that traditional gender roles are somehow natural or immutable.

The literature on family caregiving has also focused on the individual rather than on broader social and structural variables which underlie the phenomenon (Lee, 1999). This means that the fact that the majority of family carers are women has tended to be obscured (Abel, 1991), and the extent to which women absorb the cost of caring is disguised (Hooyman and Gonyea, 1995). Research on the effect of caregiving on health (e.g. Cattanach and Tebes, 1991; Pohl *et al.*, 1994) often uses the term 'family caregiver' to refer exclusively to the daughters and daughters-in-law of the elderly people being cared for; the assumption is that men do not, and should not, provide care in the family context.

A focus on the individual is once again apparent in interventions which aim to relieve this stress. Psychological interventions include psychother- apy (e.g. Gallagher-Thompson and Steffen, 1994), support groups (e.g. Peak *et al.*, 1995), and educational programmes (Magni *et al.*, 1995) to improve the performance and coping skills of caregivers, together with regular day care (e.g. Feinberg and Kelly, 1995) and occasional respite care (e.g. Caradoc-Davies and Harvey, 1995) to prevent them from collapsing under the strain. Interventions do not generally attempt to challenge the broader social structure which places intolerable demands on a powerless section of the community. The message here is clearly that the problem lies in a deficiency in the women themselves, rather than in the situation, and that it is their anger and frustration, not the situation, which is the real problem. Such approaches 'serve to deflect attention from broader struc- tural problems and from social, economic and political inequities by race, gender, age or class' (Hooyman and Gonyea, 1995: 111).

Again social inequities, by which women's choices and opportunities are restricted by the tacit assumption that women are always available to care whenever needed and without remuneration, are positioned as nor- mal, natural and unalterable, and this makes critical analysis of the situa- tion difficult within the dominant discourse of contemporary psychology (see Baker, Gibbs and Sayers, in this volume for alternative models of intervention).

The assumptions about women's and men's roles on which such research is based are not politically neutral; they serve to maintain inequalities between women and men, such as differential rates of pay, the concentration of women in poorly paid occupations and part-time work, and the feminized nature of poverty (e.g. Australian Bureau of Statistics, 1995). They also undermine the possibility of a renegotiation of social roles, either at a personal or at a social level, by positioning traditional social roles as 'normal' or 'correct'. The research literature tends to neglect, or to treat as anomalous, individuals and families who deviate from a rigidly sex-based allocation of paid and unpaid labor. While there is research which examines the working lives of role-reversed couples (Grbich, 1995), of lesbian families (Ainslie and Feltey, 1991), of single-par- ent families (Davies and Rains, 1995), and of others who attempt to devel- op their own strategies for balancing their lives, such research frequently treats these arrangements as necessarily pathological rather than as alter- native social arrangements which deserve serious consideration (Dickerson, 1995; see Mooney-Somers and Ussher, Chapter 7, and Wilkin- son, Chapter 23).

The myth of the mothering instinct, and the socially constructed assumption that women are naturally more appropriate caregivers than men, serve to restrict women's choices and their economic and social power (e.g. Badinter, 1981; Rich, 1982; Wearing, 1984). Simultaneously, this myth also denies the validity of men's interest in, and concern for, their children and serves to exclude men from emotional closeness and caring activities within their families (Carrigan *et al.*, 1985). Further, the internalization of this myth by women themselves is one factor in the high levels of guilt and exhaustion many women experience as they strive to meet social expectations in both paid employment and the domestic sphere (Phoenix *et al.*, 1991). While these issues are regularly debated within the disciplines of sociology and gender studies, a serious consideration of these and related issues is almost completely lacking in the psychological literature.

It might be argued that psychological research merely reflects social reality, but social realities have changed. The majority of women, including those with small children, are in paid employment (e.g. Australian Bureau of Statistics, 1995). Only 28 percent of U.S. households consist of 'traditional' nuclear families, with a husband in formal, paid employment, a wife in unpaid domestic employment, and one or more dependent children (Dalley, 1988). Yet psychological research seems still firmly grounded in the 1950s, in a society which no longer exists.

Alternatively, psychologists might argue that a traditional gender-based division of labor is in some sense the most desirable social arrangement, one to which everyone should aspire. But this view is clearly contradicted by evidence that women in non-traditional roles and members of non-traditional family groups (e.g. Ainslie and Feltey, 1991) generally have high levels of physical and psychological well-being, and show no interest in changing to a 'traditional' lifestyle (Grbich, 1995). Mainstream psychology generally fails to reflect on its assumptions about social contexts and arrangements, accepting particular cultural and historical circumstances as if they reflected some indisputable, unchangeable and necessary reality.

FEMINISM AND PSYCHOLOGY

A feminist approach to research in the psychology of women's health takes a perspective which differs in five main ways from traditional health psychology. Firstly, feminist women's health research focusses on health and well-being in its broadest sense, rather than on specific illnesses and illness behaviors. Secondly, it emphasizes the contexts – social, cultural and political – which shape individual choices. Thirdly, it explores diversity among groups and individuals, rather than taking the perspective that sociocultural differences simply interfere with well-designed research. Fourthly, it makes use of a range of quantitative and qualitative research methods (see Murray and Chamberlain, in this volume) to explore phenomena from different standpoints, rather than assuming that there is a single legitimate 'truth' which can only be identified by following empiricist and reductionist research methods. And finally, it is openly political.

Focus on health

In common with health psychology in general (Marks, 1996), the psychology of 'women's health' has largely been the study of women's illness.

Major texts on women's health emphasize heart disease, cancer, menstrual and reproductive disorders, and illness-relevant behaviors such as smoking, drug use and medical screening (e.g. Adesso *et al.*, 1994; Niven and Carroll, 1993; Stanton and Gallant, 1995). While these are important topics, they reflect a biological and reductionist perspective on health which does not attempt to understand the whole person in her social and cultural context.

A focus on health means addressing issues which are relevant to the everyday lives of all women throughout their lifespans (see Green, in this volume), rather than focussing on illness and specific 'health behaviors'. Investigation of women's experiences as parents, as family members, as employees and as members of society can demonstrate the inequities and social assumptions about womanhood which influence women's lives, and thus their physical and emotional health.

Women's reproductive and hormonal systems have particularly tended to be pathologized. Psychological research on menstruation, pregnancy and childbirth, and menopause has been based on the assumption that these are necessarily problematic, even in healthy women (Ussher, 1992). For example, the concept of a distressing, biologically based, premenstrual syndrome is widely accepted as fact despite a lack of consensus on its definition, symptoms, prevalence, relationship with physical and psychological well-being, or the component of the menstrual cycle with which it is associated (Klebanov and Ruble, 1994). Although the vast majority of women do not experience menstrually related distress (e.g. Rivera-Tovar and Frank, 1990), menstruation continues to be positioned as a 'problem' (Delaney *et al.*, 1988) and there is almost no research on the normal experience of menstruation (Klebanov and Ruble, 1994; see Morse, Gross, Reilly, Dye, Vaneslow, Richardson and Dell in this volume).

Similarly, with few exceptions (e.g. Ruchala and Halstead, 1994), psychological research on childbirth has tended to focus, not on the experience of a major life transition among normal healthy women, but on an assumption that any distress associated with childbirth must be abnormal and is inevitably biological in origin (Lee, 1997; see Weaver and Ennis, in this volume). Illness-focussed research which identifies a group of women as suffering from 'postpartum depression' creates a false dichotomy between normal and abnormal adjustment and implies that women who are not completely happy in the challenging role of caring for a new baby must be suffering from an 'illness'. This assumption persists despite good evidence that depression among new mothers is best explained in terms of psychosocial factors (Kumar, 1994), including life events, lack of appropriate social support, and unrealistic expectations of motherhood (see Nicolson, in this volume).

Again, there is little research on normal adaptation to motherhood, research which does not pathologize individual women but examines them in their social and cultural context (see Woollett and Marshall, in this volume). The normal experience of new motherhood involves a high workload, anxiety, fatigue and disturbed sleep (Brown *et al.*,1994; Ruchala and Halstead, 1994), and depressed mood can be seen as a normal reaction to difficult circumstances, but this is not a perspective which is taken by mainstream psychological researchers.

Research interest in the menopause is also affected by assumptions about the relationship between women's hormones and their physical and emotional well-being (Carolan, 1994). Despite the arguments of non-interventionist feminist writers (e.g. Coney, 1993; Greer, 1991), the majority of psychological research is still based on the assumption that menopause is a medical problem (see Lyons and Griffin, and Dinnerstein, in this volume). Women in their middle years typically experience substantial changes in their personal lives (Greer *et al.*, 1987), but the majority are characterized by high levels of well-being (e.g. Lee, in press) and an optimistic perspective on their futures (e.g. Mitchell and Helson, 1990; see Gannon, in this volume).

Research which focusses on health rather than illness and which puts women's health and women's lives into context, examining not only women's reactions to their circumstances but the social structures which underlie those circumstances, is likely to provide a considerably more optimistic and empowering psychology of women's health.

Focus on context

As I have already argued, psychology's tendency to focus on subjective and intra-individual causes of distress (e.g. Prilleltensky, 1989) is socially conservative. When such an approach is applied to those whose lives are constrained by social inequities, it can lead to an implicit blaming of those people for their problems (Lee, 1998b; Stanton and Gallant, 1995). Women's behavior and their health are affected in obvious ways by violence, harassment and discrimination (Rodin and Ickovics, 1990). They are also affected more subtly by a sexist and heterosexist society, and by the myths and stereotypes which maintain inequality. Women's choices are constrained by a social context which values them for their appearance, for their relationships with men, for subservience and self-sacrifice (Lee, 1998b).

The interactions between this context and any individual woman's actions regarding her health are complex, but must be understood if the psychology of women's health is to reflect this reality. Women's health research needs to take account of systemic imbalances in power and resources between women and men, as well as of sociocultural assumptions about appropriate or expected behavior for women and men. When female college students' failure to choose majors which lead to high-paying employment is blamed on their personal failings (e.g. Lapan *et al.*, 1996), for example, it is important that these young women's choices are positioned in a context which has taught them that women should not excel in science, should work in fields which are extensions of their 'natural' role as carers, and should place other people's wishes before their own. Understanding and challenging this context may be far more useful in improving the social position of women than blaming the individual for faulty decision making.

As well as the broad issues of institutionalized sexism and inequity, anti-woman stereotypes contribute to a social context in which it can be difficult for women to feel positive about their bodies and themselves (Ussher, 1992). For example, myths surrounding menstruation (e.g. Brooks-Gunn and Ruble, 1986; Lovering, 1995; Treneman, 1988) define the female body as unclean and its natural processes as disgusting and shameful. The myth that motherhood is easy, natural, and the most important thing a woman can do in her life (Ussher, 1992) makes it unsurprising that depressed mothers experience high levels of guilt and self-blame (Beck, 1992). The cultural perception of menopause as necessarily representing deterioration, decline and the end of useful life, and of ageing as a disaster for women, contributes to older women's sense that they are not appreciated as full members of society (Lennon, 1987).

Focus on diversity

Mainstream psychology assumes that subjective experience is more important and more central to understanding the individual than are social or cultural circumstances (Sampson, 1988). Psychological research often gives the impression of having been carried out in a cultural vacuum: 'the particular historical period or sociocultural context in which data have been collected is ... of little or no importance' (Spence, 1985: 1285). Cultural context, social conditions, and cultural diversity are seen as unimportant in explaining behavior, and it is assumed that findings which hold in one society will require a mere shifting of surface detail to be applied anywhere (Jahoda, 1988).

Psychological theories frequently make the assumption that ethnic, religious or racial minorities, lesbians, and people with disabilities or special needs, are basically the same as the White, middle-class, heterosexual men who are implicitly regarded as 'standard' human beings. Where people differ from the implied 'norm', they are positioned as problematic and in need of investigation and correction (Harding, 1986). Thus, gender differences in self-esteem are explained in terms of women's deficiencies, rather than men's excessive self-confidence. Homosexuality is theorized while heterosexuality is assumed to be natural and in need of no explanation (Kitzinger and Wilkinson, 1993).

Research which does look at women's experiences in different cultures and under different circumstances, however, frequently undermines the assumption that established psychological 'truths' are universal. For example, women in Asian countries do not expect to experience negative symptoms of menopause, and report much lower levels of distress than do women from Western countries (e.g. Beyene, 1986; Boulet *et al.*, 1994; Ramoso-Jalbuena, 1994; Tang, 1994).

One of the most important topics for a feminist health psychology is that of the health of 'minority' women. This includes indigenous women,

women of color, immigrant women, and women members of ethnic, religious and cultural minorities (see Marshall and Yazdani, and Lapsley, Waimarie Nikora and Black, in this volume). Indigenous people, particularly those who have been colonized by members of dominant and powerful Western cultures, experience very poor health. In Australia, for example, indigenous women's life expectancy is 16.1 years less than that of non-indigenous women (Australian Bureau of Statistics, 1995). The social impact of racism means that members of ethnic minorities have reduced educational, vocational and developmental opportunities, and its effects on health and living conditions are well documented (e.g. Funkhouser and Moser, 1990). Racism combines with sexism to mean that minority women are doubly disadvantaged, both in social opportunities and in their health and well-being (Reid and Comas-Diaz, 1990).

Women members of non-racial minorities, particularly lesbians, also experience damaging stereotypes, prejudice and feared or actual violence, both within the health care system and in society more generally (Reid, 1994). Psychological interventions with lesbian women are frequently predicated on the assumption that their sexual orientation is their 'real' problem, regardless of their stated needs or their reasons for seeking counselling or health care (Stevens and Hall, 1991; see Mooney-Somers and Ussher, in this volume).

In general, psychological research has ignored members of minorities, but there is some feminist psychological research which explores diversity without stigmatizing those whose circumstances of birth or whose life choices have placed them as members of minority groups. Research on the experiences of eating disorders among immigrant women (e.g. Mumford *et al.*, 1991) and among lesbians and women of color (Thompson, 1992); research on menopause (Rothblum, 1994), motherhood (Patterson, 1995) and aging (Deevey, 1990) among lesbians, not only explores those women's experiences but also illuminates the entire subject area from a different perspective. Non-mainstream women are forced to discover new strategies for constructing their personal lives (Brown, 1995), strategies which may be of value for other women and men attempting to renegotiate roles and responsibilities in a more equitable way.

Focus on multiple methods

While mainstream psychology adopts the principles of objective empiricism, feminist approaches to scientific epistemology are based on the assumption that human observers are necessarily biased; the social sciences in particular cannot be conducted from a position of neutrality. Feminist standpoint epistemology rejects the notion of a single universal truth, holding instead that what is true depends on the point of view of the observer. Rather than attempting to remove one phenomenon from its context and study it in isolation, the individual-in-context is taken as the basic unit of analysis, and the role of social structures, social expectations, and social constructions in the development of individual patterns of behavior are explored (Striegel-Moore, 1994).

This perspective tends to be associated with the use of qualitative and exploratory methods, such as focus groups, semi-structured interviews and participant observation, and is associated with a collaborative relationship between researcher and participants (Riger, 1992; see Murray and Chamberlain, in this volume).

While traditionally empiricist methods are valuable for approaching particular types of question, qualitative methods allow researchers to explore diversity and context, or deal with issues which have been excluded from a traditional scientific approach (Bohan, 1992). Renzetti (1995), for example, has discussed the problems inherent in conducting research which aims to understand and assist lesbians who have been the victims of partner abuse. The stigmatized nature both of relationship violence and of lesbianism means that quantitative, positivist methods are very unlikely to obtain a sample of research volunteers or encourage them to describe their experiences. A feminist participatory research model may be the only way in which it is possible to establish the extent to which a phenomenon such as lesbian partner abuse is a serious problem and, if it is, to explore the contexts in which it arises and to explore approaches to it (Renzetti, 1995).

Several psychologists (e.g. Chesney and Ozer, 1995; Stanton and Gallant, 1995) have pointed to the need for a thoughtful combination of qualitative and quantitative methods, and a selection of method on the basis of what will most appropriately address the research question. It is also important to appreciate the different biases and thus the different outcomes which will arise from different approaches. Saint-Germain *et al.* (1993), for example, investigating the low level of health care usage among older Hispanic women, used both a written survey and a series of focus groups to make a direct comparison of quantitative and qualitative methods. Focus groups, they found, provided more information on community attitudes and group norms, while the survey provided information about individual needs.

Contextualist methods have never been mainstream in psychology, although they have been used for many years (e.g. Still and Costall, 1991). Contextualist research is based on a perception that the focus of analysis should not be the individual, but the individual-in-context (Morrisl, 1988), and uses methods which range from qualitative to behavioral (Jaeger and Rosnow, 1988). Contextualist methods have been used to understand the social context of individual choices such as contraceptive use (Landrine, 1995) and cigarette smoking (Biglan *et al.*, 1990), enabling an exploration of cultural factors which may differ from those experienced by researchers who are themselves members of dominant cultures (Henderson *et al.*,1992).

Focus on political implications

As I have already argued, mainstream psychological research maintains a pretence of political neutrality, but in fact serves to maintain the status quo in many ways. Interventions which focus on the individual ignore the economic structures and the sociocultural context which pressure those individuals into difficult situations. This is as much grounded in a political perspective as is research which directly confronts these social, political and economic realities.

Feminist research in the psychology of women's health must address central issues such as the subordinate social position of women, and the difficulties which women face when they attempt to make positive health-related changes in their own and others' lives. Such research must challenge cultural assumptions such as the naturalness of women's roles as subordinates and caregivers (Gallant *et al.*, 1994), and in doing so must challenge dominant attitudes to women.

Research which ignores the social context, which treats it as a neutral background or as an inevitable aspect of an immutable reality, is politically conservative, seeking solutions to human problems in individual adaptation rather than in social change (Bailey and Eastman, 1994; Kipnis, 1994; Spence, 1985). Conversely, a psychology of women's health which starts from the perspective of the social construction of womanhood is inevitably oriented towards social explanations and social solutions.

SUMMARY

For psychology to move towards a complete understanding of the factors which impinge on women's health, a diverse range of research strategies which take as wide a range of perspectives as possible is needed. Traditional science and feminism may have a somewhat uneasy relationship, but the development of an understanding of the social and psychological issues which affect women's health requires that researchers combine the two.

The thoughtful combination of quantitative and qualitative research, and the use of developmental models and longitudinal designs, can serve to develop a psychology of women's health which sets women in their social context, which understands their health as a complex, interactive and multiply determined phenomenon, and which recognizes the diversity of women's voices and experiences.

REFERENCES

Abel, E.K. (1991) *Who Cares for the Elderly? Public Policy and the Experiences of Adult Daughters.* Philadelphia, PA: Temple University Press

Adesso, V.J., Reddy, D.M. and Fleming, R. (Eds.) (1994) *Psychological Perspectives on Women's Health.* Washington, D.C.: Taylor & Francis

Ainslie, J. and Feltey, K.M. (1991) Definitions and dynamics of motherhood and family in lesbian communities. *Marriage and Family Review,* 17, 63–85

Alessandri, S.M. (1992) Effects of maternal work status in single-parent families on children's perception of self and family and school achievement. *Journal of Experimental Child Psychology,* 54, 417–433

Australian Bureau of Statistics. (1995) *Australian Women's Yearbook 1995.* Canberra: Australian Government Publishing Office

Badinter, E. (1981) *The Myth of Motherhood: An Historical Overview of the Maternal Instinct*, London: Souvenir Press

Bailey, J.R. and Eastman, W.N. (1994) Positivism and the promise of the social sciences. *Theory and Psychology*, 4, 505–524

Bailey, W.T. (1994) A longitudinal study of fathers' involvement with young children: Infancy to age 5 years. *Journal of Genetic Psychology*, 155, 331–339

Baruch, G.K. and Barnett, R. (1986) Role quality, multiple role involvement, and psychological well-being in midlife women. *Journal of Personality and Social Psychology*, 51, 578–585

Beck, C.T. (1992) The lived experience of postpartum depression: A phenomenological study. *Nursing Research*, 41, 166–170

Beyene, Y. (1986) Cultural significance and physiological manifestations of menopause: A bio-cultural analysis. *Culture, Medicine and Psychiatry*, 10, 47–71

Biglan, A., Glasgow, R.E. and Singer, G. (1990) The need for a science of larger social units: A contextual approach. *Behavior Therapy*, 21, 195–215

Bittman, M. (1992) *Juggling Time: How Australian Families Use Their Time*. Canberra: Australian Government Publishing Service

Bohan, J.S. (1992) Prologue: Re-viewing psychology, re-playing women – an end searching for a means. In J.S. Bohan (Ed.), *Seldom seen, Rarely Heard: Women's Place in Psychology* (pp. 9–53). Boulder, CO: Westview Press

Boulet, M.J., Oddens, B.J., Lehert, P., Vemer, H.M. and Visser, A. (1994) Climacteric and menopause in seven south-east Asian countries. *Maturitas*, 19, 157–176

Brooks-Gunn, J. and Ruble, D.N. (1986) Men's and women's attitudes and beliefs about the menstrual cycle. *Sex Roles*, 14, 287–299

Brown, L.S. (1995) New voices, new visions: Toward a lesbian/gay paradigm for psychology. In N.R. Goldberger and J. B. Veroff (Eds.), *The Culture and Psychology Reader* (pp. 559–574). New York: New York University Press

Brown, S., Lumley, J., Small, R. and Astbury, J. (1994) *Missing Voices. The Experience of Motherhood*. Melbourne: Oxford University Press

Caplan, P.J. and Hall-McCorquodale, I. (1985) Mother-blaming in major clinical journals. *American Journal of Orthopsychiatry*, 55, 345–353

Caradoc-Davies, T.H. and Harvey, J.M. (1995) Do 'social relief' admissions have any effect on patients or their care-givers? *Disability and Rehabilitation*, 17, 247–251

Carolan, M.T. (1994) Beyond deficiency: Broadening the view of menopause. *Journal of Applied Gerontology*, 13, 193–205

Carrigan, T., Connell, R. and Lee, J. (1985) Toward a new sociology of masculinity. *Theory and Society*, 14, 551–604

Cattanach, L. and Tebes, J.K. (1991) The nature of elder impairment and its impact on family caregivers' health and psychosocial functioning. *Gerontologist*, 31, 246–255

Chesney, M.A. and Ozer, E.M. (1995) Women and health: In search of a paradigm. *Women's Health: Research on Gender, Behavior, and Policy*, 1, 3–26

Coney, S. (1993) *The Menopause Industry*. Melbourne: Spinifex Press

Dalley, G. (1988) *Ideologies of Caring: Rethinking Community and Collectivism*. London: Macmillan

Davies, L. and Rains, P. (1995) Single mothers by choice? *Families in Society*, 76, 543–550

Deevey, S. (1990) Older lesbian women: An invisible minority. *Journal of Gerontological Nursing*, 16, 35–37

Delaney, J., Lupton, M.J. and Toth, E. (1988) *The Curse: A Cultural History of Menstruation*. Urbana, IL: University of Illinois Press

Dickerson, B.J. (Ed.) (1995) *African American Single Mothers: Understanding Their Lives and Families*. Thousand Oaks, CA: Sage

Ellis, J.B. (1994) Children's sex-role development: Implications for working mothers. *Social Behaviour and Personality*, 22, 131–136

Feinberg, L.F. and Kelly, K.A. (1995) A well-deserved break: Respite programs offered by California's statewide system of caregiver resource centers. *Gerontologist*, 35, 701–705

Funkhouser, S.W. and Moser, D.K. (1990) Is health care racist? *Advances in Nursing Science*, 12(2), 47–55

Gallagher-Thompson, D. and Steffen, A.M. (1994) Comparative effects of cognitive-behavioral and brief psychodynamic psychotherapies for depressed family caregivers. *Journal of Consulting and Clinical Psychology*, 62, 543–549

Gallant, S.J., Coons, H.L. and Morokoff, P.J. (1994) Psychology and women's health: Some reflections and future directions. In V.J. Adesso, D.M. Reddy and R. Fleming (Eds.),

Psychological Perspectives on Women's Health (pp. 315–346). Washington, D.C.: Taylor & Francis

Grbich, C.F. (1995) Male primary caregivers and domestic labour: Involvement or avoidance? *Journal of Family Studies*, 1, 114–129

Greer, G. (1991) *The Change*, London: Penguin

Greer, J.B., McKinlay, S.M. and Brambilla, D. (1987) The relative contributions of endocrine changes and social circumstances to depression in mid-aged women. *Journal of Health and Social Behavior*, 28, 345–363

Harding, S. (1986) *The Science Question in Feminism*. Milton Keynes,U.K.: Open University Press

Hawkins, A.J., Christiansen, S.L., Sargent, K.P. and Hill, E.J. (1993) Rethinking fathers' involvement in child care: A developmental perspective. *Journal of Family Issues*, 14, 531–549

Henderson, D.J., Sampselle, C., Mayes, F. and Oakley, D. (1992) Toward culturally sensitive research in a multicultural society. *Health Care for Women International*, 13, 339–350

Henderson, K.A. (1990) The meaning of leisure for women: An integrative review of the research. *Journal of Leisure Research*, 22, 228–243

Hooyman, N.R. and Gonyea, J. (1995) *Feminist Perspectives on Family Care: Policies for Gender Justice*, Thousand Oaks, CA: Sage

Howard, G.S. (1985) The role of values in the science of psychology. *American Psychologist*, 40, 255–265

Jaeger, M.E. and Rosnow, R.L. (1988) Contextualism and its implications for psychological inquiry. *British Journal of Psychology*, 79, 63–75

Jahoda, G. (1988) J'accuse. In M.H. Bond (Ed.), *The Cross-cultural Challenge to Social Psychology* (pp. 86–95). Los Angeles: Sage

Kipnis, D. (1994) Accounting for the use of behavior technologies in social psychology. *American Psychologist*, 49, 165–172

Kitzinger, C. and Wilkinson, S. (1993) Theorizing heterosexuality. In S. Wilkinson and C. Kitzinger (Eds.), *Heterosexuality: A Feminism and Psychology Reader* (pp. 1–32). London: Sage

Klebanov, P.K. and Ruble, D.N. (1994) Toward an understanding of women's experience of menstrual cycle symptoms. In V.J. Adesso, D.M. Reddy and R. Fleming (Eds.), *Psychological Perspectives on Women's Health* (pp. 183–221). Washington, D.C.: Taylor & Francis

Koch, P.B., Boose, L.A., Cohn, M.D., Mansfield, P.K., Vicary, J.R. and Young, E.W. (1991) Coping strategies of traditionally and nontraditionally employed women at home and at work. *Health Values: Health Behavior, Education and Promotion*, 15, 19–31

Kumar, R. (1994) Postnatal mental illness: A transcultural perspective. *Social Psychiatry and Psychiatric Epidemiology*, 29, 250–264

Landrine, H. (1995) Introduction: Cultural diversity, contextualism, and feminist psychology. In H. Landrine (Ed.), *Bringing Cultural Diversity to Feminist Psychology: Theory, Research and Practice* (pp. 1–20). Washington, D.C.: American Psychological Association

Lapan, R.T., Shaughnessy, P. and Boggs, K. (1996) Efficacy expectations and vocational interests as mediators between sex and choice of math/science college majors: A longitudinal study. *Journal of Vocational Behavior*, 49, 277–291

Lee, C. (1997) Social context, depression and the transition to motherhood. *British Journal of Health Psychology*, 2, 93–108

Lee, C. (1998a) *Alternatives to Cognition: A New Look at Explaining Human Social Behavior*. Hillsdale, N.J.: Lawrence Erlbaum Associates

Lee, C. (1998b) *Women's Health: Psychological and Social Perspectives*. London: Sage

Lee, C. (1999a) Health, stress and coping among women caregivers: A review. *Journal of Health Psychology*, 4, 27–40

Lee, C. (1999b) Health habits and psychological well-being among young, middle-aged and older Australian women. *British Journal of Health Psychology*, 4, 301–314

Lennon, M.C. (1987) Is menopause depressing? An investigation of three perspectives. *Sex Roles*, 17, 1–16

Lerner, J.V. and Galambos, N.L. (1986) Child development and family change: The influences of maternal employment on infants and toddlers. *Advances in Infancy Research*, 4, 39–86

Lovering, K.M. (1995) The bleeding body: Adolescents talk about menstruation. In S. Wilkinson and C. Kitzinger (Eds.), *Feminism and Discourse: Psychological Perspectives* (pp.10–31). London: Sage

Magni, E., Zanetti, O., Bianchetti, A., Binetti, G. and Trabucchi, M. (1995) Evaluation of an Italian educational programme for dementia caregivers: Results of a small-scale pilot study. *International Journal of Geriatric Psychiatry*, 10, 569–573

Marks, D.F. (1996) Health psychology in context. *Journal of Health Psychology*, 1, 7–22

Maume, D.J. and Mullin, K.R. (1993) Men's participation in child care and women's work attachment. *Social Problems*, 40, 533–546

Mischel, H.N. and Fuhr, R. (1988) Maternal employment: Its psychological effects on children and families. In S.M. Dornbusch and M.H. Strober (Eds.), *Feminism, Children, and the New Families* (pp. 191–211). New York: Guilford Press

Mitchell, V. and Helson, R. (1990) Women's prime of life: Is it the 50s? *Psychology of Women Quarterly*, 14, 451–470

Morrisl, E.K. (1988) Contextualism: The world view of behavior analysis. *Journal of Experimental Child Psychology*, 46, 289–323

Mumford, D.B., Whitehouse, A.M. and Platts, M. (1991) Sociocultural correlates of eating disorders among Asian schoolgirls in Bradford. *British Journal of Psychiatry*, 158, 222–228

Niven, C.A. and Carroll, D. (1993) *The Health Psychology of Women*. Chur, Switzerland: Harwood

Patterson, C.J. (1995) Families of the baby boom: Parents' division of labor and children's adjustment. *Developmental Psychology*, 31, 115–123

Peak, T., Toseland, R.W. and Banks, S.M. (1995) The impact of a spouse-caregiver support group on care recipient health care costs. *Journal of Aging and Health*, 7, 427–449

Phares, V. (1992) Where's poppa? The relative lack of attention to the role of fathers in child and adolescent psychopathology. *American Psychologist*, 47, 656–664

Phoenix, A., Woollett, A. and Lloyd, E. (Eds.) (1991) *Motherhood: Meanings, Practices and Ideologies*. London: Sage

Pohl, J.M., Given, C.W., Collins, C.E. and Given, B.A. (1994) Social vulnerability and reactions to caregiving in daughters and daughters-in-law caring for disabled aging parents. *Health Care for Women International*, 15, 385–395

Price, R.H., Friedland, D. S. and Vinokur, A.D. (1998) Job loss: Hard times and eroded identity. In J.H. Harvey (Ed.), *Perspectives on Loss: A Sourcebook* (pp. 303–316). Philadelphia, PA: Brunner/Mazel

Prilleltensky, I. (1989) Psychology and the status quo. *American Psychologist*, 44, 795–802

Ramoso-Jalbuena, J. (1994) Climacteric Filipino women: A preliminary survey in the Philippines. *Maturitas*, 19, 183–190

Reid, P.T. (1994) The real problem is the study of culture. *American Psycholgist*, 49, 524–525

Reid P.T. and Comas-Diaz, L. (1990) Gender and Ethnicity: Perspectives on dual status. *Sex Roles*, 22, 397–408

Renzetti, C.M. (1995) Studying partner abuse in lesbian relationships: A case for the feminist participatory research model. In C.T. Tully (Ed.), *Lesbian Social Services: Research Issues* (pp. 29–42). New York: Harrington Park Press

Repetti, R.L., Matthews, K.A. and Waldron, I. (1989) Employment and women's health. *American Psychologist*, 44, 1394–1401

Rich, A. (1982) *Of Women Born: Motherhood as Experience and Institution*. London: Virago

Riger, S.C. (1992) Epistemological debates, feminist voices: Science, social values and the study of women. *American Psychologist*, 47, 730–740

Rivera-Tovar, A.D. and Frank, E. (1990) Late luteal phase dysphoric disorder in young women. *American Journal of Psychiatry*, 147, 1634–1636

Rodin, J. and Ickovics, J.R. (1990) Women's health: Review and research agenda as we approach the 21st century. *American Psychologist*, 45, 1018–1034

Rothblum, E.D. (1994) Transforming lesbian sexuality. *Psychology of Women Quarterly*, 18, 627–641

Ruchala, P.L. and Halstead, L. (1994) The postpartum experience of low-risk women: A time of adjustment and change. *Maternal-Child Nursing Journal*, 22, 83–89

Saint-Germain, M.A., Bassford, T.L. and Montano, G. (1993) Surveys and focus groups in health research with older Hispanic women. *Qualitative Health Research*, 3, 341–367

Sampson, E.E. (1988) The debate on individualism: Indigenous psychologies of the individual and their role in personal and social functioning. *American Psychologist*, 43, 15–22

Sarason, S.B. (1981) An asocial psychology and a misdirected clinical psychology. *American Psychologist*, 36, 827–836

Social Trends. (1995) *Social Trends on CD-ROM – Version 1.0*. London: Central Statistical Office of the U.K.

Spence, J.T. (1985) Achievement American style. *American Psychologist*, 40, 1275–1295

Stanton, A.L. and Gallant, S.J. (Eds.) (1995) *The Psychology of Women's Health: Progress and Challenges in Research and Application*. Washington, DC: American Psychological Association

Stevens, P.E. and Hall, J.M. (1991) A critical historical analysis of the medical construction of lesbianism. *International Journal of Health Services*, 21, 291–307

Still, A. and Costall, A. (Eds.) (1991) *Against Cognitivism: Alternative Foundations for Cognitive Psychology*. New York: Harvester Wheatsheaf

Striegel-Moore, R. (1994) A feminist agenda for psychological research on eating disorders. In P. Fallon, M.A. Katzman and S.C. Wooley (Eds.), *Feminist Perspectives on Eating Disorders* (pp. 438–454). New York: Guilford Press

Tang, G.W.K. (1994) The climacteric of Chinese factory workers. *Maturitas*, 19, 177–182

Thompson, B.W. (1992) 'A way outa no way': Eating problems among African-American, Latina, and White women. *Gender and Society*, 6, 546–561

Tizard, B. (1991) Employed mothers and the care of young children. In A. Phoenix, A. Woollett and E. Lloyd (Eds.), *Motherhood: Meanings, Practices and Ideologies* (pp. 178–194). London: Sage

Treneman, A. (1988) Cashing in on the curse. In L. Gamman and M. Marshment (Eds.), *The Female Gaze: Women as Viewers of Popular Culture* (pp. 153–165). London: Women's Press

Trippet, S.E. (1994) Lesbians' mental health concerns. *Health Care for Women International*, 15, 317–323

Ussher, J.M. (1992) Reproductive rhetoric and the blaming of the body. In P. Nicolson and J. Ussher (Eds.), *The Psychology of Women's Health and Health Care* (pp. 31–61). Basingstoke, U.K.: Macmillan

Wearing, B. (1984) *The Ideology of Motherhood*. Sydney: Allen & Unwin

Youngblut, J.M., Loveland-Cherry, C.J. and Horan, M. (1991) Maternal employment effects on family and preterm infants at three months. *Nursing Research*, 40, 272–275

Youngblut, J.M., Loveland-Cherry, C.J. and Horan, M. (1994) Maternal employment effects on families and preterm infants at 18 months. *Nursing Research*, 43, 331–337

CHAPTER 2

QUALITATIVE METHODS AND WOMEN'S HEALTH RESEARCH

Michael Murray and Kerry Chamberlain

INTRODUCTION

The past decade has seen a rapid growth of interest in qualitative methods of research. This can be confusing not least because the term 'qualitative methods' conceals a variety of theoretical and methodological assumptions. The aim of this chapter is to briefly review the assumptions and background of this turn to qualitative research, and discuss issues in the application of different qualitative methods to women's health research.

The growth of interest in qualitative research is part of the broader turn to language throughout the social sciences. During the past century the social and behavioral sciences have based themselves on the natural sciences. This approach contained various assumptions not least that the world exists independently of human consciousness and that it can be described objectively in terms of quantitative variables. This approach is summarized in Newton's supposed discovery that when he 'opened the book of nature, he found it was written in the language of mathematics' (see Polkinghorne, 1990). This equating of science with mathematics was reflected in all of the human sciences but especially in psychology (see Danziger and Dzinas, 1997). Smith (1997) in his history of the human sciences argues that this fascination for measurement and quantification was what united psychology as a discipline.

Admittedly, enthusiasm for this approach was not uniform and there has consistently been a minority of researchers who have adopted another approach. The debate about the nature of the human sciences has a long history. In the last century, the German philosopher Wilhelm Dilthey distinguished between two broad approaches: the natural scientific (*Naturwissenschaften*) and the human-scientific (*Geisteswissenschaften*). The former approach sought explanation (*Erklarung*) through identifying causes of events. Thus we had the link with measurement and the experimental method. This approach was the dominant approach to psychology in the English-speaking world. The latter was more concerned with understanding (*Verstehen*) and sought the meaning of events. This latter approach was dismissed as unscientific. However, the recent turn to language in the human sciences has renewed debate about the nature of science and the value of non-quantitative methods. As Polkinghorne (1990) retorted to Newton: 'When we open the book of the human realm, we find that it is written in natural language'.

APPROACHES TO QUALITATIVE RESEARCH

Within qualitative research there is a variety of theoretical perspectives. Henwood and Pidgeon (1994) identify three main approaches: empiricist, contextualist, and constructivist. The first group of researchers works within or is strongly influenced by the natural scientific approach and strives to describe in as much detail as possible people's belief systems. There is particular concern about issues of validity, reliability and generalizability of the findings. There is less concern with the social, historical or cultural context within which the accounts are generated. A popular method within this approach is that of content analysis which involved a quantification of people's accounts. This approach tends to be more descriptive than analytic.

The contextualist approach is particularly concerned with the production of inter-subjective meaning and the development of theory which integrates the detail and complexity of participant's worlds. A commonly used method is that of grounded theory (Glaser and Strauss, 1967). This method has traditionally adopted an inductive strategy which attempts to identify the underlying structure in what people have to say. This version has many similarities with the more traditional empiricist approach. A more constructionist version of this method argues that the researcher engages with the text and explicitly brings his or her assumptions to the task, in an attempt to construct, rather than discover, a meaningful account of the phenomenon in question. An example of this is the study by Costain Schou and Hewison (1998) which involved an analysis of the accounts patients gave of cancer. In reading these accounts, the authors deliberately brought previous work on coping with cancer to their interpretation.

The constructionist perspective has become increasingly influential as a framework for qualitative research. Researchers adopting this perspective draw on the methods of conversation analysis, discourse analysis, ethnomethodology, rhetoric, and narrative (Potter, 1996). All of these approaches are united by a common concern with language and its role in the construction of reality. Thus, rather than attempting to map various cognitive structures onto discourse, the constructionist considers the social usage of language. A more critical constructionism begins with an awareness of the material differences in the world particularly in terms of gender, class, and ethnicity. The aim is to link people's perspectives with their material circumstances and with the broader power structures operating in society (for examples, see Marshall and Yazdani, Malson, Mooney-Somers and Ussher, in this volume)

Admittedly, these approaches are not discrete. In particular, as researchers have become more sophisticated in the epistemological arguments they have tended to move away from the standard positivist approach and to become more sympathetic to various contextualist and constructionist approaches. For example, in the study by Costain Schou and Hewison (1998) they draw upon ideas from both grounded theory and discourse analysis.

In women's health research there has been enthusiastic usage of qualitative methods. This research can be broadly grouped into positivist/empiricist and contextualist/constuctionist. The former group included many researchers who were located in epidemiology and public health departments which historically have conducted extensive surveys of health behaviors and attitudes. Within this framework researchers often conducted qualitative work, generally based on some form of content analysis, in preparation for the surveys which were considered the 'real' work which could identify causal links. Gradually, these pilot studies became more substantial in themselves but their theoretical framework remained unchanged (see Lee, in this volume).

More recently, researchers located in social science and nursing departments have encouraged a more radical break with the natural science tradition and have embraced the various contextualist/constructionist approaches. Women have led the way in developing this form of qualitative research. This was apparent in the sex ratio of the submissions to a recent special journal issue on qualitative research (Murray and Chamberlain, 1998). There are various possible reasons for this enthusiasm, which are related to characteristics of the qualitative research endeavor. We use these characteristics to organize our following comments.

UNDERSTANDING EXPERIENCE

Qualitative research provides insights into individual perspectives that are rendered invisible in the aggregation which typifies quantitative approaches (Griffin and Phoenix, 1994), providing space for the description and interpretation of subjective experience. This is particularly important for women's health where historically the majority of health research has been conducted by men. In some cases, noticeably coronary heart disease, the research has also focussed predominantly *on* men. The reference point for health and illness has been gendered and biased towards masculinity (see Lupton, 1994a, for an overview of the historical location of women and the female body in medicine). The increasing feminization of academia has led to calls for listening to the female voice, and for investigating women's understandings of health and illness. Such an approach is obvious in the title of Freedman's (1998) article, 'Why don't they come to Pike street and ask us?' This research demonstrated that the beliefs and values of Black middle-class women differed markedly from the understandings of the dominant White medical community, and showed how this discrepancy functioned to compromise these women's health care.

Commonly, the theoretical framework underlying this approach is phenomenology, which in currently popular versions attempts to provide a detailed description of the life-world or lived experience of the individual, without contamination from the researcher's presuppositions or understandings (see Crotty, 1998, for a critique of the 'new' phenomenology and a general discussion of the assumptions underlying phenomenology). However, various methodologies have been utilized to examine subjective experience. Stevens and Doerr (1997), for example, took a narrative approach to examine women's subjective experiences of being informed that they were HIV-positive. Not surprisingly, there were differences between these women in their accounts of the impact and meaning of this event. The event was seen as a confirmation by some, an epiphany by others, and a calamity for others again. The impact of learning about their sero-status provoked changes that involved fears of transmission of the virus, increased suicidal ideation, and destabilisation of relationships and living conditions. Kearney, Murphy, and Rosenbaum (1994) used grounded theory methods to document how the experience of mothers using crack cocaine contradicted the stereotype of these women as selfish, uncaring and neglectful. Rather, their accounts revealed how they valued motherhood and worked to protect both their children and their identities as mothers from the influence of cocaine use. Studies such as these open up understandings that are ignored or avoided in non-qualitative approaches to research.

INVOLVING CONTEXT

Health and illness are not abstracted entities, but always occur within the broader context of living (Radley, 1999) and 'are made tangible when reflected through other realms or spheres of everyday life' (p. 27). Many qualitative research approaches specifically strive to account for health and illness within their context, and to incorporate the social realms of life into their explanations. For example, Mauthner (1998) argues explicitly for a relational view, taking 'relationship' as the unit of analysis, to examine post-natal depression. By examining this phenomena in the context of women's relationships to themselves, to others, and to cultural and structural opportunities and constraints, a more elaborated account of the processes of post-natal depression is available. Hallberg and Carlsson (1998) explored the experience of pain in fibromyalgia. They not only considered beliefs about the origins and nature of the pain experience, but also how pain affected family and social life for these women. Their findings authenticate Radley's argument as to how illness is reflected and presented through domains of life. Similarly, in a study of young women's accounts of sexual activity, Woollett, Marshall and Stenner (1998) located those accounts, not only within the context of their relations with young men, but also within the context of their family life. Woollett *et al.* also relate their findings to the nature of the group interview context, within which the young women co-constructed their accounts, and suggest that in their study this 'may be the reason why sexual knowledge was a common theme but sexual pleasure was rarely discussed' (p. 380). Not only are accounts constructed in a context, but the context in which they occur configures both the content and function of the account. Related to this, Costain Schou and Hewison (1998) discuss how their texts can be read 'both as constituitive of personal meaning and as social texts ... the social world both constructs and is constructed by the storying of individuals' (p. 310). Hence, although there are differences between methods in how context is drawn on, reflected, or involved in findings, it is an essential issue for qualitative research.

VALUING CONTRADICTION AND COMPLEXITY

One frequent criticism of quantitative methods is that they conceal variability and contradictions in people's beliefs and practices. The very nature of the statistical procedures used leads to a concealment of inconsistencies. Quantitative methods strive for generalizations and the construction of grand theories. Billig (1982) makes a similar claim in his discussion of the structure of ideology. Although ideological formations may strive to reduce contradictions, Billig (1987) argues that these are pervasive in everyday life and are expressed in popular rhetoric. Thus, particular accounts are not reflective of certain fixed attitudes, but rather, of a stance adopted in a particular context. Discourse analysis in particular highlights the variabilities and inconsistencies in popular accounts, and seeks to explain their functions. For example, Bransen (1992) identified three different genres of explanation that were drawn on by women to explain the role that menstruation plays in their lives: the 'emancipation' genre positioned the woman as self-assured and responsible, actively coping with any distress associated with menstruation; the 'natural' genre viewed menstruation as natural, an essential part of being a woman, and serving a cleansing function for the body; and the 'objective' genre constructed menstruation, and the body, as a separate object belonging to experts, such as medical practitioners. Although these accounts differed, Bransen notes that they are redolent with bodily separation from 'me' and all provide space for doctors to have a role in the treatment of menstrual disorders. This research reveals that there is a plurality of ways to account for menstruation, which can be drawn on in different situations to warrant and legitimate different positions.

Similarly, Lupton (1994b), in an analysis of discourses of breast cancer in the press, documents the multiple and contradictory positions created for women and the difficulties this produces for them. Press accounts only portrayed women suffering from breast cancer when they could be constructed as triumphant, brave fighters and so exemplify the benefits of early detection and medical intervention. Alongside the promotion of this 'technological imperative' ideology, a discourse of 'victim-blaming' was used to make women personally responsible both for avoiding the disease (by living an appropriate lifestyle and undergoing detection screening) and for contracting the disease (by failing to do these things). Lupton notes how these press accounts were 'underpinned by subtle messages regarding women's role in society, women's bodies, and femininity' (p. 86), and offers some speculations on how these representations affect women. Researches like these document how multiple meanings can be revealed through appropriate analyses, and also document how meanings are never absolute but are contextual, multiple, and often contradictory (see Malson, Wilkinson, and Woollett and Marshall, in this volume).

CHALLENGING ESTABLISHED POSITIONS

Critical qualitative methods are premised upon the realization that issues of power permeate all social relationships. Analyses focused on these issues regard knowledge and social practice as historically and socially located, as politically, ethnically and culturally shaped, and gendered. Sybylla's (1997) analysis of menopause, for example, argues how the 'truth' or 'reality' of menopause is historically situated, and how current understandings of menopause have been constituted by medicine. By exposing this view, Sybylla is able to argue that the 'experts' can be challenged and that women can create their own 'truth' about menopause. In Western society the dominant discourse about health and illness is that of medicine. This discourse, with all its assumptions about the biomedical nature of disease and the doctor-patient relationship, has become commonplace. As Herzlich and Pierret (1984) argue, this discourse can become disempowering.

Caught between their undecipherable physical experience and the ordered and dominating language of science, today's sufferers are often at a loss to know whether they can speak, to whom they can speak, and how they can speak. (p. xi)

Within women's health research there is particular interest in what is sometimes called post-structuralist discourse analysis. This approach, drawing its inspiration from Michel Foucault, is concerned about how everyday discourses reproduce power relations in society. Lovering (1995) provides an example of work using this approach. She was interested in how power relations were reflected in adolescents' discourse about the body. She analysed adolescents' talk about growing up and demonstrated that teenage girls found it difficult to articulate the bodily dimensions of the process. She argued that this difficulty is because 'the female body is culturally constructed as embarrassing and somehow shameful whereas the male body is not' (p. 22). In their talk, the male body was constructed as ordinary whereas the female body was extra-ordinary: 'for the boys it (menarche) seemed like some kind of amazing but 'far-fetched' female science fiction. For the girls it was more like a fascinating but frightening gothic horror story' (p. 24). The everyday language used to describe the changing female body was one of negativity whereas that for the male body was one of strength. Since language does not simply reflect reality but constitutes it, Lovering argued that these everyday adolescent discourses not only reflected the inferior position of women in society but also constituted the very identity of the teenage girls. This research project can be considered as part of the wider excavation of the oppressive nature of patriarchal sexist discourse.

In another example, Marchant-Haycox and Salmon (1997) analysed medical consultations between women, who were presenting with menstrual problems in the absence of confirmed pathology, and their gynecologists. Marchant-Haycox and Salmon specifically contrasted dialogues that either led to hysterectomy or did not. Their findings revealed that the women and doctors acted as opponents, both using specific strategies to assert their authority – women as experts on subjective symptoms and doctors as experts on the inside of the body. The findings demonstrated how different stances during the consultation led to different outcomes. Consultations leading to hysterectomy were characterized by dialogues where the women imposed a biomedical model, presented deteriorating symptoms and distress, placed responsibility on the doctor for treatment, and criticized conservative treatment. Consultations leading to conservative treatment were characterized by the doctor assessing authority to look inside the body in order to assert that it was normal. In this example we can see how power and knowledge are not simply hierarchical but are, as Foucault has argued, intertwined and threaded throughout the technologies, practices and discourses of medicine. We can also begin to see how points of resistance to established and taken-for-granted understandings emerge.

EMPOWERING PARTICIPANTS

Power in social relationships includes that between the researcher and the researched. Whereas the aim of the quantitative researcher is to maintain control, the qualitative researcher is much more flexible. The research setting becomes an opportunity for the research participant to articulate her views, and for the researcher to allow and ensure that this happens. One research strategy which specifically locates empowerment as a desired outcome is emancipatory action research. This approach, concerned particularly with interventions, seeks 'to analyse critically and to change conditions of everyday practice so that these are fairer and more equitable' (Curtis *et al.*, 1999: 203). The process involves researcher and researched as equal collaborators, focussing on shared concerns, and jointly developing desired outcomes and change. Curtis *et al.* (1999) describe how this strategy was used in promoting cervical screening for women living in caravan parks. Malterud and Hollnagel (1998) used this method within their own medical practices to develop ways of facilitating consultation talk about health resources with their women patients. Outcomes proposed from the research involved moving the forms of talk from disease to health, valuing the woman's assessment of her own situation, and accepting that options for answers were the responsibility of the patient rather than the doctor. They conclude that changes of this nature are empowering for women in general practice consultations.

PROVIDING A VOICE

Bound up with issues of valuing experience, challenge, and empowerment is a concern to provide research participants with a 'voice' – to allow the concerns of women participating in research to be heard on their own terms. It is argued by some qualitative researchers (e.g. Mishler, 1986) that this opportunity for the research participant to express her own voice is both liberating and empowering. However, other qualitative researchers are much more circumspect. For example, Bhavnani (1990) argues that without an explicitly political interpretive framework the new voice can be one of reaction and actually disempowering (see also Lovering, 1995). It is for this reason that feminist researchers adopt a more explicitly political framework for their research.

Much feminist qualitative research has attempted to subvert the dominant discourse of biomedicine by asserting the value of the female voice. However, as the contributors to a recent volume edited by Lock and Kaufert (1999) have stressed, this alternative voice is often contradictory. The challenge for the feminist qualitative researcher is to develop a perspective which is both grounded in the everyday experience of women but also critical of the power structures in society. The last decade has seen the publication of many accounts of illness, especially breast cancer, by women. In reviewing a sample of these, Murray (1997) noted that they were the beginnings of a new discourse that provided words for something which was frequently cloaked in silence. The publication of the survivors' accounts of breast cancer was the beginning of an alternative strategy. Individually, these accounts had limited impact, but together they became part of a much wider political campaign to mobilize women against breast cancer. These personal voices became part of a wider political voice. Kaufert (1998) has vividly described this transformation: 'replacing the image of the tragic victim – passive, hidden, suffering – with a woman visible, angry, demanding attention' (p. 307). The personal stories became part of a wider 'oppositional discourse' (p. 288). The work of many qualitative researchers has become part of that discourse.

While qualitative researchers have placed an emphasis on everyday discourse, they are not interested just in the actual spoken words, but in the frequent absence of words about particular issues or in particular circumstances. Such a silence can also be interpreted as a form of resistance by women rather than a sign of ignorance. In her study of working class women and cervical cancer, Balshem (1991) found that the women were initially reluctant to talk. Balshem suggested that this was a means by which the women demonstrated their opposition to the dominant biomedical culture without verbally formulating an alternative. Anthropologists have commented on the use of this form of practice which has been pathologized as passive aggression. Lock and Kaufert (1998) refer to the work of Scott (1985) in Malaysia. He described not only silence but also activities such as gossip, slander, foot-dragging and theft as 'weapons of the weak' – a means of resistance. While these strategies may be dismissed as means of accommodation with the system, the challenge to qualitative researchers is to identify alternative strategies.

SUMMARY

As we indicated earlier, there is a diversity of alternative theories and methods for qualitative research (Murray and Chamberlain, 1999). We have not tried to give a systematic account of these, although we have touched on a number in passing. Rather, we have chosen to discuss a set of issues, enmeshed in qualitative research practice, which we believe provide reasons for the popularity of qualitative approaches in women's health research. As can be seen from our discussion, these issues are highly inter-related and cannot easily be separated. It is also not surprising to find that these issues, which we have considered as integral components of qualitative research, resonate with the values and underlying assumptions shared by feminist researchers – that women are worthy of study in their own right, that a critical analysis of gender and power is essential, and that there is a need to empower women and promote change. It is because these issues *are* central that qualitative approaches will continue to be used to promote and develop research in women's health.

REFERENCES

Balshem, M. (1991) Cancer, control, and causality: talking about cancer in a working class community. *American Ethnologist*, 18, 152–172
Bhavnani, K.K. (1990) What's power got to do with it? Empowerment and social research. In

I. Parker and J. Shotter (Eds.), *Deconstructing Social Psychology* (pp. 141–152). London: Routledge

Billig, M. (1982) *Ideology and Social Psychology*. Oxford: Basil Blackwell

Billig, M. (1987) *Arguing and Thinking: A Rhetorical Approach to Social Psychology*. Cambridge: Cambridge University Press

Bransen, E. (1992) Has menstruation been medicalised? Or will it never happen? *Sociology of Health and Illness*, 14, 98–110

Costain Schou, K. and Hewison, J. (1998) Health psychology and discourse: Personal accounts as social texts in grounded theory. *Journal of Health Psychology*, 3, 297–311

Crotty, M. (1998) *The Foundations of Social Research: Meaning and Perspective in the Research Process*. Thousand Oaks, CA: Sage

Curtis, S., Bryce, H. and Treloar, C. (1999) Action research: Changing the paradigm for health psychology researchers. In M. Murray and K. Chamberlain (Eds.), *Qualitative Health Psychology: Theories and Methods* (pp. 202–217). London: Sage

Danziger, K. and Dzinas, K. (1997) How psychology got its variables. *Canadian Psychology/Psychologie canadienne*, 38, 43–48

Freedman, T. (1998) "Why don't they come to Pike street and ask us?": Black American women's health concerns. *Social Science and Medicine*, 47, 941–947

Glaser, B.G. and Strauss, A.L. (1967) *The Discovery of Grounded Theory: Strategies for Qualitative Research*. Chicago: Aldine

Griffin, C. and Phoenix, A. (1994) The relationship between qualitative and quantitative research: Lessons from feminist psychology. *Journal of Community and Applied Social Psychology*, 4, 287–298

Hallberg, L. and Carlsson, S. (1998) Psychosocial vulnerability and maintaining forces related to fibromyalgia: In-depth interviews with twenty-two female patients. *Scandinavian Journal of Caring Sciences*, 12, 95–103

Henwood, K.L. and Pidgeon, N.F. (1994) Qualitative research and psychological theorizing. *British Journal of Psychology*, 83, 97–111

Herzlich, C. and Pierrett, J. (1984) *Illness and Self in Society*. Baltimore, MD: Johns Hopkins University Press

Kaufert, P.A. (1998) Women, resistance, and the breast cancer movement. In M. Lock and P.A. Kaufert (Eds.) *Pragmatic Women and Body Politics* (pp. 287–309). Cambridge: Cambridge University Press

Kearney, M., Murphy, S. and Rosenbaum, M. (1994) Mothering on crack cocaine: A grounded theory analysis. *Social Science and Medicine*, 38, 351–361

Lock, M. and Kaufert, P.A. (Eds.) (1998) *Pragmatic Women and Body Politics*. Cambridge: Cambridge University Press

Lovering, K.M. (1995) The bleeding body: Adolescents talk about menstruation. In S. Wilkinson and C. Kitzinger (Eds.), *Feminism and Discourse: Psychological Perspectives* (pp. 10–31). London: Sage

Lupton, D. (1994a) *Medicine As Culture: Illness, Disease, and The Body in Western Societies*. London: Sage

Lupton, D. (1994b) Femininity, responsibility, and the technological imperative: Discourses on breast cancer in the Australian press. *International Journal of Health Services*, 24, 73–89

Malterud, K. and Hollnagel, H. (1998) Talking with women about personal health resources in general practice: Key questions about salutogenisis. *Scandinavian Journal of Primary Health Care*, 16, 66–71

Marchant-Haycox, S. and Salmon, P. (1997) Patients' and doctors' strategies in consultations with unexplained symptoms: Interactions of gynecologists with women presenting menstrual problems. *Psychosomatics*, 38, 440–450

Mauthner, N.S. (1998) "It's a woman's cry for help": A relational perspective on postnatal depression. *Feminism and Psychology*, 8, 325–355

Mishler, E. (1986) *Research interviewing: Context and narrative*. Cambridge, MA: Harvard University Press

Murray, M. (1997) *Narrative Health Psychology*. Visiting Scholar Series, No 7, Department of Psychology, Massey University, New Zealand

Murray, M. and Chamberlain, K. (Eds.) (1998) Special issue: Qualitative research. *Journal of Health Psychology*, 3 (3)

Murray, M. and Chamberlain, K. (Eds.) (1999) *Qualitative Health Psychology: Theories and Methods*. London: Sage

Polkinghorne, D.E. (1990) Language and qualitative research. *Theoretical and Philosophical Psychology,* 10 (2), 3–24
Potter, J. (1996) Discourse analysis and constructionist approaches: theoretical background. In J.T.E. Richardson (Ed.) *Handbook of Qualitative Research Methods for Psychology and the Social Sciences.* Leicester: BPS Books
Radley, A. (1999) Social realms and the qualities of illness experience. In M. Murray and K. Chamberlain (Eds.), *Qualitative Health Psychology: Theories and Methods* (pp. 16–30). London: Sage
Smith, R. (1997) *The Norton History of the Human Sciences.* New York: Norton
Stevens, P. and Doerr, B. (1997) Trauma of discovery: Women's narratives of being informed they are HIV-infected. *AIDS Care, 9,* 523–538
Sybylla, R. (1997) Situating menopause within the strategies of power: A genealogy. In P.A. Komersaroff, P. Rothfield and J. Daly (Eds.), *Reinterpreting Menopause: Cultural and Philosophical Issues* (pp. 200–221). London: Routledge
Woollett, A., Marshall, H. and Stenner, P. (1998) Young women's accounts of sexual activity and sexual/reproductive health. *Journal of Health Psychology, 3,* 369–381

CHAPTER 3

CHOOSING A LIFE SPAN DEVELOPMENTAL ORIENTATION

Sheila Greene

INTRODUCTION

What is meant by a developmental perspective?

In this chapter I will argue that life span developmental psychology provides a helpful knowledge base and conceptual orientation for those psychologists and allied practitioners who are attempting to effect change in women's health, whether it be physical or mental health. However, of the available developmental models, some are more satisfactory than others. I will look first at the need for a developmental perspective and what that might mean. It is in fact not at all easy to state simply what is meant by a developmental perspective: developmental psychologists cannot agree among themselves about the definition of development and thus about the subject matter of their discipline. As Overton commented in a 1997 paper, 'perhaps the only thing developmental psychologists agree upon is that their discipline is about change and some seem ambivalent about that'. *Most* will accept a minimal definition to the effect that developmental psychology is 'the study of age-related change'.

So, putting the ambivalence aside for the moment, let us concentrate on change. Change is not only the core construct for developmental psychology but also for all applied branches of psychology which entail interventionist practice. It is, of course, perfectly possible for other professionals to effect change in people's attitudes, feelings and behaviors without a psychological understanding of change and without an explicit commitment to a psychological method of effecting change. For example, change is brought about all the time by medication. Moreover some specifically psychological interventions aim to produce a change in behavior without reference to the person's life course. Behaviorist and cognitive-behaviorist therapies would be of this type. The developmental perspective, on the other hand, places change firmly in a time and life-history context.

Thus it is undoubtedly the case that change can be effected without reference to the significance of that change to the life course. I would suggest, however, that most psychologists are dealing with changes which are not of transient significance but which are embedded in the flow of a person's life and in a system of meanings which can only be fully grasped by seeing them in the context of the person's life story. Developmental psychology is unique within psychology in that it has taken as its concern the dynamic nature of human life and experience. As Jaeger and Rosnow (1988) state 'Human acts or events are active, dynamic and developmental moments of a continuously changing reality'. To a greater or lesser extent developmental psychology takes on board the consequences of our existence in time, including such issues as the expression of genetic make-up in time, the growing and aging body, the significance of the timing of events and the person's own construction of their life story and the interpretations and expectations that surround that story. For example, in relation to the individual's perspective on time and aging, the meaning of the menopause to a woman of 50 is highly dependent on her attitude to aging, her feelings about her looks, how she locates herself in time as well as on the views of the society around her. Cross-cultural studies which focus on the meaning of menopause and the meaning of aging in non-western societies inform us that in societies where menopause is the start of a socially more highly valued stage of the life cycle, negative emotions and symptoms are rarely reported (Gannon, 1999). As an example of change in meanings across the individual's life course, the meaning of disability has been shown to be very different to a child than to that same person when she becomes a teenager (Varma, 1996). Timing is another developmental issue. The 'same' event can look very different depending on the age and life situation of the person involved, thus becoming pregnant at 15 is clearly entirely different in significance in Western society to becoming pregnant at 25 or at 45 (Berryman, 1991). To take another developmental issue, the extent of continuities in attitudes and behavior from earlier to later stages of life, recent work on depression shows that by the teenage years ruminative patterns of thought, which have been found by researchers like Nolen-Hoeksema to be typical of depression in adult women and not typical of male depressives, are already emerging (Nolen-Hoeksema and Girgus, 1994). Such findings can be examined in the light of research, for example that by Gilligan and her colleagues, on adolescence as a developmental transition which has a particular meaning and resonance for girls in Western society (Brown and Gilligan, 1992).

It is important for those who set out to facilitate psychological change to do their best to understand those processes which bring about psychological change and those which prevent people from changing in ways which they or others may consider desirable. Attempting to understand patterns of change and the reasons for continuities and discontinuities, constancy and change, are central concerns to the developmentally oriented psychologist. The counselor or therapist is engaged, whether they see it that way or not, in the active manipulation of change-producing factors and therefore need to be clear as to what they think those factors are and to be working within an explicit and enabling conceptual framework. This is a point of view that would have been perfectly familiar to Freud. His developmental theory is hard to disentangle from his propositions about therapy and psychoanalysis. Most theorists who have been influential in founding different psychotherapeutic schools have either an explicit developmental theory or a theory about change at their core, and this goes for the behaviorists who are and were by their own lights anti-developmental. My argument is the theory of change best suited to the practitioner is a developmental theory or at least a theoretical orientation which incorporates a developmental perspective. Only such a theory can capture the dynamic and changing nature of women's health and the influences upon it across the life course. Experiences and cognitions which relate to the past, the present and the future contribute in important ways to determining the person's state of mind and emotional equilibrium, her attitude towards her body and her health. Behavior patterns and attitudes which are counter-productive in relation to a woman's mental and physical health can only be fully understood in relation to her pre-existing and ongoing life story. Where discontinuity exists, such as a biological catastrophe brought about by accident or illness, it must be located in the stream of events and meanings that constitute the life course

So, the developmental perspective acknowledges the time-embedded nature of existence but those who adopt this perspective do so in very different ways. There is no one developmental perspective and some developmental perspectives are, I would suggest, inadequate and misleading. They are inadequate as models of the human life course and doubly inadequate as models of the woman's life course. For example, Erikson, who is often cited as the founding father of life span psychology and set the scene for the new discipline for many years has produced interesting work, but, in many ways, has exerted an unfortunate influence on the field. His patronizing and universalizing view of the female personality was spelt out in his 1968 paper 'Womanhood and the inner space' (Erikson, 1968). In this paper he argues that a woman cannot achieve identity until she has arrived at an intimate relationship with a man, proposing that she 'holds her identity in abeyance as she prepares to attract the man by whose name she will be known, by whose status she will be defined, the man who will rescue her from emptiness and loneliness by filling the inner space'. I am not arguing, then, for the adoption of the traditional life span developmental model epitomized by theorists like Erikson.

NOT JUST ANY OLD DEVELOPMENTAL MODEL

As I have said, life span developmental theories are of varying quality and value. In order to distinguish between the different models, it is useful to employ some system for categorizing them. A number of different categorizations are possible but the most simple involves a distinction between the extent to which there is an emphasis on internal or external determinants of change. This does not map onto the old nature-nurture split, since many theories focussing on internal sources of growth and change, such as Freud's, focus on psychological rather than biological processes. Freud emphasizes intra-psychic processes and the formative role of early experience in shaping the individual's personality for the entire life course. In the developmental literature the most frequently used term to identify this type of theory is ontogenetic, which has been used by such meta-theoreticians as Featherman and Lerner (1985), Dannefer (1984) and Levenson and Crumpler (1996). I find the term ontogenetic somewhat unsatisfactory since etymologically it means development of the individual which is, after all, what developmental psychology is about, but I will use it nonetheless since it seems to be the most common term. Other theorists use different terms to label much the same approach to explaining development. For example, Lewis (1997) uses the term 'organismic' and Labouvie-Vief and Chandler (1978) 'idealistic'. It is the ontogenetic-organismic-idealistic model which is most identified with developmental psychology and is also, in my opinion, the model which is the most problematic. The central principle for ontogenetic models is that 'development is driven by and constrained by age-linked intrinsic imperatives' (Levenson and Crumpler, 1996) Ontogenetic theorists include Vaillant, Kohlberg and Erikson. Many of the child development theories which are most familiar – like Piaget's – are ontogenetic theories also. Ontogenetic theories are distinguished by their reliance on stages to describe development. They are also committed to the discovery of universal principles of development. Development is seen as progressive and as progressing towards an idealistic end-point. As Piaget pointed out – and this would apply to an ontogenetic theory specifically – 'a developmental theory does not so much rest upon its initial stage as hang from its highest one' (Piaget, 1970). So for Piaget that end-point is formal operational thinking, for Kohlberg post-conventional moral reasoning, for Erikson ego-integrity, etc.

There are numerous problems attached to this approach to the understanding of development. Amongst other things, propositions derived from it are prescriptive and normalising. They tell us what the right course should be and that those who do not follow the right path are deviant. As Jerome Bruner says 'these are developmental psychologies which assume that there is one way up, one kind of human nature that will express itself but for the fact that there are interfering injustices, degradations or differential opportunities that prevent its coming up' (Bruner, 1986). Ontogenetic theories are the main target of the critical developmental psychology movement represented by such writers as Morss (1996), Walkerdine (1988), Bradley (1989) and Burman (1994) who characterize most developmental thinking as prescriptive, reductive and permeated with biological thinking. 'Ontogenetic reductionism', Dannefer stated in 1984, is 'the practice of treating socially produced and patterned phenomena as rooted in the characteristics of the individual organism' (Dannefer, 1984).

A pressing question for those interested in a woman-centered perspective is the extent to which a model constrains and oppresses women, and it is the case that ontogenetic theorising is prone to do this as a direct result of its commitment to the idea of one true developmental path and its tendency to use the developmental path of the male as the norm. From a feminist perspective, one response to the male-centered theorizing so evident in the work of writers like Levinson, Erikson and Kohlberg is that of Carol Gilligan who was one of the first to critique developmental theorizing for its focus on men's lives and its privileging of men's values. In her book *In a Different Voice* she states: 'My goal is to expand the understanding of human development by using the group left out in the construction of theory to call attention to what is missing in this account' (1982). Since 1982 she and her co-workers have approached that goal in a number of ways but it could be argued that adding 'the missing group' is not enough. A different kind of theorizing is what is required, not the same kind of theorizing with women rather than men as the focus. Gilligan has certainly received a great deal of criticism for her essentialism, that is, seeing the psychological attributes which she describes in women as fixed attributes of all women. Much of the criticism Gilligan has received is in line with the recognition of the inherent problems to be found in developmental theories from Freud and Piaget onwards, but little attention has been paid by her critics to the possibility of working towards a developmental psychology which can offer a better understanding of women's lives. Instead, developmental theorizing has been rejected as fundamentally flawed.

There may be more potential for women in the second type of model which developmental meta-theorists counterpose to the ontogenetic type. This is variously labelled sociogenic (Featherman and Lerner, 1985; Levenson and Crumpler, 1996), contextual (Labouvie-Vief and Chandler, 1978) or contextualist (Lewis, 1997). Unlike the ontogenetic model where minimal attention is given to external factors, sociogenic models place almost total emphasis on social determinants. There are many forms of sociogenic theory, ranging from those models where development is seen as influenced by social factors working with organismic factors in a kind of add-on fashion to transactional-systemic-ecological theories such as those offered by Ford and Lerner (1992) and by Bronfenbrenner (1979) to the post-modern theories promoted by theorists like Harre and Gillett (1994) and Gergen (1991)where the person's subjectivity is seen socially constructed. According to Levenson and Crumpler the key-note of sociogenic theories is heterogeneity, both of pathways and of goals. There are no invariant sequences and no blatant value presuppositions about desirable pathways or endpoints. Some would argue that sociogenic theories are not truly developmental in that they are not concerned with universal, invariant sequences nor with the processes by which humans develop psychologically, i.e. evolve to a more advanced state. After all, the dictionary definition of development is an unfolding, a realization of inherent potential. On the other hand, I would see some sociogenic theories as developmental in the broad sense of the word, that is pertaining to age-related change, concerned with the description and explanation of diachronic processes such as growth, age, aging, history and the connection over time between different events and experiences. The developmental psychologist is also appropriately concerned with the human psychological relationship with time as it relates to the life course, and how that relationship is socially construed and structured. Thus these theories are not developmental if one uses 'developmental' in the traditional and ontogenetic sense but in the broader sense which I have outlined.

The contextual or sociogenic perspective is not without its own problems. Levenson and Crumpler identify such approaches as being 'heavily invested in social relativism'. Extreme social constructionism does land one in the wilderness of social relativism and also appears to run the risk of obliterating the unified self and the person as agent from the picture altogether. Gergen seems to see life in the post-modern world as a playground in which we can discursively, playfully construct and re-construct our multiple selves. His refusal to deal with material reality and the sometimes horrific constraints it places on people may be seen by some as unhelpful, particularly to those whose everyday reality is oppressive and/or difficult to change. Anti-developmental social constuctionists seem to want to eliminate the person's material reality and actual experiences from the picture altogether. Take as an example this statement from Lewis: 'History, as a construction, allows for the possibility that our actual histories have relatively little bearing on development. Rather, current behavior is influenced by what we think our histories were' (Lewis, 1992). A person's constructions of events are undoubtedly of great importance and people to a large extent 'story' their past, but Lewis' obliteration of personal history fails to take account of what we know about the long-term consequences of events such as, for example, child sexual abuse or educational disadvantage.

Both ontogenetic and sociogenic theories can leave certain central issues out of account such as questions of value and the bases for social action. From this point of view, ontogenetic theories can be seen as making normalizing assumptions about values and sociogenic theories eschew questions of value altogether. On the other hand, Jerome Bruner has argued that developmental psychology is inevitably engaged with issues concerning ethics and values. In fact he goes so far as to say that developmental psychology is 'a policy science' (1986). He means by this 'a science whose intrinsic object is not simply to describe but to prescribe optimal ways of achieving certain outcomes'. I have accused ontogenetic models of being prescriptive but their kind of prescriptiveness is very different from the kind of prescriptiveness acknowledged by Bruner to be at the heart of any application of developmental psychology. Erikson and like-minded theorists assume they are describing what is natural and good: Bruner, and those who follow his line of thinking, know they are describing what is constructed and that, as far as values are concerned, what is seen to be good must be negotiated – not asserted from hegemonic positions of authority. Clearly therefore, there is no one policy but our policies, our notions of what is desirable and what is undesirable for the society we live in and for its citizens inevitably influence our theorizing and practice. What we are obliged to do, once our awareness of the dangers of unexamined ideological and epistemological assumptions has been raised, is to make our assumptions clear and our politics clear and to appreciate, in the way that ontogenetic theories about universal pathways and endpoints do not, that our values may be very different from those held by others.

The other problem, perhaps, is that of personal agency. Both the ontogenetic and socio-genic models tend to see human behavior as determined by factors beyond the person's control. Both, it could be argued fail to fully take on board the possibility of the person acting to change her behavior and her life course. The concept of personal agency is also challenged by the post-modern social constructionist challenge to the idea of the unitary self. Talk of the distributed self, multiple selves, and saturated selves takes away from the traditional Western notion of personhood and challenges our respect for the dignity and uniqueness of the individual. There is of course a long tradition of reductionistic models of the person in psychology including behaviorism, mechanistic cognitivism and evolutionary theory, the last being very popular once again among psychologists, including developmental psychologists. As a counterbalance to both the determinism of ontogenetic theories and the postmodern tendency to obliterate the self and undermine notions of personal agency some developmentalists have begun to discuss counter-deterministic, liberatory or emancipatory models of human development (Teo, 1997; Levenson and Crumpler, 1996)

A critical perspective on developmental theorizing is required, one which is mindful of developmental psychology's conservative and normalizing tradition. Nonetheless, a developmental perspective is a necessary response to the reality of the dynamic, time-embedded and time-limited nature of our existence, however variously that nature is construed. A developmental perspective is needed wherever we are engaged in 'identifying and realizing the conditions under which the interests and developmental possibilities of individuals can be enhanced' (Dannefer, 1996) – anywhere where we have been invited to engage in the process of helping people to change in the way that they want to change.

SUMMARY

In recent years considerable strides have been made in challenging the view of women's health which sees physical and mental distress and difficulties only as problems which arise from deficiencies in women's constitution or psychological make-up. Social and contextual analyses which draw our attention to women's life-styles and gender roles and to the importance of public discourse in shaping behaviors and attitudes relevant to health have served as a crucial counter-balance to traditional individual-centered and medical perspectives. However, a social-contextual analysis which does not address explicitly the fact that we exist in time, personal and historical, is in danger of being static and insensitive to the dynamics of change in a woman's life.

Therapists from a variety of different persuasions have long been in the habit of paying close attention to their client's 'history' and some have explicitly drawn upon developmental theories, such as those of Erikson or Levinson. In this sense practice may be understood as arising from a developmental framework. However traditional developmental theories are both deterministic and normalizing. On the other hand, a critical contextual perspective on change across the life course can provide the therapist with a framework which increases her understanding of the possibilities for change in women's lives and the possibilities for maximizing women's health at all stages of the life course.

REFERENCES

Berryman, J. (1991) Perspectives on later motherhood. In A. Phoenix, A. Woollett and E. Lloyd (Eds.), *Motherhood: Meanings, Practices and Ideologies*. London: Sage

Bradley, B.S. (1989) *Visions of Infancy: A Critical Introduction to Child Psychology*. Cambridge: Polity Press

Bronfenbrenner, U. (1979) *The Ecology of Human Development: Experiments by Nature and Design*. Cambridge MA: Harvard University Press

Brown, L.M. and Gilligan, C. (1992) *Meeting at the Crossroads*. Cambridge MA: Harvard University Press

Bruner, J. (1986) Value presuppositions of developmental theory. In L. Cirillo and S. Wapner (Eds.), *Value Presuppositions in Theories of Human Development*. Hillsdale, NJ: Erlbaum

Burman, E. (1994) *Deconstructing Developmental Psychology*. London: Routledge

Dannefer, D. (1984) Adult development and social theory: A paradigmatic reappraisal. *American Sociological Review*, 49, 100–116

Dannefer, D. (1996) Commentary. *Human Development*, 39, 150–152

Erikson, E.(1968) Womanhood and the inner space. In E. Erikson, *Identity, Youth and Crisis*. London: Norton

Featherman, D.L. and Lerner, R.M. (1985) Ontogenesis and sociogenesis: Problematics for theory and research about development and socialization across the lifespan. *American Sociological Review*, 50, 659–676

Ford, D.H. and Lerner, R.M. (1992) *Developmental Systems Theory: An Integrative Approach*, London: Sage

Gannon, L. (1999) *Women and Aging: Transcending the Myths*. London: Routledge

Gergen, K. (1991) *The Saturated Self: Dilemmas of Identity in Contemporary Life*. New York: Basic Books

Gilligan, C. (1982) *In a Different Voice*. Cambridge, MA: Harvard University Press

Harre, R. and Gillett, G. (1994) *The Discursive Mind*. London: Sage

Jaeger, M.E. and Rosnow, R.L. (1988) Contextualism and its implications for psychological inquiry. *British Journal of Psychology*, 779, 63–75

Labouvie-Vief, G. and Chandler, M. (1978) Cognitive development and life-span developmental theories: Idealistic versus contextual perspectives. In P. Baltes (Ed.), *Life-Span Development and Behaviour*, Vol. 1. New York: Academic Press

Levenson, M.R. and Crumpler, C.A. (1996) Three models of adult development. *Human Development*, 39, 135–149

Lewis, M. (1992) Commentary on Lerner and von Eye. *Human Development*, 35, 44–51

Lewis, M. (1997) *Altering Fate: Why the Past Does Not Predict the Future*. New York: Guilford Press

Morss, J. (1996) *Growing Critical: Alternatives to Developmental Psychology*. Hove: Lawrence Erlbaum Associates,

Nolen-Hoeksema, S. and Girgus, J.S.(1994) The emergence of gender differences in depression during adolescence. *Psychological Bulletin*, 115, 424–443

Overton, W. F. (1997) Marching towards the millennium. *Human Development*, 40, 102–108

Piaget, J. (1970) *Structuralism*. New York: Basic Books

Teo, T. (1997) Developmental psychology and the relevance of a critical metatheoetical reflection. *Human Development*, 40, 195–210

Varma, V. P. (1996) *The Inner Life of Children with Special Needs*. London: Whurr

Walkerdine, V. (1988) *The Mastery of Reason*. London: Routledge

CHAPTER 4

YOUNG ASIAN WOMEN AND SELF-HARM

Harriette Marshall and Anjum Yazdani

INTRODUCTION

Epidemiological studies conducted in the U.K. suggest that the incidence of self-harm is on the increase. Self-harm has been identified as more prevalent among women than men (D'Alessio and Ghazi, 1993; Hodes, 1990). In contrast young men are thought to be at greater risk of completed suicide (Babiker and Arnold, 1997; Health of the Nation, 1994). The term self-harm is commonly used interchangeably with parasuicide to cover a broad range of behaviors which include 'self-poisoning' such as overdosing, 'external self-injury' such as cutting or burning the skin and sometimes eating 'disorders' including anorexia and bulimia (Favazza, 1987). Self-harm is usually taken as having a different set of meanings from suicide attempt where the primary aim is not self-annihilation.

The 'professionalization' of the understanding of self-harm through the reliance on academic and clinical definitions, categories and sub-divisions as above, exercises various constraints on the understanding of self-harm (Arnold, 1995; Johnstone (L), 1997; Johnstone (S), 1997; Pembroke, 1994). The conceptualization of self-harm (more often referred to in the clinical literature as deliberate self-mutilation) as psychopathology, indicative of a personality disorder (Walsh and Rosen, 1988) or a disorder of impulse control (Pattison and Kahan, 1983) is a particular construction of self-harm which warrants specific forms of interventions. For example, in focussing on the act of self-harming and on the individual as mentally ill, 'treatment' offered tends to focus on lessening the individual's self-harming behavior (through drug treatment and/or by means of behavioral modification). This can be seen in some researchers' concern with eliminating positive external reinforcement for self-harming and recommendations to health care professionals to 'reduce the level of care, empathy and concern as much as possible for the period immediately following the infliction of the wound' (Walsh and Rosen, 1988). It has been argued that clinical analyses of self-harm and recommendations such as those above serve to exacerbate rather than alleviate women's distress (Liebling *et al.*, 1997).

Alternatively it has been argued that a starting point for researchers and health carers should be to ask people who self-harm how they make sense of self-harm and what health care and support (if any) they require (Nelson and Grunebaum, 1971; Bristol Crisis Service for Women, 1995). Researchers who have taken this approach have most usually interpreted self-harm as instrumental, expressive of, and a means of coping with distress (Favazza and Rosenthal, 1993).

Hence, it has been argued that an understanding of self-harm will not be reached outside the broad sociocultural circumstances of its occurrence and without a concern for the network of relationships within which a person who is self-harming is enmeshed (Hodes, 1990; Johnstone (L), 1997). Stressful life experiences which include sexual abuse, neglect and/or emotional abuse set a context for many self-reports of self-harm (Arnold, 1995). Childhood sexual and physical abuse are frequently cited as factors leading to self-harm (for example, de Yong, 1992; Lindberg and Distad, 1985; van der Kolk et al., 1991). Other research has linked self-harm with experiences of rape and trauma in adulthood (Pitman, 1990).

CULTURAL FACTORS

Rates of self-harming according to different sub-groupings of women vary. For example, researchers argue that the incidence of self-harm is greatest among young women where pressures to conform to normative femininity, especially regarding their sexuality and roles within the family, exert conflicting demands and expectations. Young women living in the family home and lacking financial independence may experience the intersection of gender and age as combining to restrict their autonomy in ways that can be experienced as unbearable. Rates of self-harm are disproportionately high among lesbians and, as above, explanations center around the pressures to conform to heterosexuality and femininity as oppressive (Davies and Neal, 1996). Recently concern has been expressed at the incidence of self-harm among South Asian young women (in a U.K. context the ethnic category 'South Asian' refers broadly to those peoples whose familial or cultural backgrounds originate from the subcontinent of India, Pakistan and Bangladesh).

Hospital-based analyses of admissions data and surveys carried out in school settings in the U.K. suggest that Asian young women born in the U.K. are at higher risk for attempted suicide and self-harming as compared with White Caucasian and African-Caribbean young women (Handy et al., 1991; Merrill and Owens, 1986, 1988; Mumford and Whitehouse, 1988; Pendall et al., 1991). This has been explained in terms of self-harm in Asian young women in the U.K. as representing a replication of White Caucasian women's expressions of distress through a process of acculturation to Western cultures (Burke, 1976; Hodes, 1990; Merrill and Owens, 1988). Asian women born in the Indian subcontinent and living in the U.K. have a suicide rate which is approximately two to three times higher than the national average of England and Wales. One in five Asian female suicides are by self-burning, a method of suicide which is rare within the white population (Soni-Raleigh, 1996). It has been suggested that Asian-born women may bring their culturally specific patterns of suicide with them when they migrate.

A prevalent explanation for distress leading to suicide attempt and self-harm in Asian communities in the U.K. has been in terms of 'culture clash' (Bhadrinath, 1990; Merrill and Owens, 1988). This is an explanation applied to members of minority ethnic communities living in the U.K. experiencing as problematic a disjuncture between the values of 'traditional Asian' culture with those of 'British'/'Western' culture (Babiker and Arnold, 1997). 'Culture clash' explanations have been applied to Asian young women as occurring around aspects of their lives pertinent to observing Asian cultural and religious customs and traditions (see for example Bhadrinath, 1990; Merrill and Owens, 1986). It has been argued that there are specific aspects of Asian cultural traditions which place particularly high demands on young Asian women and men but that Asian women experience greater pressures than men due to 'rigidly defined roles in Indian society' (Soni-Raleigh and Balarajan, 1992: 367). In these respects explanations for self-harm and suicide invoked in relation to 'Asian' communities differ in focus from those most usually drawn on for the indigenous 'White' population.

However there are difficulties in establishing the nature of the relationship between self-harm and specific sociocultural groupings. First, there are methodological problems. The reliance on quantitative methods means that it is the researcher who conducts the coding of factors alleged to be *culturally* linked to self-harm (and coding is usually retrospective, for example by means of hospital records). Consequently research reports rarely allow any check to be made of the precision of the original notes nor examination of the move from data set to research conclusions. But in addition little or no consideration is given to the *meanings* of self-harm nor whether or how culture might be implicated for those women who are self-harming. Instead most usually it is left to the researcher to assess whether or not 'culture' is causative of self-harm.

Second, conceptually, the term 'culture' in 'culture clash' inevitably singularizes both 'Asian' and 'British'/'Western' culture. Often culture is made into a variable to allow comparisons to be made between for example 'Asian' and 'White' women. Hence, diversity within cultural grouping such as that shaped by religion, caste and class is masked (Brah, 1996, Marshall *et al.*, in press). To date, research studies on self-harm which conceptualize culture as complex, relational and diverse are few (Burman *et al.*, 1998: 233).

WHY ASIAN WOMEN SELF-HARM

Below we include some extracts from interviews conducted as part of a larger research project on young Asian women and self-harm based in the borough of Newham, East London, U.K. A full report of this research is presented elsewhere (Newham Innercity Multifund and Newham Asian

Women's Project, 1998). The context for the research was one where (mental) health and social care providers in East London have reported concerns about research suggesting that admissions for Asian women who had self-harmed were over-represented, and that their average age tended to be younger than for other ethnic groups (Howard, 1997). Clinicians note also that for various reasons not all cases of self-harm in the general population and in Asian women in particular may be reaching accident and emergency departments. Additionally, contact with (mental) health and therapeutic services tends to be at a late stage, often not until a crisis point is reached, for example, following an overdose, suggesting that Asian women do not find support services sufficiently accessible to permit earlier contact.

In our research study we took the broad category 'Asian' to include a heterogeneous population diversified along the lines of religion, class, migration patterns, language, traditions and identifications. In the context of East London, South Asian communities represent the largest sector of the minority ethnic population comprising in order of size, Indian, Pakistani and Bangladeshi communities. We utilized qualitative methods in order to explicate the meanings of self-harm as deployed by women in contact with the clinical services and with a history of self-harm (and in relation to accounts from (mental) health service providers including general practitioners (GPs), psychiatrists and counselors). In particular we examine whether, when and how various construals of self-harm are related to aspects of 'Asian' culture. In this respect the research worked, with possible relationships between two contested and somewhat 'slippery' concepts – culture as in 'Asian' young women and 'self-harm' behaviors, in order to then consider how health services might be improved for Asian women who require help for self-harm.

We present extracts from an interview with one participant referred to as 'Meena' (aged 20) who self-defined her ethnicity as Bengali and her religion as Muslim. We illustrate her various accounts of self-harm and the place of culture in Meena's narratives of circumstances of self-harm in relation to pathways to care. As in other self-reports, Meena locates meanings of self-harm within contexts characterized as distressful and emotionally painful. Within these contexts, one account of self-harming is that although it is physically painful, self-harm is associated with relief from emotional pain. In this respect the exercise of cutting the body is implicated as a vehicle for the expression and release of emotional distress.

Meena: I remember one time when I had an argument and I couldn't find anything else and I dug a screw driver into myself so badly that I made a dent into my elbow…bruising until it cut into my skin. It was really painful afterwards but it helped me to feel good…When I start cutting myself then it sort of, all my anger gets channelled into that cut and I look at the blood and I think it's a release … from emotional pain to physical, and the physical's at least over and done with. The emotional is so hard to deal with.

Self-harming is not construed as problematic in itself, but as a means of managing distressing circumstances. This account of self-harm is self-focused rather than directed towards seeking a response from others. In contrast, and present also in Meena's interview, is an account of self-harm as a catalyst of change, a means of communicating distress which serves to elicit 'outside' intervention and help.

Meena: But at least doing that [self-harm], I've got some counselling, at least I've got somewhere I can come and talk, unload a little bit. But…if I hadn't done that, I don't think I would even have had that and I would have lost all channels of contact with everyone outside.

Constructed as a trigger for the involvement of external forms of support, self-harm shows up positively as an effective means of communication. This account is qualitatively different from the interpretation of self-harm in some psychological/clinical literature as 'attention-seeking behavior' and Meena makes reference to nurses' use of this account:

Meena: When I was in hospital the nurses were saying, 'Oh, don't pay no attention to her, she's just attention seeking'.

Health carer's construal of self-harm as 'simply' attention seeking can serve to justify their withdrawal of support at a time when it is greatly needed, and hence reproduce experiences of distress on the part of women receiving care. In addition this particular categorization of self-harm as attention seeking raises issues regarding the relationship between academic/clinical analyses of self-harm and how these inform health practice. Making sense of self-harm as being a 'childish' call for attention which should be ignored undermines any understanding of self-harm as intricately entangled with issues of control: a third account of self-harm extant in Meena's interview. In this sense, located within circumstances where a lack of control is reported, the body is rendered a last site where a degree of self-determination can be exercised.

Meena: While I was cutting I felt more in control, whereas before I'd cut I sort of felt like 'Oh God', there's nothing I can control.

Control is multi-facted and also registers in terms of engaging in behaviors that others cannot control, becoming 'more' in control (as above), losing control through self-harming in order to then later get back into control. Other accounts articulate contradictions regarding self-control. While women position themselves as having agency, making decisions about the frequency, severity and extent of cutting, and hence construct the act of cutting, for example, as *taking* control they also discuss self-harming as potentially getting out of their control. A fourth account of self-harm juxtaposes self-harm through cutting with taking an overdose. Both acts are located in relation to feelings of desperation and despair, but a statement of intention of wanting to die is made in relation to the latter act. Accounts such as Meena's offer support for arguments of diverse meanings of self-harm which differ from suicide attempt. Also of note in the interviews are narratives of self-harm which, over time, include cutting, overdosing, patterns of self-imposed eating restrictions and/or starvation. This raises questions regarding the usefulness of a clinical pre-occupation with delineating and categorizing different forms of self-harm.

So far we have presented various different meanings within Meena's self-report of self-harm. Clearly we do not claim to have exhausted all potential accounts. We present the accounts above as illustrative of the complexity of self-harm, as serving different functions and as embedded within a narrative of various experiences within particular circumstances in Meena's past and present life. Articulated within contexts of abuse and distress, self-harm shows up positively as a means of managing distress. Evident across the narratives in our study are lengthy histories of sexual and physical abuse, sometimes starting in childhood, alternatively/additionally emotional and/or physical abuse from boyfriends/husbands in adulthood are enmeshed with self-harm. In this respect these narratives are not specific to Asian women and accord with the self-accounts of White Caucasian and Afro-Caribbean young women's self-reports of self-harm (Arnold, 1995; Bristol Crisis Service for Women, 1995; Pembroke, 1994; Spandler, 1996).

These patterns in the self-reports offer support for arguments for *not* starting with an expectation of cultural differences but allowing for the exploration of commonalties in the accounts of the meanings of self-harm across cultural communities. In terms of academic research, social care and mental health practice caution is called for in attending to the various factors that may play a part in accounting for Asian women's self-harm rather than privileging culture-specific explanations.

In other respects in the narratives, the articulation of self-harm with Asian culture is manifest in varying ways. Usually *particular* pressures are referenced as problematic as emanating from cultural expectations and values, many of which center around the family. For instance, the narratives make reference to traditional 'Asian' familial expectations for Asian young women to get married by a certain age as causative of pressure and distress. This is explained in terms of failure to fulfil gendered familial expectations being of issue not only for the individual or their family but related more widely to the importance of maintaining the family's good standing and honor – *izzat* – within the community.

Meena: My mother's thing is, 'So long as you've got a man there for supporting you' and my father's, 'I try to shut the community up and the community won't shut up until you get married because you're 20 now and you're not married…The family problems are still ongoing at the moment, they're probably one of my big stresses at the moment, but they believe that the answer to everything is just get married, everything will be fine, you're an Asian girl, just get married.

Culturally linked concerns for *not* bringing shame – *sharam* – to the family's reputation are imbricated in narratives of the origin and maintenance of distress and in accounting for difficulties in disclosing distress within the family (especially with regard to abuse). Consequent on the priority accorded upholding the family's reputation, 'Asian' families are construed as unwilling to admit to, and silencing of attempts to disclose, abuse and/or distress. Particular to these accounts is the consideration of obstacles facing a young woman who attempts to seek help when she is positioned within a community characterized in general terms as both 'tight knit' and 'problem/abuse free'. The narratives of pathways to care report most-usual first contact as following a crisis situation, with accident and emergency departments. This suggests particular difficulties for Asian women accessing help and support.

A further culturally linked concern relates to a cultural prescription that problems (including issues of abuse and consequent health and/or mental health problems) should be contained within the family. This has various implications. The delineation of potential sources of support in terms of 'outsiders' or 'insiders' shows up in the narratives of pathways to help and is of central importance in considering ways of developing health provision for young Asian women who are self-harming. Seeking help from 'outside' the community (whether from counselors, teachers or (mental) health carers) is designated as inappropriate. However, making contact with 'outside' support constitutes a turning point in some of the narratives of self-harm. This suggests that the development of accessible and confidential services (other than accident and emergency departments in hospitals) as initial points of contact and sources of support becomes important. These could include telephone help lines in addition to readily available information (in schools/colleges, health and community centers) about ways of accessing support and details of local services, both statutory and non-statutory. Sites for the location of support are also an issue. In the accounts, schools/colleges constitute safe places to discuss distress, self-harm, and mental health issues more generally, with school doctors and/or counselors.

Within the narratives, seeking help from 'insiders' (professionals construed as belonging within the cultural community) is often of issue but sometimes rendered limited for various reasons. For example, Meena evaluates negatively the care offered by her family doctor, a general practitioner (GP) and by an Asian psychiatrist. Construed as an 'insider', likely to take up a position and values similar to her father, advising 'go back to your family' and advocating marriage (factors that Meena associates with distress, see above), she reports their help as limited:

Meena: I went to see my GP once to ask him for anti-depressants but he's a family GP so he knows my parents pretty well, so he was... saying 'Oh go back to your family and everything will be fine, you're just being silly. He's Asian as well...Even after my suicide [attempt], you know I experienced quite a few professionals even after, whose approach of it all is just go back to your family. I even

*had one told me to get married. I was supposed to go back for a second appoint-
ment and I didn't. He [psychiatrist] was an Asian male...I didn't even want to
see him again because I knew what he was going to say and there's no point.
Because he's like my father and he understands what my father's doing and he
understands [it's for] the right reasons.*

An 'insider's' help can be characterized as 'unsafe' as they might inform
the family of the consultation. In part, issues of broken confidentiality
arise from contestation regarding whether (mental) health matters are pri-
vate/individual matters or to be shared within the family. An individual's
disclosure of abuse/distress/self-harm can be read as an act which brings
shame to the family/community and hence is not an individual but a cul-
tural/moral concern. In this respect cultural constructions of an individual's (mental) health concerns as matters to be shared within the family
raise issues regarding professional ethics. In terms of implications for
health care, the reported worries about GPs breaking confidentiality suggests the need for information on patient rights to be available in health
care surgeries, including information on how to register at another GP
practice where the family is not registered, becomes a priority.

A further and related issue is how culturally sensitive care might best
be realized in health/psychotherapeutic settings. In the accounts diverse
and complex considerations are brought to bear in formulating preferences regarding health professionals' credentials for offering good care.
These include whether Asian professionals are best suited to working
with Asian patients/clients given their understanding of cultural concerns, or limited by sharing their adherence to values/expectations linked
with distress. These discussions constitute a challenge to assumptions that
cultural matching equates with culturally sensitive care. Meena's consideration below makes reference not only to cultural background but also to
the (mental) health carer's particular views and values.

*Meena: I think I would have preferred to see somebody white, but I don't know as
long as whoever I did, if I did see someone Asian, then it had to be somebody who
looked at it with an open mind. I didn't want another… 'Go home, your family
knows best' sort of thing.*

We read these accounts as offering support for the importance of avoiding
homogenizing conceptualizations of culture within service provision.
Health and counseling services which allow for *choice* regarding ethnic
background, age group and language spoken by the service provider are
a priority. Give the account of self-harm as associated with control, the
importance of service providers leaving control in the hands of the
patient/client, not undermining their requests for help by making culturally linked or other suggestions but working with her in helping her gain
further control, becomes a priority.

Although we have identified a recurring association of aspects of Asian
culture with pressures and distress leading to self-harm, and in relation to

difficulties in accessing help and support, along with other researchers we would call for caution in concluding that Asian culture or aspects of Asian culture is indeed pathogenic. Our research was focussed on problematic concerns and our participants came from a particular clinical population, accessed through mental health services following crisis situations. Hence it is perhaps unsurprising that the accounts most usually centered around talk of Asian culture (and Asian families) as restrictive and 'closed' rather than as supportive and engaged. But also the focus placed on the family as a context of distress merits attention. The family is one prime context where contestation over young women's rights, autonomy and independence is regularly reported, regardless of cultural background. When a young woman reports arguments with her parents this does not necessarily indicate that she is involved in a culturally specific 'clash'. The dispute might relate to more general inter-generational differences. Or, as others have argued, a 'clash' might be more an expression of the political than the cultural – the restrictions on a young woman's opportunities as shaped by sexism and racism in a broader socio-political context, as expressed within the context of the family (Littlewood, 1995). In other words when working with self-reports – young Asian women's meanings of self-harm – it is important to consider broad-based gendered and/or racialized restrictions exercised on young women that may be implicated in distress rather than jumping to a conclusion that distress resides within the immediate familial relations and context.

SUMMARY

In line with this latter argument the prevalence of use of 'culture as pathogenic' in Asian young women's accounts of self-harm is unsurprising. Historically in the U.K. a culture clash explanation is widely utilized in accounting for a range of 'problems' in social science, medical/clinical literature, research and practice (some of which is cited above). Some participants reported carers' ready use of this analytic in the way they 'made sense' of Asian women's self-harm and the form of care they offered to them as patients/clients. Taking the meanings of self-harm as diverse and variously articulated with aspects of 'Asian culture' our conclusions echo those of other researchers who argue for health-training initiatives around culturally sensitive care which make clear that there is no fixed cultural template to be applied when working with Asian patients/clients requiring support for distress/self-harm. In addition, we argue for the importance of service providers attending closely to the client's agenda, her particular meanings of self-harm and health needs in supporting and caring for Asian women engaging in self-harm. This necessitates locating self-harm within the particular circumstances causing distress (which might or might not include culturally specific concerns).

REFERENCES

Arnold, L. (1995) *Women and Self-Injury: A Survey of 76 Women*. Bristol: Bristol Crisis Service for Women

Babiker, G. and Arnold, L. (1997) *The Language of Injury: Comprehending Self-Mutilation*. Leicester: BPS Books

Bhadrinath, S. (1990) Ethnic differences in self poisoning: A comparative study between an Asian and White adolescent group. *Journal of Adolescence* 13, 189–193

Bhadrinath, B. R. (1990) Anorexia nervosa in adolescents of Asian extraction. *British Journal of Psychiatry*, 156, 565–568

Brah, A. (1996) *Cartographies of Diaspora: Contesting Identities*. London: Routledge

Bristol Crisis Service for Women (1995) *Women and Self-Injury: A Survey of 76 Women*. BCSW: Bristol

Burke, A. W. (1976) Attempted suicide among Asian immigrants in Birmingham. *British Journal of Psychiatry* 128, 528–533

Burman, E., Gowrisunkur, J. and Kuljeet, S. (1998) Conceptualising cultural and gendered identities in psychological therapies. *European Journal of Psychotherapy, Counselling and Health*, 1 (2), 231–256

D'Alessio, V. and Ghazi, P. (1993) Asian women in suicide epidemic. *The Observer*, 29 August, p. 6

Davies, D. and Neal, C. (1996) *Pink Therapy*. Buckingham, Open University Press

de Yong, M. (1982) *The Sexual Victimisation of Children*. London: McFarland and Co

Favazza, A. R. (1987) *Bodies Under Siege: Self Mutilation and Body Modification in Culture and Psychiatry* (2nd edn). Baltimore: Johns Hopkins University Press

Handy, S., Chithiramohan, R.N. Ballard, C.G. and Silveira, W. R. (1991) Ethnic differences in adolescent self-poisoning: A comparison of Asian and Caucasian groups. *Journal of Adolescence*, 14, 157–162

Health of the Nation (1994) *Key Area Handbook: Mental Illness* (2nd edn). London: HMSO

Hodes, M. (1990) Overdosing as Communication: A cultural perspective. *British Journal of Medical Psychology*, 63, 319–333

Howard, M. (1997) *A Mental Health Agenda for Newham General Hospital: A Final Report of Service Developments in Relation to the Care of People Who Self-Harm or Experience Other Mental Illness*. Area 1 Community Mental Health team, Newham Community Health Services NHS Trust: Newham

Johnstone, L. (1997) Self-injury and the Psychiatric Response. *Feminism and Psychology*, 7 (3) August, 421–42

Johnstone, S. (1997) Why do medical explanations of self-harm do more harm than good? In *Managing Self-Harm: Conference Proceedings*. London: Henderson Hospital

Liebling, H., Chipchase, H. and Velangi, R. (1997) Why do women harm themselves? Surviving special hospitals. *Feminism and Psychology*, 7 (3), 427–437

Lindberg, F.H. and Distad, J. (1985) Survival responses to incest: adolescents in crisis. *Child Abuse and Neglect*, 9, 521–526

Littlewood, R. (1995) Psychopathology ad personal agency: Modernity, culture change and eating disorders in South Asian societies. *British Journal of Medical Psychology*, 68, 45–63

Marshall, H. Stenner, P. and Lee, H. (1999) Young people's accounts of personal relationships in a multi-cultural East London environment: Questions of community, diversity and inequality. *Journal of Community and Applied Social Psychology*, 9, 155-171

Merrill, J. and Owens, J. (1986) Ethnic differences in self poisoning: A comparison of Asian and White groups. *British Journal of Psychiatry*, 148, 708–712

Merrill, J. and Owens, J. (1988) Self-poisoning among four immigrant groups. *Acta psychiatry Scandinavia*. 77, 77–80

Mumford, D.B. and Whitehouse, A.M. (1988) Increased prevalence of bulimia nervosa among Asian schoolgirls. *British Medical Journal*, 297 (2), 718

Nelson, S, and Grunebaum, H. (1971) A follow-up study of wrist-slashers. *American Journal of Psychiatry*, 127, 1345–1349

Newham Innercity Multifund and Newham Asian Women's Project (1998) *Young Asian Women and Self-Harm: A Mental Health Needs Assessment of Young Asian Women in Newham, East London, A Qualitative Study*. Newham Innercity Multifund and Newham Asian Women's Project: Newham

Pattison, E.M. and Kahan, J. (1983) The deliberate self-harm syndrome. *American Journal of*

Psychiatry, 140, 867–872

Pembroke, L.R. (Ed.) (1994) *Self Harm Perspectives from Personal Experience*. London: Survivors Speak Out

Pendall, P., Hamilton, M. and Holden, N. (1991) Letter. *British Journal of Psychiatry*, 159, 441

Pitman, R.K. (1990) Self-mutilation in combat-related PTSD *American Journal of Psychiatry*, 147, 123–124

Soni-Raleigh, V. (1996) Suicide patterns and trends in people of Indian subcontinent and Caribbean origin in England and Wales. *Ethnicity and Health*, 1 (1), 55–63

Soni-Raleigh, V. and Balarajan, R. (1992) Suicide and self burning among Indians and West Indians in England and Wales. *British Journal of Psychiatry*, 161, 365–368

Spandler, H. (1996) *Who's Hurting Who? Young People, Self harm and Suicide*. Manchester: 42nd Street

van der Kolk, B.A., Perry, C. and Herman, J. (1991) Childhood origins of self-destructive behaviour,. *American Journal of Psychiatry*. 148 (12), 1665–1671

Walsh, B.W. and Rosen, P.M. (1988) *Self-Mutilation*. New York: The Guildford Press

---

CHAPTER 5

GIRLS ON 'E': SOCIAL PROBLEM OR SOCIAL PANIC?

Maria Pini

INTRODUCTION

Drawing upon data collected over the past eight years, I will look at girls' and young women's involvements within contemporary night club cultures and highlight the various strategies of self-management and care which inform social drug use here. Attention to such strategies reveals how out-dated and over-simplistic are dominant media constructions of the 'pilled up' female raver as the innocent 'prey' of 'dangerous' (either sexually predatory, or drug-pushing) men. Challenging such constructions is important not simply for our understandings of emerging modes of femininity, but also because drugs 'panics' *can* (because young people often view these as the uninformed and excessive reactions of a parental generation) actually have the effect of pushing people towards taking ever-greater risks.

Since the advent of British rave culture in the late 1980s, social drug-use has risen dramatically. Equally dramatic has been the force of public outrage which has accompanied this – with every Ecstasy-related death reported by the media escalating a general panic about youth as *endangered*. Clearly, such panic is neither entirely new nor is it limited to a British context. In Australia (where I am currently working), for example, young people's ecstasy-use has not only received a lot of media attention, but was also a central topic of debate at the 1999 New South Wales Drug Summit. Although Ecstasy use within Australia is not seen to present as significant a social problem as that posed by heroin use, it has nevertheless come to the fore of both media and parliamentary debate. And, as in the British context, so-called 'dance drugs' have become the subject of a growing moral panic about a younger generation which is seen to be both beyond *adult* control, and out of *its own* control. Recent reportage of the death of Michael Overton after he took Ecstasy at a Sydney nightclub, presents the latest example of this familiar construction of youth as uncontrollable, and in a report commenting upon the death, Dr. Gordian Fulde is quoted using a telling language as he remarks that:

Ecstasy patients, young patients, teenagers or people in their early 20's just go out of their head. They go psychotic, they go crazy, they go weird. (Sun-Herald, 25 July 1999)

If young clubbers *in general* are seen to be potentially out of control and therefore in danger, then *in particular* (and within the British context at least) it is the young *female* who is constructed as the major 'victim' of the dance and drug cultures which make up rave (Redhead, 1990; Henderson, 1997). From early press reportage of Ecstasy-related sex-crimes against young women, to the more recent U.K. press coverage of the tragic death of Leah Betts, girls have been cast as the 'innocent' prey of drug-pushers and/or dangerous and sexually predatory men. If young women are seen as the potential *sexual* 'victims' of rave, then – and along with their male counterparts – they are also seen to be *physically* and *mentally* 'endangered' by Ecstasy-use.

In this chapter, I want to comment critically upon some of the images which spring to mind when we think about the young female drug-user. In particular, I want to: highlight how the relations between drug-use and adolescent femininity have changed over the past decade; and show how very over-simplistic and out-dated are some of the images we still carry of the young female drug taker. This commentary is based partly upon data which I collected in a series of interviews carried out with young British women who rave, and take 'dance drugs' on a regular basis. What the data reveals is that although these women might valorize 'losing control', 'going mental' or getting 'completely out of it', they are also intensely aware of the potential physical, psychological and sexual dangers posed by drug-use and raving. Consequently, they can be seen to develop a variety of strategies which work towards the limitation of such risks. Recognizing such strategies is important in calming and challenging what is fast becoming an intense anxiety about drug-taking youth as what Fulde calls 'psychotic', 'crazy' and 'weird': as an urgent contemporary social problem in desperate need of a solution. Contrary to the image of 'psychotic' or reckless abandon usually associated with raving, these young women present stories in which health care and caution feature consistently and prominently.

If this data problematizes commonly held images of the young female drug user as 'victim', then it also troubles the pictures of naivety often associated with the female drug *buyer*. These women display a very sophisticated knowledge about drugs, their use and their potential effects. They are a far cry from the corrupted 'innocent' who often comes to mind when we think of girls taking drugs within the context of the nightclub.

FROM BEDROOM-CULTURE TO DRUG-CULTURE: NOW THE GIRLS ARE DOING IT TOO

Over the past decade or so, some highly significant changes have taken place around the ways in which girls and young women participate within youth cultures. It has long been accepted that traditionally, girls tended to partake of a *private* culture of the 'bedroom' whilst boys tended to cultivate more public cultures of the 'street'. Indeed, this difference in visibility has often been put forward in accounting for why the study of 'youth' has often appeared to be the study of masculinity: why for example, the early work of the Birmingham Centre for Cultural Studies tended to focus so centrally on the practices of young men (McRobbie and Nava, 1994). If male youth attracted such attention, it was because boys and men tended to be more visible, and were more likely to be involved in 'deviant' subcultures, social drug taking, and spectacular *rituals of resistance*. Girls, on the other hand, stayed within the home and the bedroom; engaging with the 'outside' world through absorbing themselves in romantic fiction, listening to records and gazing at posters of male rock and pop stars. For a variety of reasons (partly to do with personal safety and partly to do with dominant notions about 'appropriate' femininity) girls could not so easily partake of what Rumsay and Little (1989) call the 'unsupervised adventures' celebrated by youth's cultural scholars.

If in the past young women engaged with popular culture from the 'safety' of the *bedroom*, things are very different today. In the late 1990s, girls and women regularly rave, take drugs and stay out dancing all night (Pini, 1997a, b; Henderson, 1997). Even the *home* is no longer a 'safe retreat' from the *dangers* posed by the 'street'. The Betts incident demonstrated only too clearly how the 'home' (and in this case, one in which an ex-policeman and a nurse were guardians and actually present at the time) can no longer be viewed as the safe and *feminine* other to 'the street'. This incident did something to deeply threaten not only our notions about the 'innocence' of adolescent 'girl culture', but also about the safety supposedly guaranteed to women by domestic 'enclosure'. And it brought to the fore the fact that girls are now more regularly and willingly partaking of practices which have traditionally been thought of as male. Although it did not take this tragic death to inform us that social drug-use is no longer a predominantly male activity, it *did* drive home the naivety of imagining that girls just aren't interested in cultural practices associated (however problematic such an association might be) with 'adventure' and 'danger'. We have come a very long way, then, from the situation described in 1978 by Angela McRobbie who notes:

So intransigently male are the mythologies and rituals attached to regular drug-taking that few women feel the slightest interest in their literary, cinematic or cultural expressions... It would be foolish to imagine that women do not take drugs – isolated housewives are amongst the heaviest drug-users and girls in their late teens are one of the latest groups among attempted suicides by drug overdose. Instead, I am suggesting that for a complex of reasons the imaginary solutions which drugs may offer to boys do not have the same attraction for girls. One reason is probably the commonsense wisdom deeply inscribed in most women's consciousness – that boys do not like girls who drink, take speed and so on; that losing control spells sexual danger; and that drinking and taking drugs harm physical appearance. (1978, reprinted 1991: 29)

Female drug aking is no longer so heavily associated with personal pathology or with isolation (see Keane, in this volume). It has become acceptable and *social*. And as far as the perceived relations between drug taking and female physical appearance go, these too have changed dramatically. If anything, a certain 'street credibility' now attaches to looking 'out of it'. My own interview data illustrates this very clearly (Pini, 1997a, 1999), but so too did the appearance in the world of high fashion of so-called 'heroin chic'. Being 'out of it' is, for a number of reasons, no longer something which young women feel they need to avoid for fear of losing control, putting themselves in sexual danger or appearing unattractive to men. On the contrary, appearing 'out of it' is now associated by many young women with looking 'good'. As the following 19-year olds put it, for example:

If you've got a horny man that's smiling at you, it's like 'yeah'. When you're off your head, he likes it you know. I think a man loves a woman that's off her face – 'cause that's when you'll get a smile. (Jean)

Yeah, it gets much sexier when everyone looks off their face. Everyone just looks so much better and sexier and you know you do too. (Clare)

DOWN TO ACTUALITIES: RISK AND MANAGEMENT

The fact that young women are now partaking of seemingly 'risky' cultural practices which were traditionally the preserve of men, might be considered ample reason for public concern. Given that within many of today's dance cultures being 'out of it' or 'mental' are highly celebrated states, it would seem only right to be anxious about the fate of the young woman in the club environment. And because raves are often all-night, one-off events held in unfamiliar venues where drug taking is rife, it is easy to understand why there might be concern about both the immediate (physical, sexual and mental) safety of the young woman, and the long-term effects of drug taking upon her health.

    If there seems to be good reason to worry about the fate of young female ravers, then this is not simply because of media-generated 'panic'.

Actual examples of young women's lived rave activities do little to quell any worries we might have as outsiders. Sally and Jean for example, are both 19 years old, unemployed and single mothers. They regularly rave together; always taking what to an outsider would appear to be an almost lethal quantity and cocktail of 'dance drugs'. In a single night they will each take up to five Ecstasy pills and six 'speed pills', sometimes also taking an 'acid tab'. Both stress that they never buy their drugs inside an unknown venue or from somebody they do not know. They buy their drugs beforehand and where necessary 'carry' relatively large quantities into an event in condoms inserted into their vaginas. These they sell once inside, thus covering their entry costs and earning some extra money.

Angie is 19 and usually raves with her two 21-year-old friends, Kay and Chris. Like all of the other interviewees, all three of these women claim that they could not, and do not want to, 'rave straight' (i.e. without using drugs). Ecstasy is their preferred 'dance drug' although they sometimes also use 'speed' or 'acid' and more rarely, they use cocaine. At least twice a year, they attend three-day events and over this period will take up to 25 pills of Ecstasy between them.

These snap-shots appear to speak of danger and an excessive risk taking on the part of young women. And they seem to justify any concerns we might have for the health and well-being of young women ravers. However, closer attendance to the actual practices of such women indicates that health care and caution are ongoing considerations within the rave event. It is in focussing upon such practices that we can come to understand why young women like Sally and Jean can continue to rave as they do – without ever encountering any of the dangers which the media are so quick to report on. Drawing attention to such practices is clearly not about denying that deaths *have* resulted from Ecstasy use; that rapes and sex-attacks *have* taken place within events; or that consistent drug use may have serious long-term physical and psychological effects. Rather, it is about highlighting some of the work that goes into minimising potential harm, and it is about arguing – as I have done elsewhere – that despite how dangerous it might superficially appear, the rave event generally constitutes a surprisingly 'safe' environment for young women (Pini, 1997a). This is not only because the absence of alcohol and so-called 'beer-boy attitude' within a rave, seems to make for a less threatening atmosphere. It is also because – and despite its appearance as a totally hedonistic and uncontrolled activity – raving can be seen to involve its own techniques for self-care.

Of the 20 women interviewed, all spoke repeatedly of the various measures taken in order to minimize the potential dangers of Ecstasy and the potential *sexual* risks they faced within an event. Buying drugs from a regular 'dealer' before actually going to an event; staying sufficiently hydrated whilst dancing; taking breaks from dancing in order to 'chill out' and cool down; being able to 'talk yourself down' from a 'bad trip'; avoiding alcohol before and during an event; allowing a necessary 'come-down' time the following day (which in Sally and Jean's case, for example, means ensuring that child-care is available); remembering that the 'loved-up' feelings produced within an event are not a good enough reason to go home with a man and that such feelings do not guarantee personal 'safety' once outside an event; and taking a 'break' from raving if drug taking is becoming too regular or too central to ones life, are just some of the practices which figured highly within these women's accounts. Many are also very clear about which *kinds* of E are 'best' for them, i.e.. which ones agree with them physically, and fit in with their life-styles. Anna for example, is in a full-time job, and her 'pills' must allow her to get up and work the following day:

I don't like 'speedy' E where it just goes on and on and on for absolutely ages. I like mine to be, come-up fast, have a really intense bit, then come-down a few hours later and be straight again, go to sleep, wake up next day and be absolutely normal.

Clare on the other hand, prefers her E to be 'speedy':

Because I do like that real rush, and I can handle it, whereas some people can't. My mate Lou for example, gets really sick. Speed makes her nauseous and she panics if she gets too much of a thumping heart, so she doesn't touch it. Me, I can't do those 'smacky' pills. That really makes me feel sick and dizzy and once, I really thought I was going to keel over. So I just don't go near it.

It is not only *self*-care and coming to know ones *own* needs which is a prominent theme within these personal narratives. Caring for friends is also a major concern. Watching out for 'mates' – which can mean collectively challenging 'predatory' men seen to be harassing them; noting who they might go out of an event with; ensuring that they are not having a 'bad trip' by 'talking them down' and by generally coming to know their needs – is a significant and consistent theme. A familiar thread of 'keeping an eye' on each other thus runs through these accounts. In an interview with Chris, Kay and Angie for example, a very common story is repeated about the importance of having friends 'look out' for each other where either drugs or unfamiliar men are concerned:

Chris: I was really lucky to have Jo with me. She knew what to tell me, about water and stuff. And she was like right there for me and keeping an eye out and every so often – like now and then – she came and got me to see I'm alright.

Angie: Yeah, like you make sure you clock it if like... like even if I'm 'out of it', I can still clock it if like a mate's chatting with some bloke and he's trying to get her to leave or go off.

Kay: Nine times out of ten, it's just for a spliff or for a chat but ...

Angie: But you can't be sure can you?

Chris: No, we always stick together more or less. It's like you always come back to find each other.

It is not only at the level of rave *participation* that a theme of caring for women friends is evident. Two interviewees, Lisa and Michelle, are actually involved in running rave events. In both of their accounts of working at the organizational level, providing a safe environment for women appears as a major priority. Michelle, for example, speaks about the implementation of a door-security system whereby young unaccompanied women (particularly if they appear 'out of it') are escorted to waiting taxis. If these are not obviously identifiable as legitimate taxis, their number plates are noted. She also stresses that within her events, 'bouncers' have been employed to watch out for, and intervene in anything that looks like sexual harassment.

SUMMARY

This very brief discussion has hopefully made two things clear. One, that to think of young female ravers as the 'innocent' prey of dangerous men is not only over-simplistic but far removed from the realities of gender dynamics in the context of contemporary rave culture. Many of the present interviewees themselves sell drugs and have a highly developed knowledge of the drug 'market'. Two, that despite how 'risky' it may appear, raving as an activity has a certain degree of regulation or management to it. Beneath the surface of uncontrolled abandon often associated with the rave event, various operations are clearly at play which allow young women to 'go mental', and 'lose control' without putting themselves in the kind of danger conjured up by such terms. Clear themes of both self-care and care for others run alongside the emphasis placed by these women on 'letting go', 'getting completely off it', 'losing it' and so forth.

Recognizing the caution and risk-limitation that women like these exercise is an important move in contesting the public anxiety coming to surround Ecstasy use. One of the dangers with generating a drugs 'panic' is that this is very obvious to young people who have personal experience of rave culture, and to whom media coverage is *bound* to concentrate on, and exaggerate the perils. This can – as many drugs workers have pointed out – actually have the effect of driving otherwise relatively 'safe' young people to take ever greater risks with drugs.

REFERENCES

Henderson, S. (1997 *Ecstasy: Case Unsolved*. London: HarperCollins
McRobbie, A. (1991) *Feminism and Youth Culture: From Jackie to Just Seventeen*. London: Macmillan
McRobbie, A. and Nava, M. (1984) *Gender and Generation*. London: Macmillan
Newcombe, R. (1991) *Rave and Dance Drugs: House Music Clubs and Parties in North-West England*. Liverpool: Rave Research Bureau
Pini, M. (1997a) Women and the early British rave scene. In A. McRobbie (Ed.) *Back to Reality?*

Social Experience and Cultural Studies. Manchester: Manchester University Press, 1997
Pini, M. (1997b) Cyborgs, nomads and the raving feminine. In H. Thomas (Ed.) *Dance in the City*. Basingstoke: Macmillan
Redhead, S. (Ed.) (1990) *The End-of-the-century Party*. Manchester: Manchester University Press
Rumsey, H. and Little, G. (1989) Women and pop: a series of lost encounters. In A. McRobbie (Ed.) *Zoot Suits and Second Hand Dresses: An Anthology of Fashion and Music*. London: Macmillan

CHAPTER 6

WOMEN AND SUBSTANCE ABUSE: PROBLEMS OF VISIBILITY AND EMPOWERMENT

Helen Keane

Certainly the actions and the wants of women often need to be fished out of obscurity, rescued from the blanket dominance of 'man', or 'to be made visible'. But that is not all. There are always too many invocations of 'women', too much visibility, too many appellations which were better dissolved again – or are in need of some accurate and delimiting handling. Denise Riley, Am I that Name?

INTRODUCTION

This chapter considers the development of 'women and substance abuse' as a field of research, focussing mainly on recent American texts. It raises concerns about the discursive construction of women as a risk group and addresses some of the tensions within feminist therapeutic discourse and its understanding of the relationship between women and drugs.

DISCOVERING WOMEN AND DRUGS

Recent years have witnessed the development of a significant body of research and commentary on drug use and abuse among women. Not only has feminist work on women's experiences and needs been published (Ettorre, 1992; Bepko, 1991; Van Den Bergh, 1991a; Doyal, 1995; Broom, 1994), mainstream public health has also turned its attention to the female substance user (National Institute on Drug Abuse, 1998; Gomberg and Nirenberg, 1993; Addiction Research Foundation, 1996; Plant, 1990; National Centre on Addiction and Substance Abuse at Columbia University, 1996). The focus on women's drug use and the construction of women as a 'risk-group' for substance-related problems is on one hand an overdue and necessary corrective to the widespread neglect of women which characterized the drug and alcohol field for most of its history. Indeed, a central theme of feminist interventions in this field has been the invisibility of drinking and drug-using women and the need for gender sensitive perspectives to reveal the hidden realities of their lives (Ettorre, 1992: 16–18). On the other hand, a Foucauldian view of the relationship between knowledge and power encourages us to consider the possible costs as well as the benefits of the entry of the female substance abuser into public health and therapeutic discourse (see Pini, in this volume).

Ironically, the notion of women's drug use as a hidden problem has been adopted wholeheartedly by researchers, health organizations and policy makers at the same time that they are producing substantial amounts of authoritative and scientific knowledge on the topic.

The trope of revealing the hidden should not prevent us recognizing that particular truths about women are being produced in this increasingly active area, and this is true of feminist as well as mainstream accounts. Against the argument that women must be visible to gain assistance is the fact that visibility as a drug user or member of a 'high-risk group' often attracts forms of 'help' which involve intense surveillance and regulation. In an article on treatment policy for pregnant addicts, Iris Marion Young describes how a combination of expertise and care often produces 'situations of paternalistic power and discipline' (1994: 44). The status of 'health' as a pervasive regulatory norm, against which we are encouraged to judge almost every aspect of our lives, lends these issues a particular salience.

WOMEN AT RISK

Given the traditional assumption that drug abuse is a men's issue, it is not surprising that much recent work emphasizes the severity and extent of problems among the female population. Statistics are quoted to prove the high level of unrecognized harm, and this harm is often described as on the increase, as is expected in the formulaic discourse of social problems (Van Den Bergh, 1991b: 9–10; Califano, 1996, 1998; Blumenthal, 1998). Without denying the fact that policies still leave much to be desired and appropriate services for women remain scarce, the risk is that these kind of discursive strategies will construct women as a group defined and unified by suffering, physical vulnerability and powerlessness. This is particularly the case if disease models of substance abuse and addiction are combined with claims of ever-worsening rates of disorder.

The stress on women's hidden suffering needs to be considered in the context of the view that women's use and abuse of drugs can be understood as a consequence of gender oppression, in particular as a response to the low self-esteem and repressed self-identity produced by female socialization. Jahn Forth-Finegan expresses it simply, 'the cost of appropriate female gender-role behavior may well be addiction, which helps to numb the pain of powerlessness and lack of freedom and choice' (1991: 33). The arguments of British authors Doyal (1995) and Ettorre (1992) are more nuanced and less individualistic, but they still tend to view substance use as a symptom of women's inequality and lack of autonomy. For example women's smoking, drinking and use of tranquillisers can all be related to daily routines characterized by absence of control, isolation and stress.

Placing women's drug use in the context of social structures, as this argument does, is undoubtedly useful and important. It challenges the pathologization of female drug users as abnormal, immoral and 'doubly deviant' in their transgression of norms of feminine virtue (Broom and Stevens, 1991: 26). But the reading of drug use as an index of oppression easily leads to a restrictive and circular logic whereby the depth and breadth of women's drug problems serves as proof of women's oppression and the existence of oppression implies the existence of a major and growing problem. Apart from the strategic limitations of such an approach it tends to disavow differences between and within women, especially in relation to questions of pleasure. The constitution of drug and alcohol use as a form of analgesia against the pain of subordination tends to exclude women's enjoyment of substance use (Downing 1991: 48; Van Den Bergh, 1991b: 7–8; Mason, 1991: 186). Translating women's substance use into self-medication implies that women use drugs and become addicted out of lack, lack that is externally imposed, but lack nonetheless. Their substance use is constructed as reactive rather than active, stemming from a desire to quell pain rather than produce pleasure. Desire is absent from the discussion, women's drug use is constituted as a disembodied and hygienic affair. The intoxication, corporeal cravings and responses of the body are hidden away as if they would sully the picture of feminine suffering. The feminist discourse of self-medication is critical of the feminine ideal of the 'nice girl', but it is nevertheless prone to making nice girls of its own, girls who take drugs not for fun or to rebel, but to help them be good.

Understanding differences among women as categories of increased risk and vulnerability exacerbates this trend. For example, recent work on substance abuse among older women argues that these women have a magnified risk for the development of substance abuse because of their social situation, a situation characterized by isolation, loneliness, poverty, depression and pain (Rathbone McCuan et al., 1991), and because of their physiological vulnerability (National Center on Addiction and Substance Abuse at Columbia University 1998: 2). By reading older women's drinking as primarily a response to negative conditions, this literature reproduces the discourse of aging as decline and loss. The idea of a depressed older woman drinking alone in front of her television is only one possible scenario. Drinking could also take place at meals with friends and family, evidence of a continuation of social ties and involvement in community life. The construction of unified and singular subjectivities characterized by neediness and risk, such as the 'elderly woman substance abuser' or 'lesbian alcoholic' does not recognize that the subjects who occupy these spaces are formed by a constellation of forces, both restricting and enabling. Serious difficulties and predicaments are of course faced by women in these groups and intervention can be beneficial, but the rhetoric of risk excludes the capacity of women's bodies to be active producers of pleasure as well as passive sites of pain.

Another element in the development of the 'women and substance use' field which is affected by the emphasis on vulnerability and pain is the expansion of abusable substances to include those not traditionally classified as drugs. Feminists have long argued that for many women food is an addictive or at least abused substance, and it is now included in some mainstream guides to women's substance use (Addiction Research Foundation, 1996: 54). Consumption of prescribed medications and smoking have also been examined by feminist authors as significant forms of drug use, often neglected in traditional frameworks (Ettorre, 1992; Doyal, 1995; Jacobson 1986). Analysis of the politics of prescribed psychotropic drugs has been a powerful challenge to dominant views of drug use and addiction, revealing how some forms of dependence have been promoted by medical authorities while others are demonized. For women, the battles of addiction are often fought out with socially acceptable substances such as food, tranquillisers, tobacco, and alcohol in domesticated settings. However, what is made visible in the attempt to capture this reality is a broadened field of potential problems. A longer and longer list of substances and processes is made available as interchangeable indicators of personal health or sickness. In this landscape, just about everything becomes evidence of women's unhappiness and oppression, from the lighting of a cigarette to the consumption of empty calories. These behaviors then become the basis for totalized identities – 'compulsive eater', 'addicted smoker' – which require rectification, often by medical and other experts.

INTERVENTION AND EMPOWERMENT

Risk-groups are highly visible targets for intervention, their 'special needs' often justifying special measures of control. This is particularly the case in an era of what Linda Singer calls epidemic logic, in which not only transmissible diseases (namely Aids), but crime and social problems, are understood as 'epidemics'. Singer argues that the invocation of the sign 'epidemic' automatically implies that something drastic must be done to control 'the disease' and the bodies who are its agents. Epidemic logic insists that the population must be better managed and that governments must intervene to contain the threat of contagion, even if this involves the abrogation of freedoms and rights normally protected (1993: 29–31). Thus, the translation of urban decay and deprivation into an epidemic of 'crack mothers' and their 'crack babies' contains an inherent statement about an appropriate policy response focused on the policing of individuals. The fact that, at least in the United States, concern about women's alcohol consumption is commonly entwined with a moralistic and accusatory discourse of foetal welfare adds another dimension to the construction of women as a risk group. Reports on alcohol consumption among women often focus on a category called 'women of childbearing age' whose drinking is couched in terms of a threat to infant health (Bottom Line, 1994).

Feminists have been vocal critics of the focus on foetal welfare and have also condemned authoritarian treatment programs and those which enforce dominant norms of femininity. Instead, supportive and non-judgmental programs incorporating feminist principles are advocated (Morgain, 1994; Walker *et al.*, 1991; Pasick and White, 1991). Therapeutic discourse influenced by feminism often employs the notion of a natural, authentic and healthy self which pre-exists gender socialization to understand the therapeutic process. Feminist therapy is viewed as giving access to, nurturing or rediscovering this authentic female self which has been damaged or suppressed by gender socialization and the addictive process (Nol, 1991; Smith, 1991). Therapeutic intervention can thus be regarded as a process of undoing harm, rather than the moulding of a new self in line with an externally imposed image of health and wholeness.

The concept of empowerment is also frequently used to describe the overall goal of therapy and treatment, but as Young (1994) has pointed out, a focus on personal empowerment does not in itself challenge an individualized and confessional model of self-discovery and transformation. In fact, the concept of empowerment can justify the expansion of sites of improvement far beyond the client's drug use. Improving physical fitness, assertiveness and self-confidence; developing money management, parenting and interpersonal skills; learning self-defence; embarking on a path of spiritual growth; undergoing further education and vocational training; making new healthy relationships and speaking out about violence and abuse are typical elements of empowering therapy. One author describes feminist programs as encouraging clients to 'to take responsibility for making things happen in their life rather than being reactive', 'to define what is appropriate for themselves, rather than pursuing conventionally established norms' and 'to undergo an honest self-assessment' (Van Den Bergh, 1991b: 24–25). But these goals themselves promote conformity to powerful norms of autonomy, responsibility and self-examination. Whatever the underlying principles, the aim of drug and alcohol treatment is to change behavior, comportment, attitudes and desires, and this inevitably involves an exercise of power, which some 'clients' will experience as restrictive and intrusive.

Treatment programs based on collective empowerment through consciousness raising are supported by Young as an alternative to traditional individualized models of treatment (1994: 50). Ettorre advocates a similar approach in her challenge to the individual focus of traditional self-help and recovery discourse. She argues that the way forward is for substance-using women to search together for alternative means of 'preserving their integrity, exercising their autonomy and expressing their rage' (1992: 29). Feminist praxis can provide a positive and liberating alternative to both oppressive social practices and 'the debilitating effects of "comforting" substances' (p. 31). However, this framework still suggests that feminist knowledge can see women as they really are, can locate their genuine problems and needs, and can identify the paths to real empowerment and enlightenment. Moreover, feminism is still perceived as something that is already complete in its identity before it is taken up by women substance-users. Through contact with feminism, addicted and substance using women are educated and enlightened, not to mention sobered up, while feminism remains fundamentally unchanged.

The broader issue is the desire for innocent knowledge which characterizes some feminist analyses and projects. According to Jane Flax, feminist theorists who continue to operate within enlightenment metanarratives confuse two different claims – the first that certain kinds of knowledge are generated by gender-based power relations, and the second that correcting for these biases will produce better knowledge that is not generated by, and generative of, its own relations of power:

They are not content with constructing discourses which privilege some of those who have previously lacked power (at the necessary expense of others) but wish to claim discovery of ways to increase the general sum of human emancipation. These theorists assume that domination and emancipation are a binary pair and that to displace one necessarily creates new space for the other. (1992: 457)

In feminist discourses of addiction and substance use, these kinds of beliefs operate in tandem with a tension between ideals of freedom and health. On one hand, the emancipation of women, at least within a liberal paradigm, implies the expansion of choices and the reduction of 'social control'. On the other hand, promoting the health of women requires challenging the wisdom and ethical status of some of these choices and highlighting their costs. The model of innocent knowledge suggests that the truth can deliver both liberation and protection from harm, and that given true freedom, women will never make unwise or harmful or unhealthy choices. Thus innocence is installed not only within feminist knowledge, but also within the women who are its subjects and would be beneficiaries.

SUMMARY

Women's drug use has become a productive and diverse field of research which offers important insights into previously ignored experiences and problems. Feminist analyses have been particularly valuable in their attention to the broader social and cultural contexts in which drug use takes place. This chapter however has taken a critical approach to the construction of women as a risk group, arguing that there are dangers in proliferating discourses of vulnerability, suffering and oppression. It also suggests that there are tensions in feminist approaches which seek both liberation and protection for women.

REFERENCES

Addiction Research Foundation (1996) *The Hidden Majority: A Guidebook on Alcohol and Other Drugs Issues for Counsellors Who Work With Women*. Toronto: Addiction Research Foundation

Babcock, M. (1996) Does feminism drive women to drink?: conflicting themes. *International Journal of Drug Policy*, 7 (3), 158–165

Bepko, C. (Ed.) (1991) *Feminism and Addiction*. New York: Haworth Press

Blumenthal, S. (1998) Women and substance abuse: a new national focus. In National Institute on Drug Abuse, *Drug Addiction Research and the Health of Women*. Ed. by C. Worthington and A. Roman, Rockville: National Institute on Drug Abuse

Bottom Line (1994) Frequent alcohol consumption among women of childbearing age: Behavioral Risk Factor Surveillance System, 1991. *Bottom Line*, 15 (4), 63–65.

Broom, D. (Ed.) (1994) *Double Bind: Women Affected by Alcohol and Other Drugs*. St Leonards: Allen & Unwin

Broom, D. and Stevens, A. (1991) Doubly deviant: women using alcohol and other drugs. *International Journal on Drug Policy*, 2 (4), 25–27

Califano, J. (1996) Executive summary and foreword to National Centre on Addiction and Substance Abuse at Columbia University. *Substance Abuse and the American Woman*, New York: National Center on Addiction and Substance Abuse at Columbia University.

Califano, J. (1998) Foreword and accompanying statement to National Centre on Addiction and Substance Abuse at Columbia University, *Under the Rug: Substance Abuse and the Mature Woman*, New York: National Center on Addiction and Substance Abuse at Columbia University

Downing, C. (1991) Sex role setups and alcoholism. In. N Van Den Bergh (Ed.) *Feminist Perspectives on Addictions*. New York: Springer

Doyal, L. (1995) *What Makes Women Sick: Gender and the Political Economy of Health*. Basingstoke: Macmillan

Ettorre, E. (1992) *Women and Substance Use*. Basingstoke: Macmillan

Farrell, W. (1994) *The Myth of Male Power: Why Men are the Disposable Sex*. Milsons Point: Random House

Fillmore, K.M. (1984) 'When angels fall': women's drinking as a cultural preoccupation and as reality. In S. Wilsnack and L.J. Beckman (Eds.) *Alcohol Problems in Women*. New York: The Guilford Press

Flax, J. (1992) The end of innocence. In J. Butler and J.W. Scott (Eds.) *Feminists Theorize the Political*. New York: Routledge

Forth-Finegan, J. (1991) 'Sugar and spice and everything nice: gender socialization and women's addiction – a literature review. In C. Bepko (Ed.) *Feminism and Addiction*. New York: Haworth Press

Gomberg, E.L. and T. Nirenberg (Eds.) (1993) *Women and Substance Abuse*. Norwood: Ablex Publishing

Irwin, J. (1989) The liberation of males. *Men*, 4, 3–15

Jacobson, B. (1986) *Beating the Ladykillers: Women and Smoking*. London: Pluto Press

Lex, B.W. (1993) Women and illicit drugs: marijuana, heroin and cocaine. In E.L. Gomberg and T. Nirenberg (Eds.) *Women and Substance Abuse*. Norwood: Ablex Publishing

Mason, M. (1991) Women and shame: kin and culture. In C. Bepko (Ed.) *Feminism and Addiction*. New York: Haworth Press

Morgain, L. (1994) Women's addiction recovery service: a community development model. In D. Broom (Ed.) *Double Bind: Women Affected by Alcohol and Other Drugs*. St Leonards: Allen & Unwin

National Center on Addiction and Substance Abuse at Columbia University (1996) *Substance Abuse and the American Woman*. New York: National Center on Addiction and Substance Abuse at Columbia University

National Institute on Drug Abuse (1998) *Drug Addiction Research and the Health of Women*. Ed. by C. Worthington and A. Roman, Rockville: National Institute on Drug Abuse

Nol, J. (1991) Self-object search: role of addictions in a patriarchal culture. In N. Van Den Bergh (Ed.) *Feminist Perspectives on Addictions*. New York: Springer Publishing Company

Pasick, P. and White, C. (1991) Challenging General Patton: a feminist stance in substance abuse treatment and training. In C. Bepko (Ed.) *Feminism and Addiction*. New York: Haworth Press

Plant, M. (1990) *Women and Alcohol Use: A Review of International Literature on the Use of Alcohol by Females*. Geneva: WHO Publications

Plant, M. (1997) *Women and Alcohol: Contemporary and Historical Perspectives*. London: Free Association Books

Rathbone-McCuan, E., Dyer, L. and Wartman, J. (1991) Double jeopardy: chemical dependence and codependence in older women. In N. Van Den Bergh (Ed.) *Feminist Perspectives on Addictions*. New York: Springer

Singer, L. (1993) *Erotic Welfare: Sexual Theory and Politics in the Age of Epidemic*. New York: Routledge

Smith, C. (1991) Healing the feminine: a feminist residential model for treating chemical dependency. In N. Van Den Bergh (Ed.) *Feminist Perspectives on Addictions*. New York: Springer

Thom, B. (1994) Women and alcohol: the emergence of a risk group. In M. McDonald (Ed.) *Gender, Drink and Drugs*. Oxford: Berg

Underhill, B. (1991) Recovery needs of lesbian alcoholics in treatment. In N. Van Den Bergh (Ed.) *Feminist Perspectives on Addictions*. New York: Springer

Van Den Bergh, N. (Ed.) (1991a) *Feminist Perspectives on Addictions*. New York: Springer

Van Den Bergh, N. (1991b) Having bitten the apple: a feminist perspective on addictions. In. Van Den Bergh (Ed.) *Feminist Perspectives on Addictions*. New York: Springe

Walker, G. *et al.* (1991) A descriptive outline of a program for cocaine-using mothers and their babies. In C. Bepko (Ed.) *Feminism and Addiction*. New York: Haworth Press

Wilsnack, S. and Wilsnack, R. (1995) Drinking and problem drinking in US women. In M. Galanter (Ed.) *Recent Developments in Alcoholism Vol. 12: Women and Alcoholism*. New York: Plenum Press

Young, I. M. (1994) Punishment, treatment and empowerment: three approaches to policy for pregnant addicts. *Feminist Studies*, 20 (1), 33–57

CHAPTER 7

YOUNG LESBIANS AND MENTAL HEALTH: THE CLOSET IS A DEPRESSING PLACE TO BE

Julie Mooney-Somers and Jane Ussher

OVERVIEW

In this chapter we examine mental health issues in young lesbians, drawing on a recent interview study conducted with a group of Lesbian Avengers. Some of the difficulties that these young women experienced included rejection and hostility from family and friends, social isolation, and being positioned as lecherous because of being lesbian. However, we argue that mental health problems were not the inevitable result, as a number of strategies of resistance and coping were adopted. These include the positive adoption of a lesbian identity, support from other lesbians, and defiance of negative representations of lesbian sexuality.

INTRODUCTION

Women are more vulnerable to depression than men, and are more likely to be positioned as pathological within the phallocentric discourses of psychiatry and psychology (Ussher, 1991; Stoppard, 1999). Young women are increasingly vulnerable to depression at puberty, a time when they are negotiating the contradictory scripts of femininity (Ussher, 1997). What of women who are doubly deviant? What of women who identify as lesbian, dyke or queer? What of young women who negotiate femininity and sexuality outside of a heterosexual matrix? Are they saved from the double binds which tie many young women in knots – the desire to be strong and autonomous, yet not threatening to men; the desire to be sexual, yet avoid being positioned as whore; the desire to be healthy, yet maintain the feminine ideal of thinness? If women reject the discourses of femininity that lead to depression in many heterosexual women (see Stoppard, in this volume), are they not more likely to be happy and content?

If we look to mainstream research on mental health the answer is clear: adult lesbians are no more at risk of mental health problems than heterosexual women (Savin-Williams, 1990). Indeed, it appears that taken as a group, lesbians fare better than heterosexual women on measures of self - acceptance, self-sufficiency, self-confidence and general sense of well being (Savin-Williams, 1990). Looking to research on younger women, however, presents us with a different picture. Suicide and attempted suicide is disproportionately high in groups of young lesbians (Fergusson et al., 1999; Hershberger and D'Augelli, 1995). High rates of depression, and anxiety, as well as substance abuse and other self-destructive behavior, are reported by many (Nichols, 1999; Davies and Neale, 1996). The question is, why?

One answer to this question is that young lesbians are no different from any other group of young women. They are affected by all of the torments and traumas that are common at adolescence. These include difficulties with families and friends; questions about identity and subjectivity; worries about the body, about being normal; pressures to achieve and succeed; sexual violence and abuse; feelings of alienation from society; desires to take drugs, with all the consequences that this entails (see chapters by Helen Malson, Sarah Grogan, Janet Stoppard, Harriett Marshall, Maria Pini and Deborah Tolman, in this volume). Yet young lesbians are not the same as young heterosexual women. They face a range of difficulties that put them at higher risk of mental health problems if they are not able to access appropriate support. These include discrimination, rejection, verbal and physical violence, and isolation. In research conducted in North America, it has been found that nearly 50 percent of young lesbians and gay men had been victimized in school, 80 percent had experienced verbal insults, 44 percent threat of attack, 23 percent property attack, 33 percent had had objects thrown, 30 percent were chased or followed, 13 percent were spat on, 17 percent had experienced physical assault, 22 percent had experienced sexual assault, and 10 percent assault with a weapon (Hershberger and D'Augelli, 1995). Sometimes statistics can make a point more powerfully than any amount of words.

TALKING TO YOUNG LESBIANS ABOUT MENTAL HEALTH

In order to examine the way in which this can impact upon mental health, we will turn to the accounts of young women themselves, drawing on a recent research study conducted with a group of young lesbians living in London (Ussher and Mooney-Somers, 2000). Eight women, aged 17 to 24, took part in in-depth, semi-structured narrative interviews. They were all members of a non-violent direct action group, the Lesbian Avengers. This group was set up in London in 1994, and was part of an international organization, started in New York, whose central premise is action not discussion. The Lesbian Avengers carry out high profile, media friendly, 'sexy' actions to raise the awareness of lesbians. We chose to interview this particular group of young women because they had all openly and positively taken up a lesbian identity and they were willing to take part in the research.

Face-to-face semi-structured narrative interviews (Reissman, 1993; Mishler, 1986), lasting between 60 and 90 minutes, were used to explore the meanings women gave to their experiences of being lesbian and the relationship between being lesbian mental health. The research was conducted from a material-discursive-intrapsychic perspective (Ussher, 2000), using a feminist critical realist epistemology. Critical realism affirms the existence of reality, both material, psychological and environmental, but at the same time recognizes that this experience is always mediated by culture, language, and political interests rooted in factors such as sexuality, race, gender or social class (Pilgrim and Rogers, 1997; Ussher, 1996). This is an approach that allows for acknowledgment of the material, discursive and intra-psychic aspects of experience, as well as the cultural and historical context in which individual women are positioned, and in which meaning about experience is created (Ussher, 2000; see also Stoppard, and Dell, in this volume). Being grounded in a feminist standpoint means acknowledging that women's voices and experiences are silenced, distorted and obscured in a phallocentric or patriarchal culture. A less distorted view can emerge by attempting to view the world 'through our participants eyes' (Harding, 1991; 1993), in particular through attending to the narratives or accounts of women (Reissman, 1993; see Lee, in this volume). It also leads to reflexivity on the part of the researchers, and to a recognition that research is relational, in that researchers bring self-knowledge and experience into the process of designing, conducting, analysing and interpreting research.

Narrative analysis, which takes as the object of study the story itself, was used to examine the interviews. Narrative analysis assumes that the stories told do not simply mirror a world 'out there', but that they are constructed, creatively authored, rhetorical, replete with assumptions and interpretative (Reissman, 1993: 5). It was assumed that narratives act to constitute experience, meaning and reality, but that it is in the telling that we make sense of phenomena and are assumed to be doing particular 'identity work' (Ponse, 1978). However, narratives do not simply 'speak for themselves' (Reissman, 1993: 22). They are both interpretative and open to interpretation. As every text is open to several readings or inter-pretations, our analysis is aiming at 'believability, not certitude, for enlargement of understanding rather than control' (Stivers, 1993: 424). In this context, we will present an overview of two narrative themes that directly related to mental health (see Ussher and Mooney-Somers, 2000 for an analysis of issues associated with desire): discussion of the danger in being a dyke, and strategies of resistance.

THE DANGER OF BEING A DYKE

Social rejection

One of the major themes which emerged in our interviews was of secrecy around sexuality, being 'closeted', because of fears of the reactions of fam-ily, friends and society. This wasn't an unwarranted fear, as this group of young lesbians women had experienced a range of responses from ridicule through to rejection and hostility, that came from many sources. For example, one young woman, upon inviting her mother to her gradu-ation ceremony was told 'I'd rather roast in hell, you are part of my past, I want nothing to do with you'.

This reaction, although extreme, demonstrates the kind of difficulties that can be faced by young lesbians. Mother-daughter relationships play a significant role in the mental health of women, and thus this particular rejection is potentially a major risk factor for depression and anxiety. For young women having to face a world hostile to their sexuality, the support of family is an important protective factor. The absence of that cannot be underestimated.

Hostility from peers was also a common experience. As one inter-viewee commented,

sort of girls in the changing room, sort of sitting there laughing or walking out or suddenly everyone freezes and shuts up or as soon as somebody makes an anti gay remark in the school and the whole school turns around and looks at you.

Friendships with other girls and feeling part of the normative culture of the school are central to adolescent girls' subjectivity and happiness. To be excluded from this can be a very high price to pay for being openly les-bian. It thus wasn't surprising to find that for many of the interviewees, it was rejection by other girls at school that was particularly difficult.

The comments from boys I can deal with no problem. It's the comments from other girls that I find very difficult (2) cause you can see them sort of going 'awh that's disgusting, how can they do that, how can they do it, how can they feel like that, awh' that makes my skin crawl and I don't know how to deal with it.

Lesbians are lecherous

Rejection and hostility were not the only responses these young women faced. There were changes in the way they were perceived if they were 'out' about their sexuality, invariably becoming defined by their sexuality in a way that is not the case for their heterosexual peers. In a number of cases they were positioned as sexually predatory by school friends and teachers, and as a result were counseled at school to be discrete about their sexuality. This was the experience of one young woman with a nun at school:

She actually called me in and gave me this whole long talk and what it all boiled down to was her saying 'You won't attack the first years will you' (laughing).

Another talked about being shunned by friends and the need to ensure that no comment or gesture could be construed as a 'come on'.

Your friends won't even sit next to you and they won't bend down and pick up a pencil while you're near ... they run out of the changing room whenever you go there.

The implication in all of these extracts is that lesbians are positioned as predatory and lecherous; that they desire all women (or any woman). In contrast, heterosexual girls are not assumed to desire all boys, and boys are not seen as being at risk of being 'attacked' by heterosexual girls. Given this, it isn't surprising that confusion about sexuality and ambivalence about desire is commonly reported by young lesbians (Savin-Williams, 1990; Ussher and Mooney-Somers, 2000). Their sexuality marks them as other, as dangerous, as someone to be avoided or contained. Yet in actual fact, by their own accounts, being identified as lesbian was about friendship, love, desire, politics, style, power and pleasure – with sex only being one part of the equation. However, as innuendo, voyeurism and rumour were associated with their (imagined) sexual practices, sex became something that was a defining factor in their lives.

Social isolation

The reactions, rejection, hostility and ridicule can lead to feelings of isolation and being misunderstood, feeling somehow different from others. In our interviews many reported feeling alien and detached from society.

That's why I feel it's such a bloody hassle being gay, cause you don't fit in at all in society and that's one of the big things that hits you, is you are second class, and all that stuff and you just do not fit in and society doesn't want to know you and it hates you and that's a really big thing to come to terms with.

Feeling unwanted and alienated is a relatively normal, if distressing, experience at adolescence. But taking up a lesbian identity means that there are additional issues to deal with in the negotiation of subjectivity and a positive sense of self. As one woman commented,

It was so oppressive cause I knew I couldn't be myself.

Many young lesbians who feel different from others withdraw socially, thus adding further to their sense of isolation (Davies and Neale, 1996).

It was just like feeling alone, like I mean that's what most people say but I mean, that's how it felt.

This withdrawal is often preferable to the constant reminder of not being interested in 'normal' adolescent pursuits, such as boys, and can be a protective mechanism that prevents leakage of information about sexuality or subjectivity. It also means that the young woman doesn't have to try to pass as heterosexual, thus protecting her from the negative psychological outcomes associated with this strategy (Margolies *et al.*, 1987). However, being different from other girls, and not interested in boys, means missing out on the rituals of sex, love and romance that are a central part of adolescent identity development. Many young lesbians have no social network with which to discuss their desires or fantasies, and no opportunities to explore their sexuality with others who are lesbian too. As one woman commented,

When I was going through the ages of fifteen, sixteen especially high school ... everybody around me was like doing all these things discovering sex and having it and being interested in like it and I just wasn't and like and obviously I know why it was cause I'm a fucking dyke and I'm ... I don't want to be involved in that but why couldn't I like discover everything when I was fifteen like have this wild time and stuff in my high school days when I was totally free or like almost totally free or slightly freer then I probably am today.

So the normal adolescent negotiation of relationships – the trying out of different partners and exploration of sex and desire – are experiences which many of these young lesbians women never have. As the negotiation of sexuality and desire is central to the development of young women's sexual subjectivity, sense of personal empowerment and sense of entitlement (Fine, 1992; Thompson, 1995; Cowie and Lees, 1987; Tolman and Szalacha, 1999; Tolman, 1994b), this is a considerable loss.

STRATEGIES OF COPING AND RESISTANCE

There are a number of strategies available to these young women for dealing with the experiences outlined in the above extracts. The most obvious is silence – to remain closeted. Previous research has shown that young lesbians who are closeted about their sexuality, not discussing it with family or friends, live in fear of exposure and have a constant awareness that acceptance by others is based on a lie (Margolies *et al.*, 1987). Passing as heterosexual has been found to be associated with feelings of shame, depression, anxiety and awkwardness (Rotheram-Borus and Fernandez,

1995), with the most closeted individuals reporting the highest levels of social conflict, personal conflict, alienation, isolation, depression and negative self-esteem (Savin-Williams, 1990). There is also a risk of splitting and fragmentation of self, as a double life is lived. If sexuality and desire are repressed completely, there can be frustration, loneliness, guilt, feelings of self-betrayal and the living of an asexual life.

The alternative is resistance. All of the young women interviewed had chosen to adopt a lesbian identity and to do so publicly by joining the Lesbian Avengers. In the narratives presented here this was positioned as an act of resistance, of defiance, of control and a positive force for change.

These women reported a greater sense of freedom than they had experienced before, feeling that they were allowed to be themselves, be more comfortable with themselves. For this young woman, publicly naming herself removes the threat of exposure,

There was always this, rumours you know, aw, she's a dyke, she's queer, and there was me turning round saying, yeah I am, an everyone was kind of like, huh, you know cause no one, it's not some little sneaky rumour anymore.

There was also a sense of defiance in being 'out' for many.

I mean when you're labelled an abomination and a pervert, you sort of think, 'hmmm', well I've been labelled as this maybe I can do anything I want then, it's like being a lesbian. You get labelled as a lesbian and you can do what ever you want, you sleep with men, women, cats, dogs, anything you want to do because you've been labelled as a pervert so you can get away with it. I mean what more can they do to you?

I'm a dyke means I'm saying you know you're putting yourself out as well you're putting yourself further out you're not even trying to conform all their little ideas of nice little homosexuals…you're saying I'm, a dyke and I'm here and I'm gonna be loud.

There is arguably a representation of ambivalence described here in the defiant stance taken up – a sense of isolation, of being different, of being 'outside' and of facing difficulty because of this. Yet this is also an account of the acceptance of this difficulty as being an expected part of taking up a lesbian identity, and of a determination to overcome it, in having become strong, or free, through adversity. As another woman said

I got a lot more confident in myself and sort of thought let them stuff it, this is who I am and they are going to have to deal with it.

What is arguably being presented here is an argument that the investment in a lesbian identity is made stronger through the opposition of others. The importance of a positive social network to support young women after coming out cannot be underestimated. As one interviewee said:

I think it will always be difficult, but I think it won't be half as difficult as before, because now there is access into this community, which I never had before. It's part of sort of claiming an identity trying to find where you fit in ... it gives me a really nice feeling to feel part of some, this umm, this sub-culture.

Previous research has found that this support is a major protective factor against subsequent negative reactions to disclosure. At the same time, for many, feelings that were previously positioned as negative, feeling different and alien, were positioned as positive after coming out. There is thus a re-framing of the meaning of being 'other' in a heterosexual social sphere.

I can actually identify myself as something that other people aren't ... it gives me a separate identity ... something I can identify with which gives me something I can build which makes me more confident.

Contact with other lesbians is associated with good mental health (Margolies *et al.*, 1987), partly because it gives young women the opportunity to resist and reject myths and negative representations (Zitter, 1987). But it also provides a normal social network, which is an important part of adolescent development.

Heterosexually identified girls commonly group together around a shared interest in music, fashion, boys, or being a fan of a particular 'pop-star' (Garrett, 1984), forming relationships which are central to the development of their sexual subjectivity (Ussher, 1997a; Firth and Goodwin, 1984). As we have argued elsewhere (Ussher and Mooney-Somers, 2000) becoming a Lesbian Avenger arguably works in the same way for this group of young women, providing a positive social identity, a sense of group solidarity, a source of role models, friendship, and common goals. As the young women we interviewed were positioned as outsiders because of their sexuality, being a member of the Lesbian Avengers also functions to provide a social context where they are normal and accepted. It acts to reframe their lesbianism as powerful, positive and defiant – a reframing which doesn't merely take place at the level of the individual, but takes place at the level of the group.

SUMMARY

D'Augelli (1999) suggests that 'contemporary lesbian, gay and bisexual youths can emerge from adolescence without stepping into closets'. How can we, as mental health professionals and educators help young lesbian women avoid the closets, thereby avoiding the negative affects of this strategy?

In understanding the mental health of young lesbians we must take material, discursive and intra-psychic factors on board – this brief analysis of our interviews has given us just a taste of all three. There is the materiality of verbal and physical abuse, of rejection, of discrimination, of sex and desire. There is the discursive representation of the lesbian as lecherous, as other, as deviant or sick. There are intra-psychic factors such as depression, anxiety, fear, and shame – yet also desire, pleasure, power and anger. Each of these three levels is inter-twined; we can not understand one without the other. Being lesbian is a material-discursive-intrapsychic experience.

The stories told by the young women here tell of isolation, alienation, feelings of self-betrayal and fear, but also of support, validation and acceptance. These young women emphasized the importance of claiming a positive lesbian identity. They felt supported and part of something after they 'came out'. Yet they also talked of many problems at home, at school and in relationships with friends. It is important for those who are concerned with issues of women's health to take seriously the difficulties experienced by young lesbians. Young lesbians invariably face discrimination and hostility when they come out. Yet for many there is a strong desire to disclose, and positive consequences of being open about sexuality and subjectivity. Silence is not necessarily the best strategy; it can be oppressive. Support and the space to explore their sexuality in a positive and safe space can mediate against negative reactions and the ongoing difficulties of being an 'out' lesbian. Access to others who are in a similar position can also give validation.

For previous generations the negotiation of a lesbian identity was delayed until adulthood. The young women in this study, however, were negotiating their sexual identity whilst still at school or college, many were still dependent on their families for financial support, and some were still living in the family home. Educators and schools need to recognize that young lesbians face victimization and discrimination around their sexuality. Initiatives to support lesbian students can help facilitate positive mental health and positive identity development, and need to be developed. For lesbians who have other problems, the added difficulty of coming out and coming to terms with being different in an often hostile heterosexual world may mean that survival is against all odds. There are few, if any services directly targeting issues of bullying, mental health, suicide or drug and alcohol misuse in lesbian (or gay) adolescents. This is an imbalance that needs to be redressed. It is difficult to be optimistic. As Coyle and Daniels (1993) have argued, hard-pressed health authorities are reluctant to prioritize gay and lesbian mental health issues and establish specialized services. Lesbian sexual health services do exist. Does this mean that physical health initiatives are easier to deliver, or is it that mental health professionals are unaware of the needs of lesbians? It is time that this imbalance is addressed.

REFERENCES

Cowie, S. and Lees, S. (1987) Slags or drags? In Feminist Review (Eds.) *Sexuality: A Reader* (pp. 105–122)

Coyle, A. and Davies, M. (1993) Psychological wellbeing and gay identity: some suggestions for promoting mental health among gay men. In D.R Trentand and C. Reed (Eds.) *Promotion of Mental Health*. Aldershot: Avebury

D'Augelli, R.D. (1999) The queering of adolescence: implications for psychological researchers and practitioners. *Newsletter of the BPS Lesbian and Gay Psychology Section*, 3, 3–5

Davies, D. and Neal, C. (Eds.) (1996) *Pink Therapy: A Guide for Counsellors and Therapists Working with Lesbian, Gay and Bisexual Clients*. Buckingham: Open University Press

Fergusson, D.H., Horwood, L.J. and Beautrais, A.L. (1999) Is sexual orientation related to mental health problems and suicidality in young people? *Archives of General Psychiatry*, 56 (10), 876–880

Fine, M. (1992) Sexuality, schooling and adolescent girls: the missing discourse of desire. *Harvard Educational Review*, 58(1), 29–53

Firth, S. and Goodwin, A. (1984) *Rock, Pop and the Written Word*. London: Routledge

Garrett, S. (1984) Teenage Dreams. In Firth, S. and Goodwin, A. (Eds.) *Rock, Pop and the Written Word*. London: Routledge

Harding, S. (1991) *Whose Science? Whose Knowledge? Thinking from Women's Lives*. Milton Keynes: Open University Press

Harding, S. (1993). Rethinking standpoint epistemology: 'What is strong objectivity'? In L. Alcoff. and E. Potter (Eds.) *Feminist Epistemologies*. London, Routledge

Hershberger, S.C. and D'Augelli (1995) The impact of victimisation on the mental health and suicidality of lesbian and gay youths. *Developmental Psychology*, 31 (1), 65–74

Margolies, L., Becker, M. and Jackson-Brewer, K. (1987) Internalised homophobia: Identifying and treating the oppressor within. In Boston Lesbian Psychologies Collective (Ed.) *Lesbian Psychologies: Explorations and Challenges*. Urbana: University of Illinois Press

Mishler, E. (1986) *Research Interviewing: Context and Narrative*. Cambridge, MA: Harvard University Press

Nichols, S.L. (1999) Gay, lesbian and bisexual youth: understanding diversity and promoting tolerance in schools. *Elementary School Journal*, 99 (5), 505–519

Pilgrim, D. and Rogers, A. (1997). Mental health, critical realism and lay knowledge. In J.M. Ussher (Ed.) *Body Talk: The Material and Discursive Regulation of Sexuality, Madness and Reproduction* (pp. 67–82). London: Routledge

Ponse, B. (1978) *Identities in the Lesbian World: The Social Construction of Self*. Westport: Greenwood

Reissman, C.K.(1993) *Narrative Analysis. Qualitative Research Methods*, vol. 30. London: Sage

Rotheram-Borus, M.J. and Fernandez, M.I. (1995) Sexual orientation and developmental challenges experienced by gay and lesbian youth. *Suicide and Life Threatening Behaviour*, 25 (supplement), 26–34

Savin-Williams, R.C. (1990) *Gay and Lesbian Youth: Expressions of Identity*. New York: Hemisphere

Stivers, C. (1993) Reflections on the role of personal narrative in social science. *Signs: Journal of Women in Culture and Society*, 18(2), 408–425

Stoppard, J. (1999) *Women's Depression. Feminist and Social Constructionist Perspectives*. London: Routledge

Thompson, R. (1995) *Going all the Way: Teenage Girls' Tales of Sex and Romance*. New York: Hill & Wang

Tolman, D. and Szalacha, L. (1999) Dimensions of desire: Bridging qualitative and quantitative methods in a study of female adolescent sexuality. *Psychology of Women Quarterly*, 23, 7–39

Tolman, D. (1994b) Daring to desire: Culture in the bodies of adolescent girls. In J. Irvine (Ed.) *Sexual Cultures and The Construction of Adolescent Identities* (pp. 250–284). Philadelphia, PA: Temple University Press

Ussher, J.M. (1991) *Women's Madness: Misogyny or Mental Illness?* Hemel Hempstead: Harvester Wheatsheaf

Ussher, J.M. (1996) Premenstrual syndrome: Reconciling disciplinary divide through the adoption of a material-discursive epistemological standpoint. *Annual Review of Sex Research*. 7, 218–252

Ussher, J.M. (1997) *Fantasies of Femininity: Reframing the Boundaries of Sex*. London: Penguin

Ussher, J.M. (2000) Women's madness: a material-discursive-intra psychic approach. In D. Fee (Ed.) *Psychology and the Postmodern: Mental Illness as Discourse and Experience*. London: Sage

Ussher J. M. and Mooney Somers, J. (2000) Negotiating lesbian desire and sexual subjectivity: Narratives of young lesbian avengers. *Sexualities*, 3 (2) 183–200

Zitter, S. (1987) Coming out to Mom: Theoretical aspects of the mother-daughter process. In Boston Lesbian Psychologies Collective (Eds.) *Lesbian Psychologies: Explorations and challenges*. Urbana: University of Illinois Press

CHAPTER 8

FEMININITY AS A BARRIER TO POSITIVE SEXUAL HEALTH FOR ADOLESCENT GIRLS

Deborah L. Tolman

INTRODUCTION

This chapter discusses a new model of female adolescent sexual health based on feminist principles and investigates the extent to which adolescent girls' beliefs about femininity are associated with three specific elements of their sexual health. We discuss the results of a recent study in which 148 eighth grade adolescent girls completed a survey which included questions about sexual self-concept, sexual agency, attitudes towards romance conventions, femininity ideology, and demographic background. Our group found a statistically significant association between early adolescent girls' espousal of more conventional beliefs about femininity and diminished positive sexual health. To illustrate the ways in which a girl's femininity ideology interplays with her sexual health, I present the example of a 13-year-old Latina girl, whose critique of and active resistance to complying with this conventional femininity ideology offers evidence of how her femininity ideology may bolster her sexual health.

Adolescence is a time of enormous change in girls' bodies, relationships, emotions, and experiences – changes that include the development of adult sexuality. Traditionally, the sexual health of adolescent girls has been evaluated in terms of their participation in heterosexual intercourse. Two primary questions have been regularly asked and answered: have adolescent girls ever had sexual intercourse or, alternately and more popular of late, have they been abstinent? If they have had sexual intercourse, did they use effective contraception to protect against pregnancy, and in recent years, did they use condoms to protect as well against sexually transmitted diseases (STDs), specifically human immunodeficiency virus (HIV)?

These questions have a number of shortcomings. More often than not, they are asked of girls of color and girls living in poverty, with the not-so-subtle insinuation that only these girls are sexual. They maintain the invisibility of lesbian adolescents, as the only form of sexual behavior that they acknowledge is sexual intercourse. They reflect a model of adolescent sexuality in which 'the discursive focus is on behavioral rates rather than an elaboration of the cultural logics of adolescent sexuality' (Irvine, 1994: 3). Yet these questions have traditionally defined what we know about

adolescent sexuality. The most recent data suggest a trend of more absti-
nence and less unprotected sex: pregnancy rates among all adolescents
declined by 13 percent from 1991 to 1995 (Kaufmann *et al.*, 1998), more
than half of U.S. girls have not begun to have sexual intercourse by the age
of 18, and condom use among U.S. adolescents has increased 23 percent
since 1991 (Centers for Disease Control and Prevention, 1998). With the
physically most risky qualities of behavioral expressions of sexuality on
the decline, it is prudent to ask: does this mean that these adolescent girls
are sexually more healthy?

In 1995, the National Commission on Adolescent Sexual Health
released a consensus statement in the United States, endorsed by 48
national organizations including the American Medical Association,
declaring that becoming a sexually healthy adult is a key developmental
task for adolescents (Haffner, 1995). This statement extended the conception of sexual health beyond pregnancy prevention and the avoidance of
contracting STDs. The Commission incorporated into its conception of
sexual health the ability 'to develop and maintain meaningful interpersonal relationships' and to 'express affection, love, and intimacy in ways
consistent with one's own values' (Haffner, 1995: 4). To be considered
healthy, they declared, sexual relationships and the expression of sexuality in behavior must be 'consensual, nonexploitative, honest, pleasurable
and protected against unintended pregnancies and STDs, if any type of
intercourse occurs'(Haffner, 1995: 4). This statement represents a crucial
step toward a positive conception of sexuality for adolescents, bypassing
the notion that simply avoiding sexual intercourse or avoiding its negative
consequences is good enough. Sexual health, then, goes beyond the physical consequences of sexuality and incorporates experiential, psychological and relational dimensions as well.

Although a step forward, this statement is not sufficient, because it
assumes an archetypal adolescent who does not exist in reality. It does not
acknowledge the very real dimensions of gender, race, ethnicity or class
which organize adolescent sexuality in important ways. Feminist analysis
reveals that sexuality is not gender neutral, because the meanings and
realities associated with male and female sexuality are culturally constructed to be profoundly different and based on male privilege (hooks,
1981; Koedt, 1972; Rich, 1983; Vance, 1989). Feminists have also fleshed out
the ways in which race, ethnicity, sexual orientation and class create sexual hierarchies among women (Collins, 1990; Wyatt, 1997; Espin, 1999;
Tolman, 1996; Walkerdine, 1997). Despite the sexual revolution of the
1960s, society's conception of sexuality for adolescent girls who want to be
considered good, normal, and acceptable remains constrained. Good girls
are still supposed to 'just say no', not supposed to feel intense sexual
desire, and remain responsible for the sexual desire of boys and for protecting themselves from harm. Good girls are still assumed to be white
and middle class. Sexual violence, and the threat of violence, remain a real
and pervasive feature of the terrain of female sexuality (Kelly, 1988). Girls
are still expected to conform to the conventions of romance that organize

and assume heterosexuality, including needing to have, please, and keep a boyfriend, and the media continue to incite and naturalize girls' desire for these trappings of heterosexuality (Carpenter, 1998; Durham, 1998). Real, live adolescent girls must negotiate these constructions in working out their own conceptions of sexuality by and through which they express their own feelings, desires, and beliefs. The process by which girls create their sexual biographies is profoundly relational, carried out within the institutional and cultural spaces of their lived experience – in their schools, churches, synagogues, and mosques; in their neighborhoods, in clinics or doctors' offices; and within their racial and ethnic histories.

Feminist scholarship offers direction for the development of a model of positive sexual health for adolescent girls that recognizes how our society denies and diminishes female sexuality (Rich, 1983; Vance, 1989; Fine, 1988; Tolman and Szalacha, 1999) and that incorporates forms of resistance that enable girls to become sexually healthy. If girls are not supposed to acknowledge their own sexual desire or be assertive on behalf of their own wishes, and if they are supposed to comply with conventions of hetero-sexual romance, then it may be especially difficult for them to engage in sexual relationships that are 'consensual, nonexploitative, pleasurable, honest and protected' from pregnancy and disease. To develop such rela-tionships, both participants must have a sense of entitlement to say no and to say yes to forms of sexual expression, to know and have agency in rela-tion to their own feelings, to acknowledge their own sexuality, and to be free from violence.

Feminist analysis has also suggested that sexual health is multidimen-sional. Together with my staff at The Gender and Sexuality Project at the Center for Research on Women at Wellesley College, I am currently devel-oping such a model of sexual health for female adolescents (Figure 1), in which I identify four domains: 1) the individual girl, including her knowl-edge and attitudes, sense of entitlement to self pleasure (i.e., through mas-turbation, sexual fantasy) and sexual self-concept; 2) romantic/sexual relationships, including use of condoms and some forms of contraception, avoiding or leaving abusive partners when possible, and adopting a criti-cal perspective on romance conventions; 3) social relationships, including having support to work through confusion and questions about sexuality, to communicate with others about sexuality and to evaluate the quality of relationships; and 4) the sociopolitical dimensions of girls' sexuality, including access to and freedom to use reproductive health care, informa-tion and materials to sustain sexual health, and images of girls' sexuality as normal and acceptable.

Three elements of this model – accepting one's sexuality, feeling enti-tled to positive sexual agency and holding a critical perspective on con-ventions of romance – have not yet been identified or investigated as pos-sible key features of positive sexual health for adolescent girls. We began to assess this model by studying how these qualities help girls make healthy choices about their sexuality. We selected these constructs in part because they represent how individual girls negotiate the conceptions of

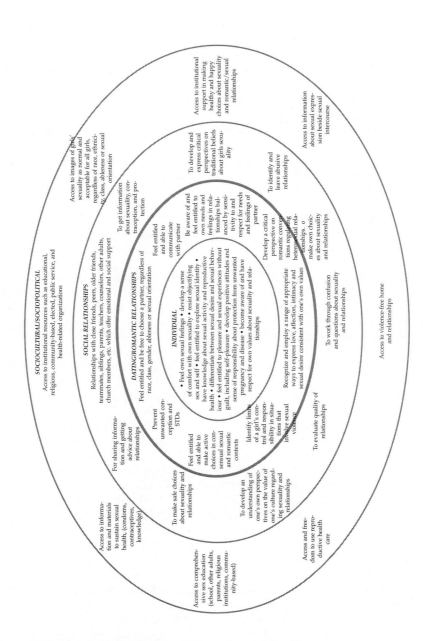

Figure 1. A model of female adolescent sexual health.

sexuality available to them. Future analyses will evaluate the many other features of this model.

Holding conventional beliefs about femininity and endorsing or engaging in stereotypic feminine behaviors have been associated with health risks and outcomes in women, including eating problems, risk for HIV, smoking, and breast reduction or augmentation (Birtchnell *et al.*, 1990; Brazelton *et al.*, 1998; Murnen and Smolak, 1997; Hansel *et al.*, 1993; Waldron, 1991). We investigated the ways in which early adolescent girls' beliefs about femininity might be associated with these three aspects of their sexual health in early adolescence. It is at early adolescence that girls first engage in romantic relationships and expressions of sexuality and develop the scripts that organize these experiences. It is also at early adolescence that beliefs about gender begin to intensify and to take their adult forms (Katz and Ksansnak, 1994; Galambos *et al.*, 1990). Because these processes occur simultaneously, an examination of the relationship between femininity and sexual health at this developmental moment is warranted.

METHODS

We employed a universal sampling technique and studied all eighth grade girls (n=148) in one north-eastern urban school district in the United States who are participating in a longitudinal study of gender ideology and its relationship to both risk of unintended pregnancy and sexual health. The response rate was very high (93 percent for the district).

The participants completed a survey that included demographic questions; questions about their sexual behavior, sexual health, and risk of unintended pregnancy; and standardized scales measuring their beliefs about femininity. Written permission was obtained from each child's parent or guardian, and the survey was available to bilingual students in Spanish, with a Spanish-speaking researcher present. A subset of 46 girls with high and low scores on measures of beliefs about femininity was selected and interviewed individually about their experiences with relationships, dating, and sexuality, using a clinical, semi-open interviewing technique designed to elicit narratives.

Beliefs about femininity were measured using two different scales. The Aodolescent Femininity Ideology Scale (AFIS) is a 20-item scale using a 6-point response scale (strongly agree to strongly disagree) which measures the extent to which adolescent girls have internalized dominant cultural conventions of femininity associated with how they feel and act in relationships with others and how they relate to their own bodies (Tolman and Porche, forthcoming). It is comprised of the Inauthentic Self-in-Relationship (ISIR) subscale and The Objectified Relationship with Body (ORWB) subscale. This scale was developed by our staff with diverse adolescent girls and incorporates the norms of femininity they perceive to regulate their behavior and identities as described by them in focus groups. High scores indicate internalization of a more conventional femininity ideology. The 12-

item Attitudes Toward Women Scale for Adolescents (AWSA) was used to measure girls' beliefs about feminine gender roles (Galambos *et al.*, 1985). Participants indicate their endorsement of more conventional and less traditional beliefs about how women should behave using a 4-point, Likert-type agree-disagree scale. High scores indicate less conventional attitudes toward women's roles and rights.

Girls' acceptance of their emerging sexuality was measured by the Sexual Self Concept Scale (SSC), which contains 14 items answered on a Likert-type agreement scale (Winter, 1988). Sexual self-concept is defined as an individual's evaluation of her own sexual feelings and actions. The scale was found to be internally consistent (standardized alpha coefficient= .90) for a college population and modified for our use with this early adolescent sample. In addition, our group developed two additional measures of positive sexual health for this study. The Index of Romantic Conventions includes 12 items answered on a 4-point, Likert-type scale, which demonstrated acceptable internal consistency (standardized alpha coefficient=.75). Based on research on girls' sexuality (Tolman, 1994; Lees, 1993; Thompson, 1995) and feminist analyses of romance (Lees, 1993; Thompson, 1995; Christian-Smith, 1990; Radway, 1984), these items reflect norms regulating heterosexual relationships and center on girls identifying and meeting boys' needs, including their sexual desires, and encouraging girls to seek and maintain these relationships at the expense of their own needs and desires. Finally, girls' perceptions of their sexual agency was measured by a composite of two single items (1) 'If I were uncomfortable I know I could refuse a sexual experience that my boyfriend/girlfriend wanted me to try'and (2)'I'm sure I could ask someone I was having sex with to use protection (condoms or birth control).'

Our team performed correlational and simple regression analyses to evaluate the strength and statistical significance of possible associations between early adolescent girls' beliefs about femininity and their sexual health. In addition, we investigated the role of ethnicity in these associations. Class differences that may also be compelling in understanding these associations are not presented at this time. The multiracial subset was not included due to the difficulty in interpreting such analyses.

RESULTS

The girls in the sample were 13 to 14 years old. Fifty-two percent were white, 20 percent Latina, and 17 percent bi-racial or multi-racial. Fifty-two percent reported that their families had ever received public assistance, while 29 percent reported current assistance of some sort, including participation in a free lunch program. Only a third (36 percent) reported that their mothers had college degrees or higher. These girls reported a range of sexual experiences: 82 percent had held hands, 68 percent had kissed on the mouth, 24 percent had touched someone under their clothes or with no clothes on, 28 percent had been touched under their clothes or with no

Table 1. Estimated Correlations Between Adolescent Girls' Beliefs About Femininity and Sexual Health

Variable	Sexual Agency	Romance Conventions	Sexual Self-Concept	Mean (sd)
Beliefs About Femininity				
AFIS–Inauthentic Self in Relationship (ISIR)				
Full Sample (n=148)	-0.21 †	0.24 †	0.01	3.27 (.73)
White Girls (n=77)	-0.16	0.22	0.08	3.31 (.77)
Latina Girls (n=29)	0.03	0.16	-0.22	3.40 (.75)
AFIS–Objectified Relationship with Body (ORWB)				
Full Sample (n=145)	-0.12	0.41‡	0.03	3.10 (.67)
White Girls (n=76)	-0.18	0.53‡	0.08	3.15 (.72)
Latina Girls (n=29)	-0.01	0.19	-0.04	3.23 (.69)
Attitudes Toward Women (AWSA)				
Full Sample (n=148)	0.37‡	-0.22 †	0.22 †	3.45 (.44)
White Girls (n=77)	0.13	-0.29*	0.29*	3.61 (.30)
Latina Girls (n=29)	0.33	-0.11	0.50 †	3.03 (.50)
Mean(s.d.) Full Sample	3.55 (.67)	2.27 (.48)	3.29 (.54)	
Mean(s.d.) White Girls	3.64 (.52)	2.30 (.47)	3.31 (.52)	
Mean(s.d.) Latina Girls	3.21 (.90)	3.37 (.58)	3.21 (.57)	

* p<.05 † p<.01 ‡ p<.001

clothes on, 7 percent had had sexual intercourse, and 14 percent reported other forms of sexual experience.

Accepting one's emerging sexuality, feeling entitled to positive sexual agency and holding a critical perspective on conventions of romance correlated with various forms of beliefs about femininity (see Table 1). We found statistically significant associations between early adolescent girls' espousal of more conventional beliefs about femininity and diminished positive sexual health. For the full sample, girls with higher scores on the Index of Romance Conventions had higher scores on the ISIR subscale of the FIS (r=.24, p<.01), that is, tended to be inauthentic in relationships, and had higher scores on the RWB subscale of the FIS (r=.41, p<.001), that is, tended to relate to their bodies as objects. Girls with lower scores on the sexual agency composite had somewhat higher scores on the SIR subscale of the FIS (r=-.21, p<.01) and lower scores on the AWSA (r=.37, p<.001), that is, girls who felt less sexual agency tended to be inauthentic in relationships and have more conventional beliefs about women's roles and rights. Finally, girls who scored lower on the Sexual Self Concept Scale had lower scores on the AWSA (r=.22, p<.01), that is, girls who tended towards less acceptance of their sexuality had more conventional beliefs about women's roles and rights.

When we compared these associations for white girls and Latinas, different patterns emerged in the association between beliefs about femininity and sexual health. There was a strong association between romance conventions and how girls relate to their bodies among White girls (r=.53, p<.001), and no significant correlation between these two variables for the Latina girls. We found a strong correlation between sexual self-concept and scores on the AWSA for Latina girls (r=.50, p<.001) and a moderate correlation between these two variables for white girls. In a simple regression analysis, the AWSA explained 9 percent of the variation in sexual self-concept for white girls [F(1,75)=6.99, p<.01], and 25 percent of the variation for Latina girls [F(1,27)=9.01, p<.006]).

CASE ILLUSTRATION

A subset of this sample (n=46) was interviewed individually about their experiences with relationships and sexuality. I present here a 13-year-old Latina girl who has appropriated a male persona, calling herself 'Will Smith'. She was chosen because her stories illustrate how femininity ideology can organize, limit and challenge girls' attempts at sexual health within a particularly traditional social context. Will Smith exemplifies a pattern identified in these interviews that girls who articulated a critical perspective on unequal gender arrangements and norms of femininity were better able to answer questions about how being a girl affected the choices they made in their relationships. She was interviewed by a Latina woman in both Spanish and English.

When asked about how she's supposed to act or be in a relationship because she is a girl, she replied:

The girl is down to like 5 percent and the boy is like 95 percent. Like the boy has the right to go out but the girl needs to stay home cleaning the house ... I don't agree with that, cause like if I see my boyfriend talking to a girl and I get mad at him, he'll be saying 'Well, it's different, cause you're a girl and I'm a boy.' I'll be like, 'What's the difference?'

Int: So if you don't behave the way you have just described you would...

I would be a so-called hoochie [a colloquialism for 'whore']... I think it's disgusting to tell you the truth... in the Dominican Republic, the thing is boys can have as many girls as they want. And you know that's not a problem....I was straight up with my boyfriend with that too. I was like, 'If you think you're gonna be going on like from me to another girl and then another girl and stuff, you must be buggin, cause it ain't gonna be like that with me.'

Will refuses to participate in the conventions of romance and femininity ideology that would have her put up with a double standard enabling boys to treat – and mistreat – girls as objects. She understands and is willing to live with the consequences of possibly losing her boyfriend by taking this stand.

She articulated her awareness of and resistance to being objectified:

You need to worry what your breast size are. How your butt is formed. For a boy to like you, you have to have like the features ... First it's like the way you act around them [boys], then it's your body and THEN comes like what's inside, you know what I mean. I don't like that.

Sensing that being objectified renders her agency, feelings and desires irrelevant, Will demands that she be acknowledged and desired for 'who I am'. In refusing to be constructed as an object, she is less vulnerable to being used as an object.

Having asked her boyfriend out, Will was willing to be an active agent, taking the initiative in starting a relationship she wants, rather than waiting to be noticed by a boy, and defining its terms. In negotiating her relationship and her sexuality with her boyfriend, Will told him 'straight out':

If you want me because of sex you better be going opening the door and walking away cause it ain't gonna happen ... I don't want to, nothing of that, not until I'm ready ... The kissing is going to be done if I like it and if I don't like it, then it's off. And if you don't like that, well that's too bad, you're leaving.

Will feels empowered to include her own feelings in her decisions about sexual expression, as well as to demand that her boyfriend honor her decisions as well.

Will's stories offer a number of insights into how her femininity ideology shapes and, in her case, contributes to her sexual health. On the one hand, she has taken in the message that she has to fend her boyfriend off from doing sexual things to her, which creates a kind of negative sexual agency. However, she also voices a sense of entitlement to her own desire as an important ingredient in her sexual experiences. She also explicitly ties being used sexually and being sexually passive with more traditional ideas about both femininity and masculinity, ideas that she rejects. While Will is not risk free – she shows some signs of risk of unintended pregnancy, her self-esteem is low and she is depressed – her ability to see, know, and understand how girls are positioned as sexually vulnerable by cultural norms about femininity constitutes a strength that needs to be recognized and built upon. Without support for this vision, she is at risk of losing what may be keeping her depression and low self-esteem from becoming diminished sexual health.

SUMMARY

Rather than simply striving to diminish and eliminate the risks associated with sexual intercourse, this work contributes to an expanding conception of sexual health for adolescent girls. Based on feminist scholarship and the obstacles facing girls and women in negotiating sexuality, we inquired about three components of positive sexual health for adolescent girls: accepting one's sexuality, having a sense of positive sexual agency, and rejecting romance conventions. Girls' beliefs about different aspects of femininity were associated with these three features of sexual health. How girls relate to their bodies was not pertinent to sexual agency, but their attitudes toward women and their inauthenticity in relationships were. Only their attitudes toward women related to their sexual self-concept.

Romantic conventions emerged as pervasively related to girls' beliefs about femininity, correlating with all three measures. Some of these associations were stronger for the white or Latina girls in the sample.

While causality has not been established, and while all forms of femininity measured did not correlate strongly or significantly with all three aspects of sexual health, this correlational study does suggest that holding conventional beliefs regarding femininity is a barrier to positive sexual health for girls and needs further investigation. One interpretation of these results is that girls' beliefs about femininity extend into their sexual beliefs and practices, that is, that their femininity ideology incorporates cultural norms regulating their negotiation of sexuality. Because the girls in this study were early adolescents, many of whom have limited actual sexual experience, it will be important to see how their femininity ideology relates to their sexual health as they mature (Brown and Gilligan, 1992).

These moderate correlations suggest that femininity ideology is only one factor that supports or undermines female adolescent sexual health and that ethnicity is an important factor in the relationship between girls' beliefs about femininity and their sexual health. This relationship needs to be investigated for African-American, Asian, Native-American, and biracial girls. The intersections and interplay between and among multiple identities, including race, ethnicity, socioeconomic class, religion, religiosity, ableness, and sexual orientation, need to be explored; some will be addressed in future analyses by our group at the Gender and Sexuality Project.

This study is the beginning of an empirical approach to female adolescent sexuality which connects sexual health with the multifaceted experiences of sexuality that may be part of female adolescence. The model of female adolescent sexual health from which this study is drawn identifies the various relationships and social contexts in which girls negotiate their sexuality. In so doing, our group hopes to shift away from a blaming – as well as 'fixing' – the victim approach to girls' sexuality and toward examining and intervening in the relational and social circumstances of girls' lives in order to engender and sustain their sexual health.

This study suggests that conventional femininity ideology may function as a barrier – and, conversely, that critique of femininity ideology may offer a booster – to adolescent girls' sexual health. Girls are under pressure in their families, in their relationships, in their schools, from the media, and perhaps even from service and care providers to capitulate to conventions of femininity that may diminish their sexual health. These social institutions should be subject to the frequent and vocal scrutiny of adults who care for and about adolescent girls. Based on this and other studies in which girls have been interviewed about their lives, it is likely that many girls have never heard a critical perspective on femininity or on how society encourages them to think about their own sexuality. Equally important, girls who have had access to such critiques seem to be more likely to feel empowered and entitled to make healthy and safer choices and to have more positive experiences with sexuality (Fine, 1988; Tolman, 1994; Thompson, 1995). Helping adolescent girls identify and question conventions of femininity and to consider that they are entitled to their own sexuality can offer the initial spark needed to begin a process of critical thinking about these aspects of their lives and identities.

ACKNOWLEDGMENT

This research was supported by a grant from the Ford Foundation. The Gender and Sexuality Project currently includes Michelle Porche, Renee Spencer, Myra Rosen-Reynoso, Judy Chu, and Darce Costello. The author wishes to thank them for their assistance and contributions to this article, and also the three anonymous reviewers who offered thoughtful and helpful comments.

REFERENCES

Birtchnell, S., Whitfield, P. and Lacey, J.H. (1990) Motivational factors in women requesting augmentation and reduction mamaplasty. *Journal of Psychosomatic Research*, 34, 509–514

Brazelton, E. W., Greene, K. S., Gynther, M. and O'Mell, J. (1998) Femininity, bulimia, and distress in college women. *Psychological Report*, 83, 355–363

Brown, L. M. and Gilligan, C. (1992) *Meeting at the Crossroads*. Cambridge, MA: Harvard University Press

Carpenter, L. (1998) From girls into women: Scripts for sexuality and romance in *Seventeen* magazine, 1974–1994. *Journal of Sex Research*, 35, 158–168

Centers for Disease Control and Prevention (1998) Trends in sexual risk behaviors among high school students – United States, 1991-1997. *M MW R*, 47, 749–752

Collins, P. H. (1990) *Black Feminist Thought*. New York: Routledge

Christian-Smith, L. (1990) *Becoming a Woman Through Romance*. New York: Routledge

Espin, O. (1999) *Women Crossing Boundaries*. New York: Routledge

Fine, M. (1988) Sexuality, schooling, and adolescent females: The missing discourse of desire. *Harvard Educational Review*, 58, 29–53

Durham, M. (1998) Dilemmas of desire: Representations of adolescent sexuality in two teen magazines. *Youth and Society*, 29, 369–389

Galambos, N., Almeida, D., and Petersen, A. (1990) Masculinity, femininity, and sex-role attitudes in early adolescence: Exploring gender intensification. *Child Development*, 61, 1905–1904

Galambos, N., Petersen, A., Richards, M. and Geitelson, I. (1985) The Attitudes Towards Women Scale for Adolescents: A study of reliability and validity. *Sex Roles*, 13, 343–356

Haffner, D. (Ed.) (1995) *Facing facts: Sexual health for America's Adolescents*. New York: Sexuality Information and Education Council of the United States (The Report of the National Commission on Adolescent Sexual Health)

Hansel, N.K., Weeks, M.E., Ryan, J.G., and Fowler, G.C. (1993) The female role in the transmission of HIV infection. *Archives of Family Medicine*, 2, 870–873

hooks, b. (1981) *Ain't I a Woman*. Boston: South End Press

Irvine, J. (1994) Cultural differences and adolescent sexualities. In J. Irvine, (Ed.) *Sexual Cultures and the Construction of Adolescent Identities*. Philadelphia: Temple University Press

Katz, P. and Ksansnak, K. (1994) Developmental aspects of gender role flexibility and traditionality in middle childhood and adolescence. *Developmental Psychology*, 30, 272–282

Kaufmann, R.B., Spitz, A.M., Strauss, L.T. *et al.* (1998) The decline in the US teen pregnancy rates, 1990–1995. *Pediatrics*, 102, 1141–1147

Kelly, L. (1988) *Surviving Sexual Violence*. Cambridge, MA: Polity

Koedt, A. (1972) *Radical Feminism*. New York: Quadrangle

Lees, S. (1993) *Sugar and Spice: Sexuality and Adolescent Girls*. London: Penguin Books

Murnen, S.K., and Smolak, L. (1997) Femininity, masculinity, and disordered eating: A meta-analytic review. *International Journal of Eating Disorders*, 22, 231–242

Radway, J. (1984) *Reading the Romance*. Chapel Hill: University of North Carolina Press

Rich, A. (1983) Compulsory heterosexuality and lesbian existence. In A. Snitow, C. Stansell and S. Thompson (Eds.) *Powers of Desire*. New York: Monthly Review Press

Thompson, S. (1995) *Going All The Way: Teenage Girls' Tales of Sex, Romance and Pregnancy*. New York: Hill and Wang

Tolman, D.L. (1996) Adolescent girls' sexuality: Debunking the myth of the urban girl. In B. Leadbeater and N. Way (Eds.) *Urban Girls* (pp. 255–271). New York: New York University Press

Tolman, D.L. (1994) Daring to desire. In J. Irvine (Ed.), *Sexual Cultures and the Construction of Adolescent Identities* (pp. 250–284). Philadelphia: Temple University Press

Tolman, D.L. and Porche, M.V. (forthcoming) The Adolescent Femininity Ideology Scale: Development and validation of a new measure for girls. *Psychology of Women Quarterly*

Tolman, D.L., and Szalacha, L.A. (1999) Dimensions of desire: Bridging qualitative and quantitative methods in a study of female adolescent sexuality. *Psychology of Women Quarterly*, 23, 7–39

Vance, C.S. (1989) Pleasure and danger: Toward a politics of sexuality. In C.S. Vance (Ed.) *Pleasure and Danger*. London: Pandora Press

Waldron, I. (1991) Patterns and causes of gender differences in smoking. *Social Science Medicine*, 32, 989–991

Walkerdine, V. (1997) *Daddy's Girl*. Cambridge, MA: Harvard University Press

Winter, L. (1988) The role of sexual self-concept in the use of contraceptives. *Family Planning Perspectives*, 20, 123–127

Wyatt, G. (1997) *Stolen Women*. New York: John Wiley & Sons

CHAPTER 9

'I COULDN'T IMAGINE HAVING SEX WITH ANYONE ELSE': YOUNG WOMEN'S EXPERIENCE OF TRUSTWORTHINESS IN HETEROSEXUAL RELATIONSHIPS

Niamh Stephenson, Susan Kippax and June Crawford

INTRODUCTION

This chapter interrogates one particular notion of trustworthiness as it arose in young women's discussions of (monogamous) heterosexual relationships: being trustworthy involves more than simply having sex with only one partner, it amounts to *desiring* no one other than one's partner. We examine this notion of trust as it is constituted through a discourse of sexuality in which sexual intimacy is thought to lead to true knowledge of the subject (Foucault, 1984). Here, women's trustworthiness is cast as a necessary foundation for monogamous heterosexual relationships, something that will inevitably be known. We then draw on a psychoanalytically informed account of heterosexuality to consider how *women's* trustworthiness shores up a fantasy of masculine subjectivity as autonomous, bounded and self-identical. We consider how the figure of the untrustworthy (unclean) woman is cast as a site for the merging of one man's bodily fluids with those of another man. This constitutes a threat to the fantasy which demarcates heterosexual masculinity (as opposed to femininity or is homosexuality). Thus, young women's trustworthiness can serve to shore up a phallocentric fantasy of heterosexual masculinity (see Segal and Teifer, in this volume).

A BEDROCK OF TRUST

Monogamy is commonly employed as a HIV/AIDS prevention strategy by heterosexual men and women, which means that trust in heterosexual relationships arises as a health issue (Kippax *et al.*, 1994). In this chapter we focus on young women's lived experience of being trustworthy heterosexual partners. We examine the discursive practices and psychical fantasies through which women's experience of a particular notion of trustworthiness is constituted and lived. Our analysis draws on the data collected by the National Centre for HIV Social Research (NCHSR) as part of a project about heterosexuality and HIV prevention. Here, we focus on the interviews (27) and focus groups (13) conducted with heterosexual women. The majority of participants were young women who were recruited through university or through youth centers.

We are concerned with women's talk about their experience of themselves as trustworthy sexual partners. When invoked in conversation and interview situations, young women's understandings of themselves as trustworthy can serve to curb discussion of trust in relationships. Trustworthiness might be experienced in an infinite number of ways, and discussion of such is critical. Here, however, we focus on a particular configuration of trust, i.e. trust as the unquestionable foundation of heterosexual relationships, a foundation which appears to preclude sexual interest in anyone other than one's partner.

In addressing the relationship between the 'marital discourse' and condom use (or lack of it), Willig (1995) points to the fundamental role of trust in heterosexual relationships. Within this discourse, trust is understood as requiring constant *re-creation*. A range of practices become subject to the demands for re-creating trust in heterosexual relationships, such as the decision to conceive (implying trustworthiness), or the reluctance to discuss sex with partners for fear that it might signal a problem, and untrustworthiness. This notion of trust, as something requiring ongoing maintenance, is less evident in the talk of many of the young women who participated in this project. Trust is described as the *bedrock* of their relationships. Without trust there simply wouldn't be a relationship. The absence of trust signifies the end of a relationship, rather than the need to negotiate, rethink, or change aspects of the relationship. In order to elucidate this configuration of trust, we consider the relationship between trust and discourses of sex, intimacy and knowledge, distinguishing a sexually specific meaning of trustworthiness in the talk of young women.

BEING TRUSTWORTHY

Many of the young women professed that desire for their partners in their current relationships precluded desire for another. This was not the case for all participants. But we would suggest that it is a dominant meaning and living other forms of desire is no easy matter. This is illustrated in Amanda's explanation of her failure to follow up on her desire to have sex with other men, even though her partner had encouraged her to branch out.

But even if I did that, and I'm glad I didn't, but even if I did … yeah, it would eventually end because of the guilt I felt. So I'm glad I didn't … I think it's better this way. 'Cause I've got no guilty conscience at all.

Deception is not the problem here; simply going against the grain of monogamy invokes guilt.

This configuration of desire is of interest because it illustrates that being monogamous entails more than following rules or scripts. Having sex with other people is not even the issue. What one is expected to do, what one does and what one desires are often all conflated in the talk of many of these young women. So monogamy is cast as unproblematic. Here, trust is not simply about telling the truth, it is about *being* true. When contemplating the possibility of unfaithfulness, Laura remarks:

I would tell him straight away anyway. There's no way. You wouldn't be able to keep it from him anyway.

Honesty is seen as necessary because he would automatically know. Laura credits men with a profound insight into their individual partners' lives. It is this assumed continuum between her thoughts and actions and his knowledge of her action and thoughts which, we argue, constitutes the lived experience of many young heterosexual women's understanding of themselves as trustworthy.

POLICING TRUST

When we consider the meanings of masculine sexuality afforded by 'the male sex drive' discourse, men are constructed as philanderers in constant pursuit of sexual experience (Hollway, 1989). Because men are thought to be driven to sex, they have diminished responsibility for how and with whom they have sex, rendering men's trustworthiness problematic. Women, by comparison, are constituted as relatively trustworthy. Such an understanding of trust and fidelity in heterosexual relationships is 'common-sense'. Yet a conflicting common-sense notion, is that women are intrinsically untrustworthy and their sexuality demands surveillance.

The processes through which women become 'woman' are ones of objectification and policing (de Beauvoir, 1973). Surveillance of women's sexuality is part of women's lived experience, and it isn't simply a matter of something men do to women. This is evident in the talk of these young women. In the following exchange, knowledge of women's trustworthiness (or lack of) is cast as problematic, something which may possibly elude policing. Interestingly, the discussion arrives at this point after Sarah describes the problems of actually knowing *men's* fidelity:

Sarah: *[You can] never be sure even if they swear [that they are faithful] and you really believe it, even if, you can never be sure.*

Wendy: *Not just that, the girls they've been with before you.*

Interviewer: *And who have they been with?*

Sarah: *Yeah, you never know.*

Wendy: *They might think she's pure and innocent but she could be the big slut of wherever they were.*

Women's own complicity in the reproduction of the need to control (other) women's risky sexuality is evident in the talk between Sarah, Wendy and the interviewer (also a woman). Experiences of being trustworthy are one means through which this control is lived by some young women.

There is a paradoxical freedom to be found in committed monogamous relationships, a freedom from demands to explain and account for oneself. Foucault argues that with the 'discursive explosion of the eighteenth and nineteenth centuries … nothing further was demanded of it [heterosexual monogamy] than to define itself from day to day' (1984: 38). The heterosexually monogamous are constituted as the grounds from which others deviate. It is easier to simply shore up monogamy than it is to question or explain it, and this is evident in our interviews with young women about heterosexuality. Trust between others (including themselves and their past partners) may be nebulous. But, as mentioned above, in the talk of many of these young women, often their own trustworthiness is accounted for in terms which exclude wayward desires:

Maria: It's the ultimate taboo really. To want to sleep with anybody else, because that's what a relationship's really all about, an involved relationship is being able to trust somebody else. And we – our whole relationship's based on trust, a very open trust.

This unproblematic stress on fidelity, explained in terms of (excluded) desire, means that trust is constructed as unquestionable.

THE CONSTRUCTION OF TRUST IN THE DISCOURSES OF SEX, INTIMACY AND KNOWLEDGE

The conflation of sex and knowledge in the talk of these young women is evocative of Foucault's claim that in Western culture, sex has been constituted as a problem of truth. The link between sex and truth is implicated in two processes: Not only do we seek out the truth of sex, but 'we demand that it tell us our truth … the deeply buried truth … about ourselves which we think we possess in our immediate consciousness' (1984: 69). Like knowing someone intimately, knowing someone sexually is considered an inherently more truthful way of knowing.

Shotter (1993) discusses the association between self-knowledge and the experience of intimacy in committed sexual relationships, invoking the public/private binary to argue that private modes of speech constitute the experience of an 'intimate' knowledge of ourselves and of others. Without reifying the public/private binary, following Shotter, we contend that the discourses of public and private talk can constitute different ways of experiencing both our relationships and ourselves. This connection between ways of talking, intimacy and knowledge is evident in the following:

Laura: *It's knowing your partner to the extent …. You can talk about anything.*

Ann: *You can talk about – a good relationship is like talking to him like you would talk to no-one else at all.*

Cath: *Like you wouldn't even talk to your mother [laugh]. Sorry! You wouldn't even talk to your mother. That's sort of like how I feel, if you … trust someone enough to do that, then the relationship's going to go far.*

The talk of Laura, Ann and Cath suggests that intimate ways of knowing people are understood as intrinsically more truthful. The differences between public and private modes of speech are not only evident in how one addresses others but are inherent in one's relationship to oneself: intimate speech genres which constitute personal relationships can 'open up' new realms of self-consciousness (Shotter, 1993). But, what is divulged is not a unique individual essence. Rather the aspect of self being revealed is constructed in the mode of talk.

There is a confessional aspect to intimate talk. Intimacy involves trusting both oneself and the other to be honest as well as attributing oneself and the other with a particular form of self-knowledge. Through intimate talk people can come to understand themselves, and their partners, as incapable of having stray sexual desires or of acting on those desires:

Trish: *Because we're so open with each other, there'd be this breakdown before you'd even want to be going out and sleeping with anybody else.*

Being 'open' is incompatible with a breach in trust. In Trish's talk, infidelity then can only occur following a breakdown in communication – it would not come as a surprise. This shores up the notion of trust as unproblematic, if trust wasn't warranted one would know before 'you'd even *want*' to be unfaithful. These discourses, of sexuality and intimacy, constitute the experience of 'knowing' and trusting not only one's partner but also oneself. Through the practice of intimate talk in committed sexual relationship, young heterosexual women can 'learn' that they are trustworthy individuals and that *they* are not 'sluts' whose sexuality poses a dangerous threat to the social order.

SELF-IDENTITY, BODY FLUIDS AND TRUST

In giving a discursive account of heterosexuality, we have examined the role of language in constituting the lived experience of young, heterosexual women. What emerges is the importance of the clean/unclean dichotomy. Another way of approaching this dichotomy is to draw on a psychoanalytically informed account of heterosexuality, foregrounding the importance of fantasy (e.g. Irigaray, 1985). Here, we are turning on psychoanalysis, not in order to speak the truth of feminine subjectivity, but as *a* cultural form through which experience is constituted (Parker, 1996; Sofia, 1992).

Experience and subjectivity are constituted in and through phantasies, phantasies have real effects (Walkerdine and Lucey, 1989). But the relationship between phantasy and reality is not a straightforward, deterministic one. Sexual difference feminists argue that to understand the way subjectivities are constituted, we need to understand the process of identification. The symbolic order is the field through which subjectivity is constituted. Identification involves the projection of the bodily ego onto one of two stable points in the symbolic order – masculine or feminine (Butler, 1993). Luce Irigaray argues that subjectivity, as it is constituted in the symbolic order, is phallocentric: i.e. although there are both masculine and feminine points of identification, *both* reflect and represent a singularly masculine understanding of experience. There is another, non-phallocentric, version of the feminine (often described in terms of excess) which does *not* take the masculine as its starting point. This second version of the feminine is repressed in the symbolic.

The masculine subject, as it is instituted through the symbolic realm, is fantasized as self-identical, as capable of announcing, elaborating, embellishing and expanding himself; he is imagined as active, rational, unitary and self-contained (Grosz, 1989; Henriques *et. al.*, 1984). This does not mean that all men (or women) necessarily consciously experience themselves as active, elaborating, unitary, etc. What is critical, for masculine identification, is a fantasy of the subject as self-grounded. Feminine subjectivity is represented and fantasized, in the symbolic realm, as the negative term of masculinity. Whilst the masculine is affiliated with activity, autonomy and the mind, for example, feminine identification involves an alignment with passivity, dependency and the body.

There is more to women's (and men's) experience than these phallocentric fantasies of subjectivity. Irigaray (1985) argues that the feminine terms of fluidity, ambiguity, plurality and elusiveness (which are repressed, yet preserved, in the symbolic order) threaten to reveal the phallocentrism of subjectivity and the symbolic realm. So there are two versions of the feminine. The first can be articulated within the terms of a phallocentric symbolic order, it shores up phallocentric masculinity. And the second, the repressed (excess) feminine, potentially undermines or disrupts the ways in which women are commonly represented, for example, as either 'nice' or 'a slut'. Women's lived experience of heterosexuality is constituted in the tension between these different versions of the feminine – without being inevitably constrained to one of these two positions.

Fantasies of subjectivity are neither stable nor concrete. Although repressed, the (excess) feminine 'is *always already there* in any adult sexual pleasure (men's as well as women's)' (Grosz, 1989: 117). Phallocentric subjectivity is constantly under threat. Strategies for keeping the (excess) feminine at bay include negation and denigration of the feminine and policing and vilifying women. In what follows, we argue that women's trustworthiness can act to guard against the threat to masculine self-identity. For a young heterosexual woman, being trustworthy can serve the dual purposes of demarcating oneself from excessive femininity and shoring up phallocentric masculinity.

Drawing on Bersani (1988), Waldby *et al.* (1993) argue that women's bodies can threaten heterosexual masculine subjectivity, because it is through the bodies of women that men risk coming in contact with other men's body fluids. The menace of body fluids is that they 'attest to the *permeability* of the body, its necessary *dependence* on an outside, its liability to *collapse* into this outside (this is what death implies) ... They affront a subject's aspiration toward *autonomy* and *self-identity*' (Grosz, 1994: 193, emphasis added). Grosz continues to argue that this threat to heterosexual masculine subjectivity is contained in the demarcation of men and women's body fluids. In contrast to women's body fluids (indicative of lack of control), men's bodies are imagined as phallic and impermeable, and semen is phenomenologically experienced as a solid. The value of semen is understood in terms of where it goes and what it does (Roberts *et al.* 1996). In the phallic economy semen can be a mark of appropriation of women's bodies, affirming masculine self-identity by extending the realm under a man's control. Alternative representations of semen may be experienced as threatening or undermining, by heterosexual men. For example, when Jack is asked about semen he is reminded of his 'phobia':

Interviewer: *What about semen, what do you think about semen?*

Jack: *Ahh, I must say I find it a little bit repulsive ... I mean – having kissed girls who have just given you a head job [pause]. You're more worried about what it might taste like rather than what it does taste like ... There's a certain phobia about it, that's for sure.*

Whilst semen is, or is imagined to be, in its 'proper' place inside women's bodies it can confirm men's autonomy and impermeability (Roberts *et al.*, 1996). Women's permeable bodies are represented as out of control and their body fluids as polluting and dangerous. This is evidenced in the early HIV prevention campaigns aimed at heterosexuals. Although either a man or a woman can transmit HIV, these campaigns targeted women, constituting women's bodies as potential contaminants of 'the public' (Waldby *et al.*, 1993). The division between the affirmation and the menace afforded by men's and women's body fluids is simultaneously upheld and undermined by men's fear of their own semen being mixed with those of other *men*, in the bodies of 'promiscuous' women. Such an event joepardizes the demarcation upon which heterosexual masculine subjectivity is premised. Bersani (1988) argues that, for heterosexual men, to lose one's identity in sex is to be like a woman. Penetrability is central to this division in that only women's bodies are understood as penetrable, thus requiring surveillance.

Heterosexual men invoke the distinction between clean and unclean women to contain this threat to their subjectivity (Waldby *et al.*, 1993). With regard HIV/AIDS prevention, this easily translates into the strategy of: use a condom if she's sleazy, but not if she's choosy. The relevance of this argument is that the importance of a woman's fidelity, for a hetero-sexual man, is understood in terms of her penetrability. It arises out of her penetrability. A woman's fidelity serves to maintain the boundaries of a man's identity. As long as she is faithful, he can penetrate her without coming into contact with other men's body fluids, and without the fear of losing himself, losing his self-identity.

The hegemonic meaning of heterosex is that a man penetrates a woman, or that she is penetrated by him. As Gill and Walker put it:

The 'real' woman of the 1990s is the Madonna and the Whore ... is sexually hun-gry for penetrative sex. She can 'have it all' but never dreams of having anything different ... everything other than penetration remains treated as 'foreplay' ... The discourse says ... 'anything goes', but try actually doing anything and we know we've transgressed some unbroken rule. (1993: 70)

This explains the double meaning of having it. It means both having the look which signifies penetrability (being sexy) and having a penis (being penetrated). Gavey (1993) points to the problems women experience in negotiating this continuum between having it and having it. She high-lights how women can often experience recognition of their attractiveness as an obligation to make themselves available sexually. So, if women enjoy a flirt, they may feel duty bound to pay out. Such compulsion is not sim-ply a matter of an interaction between two people, it is constituted at the level of the symbolic order. An important attribute of the first version of the feminine (which belongs with*in* the symbolic realm) is penetrability. Appearing any other way constitutes a potential threat to phallocentric masculinity, it involves the risk of being overlooked as a subject. The importance of having it is not only tantamount to being penetrable, but to being a subject in the symbolic realm.

BEING TRUSTWORTHY: CONTROL AND SELF-IDENTITY, POWER AND PLEASURE

As noted above, the distinction between clean and unclean women is of fundamental importance to heterosexual masculine subjectivity. To be seen as clean or good, a woman has to be seen as trustworthy. For 'nice' girls, the dilemma (which cannot be successfully resolved) is to be both trustworthy and penetrable. Clean women shore up phallocentric fan-tasies of their male partners as autonomous subjects. In the context of het-erosexual relationships, women's embodiment of trustworthiness works to contain the danger posed to heterosexual masculine subjectivity by the possibility of merging one's body fluids with those of another man. In this sense, women's trustworthiness can be understood as an element in 'the process of meaning constitution [which] requires that women reflect that masculine power and everywhere reassure that power of the reality of its illusory autonomy' (Butler, 1990: 45).

Through the discursive practices of sex and intimacy, in monogamous relationships, heterosexual women may come to know themselves as trustworthy and 'clean'; a form of self-knowledge which serves to uphold a notion of masculine self-identity in which the subject is thought to be autonomous, knowledgeable and in control. In being penetrable women are afforded the culturally valued experience of knowing oneself and one's sexual desires. In being trustworthy, women not only reflect back to men a culturally valued subjectivity, but in so doing assume it for themselves. That is, the kind of trustworthiness adopted by these young women, places them firmly within the symbolic order, where women are either 'nice', or 'sluts'. 'Clean' women, then, are trustworthy *because* they don't entertain 'taboo' desires. What goes against the logic of phallocentrism is the idea that practicing trustworthiness doesn't have to involve sorting desire into what is permissible and what isn't and then disavowing what isn't.

SUMMARY

A discursive approach to the notion of trustworthiness we are exploring here foregrounds the importance of the clean/unclean dichotomy. Irigaray uncovers what is submerged in dominant discourses to explore the feminine and to show that although these discourses are thought to be universal, they are isomorphically related to masculine sexuality. In this chapter we have examined the relationship between the discourses of sexuality and intimacy, phallocentric subjectivity and women's experience of being trustworthy. Our intention is neither to renounce women's trustworthiness, nor to repudiate trust as always and essentially phallocentric. In deconstructing young women's sense of trustworthiness, we have attempted to elucidate how, when heterosexual women posit trust as an unquestionable bedrock of sexual relationships they may foreclose on the articulation of desire, and the possibility of engaging in other forms of sexual relationships (monogamous or otherwise). In discussing the relationship between phallocentrism and young heterosexual women's experience we are opening up the notion of trust. Through questioning the foundational nature of trust we hope to contribute to ways of rewriting and elaborating on alternative ways of practicing trustworthiness – or not (Butler, 1992).

REFERENCES

Bartky, S. (1990) *Femininity and Domination: Studies in the Phenomenology of Oppression*. New York: Routledge
Bersani, L. (1988) Is the rectum a grave? In D. Crimp (Ed.) *AIDS: Cultural Analysis, Cultural Activism*. Cambridge: MIT Press
Butler, J. (1990) *Gender Trouble: Feminism and the Subversion of Identity*. New York: Routledge
Butler, J. (1992) Contingent foundations: feminism and the question of 'postmodernism'. In J. Butler. and J. Scott (Eds.) *Feminists Theorize the Political*. New York: Routledge
Butler, J. (1993) *Bodies that Matter: On the Discursive Limits of 'Sex'*. New York: Routledge
de Beauvoir, S. (1973) *The Second Sex*. New York: Vintage

Foucault, M. (1984) *The History of Sexuality Volume 1*, translated by Robert Hurley. Harmondsworth: Penguin

Gavey, N. (1993) Technologies and effects of heterosexual coercion. In S. Wilkinson and C. Kitzinger (Eds.) *Heterosexuality: A Feminism and Psychology Reader*. London: Sage

Gill, R. and Walker, R. (1993) Heterosexuality, feminism, contradiction: on being young, white, heterosexual feminists in the 1990s. In S. Wilkinson and C. Kitzinger, (Eds.) *Heterosexuality: A Feminism and Psychology Reader*. London: Sage

Grosz, E. (1989) *Sexual Subversions: Three French Feminists*. Sydney: Allen and Unwin

Grosz, E. (1994) *Volatile Bodies: Towards a Corporeal Feminism*. Sydney: Allen and Unwin

Henriques, J., Hollway, W., Urwin, C., Venn, C. and Walkerdine, V. (1984) *Changing the Subject: Psychology, social regulation and subjectivity*, London: Methuen

Hollway, W. (1989) *Subjectivity and Method in Psychology*. London: Sage

Irigaray, L. (1993) *Sexes and Genealogies*, translated by Gillian Gill. New York: Columbia University Press

Irigaray, L. (1985) *This Sex Which Is Not One*, translated by Catherine Porter with Carolyn Burke. Ithaca: Cornell University Press

Kippax, S., Crawford, C. and Waldby, C. (1994) Heterosexuality, masculinity and HIV. *AIDS* 8, (suppl 1) S315–S323

Parker, I. (1996) Psychology, science fiction and postmodern space. Paper presented at the Discourse and Cultural Practice Conference, Adelaide, 1996

Roberts, C., Kippax, S., Spongberg, M. and Crawford, J. (1996) 'Going down': oral sex, imaginary bodies and HIV. *Body and Society*, 2, 107–124

Rose, J. (1986) *Sexuality in the Field of Vision*. London: Verso Press

Shotter, J. (1993) *Cultural Politics of Everyday Life*. Buckingham: Open University Press

Sofia, Z. (1992) Hegemonic irrationalities and psychoanalytic cultural critique. *Cultural Studies*, 6, 376–394

Waldby, C., Kippax, S. and Crawford, J. (1993) *Cordon sanitaire*: Clean and unclean women in the AIDS discourse of young heterosexual men. In P. Aggleton, G. Hart and P. Davies (Eds.) *AIDS: The Second Decade*. Lewes: Falmer Press

Walkerdine, V. and Lucey, H. (1989) *Democracy in the Kitchen: Regulating Mother's and Socialising Daughters*. London: Virago Press

Willig, C. (1995) 'I wouldn't have married the guy if I'd have to do that': heterosexual adults' constructions of condom use and their implications for sexual practice. *Journal of Community and Applied Social Psychology*, 5, 75–87

CHAPTER 10

RECLAIMING WOMEN'S SEXUAL AGENCY

Lynne Segal

INTRODUCTION

Increasing women's sexual satisfaction, health and safety has always meant freeing women from the dangers of sexual coercion, the infliction of unwanted pregnancy and the injuries of sexually transmitted disease – most recently from the threat of HIV and AIDS. One of the main obstacles to achieving these goals, world-wide, remains women's subordinate social status compared to men: a subordination characteristically symbolized in men's sexual dominance of women. Even in these supposedly post-femi-

nist times (at least in the developed world), many researchers still suggest
that it remains hard to find either a language, or practice, which does not
privilege men's sexual agency in heterosexual encounter – especially
among young women (see Stephenson *et al.*, in this volume). Here I trace
out the difficulties of trying to overturn notions of the inevitability of
men's dominance of heterosexuality in order to encourage a sense of
women's sexual agency.

Think sex, and we tend to think about male sexuality. And when we
think about male sexuality we tend, still, to think of instinctual forces and
overpowering drives. Such unthinking associations were challenged time
and again throughout the twentieth century: by sexologists emphasizing
the role of learning in sexual behavior; by psychoanalysts, illustrating the
deep disturbances in the assumed links between gender identity and sexuality; by sociologists highlighting the overriding significance of cultural
contexts and symbolic meanings; by anthropologists, stressing cultural
specificities; by feminists pointing to the primacy of the gendered power
relations in fashioning those meanings as intractably phallocentric conceptions of sexuality; by gay and lesbian scholars pointing to the lifelong
coercive policing of sexual deviancy, seemingly necessary for the maintenance of heterosexual norms. Where has all this criticism led us?
Seemingly, full circle. At least in the most popular consumption of sexual
knowledge at the close of the twentieth century, we are back to where we
all began at the last *fin de siecle*: hearing again old tales of the hyperactive
male blindly programmed by his genes to seek 'reproductive advantage'
through voracious sexual pursuit; of the hesitant female, adapted to hold
back from sexual engagement in order to select a 'mate' with resources. A
very old story posing as 'new' evolutionary theory.

ELABORATING SEXUAL DIFFERENCE

The rapid rise and media promotion of 'evolutionary psychology' in offering itself as a new paradigm for the discipline has strengthened traditional notions of fundamental contrasts between male and female sexuality
along traditional normative lines. Thus David Buss has produced a plen-
tiful body of research on what he calls 'mating strategies' in the U.S.A,
Britain, and 35 other cultures, all showing that men declare themselves to
be far more promiscuous than women, and readier to have sex with any
female strangers, so long as they are young and attractive. Women, in contrast, are universally said to report desiring (or 'mating' preferences for)
ambitious, industrious men, with good financial resources (Buss, 1994).
Buss is researching the same furrow as a majority of other evolutionary
psychologists, who also assure us of the reality of men's predetermined
sexual promiscuity which (together with their greater predisposition for
violence and risk taking) is one of the most repeated claims of evolutionary theorists (Symons and Ellis, 1989). But this, of course, is precisely what
those who stress the cultural rather than the biological basis of contrasting
sexual conduct themselves predict, whether via individually based 'learn-

ing theory' or discursively mediated 'social construction' perspectives: in male-dominated societies boys learn to see heterosexual activity as a confirmation of masculinity (and certainly know that boasting about their desire to perform it, is the single easiest way of proclaiming their 'virility': 'whoooa!'); girls learn to value committed relationships over casual sex (or, at least, certainly discover that they ought to say they value them if they are not to be thought whatever is the local vernacular for 'slag', and thereby avoid the assaultive behavior such labelling condones).

The humorous side to the shallowness of this research is that were men's promiscuous boasts, and women's prudent protestations, to be accepted as indicative of selectively evolved behavior patterns, rather than – in line with my own sceptical hypothesis – gender differentiating, cultural 'identity work', a tiny minority of enormously hyperactive 'young and attractive' women would have to be obliging an army of dedicatedly randy men. As Dorothy Einon suggests in regard to her own research, in which heterosexual men reported having three or four times the number of sexual partners that women did, the figures just don't compute (Einon, 1998). In fact, the one constant feature of changes in the pursuit of human sexual pleasure is their negative correspondence with reproductive ends (Janus and Janus, 1993; Laumann et al., 1994; Wellings et al., 1994). Any overview of the problems women face asserting their own sexual agency, and hence feeling confident in assuming a measure of control over their sexual lives, from its pleasures or dangers to its health risks or benefits, thus immediately engages us with the disputes still being waged between those who believe that 'sexuality' involves doing 'what comes naturally' and those who are just as certain that in the domain of the sexual we all perform 'what comes socioculturally'. This debate expands into another, between those who stress the idea of fixed sexual identities and those, often influenced by psychoanalysis and recent Foucauldian theory, who describe the prevalence of unstable sexual pluralities. Only by engaging with, and critically assessing, the debates and controversies stimulated by conflicting perspectives on sexuality can we produce an agenda for understanding and connecting with the diversity of problems in women's sexual lives today; or, indeed, in men's. To do so we have, once again, to problematize all that is most taken for granted about sexuality, to go beyond what endures as commonplace knowledge, no matter how often it is challenged, repudiated, or revealed as downright ridiculous. For in a way which really is unique, almost everything connected to sexuality seems to thrive on its own contradictions, as any summary of the history of 'sexuality' can highlight.

As most readers will know, nineteenth-century sexologists saw male and female sexuality as fundamentally opposed instincts: male sexuality was viewed as aggressive and forceful; female as passive and responsive. They thereby equated the three concepts – 'sex', 'gender' and 'sexuality' – through a parallel set of oppositions – 'male/female', 'masculine/feminine', 'active/passive'. With the re-emergence of reductive biologism today, this is exactly what we hear again: some scientists searching in the hypothalamus for distinct neural patterns, others hunting down possible sources of genetic variation in the chromosomes, which might tie in with supposedly clearly differentiated male and female sexual patterns. Any reported correlation of biological data with sexual behavior receives immediate international media attention, no matter how speculative (see Hamer *et al.*, 1993), while more sophisticated analysis of the cultural shaping of sexuality remains confined to elite publications.

INTRODUCING CULTURE

Yet, sexologists had begun to turn the tables on their founding fathers' most basic assumption – the opposed sexual natures of women and men – by the mid-twentieth century. Armed with their new empirical tools, the mass sexual survey, soon augmented by carefully measured laboratory recordings and the influential research of both Kinsey and Masters and Johnson, stressed the role of cultural 'conditioning' in creating distinct sexual patterns, downplayed the contrasts between 'normal' and 'abnormal' sexual behavior, while insisting upon the overriding similarities between male and female sexuality. However, although emphasizing the conditioned malleability of human sexuality, these behavioristic researchers never problematized the notion of 'sexuality' itself, assuming they were, in the end, dealing with different ways of satisfying some biological need, akin, say, to hunger, and the diversity of food preferences with which we might satisfy it.

Indeed, it was only when the two sociologists John Gagnon and William Simon took over the Kinsey Institute in the USA in the late 1960s, and published their influential Sexual Conduct in 1973, that the new sociological perspective on sexuality came into its own. Moving decisively away from any biomedical model, Gagnon and Simon (1973) argued that sexuality is primarily culturally determined. It is 'socially constructed', via the learning of 'sexual scripts', and this includes the great importance we attach to sexuality itself in any culture. What would prove most compelling about this analysis was its claim that the acquisition of gender identity is prior to, and determining of, the contrasting sexual scripts which shape boys' and girls' entry into the experience of sexuality. Whether studying mass culture, or interviewing men and women, it was clear that the 'masculine' script is tied to, and confirmed by, sexual performance itself; the 'feminine' is tied to, and confirmed by, a sexual relationship or marriage. Sexual patterns, it is therefore argued, reflect not some inner sexual need, but rather desire for the confirmations of gender identity. But, it is in particular 'masculinity' which has been revealed – in all manner of ways – to lean so heavily upon confirmations of manhood through penile performance. For recent evidence, one need only look at men's race for Viagra (said to be the fastest takeoff for any new drug that pharmacists can recall when it was launched in the U.S.A in 1998): a rush for a drug first developed for heart medication, one which has no biological properties linked to sexual arousal, is known to cause headaches, cer-

tain visual distortions and blackouts, but which effects penile performance by assisting arteries to remain fully dilated (Handy, 1998).

GENDERED POWER IN HETEROSEXUAL RELATIONS

Social construction theory was further elaborated by feminists who saw
sexuality as a key site of men's power over women (Tiefer, 1995). The cultural links between gender and sexuality threw crucial light on the troubling issue of men's sexual violence, and its occurrence not so much in the
service of sexual needs as in the often compulsive pursuit of proofs of
'masculinity', not infrequently, through coercive sexuality. The implications of many men's determination to pressurize women for sex only
became all the more troubling for feminists with the advent of AIDS,
adding to their awareness of women's already greater vulnerability to the
possibly of unwanted pregnancy, or violence, through sex with men. It
should be obvious that any culture which encourages men to prove their
masculinity through sexual performance helps legitimize male sexual
coerciveness, and makes it harder for women to enjoy the space to sort out
and express their own wishes. In line with social constructionism, an
upsurge of research, now often referred to as the new 'sociology of the
body', began mapping the ways in which bodily activities are invested
with – or denied – sexual meaning.

To take just one example, a host of recent studies have shown the contrasting symbolism of young men's and women's first encounters with
genital heterosexuality. Interestingly, while both often recall the experience as involving anxiety, nervousness, even disappointment, almost all
the men (of whatever age) saw it as an important 'achievement' on the
way to manhood, something to exult in, even when they didn't much
enjoy the experience itself: 'Now I'm a man, I am a man'; 'My ego just
went WHOOMPH', is overwhelmingly the type of male reaction reported
(Rubin, 1991; Connell, 1995; Holland *et al.*, 1998).

Yet women have no such parallel exaltation over their first sexual experience as 'defining of womanhood'. In contrast, women recall the far more
ambiguous, often embarrassing, significance given to their first period or
menstruation as symbolizing their entry into 'womanhood' (Prendergast,
1989).

DISCURSIVE LIMITATIONS

However, this research on the social construction of sexuality, tied to the
creation and maintenance of gender hierarchy, has limitations as well as
strengths. It courts the danger of replacing biological reductionisms with
new forms of cultural reductionism. For while sexual identities and practices are indeed social, they are exceedingly complex – both psychologically and culturally. In focussing their analysis on symbolic systems and
what Foucault (1979) called discursive regimes, social construction theory
can easily erase the nuances of subjective conflict and ambivalence. It usu-

ally eschews the critical appropriation of key psychoanalytic insights which, drawing upon clinical data and detailed biographical observation, can open our eyes to the contradictory and disruptive particularities of psychic life in relation to culture and history (Freud, 1977). Whereas social construction theories predict the successful moulding of gender identities (with occasional resistance), psychoanalytic reflections point us towards the chronic failure of psychic life to reflect consciously learned norms. For example, many sex researchers (from the time of Kinsey) have suggested that 'the largest single category of homosexual men are heterosexually married' (Harrison, 1995: 375). Only through some understanding of the frequent failure of the inner world to reflect cultural norms does it become easier to see why it should be men who, although the favored and most powerful sex, and despite the continual and ubiquitous policing of any 'effeminate' deviance, should so far outnumber women in seeking sex changes.

Sexual identities and practices are generated in social contexts which are also increasingly dynamic and shifting, drawing upon a plurality of signifying practices and competing cultural narratives. Social construction frameworks have tended to limit the diversity of cultural meanings which gender encodes, as well as the instabilities of even the most established social relations. Attentive to the fissures and disruptions of personal biographies as they unfold within very specific, often shifting subcultural and political contexts, Australian sociologist Bob Connell (1995), for example, depicts heterosexual men (influenced by feminism) who are uncomfortable unless women take the sexual initiative, and control the relationship; or the homosocial bonds which are consolidated through queer baiting – just as so many other studies have revealed the extent to which heterosexual pursuit can be primarily an affair between men: as one 17-year-old man explained to British researchers recently: 'men just see [sex] as something that has got to be done, that's what I think, so men don't tease you' (Holland *et al*. 1998: 162).

THE INSTABILITIES OF SEXUAL EXPERIENCE

It should be obvious that, for all the psychic and cultural pull of dominant binaries of heterosexuality, its codings have never been secure. Indeed, as I argued in my book, *Straight Sex*, it has always been in desired sexual encounter, of whatever kind, that the presumed polarities of gender can be felt to falter and blur. Sexual pleasure – taking us all the way back to the fears and longings of childhood attachments – is as much about letting go and losing control for men as it is women. Just as it can be as much about asserting control for women, as it is for men. Where does this leave us? Influenced by Foucault, the growth of 'queer theory' in recent lesbian and gay scholarship has celebrated strategies of disruptive resistance, seeking to transgress all the old binaries chaining sexuality to gender (Butler, 1990). In what some see as these postmodern, post-feminist, post-gay times of flexible bodies, the latest sexual vanguard suggests that it is time to liberate ourselves from all the old sexual identities, moving on to fashion our sexual performances in whatever way we choose. But, the idea that we are, or may soon become, post-gender, exists alongside the continuing potency of the narrative of basic gender polarity.

Queer theory's semiotically driven reflections rarely address the ways in which, throughout our lifetimes, we move in and out of the identifications, pleasures and vulnerabilities of gender settlements, structures of desire, and management of bodily capabilities with health, age, and a myriad other belongings and exclusions, playing a central role. We are never simply subject to (or in rebellion against) sexual and gender norms or normativities. Against Foucauldian framings, the complexity of both psychic life and bodily investments are not homologous with polarizing gender discourses, or the social injunctions which render them intelligible. On the one hand, psychic life has an autonomous complexity which sexual difference, or gender identity, does not exhaust. On the other hand, the external namings and rules which solicit gender and sexual performativity are not themselves seamless and unchanging. Gender is thus not internalized as a single entity, but rather it operates subjectively within an array of often conflicting mental representations and self-perceptions (Segal, 1999).

Since the cultural dynamics of gender mean that it is never simply an elaboration of anatomical sexual difference, it will always be possible to question the meaning of 'masculinity' and 'femininity', and point to their uncertain content, both psychically and socially. The most healthy option, surely, is the hope that we might feel better able to acknowledge and indulge real gender ambiguities, rather than feel driven to reify or eliminate them. For those wishing to empower women sexually, the question is how it is possible to register women's specific needs and interests in relation to current gender structures and meanings, while still rendering notions of gender *less* rather than *more* controlling. As I see it, this cannot be done without the careful attention to the ways in which gender and sexuality operate together at any historical moment, in all their psychic complexity, and as a structure of social relations and symbolic contrasts.

CHALLENGING THE OBSTACLES TO WOMEN'S SEXUAL AUTONOMY

The way to fight the idea of sex, and its rigidly conceived ties to gender or sexuality as the core of our being is thus not to negate or eliminate our own complex psychic investments and social negotiations as gendered and sexually desiring beings. It is rather to highlight their complexity, and potential fluidity. As many feminist visions already suggest, sexual difference can be re-conceived and enacted in ways which work to undermine, rather than to shore up, strictly hierarchical conceptions of gender centered on affirming active/heterosexual/masculine dominance (symbolized as phallic). But this means challenging other forces which are also at work to preserve the traditional codings.

For example, in the U.S.A, just when queer theory and transgression gained academic modishness, the most significant, most modest, most easily bestowed choices which might have been made available to young women entering adult sexual engagements were being systematically withdrawn. The encouragement of sexual self-confidence and knowledge, information about sexually transmitted diseases and reliable contraceptive resources were officially forbidden in the public arena of teenagers. In 1997 The Adolescent Family Life Act became federal law in the U.S.A., making available a $100 million a year funding for 'sex education', with an exclusive 'abstinence only' focus, which prohibited information about contraception or safer sex techniques, despite ample knowledge (even admitted by its promoters) that its chastity lessons meet none of its intended goals: to reduce teenage pregnancy and HIV transmission, and to raise the age at which young people become sexually active (Haffner, 1997). One survey reported that students enrolled in an abstinence-only programme engaged in more sex than those in a control group which, although publicized, failed to prevent the Clinton Administration from making such courses the single top priority of its National Campaign to Prevent Teen Pregnancy' (Flinn, 1997: 18). This is in line with figures from the Netherlands, where teenage pregnancy rates are over 13 times lower than in the U.S.A., and the average age of first intercourse is higher (Bright, 1999: 9).

Overwhelmingly targeting and intimidating young women, the transparent aim of abstinence-only sex-education is to promote fear and ignorance about sexual activity. In her chilling account of the injurious effects of these pro-abstinence educational packages, Judith Levine illustrates their chronic dishonesty, and the callous perpetuation of falsehoods about the dangers of all contraceptives, and of even the safest sexual practices (like kissing!). As she notes mournfully, the desiring body, and pleasurable, consensual sex acts, were just nowhere to be found in sex education in the U.S.A. in the 1990s. Their anti-sex message is matched only by their rigid notion of gender roles: 'the peers who pressured were invariably male, and those who refused and delayed were female' (Levine, forthcoming). However transgressive they may wish to be, many young American girls are still terrifyingly coerced by the necessity to avoid pregnancy, and the scapegoating and potential financial penalties they face should they choose to mother, alone. Meanwhile, the teenage pregnancy rate in England and Wales is only sightly lower than that in the U.S.A.: rivalling the very poorest parts of Western Europe; a startling seven times above that of the Netherlands; and far higher than any other EEC country (Bright, 1999: 9). In Britain, as in the U.S.A., social inequality and inadequate sex education are a significant part of the problem, as British politicians are just beginning to admit.

PROMOTING WOMEN'S SEXUAL HEALTH

Even in a post-phallic world some forms of gendered bodily difference are likely to be marked, although in different ways, at different times. But the battles we currently wage to empower women sexually, with knowledge and with new narratives of desire and self-worth, can help to ensure greater safety and sexual health for women. The forces which have tried to silence women's sexual choices have not succeeded in their ultimate goals, even if they have often made life harder for the most vulnerable women. In Western countries, the popular press remains deeply ambivalent about women's sexuality. On the one hand, it often greets young women's sexual assertiveness with derision, if not contempt, seen, for example, in its contradictory attitude towards its own invented notion of 'girl power' (to refer to the growing fame and fortune of 'pop' goups like the Spice Girls) or TV's latest, partially self-mocking, 'Ladettes'. On the other hand, cultural studies researchers, like Angela McRobbie, have for some time been celebrating the growing acceptance of women's sexual pleasure in the popular culture enjoyed by young women (McRobbie, 1996). Unsurprisingly, this ambivalence in popular culture is reflected in young women's own responses to sexuality and pleasure (Holland, *et al.*, 1998).

SUMMARY

Writing of the continuing existence of power relations in heterosexuality, most researchers suggest that young women, in particular, still find it hard to find either a language, or practice, which does not privilege men's sexual agency in heterosexual encounter. However, as British researchers Janet Holland and her associates suggest, there is both conformity and resistance to what they call the 'male-in-the-head', or 'women's collusion in male dominance of heterosexuality'. Having interviewed women and men between the ages of 16 and 21 over a number of years, trying to discover how to increase sexual health and safety to prevent the transmission of HIV and AIDS, they remain cautiously optimistic:

While we have shown that the demands of heterosexuality pull against the demands of sexual safety, it may be that the challenges posed by safer sex also provide a mechanism through which the 'male-in-the-head' can be called to account. The asymmetry of heterosexuality, while powerful and enduring, has nevertheless to be constantly recreated ... As young people seek to create their own gendered identities, they do have some space to negotiate their own version of heterosexualities. (Holland et al., 190, 1998)

On a theoretical level, psychologists wishing to empower women sexually will need to keep on insisting, against a popular diversity of competing voices, that there is no fundamental blueprint dictating our sexual lives. On a psychological and social level, we need to continue to seek out ways of helping to make women everywhere more confident that they have a right to sexual pleasure, on their own terms, if we are to encourage safety and satisfaction in women's sexual lives.

REFERENCES

Bright, M. (1999) U.K. eyes Dutch sex lessons. *The Observer*, 21 February

Buss, David (1994) *The Evolution of Desire: Strategies of Human Mating*. London: HarperCollins

Butler, J. (1990) *Gender Trouble*. London: Routledge

Connell, R.W. (1995) *Masculinities.*, Cambridge: Polity

Einon, D. (1998) How many children can one man have? *Evolution and Human Behavior*, 19, 413–426

Flinn, S. (1997) The Clinton Administration's Adolescent Pregnancy Prevention Program: ignorance does not equal abstinence. *Siecus Report*, 25 (4), April/May, 18

Foucault, M. (1979) *The History of Sexuality, Vol 1: An Introduction*. London: Allen Lane

Freud, S. (1977) *Three Essays on Sexuality, The Pelican Freud Library* (1905) (PFL), vol 7, Harmondsworth: Penguin

Gagnon, J. and Simon, W. (1973) *Sexual Conduct: The Social Sources of Human Sexuality*. New York: Aldine

Haffner, D. (1997) What is wrong with abstinence-only sexuality education programs. *Siecus Reports*, 25, April/May

Handy, B. (1998) The Viagra craze. *Time*, 4 May, 50–57

Harrison, J (1995) Roles, Identities and sexual orientation: homosexuality, heterosexuality, and bisexuality. In R. Levant and W. Pollack (Eds.) *A New Psychology of Men*. New York: Basic Books

Holland, J *et al.* (1998) *The Man in the Head: Young People, Heterosexuality and Power*, London: The Tufnell Press

Janus, S. and Janus, C. (1993), *The Janus Report of Sexual Behavior*. New York: John Wiley

Laumann, E. *et al. The Social Organization of Sexuality: Sexual practices in the United States*. Chicago: University of Chicago Press

Levine, J. (forthcoming) *Harmful to Minors: How Sexual Protectionism Hurts Children*

McRobbie, A. (1996) More! New sexualities in girls and women's magazines. In J. Curran, D. Morley, and V. Walkerdine (Eds.) *Cultural Studies and Communication*. London, Arnold

Prendergast, S. (1989) Girls Experience of Menstruation in Schools. In L. Holly (Ed.) *Girls and Sexuality*. Milton Keynes: Open University Press

Rubin, L. (1991) *Erotic Wars: What Happened to the Sexual Revoluion?*. New York: HarperCollins

Segal, L. (1994) *Straight Sex: The Politics of Pleasure*. London: Virago

Segal, L. (1999) *Why Feminism? Gender, Psychology, Politics*. Cambridge: Polity Press

Symons, D. and Ellis, B. (1989) Human male-female differences in sexual desire in A.S. Rasa *et al.* (Eds.) *The Sociobiology of Sexual and Reproductive Strategies* (pp. 131–146) New York: Oxford University Press

Tiefer, L. (1995) *Sex Is Not a Natural Act*. Boulder: West View Press

Wellings K. *et al.* (1994) *Sexual Behaviour in Britain*. Harmondsworth: Penguin

THE SOCIAL CONSTRUCTION OF WOMEN'S SEXUALITY: THE DANGERS OF PHARMACEUTICAL INDUSTRY INTEREST

Leonore Tiefer

INTRODUCTION

Analysing the social control of women's sexuality has been at the center of feminist scholarship; promoting women's sexual self-determination has been in the forefront of feminist politics (see Segal, in this volume). Both of those projects make us concerned about the sudden attention being paid to women's sexuality by biomedicine and the pharmaceutical industry in the late 1990s. A tide of new research, new diagnostic nomenclature, new assessments of 'risk', and all the other pseudo and semi-scientific medicalizing that accompanies pharmaceutical industry attention is beginning to roll forward from public relations departments to the media, into subsidized conferences, and into professional journals. Feminists must redouble their efforts to develop and publicize a social constructionist analysis of sexuality in the face of this latest wave of biological reductionism and essentialism (i.e. phallocentrism).

TODAY'S EXAMPLE

Here is just one small example to show how commercial forces are shaping people's knowledge of sexuality. The Internet is rapidly becoming an important source for all sorts of information, especially health information. Because of anxieties and inhibitions, people with sexual questions may be even more likely to go to the Internet than a public library or their friends. On 26 April 1999, the well-respected diabetes research and treatment center, the Joslin Center of Boston, issued a press release announcing a new sexual dysfunction section of their general information website which would offer sexuality information for both men and women. Upon opening the website (*www.joslin.org/education/library/sexual_dysfunction.html*), one first sees the page name, 'Sexual dysfunction – Sponsored by Viagra™ – Joslin Diabetes Center'. At the bottom of each page of sexual quiz and information, one finds, 'This site is sponsored in part through an unrestricted educational grant from Pfizer, Inc.' together with the Pfizer logo. And what kind of information is provided? It's the same fragmented and medicalized information pharmaceutical-sponsored studies of men's erectile function have promoted for years. Women's sexual problems are assessed by Yes/No answers to the following: 'Have any of these been a problem for you in the last month? Lack of interest in sex, Unable to relax and enjoy sex, Difficulty in becoming sexually aroused, Difficulty in having an orgasm.' There are no definitions of sex or sense that there are many ways to be sexual. There is nothing about sensuality, the state of one's relationship, techniques or attitudes of partners, the woman's own emotions, or sex from the point of view of pleasure. It's all about sex as a normative genital performance, in fact, the performance of intercourse. I called Joslin's Public Relations department and learned that their website was developed with Pfizer money by a computer company with input from one endocrinologist and one social worker. Public Relations didn't know if Pfizer had given the company information, and didn't realize that 'Viagra™' was on the website. They promised to have it removed, but they rejected suggestions for expanding the sexuality information. Later communications indicated that Pfizer had not contributed content for the website, but they still rejected suggestions to refocus the material.

SEXOLOGICAL MODEL OF SEXUALITY

The pharmaceutical industry capitalizes on 'the sexological model of sexuality', which continues to dominate sexuality theory and research despite persistent efforts of feminists and humanists (Tiefer, 1999). Five of its central tenets are:

1. Sex is 'a material phenomenon which involves an extended series of physical, physiologic, and psychologic changes [which] could be subjected to precise instrumental measurement if objectivity among scientists and public respect for scientific research allowed such laboratory investigation' (Kinsey et al., 1948: 157).
2. There are important and natural differences between the type and extent of sexual interests and experiences of women and men.
3. Heterosexual impulses are the norm, including desire for sexual arousal and orgasm through coitus, as a result of evolution. Boundaries can be drawn between healthy/normal and abnormal/pathological manifestations.
4. Everyone has a sexual identity – heterosexual, homosexual or bisexual, and a gender identity – girl/woman/female or boy/man/male.
5. Sexuality exists in individuals, i.e. it is an intrinsic quality of personality. Much of this model expresses vague naturalized Judao-Christian values, albeit dressed up in empirical language.

TRADITIONS OF SEX RESEARCH

Sex research throughout the twentieth century has focussed on details and mechanisms for this sexological model rather than questioning or examining its basis. Which hormones are most active; how best to measure sex differences; what factors contribute to abnormality, etc. This tradition developed in large part because, prior to Alfred Kinsey's survey work in the 1940s and 1950s, research on sexuality was a scandalous area. Researchers were prevented by public opinion and professional peer-pressure from studying human sexuality, so they used laboratory animals instead. While they admitted that animal studies could not address the human situation precisely, they believed 'animal models' permitted helpful simplification and better control of variables (cf. Beach, 1977). Decades of studying mechanisms and patterns of animal mating have left their mark on sex research. It is easy, now, to assume without reflection that sexuality is something animals and people have in common, and that concepts like sexual attraction or inhibition, categories like heterosexual or male, or physiological mechanisms such as hormones or brain sites, are unproblematic terms which mean something similar in the sex lives of animals and human beings. Issues like sexual violence, body image, diverse subjective meanings, or sexual identity and role were sidelined to clinical and anthropological discussions of 'influences' which culture and individual life experience added to 'basic' sexual patterns.

SEXOLOGY TAKES A MEDICAL TURN

Some feminist authors feel that twentieth-century sexology has been medicalized ever since nineteenth-century doctors such as Kraft-Ebing defined the barriers around sexual 'normality' (Irvine, 1990). However, a new phase began when, as a result of converging economic, medical, demographic, and cultural factors in the 1970s, urologists became interested in men's erectile problems (Tiefer, 1995). Aided by new health and science media, they built a reputation as sexuality 'experts' despite their failure to understand sex as anything more than the operation of physical organs. Long used to commercial research sponsorship, urologists have lately recruited sex researchers to collaborate on drug studies. The longstanding shortage of sex research financing (due to sexuality's 'scandalousness') has attracted many of the most active researchers to the new collaboration. The research paradigm, however, stays strictly limited to biomedical sexuality.

LOSSES FOR SEXUALITY OF THE PHARMACEUTICAL TAKEOVER

There are at least four ways that sexuality research is diminished and threatened as a result of pharmaceutical industry domination.

It bypasses the psychological and relational complexity of sexuality: Very little attention is paid to the person or the couple attached to the genitals in the sexological model. Industry research aims at a product for an individual, and thus avoids the psychosocial context of sexuality. Feminists and relationship theorists, by contrast, would argue that individualistic measurement of sexual organ function in the laboratory, or even self-report of organ function in the home setting, offers a biased and incomplete picture of sexuality. Wise (1999) recently published two cases in which a couple's marital situation deteriorated following the prescription of Viagra. In neither case was the wife involved in any way in the prescription process. My impression is that psychological and relational issues are avoided in sexuopharmacological research because they introduce complications which could add bad news and slow down the process of drug approval.

It masks gender and other sociocultural factors. Sexual function is treated as universal and biological in the pharmaceutical industry model, downplaying variations. In the past, sex researchers have examined power dynamics of sexuality, developmental continuities and discontinuities of sexuality, the embeddedness of sexuality within cultural systems of gender meaning, the connection of sexuality to leisure, the social construction of the body, and shifting notions of sexual orientation and gender identity. All of these issues are dismissed in sexuopharmaceutical reductionism. In the wake of the successful research on erectile dysfunction, new pelvic vascular sexual dysfunctions in women have recently been announced by urologists and proclaimed as serious public health problems, requiring research and 'treatment' (Goldstein and Berman, 1998; Park *et al.*, 1997). The only way gender plays in sexuopharmacology is as a source for new patients.

It denies sex is socially constructed. Pharmaceutical industry-sponsored research relies on brief, fixed-alternative, self-report questionnaires which ignore social processes through which sexual experiences acquire meaning. Sexologists know that research questionnaires themselves contribute to the social construction of sexuality when they assume that language like 'intercourse', 'sexual satisfaction', and even 'get an erection' or 'attempt sexual intercourse' is unproblematic. For example, the first question of the much-used International Index of Erectile Function (IIEF) (Rosen *et al.*, 1997) asks, 'How often were you able to get an erection during sexual activity during the past four weeks?' Is anyone concerned about how the respondent decides whether a particular moment in a kitchen, a bedroom, or a car constitutes 'sexual activity'? Is anyone interested in the partner's role or feelings? Is anyone interested in how participating in a sex research study affects the sexual activity being counted?

In other words, by focusing on the presumably naturalized actions of specific bodies, IIEF-type research disguises how sexual activity is produced and experienced by the participants, how such negotiation and experience fits into larger social contexts, and the role of the researchers themselves in perpetuating particular sexual scripts

(Gagnon and Parker, 1995). The impact of Viagra, for example, in accentuating phallocentrism is unlikely to be examined in any research funded by the pharmaceutical industry (Tiefer, 1994).

It disguises the connections of sex to politics. Of immense importance to feminists is the way sexuopharmacology participates in sexual and gender politics. Schmidt (1993) suggest that:

gazing at the diligence with which urologists, andrologists, surgeons and physiologists pursue the dream of the 'perfect penis' against the backcloth of the social upheavals and the profound changes in gender relations and sexual conduct of the last 20 years, one could conclude that the struggle is not about restoring one man's potency, but a desperate effort to re-establish western male potency in general. In fact it looks like a magic rite symbolically guaranteeing the phallus's immunity from danger in the face of a (slightly) changing power balance of the sexes. (p. 264)

Sex researchers have often allied themselves with a liberatory sexual politics that endorsed sexual diversity and self-determination by highlighting the damaging effects of sexual restrictiveness and puritanical values on people's lives (e.g. Brecher, 1969). Feminism has continued this tradition by showing how sexual double standards limit women's sexual self-determination regarding sexual pleasure, contraception, and disease (e.g. Segal; 1994, Heise, 1995). The focus of the pharmaceutical industry on the decontextualized performance of intercourse and orgasm will hinder women's sexual emancipation.

SUMMARY

Authority on sexual matters within dominant culture has been increasingly conferred by mass media and the public on experts with medical or health perspectives. Feminists must take action to reframe sexuality as a matter of history, ethics, and politics in order to proceed with women's sexual empowerment.

REFERENCES

Beach, F.A. (1977) Cross-species comparisons and the human heritage. In F.A. Beach (Ed.) *Human Sexuality in Four Perspectives* (pp. 296–316). Baltimore: Johns Hopkins University Press
Brecher, E.M. (1969) *The Sex Researchers*. Boston: Little, Brown & Co
Irvine, J. (1990) *Disorders of Desire: Sex and Gender in Modern American Sexology*. Philadelphia: Temple University Press
Gagnon, J.H. and Parker, R.G. (1995) Conceiving sexuality. In R.G. Parker and J.H. Gagnon (Eds.) *Conceiving Sexuality: Approaches to Sex Research in a Postmodern World* (pp. 3–16). New York: Routledge
Goldstein, I. and Berman, J.R. (1998) Vasculogenic female sexual dysfunction: Vaginal engorgement and clitoral erectile insufficiency syndromes. *International Journal of Impotence Research*, 10, suppl 2, S84–90
Heise, L. (1995) Violence, sexuality and women's lives. In R.G. Parker and J.H. Gagnon (Eds.)

Conceiving Sexuality: Approaches to Sex Research in a Postmodern World (pp. 109–134). New York: Routledge

Jackson, M. (1994) *The Real Facts of Life: Feminism and the Politics of Sexuality (1850–1940)*. London: Taylor & Francis

Kinsey, A.C., Pomeroy, W.B., Martin, C.E. and Gebhard, P.H. (1948) *Sexual Behavior in the Human Male*. Philadelphia: W. B. Saunders

Park, K., Goldstein, I., Andry, C., Siroky, M.B., Krane, R.J., and Azadzoi, K.M. (1997) Vasculogenic female sexual dsyfunction: The hemodynamic basis for vaginal engorgement insufficiency and clitoral erectile insufficiency. *International Journal of Impotence Research*, 9, 27–37

Rosen, R.C., Riley, A., Wagner, G., Osterloh, I.H., Kirkpatrick, J. and Mishra, A. (1997) The international index of erectile function (IIEF): A multidimensional scale for assessment of erectile dysfunction. *Urology*, 49, 822–830

Schmidt, G. (1993) A backlash disguised as progress. *International Journal of Impotence Research*, 5, 263–264

Segal, L. (1994) *Straight Sex: The Politics of Pleasure*. London: Virago Press

Tiefer, L. (1994) The medicalization of impotence: Normalizing phallocentrism. *Gender and Society*, 8, 363–377

Tiefer, L. (2000) The social construction and social effects of sex research. In C.B. Travis and J.W. White (Eds.) *Sexuality, Society and Feminism*. pp. 79–107. Washington, D.C.: *American Psychological Association*

Wise, T. N. (1999) Psychosocial side effects of sildenafil therapy for erectile dysfunction. *Journal of Sex and Marital Therapy*, 25, 145–150

CHAPTER 12

RAPE: CULTURAL DEFINITIONS AND HEALTH OUTCOMES

Nancy Felipe Russo, Mary P. Koss and Luciana Ramos

INTRODUCTION

Rape is a significant problem for women around the world and has been identified as a critical health and human rights issue (Koss *et al.*, 1994). In the context of increasing globalization of the world's economies, including the health-related sectors of those economies, it becomes ever more important to consider how culture shapes the meanings and consequences of rape to its victims in ways that have profound health implications. A full picture of the health-related physical, mental, and social consequences of rape requires examining the differential impact of different forms of rape on women's health in different cultural contexts.

No one chapter can do justice to the myriad of rape aims, forms, and contexts and we do not attempt to do so here. Here we have three goals: to increase appreciation of the diversity of forms and cultural definitions of rape; to encourage increased understanding of how cultural definitions can affect rape consequences, and to identify some of rape's physical and mental health outcomes.

CULTURAL DEFINITIONS OF RAPE

Rape, from a woman's point of view, is not prohibited, it is regulated
Catherine MacKinnon, 1983: 651

Definitions of rape vary across cultures and within cultures across time. Behaviors that are labeled as 'rape' or 'abuse' and punished in some cultures may be ignored or condoned in others (Koss *et al.*, 1994; Rozeé, 1993; Williams and Holmes, 1981). Whatever the situation, however, every society has mechanisms that 'legitimize, obfuscate, deny, and thereby perpetuate violence' (Heise, Pitanguy, and Germain, 1993: 1). How rape is culturally defined and whether it is socially defended, ignored, or punished can have profound implications for the physical and mental health of rape victims.

Rape is a penetration of the mouth, anus, or vagina by the penis, fingers, or objects, without consent, through force or nonforcibly if the victim is unable to consent. Rape can be classified into two major categories: *transgressive* or non-normative is uncondoned, illicit genital contact that violates both the will of the victim and social norms; and tolerated or *normative* rape, which encompasses rapes that are unwanted by the woman yet do not violate norms for acceptable behavior that are held by self-isolated groups or subcultures, institutions, and even nations (RozJe, 1993).

Transgressive rape is a narrow category that represents the typical view of rape as forced sex by a complete stranger. Even though not condoned, in some nations, statutes restrict legal remedy for this type of rape only to those women with a respectable reputation and/or impose penalties for rape of children that phase out as womanhood is attained (Heise *et al.*, 1993). Class also may determine the 'value' of the woman who is raped and affect punishment of the rapist. For example, in Sri Lanka, if a virgin under age 18 is raped by a man of lesser caste or class he will be punished; but women who are lower class and independent, of middle age, and raped by an acquaintance, are advised 'to nurse your wounds at home' (Coomaraswamy, 1992: 51). In some societies, punishment for rape varies depending on the means available to 'repair' the damage to the women and the family 'caused' by the rape. For example, in Palestinian society, as well as Chile, Guatemala, and Peru, a man who rapes a minor is exonerated if he agrees to marry her (Heise *et al.*, 1993; Shalhoub-Kevorkian, 1999). In Jordan, rape offenders may be executed if convicted; if the rape can be construed as a crime of honor. However, killing the rape victim can 'cleanse the disgrace brought on the family by the rape, thus mitigating damages' (Shalhoub-Kevorkian, 1999).

Normative rape is a diverse category that encompasses a wide range of enforced genital contact including that occurring as part of cultural defloration rituals, child rapes occurring under the guise of arranged marriage, rapes by acquaintances or dates, marital rape, punitive rape to control activists, gynecological rapes including forced virginity examinations. It may also include sexual torture that can entail sexual humiliation, threats, violence toward sexual organs, and/or sexual assault as forms of discipline or interrogation by state security forces, forced prostitution, sexual slavery, and rape of refugees (e.g. Amnesty International, 1992; Human Rights Watch, 1992a; Rozeé, 1993).

Rape is a weapon of war that includes the deliberate degradation of women to break the spirit of the male enemy, as well as genocidal rape designed to destroy cultures and 'cleanse' bloodlines by impregnating women or by raping them to death (Human Rights Watch, 1993b). The Japanese government has acknowledged its sexual slavery of Korean women during World War II to 'comfort' the Japanese troops (see Swiss and Giller, 1993). More recently, there has been massive raping of women in Bangladesh, Cambodia, Liberia, Uganda, Peru, Cambodia, Somalia, and Bosnia (Koss et al., 1993).

Rape is also used to punish and control women in times of peace. For example, in Latin America, feminists charge that rape is used to turn 'Madonna into whore' and to warn women to stay in their traditional domain (Bunster, 1986: 307, cited in Lykes et al., 1993: 535). In India, a woman leader was gang raped in front of her husband by a group of men who disapproved of her organizing against child marriage. He was warned 'keep your wife in line or we'll rape her again' (Koss et al., 1994). In Iran, women who were to be executed for supporting the Shah were first raped to 'prevent them from going to heaven' (Shalhoub-Kevorkian, 1999: 168). Recently in the Middle East, in response to the 'damage to his manhood' that resulted when a 20-year-old woman attempted suicide rather than be forced to marry him, the fiancé and his brothers kidnapped her, savagely raped her, and poured acid on her face and body to leave permanent scarring (Shalhoub-Kevorkian, 1999).

Cultural definitions of rape have important implications for the physical and mental health of rape victims because they can shape responses to rape in a variety of ways. They reflect cultural myths about rape, including notions such as the victim provoked the assault, she enjoyed it, only promiscuous women get raped, and raped women are 'damaged goods', that can shape the victim's perceptions of the event and exacerbate feelings of self-blame, guilt, and shame. They can affect whether a woman who is raped seeks services at a rape crisis center or obtains victim assistance to which she is entitled as a victim of crime. They also shape the responses of other people – family, friends, health professionals, and other community members – such that rape becomes traumatic 'not only by the terrifying experience of the assault, but also by public attitudes that affect the perception and treatment of the rape victim by others' (Lefley et al., 1993: 623; also see Wyatt, 1992). In particular, minimizing the importance and severity of the experience can have a profound and negative impact on the rape victim. Indeed the inappropriate, insensitive, and sometimes even brutal ways rape victims have been treated help to explain women's silencing around their rape experience.

In societies such as in the Middle East and parts of Asia the stigma of rape confers severe social and health consequences. Women may be ostracized by their families and the community, divorced by their husband, and even killed to preserve family 'honor' (Ben Baraka, 1993). One woman described the need to keep silent:

If the mukhtar (clan leader) ever finds out, not only will I be killed, but all my sisters will pay the price of my mistake. Everyone in the village will refuse to marry any of the girls in the family, and that's in addition to the high probability that my father will divorce my mother ... and God knows who else will be divorced. (Shalhoub-Kevorkian, 1999: 165)

Hymen repair surgery becomes perceived as a necessity. Shalhoub-Kevorkian (1999) describes a case in which a 10-year-old Palestine girl was raped and the doctor subsequently told her father that it was impossible to perform the surgery to repair her hymen. His response: 'There are only two ways to hide the calamity: one is to kill my daughter; the other is to perform the hymen repair and not tell anybody about the incident. If you won't do the hymen repair, you'll be the reason for her death' (p. 162).

The criminal justice system response to rape victims also can play a significant role in exacerbating rape's trauma. Bias against rape victims reaches unspeakable heights in Pakistan, where women's testimony is considered worth only half of a man's. Under the Zina Ordinance, which makes sex outside of marriage a crime against the state, if a woman charges a man with rape and fails to meet the high standard of evidence needed to prove the charge, she can be imprisoned based on the fact she admitted she had illegal intercourse with the rapist (Human Rights Watch, 1992b). As part of the proceedings, in order to establish the women's virtue (the word of virtuous women has more weight), a finger test is applied. If the woman's vagina accommodates two fingers easily, sex is considered to have been habitual, and her testimony is discounted (Jahangi and Jalani, 1990).

Pakistan provides just one example of how negative responses to rape can be shaped by how a culture constructs female sexuality (including whether it emphasizes female purity, virginity, and fidelity, stresses family relationships, and defines family gender roles of husband, wife, father, and mother separately and rigidly) (Ramos *et al.*, 1999). Religious ideology and institutions in particular can play a powerful role in shaping responses to rape in ways that foster negative reactions to rape victims and cut women off from support from their religious community as well as from their family (Williams and Holmes, 1981). In both Muslim and Catholic traditions, the notion of injury caused to kinsmen has been important, not only because males are considered responsible for women, but also because a chaste woman represents significant 'symbolic wealth' for the family (Giraud, 1987). Thus men may seek revenge for a woman's rape – sometimes by blaming and killing the woman – because they themselves have suffered an injury and must defend their honor (Shalhoub-Kevorkian, 1999). In such contexts, a woman who has been raped thus fails her religious obligations as well as in her duty to her husband and family.

Demands for hymen repair in Middle Eastern rape victims is only one of the results of the rigid emphasis on chastity in Arab society. The health-threatening lengths to which Muslim women will go to protect their hymen is found in the case of a 15-year-old Palestinian girl who was raped without penetration sufficient to break her hymen. She became pregnant, and in order to 'rescue the hymen', the doctor aborted the pregnancy by caesarean section (Shalhoub-Kevorkian, 1999: 163). In this cultural context, some rape victims, when faced with the shame and disgrace of loss of virginity, attempt suicide before they can be ostracized or killed by others. Honor works differently in Middle Eastern and Latin American societies. In Latin America, members of a woman's family may avenge the dishonor by attacking the perpetrator and presumably the threat of vengeance somewhat deters such aggression.

Unfortunately, cross-cultural data on health outcomes are lacking. Thus we primarily focus on rape as it has been defined and studied in developed Western countries. Keep in mind that factors differ across cultures that can affect both the meaning of the rape experience to the women and her resources for dealing with rape's physical, psychological, and social aftermath. Most of the findings reported below are based on studies focussing on single episodes of rape occurring in peacetime (Swiss and Giller, 1993). It should always be kept in mind that a full understanding of rape and sexual assault requires understanding the meanings, definitions, and contexts of rape experiences

THE U.S. CONTEXT

MacKinnon's (1983) observation above is exemplified in the ways rape has been defined in the United States. Legal definitions of rape in the U.S. (one expression of culture) have undergone profound changes in the last two decades, and have literally transformed the acts that are viewed as rape (Koss et al., 1994). Today, rape is usually defined legally as 'nonconsensual sexual penetration of an adolescent or adult obtained by physical force, by threat of bodily harm, or at such time when the victim is incapable of giving consent by virtue of mental illness, mental retardation, or intoxication' (Koss et al., 1994: 159). In particular, there has been a radical change in views on marital rape. Only a few states continue to exclude spouses as perpetrators in their rape laws.

Rape is the most underreported crime (Bureau of Justice Statistics, 1997). When police reports and community surveys are compared, only about one in three of rape/sexual assaults involving young adult women (aged 12 to 34 years) are reported; for women aged 50 to 64 the figure is even lower (26.8 percent). Multiple factors underlie this 'silencing' of women in the Western context, but one is the fact a woman may not conceptualize her experience as rape even though it may meet the legal definition of rape. For example, Koss et al. (1988) found that among women who had experienced events meeting the legal definition of rape, only 27 percent actually conceptualized those experiences as such. Thus, rape –

particularly marital, date, and acquaintance rape – continues to be under-reported and unlikely to be prosecuted, and thus is functionally condoned.

Cultural definitions and attitudes related to rape within the U. S. vary with ethnicity, but have not been extensively studied. Some research suggests that African-American women may not perceive their experiences as 'real rape', but even when they do may perceive a variety of barriers to disclosure and help seeking (Wyatt, 1992). Other research has found that Mexican-Americans, in comparison to Anglo- or African-Americans are more likely to question the legitimacy of rape accusations and express unwillingness to prosecute assailants. In particular, Mexican-Americans holding traditional female role conceptions were more likely than others to hold conservative attitudes toward rape, viewing rape as a shameful secret, to be shared only within the immediate family. Males were less victim-supportive than females, and victims tended to use the legal, medical and judicial support systems less than other groups (Williams and Holmes, 1984).

HEALTH OUTCOMES OF RAPE

The health costs of rape to women and society are now being recognized (Koss *et al.*, 1994). A substantial body of research documents the physical, psychological, and social consequences of rape (e.g. Brener *et al.*, 1999; Golding, 1999; Golding *et al.*, 1997; Goodman *et al.*, 1993a, b; Foa and Rothbaum 1998; Koss, 1993; Koss *et al.*, 1994; Koss and Mukai, 1993; Lefley *et al.*, 1993; McCauley *et al.*, 1997; Williams *et al.*, 1997).

Physical Outcomes

Between 30 and 50 percent of rape victims experience physical trauma, some with permanent disability. Of those who are injured, only about one-half receive formal medical care (Koss *et al.*, 1991). Nearly one-third of rapes involve oral or anal penetration in addition to vaginal contact, and half of rape victims seen in trauma centers have vaginal and perineal trauma (Woodling and Kossoris, 1981). An estimated 15 percent of raped women have significant vaginal tears, and 1 percent require surgical repair (Cartwright, *et al.*, 1987). Anorectal injuries can be produced by penetration by the penis as well as by digits, hands, blunt objects and other foreign bodies into the rectum (Chen *et al.*, 1986).

About four in ten rape victims experience injuries outside the genital area. These include abrasions of the head, neck and face, the extremities, and the trunk region, with severe injuries encompassing multiple traumas, major fractures, and major lacerations. Skeletal muscle tension in rape victims results in sleep disturbances, fatigue, and tension headaches. Other common problems include chronic pelvic pain and gastrointestinal irritability (e.g. irritable bowel, stomach pains, nausea, no appetite, and inability to taste food) (Golding, 1999; Koss and Heslet, 1992).

Sexually transmitted diseases (STDs) have been estimated to occur in 4 to 30 percent of rape victims (Forster *et al.*, 1991; Koss and Heslet, 1992). Of the 15 STDs identified, gonorrhea, chlamydia, trichomonal infections, and syphilis are the most common, but transmission of life-threatening hepatitis B and HIV infection also occur. Twenty-six percent of rape victims who are interviewed within three months of rape spontaneously express concern about AIDS (Baker, Burgess, Brickman, and Davis, 1990). Rape results in pregnancy in about 5 percent of cases in the U.S. (Koss *et al.*, 1991).

Among raped women who seek medical intervention, many fail to receive the emergency care recommended by standard rape protocols. In one national study, 60 percent of victims had no pregnancy testing or prophylaxis, and 73 percent reported they had no information or testing for exposure to HIV (NVC, 1992).

Rape can have long-lasting health consequences (Koss, 1991; Felitti, 1998). A number of persisting conditions are disproportionately higher among rape victims, including chronic pelvic pain, gastrointestinal disorders, headaches, psychogenic seizures, and premenstrual symptoms (Koss and Heslet, 1992; Golding 1999). Rape victims are more likely to experience chronic pain, including chronic pelvic pain, headaches, and fibromyalgia (Collett *et al.*, 1998; Ehlert *et al.*, 1999; Golding, 1999). Headaches are particularly associated with injurious assaults. It is not surprising that longitudinal research has found adult victims of sexual assault to seek help from physicians twice as frequently as other women, with the largest increases in health care use delayed until the second year after being victimized (Koss *et al.*, 1991).

Because of such findings, the American Medical Association (Council on Scientific Affairs, 1992) adopted a policy urging physicians to undertake routine screening for victimization by violence at health care system entry points, validate disclosures of victimization, and link patients to resources in the community designed to serve rape victims.

Emotional, Cognitive, and Behavioral Outcomes

Rape victims incur a wide range of emotional, cognitive, and behavioral outcomes depending on a variety of factors related to characteristics of the victim and of the rape experience. These include the age of the victim when it occurred, the relationship between the victim and the perpetrator, history of physical and sexual abuse, other sources of life stress, and frequency, severity, form, and duration of the rape experience (Kilpatrick *et al.*, 1987; Koss, 1988, 1993). An individual's psychological resources and coping ability prior to being raped and the nature of the recovery environment play key roles in shaping rape outcomes.

During and just after the assault, rape victims focus on physical and emotional survival, attempting to cope with the situation by such things as talking with or fighting the perpetrator or otherwise trying to escape, remaining calm, praying, and attempting to remember advice on how to deal with rape. However, if the woman perceives escape as impossible, she may attempt to dissociate (Burgess and Holmstrom, 1979a, 1979b).

Shock, intense fear, numbness, confusion, extreme helplessness and/or disbelief may follow the experience (Burgess and Holmstrom, 1979a, 1979b, 1979c; Koss and Harvey, 1991; Kilpatrick *et al.*, 1979). Other common outcomes include anxiety, depression, phobias/panic disorder, and sexual dysfunction (NVC, 1992). Victims may exhibit nightmares, catastrophic fantasies, and feelings of alienation and isolation (Koss and Harvey, 1991). Feelings of vulnerability, loss of control, and self-blame may persist (Burgess and Holmstrom, 1979a, 1979b; Kilpatrick *et al.*, 1985; Resick *et al.*, 1981).

Depressive symptoms found in rape victims include sleep and appetite disturbance, loss of interest and pleasure in normal activities, and decreased concentration (Becker *et al.*, 1984). Rape victims may withdraw from people and activities (Burgess and Holmstrom, 1979) and self-blame is often severe (Burgess and Holmstrom, 1979; Miller and Porter, 1983). Among U.S. women in the community not in treatment, an estimated 17 percent to 19 percent of rape victims have attempted suicide (Kilpatrick *et al.*, 1985). In societies where rape victims are ostracized, the figures are most certainly higher (Shalhoub-Kevorkian, 1999).

Women may fear that their rapist will return and harm them further as well as fearing retaliation if they contact the police. Victims of rape by intimates or acquaintances may be stunned that someone trusted could attack them (Browne, 1991). In particular, when women are raped by a partner, the may experience shame and humiliation so intensely they find it difficult to disclose the fact they were raped (Finkelhor and Yllö, 1983; Russell, 1983). It has been argued that abortion for pregnancies resulting from rape should be prohibited unless the rape is immediately reported. This argument is ill-informed about the context and aftermath of rape.

The diagnosis of post-traumatic stress disorder (PTSD) has provided conceptualization of many of the psychological sequelae for rape. PSTD is characterized by intrusive re-experiencing of the traumatic experience, and symptoms include denial, increased arousal, irritability, angry outbursts, hypervigilance, and sleep disturbances (American Psychiatric Association, 1994). The PTSD construct reflects findings from research that has identified common emotional reactions to stress from diverse sources, including crimes, accidents, war, and natural disasters. These include anger, shock, disbelief, confusion, fear, anxiety, helplessness, insecurity, suggestibility, passivity, and difficulty in making decisions and in functioning alone (Figley, 1985).

Most rape victims evaluated at a trauma center in the immediate aftermath of rape meet symptom criteria for post traumatic stress disorder (PTSD). For example, an average of 12 days following assault, 94 percent of rape victims met PTSD symptom criteria; 46 percent still met the criteria three months later (Rothbaum *et al.*, 1992). Other studies in France, New Zealand, and the U. S. have found PSTD in 50 percent to 90 percent of victims (Bownes *et al.*, 1997; Breslau *et al.*, 1998). Rape is more likely to induce PTSD than is a range of traumatic events affecting civilians, including robbery, physical assault, tragic death of a close friend or family member, or natural disaster.

The nature of the attack itself can affect its psychological consequences. The greater the physical threat, and the greater the probability of intercourse, the greater the trauma (Stein *et al.*, 1987). Interestingly, absence of violence may decrease post-rape functioning. When rape includes fondling and caressing, victims may associate subsequent displays of physical affection with the coerced caresses of the rapist, evoking anxiety and other symptoms (McCahill *et al.*, 1979).

Fear responses may be triggered by a variety of stimuli directly associated by the attack itself, by potential consequences of the rape (e.g. testifying in court, contracting an STD, or by situations that appear to pose a new threat of attack (Kilpatrick *et al.*, 1981). Even when specific triggers are lacking, anxiety can become generalized, leading to 'jumpiness', sleep disruptions, lack of concentration, and distrust or fear of men (Burgess and Holmstrom, 1979a, 1979b; Nadelson *et al.*, 1982; Finkelhor and Yllö, 1985).

Victimization assaults the survivors 'world of meaning' (Conte, 1988: 325). Beliefs are potentially challenged by rape, including safety, power or efficacy, trust, esteem, and intimacy (McCann and Pearlman, 1990). In addition, lesbian victims assaulted by men must also confront the effects of victimization on their sexual identity (Garnets *et al.*, 1990). A woman whose body is violated, particularly by an intimate partner, may cease to believe that she is secure in the world, that she is a person of worth, and that the world has order and meaning (Janoff-Bulman and Frieze, 1983). In particular, when women are assaulted in 'safe' environments, such as when they are with someone they trust, their symptoms of fear and depression are more severe (Burge, 1989). Despite the fact that cognitive changes after rape are intense and salient, they are ignored in the diagnostic criteria for PTSD, which focus on memory intrusions, emotional arousal, and avoidance behavior.

Victims of sexual assault may suffer from a variety of sexual dysfunctions including fear of sex, arousal dysfunction, and decreased sexual interest (Becker *et al.*, 1986; Ellis *et al.*, 1980). Victimization in childhood is associated with higher risk for unwanted pregnancy and abortion as well as subsequent revictimization (Deitz *et al.*, 1999; Russo and Denious, 1998). High risk sexual behavior (including multiple partners and trading sex for money and drugs) as well as serious alcohol and drug-related problems have been found to be correlated with a history of sexual victimization, but the direction of the relationships are unclear (Burnam *et al.*, 1988; Frank *et al.*, 1981). Recent longitudinal research (Kilpatrick *et al.*, 1997) examining violent assault and substance use in women over two years, found that at time 1, use of drugs, but not abuse of alcohol, increased odds of subsequent assault. Further, if a new assault occurred in the subsequent period, odds of both alcohol abuse and drug use significantly increased, even among women with no previous use or assault history. For illicit drug use, findings revealed a 'vicious cycle relationship in which substance use increases risk of future assault and assault increases risk of subsequent substance use' (p. 834).

Rape victims typically show very high distress levels within the first week with this distress peaking in severity approximately three weeks after the assault. It continues at a high level for the next month, beginning to improve by two to three months post assault (Rothbaum *et al.*, 1992). Research suggests that mental health status at the end of the third month is a good indicator of long-term adjustment (Burgess and Holmstrom, 1974). However, for some women symptomatology returns from two weeks to several months after the assault (Forman, 1980). At this time the woman may seek help for these symptoms without informing service providers about the rape experience underlying them (Browne, 1991).

Approximately a quarter of rape victims continue to experience negative effects, some continuing several years after being raped (Hanson, 1990). Even many years later, rape survivors are more likely to receive a variety of psychiatric diagnoses, including depressive disorders, alcohol abuse and dependence, drug abuse and dependence, generalized anxiety, obsessive-compulsive disorder, and post-traumatic stress disorder (PTSD); Burnam *et al.*, 1988; Golding *et al.*, 1997; Kilpatrick *et al.*, 1985).

Finally, the impact of fear of rape on women's mental health must be included in any portrait of rape's impact on women's health and well-being. As RozJe (1993) has observed, when women's choice is the defining feature for rape, there is little evidence of the existence of the idea of a rape-free culture. Even if rape is rare the very fact it is possible means it can be used to threaten and socially control women, serving as a formidable barrier to their full participation in public life (RozJe, 1993, 1996). In addition to direct effects on psychological well-being, fear of rape can affect the health of a woman and her family by damaging her ability to work and to feed, clothe, and shelter them.

SUMMARY

In summary, rape is widespread around the globe, and has many forms. Cultural definitions of rape vary widely within and across cultural contexts, and such definitions have profound implications for women's physical and mental health. Severe physical consequences of rape include death, injury, and lingering risk for a variety of illnesses. Emotional, cognitive, and behavior responses vary depending on the woman's psychological and social coping resources and the nature of the assault, but can include fear, anxiety, depression, sexual dysfunction, and post-traumatic stress disorder, significant changes in a women's view of her world and of her self, and changes in important health behaviors, including alcohol and drug abuse. Clearly women's rights and ability to maintain their bodily integrity involve survival issues and have substantial public impact (Koss *et al.*, 1994). We hope that this chapter will stimulate interest in the study of the health effects of multiple forms of rape across cultural boundaries. We also hope it will motivate readers to work more actively to eliminate rape and other forms of violence against women around the world. Although the bulk of research presented here on the physical and mental health of rape victims reflects the Western context, we must never forget that in many parts of the world dishonor, disgrace, beatings, imprisonment, suicide, and death continue to be health-related consequences of being raped.

ACKNOWLEDGMENT

International collaboration was possible through a National Council of Science and Technology in Mexico (CONACYT) Post-doctoral Grant to the third author.

REFERENCES

Amnesty International (1992) Sexual torture of political prisoners: An overview. *Journal of Traumatic Stress*, 2, 305–318

American Psychiatric Association (1994) *Diagnostic and Statistical Manual of Mental Disorders* (DSM-IV). Washington, D.C.: American Psychiatric Association

Baker, T.C., Burgess, A.W., Brickman, E. and Davis, R.C. (1990) Rape Victims' concerns about possible exposure to HIV infection. *Journal of Interpersonal Violence*, 5, 49–60

Becker, J.V., Skinner, L.J., Abel, G.G. and Treacy, E.C. (1982) Incidence and types of sexual dysfunction in rape and incest victims. *Journal of Sex and Marital Therapy*, 8, 65–74

Becker, J.V., Skinner, L.J., Abel, G.G., Axelrod, R. and Treacy, E.C. (1984) Depressive symptoms associated with sexual assault. *Journal of Sex and Martial Therapy*, 10(3), 185–192

Becker, J.V., Skinner, L.J., Able, G.G. and Cichon, J. (1986) Level of post-assault sexual functioning in rape and incest victims. *Archives of Sexual Behavior*, 15, 37–49

Ben Baraka, M. (1993, November) Defloration in Algeria: A case study of force during sexual initiation. Paper presented at the United National Population Council Meeting, Sexual Coercion and Women's Reproductive Health, jointly sponsored by the Population Council and the Pacific Institute for Women's Health, New York

Bownes, I.T., O'Gorman, E.C. and Sayers, A. (1997) Assault characteristics and posttraumatic stress disorder in rape victims. *Acta Psychiatrica Scandinavica*, 83 (1), 27–30

Breslau, N., Kessler, R.C., Chilcoat, H.D., Schuitz, L.R., Davis, G,C., and Andreski, P. (1998) Trauma and posttraumatic stress disorder in the community: The 1996 Detroit Area Survey of Trauma. *Archives of General Psychiatry*, 55, 626–632

Brener, N.D., McMahon, P.M., Warren, C.W., and Douglas, K.A. (1999) Forced sexual intercourse and associated health-risk behaviors among female college students in the United States. *Journal of Consulting and Clinical Psychology*, 67, 252–259

Browne, A. (1991) The victim's experience: Pathways to disclosure. *Psychotherapy*, 28, 150–156

Bunster, X. (1986) Surviving beyond fear: Women and torture in Latin America. In J. Nash and H. Safa (Eds.) *Women and Change in Latin America* (pp. 297–325). South Hadley, MA: Bergin and Garvey

Bureau of Justice Statistics (1997) *Criminal Victimization in the United States: 1994. NCJ-162126.* Washington, D.C.: U.S. Department of Justice

Burge, S. K. (1989) Violence against women as a health care issue. *Family Medicine*, 21 (September-October), 368–373

Burgess, A.W. and Holmstrom, L. (1979a) Adaptive strategies and recovery from rape. *American Journal of Psychiatry*, 136, 1278–1282

Burgess, A. W. and Holmstrom, L. (1979b) *Rape: Crisis and Recovery.* Bowie, MD: Robert J. Brady

Burgess, A.W. and Holmstrom, L. (1979c) Rape: Sexual disruption and recovery. *American Journal of Psychiatry*, 133, 648–657

Burgess, A.W., Holmstrom, L.L. (1974) Rape trauma syndrome. *American Journal of Psychiatry*, 131, 981–986

Burnam, M.A., Stein, J.A., Golding, J.M., Siegel, J.M., Sorenson, S.B., Forsythe, A.B. and

Telles, C.A. (1988) Sexual assault and mental disorders in a community population. *Journal of Consulting and Clinical Psychology*, 56, 843–850

Cartwright, P.S. and The Sexual Assault Study Group (1987) Factors that correlate with injury sustained by survivors of sexual assault. *Obstetrics and Gynecology*, 70, 44–46

Chen, Y.M., Davis, M., Ott, D.J. (1986) Traumatic rectal hematoma following anal rape. *Annals of Emergency Medicine*, 15, 122–124

Collett, B.J., Cordle, C.J., Stewart, C.R., and Jagger, C. (1998) A comparative study of women with chronic pelvic pain, chronic nonpelvic pain, and those with no history of pain attending general practitioners. *British Journal of Obstetrics and Gynaecology*, 105(1), 87–92

Conte, J. R. (1988) The effects of sexual abuse on children: Results of a research project. *Annals of the New York Academy of Sciences*, 528, 311–326

Coomaraswamy, B. (1992) Sri Lanka -Of Kali born: Women, violence, and the law. In M. Schuler (Ed.) *Freedom from Violence: Women's Strategies from Around the World* (pp. 49–61). New York: UNIFEM WIDBOOKS

Council on Scientific Affairs (1992) Violence against women: Relevance for medical practitioners. *Journal of the American Medical Association*, 257, 3184–3189

Deitz, P.M., Gazmaranian, J.A., Goodwin., M.M., Bruce, F.C., Johnson, C.H., and Rochat, R. W. (1999) Unintended pregnancy among adult women exposed to abuse or household dysfunction during their childhood. *Journal of the American Medical Association*, 282, 1359–1364

Drossman, D.A., Lesserman, J., Nachman, G., Li, Z., Gluck, H., Toomey, T. C. and Mitchell, M. (1990) Sexual and physical abuse in women with functional or organic gastrointestinal disorders. *Annals of Internal Medicine*, 113, 828–833

Ehlert, U., Heim, C. and Hellhamer, D.H. (1999) Chronic pelvic pain as a somatoform disorder. *Psychotherapy and Psychosomatics*, 68 (2), 87–94

Ellis, E.M., Calhoun, K.S. and Atkeson, B.M. (1980) Sexual dysfunctions in victims of rape: Victims may experience a loss of sexual arousal and frightening flashbacks even one year after the assault. *Women and Health*, 5, 39–47

Felitti, V.J. (1998) Long-term medical consequences of incest, rape, and molestation. *Southern Medical Journal*, 84 (3), 328–331

Figley, C.R. (Ed.) (1985) *Trauma and Its Wake: The Study and Treatment of Post-Traumatic Stress Disorder*. New York: Brunner/Mazel

Finkelhor D. and Yllö, K. (1983) Rape in marriage: A sociological view. In D. Finkelhor, R. J. Gelles, G.T. Hotaling, and M.A. Straus (Eds.) *The Dark Side of Families: Current Family Violence Research* (pp. 119–31). Beverly Hills, CA: Sage

Finkelhor D. and Yllö, K. (1985) *License to Rape: Sexual Abuse of Wives*, New York: Holt, Rinehart, and Winston

Foa, E.B. and Rothbaum, B.O. (1998) *Treating the Trauma of Rape*. New York: Guilford Press

Forman, B. (1980) Psychotherapy with rape victims. *Psychotherapy: Theory, Research, and Practice*, 17, 304–311

Forster, G.E., Estreich, S., Hooi, Y. S. (1991) Screening for STDs. Letter to the editor. *Annals of Emergency Medicine*, 324, 161–162

Frank, E., Turner, S.M., Stewart, B.D., Jacob, J. and West, D. (1981) Past psychiatric symptoms and the response to sexual assault. *Comprehensive Psychiatry*, 22, 479–487

Garnets, L., Herek, G. M. and Levy, B. (1990) Violence and victimizations of lesbians and gay men: mental health consequences. *Journal of Interpersonal Violence*, 5, 366–383

Giraud, Francois (1988) La reacción xocial ante la violación: del dicurso a la práctica (Nueva España, siglo XVIII. [The social reaction towards rape from discourse to practice (New Spain, 18th century)] In Seminario de Historia de las Mentalidades: El placer de pecar & el efán de normar (pp. 295-352). Mexico City: Joaquín Mortiz/Instituto Nacional de Antropologia e Historia

Golding, J.A., Cooper, M.L., and George, L.K. (1997) Sexual assault history and health perceptions: seven general population studies. *Health Psychology*, 15, 417–425

Golding, J.M., Stein, J.A., Siegel, J.M., Burnam, M. and Sorenson, S.B. (1988) Sexual assault history and use of health and mental health services. *American Journal of Community Psychology*, 16, 625–644

Goodman, L.A., Koss, M.P., and Russo, N.F. (1993) Violence against women: Physical and mental health effects. Part I: Research findings. *Applied and Preventive Psychology: Current Scientific Perspectives*, 2, 79–89

Hanson, R.K. (1990) The psychological impact of sexual assault on women and children: A review. *Annals of Sex Research*, 3, 187–232

Heise, Lori, Pitanguy, J. and Germain, A. (1993) *Violence Against Women: The Hidden Health*

Burden. Washington, D.C.: The World Bank

Jhangi, A. and Jalani, H. (1990) *The Hudood Ordinances: A Divine Sanction?* Lahore, Pakistan: Rhotas Books

Koss, M.P., Dinero, T.E., Seibel, C. and Cox, S. (1988) Stranger, acquaintance, and date rape: Is there a difference in the victim's experience. *Psychology of Women Quarterly*, 12, 1–24

Human Rights Watch (1993a) *War Crimes in Bosnia-Herzegovina: Volume 2*. New York: Author

Human Rights Watch (1993b) *Widespread Rape of Somali Women Refugees in NE Kenya*. New York: Author

Human Rights Watch (1993c) *Rape in Kashmir*. New York: Author

Janoff-Bulman, R. and Frieze, I.H. (1983) A theoretical perspective for understanding reactions to victimization. *Journal of Social Issues*, 39, 1–17

Kilpatrick, D.G., Best, C.L., Veronen, L.J., Amick, A.E., Villeponteaux, L.A. and Ruff, G.A. (1985) Mental health correlates of criminal victimization: A random community survey. *Journal of Consulting and Clinical Psychology*, 53, 866–873

Kilpatrick, D. G., Resick, P. A. and Veronen, L. J. (1981) Effects of a rape experience: A longitudinal study. *Journal of Social Issues*, 37, 1050–121

Kilpatrick, D.G., Saunders, B.E., Amick-McMullan, A., Best, C.L., Veronen, L.J. and Resnick, H.S. (1989) Victim and crime factors associated with the development of crime-related posttraumatic stress disorder. *Behavior Therapy*, 20, 199–214

Kilpatrick, D.G., Saunders, B.E., Veronen, L.J., Best, C.L., Von, J. M. (1987) Criminal victimization: lifetime prevalence, reporting to police, and psychological impact. *Crime and Delinquency*, 33, 478–489

Kilpatrick, D.G., Veronen, L.J. and Best, C.L. (1985) Factors predicting psychological distress among rape victims. In C.R. Figley (Eds.). *Trauma and Its Wake: The Study and Treatment of Post-Traumatic Stress Disorder* (pp. 113–41). New York: Brunner/Mazel

Kilpatrick, D.G., Veronen, L.J. and Resick, P.A. (1979) Assessment of the aftermath of rape: Changing patterns of fear. *Journal of Behavioral Assessment*, 1, 133–148

Kilpatrick, D.G., Veronen, L.J., Saunders, B.E., Best, C.L., Amick-McMullan, A. and Paduhovich, J. (1987) *The Psychological Impact of Crime: A Study of Randomly Surveyed Crime Victims*. Final report on grant No. 84–IJ-CX-0039 submitted to the National Institute of Justice

Kilpatrick. D.G., Acierno, R., Resnick, H.S., Saunders, B.E. and Best, C.L. (1997) A 2–year longitudinal analysis of the relationships between violent assault and substance use in women. *Journal of Consulting and Clinical Psychology*, 65, 834–847

Koss, M.P. (1991) The impact of crime victimization on women's medical use. *Journal of Women's Health*, 2, 67–72

Koss, M. P. (1985) The hidden rape victim: Personality, attitudinal, and situational characteristics. *Psychology of Women Quarterly*, 9, 193–212

Koss, M.P. (1988) Women's mental health research agenda: Violence against women. *Women's Mental Health Occasional Paper Series*. Washington, D.C.: National Institute of Mental Health

Koss, M.P. (1990) The women's mental health research agenda: Violence against women. *American Psychologist*, 45, 374–80

Koss, M.P. (1993) Rape scope, impact, interventions, and public policy responses. *American Psychologist*, 48, 1062–1069

Koss, M.P., Goodman, L.A., Browne, A., Fitzgerald, L., Keita, Koss and Russo, N.F. (1994) *No Safe Haven: Male Violence Against Women at Home, at Work, and in the Community*. Washington, D.C.: American Psychological Association

Koss, M.P., Heise, L. and Russo, N.F. (1994) The global health burden of rape. *Psychology of Women Quarterly*, 18, 509–530

Koss, M.P, Dinero, T.E., Seibel, C. and Cox, S. (1988) Stranger, acquaintance, and date rape: Is there a difference in the victim's experience? *Psychology of Women Quarterly*, 12, 1–24

Koss, M.P. and Harvey, M. (1991*)* *The Rape Victim: Clinical and Community Approaches to Treatment*. Lexington, MA: Stephen Greene Press

Koss, M.P. and Heslet, L. (1992) Medical Consequences of Violence Against Women,

Koss, M.P, Koss, P.G. and Woodruff, W. J. (1991) Deleterious effects of criminal victimization on women's health and medical utilization. *Archives of Internal Medicine*, 151, 342–347

Koss, M.P., Woodruff, W.J. and Koss, P.G. (1991) Criminal victimization among primary care medical patients: Incidence, prevalence, and physician usage. *Behavioral Science and the Law*, 9, 85–96

Koss, M., Goodman, L., Fitzgerald, L., Keita, G., and Russo, N.F. (1993) Male violence women: Current research and future directions. *American Psychologist*, 48, 1054–1058

Lefley, H.P.; Scott, C.S.; Llabre, M. and Hicks, D. (1993) Cultural beliefs about rape and victims' response in three ethnic groups. *American Journal of Orthopsychiatry*, 63, 623–632

Lykes, B., Brabeck, M.M., Ferns, T. and Radan, A. (1993) Human rights and mental health among Latin American women in situations of state-sponsored violence. *Psychology of Women Quarterly*, 17, 525–544

MacKinnon, C. (1983) Feminism, Marxism, and the State: Toward feminist jurisprudence. *Signs: Journal of Women in Culture and Society*, 8, 635–658

McCahill, T.W., Meyer, L.C. and Fischman, A.M. (1979) *The Aftermath of Rape*, Lexington, MA: D.C. Heath & Co

McCann, I.L. and Pearlman, L.A. (1990) *Psychological Tauma and the Adult Survivor: Theory Therapy and Transformation*. New York: Brunner/Mazel.

McCauley, J., Kern, D.E., Kolodner, K., Dill, L., Schroeder, A.F., DeChant, H.K., Ryden, J., Derogatis, L.R., and Bass, E.B. (1997) Clinical characteristics of women with a history of childhood abuse: Unhealed wounds. *Journal of the American Medical Association*, 277, 1362–1368

Miller, D.T., and Porter, C.A. (1983) Self-blame in victims of violence. *Journal of Social Issues*, 39, 139–152

Nadelson, C., Notman, M., Zackson, H. and Gornich, J. (1982) A follow-up study of rape victims. *American Journal of Psychiatry*, 139, 1266–1270

National Victims Center (NVC) (1992, April) *Rape in America: A Report to the Nation*. Arlington, VA: Author

Ramos Lira, L., Koss, M.P. and Russo, N.F. (1999) Mexican-American women 's definitions of rape and sexual abuse. *Hispanic Journal of Behavioral Sciences*, 21(3), 236–265

Resick, P.A., Calhoun, K., Atkeson, B. and Ellis, E. (1981) Adjustment in victims of sexual assault. *Journal of Consulting and Clinical Psychology*, 49, 704–712

Rothbaum, B.O., Foa, E.B., Riggs, D.S., Murdock, T. and Walsh, W. (1992) A prospective examination of post-traumatic stress disorder in rape victims. *Journal of Traumatic Stress*, 5455–5475

RozJe, P.D. (1993) Forbidden or forgiven? Rape in cross-cultural perspective. *Psychology of Women Quarterly*, 17, 499–514

RozJe, P.D. (1996) Freedom from fear of rape: The missing link in women's freedom. In J.C. Chrisler, C. Golden and P.D. RozJe (Eds.) *Lectures on the Psychology of Women* (pp. 309–322). New York: McGraw-Hill

Russell, D.E.H. (1983) The prevalence and incidence of forcible rape and attempted rape of females. *Victimology: An International Journal*, 7, 81–93

Russell, D.E.H. (1990) *Rape in marriage: Expanded and revised edition*. Bloomington: Indiana University Press

Russo, N.F. and Denious, J. (1998) Understanding the relationship of violence against women to unwanted pregnancy and its resolution. In L.J. Beckman and S.M. Harvey (Eds.) *The New Civil War: The Psychology, Culture, and Politics of Abortion* (pp. 211–234). Washington, D.C.: American Psychological Association

Shalhoub-Kevorkian, N. (1999) Towards a cultural definition of rape: Dilemmas in dealing with rape victims in Palestinian society. *Women's Studies International Forum*, 22, 157–173

Stein, J.A., Golding, J.M., Siegel, J.M., Burnam, M.A. and Sorenson, S.B (1988) Long-term psychological sequelae of child sexual abuse: The Los Angeles Epidemiologic Catchment Area study. In G.E. Wyatt and G.J. Powell (Ed.) *Lasting Effects of Child Sexual Abuse* (pp. 135–154). Newbury Park, CA: Sage Publications

Swiss, S. and Giller, J.E. (1993) Rape as a crime of war: A medical perspective. *Journal of the American Medical Association*, 270(5), 612–615

Williams, J.E. and Holmes, K.A. (1981) *The Second Assault: Rape and Public Attitudes*, Westport, CT: Greenwood Press

Woodling, B.A. and Kossoris, P.D. (1981) Sexual misuse: Rape, molestation, and incest. *Pediatric Clinics of North America*, 28, 481–499

Wyatt, G.E. (1985) The sexual abuse of Afro-American and White-American women in childhood. *Child Abuse and Neglect*, 9, 507–519

Wyatt, G.E. (1990) Sexual abuse of ethnic minority children: Identifying dimensions of victimization. *Professional Psychology: Research and Practice*, 21, 338–343

Yllö, R. and Bograd, M. (Eds.) (1988) *Feminist Perspectives on Wife Abuse*. Newbury Park: Sage

CHAPTER 13

SEXUAL ASSAULT AND DOMESTIC VIOLENCE: IMPLICATIONS FOR HEALTH WORKERS

Sue Lees

INTRODUCTION

This chapter begins by outlining the risks that women and children can face on the breakdown of relationships with abusive men, and the effects, both direct and indirect, of both experiencing and witnessing violence on their physical and psychological health. Recent government interventions in both developing guidelines on improving recognition of, and treatment for, the effects of domestic violence, are outlined. The need for special innovative programmes to deal with the particular needs of ethnic groups are proposed. The lack of formal courses on domestic violence on training courses in Britain is contrasted with the national provision in the United States.

On 4 August 1998 three children were found dead in a smouldering Ford Capri, killed by their father because he feared his wife had walked out on him. The father hung himself. Police identified the three children as Lucy aged 7, Thomas, aged 4 and Hollie, 3 (*The Guardian*, 4 August 1998). On 20 March 1999 Peter Hall was sentenced for stabbing his girl friend, Celeste Bates, aged 31, and killing her two children. He first murdered her before collecting her 17-month-old son, Milo, from his nursery and taking him to her home, where he killed him with a pickaxe handle. He then collected 8-year-old Daniel from his childminder and killed him the same way. After the killings he went to a pub and told drinkers: 'I am going to be famous'. Sentencing Hall at Manchester Crown Court, Mr Justice Forbes said 'None of your victims had done you the slightest harm … Together they formed a decent, happy, loving family unit … which fell victim to your jealous rage' (*The Guardian*, 20 March 1999).

These two tragic cases illustrate the danger that women and children fleeing from abusive fathers face. The effect of recent legislation awarding fathers more rights of access to children has put women escaping violence more at risk. Men can apply for contact orders under the Children Act 1989 and use court procedures to track down their victims. Hester and Radford (1996) reviewed developments regarding contact between children and parents after separation and divorce. They outline the tactics used by men in custody cases such as using children as hostages to force women to return, manipulation of legal procedures relating to child care in attempt to involve courts and law to continue the harassment. They point out that the concept of 'parental responsibility' by which men are encouraged to have more contact with their children does not take into consideration the harassment women and children suffer; violence on children is not taken into account in judicial settlements of child contact post-separation.

Domestic violence, both sexual and physical, can have both direct and indirect effects on women's and children's physical and mental health. Even the direct effects are not always recognized and it is only recently that the indirect effects of the witnessing of violence by children is beginning to be appreciated. This chapter outlines some of the known effects of sexual assault and domestic violence and discusses how health workers can contribute to meeting this challenge.

Contrary to public opinion, women and children are much more likely to be assaulted in the home than outside it. Data from the U.S.A, the U.K., Australia and New Zealand all confirm that interpersonal violence, whether homicide, sexual assault or physical assault, is largely committed by those known to the victim. Half of the women murdered worldwide are killed by husbands, partners or lovers. Children are also at risk at this time. Roughly two thirds of children under 16 murdered by parents are killed by their fathers or stepfathers. The most dangerous time is after a couple have broken up.

PREVALENCE OF DOMESTIC VIOLENCE

In the 1970s Britain was one of the first countries to set up crisis centers and refuges where women could escape from violence by their partners, or other relatives. In 1997–1998 there were 54,000 women and children staying in 240 refuges in England and a further 145,000 sought advice and help from Women's Aid services (Women's Aid Annual Report 1998). The demand for such services reflected the widespread prevalence of domestic violence

A number of reports (Mooney, 1994; Dominy and Radford, 1996) including one from the British Medical Association (1998) estimated that as many as one in four women have been affected by domestic violence. Homicide statistics worldwide inform us that women are most likely to be killed by current or former husbands or partners or lovers (Daly and Wilson, 1988). The costs and consequences have been documented by the World Bank and the United Nations. Major challenges still face us in recognizing the effects of violence on the lives of women and children.

In the 1990s the harmful effects of witnessing domestic violence on children have been recognized and the links between child abuse and abuse of women documented (Mullender and Morley, 1995; Anderson, 1997, Hester and Pearson, 1998). The setting up and expansion of ChildLine, a helpline which children can ring anonymously, has revealed the widespread incidence of such abuse. An analysis of calls made to

ChildLine (Epstein and Keep, 1995) indicated how children describe feeling responsible both for causing the violence and for preventing it, and this in turn engenders an overwhelming sense of helplessness. Over a third of the sample had been physically abused themselves.

Additionally, UNICEF calculates that trafficking in children is the third most lucrative illegal trade in the world, after drugs and weapons, and is a multi-billion dollar business. It is estimated that 5,000 children work in the sex trade in Britain and are the victims of family abuse, career paedophiles, prostitution, sex tourism and pornography. Prostitution of young women under 16 is a question of growing concern (see Kelly *et al.*, 1995; Barrett, 1997; Barnardos, 1998).

THE EFFECTS OF SEXUAL ASSAULT ON HEALTH

Research studies on rape in the U.S.A., Canada and Britain reveal that women are far more likely to be assaulted by men they know or are related to than by strangers. The rates of assault are high (see Russo, Koss and Ramos, in this volume). Between one in five and one in seven women report having been victims of rape, with girls under 15 years of age being those most at risk. In research I conducted for the TV Dispatches programme *Getting Away with Rape* (1993), out of 100 victims, one in five lost their virginity as a result of the rape, seven became pregnant and seven caught a sexually transmitted disease (see Lees, 1997; Gregory and Lees, 1999) and most feared HIV.

One woman described the effects as follows:

shock, numbness, humiliation, degradation, disbelief, guilty, self blame and anger which led to me mutilating myself, embarrassment, loss of control, severe depression (I take antidepressants) irritability, mood swings, fear of being alone, crying a lot, inability to sleep, nightmares, relationship problems with family and friends, no enthusiasm for life, anorexia, loss of concentration, feelings of being dirty, defiled, contaminated (constantly washing), loss of self trust, safety and independence.

During the 1980s research has advanced our knowledge about the short- and long-term effects of rape – often referred to as the rape trauma syndrome, a post traumatic stress response (see Holmstrom and Burgess, 1978; Hall, 1985; Newburn, 1993; for a discussion of the effects of sexual harassment see Thomas, in this volume). Typical reactions include helplessness, sleeplessness, flashbacks, nightmares, anger, suicidal feelings, phobic reactions, depression, mood swings, fear of being alone, relationship problems (in particular not enjoying sex), anorexia, loss of concentration and self-esteem and blaming oneself. Personal relationships are often disrupted, and sexual relationships often break up. A finding of crucial importance is that such reactions are often delayed or 'blocked out'. Complainants may appear calm and controlled, or they may be angry rather than distraught.

The use of a medical term, rape trauma syndrome, to describe such symptoms carries some disadvantages. Absence of particular symptoms can be used maliciously by defence doctors for example, as evidence that the complainant is making false allegations. One of the ironies is that the very qualities that help women survive are the ones that are most inappropriate for obtaining a conviction; the rape victim is expected to display emotion even many months after the event and in public. The use of medical terms can also reduce the complexity of the woman's experiences to a set of 'individual symptoms' which once understood, can be cured by the medical profession alone.

THE IMPACT OF HEALTH WORKERS

Research indicates that doctors and nurses can have a marked effect on a victim's recovery, and can determine whether she is helped in the recovery process or undergoes further trauma (Burgess and Holmstrom, 1974). In my study of the police treatment of rape victims, 11 women interviewed had been medically examined (Lees, 1997); all but one had requested to see a woman doctor, but in only two cases was a woman available. The medical examination was described by seven of the women as a stressful experience, some saw it as an endurance test, and three described it as utterly degrading, in one case as bad as the rape itself.

Three doctors appeared to have been callously unsympathetic, even cruel. Others may not have been deliberately heartless, but did not appreciate the acute sensitivity of victims. Forensic requirements were often put into effect with little flexibility. The following descriptions give one little confidence in the service:

So I got examined by the doctor. She wasn't very nice. It was terrible. She gave me the morning after pill and she didn't explain anything about it. I was throwing up. I didn't know I'd be throwing up for nothing. She wasn't the slightest bit sympathetic or anything like that. She didn't care. She was just doing her job

I looked down at myself with this sheet wrapped around me and he [the medical officer] turned to the WPC and said 'Cover her up will you?'. I felt like a piece of something on a slab – cover that up we should not be looking at that.

Another woman, herself a medical professional working in a local hospital, was very unhappy with her treatment:

The one thing I didn't like was the police surgeon. I don't think the police told him I was the victim and he seemed to treat me as if somehow I was a criminal. I ended up in tears. He just seemed so rude to me, all the time, and he wanted me to spit in a pot and I couldn't and every time I tried to spit I wanted to be sick. It was really horrible the way he treated me. Because of being in the medical profession I notice things like that as I'm into training doctors and that one was not one of mine. I'm sure no-one told him that this is a victim not a criminal. I'm sure no one said anything to him.

Part of the difficulty appears to be the undue concentration on the investigatory aspects to the neglect of humane considerations. The inflexible implementation of procedures may sometimes override common sense and lead to the victim's unnecessary discomfort. One complainant was not allowed to drink for five hours after a major assault, although she had not had oral sex. Forensic evidence is, of course, relevant only in establishing that intercourse took place, not whether it took place with or without consent. However, there is a great deal of fuzzy thinking and forensic evidence can be used against rather than for the complainant in a number of ways. For example, in the absence of vaginal injuries, forensic evidence can be used by the defence to argue that the woman consented. Arguments about whether the woman 'lubricated' are particularly pernicious. One police officer interviewed, who had been on the special course on sexual assault at the Hendon Police Training College in London, insisted quite fallaciously that forensic tests could ascertain from the fluids whether or not the complainant had consented. If some trained police officers believe this, it is not surprising that jurors are often confused.

We are only beginning to understand the effects of rape and its aftermath. The difficulties of undertaking research in this area, and the need for greater sensitivity of health professionals, is discussed at greater length by Temkin (1996, 1997) and Lees (1997).

COMMUNITY NURSING AND CARE IN PREGNANCY

Nurses work in a variety of health and community settings and may often be the first outside the family to know that abuse is occurring. School nurses may be crucial in preventive work. Health visitors, nurses in accident and emergency departments and community nurses are uniquely positioned. Mezey *et al.* (1998) found that women attending GP surgeries were more likely to disclose domestic violence to their health visitor.

Domestic abuse often starts or escalates in pregnancy. Relatively few women die during pregnancy or childbirth, but, when pregnant, women are more likely to suffer domestic violence at the hands of their partner and are more likely to commit suicide. An Enquiry into Maternal Deaths, which reports every year, noted in 1998 the failures of some junior medical, obstetric, accident and emergency staff, GPs and midwives to diagnose dangerous conditions or refer the women to specialists who would identify them. To remedy this, it recommended that:

- ante-natal clinics have procedures for identifying women who may become depressed to be aware of the signs that a woman is being battered or is falling into a potentially suicidal depression (Boseley, 1998)
- details of psychiatric disorder, substance abuse or previous self-harm should be taken when a woman books into hospital.
- all pregnant women should have at least one consultation with the lead professional involved in pregnancy care which is not attended by her

partner or any family member and that a set of confidential notes should be kept separate from those held by the patient (BMA 1998).

In November 1997 the Royal College of Midwives produced guidelines entitled *Domestic Abuse in Pregnancy* to help midwives recognize and deal with it. The guidelines point out that the links between domestic abuse and adverse pregnancy outcomes suggest that midwives should assume a greater role in its detection and management. The guidelines outline how to identify domestic violence, the importance of documenting the abuse, and the need to inform women of their options. The guidelines emphasize that discussing domestic abuse can be difficult and embarrassing and argue that it is best to ask direct questions rather than hedge around the issue.

NATIONAL INTERVENTIONS

Until recently government bodies have failed to give any guidance about treating domestic violence. In 1997 the Department of Health issued a circular on the new Family Law Act which included limited guidance on both general issues and on interagency initiatives. Currently, however, there is little coordination of strategic responses of health services to domestic violence at either national or local level. Women have difficulty in gaining physical access to services and there is a need to raise public awareness, and for the monitoring of services.

Recent studies (see Henderson, 1997; BMA, 1998) found that health services were among the least likely of all services to disseminate any information on domestic violence. It is not only doctors, community health workers, and hospital accident and emergency services, but also staff from specialities as wide ranging as palliative and paediatrics, geriatric medicine and genito-urinary services that need training (see Mullender and Morley, 1996: 130).

Since accident and emergency departments are available in some hospitals on a 24-hour basis and do not require appointments, they are often the place where women go if they are injured. Research indicates that domestic violence is frequently not audited or even recorded and staff are not generally trained to recognize or to respond effectively to it (see McWilliams and McKiernan; 1993, Roberts *et al.*, 1997). Women who had been treated were interviewed by McWilliams and McKiernan. The majority of women interviewed believed that the hospital staff should question them more and thought that if approached with sensitivity, women,would be prepared to talk. They also expressed the need for advice and information. By treating the injuries and ignoring the context in which the injuries occurred, health service professionals could easily exacerbate the difficulties women faced. Insufficient time and lack of awareness of the problem means that staff are not identifying the cause of the problem at an early stage. Confidentiality between doctor and patient is regarded as the prime concern and doctors have no legal responsibility to contact the police unless the patient agrees, unlike in France where this is obligatory.

Some local authorities are trying to provide a more coordinated service and to provide training. For example, the Accident and Emergency Department of Leeds General Infirmary is part of coordinated community care planning and inter-agency network to meet the needs of women experiencing violence. Another project in Glasgow involved a full-scale audit to ascertain the current proportions of abused women using services and what responses they received. There is some evidence that doctors are considerably more helpful than other health workers but training for them is still lacking.

BMA REPORT 1998

The British Medical Association (1998) report, *Domestic Violence: A Health Care Issue,* is a comprehensive but accessible discussion document to raise awareness of the nature and prevalence of domestic violence, outlining the role of health care workers in identifying domestic violence and suggesting strategies to help manage and reduce the problem. The report points out that health professionals do not need to prove the existence of violence (like legal professionals), but need to identify and acknowledge it when it does occur. Confidentiality must be discussed with patients, but doctors should underline that secrecy cannot always be guaranteed. It points out that it is important that health workers recognize symptoms of escalating domestic violence, especially those with possible homicidal outcome. Such factors include rising severity and frequency of domestic violence, sexual assault, alcohol or drugs use by perpetrator, and past suicidal attempts by women – all of these should be monitored. It is important to provide women with a supportive environment. Posters and pamphlets in surgeries giving information about where to find help can be useful.

The report also argues that following disclosure, a woman's description of what has happened should be respected. The current safety of woman and children should be gauged and the doctor should encourage her to make her own decisions rather than tell her what to do. The importance of keeping detailed records is stressed as subsequent evidence of violence may be requested – body maps to illustrate injuries, photographs, GP records confirming effects of violence and mental health problems. Patients should also keep a record of the violence. A seven-step overall approach is recommended which includes privacy and confidentiality; questioning; respect and validation; assessment and treatment; record-keeping and concise documentation; information giving; and support and follow up.

The training for health professionals is improving, yet little information is available on what exactly is covered. No formal studies have been undertaken nationally in the U.K. on the extent of education received by medical students and doctors at undergraduate or postgraduate level, unlike in the U.S. where such training is well established. A survey in 1986 of accredited U.S.A. and Canadian medical schools found that just under half of those who replied were providing some instruction on domestic violence. By 1994 this had increased to 87 percent of U.S. medical schools. The *Journal of the American Medical Colleges*, recently produced a 115-page supplement entirely devoted to the subject of educating the nation's doctors about family violence and abuse. This included the importance of acquiring knowledge and skills as well as developing new knowledge and learning to work in partnership with community groups. In the U.K., on the other hand, domestic violence is considered a peripheral issue. A survey of 254 doctors in the Midlands found that a mere 10 percent had received some training either at undergraduate or postgraduate level (British Medical Association 1998: 41).

NEED FOR MORE TRAINING FOR COMMUNITY NURSING

Training courses for nurses, midwives and health visitors usually consider gender issues and domestic violence, but there are large individual variations between courses and few concentrate on domestic violence (Pahl, 1995). According to the report commissioned by the Department of Health and Social Services in Belfast, Northern Ireland (McWilliams and McKiernan, 1993) the response of statutory agencies was often to ignore or minimize the violence, appearing to give legitimation to its use. Social workers sometimes made judgments against wives because they were 'in a refuge' while their husbands were 'living in a nice home' which inadvertently led to several women losing custody of all or some of the children. Community psychiatric nurses estimated that 8 to 10 percent of their current cases related to domestic violence

The 1990s have seen considerable public policy and professional concern about domestic violence as the consequences for mothers and children have begun to be recognized. The Department of Health commissioned the development of a reader, *Making an Impact*, and a Training Resource pack to increase awareness about the impact on children of domestic violence and to develop professional understanding of how best to offer help and support (Hester and Pearson, 1998). The materials were devised by Barnardo's, the NSPCC, and the Domestic Violence Research Group of the University of Bristol with the assistance of a multi-disciplinary team. There is some evidence that social work responses still often adhere to pathologizing or a family systems model. According to this model women in violent relationships are seen as 'clients in need of therapy, rather than people in need of alternatives and choices' (Dobash and Dobash, 1992: 234).

DEVELOPMENT OF GUIDELINES

The following guidelines have been developed and are useful for training purposes: The West London Health Promotion Agency (1997) published a pack containing the first guidelines on domestic abuse in pregnancy by the Royal College of Midwives. *Good Practice Guidelines on Domestic Violence* was produced by the Leeds Inter-Agency Project where a training pack for 'Training For Trainers' has also been developed. This is to support and enable participants to offer a training program and should be used in conjunction with the pack. Trained trainers will undertake four days of training in total. The basis of this program has been used extensively throughout the U.K. Peer assessment and feedback is an essential aspect of the program. Facilitators are advised to be aware of the potential for insensitive feedback and negativity from participants. Establishing ground rules clearly at the beginning is important. (The pack was written by Andrea Tara-Chand and is available from LIAP, CHEL, 26 Rounday Rd, Leeds LS7 IAB. It was funded by the Home Office Programme Development Unit.)

Good practice guidelines have also been developed by some local authorities to encourage work with ethnic minorities. Domestic violence response units were set up in Haringey and Lambeth, both in the heart of Black communities. UJIMA a Black housing association set up the first refuge for Black women in 1988. By 1997 about 40 of the 240 refuge services in England ran specialist refuges. Rai and Thiara (1997) documented the living experiences of Black women's use of refuge support services.

Sen's (1997) study of the needs of ethnic minorities undertaken for the Camden Equalities Unit highlights the frequent exclusion of ethnic minority women (in this case Bangladeshi, Chinese and Horn of Africa women) from initiatives on domestic violence and stresses the need to provide appropriate services to women from these communities. She found that cultural constraints do not prevent women from minority groups from using the services, and that where appropriate services are provided, women will use them. She recommends development of further specific services taking account of ethnic minority women's needs.This requires more ethnic minority staff, monitoring of ethnic users, keeping centralized records and providing further training on the impact of domestic violence on children.

Finally Jackson (1996) documents how deeply racism is affecting the provision of support and care for the abused Black child. She argues that child abuse is taken less seriously if the child is from an ethnic minority and points to the lack of monitoring of ethnic children in care.

SUMMARY

Domestic violence can have both direct and indirect effects. The direct effects, at the extreme, result in death, but also involve serious injuries which can lead to long-term disability. Additionally, pregnancy is known to render women particularly vulnerable to abuse; injuries to the foetus can result. Indirect effects include suicide and self-harm, post-traumatic stress, depression and eating disorders. Research has also established that witnessing violence can have a damaging effects on children's health, both physical and mental.

The effect of doctors and health workers on recovery is well established. The failure of some forensic medical examiners to treat rape and sexual assault victims sensitively needs addressing, as well as the need for guidelines on developing more awareness among health workers more generally. For example, health professionals working in the community are in a key position to assist women and children to escape from violence, and to provide services to address the effects. Similarly, doctors working in accident and emergency departments are in a key position to effectively diagnose injuries resulting from assaults.

At present there is little coordination of strategic responses of health services to domestic violence at either national or local level. The British Medical Report 1998 *Domestic Violence: A Health Care Issue* provides a landmark in calling for national guidelines on both the recognition and treatment of domestic violence. The report calls for coordination of strategic responses of health services to domestic violence at national and local levels.

Training is improving, but is patchy and there is a striking lack of formal courses on domestic violence, unlike in the United States where such courses are well established and an integral part of training in medical education, for both doctors and nurses. Various innovative developments are outlined. Resource training packs, such as the Department of Health's, *Making an Impact* have been commissioned, and guidelines to address the needs of ethnic groups and pregnant women (Royal College of Midwives, 1997), have been developed in a few areas.

Overall research indicates that the response of statutory services is often to ignore or minimize violence. Failure to address the problem and take it seriously is to legitimize it. There is therefore a need for a national strategy both on education and training and on improvement in diagnosis and intervention.

REFERENCES

Anderson, L. (1997) Contact between children and violent fathers: in whose best interests? *ROW Bulletin*, Summer

Barnardos (1998) *Whose Daughter Next? Children Abused through Prostitution.* Available from Tanners Lane, Barkingside, Ilford, Essex IG6IQC

Barrett, D. (Ed.) (1997) *Child Prostitution in Britain.* London: Children's Society

Boseley, S. (1998) Abuse Risk Higher during Pregnancy, *The Guardian*, 24 November

British Medical Association (BMA) (1998) *Domestic Violence: A Health Care Issue?* London: BMA

Burgess, A. and Holmstrom, L. (1974) Rape trauma syndrome and post traumatic stress response. In A. Burgess (Ed.) *Research Handbook on Rape and Sexual Assault* (pp. 46–61). New York Garland

Daly, M. and Wilson, M. (1988), *Homicide.* New York: Aldine De Gruyter

Dispatches (1993) *Getting Away with Rape.* First Frame, Channel 4 Television, London

Dobash, R. and Dobash, R. (1992) *Women. Violence and Social Change.* London: Routledge

Dominy, N. and Radford, L. (1996) *Domestic Violence in Surrey: Developing an Effective Inter-Agency Response.* University of Surrey

Epstein, C. and Keep, G., ChildLine, in Saunders, A. (Ed.) What children tell ChildLine about domestic violence. In *It Hurts Me Too*, London: ChildLine

Gregory, J. and Lees, S. (1999) *Policing Sexual Assault.* London: Routledge

Hall, R. (1985) *Ask Any Woman: A London Enquiry into Rape and Sexual Assault.* Bristol: Falling Wall Press

Henderson, S. (1997) *Service Provision to Women Experiencing Domestic Violence in Scotland.*

London: Scottish Office Central Research Unit

Hester, M. and Radford, L. 1996 Domestic Violence and Access arrangements in Denmark and Britain. *Journal of Social Welfare and Family Law*, 1, 57–70

Hester, M. and Pearson, C. (1998) *Making an Impact*. Bristol: Policy Press

Holmstrom, L. and Burges, A. (1978) *The Victim of Rape: Institutional. Reactions*. New York: Wiley

Jackson, V. (1996) *Racism and Child Protection: The Black Experience of Child Sexual Abuse*. London: Cassell

Kelly, L., Wingfield, R., Burton, S. and Regan, L. (1995) *Splintered Lives: Sexual Exploitation of Children in the Context of Children's Rights and Child Protection*. London: Barnardo's

Lees, S. (1997a) *Carnal Knowledge: Rape on Trial*. London: Penguin

Mezey, G., King, M. and MacClintock, T. (1998) Victims of Violence and the General Practitioner. *British Journal of General Practice*, 48, 906–908

McWilliams, M. and McKiernan, J. (1993) *Bringing it Out in the Open: Domestic Violence in Northern Ireland*. Centre for Research on Women, University of Ulster

Mooney, J. (1994) *The Hidden Figure: Domestic Violence in North London*. Borough of Islington Police and Crime Prevention Unit

Mullender, A. and Morley, R. (Eds.) (1995) *Children Living with Domestic Violence*. London: Whiting and Birch

Mullender, A. and Morley, R. (1996) *Preventing Domestic Violence to Women*. Police Research Group, Crime Prevention Unit Series Paper 48

Newburn, T. (1993) *The Long-term Needs of Victims: A Review of the Literature*. London: Home Office Research and Planning Unit, Paper 80

Pahl, J. (Ed.) (1995) Health professionals and violence against women. In P. Kingston and B. Penhale (Eds.) *Family Violence and the Caring Professions*. London: Macmillan

Radford, L., Hester, M. Humphries, J. and Woodfield, K (1997) *For* the sake of the children: the law, domestic violence and child contact in England. *Women's Studies International Forum*, 20 (4), 471–482

Rai, D. and Thiara, R. (1997) *Redefining Spaces: The Needs of Black Women and Children in Refuge Support Services and Black Workers in Women's Aid*. Women's Aid Federation, PO Box Bristol BS99 7WS

Roberts, G.L., Lawrence, J.M., O'Toole B, Raphael B. (1997) Domestic violence in the emergency department: two case-control studies of victims *General Hospital Psychiatry*, 19; 5–11. Quoted in BMA report 1998

Royal College of Midwives (1997) *Domestic Abuse in Pregnancy*, Available from Royal College of Midwives, 15 Mansfield St, London W1M OBE

Sen, P. (1997) *Searching for Routes to Safety: A Report on the Needs of Ethnic Minority Women Dealing with Domestic Violence*. London: Camden Equalities in Action

Temkin, J. (1996) Doctors, rape and criminal justice. *Howard Journal*, 35 (1) 1–20

Temkin, J. (1997) Plus ca change. *British Journal of Criminology*, 37, 507–527

Women's Aid Federation Annual Report 1998. Available from Women's Aid Federation, PO Box Bristol BS99 7WS

CHAPTER 14

NAMING ABUSE AND CONSTRUCTING IDENTITIES

Rosaleen Croghan and Dorothy Miell

INTRODUCTION

Women's experience of childhood abuse and domestic violence has traditionally been conceived of in terms of individual victimology. The literature on responses to traumatization or victimization has tended to be located within clinical and mainstream social psychological frameworks including attribution theory and information processing with little attention to social and political factors that might inform such constructs (McCann and Pearlman, 1990). Such approaches emphasize the distinguishing features of both 'victims' and their abusers positioning them as distinct groups with characteristic features. For example Dobash and Dobash (1992) list 30 traits generated by various theorists that supposedly differentiate between abused and non-abused women ranging from an inability to cope to introspection and masochism. Victimology has thus been historically associated with a conservative set of assumptions that sought to implicate victims as co-authors or co-conspirators in their own subjugation (Newburn and Stanko, 1994; Caplan, 1990). There has for example been a great deal of focus on the mother's role in father-daughter incest, in which she has been cast as an 'active non participant' and on the daughter's contribution to her own abuse either through seduction or as a means of revenge Fairclough (1986).

WOMEN'S ACCOUNTS OF ABUSE

Women's accounts of their experience of sexual violence and abuse, for example those of Angelou (1971), Armstrong (1979), Brownmiller (1975), and Spring (1981), take issue with these constructions of their identity as passive victims or as co-participants in their own victimization. Such accounts draw attention both to the relationship of power that make such victimization possible and to the ways in which women have triumphed over their adversity, often in spite of rather than because of expert help. 'Battered women are survivors in a struggle for our lives. We are not helpless, not weak, we are courageous strong women. We are women who never stop hoping, fighting or dreaming for our sanity' (Mary Zavala, quoted in Kelly (1988).

This emphasis on abused women's identity as survivors rather than as victims was a feature of the self-help groups that began to emerge among women who had experience of sexual violence (for example the Incest Survivors Network founded in London in 1982). Such groups emphasized values of self-reliance and the reciprocity and reassurance that comes from mutual support and insisted on their credentials as expert witness to their own experiences and their ability to define their own needs and the appropriate response to them (Lloyd, 1992).

Feminist approaches to women's accounts of abuse have focussed on the ways that women's identities have been, and continue to be defined and appropriated in ways that increase their victimization (Kelly, 1984, 1988; Hooper, 1987; McCleod and Saraga, 1988; Nelson 1987; see also Thomas and Russo *et al.*, in this volume). These studies have looked at the ways in which women have been ascribed a contradictory and negative victim identity which inscribes their experience within a discourse of passivity and lack of control and which reconstitutes women's elective choices, for example their choice of same-sex relationships as evidence of their pathology rather than a conscious exercise of rational choice. Wood and Rennie (1994) have argued that definitions of rape continue to be dependent on a paradigm in which women are assigned the position of passive victim, and the medical and legal professions are positioned as arbiters of the act. Similarly Eagle (1998) has shown how gender-typical ascriptions of male aggression, and female passivity and acquiescence are likely to have real effects on the perception of the victim's identity in ways that are problematic for both sexes, in that women's strategies for resistance are likely to be underestimated while men's are overestimated. Kelly *et al.* (1988) suggest that the current orthodoxy of representing children as victims and adults as survivors consistently underestimates the coping and survival strategies used by those who are abused and suggests that an understanding of such strategies is important for work both with children and adults.

A number of studies have focussed on women's accounts of their experience of abuse as contested sites in which women's attempts to redefine their identities in positive ways are constantly vulnerable to re-appropriation. Here it is argued that the credibility of abused women is constantly under attack and that this can be seen in a number of contemporary controversies from the debate over false-memory syndrome, to disputes over diagnosis, to doubts over the status of the child witness (Richardson and Bacon, 1988; Westcott, 1992).

Barry (1978) argues that both survivors' accounts and feminist academic attempts to draw attention to the extent and seriousness of women's victimization and the adverse effects of abuse on women's health have been re-appropriated within a professional discourse of 'victimism' which dismisses any question of the abused woman's agency and initiative. Similarly Armstrong (1991) argues that women's revelations of sexual abuse and their claim to authority over their own experience were quickly appropriated by experts within a thriving 'incest industry' in the

1980s and 1990s and that psychological explanations were used to appropriate feminist rhetoric and to erase feminist questions about the implications of sexual violence. She writes 'we spoke of male violence and deliberate socially accepted violation, they spoke of family dysfunction. We spoke of rage, they named rage a stage. We spoke of social change, they spoke of personal healing. We spoke of political battle, they spoke of our need to hug the child within'.

In addition, Kitzinger (1993) argues that the resistance implicit in the construction of the survivor identity has been re-appropriated and subverted in a number of recently published self-help books in which the rhetoric of self-realization is used to re-affirm the abused woman's individual responsibility for her recovery.

DISCURSIVE APPROACHES TO IDENTITY

Because of this insight into the ways in which women's accounts of their abuse are liable to appropriation, recent discursive approaches to victimization and women's health have focussed on such accounts as sites of both resistance *and* accommodation. A recent study by Croghan and Miell (1999) examines abused women's resistance to the notion that because of their abuse in childhood they are likely to become either abusive in adulthood or victims of abuse (the so-called 'inter-generational hypothesis'). However, while they suggest that abused women actively resist the negative identity ascription applied to them, for example by presenting themselves as receptacles of privileged knowledge and as thus more able to protect their *own* children, they do so within the parameters of the interpretative repertoires available to them (Potter and Wetherell, 1987).

Thus in trying to establish their credentials as mothers they are forced to accommodate to existing negative constructions of their identity in order to establish their right to be heard. Croghan and Miell suggest that psycho-dynamic discourses of unconscious damage are particularly damaging to women who have experience of abuse in that they undermine the woman's claim to personal insight and therefore her ability to effect positive identity transformations without recourse to expert therapeutic help.

As the following extracts suggest, this discourse provides a framework for the interpretation of childhood abuse in terms of long-term damage, and the determinism implicit in this construction creates problems for women in constructing a positive and agentive life narrative.

S: *It is important that if you've been through an experience you know it's a bad experience ... but saying that if you've if something bad has happened to you and you don't want to experience it again but yet it crops up again ... um I still think you're going to go through and do it.*

It is also a discourse which has wide currency within the caring professions and can, as in the following extract be used as an assessment tool in determining the risk that mothers pose to their children.

Swk 1: *I think you see they might be all right until they are put under stress and when they are under stress then the old patterns will emerge um unless they get any effective therapy.*

However, women do not passively accept these constructions of their experience. Instead they actively engage with them and try to subvert them, as in the extract below in which the speaker subverts the notion of *unconscious* motivation implied in the discourse of psychological damage and instead emphasises her personal agency and her ability to transform her past.

A: *They say they will do it if they grow up in a family where they have been hit but then again I mean I grew up in a family where my dad hit me and I didn't want to hit my kids. It makes you want to go the opposite well for me it did. It made me think I am never going to hit my kids when I grow up.*

Discursive approaches to identity which underline the need to pay close attention to the socially mediated narratives or 'texts of identity' (Shotter and Gergen, 1987) and to the opportunities they afford to women for self definition have recently begun to be adopted in postmodernist approaches to therapy (for example, in the approaches formulated by White and Epston, 1990; Mcleod, 1997; Rennie, 1994). These approaches have moved away from the traditional therapeutic focus on talk as representative of inner states and on a univocal expert interpretation, to an approach which affords individuals the opportunity to negotiate new and agentive narratives. Such approaches would see both victim and survivor identities as just two of many possible self-narratives which could be used strategically and contingently to emphasize different aspects of women's experience and to fulfill specific ends, rather than as fixed or immutable truths about women's experience. Thus a narrative of victimology might be used positively as a means of drawing attention to women's structural disadvantage and vulnerability and negatively as a source of personal disempowerment. Similarly a survivor narrative could be used positively as a source of strength and self-determination or negatively as a means of blaming the victim. However, as Lynch (1998) points out, such an approach does not solve the problem of the basis on which narratives are chosen as adequate or beneficial, or the problem of the value systems inherent in therapeutic communities and practices which may be out of sync with those of their clients. Nor does it solve the problem of the tension between what is attributed to the inner state of the client and what is attributed to the material and social conditions in which the client lives. All these questions are likely to have a bearing on the kind of identities made available to survivors within the therapeutic relationship.

There have as yet been few studies that look at the nature and causes of positive narrative shifts in those who have survived abuse, though studies of self-help groups tend to suggest that such shifts most often come about in informal settings in which there is mutual support and an open approach to what does and what does not constitute a valid form of identity (Kappela, 1995; Lloyd, 1992; Simonds, 1992). The empirical research into the long-term outcome for the abused underlines the importance of creating a fully agentive version of the self which integrates the experience of abuse (Ferguson *et al.*, 1993; Kelly *et al.*, 1992; Bart and O'Brien, 1986). Because of this Lynch (1998) recommends a paradigm shift in therapeutic practice in which therapy is seen as a two way process in which both parties possess expertise and insight.

SUMMARY

Survivors' accounts tend to suggest many different routes towards the accommodation both of the experience of abuse and the negative positioning occasioned by it. However, they do suggest that a positive re-working of the experience of abuse depends both on gaining access to alternative discursive frameworks and on an accurate appraisal of the material practices that foster women's victimization. Feminist approaches to therapy would also emphasize the need to take into account the connections between material and discursive positioning and would argue that narratives are likely to be only as effective as the ability to put them into practice. In other words, that identities negotiated in therapy are unlikely to survive long in the world outside the therapist's office without some form of corroboration (Hall and Lloyd, 1993).

We would suggest that there appears to be some potential for linking previous research which has focussed on cognitive schema and coping mechanisms with narrative and feminist post-structural accounts. For example, research which suggests that universal rather than individual perceptions of vulnerability are instrumental in reducing self-blame in those who have suffered abuse (Perloff, 1981) might be adapted to include an understanding of the interplay between personal identity and the structural conditions which make *all* women vulnerable. Similarly work on the role of normative standards in coping with victimization (Taylor *et al.*, 1981) which emphasizes the importance of social comparisons in making sense of trauma might be adapted to include an understanding of the social construction of identities and women's positioning within cultural repertoires. In addition Janoff-Bulman's classic (1979) distinction between situational and characteriological self-blame, which suggests that a focus on the situations that precipitated the abuse rather than on the character of the victim is an important aid to women's sense of mastery in coping with trauma, might be adapted to a feminist model which is grounded in a realistic appraisal of risk and risk avoidance. As Kelly (1988) has noted, any approach to women's accounts of abuse and the negotiation of identities needs to include an understanding of abuse as a common feature of women's experience rather than as the province of a special category of women. Thus women's accounts of abuse need to be understood both as a means of individual survival and as a means of collective resistance.

REFERENCES

Angelou, M. (1971) *I Know Why The Caged Bird Sings*. New York: Bantam

Armstrong, L. (1991) Surviving the incest industry. *Trouble and Strife*, 21, Summer

Armstrong, 1979, *Kiss Daddy Goodnight*. New York: Hawthorn Books

Barry, K. (1979) *Female Sexual Slavery*. San Francisco: Prentice-Hall

Bart, P.A. (1981) Study of women who were both raped and avoided rape. *Journal of Social Issues*, 37 (4), 123–137

Bart, P. and O'Brien, Patricia (1986) *Stopping Rape: Successful Survival Strategies*. Oxford: Pergamon Press

Brownmiller, S. (1975) *Against Our Will: Men Women and Rape*. New York: Simon and Schuster

Caplan, P. (1990) Making mother blame visible: The emperor's new clothes. *Women and Therapy*, 10, 112, 61–70

Croghan, R. and Miell, D. (1999) Born to abuse? Negotiating identity within an interpretative repertoire of impairment. *British Journal of Social Psychology*. 8, 315–355

Dobash, R.E. and Dobash, R.P. (1992) *Women, Violence and Social Change*. London: Routledge and Kegan Paul

Eagle, G. (1998) The constructions of experience in response to location in contradictory subject positions: The case of male crime victims. Proceedings International Conference on Discourse and the Social Order, Rose Forrester and Carol Percy (Eds.) Aston Business School (pp. 3–19)

Fairclough, E. (1986) Responsibility for incest: a feminist view. *Social Work Today*, UEA Social Work Monographs No 16

Ferguson, H.R., Gilligan, R.R. Torode (Eds.) 1993 *Surviving Childhood Adversity*. Dublin: Social Studies Press

Hall, S. and Lloyd, S. (1993) *Surviving Sexual Abuse*. London: Falmer

Hooper Carol Ann (1987) Getting him off the hook: the theory and practice of mother blaming. *Trouble and Strife*, 12.

Janoff Bulman (1979) Characteriological versus behavioural self blame: Inquiries into depression and rape. *Journal of Personality and Social Psychology*, 37, 1798–1809

Kappela, Susan (1995/96) Survivors and supporters working on ritual abuse. *Trouble and Strife*, Winter, 40–52

Kelly, L. (1988) *Surviving Sexual Violence*. Cambridge: Polity Press

Kelly, L., Regan, L. and Burton, S. (1992) Beyond victim to survivor: the implications of knowledge about children's resistance and avoidance strategies. Paper presented to the conference Surviving Childhood Adversity. July, Trinity College Dublin

Kelly, L. (1984) Effects or survival strategies? The long term consequence of the experience of sexual violence. Paper presented at the Second International Conference for Family Violence Researchers, August, University of New Hampshire

Lloyd, Siobhan (1992) Facing the facts: self help as an empowering response to sexual abuse Paper presented to the Conference Surviving Childhood Adversity. Dublin

London Rape Crisis (1987) *Strength in Numbers*. London: LRC

Lynch, G. (1998) Counselling and the dislocation of representation and reality. *British Journal of Guidance and Counselling*, 26 (4)

McCleod, M. and Saraga, E. (1988) Challenging the orthodoxy: towards a feminist theory and practice. *Feminist Review*, 28, 16–55

McCleod, J. (1996) The emerging narrative approach to counselling and psychotherapy. *British Journal of Guidance and Counselling*, 24, 173–184

McCann, L. and Pearlman, L.A.(1990) *Psychological Trauma and the Adult Survivor*. New York: Bruner Mazel

Nelson, S.I. (1987) *Incest: Fact and Myth* (2nd edn). Edinburgh: Stramullion Press

Newburn, T. and Stanko, E. (1994) *Just Boys Doing Business: Men, Masculinity and Crime*. London: Routledge and Kegan Paul

Perloff, Linda (1981) Perceptions of vulnerability to victimisation. *Journal of Social Issues*, 2 83 vol. 39, 41–61

Potter, M. and Wetherell, M. (1987) *Discourse and Social Psychology*, London: Sage

Rennie, D. (1994) Story telling in psychotherapy: the client's subjective experience. *Psychotherapy*, 31, 234–243

Richardson, S. and Bacon, H. (Eds.) (1988) *Child Sexual Abuse: Whose Problem? Reflections from Cleveland*. Birmingham: Venture Press

Shotter, J. and Gergen, K.J. (Eds.) (1987) *Texts of Identity*. London: Sage

Simonds, W. (1992) *Women and Self Help Cult*ure. New Brunswick, NJ: Rutgers University Press

Spring, J. (1987) *Cry Hard and Swim*. London: Virago 1987

Taylor, S.E., Wood, J.V. and Lictman (1981) It could be worse: Selective Evaluation as a response to vicitmisation. *Journal of Social Issues* 2 83 vol. 39, 19–40

Ussher, J.M. and Dewberry C. (1995) The long-term effects of childhood sexual abuse: a survey of adult women survivors in Britain. *British Journal of Clinical Psychology*, 34, 177–192

Westcott H.L. (1992) The 1991 Criminal Justice Act: research on children's testimony. *Adoption and Fostering*, 16 (3), 7–12

Wood, L.A. and Rennie, H. (1994) The discursive construction of victims and villains. *Discourse and Society*. 5 91 0 125–148

White, M. and Epston, D. (1990) *Narrative Means to Therapeutic Ends*. New York: Norton

CHAPTER 15

SEXUAL HARASSMENT AND STRESS: HOW WOMEN COPE WITH UNWANTED SEXUAL ATTENTION

Alison M. Thomas

INTRODUCTION

This chapter examines recent evidence from clinical and survey research of the various ways in which sexual harassment can affect women's health and well-being. Starting with a brief review of feminist theorizing of 'unwanted sexual attention', it outlines the different forms that harassment may take and discusses the range of stress effects, both psychological and physiological, that have been associated with it. From this it is apparent that an important, yet often unacknowledged, issue is the way in which the effects of sexual harassment are mediated by how women choose to label and respond to their experience. This, it is argued, is something which warrants further research, since it has important practical implications for the provision of sexual harassment education, and information and support networks.

Interest in sexual harassment – in academia, in the legal context and in the mass media – has grown significantly throughout the 1980s and 1990s, since it was first named and publicly problematized in the late 1970s by feminists such as Lyn Farley (1978) and Catherine McKinnon (1979). Over the last two decades increasing concern about sexual harassment has resulted in the widespread development of anti-harassment policies in the workplace and in educational settings, as well as in the publication of numerous books and academic papers on the subject.

This attention to a problem that was for so long ignored is of course very welcome; however, the vast majority of this work has been limited to a narrow focus on just two main issues – problems of definition and perception, and incidence rates. Disagreement regarding definitions of sexual harassment has inevitably called into question much of the research on its prevalence and, in the absence of agreement on this, many appear to have concluded that sexual harassment is not an important social problem (cf. Kitzinger and Thomas, 1995).[1] This has in turn had the effect of stalling the development of research to examine the impact of harassment: Gutek and Koss (1993) point out that there has been very little funded research in this area, resulting in 'an appalling lack of empirical data' on it.

Nonetheless, reviews of the accumulated findings of those studies that exist concur in suggesting that as many as 50 percent of women may experience some form of sexual harassment during their working lives, and that the majority of those who do will experience a range of negative effects as a result, both psychological and, in many cases, also physical (e.g. Fitzgerald and Ormerod, 1993; Koss et al., 1995; see Lees, Russo, Koss and Ramos, in this volume). Such findings thus suggest that this is indeed a significant problem in women's lives, although as Gutek and Koss (1993) observed, they also reveal through their limitations that a lot more research is needed.

Before proceeding with this review of research on the effects of sexual harassment, it is first necessary to provide a brief outline of how it has been theorized, in so far as this is important in clarifying the significance of its effects on women's health.

WHAT IS SEXUAL HARASSMENT?

A major theme emerging from the early work of Farley (1978), and further developed in subsequent feminist theorizing of sexual harassment (e.g. Wise and Stanley, 1987), has been the analysis of harassment as a means whereby men use sexuality in order to exercise power over women – to 'put women in their place'.[2] This can be seen as the common denominator in a whole spectrum of behaviors (see Russo, Koss and Ramos, in this volume), ranging from acts that are universally recognized to be both offensive and inappropriate (such as a male employer threatening a female employee with the loss of her job unless she responds to his sexual advances; see Lawthom, in this volume) to those that may appear innocuous to some (such as a single incident of wolf-whistling in a public place). From this analytic perspective, any and all such acts represent ways in which men attempt to assert their power over women, whether those with whom they work, or those they simply encounter walking down the street. The validity of this analysis is strongly supported in women's accounts of their experiences of sexual harassment, in which a common refrain is the sense of powerlessness it engenders, and consequent feelings of anger and frustration (e.g. see Sumrall and Taylor, 1992).

A second theme of major importance has been the recognition that what is crucial in identifying an act as one constituting sexual harassment is that it is 'unwanted attention' for the person receiving it (see for example the definitions provided by the European Commission in its Code of Practice, 1991; and by the U.S. Equal Employment Opportunity Commission, 1980). This stipulation is necessary since, as already noted, sexual harassment may include a multitude of different behaviors which in other contexts might not be deemed to be harassing – for example, suggestive looks, verbal comments and sexual touching, all of which may be exchanged on a mutually consenting basis between a couple.

Together, these two themes have been important in developing analyses of sexual harassment, both politically and for practical purposes; both also have significant implications for any discussion of how sexual harassment affects those who experience it.

With regard to the first theme, the development of the analysis of sexual harassment as 'doing power' has generated a considerable body of research on the power relations in situations in which harassment occurs (e.g. Hearn and Parkin, 1987), and this in turn has been influential in guiding the formulation of sexual harassment policies in which power is an explicitly recognized aspect of the problem (e.g. Collier, 1995; Rubenstein and De Vries, 1993). Moreover, once we acknowledge that sexual harassment is primarily to do with an abuse of power, it becomes possible to see the similarities between this and other assertions of male power over women, and thus to identify it as part of a continuum of male violence against women (whether subtle and psychological or crudely physical). This has been an important theme in the work of a number of feminists such as Kelly (1987), Kissling and Kramarae (1991) and Stanko (1993). Researchers such as Salisbury *et al.* (1986) have pointed out that many of the effects reported by victims of sexual harassment are indeed similar to those reported by women who have experienced other forms of violence.

In the case of the second theme, the consequences of asserting that it is a woman's labelling of her experience as 'unwanted' that serves to confirm it as sexual harassment have been complex and often problematic: although in principle this has been politically empowering for women, at the same time it has often proved disabling in practice. For even though the purpose of this redefinition was to render irrelevant the question of the intentions of the alleged harasser, and to emphasize how his actions are perceived by his 'victim', many women may still hesitate to define a situation as harassment if they believe the man to have been an 'innocent' offender, unaware that his actions were causing offence (Thomas and Kitzinger, 1994).

Furthermore, as many feminists have argued, following Rich's analysis of 'compulsory heterosexuality' (Rich, 1980), in any society in which heterosexual flirtation is an expected and accepted part of everyday life, and in which women are generally socialized to accept all forms of attention from men as flattering, whether they appreciate them or not, it can be difficult for them to draw a clear line between what is 'wanted' and what is 'unwanted'. Any resulting hesitation is then itself a critical factor: in situations in which a woman does not immediately react by indicating that this was unwanted behavior she may fear that she is in some way to blame for allowing the situation to continue, and as we shall see, self-blame all too frequently emerges as a complicating factor in many women's experiences of sexual harassment (Salisbury *et al.*, 1986).

THEORIZING THE EFFECTS OF SEXUAL HARASSMENT

Pursuing the feminist analysis of sexual harassment as a situation in which a man exercises power over a woman in a sexualized context, and against her wishes, it is not hard to see why this should potentially have a number of negative psychological effects. Psychological theory and research indicate that a positive sense of self and individual agency are key elements of healthy adjustment (Wylie, 1974/1979), and hence we should expect threats to these (such as arise in a harassing situation when a woman experiences unwanted attention) to have potentially damaging consequences for the individual's psychological well-being. This is indeed what researchers have found, with claims that sexual harassment leads, cumulatively, to a reduction in a woman's sense of agency (Cairns, 1997) and to the erosion of her self-confidence (Larkin, 1997).[3]

While all women might be expected to be affected by a momentary loss of self-confidence following any incident of sexual harassment, however 'trivial' it may seem, the extent and long-term impact of the effects they experience will depend, however, on the particular circumstances in which the harassment takes place, the form it takes and its duration. In addition, the direct effects of any form of harassment will frequently be compounded by its indirect after-effects – for example, how both the woman herself and others react to it, including whether she even identi-fies it as harassment and herself as a 'victim' (Salisbury *et al.*, 1986).

In many cases the strain of coping with ongoing harassment is also liable to provoke additional stress symptoms, physiological as well as psychological (Koss, 1990). Thus a variety of studies have shown that in cases of prolonged harassment women report a range of negative psy-chological effects, including chronic anxiety and depression, as well as physiological symptoms such as headaches, sleeplessness, stomach prob-lems and nausea (e.g. see Crull, 1982; Loy and Stewart, 1984; Salisbury *et al.*, 1986). In the most severe cases, the symptoms experienced by victims of harassment may resemble those characteristic of Post Traumatic Stress Disorder (see Gutek and Koss, 1993). Not surprisingly, symptoms of stress of these kinds also frequently affect the individual's work, resulting in loss of motivation, and avoidance of the harassment situation through increased absenteeism (U.S. Merit Systems Protection Board, 1981, 1987). Gutek and Koss (1993) thus note that effects may be seen in various areas of a person's life:

Measuring the impact of harassment involves outcomes within three domains: somatic health, psychological health, and work variables including attendance, morale, performance, and impact on career track. In short, there is no single impact of sexual harassment. (Gutek and Koss, 1993: 30)

From this it should be apparent that it is no simple task to outline the effects of experiencing sexual harassment, since they are invariably complicated by a variety of factors. For the purposes of this overview, however, I shall identify some of the important distinctions that can usefully be made in assessing what is known.

ISOLATED INCIDENTS VERSUS PROLONGED HARASSMENT

It has become clear from the gradual accumulation of survey research and women's own accounts that for most, their main experience of sexual harassment over their lifetime will consist of isolated incidents of the mundane 'dripping tap' variety (Canadian Human Rights Commission, 1983; Gardner, 1980; Larkin, 1991).[4] Such incidents commonly occur in public places, in which the harassment comes from strangers and typically takes the form of whistling, grunts and other noises, and verbal comments – such as sexist remarks or sexual innuendo. These kinds of sexual harassment are often not even acknowledged as harassment because of their very frequency, and although they may on occasion be alarming, more often they prompt little more than irritation in the recipient.

It is probably for both of these reasons that there has been little research attention to this kind of harassment and its effects, with the exception of the work of a few feminist researchers such as Gardner (1980, 1995) and Larkin (1997), who have taken seriously the implications for women of having to tolerate these everyday forms of unwanted attention from men. Both have argued that just like the 'dripping tap', these daily hassles can have the cumulative effect of adding unnecessary stress into women's everyday lives. They have also made the important point that even apparently innocuous incidents could always transform into a situation involving physical threat (and sometimes do), and that fear of what might happen is therefore always at the back of women's minds. This may mean that a woman out jogging who has in the past been raped will react quite differently to a wolf-whistle from a man on the street-corner than one who has not. (This of course highlights one of the many problematic aspects of research in this area – that trying to place incidents of sexual harassment on some kind of sliding scale of severity is often a futile exercise, given that the context in which the harassment occurs has so much influence on how it is experienced.)

The other main form of sexual harassment that women experience occurs much less frequently but, because it generally occurs over a lengthy period of time and in circumstances which may make it hard to avoid, it is generally recognized to have more damaging effects. This is harassment which occurs in situations such as the workplace and comes generally from somebody known to the victim. It may take many forms, encompassing the whole spectrum of harassing behaviors, but for legal purposes has come to be classified in terms of the general way in which it affects its victims, with two principal categories emerging: explicitly coercive behaviors ('quid pro quo' harassment) and those behaviors which create a 'hostile environment' for the victim (Aggarwal, 1987).[5]

Most of the research on the effects of sexual harassment has dealt with prolonged harassment of these two kinds, occurring either in the workplace or in educational settings such as universities, and it is therefore to this body of work that I will now turn for a more detailed review of its findings.

RESEARCH ON THE EFFECTS OF SEXUAL HARASSMENT

Although many women have written graphic and emotionally powerful accounts of their experiences of sexual harassment (for example, those in Sumrall and Taylor's (1992) collection), it is striking that by comparison with the extensive body of work on other forms of violence against women (such as rape, child sexual abuse or domestic violence, see Russo, Koss and Ramos, Lees, and Croghan and Meill, in this volume), there has been so little systematic research attention to the range of psychosomatic effects experienced by victims of harassment.

What limited information we do have on this comes from two main sources, which provide us with different but complementary information. Firstly, we have data from questionnaire-based research surveys on sexual harassment and its consequences (e.g. Loy and Stewart, 1984; Gruber and Bjorn, 1988; Schneider *et al.*, 1997); and secondly, a number of counselors have reported on the effects of sexual harassment, based on their work with clients who have experienced it (e.g. Crull, 1982; Salisbury *et al.*,1986).

The survey approach typically yields a variety of different experiences of sexual harassment. Many of these prove to be isolated and relatively mild incidents, while others may be part of an ongoing pattern and thus correspond to the definition of a 'hostile environment' outlined earlier; generally only a small minority involve 'quid pro quo' harassment (Loy and Stewart, 1984). By contrast, the majority of the harassment cases discussed in reports from counselors are likely to fit one of these two legal definitions of sexual harassment and, self-evidently, to have been sufficiently severe to prompt the victim to seek professional help. Taken together, these two sources provide ample evidence that sexual harassment can have very serious consequences for those who experience it.

SURVEY FINDINGS

Methodological discrepancies make it difficult to arrive at any reliable estimates of the overall proportion of women who experience different physical and/or psychological effects as a consequence of their harassment experience.[6] Nevertheless, most surveys find that nervousness, irritability, and anger are frequently reported outcomes, often accompanied by disturbed sleep patterns, various eating disorders and stomach problems (Gutek and Koss, 1980). Loy and Stewart (1984) found that overall, 75 percent of their sample reported one or more symptoms of this kind, rising to 80 percent in cases which were identified as more serious, such as those involving 'quid pro quo' harassment.[7]

This claim – of a positive correlation between the severity of the harassment and the severity of its effects – seems intuitively plausible, and has indeed been supported by others (e.g. Schneider *et al.*, 1997); it also coincides with the findings from the clinical literature (see Koss, 1990). Many studies have likewise found that the worse the harassment, the greater the likelihood of it prompting an active rather than passive response (e.g. Gruber and Bjorn, 1988). It seems that women often choose to ignore the milder forms of sexual harassment, such as gender harassment, and only respond with direct action (whether confronting the harasser or reporting the harassment to someone in authority) when the harassment becomes more severe, either through its cumulative effect or as a result of one particularly upsetting incident – such as one involving sexual assault (Gruber and Bjorn, 1982; Loy and Stewart, 1984).

More systematic efforts to clarify the relationship between specific types of sexual harassment, their effects and women's responses have been problematic, however, for a number of reasons, both conceptual and methodological. Firstly, it is necessary to remember that survey data such as these are typically derived from responses to a checklist of behaviors identified as harassing by the researcher. This is important, because many survey findings have failed to take account of possible differences between the researcher's definitions of sexual harassment and the respondents' own perceptions of their experiences. In fact, where respondents have been asked whether or not in their view the incident they reported was 'sexual harassment', it has often been found that only a minority will label it thus – for example, 30 percent in the Canadian Human Rights Commission study (1983); and 28 percent across two linked studies by Schneider *et al.* (1997).

Secondly harassment 'checklists' may not allow for multiple responses, nor ask whether the incident(s) reported occurred on more than one occasion. In other words, many studies have neglected to differentiate sufficiently between those cases of sexual harassment that are isolated incidents and those that represent part of a systematic pattern of harassment over time. In so doing they have thereby often served to obscure rather than clarify the relationship between particular forms of harassment and their effects. For example, what might in itself appear to be a relatively 'trivial' incident – as reported in the course of a survey – could appear to have prompted a disproportionately severe reaction, due however not so much to the intrinsic nature of that one incident but to the fact that it represented just the latest in a series of similar incidents over a period of time, whose accumulated effect provoked that reaction.

In fact, those surveys that do allow for multiple responses have tended to find that many women experience both more than one incident and more than one type of harassment. For example, Schneider *et al.* (1997) reported that although the largest single category of behaviors reported in their study was that of 'gender harassment' (sexist behavior, crude comments or jokes), a significant proportion of women also reported experiencing unwanted sexual attention (pressure for dates, unwanted touching), thus making it difficult to separate out the effects of the two kinds of harassment.

It is thus apparent that survey research has so far been unable to do much to clarify the complex effects of sexual harassment, or to capture the cumulative nature of the stresses that result from prolonged harassment. However, here we are able to turn instead to the findings from various clinical studies, which are more helpful in this regard.

CLINICAL LITERATURE

Even though reports from counselors are based on the experiences of only a minority of victims of harassment, and tend to represent the most severe cases, the few that we have (most notably Crull, 1982, 1990; Salisbury *et al.*, 1986) have been valuable not only in depicting the extremely traumatic effects of harassment in such cases, but also in providing us with some insight into the sequencing of the harassment process. By the time women reach the point at which they feel it necessary to seek professional help in dealing with their distress, the harassment has typically been going on for some time and, based on their work with victims, Salisbury *et al.* (1986) were able to outline a common sequence of four stages that all had gone through, each characterized by different psychological and physical symptoms.

These stages are, firstly, a period of confusion/self-blame, during which the individual may find the situation ambiguous and be uncertain how to respond. This gives way to a period of fear/anxiety, as she is forced to acknowledge that this is harassment and that it is continuing, in spite of any efforts she may have made to stop it. She may feel trapped and helpless to act because of fear of the possible consequences, and her response at this stage may therefore be to seek medical treatment for her stress symptoms and/or counseling. The third stage is characterized by depression/anger, as the situation worsens and this may drive her to crisis point. The authors claim that anger erupts as the individual realizes that she is not to blame for the harassment, and this is the stage at which she may therefore make a formal complaint within her organization. However, while this should ideally represent a positive step in the recovery process, in practice it can often lead to a deterioration in the work situation as she risks being perceived as a 'trouble-maker' and thereby losing the support of co-workers. This can lead to the fourth and final stage of disillusionment, in which the woman may feel let down by the formal complaint process and lose her confidence in it, leading often to a general questioning of long-held beliefs in fairness and justice; loss of support from others may also damage her ability to trust others, especially men.

This identification of the sequencing of reactions, responses and their effects clearly highlights the complexity of the consequences of harassment, and the need for recognition of the significance of all those factors that may mediate its effects, such as the availability of workplace harassment policies, and factors that encourage or inhibit women from taking advantage of support systems such as these. In particular, it suggests the importance of differentiating between the initial effects of harassment and those that may result from making a complaint or otherwise 'making an issue of it'.

UNANSWERED QUESTIONS

To date, the findings from both the survey data and the clinical literature present few answers, but raise a number of questions, one of which appears particularly crucial. As noted here, Salisbury *et al.* (1986) have claimed that one of the most important ways of dealing with the stress of harassment is by recognizing it as such, so as to escape the damaging effects of self-blame; they suggest that this generally represents a 'turning-point' in a woman's response to the harassment situation and helps restore a sense of control. This certainly makes sense in light of the literature on 'learned helplessness' (Seligman, 1974), which associates perceived lack of control with depression, and has been applied similarly to analyses of how women cope with the psychological consequences of rape (Meyer and Taylor, 1986).

However, the same psychological theory has also been employed to explain the opposite behavioral strategy of resisting labelling an incident as sexual harassment. Qualitative research such as the interview study conducted by Kitzinger and Thomas (1995) suggests that one way in which women are able to protect themselves from distress in less severe cases of harassment is by downplaying, dismissing or ignoring it. Refusing to identify it as 'harassment' may enable some women to retain their own sense of control over the situation, in so far as they thereby resist taking on the status of 'victim' (Janoff-Bulman and Frieze, 1983; Rabinowitz, 1990).

Judging by the available survey data it would appear that this is a coping strategy adopted by many women. For example, Schneider *et al.* (1997) found that just under 70 percent of respondents in two linked surveys reported minimizing the incident by telling themselves that it was unimportant, and only 28 percent actually chose to identify the incident concerned as one involving sexual harassment.

Nevertheless, Schneider *et al.* noted that even the majority of women who chose not to label their experience as harassment still reported finding it upsetting, and reported negative effects following from it. In their words, 'experiencing harassment appears to be more important in determining outcomes than labelling oneself as a victim of harassment' (Schneider *et al.*, 1997: 413).

How then are we to make sense of such contradictory findings? Does labelling an incident sexual harassment alleviate or actually increase the stress of coping with it? It seems likely that a woman's responses will vary according to the kind of harassment that is involved, the stage at which the situation is labelled, and the response options available to her – which may or may not enhance her feelings of being in control of the situation (cf. Thacker, 1992). In the case of relatively mild incidents which are not repeated, it is probably easier and more satisfactory for women to dismiss the incident. However, in more serious cases of prolonged harassment, the evidence from Salisbury *et al.*'s counseling observations suggests that such a strategy is not advantageous, and their work would indicate the psychological benefits of recognizing the situation as one involving sexual harassment. Indeed, they argue that acknowledging this and taking action in response is an important way in which women can regain a sense of control over the situation.

Clearly, this is one of several areas in which further research is needed. Paying closer attention to how women themselves label particular incidents will hopefully yield some insights into how this affects their responses, and thereby help clarify how we can best help women to cope with harassment – for example by providing better education and information about it, and better support networks.

SUMMARY

What, then, can we conclude from this necessarily brief overview of research on the effects of sexual harassment? As seen here, there is evidence of the diverse ways in which sexual harassment affects the significant numbers of women who experience it – affecting both physical and emotional health and, in the longer term, leading to potentially damaging changes in self-perception (Cairns, 1997; Koss, 1990; Salisbury *et al.*, 1986).

However, as Gutek and Koss (1993) comment in their own review of this field, the available research has a number of serious shortcomings, both conceptual and methodological. As a consequence, while it has yielded a lengthy 'laundry list of effects and responses', offering various pointers for future research, it has so far done little to clarify the critical features of the harassing situations that provoke such reactions.

One issue in particular which clearly warrants further attention is the question of how the effects of sexual harassment and women's responses to it are mediated by how they perceive and label it.

While in an ideal world we would simply not have to deal with sexual harassment, as things stand we have to find ways of minimizing the stress it causes in women's lives. Understanding more about this process will hopefully aid us in doing so.

NOTES

1. While a full discussion of these various problems and the debates they have provoked is beyond the scope of this chapter (see Thomas and Kitzinger 1997 for a review of some of the salient issues), it should be noted here that survey-derived estimates of the prevalence of sexual harassment have varied considerably, with some of this variability being attributed to these problems of definition and some being blamed on other methodological problems (see Arvey and Cavanaugh, 1995; Lengnick-Hall, 1995; also Gillespie and Leffler, (1987).
2. Throughout this chapter I am dealing exclusively with women as victims of sexual harassment, and referring mostly to studies in which men have been the harassers. While this is statistically typical of the majority of harassment cases (Collier, 1995), this is not to deny that men can themselves be the victims of sexual harassment, and that both men and women may be victimized by their own as well as the other sex. (See Epstein (1997) for a discussion of the harassment of gay men and lesbians as a means of enforcing heterosexuality.)
3. Herbert (1989) has indeed gone so far as to argue that sexual harassment, by damaging women's sense of ownership of their own bodies, is psychologically 'crippling' for women in contemporary societies, just as the ancient practice of foot-binding was literally so for Chinese women in the past
4. So named by Wise and Stanley (1987) because while such incidents are individually often trivial and as such may hardly impinge on our consciousness, they nevertheless form a constant background 'noise' in our lives, and together end up accumulating into something more significant
5. In legal rulings and workplace harassment policies across North America and Western Europe there is now a general consensus regarding the formal identification of these two principal categories of harassment – 'quid pro quo' harassment and 'hostile environment' harassment. The first refers to a situation in which one person (typically in a position of relative power) pressures someone less powerful to comply with their sexual demands, via the use of promises (of various rewards or favors) or threats (of adverse consequences) which will follow compliance or non-compliance. The second and far broader category encompasses any unwanted and offensive behaviors which, cumulatively, have the effect of creating an environment in which it is made difficult for the victim to work or study
6. According to the review by Koss (1990), 'between 21–82 percent of women reported that their emotional or physical condition worsened as a result of harassment' – a very approximate figure indeed!
7. Most studies have found that women generally tend to identify coercive 'quid pro quo' harassment as more serious (and more stressful) than 'environmental' harassment; likewise, that harassment from a supervisor is regarded as more serious than harassment that comes from a co-worker of equal status. In both cases this confirms the significance of the power dimension in sexual harassment.

REFERENCES

Aggarwal, A.P. (1987) *Sexual Harassment in the Workplace*. Toronto: Butterworths

Arvey, R.D. and Cavanaugh, M.A. (1995) Using surveys to assess the prevalence of sexual harassment: Some methodological problems. *Journal of Social Issues*, 51 (1), 39–52

Cairns, K. (1997) 'Femininity' and women's silence in response to sexual harassment and coercion. In A.M. Thomas and C. Kitzinger (Eds.) *Sexual Harassment: Contemporary Feminist Perspectives*. Buckingham: Open University Press

Canadian Human Rights Commission (CHRC) (1983) *Unwanted Sexual Attention and Sexual Harassment: A Survey of Canadians*. Ottawa: CHRC/Research and Special Studies Branch

Collier, R. (1995) *Combatting Sexual Harassment in the Workplace*. Buckingham: Open University Press

Crull, P. (1982) Stress effects of sexual harassment on the job: Implications for counselling. *American Journal of Orthopsychiatry*, 52 (3), 539–544

Epstein, D. (1997) Keeping them in their place: Hetero/sexist harassment, gender and the enforcement of heterosexuality. In A.M. Thomas and C. Kitzinger (Eds.) *Sexual Harassment: Contemporary Feminist Perspectives*. Buckingham: Open University Press

Equal Employment Opportunities Commission (1980) *Guidelines on Discrimination because of Sex*, Washington, D.C.: EEOC

European Commission (1991) Code of practice on sexual harassment. Reproduced in *Equal Opportunities Review*, 41, 39–42

Farley, L. (1978) *Sexual Shakedown: The Sexual Harassment of Women on the Job*. New York: Warner Books

Fitzgerald, L.F. and Ormerod, A.J. (1993) Breaking silence: The sexual harassment of women in academia and the workplace. In F. Denmark and M. Paludi (Eds.) *Psychology of Women: A Handbook of Issues and Theories*. Westport, CT: Greenwood Press

Gardner, C.B. (1980) Passing by: Street remarks, address rights and the urban female. *Sociological Quarterly*, 50 (3/4), 328–356

Gardner, C.B. (1995) *Passing By: Gender and Public Harassment*, Berkeley, CA: University of California Press

Gillespie, D.L. and Leffler, A. (1987) The politics of research methodology in claims-making activities: social science and sexual harassment. *Social Problems*, 34 (5), 490–500

Gruber, J.E. and Bjorn, L. (1988) Women's responses to sexual harassment: an analysis of sociocultural, organizational, and personal resource models. *Social Science Quarterly*, 67, 814–826

Gutek, B.A. and Koss, M.P. (1993) Changed women and changed organizations: Consequences of and coping with sexual harassment. *Journal of Vocational Behavior*, 42, 28–48

Hearn, J. and Parkin, W. (1987) *Sex at Work: the Power and Paradox of Organisation Sexuality*, Brighton: Wheatsheaf

Herbert, C. (1989) *Talking of Silence: The Sexual Harassment of Schoolgirls*. London: Falmer

Janoff-Bulman, R. and Frieze, I.H. (1983) A theoretical perspective for understanding victimization. *Journal of Social Issues*, 39, 1–17

Kelly, L. (1987) The continuum of sexual violence. In J. Hanmer and M. Maynard (Eds.) *Women, Violence and Social Control*. London: Sage

Kissling, E. and Kramarae, C. (1991) Stranger compliments: The interpretation of street remarks. *Women's Studies in Communication*, 4 (1), 75–93

Kitzinger, C. and Thomas, A.M. (1995) Sexual harassment: A discursive approach. In S. Wilkinson and C. Kitzinger (Eds.) *Feminism and Discourse: Psychological Perspectives*. London: Sage

Koss, M.P. (1990) Changed lives: The psychological impact of sexual harassment. In M.A. Paludi (Ed.) *Ivory Power: Sexual Harassment on Campus*. Albany: SUNY Press

Koss, M.P., Goodman, L.A., Browne, A., Fitzgerald, L.F., Keita, G.P. and Russo, N.F. (Eds.) (1995) *No Safe Haven: Male Violence against Women at Home, at Work and in the Community*. Washington, D.C.: American Psychological Association

Larkin, J. (1991) Sexual harassment: From the personal to the political. *Atlantis*, 17 (1), 106–115

Larkin, J. (1997) Sexual terrorism on the street: the moulding of young women into subordination. In A.M. Thomas and C. Kitzinger (Eds.) *Sexual Harassment: Contemporary Feminist Perspectives*. Buckingham: Open University Press

Lengnick-Hall, M.L. (1995) Sexual harassment research: a methodological critique. *Personnel Psychology*, 48, 841–864

Loy, P.H. and Stewart, L.P. (1984) The extent and effects of the sexual harassment of working women. *Sociological Focus*, 17 (1), 31–43

McKinnon, C. (1979) *Sexual Harassment of Working Women: A Case of Sex Discrimination*. New Haven, CT: Yale University Press

Merit Systems Protection Board (1981) *Sexual Harassment in the Federal Workplace: Is it a Problem?* Washington, D.C.: U.S. Government Printing Office

Merit Systems Protection Board (1987) *Sexual Harassment of Federal Workers: An Update*, Washington, D.C.: U.S. Government Printing Office

Meyer, M.C. and Taylor, S.E. (1986) Adjustment to rape. *Journal of Personality and Social Psychology*, 5, 1226–1234

Rabinowitz, V.C. (1990) Coping with sexual harassment. In M.A. Paludi (Ed.) *Ivory Power: Sexual Harassment on Campus*. Albany: SUNY Press

Rich, A. (1980) Compulsory heterosexuality and lesbian existence. *Signs: Journal of Women in Culture and Society*, 5, 631–660

Rubenstein, M. and De Vries, I. (1993) *How to Combat Sexual Harassment at Work: A Guide to Implementing the European Commission Code of Practice*. Luxembourg: Commission of the European Community

Salisbury, J., Ginorio, A.B., Remick, H. and Stringer, D.M. (1986) Counseling victims of sexual harassment. *Psychotherapy*, 23 (2), 316–324

Schneider, K.T., Swan, S. and Fitzgerald, L.F. (1997) Job-related and psychological effects of sexual harassment in the workplace: empirical evidence from two organizations. *Journal of Applied Psychology*, 82 (3), 401–415

Seligman, M. (1974) Depression and learned helplessness. In R. Friedman and M. Katz (Eds.) *The Psychology of Depression: Contemporary Theory and Research*. Washington, D.C.: Winston-Wiley

Stanko, E. (1993) Ordinary fear: Women, violence and personal safety. In P. Bart and E. Moran (Eds.) *Violence Against Women: Bloody Footprints*. London: Sage

Sumrall, A.C. and Taylor, D. (Eds.) (1992) *Sexual Harassment: Women Speak Out*. Freedom, CA: The Crossing Press

Thacker, R.A. (1992) A descriptive study of behavioral responses of sexual harassment targets: Implications for control theory. *Employee Responsibilities and Rights Journal*, 5, 155–171

Thomas, A.M. and Kitzinger, C. (1994) 'It's just something that happens': The invisibility of sexual harassment in the workplace. *Gender, Work and Organisation*, 1 (3), 151–161

Wise, S. and Stanley, L. (1987) *Georgie Porgie: Sexual Harassment in Everyday Life*. London: Pandora Press

Wylie, R.C. (1974/1979) *The Self Concept*. Lincoln, NE: University of Nebraska Press

CHAPTER 16

WOMEN'S SEXUAL HEALTH: AN OVERVIEW

Sylvia Smith

INTRODUCTION

This chapter begins by celebrating some of the changes which have allowed women to become more active, autonomous agents in their sex lives, able to acknowledge what does and does not produce pleasure. It takes a close look at some of the decisions, risks, and dilemmas which women face in their sexual activities, covering issues such as sexually transmitted infections, contraception, and gynaecological cancers. Inevitably it points to some of the inequalities in sexual relationships which still obtain for many women, and to the andocentrism still pervading much research on these issues, which at times proves hazardous to women's health.

The latter half of the twentieth century has witnessed sweeping changes in attitudes towards sexuality, the essence of which is liberalization, and an emphasis on pleasure. Most important for *women* has been the validation of their desire and right to actively attain sexual satisfaction. This has not always been the case. From 1750 to the end of the nineteenth century sexual behavior was the subject of scientific study within the rubric of medical and biological science, and was considered a necessary means of fulfilling the biological function of reproduction, a drive under the control of men (see Segal, and Teifer, in this volume). Anything performed outside of this context, aimed at heightening sexual pleasure, such as masturbation, homosexuality, use of prostitutes, or sex toys, was regarded as depraved, abnormal and immoral. This approach was at its height in Victorian England, when even table legs were covered in respectable houses, for fear of exciting the passion of the men folk! 'Nice' women were regarded as passive sexual partners, and the need for men to attempt to make sex pleasurable for women was not acknowledged. Throughout this time women were regarded as creatures of purity, undefiled by sexual needs, whose marital duty was to oblige their husbands.

The twentieth century has witnessed a significant change in attitudes towards sex generally, and for women in particular. The emphasis is now on the activity of sex, rather than on its reproductive function, and it is socially acceptable for women to expect their sexual activities to be pleasurable. Helped by Kinsey's work in 1948, which declared that sex should be pleasurable for women and men, Masters and Johnson (1966), conducted a comprehensive study of sexual activity, including both male and female orgasm. They described a sexual response cycle which showed gender similarities, and identified a legitimate role for excitement and pleasure in sex for women as well as men. For the first time in history female desire, and its fulfillment, was legitimized.

Since the Hite reports on male and female sexuality (1976, 1981, 1987), this view of sex as pleasurable has polarized further, towards sex as a leisure activity, with open publication of sex manuals and videos, and explicit sexual activity being shown by the media. Perhaps the biggest change for women has been the removal of the taboos which forbade them to talk about their sexuality, to demand their share of the sexual attention which would bring them to orgasm, and to take responsibility for their own sexual needs. In addition attitudes towards homosexuality have liberalized somewhat, helped by legislative changes in Britain and America.

These changing attitudes have allowed people greater freedom of sexual expression. Indeed the WHO (1996) identify a role for a fulfilling sex life in the promotion of health and well-being, emphasizing the need for sex to be without guilt or shame. However this freedom has brought into focus the *risk* associated with sexual activity in terms of unwanted pregnancy and sexually transmitted diseases, including HIV and AIDS. Consequently attention has focussed on the promotion of safe and healthy sex, and there is now an extensive literature on the psychology of preventative behavior.

WOMEN AND SEXUALLY TRANSMITTED INFECTIONS

In addition to HIV and AIDS the incidence of other STIs has been rising in both the U.S.A. and Britain. For women an untreated STI, e.g. chlamydia, can damage their reproductive system, with resulting infertility. The problem is exacerbated by the asymptomatic nature of chlamydia and other STDs.

Young women, aged 16 to 25, are particularly vulnerable, and more so than their male counterparts. Increased experimentation with drugs, alcohol and sex increases the risk for this age group, and studies of college women reveal very low perceptions of risk. In the shadow of AIDS many people think of sexual risk only in terms of HIV infection, and those who are not gay men or injecting drug users often feel safe, forgetting the risk of the classic STIs. Hale and Trumbetta (1996) make a plea for interventions which concentrate on improving women's self-efficacy, seeing this as a much more powerful aid to safer sex than mere knowledge. Beliefs about one's ability to refuse unsafe sex, and to use condoms have been found to effectively predict safer sex in several studies (e.g. Kasen *et al.*, 1992).

The principles of safer sex which apply to the prevention of HIV also apply to *STDs*. Condoms offer the best protection, but are not unproblematic for women. They are male controlled, and since many men are unwilling to use them, and women rarely hold equal power in sexual decision making, they may be at risk. In any case, constant emphasis on condoms reinforces the male view that good sex is penetrative sex. Given the high risk of infection associated with unprotected vaginal sex, and the fact that many women enjoy non-penetrative sexual contact, interventions which re-educate men to sometimes consider alternatives to intercourse might reduce the risk of infection, and give women more of what they enjoy.

CONTRACEPTION

Contraceptive devices and potions have been around for thousands of years, although most of them were probably ineffective or dangerous. Szarewski and Guillebaud (1998) describe how women in China were advised to swallow live tadpoles, and in India large quantities of three year-old molasses were recommended daily for two weeks! Happily we've made some progress, but even now the perfect contraceptive has not been invented, and all have their pros and cons. Generally speaking the more reliable a contraceptive method the greater the chance of its being risky to health or having side effects. Safer methods, such as natural family planning are less guaranteed to prevent pregnancy. However there is enormous choice, and although contraception should ideally involve both partners, it is often the woman who takes responsibility. She must therefore seek advice, and carefully select the method which is best for her (see chapter 17 by Beth Alder, in this volume, for further discussion of contraceptive choice).

Hormonal contraception

The most effective contraceptives are those which act upon women's hormones, such as the combined pill, the 'mini-pill', injectable progestogens, and implants. Refinements in knowledge and products have reduced the side effects of this method over the last ten years, and indeed significant health benefits have been recorded. When used correctly it offers high reliability for women who are sure that they do not wish to become pregnant.

Hormonal contraception, such as the pill, is not a new idea. Almost every culture has used plant derivatives in an attempt to prevent contraception, some of which contained substances likely to have induced miscarriage. In 1941 a progesterone-like substance, found in the roots of the Mexican yam, formed the basis of the modern pill. Within ten years an oral contraceptive pill was available, containing oestrogen and progestogen, which stopped ovulation. Progestogen is a synthetic compound resembling progesterone, used because natural progesterone is destroyed in the stomach, and cannot be taken orally. Testosterone is the main source of progestogen, and early preparations suffered from difficulties in removing all the 'male' characteristics, which could have androgenic effects, such as acne and excess hair growth on women taking the pill. It could also cause weight gain and loss of libido, so there was a price to be paid by women taking these early medications. In addition the early progestogens raised LDL cholesterol and lowered HDL cholesterol, increasing the risk of heart attack and stroke. The risk of thrombosis led to the development of much lower dose pills, and refinement of the hormones used. Happily in recent years a new generation of progestogens have been developed which eliminate the androgenzing character of the earlier versions, and the cardiovascular risks. Nowadays more than sixty million women world wide take the contraceptive pill.

Since those early days massive amounts of research have been done, and both the health risks and benefits are much more clearly understood. Smoking substantially increases the risk of vascular problems. During the 1960s and 1970s it was fashionable for women to both smoke and take the pill, as a sign of their new-found liberation and sophistication. It is not therefore surprising that thrombosis was such a problem. Research has since demonstrated that if smoking is taken out of the equation, the risk of pill-related cardiovascular disease diminishes, and for women under 35 almost disappears. However women over 35, who smoke, may be advised not to take the pill.

HEALTH BENEFITS OF THE COMBINED OESTROGEN AND PROGESTOGEN PILL

Any slight increase in risk to health must be weighed against the tremendous benefits of the contraceptive pill: a 50–75 percent reduction in benign breast lumps, 30 percent lower incidence of fibroids, and more easily controlled endometriosis. But most impressive is the reduction in the chances of developing both endometrial cancer (by 50 percent) and ovarian cancer (by 40 percent). The risk reduction for both is effective after only one year of medication, and lasts for up to 15 years after stopping when women are likely to be entering middle age. The benefits are therefore doubly sweet as the risk of both cancers is greater in women over 50.

Alternatives to the combined oestrogen and progestogen pill

THE 'MINI-PILL'

The so called 'mini-pill' contains progestogen-only, and works by preventing ovulation in 20 percent of women, and disrupting it in a further 40 percent. For the other 40 percent who keep ovulating progestogen thickens the cervical mucus, forming a mesh-like net which acts as a barrier to sperm trying to enter the uterus. With a 0.5 to 4 percent failure rate it is not quite as reliable as the combination pill, but for women over 35 who smoke or have a history of thrombosis, and who should not therefore take oestrogen, it is a good substitute. However it is absolutely imperative to take the pill within three hours of the same time each day, because the mucus thickening effects wear off within 27 hours.

PROGESTOGEN INJECTIONS AND IMPLANTS

Injections are given intramuscularly every eight or twelve weeks. They work by preventing ovulation in *all* women, because of the higher dose, thickening the cervical mucus so that it is impermeable to sperm, and thinning the lining of the uterus, so that a fertilized egg would be unable to implant itself.

Progestogen implants are inserted as a capsule under the skin of the arm, and slowly release a low dose of hormone. Norplant is widely used in the U.S.A, and was introduced into the U.K. in 1993. It lasts for five years, after which the capsule must be removed. It is therefore good for women who have difficulty remembering to take a daily pill. However Norplant still uses the older type of androgenizing progestogen, and a new product called Implanon, which contains the new progestogen, should be available soon.

Intrauterine devices (IUDs)

These are plastic loops or coils, often covered with copper or silver wire, which are inserted into the uterus, and used by about 5 percent of women. They can remain in-situ for five years if they are copper, longer if they are plastic, and have the advantage that contraception can be virtually forgotten about for that duration. They work by setting up an inflammatory response; large numbers of white blood cells gather around the IUD, and are a constant presence as long as it is in-situ. The function of these cells is to 'swallow' bacteria, but in this situation they ingest sperm, and possibly the egg when it reaches the womb. The white cells also make the lining of the womb a hostile environment for any eggs which do manage to get fertilized.

Fitting the IUD will be done by a doctor, and can be painful, especially for women who have not had children, so it is usual practice to administer a painkiller before the procedure. The failure rate is 0.3 to 2 percent, with rates for women below 30 being at the higher end, probably because they ovulate more frequently, whilst the over thirties have the lower failure rates, which are as good as the combined pill.

PROBLEMS WITH IUDS

There can be problems with heavy, prolonged and painful periods; the presence of the IUD stimulates the production of prostaglandins in the uterus, which cause muscular contractions and bleeding. In addition there is a higher incidence of ectopic pregnancy and pelvic infection, which may cause narrowing of the Fallopian tubes. It is most important that women considering this form of contraception are informed of these potential problems, and the reader might be forgiven for wondering whether any woman would seriously risk putting her body through this. And do we need to ask whether men would tolerate such painful and potentially serious side effects, even for sex. The reader is asked to excuse this hint of cynicism, fuelled by the author's memories of being told by her male gynaecologist, when she complained of two-week long flooding periods combined with intense pain, that 'a small price had to be paid for pleasure'. Needless to say a more sympathetic doctor was found, who agreed to remove the device. Apparently new developments include a hormone-releasing version of the IUD, which should avoid many of these problems.

Diaphragms

The idea of blocking the entrance of sperm into the cervix has been around for thousands of years. The Ancient Egyptians used pessaries made from honey and crocodile dung. Thank heavens for progress and for plastics! The first modern diaphragms and caps were made in the nineteenth century in Germany and Holland, hence the name 'Dutch Cap'. They became widely used in the first half of this century, probably because there were few alternatives, and they did offer women the opportunity to have some control over their fertility. They have been largely superceded by the more reliable pill and IUD, but 2 percent of British women still use them, in conjunction with spermicidal foams or gels. Failure rates in young women are unacceptably high, at 10 to 15 percent, but for older women failure rates are as low as 3 percent.

The female condom, or 'femidom'

The female condom has been available over the counter since 1992. It consists of a polyurethane sheath that lines the vagina, and covers the cervix, preventing sperm from entering the uterus. It is inserted before intercourse, rather like a diaphragm, and is lubricated with a silicone, non-spermicidal lubricant. There have been few studies as yet, but initial failure rates are around 12 to 15 percent, comparable to other barrier methods. It has received mixed reactions, and allegedly a sense of humor helps to improve its acceptability! The penis can apparently 'miss' the correct route, and some couples have found it aesthetically unattractive. The outer rim, which remains outside the vagina, is easily visible and over half the couples in a British trial dropped out because they found it aesthetically displeasing, but a third liked it and said they would carry on using it.

Natural Family Planning

This is often called the rhythm method because it requires the woman to chart the natural rhythms of her body. Women chart their early morning temperature, and examine cervical changes and mucus in order to pin-point ovulation. Explicit training is required to do this. Intercourse should be restricted to infertile periods, and therefore around 20 days of absti-nence each month is required. Clearly a high level of vigilance is neces-sary, and for those in stable relationships who wish to avoid other contra-ceptive methods because of aesthetic or religious beliefs, it can work well, and involves the man closely in the contraception process. It is now pos-sible to buy the 'Persona', a small computer, which incorporates a mini-laboratory to measure hormone levels in urine, and allows a more precise monitoring of ovulation time.

GYNAECOLOGICAL CANCERS

The thought of having cancer in any part of her reproductive system will strikes a note of terror for most women. Gynaecological cancer refers to cancer of the cervix, uterus, endometrium, and ovary. Endometrial cancer is the most common, and ovarian the most lethal. There are 75,200 cases of gynaecological cancers in the U.S.A. each year, with 25,200 deaths. Of these, uterine cancers account for 7.9 percent of cases (5.3 percent deaths) and ovarian for 4.1 percent of cases (4.1 percent deaths) (American Cancer Society, 1984). In the U.K. there are 15,390 cases of gynaecological cancers annually, of which uterine cancers account for 27.3 percent of cases (11.7 percent deaths), ovarian for 38.6 percent cases (61.4 percent deaths) and cervical 28.2 percent cases (21.2 percent deaths) (Cancer Research Campaign Scientific Yearbook, 1996–97). Older women and women from lower socio-economic groups are more like to develop and die from these diseases, probably because of risk factors such as smoking, obesity and less access to information, detection and treatment facilities.

The very word cancer evokes a conditioned fear response, despite the fact that advances in knowledge now make many cancers curable, and sur-vival times longer. Much of this advance is due to screening – the early detection of malignancy at an asymptomatic stage, when opportunities for treatment, and the possibility of cure are optimal. (See the chapter by Julie Fish and Sue Wilkinson, in this volume, for a discussion of cervical screen-ing.)

SCREENING FOR UTERINE AND OVARIAN CANCERS

High risk women should be screened regularly for these cancers. Risk fac-tors for endometrial cancer are obesity, diabetes, infertility, breast cancer, adenomatous uterine hyperplasia and chronic anovulation. The recom-mendation of the American Cancer Society (1995) is that high risk women over 50 should undergo screening with endometrial curettage or aspira-tion at the time of their menopause, with follow-up tests at intervals rec-ommended by their doctor. Several studies are currently investigating the effectiveness of vaginal sonography in early detection of endometrial cancer. Clearly the increasing variety and sophistication of testing procedures is to be welcomed.

The poor prognosis of ovarian cancer must cause women who are at high risk due to family history, having no children, pelvic irradiation, or a history of breast, colon or endometrial cancer, a great deal of anxiety, and an annual pelvic examination is imperative for them. However this examination can easily miss smaller, curable lesions, and it is essential that newer techniques are pioneered: currently the use of biomarkers, trans-vaginal sonography, and trans-vaginal color Doppler are being explored as screening tools, but they are not yet recommended for general use. This lack of proven screening tests for ovarian cancer causes severe psychological distress to women at high risk. Paskett *et al.* (1994) attempted to validate new screening methods with 31 high risk women, many of whom had watched their mother or sister die painful deaths from this 'silent killer'. Not surprisingly they displayed high levels of fear, anxiety, sleeplessness, depression, and reduced sexual functioning. Several of them were considering radical bilateral opherectomy as prophylaxis, because of the fallibility of the available screening technology. Such distressing cases must heighten our awareness of the priority which must be given to funding developments which can tighten up the accuracy of screening procedures, so that women in high risk groups can make informed decisions about their lives and their treatments.

REFERENCES

American Cancer Society (1995). *Cancer Facts and Figures*. Atlanta, GA: Author

Burman E (Ed.) (1990) *Feminist and Psychologist Practice*. London: Sage

Cancer Research Campaign *Scientific Yearbook, 1996–97*

Centers for Disease Control and Prevention (1992). 1993 revised classification system for HIV infection and expanded surveillance case definition for AIDS among adolescents and adults. *Morbidity and Mortality Weekly Report, 41* (whole no. RR-17)

Davies, V. (1995) *Abortion and Afterwards*. Bath: Ashgrove Press

Hale, P.J. and Trumbetta, S.L. (1996) Women's self-efficacy and sexually transmitted disease prevention behaviours. *Research in Nursing and Health, 19*, 101–110

Health Update: Sexual health (1997). Second Edition. Health Education Authority, Hamilton House, Mabledon Place, London WC1 H9TX

Hite, S. (1976) *The Hite Report*. New York: Macmillan

Hite, S. (1981) *The Hite Report on Male Sexuality*. New York: A.A. Knopf

Hite, S. (1987) *The Hite Report on Women and Love*. London: Penguin

International Perinatal HIV Group (1999) released before scheduled publication date on 1 April. The mode of delivery and the risk of vertical transmission of Human Immunodeficiency Virus Type-1. A Meta-Analysis of 15 Prospective Cohort Studies. *New England Journal of Medicine*

Kasen, S., Vaughan, R.D. and Walter, H.J. (1992) Self-efficacy for AIDS preventive behaviour among tenth grade students. *Health Education Quarterly, 19*, 187–202

Masters, W. and Johnson, V. (1966) *Human Sexual Response*. Boston, MA: Little, Brown

Morokoff, P. J. (1992, August) AIDS prevention in women: behavioural change efforts and public policy. In S.M. Czajkowski (Chair), Biobehavioural Influences on Women's Health: Research and Policy Perspectives. Symposium conducted at the meeting of the American Psychological Association, Washington, D.C.

Morokoff, P.J., and Harlow, L.L. (1993). The Role of Sexual Assertiveness in the Primary Prevention of AIDS in Women. In P.J. Morokoff (Chair). Primary and Secondary Prevention of AIDS in Women. Symposium, conducted at the meeting of the American Psychological Association, Toronto, Canada

Paskett, E.D., Phillips, K.C. and Miller, M.E. (1995) Improving compliance among women with abnormal Papanicolaou smears. *Obstetrics and Gynecology*, 86, 353–359

Patton, C. (1991). Containing safe sex. In Andrew Parker, Doris Somer, May Russo, and Patricia Yaeger (Eds.) *Nationalism/Sexualities*. New York: Routledge

Squire C. (Ed.) (1993) *Women and AIDS: Psychological Perspectives*. London: Sage

Szarewski, A., and Guillebaud, J. (1998) *Contraception: A User's Handbook*. Oxford: Oxford University Press

Ward, C. (1999) HIV Testing in pregnancy: Changing the policy to universal recommendations. *Practising Midwife*, 2 (2)

CHAPTER 17

CONTRACEPTION CHOICE: A BIOPSYCHOSOCIAL PERSPECTIVE

Beth Alder

INTRODUCTION

The biopsychosocial perspective considers that our understanding of behavior results from an integration of biological, psychological and social factors. The biological perspective is often given less attention in discussions of contraception and sexuality but most methods of contraception involve medical intervention and oral contraception, in particular, has a direct physiological influence on women's bodies. Models of health behavior have been applied to contraceptive choice although contraceptive decision-making behavior is likely to be complex when the physical effects and the sexual implications of the method chosen are considered. Oral contraception is widely used throughout the world, and has been the focus of research into issues of side effects, sexuality and compliance. Contraception use is inextricably related to sexuality and contraceptive choice is both affected by, but also may influence, sexual interest and behavior.

Control over fertility was one of the most significant developments in women's lives in the twentieth century and will probably be taken for granted in the twenty-first century. Control over fertility has liberated women from the fear of unwanted pregnancy. It has reduced maternal morbidity resulting from multiple pregnancies, and enabled women to space their pregnancies to fit in with their lifestyle and economic circumstances.

If women can control their fertility there is no justification for limiting their opportunities for education and employment. However, there are still striking differences in contraceptive use and control across the world. The development of effective and safe contraception has had a major impact on the liberation of women, and the change in their role in society. In spite of the impact of the development of the oral contraceptive pill, women may be seeking to avoid medical control over their fertility and there is no longer an assumption that it should be the responsibility of women alone to use effective contraception. In a report based on 1992 surveys, Oddens (1996) suggests that attitudes towards the perceived medical nature of some contraceptive methods (oral contraceptives, sterilization and IUDs) influence contraceptive use.

In this chapter I will consider the biological background to contraception and how contraceptive choice is related to cognition and to social influences. It will concentrate on research on contraception in industrialized countries, using a biospsychosocial perspective (see also Smith, in this volume).

THE BIOPSYCHOSOCIAL PERSPECTIVE

The choice of contraceptive method may have an influence on sexual behavior but it may also influence health. Health is a continuum and following Antovosvky's' model we continually move from a state of health to a state of unwellness (Antonovsky, 1979). Contraception, particularly hormonal contraception, can influence our health as described in this model. On the illness side of the continuum we may be aware of physical signs in our bodies. These may be minor such as fluid retention or nausea, or severe such as thrombosis. On the wellness side we may have an elevation of mood or feelings of energy.

The biopsychosocial perspective (Sarafino, 1994) suggests that if we want to consider the effects of using a given contraceptive on behavior, emotions and cognitions we need to consider many factors.

The biological perspective

The biological perspective includes the physiology of a person. The physiology of an adult depends on genetic factors and early environmental factors such as nutrition. It is influenced by current behavior such as alcohol intake and smoking habits. The body is efficient and has evolved to cope with infections, damage to tissue, and variations in temperature and diet. There is also an underlying aging process and the body of a prepubertal girl will be very different from a post-menopausal woman.

In considering the psychological effects of contraception we need to take into account this biological background. For example, if we consider a hypothetical association between oral contraception and weight gain we need to look at different pathways. To say that hormones cause weight gain may be too simplistic if we do not consider mechanisms. Weight gain may be actual or perceived. Many women 'feel fat' when they retain fluid and in some women, fluid retention leading to feelings of bloatedness is associated with the menstrual cycle. Weight gain may also occur because of an increase in food intake and in young women food intake may be related to mood or self-esteem. In this instance, the hormones may be related either to appetite control directly or to a change in self-esteem. If we add to this the possible effects of fluid retention on self-esteem it can be seen that a link between oral contraception and weight gain could be very complicated.

Contraception and behavior

Apart from those using modern reproductive technology, there is a high risk of pregnancy occurring as a result of an act of sexual intercourse. However, as not all unprotected sexual intercourse results in pregnancy, there is a poor correlation of behavior and outcome. If most young couples are sexually active, and most of them are not infertile, lactating, or pregnant, we can assume that they are using contraception. This implies that contraceptive behavior is widely practised. In industrialized countries contraceptive advice and supplies are accessible and contraceptive methods are safe, reliable and relatively inexpensive. In spite of this, the abortion rate in Scotland in 1996 was 11.2 per 1000 women aged 15 to 44. (Scottish Health Statistics, 1997, 1998). Not all unplanned pregnancies result in abortion and as not all sexual intercourse results in pregnancy, it seems likely that the abortion rate represents a considerable amount of sexual activity occurring without contraception. If contraception is accessible and in many countries free or relatively inexpensive, what is the reason for not using contraception? This question has been surprisingly little studied by psychologists (apart from an interest in condom use, stimulated by the concern about the transmission of HIV infection, not prevention of pregnancy).

MODELS OF CONTRACEPTIVE CHOICE

Career model

The contraceptive career model suggests that the choice of contraception depends on the circumstances at the time and this changes with age, the stage of relationship of the couple and their plans for parenting (Lindemann, 1977). The contraceptive career has three stages. In the natural stage, sexual intercourse is relatively rare and unplanned and the woman does not perceive herself as a sexual being; she neither uses contraception nor takes responsibility for it. In the peer prescription stage there is more frequent sexual activity and a moderate acceptance of sexuality. At this stage she may seek information from intimate women friends but not from outside agencies. In the expert stage she has incorporated sexuality into her self-concept and so is more willing to use contraception that requires pre-planning, and to seek contraceptive advice. This sequence of behavior may not describe the contraceptive career today when at the second stage she may be exposed to health promotion programmes to encourage use of contraception and safer sex. Whitely and Schofield (1986) carried out a comprehensive meta analysis of 134 studies of the use of contraception by adolescents. They found strong support for the contraceptive career model for women but not for men. In a population survey in the U.K. and Germany, patterns of contraception use were found to be closely related to variables such as age, parity, marital status and intention to have children (Oddens, 1996). Sexual self-acceptance was a major variable for both men and women. Other important variables were frequency of intercourse, self-esteem and rejection of traditional sex roles.

Decision model

The decision model suggests that the decision to use contraception is made on a costs/benefit analysis, and it received good support for women in Whitely and Schofield's review. The perceived risk of pregnancy (not surprisingly) was highly associated with contraceptive use. The more positive women felt about the benefits of contraception and its perceived importance, the more likely it was that they would use contraception. Contraceptive use by young women depends on how psychosexually mature they are. The decision will also depend on the amount and quality of information that they have (related to their career stage), their perceived social norms (how acceptable contraceptive behavior is), and the stage that a relationship has reached. Contraception is more likely to be used if there is a stable sexual relationship.

Transtheoretical model

The transtheoretical model of behavior change suggests that people progress through stages of precontemplation, contemplation, preparation, action and maintenance, that people balance the advantages and disadvantages of change and that their behavior is related to self-efficacy (Prochaska et al., 1992). It was used to predict general contraceptive use and condom use in 248 heterosexually active college-age men and women (Grimely et al., 1995). No sex differences were found for general contraceptive use, condom use with casual partners and condom use with main partners, but men and women did differ on the disadvantages and advantages and levels of self-efficacy.

Health Belief Model

Mahoney et al. (1995) tested the Health Belief Model in college students in relation to condom use and HIV infection. Sporadic users differed from both consistent and non-users in the number of sex partners in the previous year and frequency of drunkenness during sexual intercourse, but only perceived susceptibility to infection and self-efficacy differed between the groups. In a longitudinal study of condom use over one year among 16- and 18-year-olds, HBM variables were not found to predict condom use (Abraham, 1996).

The choice of contraceptive method may depend on the perceived attributes of different contraceptive methods. Harvey *et al.* (1991) compared 330 vaginal sponge users with 330 oral contraceptive or diaphragm users drawn at random from the same geographical areas and interviewed over the telephone. Effectiveness and safety were rated most highly. Each user group emphasized those attributes that characterized their chosen method. Convenience of use and interference with sexual activity were the least emphasized. The relative undesirability of other methods (for example side effects of the pill) was important.

This application of models suggests that the choice of a method of contraception is a rational decision-making process. However, if the method requires an action such as putting on a condom (possibly in an emotionally charged sexual interaction), the actual behavior may not match the intention. Using contraception may differ from other health behaviors because it may involve both partners. The oral contraceptive pills and IUDs differ from barrier methods in that they are to some extent under the control of the woman independent of negotiations with her partner. One of the few research studies on couples' contraceptive choice studied 40 couples over a four-year period (Miller and Pasta, 1996). They distinguished between method-choice and method-use in decision-making. Method-choice is about continuing with the present method or changing to a new one. Method-use is the actual use of the selected method, e.g. taking the oral contraceptive pill daily or inserting a diaphragm. They found that husbands and wives appeared to have equal influence on method-choice but intentions depend on their own preference. This suggests that the final choice is based on sharing information and preferences, perhaps on a cost-benefit basis.

ORAL CONTRACEPTION

The oral contraceptive pill has become the gold standard for pregnancy prevention, against which other methods may be compared. Its ease of use, reliability, lack of side effects and availability has undoubtedly raised the general expectations of contraceptive methods. Oral contraception does not interfere with the act of sexual intercourse and gives women control over their fertility.

The most common type of pill used today is the combined pill which contains between 30 and 50 mg of oestrogen and varying amounts of progesterone. It works by inhibiting ovulation by suppressing the production of gonadotrophins from the anterior pituitary gland. It has a pregnancy rate of 0.18 per 100 woman years. The progesterone also causes changes in the reproductive tract so that the cervical mucus is thicker and sperm are less able to travel to the fallopian tubes.

Oral contraception use

Guillebaud (1991) estimated that 70 million women worldwide take the oral contraceptive pill every day. Oral contraceptives tend to be the first choice of contraception: 39 percent of women aged between 16 and 35 used the pill (Social Trends 1995). The decline in the use of oral contraceptives with age has been related to perceptions of health risks, although the risks to health are low. In 1989 a 'pill scare' in Germany associated certain pills with an increased risk of thromboembolism and this was followed by a fall in the number of oral contraceptive users. This happened again in the U.K. in October 1995. Women's perception of an increase of risk may have prompted them to change their behavior or to seek advice to change their type of pill or to stop taking oral contraceptives altogether. Previous pill scares in thrombosis (1967), arterial disease (1977) and cancer (1983) were followed by a fall in pill use, but the evidence is indirect (Wellings, 1985). The British Pregnancy Advisory Service reported an increase in abortions following the scare when comparing the same periods in the two previous years. They found that many women changed their behavior following the announcement, but this was based on a questionnaire study of 330 women who had approached the clinic for advice (Ramsay, 1996). Many women have difficulty in complying with the regimen of oral contraception and nearly half (47 percent) of women miss at least one pill per cycle (Rosenberg and Waugh, 1999). Condon *et al.* (1995) carried out a retrospective study of 145 women using the oral contraceptive pill and found that nearly half reported side effects and most changes in well-being were perceived as negative. It is difficult to carry out good prospective studies of pill users because of ethical difficulties and high attrition rates. Women who have side effects may stop using the pill, and those who continue and become long-term users are less likely to report side effects. Women who take the pill probably do so because it is very important to them to have a safe form of contraception, and they may be more likely to tolerate side effects for the sake of a high level of protection. Women who use oral contraceptives may differ in their sexual behavior from those using other methods. They may wish to avoid interference with the act of sexual intercourse.

Psychological effects of oral contraception

The psychological effects of oral contraception may arise from a direct effect of the hormones but there could also be indirect effects. The very safety which eliminates the risk of pregnancy, may make intercourse unexciting for some women, or may induce feelings of guilt if there are religious objections. The biopsychosocial perspective is very evident and it is important that causal relationships between hormones and behavior or mood change are not made without considering possible psychological mechanisms. Similarly the psychological effects of the pill cannot be understood without considering the physiological effect of these hormones. There are also physical beneficial effects of the pill. Menstrual blood loss is light, menstrual periods are predictable, and less painful.

SEXUALITY AND ORAL CONTRACEPTION

Taking the biopsychosocial approach into sexuality means that we need to consider the biological background to sexuality as well as the psychological and social factors considered by Smith (see Chapter 19, in this volume).

Evolution and sexuality

There is an evolutionary argument for different sex patterns of sexual behavior in males and females. Dawkins (1976) discusses the evolution of behavior and suggests that selection acts on our genes. Any behavior that ensures the survival of our genes, whether carried by us or members of our family, will have adaptive value. Any behavior that makes it more likely that genes will be passed on will have a selective advantage. For instance, it is in the interest of the male mammal to impregnate as many females as possible (providing that he establishes that they will make good mothers). It is in the interest of the female to be more selective. She must ensure that any male who fertilizes her eggs carries genes that are likely to contribute to survival of the offspring and so ensure the survival of her genes.

The social aspects of control over sexual behavior also have an evolutionary perspective. There are wide variations in sexual receptivity in female mammals. In many species the female is only receptive at certain times. These may be regulated by the oestrous cycle. In some species the female will only ovulate at certain times of the year (e.g. deer); in others ovulation is stimulated by copulation (e.g. badger); and in others ovulation occurs every three or four days (e.g. mice). Sexual activity in humans occurs throughout the year. In women sexual interest may be related to the time of the menstrual cycle. Sexual arousal may be considered to be a drive like hunger, and sexual appetite is like feeling hungry. Sexual desire or appetite results from a complex interaction between cognitive processes, neurophysiological mechanisms and mood state. People learn through experience what it is that they find arousing, and this varies between individuals. The physiological state of the person may influence arousal. Alcohol may increase sexual appetite but depress sexual arousal, and fatigue in a new breastfeeding mother may lead to lack of interest in sexual activity. A depressed mood may lead to low sexual arousal. Loss of libido is recognized as a symptom of clinical depression. On the other hand positive mood or happiness may increase the chance of enjoyable sex and enjoyable sex can make for happiness.

Side effects of oral contraception

The early high oestrogen oral contraceptive pills were reported to have side effects of reduced sexual interest and depression. Bancroft and Sartorius (1990) in a literature review concluded that oral contraceptives decreased pre-menstrual symptoms and suggested that a small group of women, number unknown, are adversely affected. In a study of readers of a monthly women's magazine, Warner and Bancroft (1990) asked about the level of well-being and sexual interest in 'the week before the period', 'during the period', 'the week after the period', 'other times' or 'never'. Women taking the pill were less likely to report highs and lows in well-being overall than non-pill-taking women. They were more likely to report high sexual interest 'during the period' or 'before', but this did not relate to changes in well-being. These findings suggest that there may be a direct effect of the pill on sexuality, independent of its effects on mood. Bancroft (1988) suggests that oral contraceptives may have an adverse effect on mood initially but some women then settle down, whereas other women will change their brand of pill or abandon oral contraceptives altogether.

EMERGENCY CONTRACEPTION

Hormonal post-coital contraception can prevent pregnancy in nearly 100 percent of cases, and yet few women presenting for termination of pregnancy have attempted to use this form of contraception (Smith et al., 1996). In a population-based survey of 1214 women in Grampian, Scotland (65 percent response rate), Smith and colleagues found that although most women (94 percent) were aware of emergency contraception only 39 percent knew the correct timing for its use. Two pills need to be taken 12 hours apart within 72 hours of unprotected sexual intercourse. The morning after pill may have had a negative image in the media and there is debate about the advisability of deregulation (Glasier, 1993). The so-called once-a-month pill (the anti progesterone, RU486) is taken at about the time of the expected menses and induces menstrual like bleeding and/or abortion. In a survey of attitudes in Scotland, Romania and Slovenia it was found that 72 percent, 81 percent, and 94 percent of women respectively, felt positive to the idea of a pill which inhibited ovulation (Rimmer et al., 1992). Over 50 percent thought that a pill which inhibited or interfered with implantation was an acceptable idea. A pill which was taken only if menstruation was delayed by one or two days was acceptable by only 24 percent in Scotland, but 80 percent in Romania and 80 percent in Slovenia. Attitudes to abortion, availability of contraception and religious beliefs are likely to be important. Post-coital contraception may produce nausea and vomiting but because they are of short-term use they are unlikely to have psychological effects mediated directly by the hormones. Psychological benefits may arise from its very early use and there is potential for wider distribution and demedicalization.

STERILIZATION

Vasectomies in men and laparoscopic sterilization in women are the most widely used methods of contraception worldwide. The procedures are safe and effective, but they are effectively irreversible. Regret may lead to requests for reversal, and these usually follow remarriage after divorce, death of one or more children, change in family circumstances or psychological problems related to infertility. Men are potentially capable of fathering children into their sixties, and some men do not want to end their fertility prematurely (Hunter, 1994). Some men may be reluctant to undergo an operation on their genitals. It could be argued that the ending of fertility in their thirties has different psychological implications for men than for women whose fertility declines naturally in their mid-thirties. However most studies find that both procedures are very successful and are followed by positive adjustment. In a retrospective study Alder et al. (1981) interviewed a sample of 45 women who had been sterilized and a matched group of women whose partners had had a vasectomy. We found that women who had been sterilized reported more menstrual changes both positive and negative than those whose husbands had had a vasectomy. Six women expressed some regret. Laparoscopic sterilization in women is a simple, safe and effective surgical procedure. Regret rates of up to 15 percent were reported in early studies, but prospective studies have found much lower rates of nearer 5 percent (Alder, 1984). A prospective study of 115 Chinese women followed up over a year found that there was no adverse effect on sexual adjustment and that their mental health measured by the GHQ (Goldberg, 1978) significantly improved. The regret rate after one year was 3.4 percent (Tang and Chung, 1997). There is some evidence that young women may be more likely to regret sterilization, but this is probably because there is an increased risk of marital breakdown associated with early marriages. Post-partum sterilization may be followed by a higher rate of physical and psychological problems than sterilization, which is carried out at least three months after delivery (Oates and Gath, 1989).

SUMMARY

Few new methods of contraception have been developed recently, possibly because of fear of potential litigation. Most research appears to be directed at reducing the side effects of oral contraceptive pills. There is a renewed interest in natural family planning (see Smith, Chapter 19, in this volume). Female condoms have recently been introduced and appear to be acceptable. The male pill is another possible development, but there is some doubt about whether women would trust men to take it regularly (Guillebaud, 1991).

Men and women may differ in their relative influence on the choice of contraceptive method. It has been assumed that women primarily influence contraceptive behavior within marriage and much family planning advice is directed at women. Patterns of contraception choice are likely to change with each succeeding generation. Expectations change, awareness of medical risks may increase and availability depends on economic development. It seems unlikely that, once discovered, women are going to reject the benefits of safe, effective contraception but they may become more discerning in their choice and contraceptive advice must be tailored to the needs of individual women and their stage in their reproductive career.

REFERENCES

Alder, E. (1984) Sterilisation. In A. Broome and L. Wallace (Eds.), *Psychology and Gynaecological Problems*. London: Tavistock

Alder, E.M., Cook, A., Gray, J., Tyrer, G., Warner, P., and Bancroft, J. (1981) The effects of sterilisation: a comparison of sterilised women with the wives of vasectomised men. *Contraception*, 23, 45–54

Antonovsky, A. (1979) *Health, Stress and Coping*. San Francisco Josey-Bass

Bancroft, J. (1989) *Human Sexuality and Its Problems* (2nd edn). Edinburgh: Churchill Livingstone

Bancroft, J. and Sartorius, N. (1989) The effects of oral contraceptives in well-being and sexuality. *Oxford Review of Reproductive Biology*, 12, 57–59

Condon J.T., Need, J.A., Fitzsimmons, D. and Lucy, S. (1995) University students' subjective experiences of oral contraceptive use. *J Psychosom Obstet-Gynaecol*, 16, 37–43

Dawkins, R. (1978) *The Selfish Gene*. Oxford: Oxford University Press

Glasier, A. (1993) Emergency contraception: time for deregulation? *British Journal of Obstetrics and Gynaecology*,100, 611–612

Goldberg, D. (1972) *The Detection of Psychiatric illness by Questionnaire*. Oxford: Oxford University Press

Grimely, D.M., Prochaska, J.O., Velicer W.F., and Prochaska, G.E. (1995) Contraceptive and condom use adoption and maintenance: a stage paradigm approach. *Health Education Quarterly*, 22, 20–35

Guillebaud, J.(1991) *The Pill*. Oxford: Oxford University Press

Harvey, S.M., Beckman, L.J. and Murray, J (1991) Perceived contraceptive attributes and method choice. *Journal of Applied Social Psychology*, 21, 774–790

Hunter, M. (1994) *Counselling in Obstetrics and Gynaecology*. Leicester: BPS

Lindemann, C. (1977) Factors affecting the use of contraceptives in the non marital context. In R. Gemme and C. Wheeler (Eds.) *Progress in Sexuality*. New York: Plenum

Mahoney, C.A., Thombs, D.L. and Ford, O.J. (1995) Health belief and self efficacy models: their utility in explaining college student condom use. *AIDS Education and Prevention*, 7, 32–49

Miller, W.B. and Pasta, D. (1996) The relationship of husbands and wives on the choice and use of contraception, a diaphragm and condoms. *Journal of Applied Social Psychology*, 26, 1749–1774

Oates, M. and Gath, D. (1989) Psychological aspects of gynaecological surgery. *Bailliere's Clinical Obstetrics and Gynaecology*, 3, 729–749

Oddens, B.J. (1996) *Determinants of Contraceptive Use*. Amsterdam: Euburon Publishers

Prochaska, J.O., DiClemente, C.C. and Norcross J.C. (1992) In search of how people change: applications to addictive behaviours. *American Psychologist*, 47 1102–1114

Ramsay, S. (1996) U.K. 'pill scare' led to abortion increase. *Lancet*, 347, 1109

Rimmer, C., Horga, M., Cerar, V., Alder, E. M., Baird, D. T. and Glasier A. (1992) Do women want a once-a-month pill. *Human Reproduction*, 7, 608–611

Rosenberg, M. and Waugh, M.S. (1999) Causes and consequences of oral contraceptive non-compliance. *American Journal of Obstetrics and Gynecology*, 180, s276–s279

Sarafino, E.P. (1994) *Health Psychology: Biopsychosocial Interactions*. New York: John Wiley

Scheeran, P. and Abraham, C. (1996) The Health Belief Model. In M. Conner and P. Norman (Eds.) *Predicting Health Behaviour*, Buckingham Open University Press

Scottish Health Statistics 1997 (1998) Edinburgh: ISD Scotland

Smith, B.H., Gurney, E. Aboulela, and Templeton, A. (1996) Emergency contraception: a survey of women's knowledge and attitudes, 103, 1109–1106

Social Trends 1995. London: HMSO

Tang, C.S-K. and Chung, T.K.H. (1997) Psychosexual adjustment following sterilization: a prospective study on Chinese women. *Journal of Psychosomatic Research,* 42, 187–196

Warner, P. and Bancroft, J. (1990) Factors relating to self-reporting of the pre-menstrual syndrome. *British Journal of Psychiatry,* 157, 249–260

Wellings, K. (1985) Help or hype: an analysis of media coverage of the 1983 'pill scare'. *British Journal of Family Planning,* 11, 92–98

Whitely, B.E. and Schofield, J.W.(1986) A meta-analysis of research on adolescent contraceptive use. *Population and Environment,* 8, 173–203

CHAPTER 18

MENOPAUSE AND SEXUALITY

Lorraine Dennerstein

INTRODUCTION

Clinicians have long been concerned about the effect of menopause on female sexual functioning. A high incidence of sexual problems is reported by women attending menopause clinics (Sarrell and Whitehead, 1985). This would seem to suggest that menopausal status (and underlying hormonal change) may be linked to adverse effects on sexuality. Most surveys of sexual activity in women have used readers of women's magazines who have responded to questionnaires, or highly selected samples obtained through clinics, advertisements or personal contacts. The main disadvantage is the lack of generalizability of findings to the general population. Population-based surveys can help address the question of any link between menopause and sexuality. Yet relatively few of the population studies of the menopausal transition in mid-aged women have inquired about sexual functioning. Even fewer have used a validated questionnaire to assess the different aspects of sexual functioning. The role of aging per se has to be disentangled from that of menopause, with which it is often confounded. The menopausal transition is a time of psychosocial as well as biologic change. If there are adverse changes in sexuality does it reflect ill-health, the hormonal change or psychosocial factors? Longitudinal studies of samples derived from the general population are in the best position to sort out whether there is a change in sexual functioning, and if so whether this reflects aging, health status, hormonal or psychosocial factors. This chapter utilizes the results of population-based surveys to explore the relative role of the menopause in midlife female sexual functioning (see also Gannon, this volume).

EFFECTS OF AGING

Aging and length of the relationship are known to affect sexual functioning of both men and women. For example, James (1983) used cross-sectional and longitudinal data to show that coital rate halved over the first year of marriage and then took another 20 years to halve again. A number of studies report that an additional decrement in aspects of sexual functioning occurs in mid-age. The early work of Pfeiffer and Davies (1972) using cross-sectional data from the Duke University study, found a pattern of declining sexual activity in both men and women, but the decrement was larger for women than for men of the same age and the sharpest increase in decline in sexual interest for women occurred around the mean of age of menopause (Pfeiffer et al., 1972). The Swedish cross-sectional and longitudinal studies of Hallstrom (1977) and Hallstrom and Samuelsson (1990) found a dramatic decline in sexual interest, capacity for orgasm and coital frequency with increasing age. Not all women reported a decrease but the majority of the postmenopausal women did. The number reporting increase in interest or orgasmic capacity was small and less likely with rising age. The Oxford studies of women aged 35 to 59 again found that the older women had less frequent intercourse, orgasm and enjoyment of sexual activity (Hawton et al., 1994) and increased sexual dysfunction (Osborn et al., 1988).

The Melbourne Women's Midlife Health Project introduced into the longitudinal study, a detailed sexuality questionnaire, the Personal Experiences Questionnaire. This was adapted from the McCoy Female Sexuality Questionnaire (McCoy and Matyas, 1996). Using cross-sectional analysis of data from the fourth year of the longitudinal study we found adequate internal consistency as measured by Cronbach's alpha, (0.71) (Dennerstein et al., 1997). Six factors were found on principal components factor analysis. Of the six factors, two are considered as determinants of sexual functioning (Factor 1, Feelings for Partner; and Factor 5, Partner Problems). The remaining four factors are considered as dependent or outcome variables: Factor 2, Sexual Responsivity, Factor 3, Frequency of Sexual Activities, Factor, 4 Libido and Factor 6, Vaginal Dryness/Dyspareunia. Using data collected annually for six years we found the following factors significantly diminished (p<0.001) with time (years in study): Feelings for Partner; Sexual Responsivity; Frequency of Sexual Activities; Libido. The following factors significantly increased (p<0.001) with time (years in study): Vaginal Dryness/Dyspareunia; Partner Problems (Dennerstein et al., 1999).

Aging versus menopausal status

Most population surveys which addressed this issue find an additional adverse effect of menopausal status on sexual functioning over that of aging per se (Pfeiffer and Davis, 1972; Hunter et al., 1986; Dennerstein et al., 1994). The Swedish study of 800 women was in a better position than most cross-sectional studies to disentangle the effect of age on women's sexuality as it was age stratified instead of having age groups (Hallstrom, 1977). Within each age group of women aged 38, 46, 50, and 54 were pre, peri and postmenopausal women. When age was controlled the relationship between menopausal status and decreased sexual functioning remained highly significant but when climacteric phase was held constant the relationship between age and sexual functioning was not significant. These findings indicate a contribution from the climacteric independent of age factor alone.

The Melbourne Women's Midlife Health Project is one of the few population-based studies to follow women through the menopausal transition with validated rating scales (the Personal Experiences Questionnaire), interviews and physical measures including hormone assessments.

Cross-sectional data was reported from the initial baseline study of a population sample of 2001 randomly selected Australian-born women aged between 45 and 55 years (Dennerstein *et al.*, 1994). The major outcome variables (obtained in a telephone interview) were: responses to questions relating to changes in sexual interest over the prior 12 months, reasons for any changes, occurrence of sexual intercourse, and of unusual pain on intercourse. Although the majority of women (62 percent) reported no change in sexual interest, 31 percent reported a decrease. Reduction in sexual interest was significantly associated with natural menopause rather than age, decreased well-being, lower education, lack of paid employment and increased symptomatology. This initial study was limited by using only four questions about sexual functioning rather than a valid, reliable measure of sexual functioning. The analysis related to sexual interest included women who did not have a current partner. Hormone levels were not assessed at baseline but were introduced into the longitudinal study.

Preliminary analysis from the initial five years of follow-up was carried out for data from the 255 women who were in the natural menopausal transition using as the outcome variable: Factor 4: Libido (reflecting female autoerotic activity). Analysis of variance found a significant adverse effect on libido of age and the menopausal transition. The marked decrease in libido occurred about three years before prolonged amenorrhoea was first reported by the women (Dennerstein *et al.*, 2000).

MENOPAUSE: HORMONAL CHANGE OR PSYCHOSOCIAL FACTORS?

Population-based surveys have found many factors impact significantly on female sexual functioning in midlife (Pfeiffer and Davis, 1972; Hallstrom, 1977; Hallstrom and Samuelsson, 1990; Hawton *et al.*, 1994; Osborn *et al.*, 1988; Koster and Garde, 1993; Dennerstein *et al.*, 1994). These include presence of a sexual partner, partner's age and health, length of the relationship, feelings towards the partner, level of past sexual functioning, social class, educational level, experience of physical or psychological ill-health, stressors, employment, personality factors, and negative attitudes towards the menopause.

Further analysis of data from the longitudinal phase of the Melbourne Women's Midlife Health Project assessed the relative contributions of menopausal status, hormone levels and feelings toward the partner. The three hormones measured (FSH, estradiol, and inhibin) varied significantly with age and menstrual status, were highly intercorrelated and could be aggregated into a latent variable l. Multivariate analysis of variance found significant effects on Libido of l (p = 0.02). The effect of menstrual status and age were then no longer significant. Feelings for partner (Factor 1) had an even more powerful effect on libido (p = 0.003) (Dennerstein et al, 2000). [See Figure 1.]

Using data from six years of annual follow-up in the Melbourne Women's Midlife Health Project (sample = 354 women), we tried to fit in one global model the sexual outcome factors measured by the PEQ, and possible determinants: aging, menopausal status, HRT use, symptoms, hormone levels, social factors (education, paid work, stress, daily hassles), well-being, Feelings about Partner and Partner Problems (Dennerstein *et al*., 1999). The aim of this analysis is to depict in a systematic way all the interrelationships.

The best fit model is shown in Figure 2. The goodness of fit test did not reject this model (p=0.06), and the Normal Fit Index was 0.92, which means that the fit was not too far from the perfect fit, taking the independence model as the zero fit. Rectangles represent the measured variables. The circle denotes the latent variable (ovarian functioning) and arrows designate a causal path and its direction. Two-directional arrows indicate covariance between two variables. Age was confounded with menopausal status and had no independent effects and has thus not been included in Figure 2. Menopausal status does affect two aspects of sexual functioning (Vaginal Dryness/Dyspareunia and Sexual Responsivity). The effect on Sexual Responsivity appears to be indirect, with significant effects of menopausal status on symptoms, which then affect well-being, which in turn influences Sexual Responsivity. No direct effects of hormonal variables or HRT on sexual outcome measures is evident.

Social factors such as stress, daily hassles, educational level and paid work have only indirect effects on sexual functioning, through effects on well-being and experience of problematic symptoms, both of which affect parameters of sexual functioning. Women's increasing positive Feelings for Partner have significant and powerful positive effects on their Libido, Sexual Responsivity, and well-being and protect against experience of symptoms. The covariance between Feelings for Partner and menopausal status may indicate a vulnerability during the menopausal transition. This close relationship during the menopausal transition is also evident for experience of stress. Similarly covariance is evident between stress and daily hassles, stress and paid work, and paid work and educational status. Decreasing Sexual Responsivity and increasing Vaginal Dryness/ Dyspareunia increase partner problems. The presence of Partner Problems leads to lower Frequency of Sexual Activities but increased Libido (a measure of autoeroticism). Increasing Vaginal Dryness/Dyspareunia has

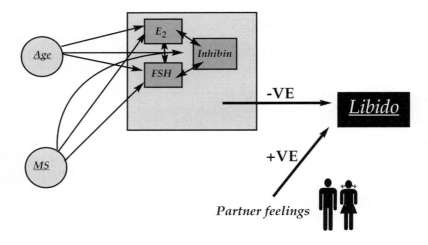

Figure 1. Effect on libido of hormones, age and feelings about partner.

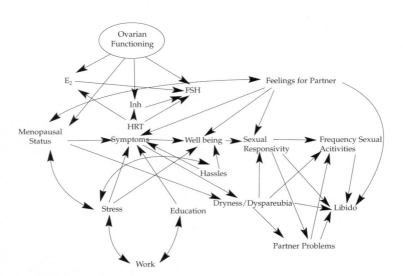

Figure 2. Global model of factors affecting sexual functioning (reprinted from CLIMACTERIC 1999; 2: 254-262 with permission).

a significant negative effect on Sexual Responsivity, Libido, and Frequency of Sexual Activities.

Thus this global modelling shows the way in which biological, health status and psychosocial factors interact to affect different aspects of sexual functioning. The effects of the hormonal changes of the menopausal transition are relatively weak in their effects on well-being and sexuality. The major factors affecting women's sexuality during the mid-life years are feelings for the partner, partner problems, well-being and experience of a number of symptoms. Vaginal dryness and dyspareunia are directly affected by menopausal status.

SUMMARY

Population-based studies suggest a decrement in several aspects of female sexual functioning associated with the midlife years. There is growing evidence that this reflects hormonal changes of the menopausal transition. However hormonal change is only one aspect of the many factors that impact on sexual functioning. These include the woman's own premorbid level of sexual functioning, her personality, educational level, stress, physical and psychological health status, and the presence and quality of a sexual relationship.

When mid-aged women report sexual problems the clinician must explore all these aspects in detailed history taking involving the woman and her partner. Given the range of factors affecting sexual functioning and the significantly more powerful effect of partner factors over that of hormonal factors, a broadly based biopsychosocial approach is needed. Hormonal prescription alone is rarely enough!

REFERENCES

Dennerstein, L., Dudley, E. and Burger, H. (1997) Well-being and the menopausal transition. *Journal of Psychosomatic Obstetrics and Gynecology*, 18(2), 95–101

Dennerstein, L., Lehert, P., Burger, H. and Dudley, E. (1999) Mood and the menopausal transition. *Journal of Nervous and Mental Disease*, 187(11), 685–69

Dennerstein, L., Lehert, P., Burger, H. and Dudley, E. (2000) Biological and psychosocial factors affecting sexual functioning during the menopausal transition. In F. Bellino (Ed.) *Biology of Menopause*. New York: Springer-Verlag

Dennerstein, L., Smith, A., Morse, C. and Burger, H. (1994) Sexuality and the menopause. *J. Psychosom. Obstet. Gynecol.*, 15, 59–66

Hallstrom, T. (1977). Sexuality in the climacteric. *Clinics in Obstetrics and Gynaecology*, 4 (1), 227–239

Hallstrom, T. and Samuelsson, S. (1990) Changes in women's sexual desire in middle life: the longitudinal study of women in Gothenburg. *Archives of Sexual Behavior*, 19 (3), 259–268

Hawton, K., Gath, D. and Day, A. (1994) Sexual function in a community sample of middle-aged women with partners: effects of age, marital, socioeconomic, psychiatric, gynecological, and menopausal factors. *Arch Sex Behav.*, 23 (4), 375–395

Hunter, M., Battersby, R. and Whitehead, M. (1986) Sexual dysfunction among middle aged women in the community. *Maturitas*, 7, 217–228

James, W. (1983) Decline in coital rates with spouses' ages and duration of marriage. *J. Biosoc. Sci.*, 15, 83–87

Koste, A. and Garde, K. (1993) Sexual desire and menopausal development. A prospective study of Danish women born in 1936. *Maturitas*, 16, 49–60

McCoy N. L. Matyas, J. R. (1996) Oral contraceptives and sexuality in university women. *Archives of Sexual Behavior*, 25 (1), 73–90
Osborn, M., Hawton, K. and Gath, D. (1998) Sexual dysfunction among middle aged women in the community. *BMJ*, 296, 959–962
Pfeiffer, E. and Davis, G. (1972) Determinants of sexual behavior in middle and old age. *J. Am. Geriatr. Soc.*, 20 (4), 151–158
Pfeiffer, E., Verwoerdt, A. and Davis, G. (1972) Sexual behaviour in middle life. *Amer. J. Psychiat.*, 128 (10), 1262–1267
Sarrel, P. M. Whitehead, M.I. (1985) Sex and menopause: defining the issues. *Maturitas*, 7, 217–224

CHAPTER 19

LIVING ON THE EDGE: WOMEN WITH LEARNING DISABILITIES

Jan Burns

INTRODUCTION

Women with learning disabilities have largely remained invisible within the discourses of psychology, health, gender and feminism. Their position is not that of many other women wishing to challenge the patriarchal, Westernized construction of gender roles. Their battle is much more remote, crude and often desperate. Historically, the battle has been as basic as to gain the status of human. However, this entry into the human race is only partial and carefully regulated. One way it has been regulated is by the portrayal of people with learning disabilities as asexual and genderless beings (Burns, 1993). Nevertheless, over the last decade there has been a small, but growing literature on women and learning disabilities (e.g. Noonan-Walsh, 1988; Burns, 1993; McCarthy, 1993; Clements, Clare and Ezelle, 1995; Brown, 1996; McCarthy, 1999). Prior to this time virtually nothing was written. This is in stark contrast to the literature on women and mental health and even women and physical disabilities (e.g. Chesler, 1972; Ussher, 1991; Fine and Asch, 1988; Morris, 1991). Whilst this stream of work continues to grow, the bulk of research with in the area of learning disabilities remains untainted by any acknowledgement of gender. Where the gender of the individual with learning disabilities has been acknowledged it has usually been in relation to sex and problematized (e.g. Brown, 1994). The phenomenology of being a woman or man with learning disabilities remains largely untold. The field of learning disabilities is now encapsulated in a rhetoric of individual rights, opportunities and integration. Nevertheless, behind this politically correct ideology women and men with learning disabilities still hold a sanitized, asexual, de-gendered position – 'the third sex' (Burns, 1999). The de-gendering of women with learning disabilities is nowhere better illustrated than in relation to their health care.

HEALTH PROMOTION

Despite the fact many women with learning disabilities spend a large part of their lives within hospitals cared for by, among others, doctors and nurses, their health care is poor. They have been, and continue to be, routinely discriminated against within primary care. A recent British survey firmly identified such inequality (MENCAP, 1998). In terms of routine health screening it was found that breast screening for women with learning disabilities aged 50 and over in Britain averaged a 50 percent uptake rate compared to the national figure of 76 percent. Interestingly, given the drive towards community care, this was significantly worse for women with learning disabilities living within family care where uptake was only 17 percent. Worse still are the figures for cervical smears where women with learning disabilities averaged an uptake of 3 to 17 percent compared to the national U.K. figure of 86 percent.

Such statistics betray a new form of eugenics based on ignorance, myth and misinformation. Studies looking at the attitudes towards people with learning disabilities by General Practitioners and other medical professions routinely uncover ignorance and prejudice (Barker and Howells, 1990; Minihan et al., 1993; Bond, Kerr et al., 1997). In Britain, one of the few studies to be carried out in this area examined health care workers' attitudes to the provision and use of cervical screening for women with learning disabilities (Nightingale, 1999). This study starkly illustrated some of these attitudes. For example, a local health care policy explicitly suggested that 'mentally subnormal patients' be routinely excluded from screening lists. The reasons given for such exclusion were largely based on the premise of sexual inactivity. A poor premise in itself as although diminished there is still a risk of cervical cancer among celibate women (MENCAP, 1998). Other explanations given by those surveyed included:

'If a woman takes her pants off and gets on the couch, then she is sexually active. If she sits on the couch with her hands around her knees then she probably isn't'. [Practice nurse]

'I did have a Down's syndrome from a residential home ... she didn't look as though she was [sexually] active.' [Practice Nurse]

'Certain classes are more promiscuous such as Down's syndrome.' [General Practitioner]

'They are not high risk at home, not promiscuous, no access to sex.' [General Practitioner] (Nightingale, 1999)

The confusion displayed by these workers is not confined just to primary care. All levels of health care, specialist and generic are suffused by it and it is in the expression of sexuality that such confusion is best displayed.

SEXUALITY

The narrative that surrounds the sexual development of people with learning disabilities echoes that of childhood development up to the brink of adolescence. Individuals should be protected until they reach an age of understanding and bodily changes when education is then provided. Theoretically, this education parallels the psychological and physical development and maturation of the individual, assisting the individual to safely explore their sexuality, develop meaningful and long-term relationships, prepare for parenthood and then in turn be prepared to facilitate this cycle for their own offspring.

The reality for women with learning disabilities is very different from this. Historically, they are unlikely to leave home at the same time as other women their age, they are unlikely to have long-term relationships, co-habit or marry, become pregnant, give birth to a baby and care for a child (Booth and Booth, 1994; Brown, 1994). They are likely to have had some sex education, but this was probably mostly focussed on protection and 'saying no' and is unlikely to have included information about less traditional sorts of sexually fulfilling relationships such as lesbianism (Burns, 1993). Such a developmental history presents a falsely innocent picture. The other reality is that women with learning disabilities are much more likely to be sexually and physically abused than other women (Furey, 1989; Turk and Brown, 1992; Carlson, 1998). They are likely to experience sex as painful and for it to be totally constructed around a male perspective equalling penetration, with little likelihood of accompanying positive emotions such as love, care and tenderness (McCarthy, 1999).

Yet again the motif of woman as both virgin and whore is played out. These images of people with learning disabilities as either holy innocents or sexual menaces continuously surface within the literature documenting the history of services for people with learning disabilities (e.g. Wolfensberger, 1972; Ryan and Thomas, 1980; Sinason, 1992). It is perhaps not surprising that such duplicity of representations of women with learning disabilities causes confusion in terms of service reactions. On the one hand we have the de-sexing of women with learning disabilities, and then on the other we have a history of enforced sterilization, premised on fears of outrageous sexual appetites, unbounded fertility, and routine abortion through ill-founded beliefs of inheritance of disability (Park and Radford, 1998).

OBJECTIFICATION

The theme of people with learning disabilities being objectified is well articulated in the literature. The move away from terms such as 'spastic',

'Down's', 'the mentally handicapped', emphasizing difference, to more inclusive terms such as 'people with learning disabilities', emphasizing similarity is evidence of a raised consciousness about this issue. The shift to a greater emphasis on advocacy, representation and integration within government policy making also demonstrates a more inclusive attitude (DOH, 1998). This perhaps parallels earlier movements including the emancipation of women (Hanna and Rogovsky, 1991). At first glance the need to fight objectification appears common ground to such movements. However, the subjective experience of that objectification is very different for women with learning disabilities. It is to be objectified in a much wider sense. It is not exclusion, marginaliztion and de-valuation predicated on gender, it is predicated on exclusion from the human race. To be an asexual object that is talked about, moved, washed, fed and set aside, is objectification at a grosser, more primitive level. It is an attack on one's very personhood. Construed as an hierarchical ladder, to be objectified as a women is at least to get both one's personhood and gender recognized. Talking about physical disability, but equally relevant here, Cole (1988) suggests that:

Most able-bodied women experience problems in being treated as a sexual object, whereas many disabled women experience being treated as an asexual object ... [and] may never have had the experience of flirting ... being harassed, or objectified. (Cole, 1988: 284, cited in Kallianes and Rubenfeld, 1997)

As Kallianes and Rubenfeld (1997) note, this might exempt women from many sexist attitudes, but it also exempts them from the identity and role of 'woman', leaving them with the primary identity of disability, as sexless, genderless, and being totally characterized and identified by their deficiencies. It is not hard to see why such a position is almost intolerably painful and to exchange it for the position of 'woman', no matter how devalued itself, would be an opportunity readily grasped. To be harassed as a woman may be far preferable to being ignored as a disabled person. Understanding this need to identify as a woman sheds some light upon the readiness with which many women with learning disabilities embark upon the unfulfilling and sometimes dangerous sexual relationships described in some research (Carlson, 1998; McCarthy, 1999).

It is here that we see a paradox, one that has previously been noted in the women and physical disability literature (e.g. Fine and Asch, 1988). Kallianes and Rubenfeld (1997: 205) put it succinctly as:

the issues for which feminists have struggled – for women not to be defined sexually, for the right to roles other than mothers – appear to be the opposite of what disabled women demand.

Whilst it must be recognized that many parallels may be drawn with the experience of physically disabled women, one major difference must be acknowledged. Physically disabled women are better able to advocate for themselves. Many women with learning disabilities are not so able and have to use non-disabled women as their conduits. It is also perhaps interesting to note that the interest in writing about the experience of women with learning disabilities has been lead by feminists who have quickly drawn parallels with other minority groupings (e.g. Burns, 1993; McCarthy, 1993; Brown, 1994). As such it is easy to then find oneself in this paradox, where a women with learning disabilities is very clearly asking one to support her in a lifestyle that you as a feminist may have rejected. It is perhaps worth bearing in mind Finger's (1984) cautionary note: 'no progressive social movement should exploit an oppressed group to further its ends' (Finger, 1984: 287).

MOTHERHOOD

Women with learning disabilities do want to engage in activities that dominate other women's lives, they want to have relationships, they want traditional roles such as marriage and they want to be mothers (Booth and Booth, 1994; Brown, 1996). In the same way that the construction of gender around sexual relations and women with learning disabilities has been ignored, the construction of motherhood also remains relatively unexplored. Undoubtedly, women with learning disabilities experience the same needs and desires to have children as women in mainstream society. However, the very experience of growing up as a women with learning disabilities may well propagate other emotional needs which are expressed through the desire of motherhood. People with learning disabilities are well aware of the harsh and pejorative cultural messages around them. Such messages might include imperfection, rejection, regret and error (Kallianes and Rubenfeld, 1997). The cultural icons and motifs that surround learning disabilities include shame, menace, pity and charity. The focus of medicine and habilitative services on the eradication and annihilation of the differences experienced by people with learning disabilities provides a very powerful message about value and worth. In terms of finding an acceptable reason for actually existing and compensating for 'being a problem', motherhood presents an attractive route for women with learning disabilities. Finger (1984) captures this emotion most eloquently when she described herself in relation to childbirth as 'wanting something perfect to come out of my body' (cited in Kallianes and Rubenfeld, 1997).

The complexity of emotional needs around motherhood for women with learning disabilities has been a long neglected area. We are now facing a time when policy is ahead of theory, where many more women with learning disabilities are becoming pregnant, having their children and fighting to care for them. Services are struggling to juggle the needs of the child with the need to protect the parent. This is in the context of a dearth of literature to aid policy making and service provision. What has been written is largely reactive, focussing on how we manage, assess and intervene when women with learning disabilities enter the reproductive arena

(Baum, 1994; McGaw, 1996). Some sociological and ethnographic work in this area is starting to be published (Booth and Booth, 1994), but in terms of the psychological literature concerning the meaning that motherhood has for these women little has been written (Edmonson, 1999).

WOMEN'S BODIES

This lack of literature is not confined to motherhood. If we are to look to other areas within the psychology of women and health the literature is equally sparse. For example, the now mainstream area of research into the menstrual cycle has hardly penetrated the learning disabilities literature. The debates around the influence of menstruation on mood and cognitive abilities leaves women with learning disabilities untouched. Clinically, data is routinely gathered on women's menstrual cycles and used to explain behavior ranging from mood swings (Kaminer *et al.*, 1988) to physical aggression (O'Dwyer *et al.*, 1995). The controversies that rage around 'pre-menstrual syndrome', it's very existence, it's definition and form have no place in the reductionist discourse that surrounds women with learning disabilities.

The potential richness of crossing into the ghetto of learning disabilities is well demonstrated by the only two existing papers on the menarche in women with learning disabilities. Carr and Hollins (1993) in a study of women with learning disabilities in inner city London showed that they actually experience the menopause earlier than other women in the general population, and this difference was even more marked for women with Down's syndrome. This was later replicated by Schupf *et al.* (1997) in New York. The significance of such findings are twofold, aiding both practice and theory. To understand that women with learning disabilities may be going through the menopause at an earlier age allows recognition of symptoms that may well have been ignored or misinterpreted otherwise. Theoretically such a finding also has serious implications for the premature aging hypothesis in learning disabilities. This hypothesis largely fuelled by the link found between dementia and Down's syndrome suggests that physiologically the aging process proceeds more rapidly for people with learning disabilities. Such findings clearly add some very useful evidence to support this hypothesis.

SUMMARY

Given even very traditional examples such as those discussed, it is surprising why gender research within learning disabilities remains such a fallow field. Perhaps we need to reflect upon ourselves as researchers and the voices that serve to shape our psychological knowledge base to understand this. Those writing about women, health and psychology may all experience times of psychological distress, ill-health, oppression, prejudice, we may also experience what it is like to be a mother, a partner, a sexual object. Our research into these issues will resonate somewhere with our own experience. We cannot by definition experience what it is like to have learning disabilities. Women with learning disabilities are unlikely to write papers for journals, or read and comment on the literature. The responsibility hence lies upon the researchers and practitioners to act as fair and honest intermediaries and facilitate the inclusion of women with learning disabilities' experience into psychological knowledge. Women with learning disabilities are willing to be involved in research if asked and have clearly much to teach us.

REFERENCES

Barker, M. and Howells, G. (1990) The medical needs of adults: primary care for people with a mental handicap. *Occasional Paper 47*, London: Royal College of General Practitioners

Baum, S. (1994) Intervention with a pregnant woman with severe learning disabilities: a case example. In A. Craft (Ed.) *Practice Issues in Sexuality and Learning Disabilities*. London: Routledge

Bond, L., Kerr, M. and Thapar, A. (1997) Attitudes of general practitioners towards health care for people with intellectual disability and the factors underlying these attitudes. *Journal of Intellectual Disability Research*, 41 (5), 391–400

Booth, T. and Booth, W. (1994) *Parenting Under Pressure: Mothers and Fathers with Learning Disabilities*. Buckingham: Open University Press

Brown, H. (1994) 'An ordinary life?': a review of the normalisation principle as it applies to the sexual options of people with learning disabilities. *Disability and Society*, 9 (2), 123–144

Brown, H. (1996) Ordinary women: issues for women with learning disabilities – A Keynote Review. *British Journal of Learning Disabilities*, 24, 47–51

Brown, H. and Smith, H. (1989) Whose 'Ordinary Life' is it Anyway? *Disability, Handicap and Society*, 4 (2), 105–119

Burns, J. (1993) Sexuality, sexual problems, and people with learning difficulties. In J. Ussher and C. Baker (Eds.) *Psychological Perspectives on Sexual Problems: New Directions in Theory and Practice*. London: Routledge

Burns, J. (1993) Invisible women: women who have learning disabilities. *The Psychologist: Bulletin of the British Psychological Society*, 6, 102–105

Burns, J. (in press) Gender identity and women with learning disabilities – the third sex. *Clinical Psychology Forum – special edition ' Waiting to be asked – women with learning disabilities'*

Carlson, B. (1998) Domestic violence in adults with mental retardation: reports from victims and key informants. *Mental Health Aspects of Developmental Disabilities*, 1 (4), 102–112

Carr, J. and Hollins, S. (1995) Menopause in women with learning disabilities. *Journal of Intellectual Disability Research*, 39 (3), 137–139

Chesler, P. (1972) *Women and Madness*. New York: Doubleday

Clements, J., Clare, I.C.H. and Ezelle, L.A. (1995) Real men, real women, real lives? Gender issues in learning disabilities and challenging behaviour. *Disability and Society*, 10 (4), 425–437

Cole, S.S. (1988) Women, Sexuality, and Disabilities. *Women and Therapy*, 7 (2), 277–294

Deegan, M.J. and Brooks, N.A. (Eds.) (1985) *Women and Disability: The Double Handicap*. New Brunswick, NJ: Transaction

DOH (1998) *Signposts for Success in Commissioning and Providing Health Services for People with Learning Disabilities*. London: Department of Health

Edmonds, J. (2000) On being a mother: a positive identity in the face of adversity. *Clinical Psychology Forum – special edition ' Waiting to be asked – women with learning disabilities'*

Fine, M. and Asch, A. (Eds.) (1988) *Women with Disabilities: Essays in Psychology, Culture, and Politics*. Philadelphia: Temple University Press

Finger, A. (1984) Claiming all of our bodies: reproductive rights and disability. In R. Arditti, R.D. Klein and S. Minden (Eds.) *Test-Tube Women: What Future for Motherhood?* London: Pandora Press

Furey, E.M. (1989) Abuse of persons with mental retardation: A literature review. *Behaviour, Research and Treatment*, 4, 143–154

Hanna, W.J. and Rogovsky, B. (1991) Women with disabilities: two handicaps plus. *Disability, Handicap and Society*, 6 (1), 49–63

Kallianes, V. and Rubenfeld, P. (1997) Disabled women and reproductive rights. *Disability and Society*, 12 (2), 203–221

Kaminer, Y., Feinstein, C., Barrett, R., Tylenda, B. and Hole, W. (1988) Menstrually related mood disorder in developmentally disabled adolescents: review and current status. *Child Psychiatry and Human Development*, 18, 239–249

Lennox, N.G., Diggens, J.N. and Ugoni, A.M. (1997) The general practice care of people with intellectual disability: barriers and solutions. *Journal of Intellectual Disability Research*, 41 (5), 380–390

McCarthy, M. (1993) Sexual experiences of women with learning difficulties in long-stay hospitals. *Sexuality and Disability*, 11 (4), 277–285

McCarthy, M. (1999) *Sexuality and Women with Learning Disabilities*. London: Jessica Kingsley

McGaw, S. (1996) Services for parents with learning disabilities. *Tizard Learning Disability Review*, 1 (1), 21–28

MENCAP (1998) *The NHS: Health for All? People with Learning Disabilities and Health Care*. London: Royal Society for Mentally Handicapped Children and Adults

Minihan, P. M., Dean, D.H. and Lyons, C.M. (1993) Managing the care of patients with mental retardation: a survey of physicians. *Mental Retardation*, 31, 239–246

Morris, J. (1991) *Pride Against Prejudice*. London: Womens Press

Nightingale, C. (2000) Barriers to health access: a study of cervical screening for women with learning disabilities. *Clinical Psychology Forum – special edition 'Waiting to be asked – women with learning disabilities'*

Noonan-Walsh, P. (1988) Handicapped and female: two disabilities. In R. McConkey and P. McGinley (Eds.) *Concepts and Controversies in Services for People with Mental Handicap*. Dublin: St Michael's House

O'Dwyer, J.M., Holmes, J. and Friedman, T. (1995) Menstruation and aggression in a population of women with learning disabilities. *British Journal of Learning Disabilities*, 23, 51–55

Park, D. and Radford, J. (1998) From the Case Files: reconstructing a history of involuntary sterilisation. *Disability and Society*, 13 (3) 317–342

Ryan, J. and Thomas, F. (1980) *The Politics of Mental Handicap*. Middlesex: Penguin

Schupf, N., Zigman, W., Kapell, J. Kline, J. and Levin, B. (1997) Early menopause in women with Down's syndrome. *Journal of Intellectual Disability Research*, 41 (3), 264–267

Sinason, V. (1992) *Mental Handicap and the Human Condition: New Approaches*. London: Tavistock Free Association Books

Turk, V. and Brown, H. (1992) Sexual abuse and adults with learning disabilities. *Mental Handicap*, 20 (2), 56–58

Ussher, J.M. (1991) *Women's Madness: Misogyny or Mental Illness*. London: Harvester Wheatsheaf

Wolfensberger, W. (1972) *The Principle of Normalization in Human Services*. Toronto: NIMR

PHYSICAL HEALTH AND ILLNESS

CHAPTER 20

WOMEN LIVING WITH HIV IN BRITAIN

Corinne Squire

INTRODUCTION

This chapter examines how HIV positive women in Britain, a relatively small group but one that encompasses significant diversity, live with the epidemic. It tries to understand the psychological characteristics of these lives within their physiological, epidemiological and social matrices. It draws on contemporary research, including the author's own research on HIV and support, as well as on writing from within communities of HIV-affected women in Britain. Finally, it presents a wish-list of future policy and provision for HIV positive women in Britain.

WOMEN IN BRITAIN AND THE TRANSNATIONAL EPIDEMIC

Women constitute 14.8 million of the 33.6 million people worldwide known to be HIV positive. Around 70 percent of present and new infections occur in Africa south of the Sahara, where prevalence is highest among women (*www.unaids.org*, April 2000). Issues around women are thus at the center of the epidemic worldwide. At the same time, within health psychology in general, there is increasing recognition of gender's critical significance for health and illness (Hunt and Annendale, 1999). Both these factors mean that women's relation to HIV is a key and expanding area of health-psychological study.

Britain has low HIV infection rates compared to other European countries. By September 1999, there had been 16,612 recorded AIDS cases, one in women for every nine in men, and 39,444 HIV diagnoses, one in women for every six in men. While at first the epidemic was concentrated among gay men, rates of new HIV and AIDS diagnoses are falling in this group. These rates are also falling among women. Still, by 1998, women constituted 37 percent of new diagnoses (PHLS, 1999a, 1998; WHO Weekly Epidemiological Record, October 1998). At the start, British women's HIV infection arose mainly from unsafe intravenous drug use or unprotected sex with HIV positive male drug users. But HIV prevalence and new infections among intravenous drug users have fallen dramatically (Rhodes *et al.*, 1998; Wellings and Field, 1996). The present increase is mostly among heterosexual women with no drug-associated risk, particularly – because of age patterns in heterosexual relationships – in younger women of 20–34 years (PHLS, 1998).

During the past ten to 15 years, migrations from African countries devastated by civil unrest and political repression, as well as the continuing presence of African visitors and students, have helped shape the British epidemic. HIV exposure in Africa now accounts for nearly a third of British HIV diagnoses (PHLS, 1998; *www.phls.co.uk*, March 1999). Almost half of all women with HIV cite exposure in Africa as their most likely transmission mode, and transmission continues within African communities (Mukasa, 1997). Other migrations into and across Europe may also affect HIV prevalence in as yet unevaluated ways. For instance, the steepest increase in HIV reports came in 1999 from injecting drug users in countries of the former Soviet Union, particularly Ukraine, and it is likely that such increases will both impact the broader population and, at a time of high intra-European mobility, affect people in other countries (*www.unaids.org*, April 2000).

This situation is not unique. Many other overdeveloped countries and countries in the developing world exhibit large shifts in population which change national HIV profiles. The transnationalism of the HIV epidemic is, though, particularly marked in Britain, compared to other European countries, because Britain has historical links through colonialism with countries badly hit by the epidemic first in east, then in southern Africa, such as Kenya, Uganda, Zambia, Zimbabwe and South Africa. The epidemic's recent recorded upturn in west African countries, notably Nigeria, may also affect Britain's HIV profile (PHLS, 1999a).

WOMEN LIVING WITH HIV: GENDER SIMILARITIES

What are HIV's psychological effects on women, and to what extent are they gender-specific, or determined by factors other than gender and shared with men? I shall concentrate here on women infected with HIV, though many HIV negative women who are relatives and friends of people living with HIV, or workers, volunteers or activists, are also deeply affected (Rieder and Ruppelt, 1989).

For both women and men, living with HIV means coming to terms with a chronic, probably fatal illness, heavily stigmatized through its connections with transgressive sexualities and, in the West, with drug use and racial 'otherness'. This illness has dramatic implications for people's economic status, social relations and personal lives. It is characterized by medical, personal and social uncertainties (Weeks, 1995), but it provokes emotional reactions of some commonality. Reactions typically include shock, shame and fear, anger and guilt, denial, grief, depression and acceptance (Hedge, 1996; Herek and Greene, 1995; Pierret, 2000). In my longitudinal interview study on HIV and support, for instance, Sally (all interviewees' names have been changed), an HIV positive white European woman, provided an account similar to that of many gay men in this and other studies.

It was so big a shock ... I was so scared. And then I kind of got over it because you can't be worried all the time, you learn to live with the virus. But if I start to get sick or something, then it's like I'll have to got through things again. But there's a lot of hope, they can find out medicines.

Often, variables in HIV experience such as time since diagnosis, illness history and current state of health seem more powerful predictors of psychological state than gender (Herek and Greene, 1995).

Representations and experiences of HIV also depend strongly on sexuality. Lesbian and bisexual women have been by turns assimilated to gay men, and treated as invisible in research and in popular accounts of the epidemic (Boffin, 1990) – a neglect that is distinct from the alternate ignoring of and fascination with heterosexual HIV positive women. HIV positive heterosexual women and men and lesbians often have unsupportive kin and friendship networks, and feel alone. Heterosexual women and men who are at high HIV risk through their drug use or partners often rate the emotional value of unsafe sex above its HIV risk (O'Sullivan and Ardill, 1996; Rhodes *et al.*, 1998; Rhodes and Cusick, 2000). In my study, one interviewee, Samantha, a white British woman, provided a dramatic example when she described how she and her HIV positive male partner had sometimes had unsafe sex – with the result that she was now HIV positive – not to show love or share his condition, but simply because sex was important in their relationship but rarely happened unless it was spontaneous.

HIV positive gay men may suffer the same neglect, isolation and invisibility as HIV positive heterosexuals and lesbians. They may make similar calculations about safety and intimacy to those made by HIV positive heterosexual women and men (Joffe, 1997; Smith *et al.*, 1997: 81–6). But in the West, HIV positive gay men have benefitted most from a series of campaigns and voluntary services directed at improving treatments, preventing transmission and reducing discrimination, and from a more general commitment to supporting them, expressed first and most strongly by other gay men and lesbians (Brown, 1997; Crimp, 1988; Herek and Greene, 1995; Oppenheimer and Reckitt, 1997; Saalfield and Navarro, 1991; Watney, 1994).

Finally, living with HIV is also a matter of *where* you live. In the developing world, a high proportion of people face poverty and malnutrition, war, political violence, inadequate medical, social and educational services, and immediately life-threatening illnesses that overshadow HIV. In the West, HIV is also associated with social exclusion, with economic disadvantage and social disempowerment, but less frequently and to a lesser degree. Men and women, gay and straight alike, live with these differences.

WOMEN LIVING WITH HIV: GENDER DIFFERENCES

HIV is, however, lived differently by women, regardless of their HIV history, their sexuality or where they live. The physiology of the disease is gendered. Women are more easily infected through vaginal intercourse than their male partners, and sexually transmitted infections increase this likelihood more for them. Thus an HIV positive woman in a relationship with an HIV positive man is more likely to have been infected by him than vice versa. This asymmetry may produce gendered patterns of guilt and blame, as well as the mutual concern and fear such relationships inevitably carry. HIV positive women are also more likely to be reinfected in new relationships with HIV positive men, so even these relationships are fraught with extra transmission risk for them.

In HIV-discordant heterosexual relationships, HIV positive partners are usually most concerned about transmission risk (van der Straten et al., 1998). Nevertheless, an HIV positive woman in a relationship with a man who is negative or does not know his status may have to negotiate very carefully for that relationship's continuance. Women's economic dependency and their likelihood of experiencing men's violence around HIV distinguishes such negotiations from those conducted by men. Actual and threatened violence is indeed central to any consideration of HIV and AIDS among women (*www.hiv.unaids.org.*, March 1999; Maman et al., 2000). In the HIV support study, one interviewee, Rose, spent four years educating her partner about HIV, going to couples counseling, and living with episodes of his drinking and physical abuse – during which time she told no one besides HIV service workers about her status – in order to negotiate his acceptance. HIV positive women often find such negotiations too difficult. Sally, for instance, said of her past attempts at relationships with HIV negative men,

I start feeling I can't even see them any more because I should tell them. I don't know how I'm going to tell them … they get so scared.

Gay and heterosexual HIV positive men also find problems in negotiating relationships with HIV negative people, but with women there seems to be a gendered anxiety at work: stereotypes of women's terrorizing 'feminine' infectiveness more than make up for the lower transmission risk that vaginal intercourse statistically has for men.

Women can transmit HIV to children, and pregnancy and childbirth may dramatically affect the course of their disease, so reproduction carries a double load of concerns. Sally, who had one HIV negative child, described her reluctance to get pregnant with her second husband, an HIV positive man whose first wife and child had died of AIDS. He was the best thing that had happened to her since her diagnosis, and she understood his desire for a child, but the potential harm to her health, the agony of waiting to know a child's status and the possibility of an HIV positive child, were, together, too much for her:

We want a child now ... even if it would be sick or anything, he wants the child, and then I feel, because he's there, I could maybe handle it ... But what if the medicine would stop working when I'm pregnant? Like the virus would get very aggressive again. So I don't know. It's very difficult.

While HIV positive women are subject to some of the highly specific infections that initially defined AIDS, their HIV disease and AIDS are now defined by gynecological conditions that HIV negative women exhibit too, though with less severity and frequency – for instance, invasive cervical cancer, pelvic inflammatory disease and yeast infections. Such non-HIV-specific conditions may lead women, and clinicians, to underestimate their illness. One participant in the support study claimed her GP's treatment of her new herpes infection was not aggressive enough and she had to make an emergency hospital visit – with the result that her interview was conducted in an outpatient clinic.

Women's HIV diagnosis, treatment and prognosis differ markedly from men's. Women are tested and receive treatment later – though as with heterosexual men this is sooner now than in earlier years of the epidemic; they receive less treatment for the same condition – TB, for instance (*AIDS Weekly Plus*, 14 July 1997); they have more symptoms for longer; they die sooner after an AIDS diagnosis (Ravas *et al.*, 1998), and combination therapy, or Highly Active Antiretroviral Therapy (HAART), is reducing their death rates less than those of gay men (*www.phls.co.uk*, March 1999; PHLS, 1999b).

The discrepancies can be explained variously. Women's gender-specific but non-HIV-specific symptomatology could be partly responsible. Epidemiology may also play a part. In western countries, outside neighborhoods with significant numbers of African migrants or high levels of IV drug use, women patients and clinicians are unlikely to think of HIV; women do not 'fit the category' (Lawrence and Kanabus, 1999). Moreover, the population of HIV positive women in Britain, mostly infected later than HIV positive gay men, is less likely to have been ill and therefore more likely to be holding off from treatment and service involvement as asymptomatic HIV positive men, too, do; not having symptoms is often a reason women advance for not seeking diagnosis or treatment (Ravas *et al.*, 1998). HIV positive people of African origin also benefit less from HAART and have worse prognoses, and this difference is likely often to be compounded by gender. Among people infected with HIV through drug use, too, women's health is worse and their use of HIV services less, perhaps partly because of their more privatized drug use and lesser recourse to drug services (McKegany *et al.*, 1998).

Women themselves emphasize psychological reasons – anxieties and fears about death, denial, and feeling reassured by the absence of symptoms – for their delays in seeking help (Ravas *et al.*, 1998). But these factors cannot be understood outside their social context. Overall, women living with HIV in the West have fewer educational and economic resources than HIV positive men. They may find information about HIV inaccessible, making them specially liable to the psychological factors they cite. They may be unable, for financial or family reasons, to get to diagnostic and treatment facilities. They may be economically, socially and personally dependent on sexual relationships, or sex work, with men, that would cease or become violent if fidelity or condoms were discussed or HIV or other sexually transmitted infections mentioned, as happened to Rose.

In the West, HIV positive women are often poor and of color. They include a significant number of injecting drug users and their partners, sex workers, women with histories of sexually transmitted infections (Stein and Kuhn, 1996; Vuylsteke *et al.*, 1996), women, especially younger women, with histories of abuse (Friedman *et al.*, 1997; Hoffman and Futterman, 1996; Miller, 1999; Perez *et al.*, 1995; Sherr, 1997a; Weissman and Brown, 1995), women with mental health problems, and recent migrants of unsettled citizenship status who are often refugees from war zones or political violence, and who may have suffered multiple bereavements through these events, as well as through AIDS. All these women may find HIV hard to deal with because of other problems in their lives. Mina, for instance, a young HIV positive African refugee in the HIV support study, had had extensive counseling after coming to Britain, to deal with her rape and experiences of civil unrest. She was brought to consider her HIV status only later, and when she was tested she used her earlier counselor, rather than HIV services, for support:

I lost my family back in my country. At the same time as I was raped, one of my brothers died, I lost a few brothers. And then I came here, you know, for a year I couldn't talk to anybody, then I was abused from here, then I ended up in a refuge here. They say, 'you better see a counselor', first for all those other things, and then in the process I started thinking about HIV as well ... my counselor is like my mother, she took me to get my results.' For other women, life problems such as drug use may even be a refuge from HIV, as with many intravenous drug users who describe numbing their emotions after diagnosis with drugs. (Ravas et al., 1998)

Such life problems are of course lived through by HIV positive men as well as women, but the relative paucity of services appropriate for and accessed by women, combined with women's specific, gendered experiences of, for example, physical and sexual violence and drug use, may make many HIV positive women especially unlikely to look beyond these problems, to HIV itself.

Another reason for gender discrepancies in HIV diagnosis, treatment and prognosis in the West is that services for women have followed, with some lag and considerable inappropriateness, the model set by services oriented towards gay men. (This is also true for heterosexual men, though services oriented at drug users and hemophiliacs in the second wave of provision were targeted implicitly at this group.) Services have, too, often seemed biased against women – and against all people of color, though it is beyond the scope of this chapter to consider this bias fully. The initial definition of AIDS left out common female symptoms; early clinical drug trials excluded women, whose reproductive biology it was thought introduced a confusing factor; some pregnant women still feel forced into AZT treatment and Caesarean sections (Ward, 1997). New tests and drugs, like the viral load test and HAART, came late and in unsuitable forms, to hospitals outside large metropolitan centers, and to hospitals in poor city areas serving significant African populations. The medical profession has sometimes been seen as conducting Tuskegee-type 'experiments' with people of African origin; anonymous testing of pregnant women for epidemiological data is opposed by a significant minority of pregnant women (Sherr et al., 1996), and the offering of HIV tests to women simply on the basis of African origin has been viewed with deep suspicion. As with gay men earlier in the epidemic, African women in Britain – Mina was an example – also allege hospitals have tested them despite their withholding consent (Mukasa, 1997).

Support services originally set up by and for white gay men, and even those designed later for gay men of color, lesbians, and heterosexual women and men, but using the original model, often failed to meet their users' requirements. For instance, women want drop-ins more than support groups, and need specific services for children, not just a crèche. Lacking social support networks, they also want ongoing links with particular workers, not time-limited, task-specific relationships, and they are very concerned about confidentiality and stigma (Ravas et al., 1998). African service users are often especially concerned about confidentiality, are unlikely to see psychological counseling as helpful, find social workers ignorant of their preferred modes of family and community life and respond better to services provided through social rather than educational channels (Mhereza, 1998; Mukasa, 1997). Women and men who are IV drug users are fatalistic about their health and conservative about sexual practices in ways that gay-oriented education programmes do not expect and, again, want long-term relationships with support workers (Mulleady, 1992: 75, 98–100; Rhodes and Malotte, 1997; Rhodes et al., 1998).

Comparisons between HIV positive women and men are thus comparisons not simply between genders, but across a multiplicity of physiological, epidemiological and social differences. Yet some more general gender differences seem to emerge from the data, and it is to these differences that this chapter now turns.

WOMEN, HIV AND STIGMA

Stigma was early identified as an unavoidable concomitant of living with HIV (Herek, 1990; see also Pierret, 2000) and in Britain it retains a very powerful and often now a racialized place in HIV positive women's experiences. Women's issues around HIV are especially likely to be seen as *African* women's issues – a perspective that should help direct much-needed resources at an under-served constituency, but that in practice stigmatizes HIV in African and other women (Mukasa, 1997). What seems to be happening is a racialized version of the earlier 'queering' of every-one infected or affected by HIV through the stigma of the 'gay plague' (Gorna, 1997; Patton, 1990; Treichler, 1988). HIV's stigma was confronted and to a large extent dismantled by gay men – but it is naïve to imagine it has disappeared (Squire, 1997). HIV in Britain has come to seem a treat-able and declining illness that white middle class gay men live with, with humor, bravery and skill, and that affects small numbers of drug users, their partners, and hemophiliacs. However, the virus's association with people of African origin is a new ground for stigma, and everyone living with HIV in Britain runs the risk of being consigned to the closet by the racialized as well as the sexualized stigma that now characterizes the epi-demic (Lear, 1997: 163). HIV is turning into a disease of racialized as much as social exclusion.

HIV among people of African origin often stigmatizes women rather than men. HIV prevalence studies suggesting high rates in African com-munities are performed on women and their new-borns, and HIV positive African women use services more than HIV positive African men, so the public 'face' of HIV among people of African origin in Britain tends to be female. Stigma is acute even within African communities, where large fractions of people may be HIV positive but being 'out' about your status is frightening rare, and especially for women, shameful (Ssanyu-Sseruma, 1999). The anonymous winner of the magazine *Positive Nation*'s 'Positive Woman of the Year' award for 1998, 'A', an African woman, declined the award for this reason (*Positive Nation*, March 1999: 15). Such stigma makes it difficult to take medication or even to behave safely by using condoms or bottle-feeding your babies. Not having children, or having ill children or children who die, is especially problematic in many African communi-ties and is strongly associated with the stigma of HIV (de Freitas, 2000). Even using locally provided HIV services can be difficult (Squire, 1999). One woman in the HIV support study for instance refused an HIV-dedi-cated home help she needed because her friends had seen this worker at the house of a neighbor known to have died of AIDS.

African women in Britain are not the only group of women to experi-ence specific forms of stigma. Female injection drug users report feeling more stigmatized by their behavior than male injectors (McKeganey *et al.*, 1998), a difference that may relate to their later diagnosis, lesser treatment, worse prognosis and lower service use. But all HIV positive women live with shared stigmas, too. Though sometimes pictured as unwitting vic-tims of HIV-infected men, women with HIV are also consistently viewed as repositories of a specifically feminine threat, the 'always already infect-ed' (Patton, 1994: 108). As with other behaviorally, especially sexually transmitted, conditions, they are represented as unthinking biological vec-tors, carrying HIV from gay or bisexual men and male injection drug users into the rest of the population and infecting the next generation while uncontrolledly pursing their desires for chemical, reproductive and sexual pleasures. 'Sex=women=disease=chaos', as Tamsin Wilton (1997: 139) puts it. Women in the HIV support study who described a shamed, fearful withdrawal from the world after diagnosis, and an intensified sense of repulsion at their bodies, demonstrated the effects of this equation.

HIV AS PART OF WOMEN'S LIVES

A second general factor in women's reactions to the epidemic, is that they are more likely to see the virus as outweighed in their lives by other factors – not just drug use, general ill-health and poverty, which might also apply to male drug users and to men with few economic resources – but also relationships with partners and children. This relational self-perception de-emphasizes HIV, which can be a helpful response (Schwarzberg, 1993). But it can also consign women to 'feminine' caring for others at cost to themselves. It can be a denial of HIV in response to stigma, for such bracketing off of HIV turns a 'bad' girl into a 'good' one. In the HIV support study, Samantha, for instance, who had become HIV positive from known high-risk activities, was planning not to seek treatment that she thought would harm her relationship by reminding her partner he had infected her. Seeing pills around the whole time, she said, would make him feel terrible. Women may restrict their negotiation of safer sex in personal relationships, or their HIV status disclosure and service seeking, out of concern for how they are viewed as women, particularly in terms of their sexuality. They may situate themselves as carers for men and children, including HIV positive men and children, whose lives revolve round discharging these responsibilities, rather than as HIV positive and in need of care for themselves (Lucas, 1995). One interviewee, Laura, who had an HIV positive boyfriend, spent her time working and looking after him, and used HIV services only sporadically, although she described quite severe symptoms of her own. She also spent considerable time visiting other, sicker women who she had met through HIV services:

I feel lucky you know to be well and ok, and that I can visit other people that are sick, you know, it just makes me feel happy.

Another interviewee, Halina, who like many HIV positive asymptomatic people said she often 'forgot' her positive status, discussed her possible future illness and death almost entirely in terms of her concerns about how her son would manage and who would look after him.

Again, there can be confounding factors. HIV positive gay and heterosexual men who are carers may similarly underplay their own HIV status. Women, though, are more likely to be caring for partners and children. They are also socially enmeshed in such roles through notions of 'feminine' nurturance and care that affect gay and heterosexual men less. In heterosexual relationships, particularly where there are children, women

are, too, likely to bear most domestic responsibilities. Of course, HIV positive men are concerned about their children's actual or potential HIV status and, more than women, about their parenting abilities (Mukasa, 1997).
HIV positive single parents, both women and men, encounter difficulties
making provision for their children's possible futures (Salter Goldie *et al.*,
1997). Family and legacy have special significance for women and men in
disempowered ethnic minority communities (Amaro, 1988). Yet HIV positive women are, like other women, more fundamentally imbricated in
discourses that define them as parents. For women who are drug users,
children may indeed be the only source of feelings of self-worth, and may
represent a window of opportunity for change (Mulleady, 1992: 108, 120;
O'Sullivan and Thomson, 1996).

A gender difference that seems at first to tend in the opposite direction,
suggesting HIV positive women are *more* psychologically engaged with
their HIV status than HIV positive heterosexual men, is that they are more
involved with HIV services and treatment. Women's lack of support networks, compared for instance to gay men, may be partly responsible
(London *et al.*, 1998). Women often also act as conduits of information and
support to heterosexual male partners and friends. This trend has been
noticed particularly in relation to HIV positive African women. Advocacy
organizations sometimes declare the greatest help the women could get
would be services targeted at African men. We could then see women's
greater involvement with HIV services as part of their classic gatekeeper
function in public health programmes. In addition to gaining support
from these services for themselves, they are implicitly expected to educate
and support the 'hidden' population of HIV positive heterosexual men,
thus doing, for free, work that formal services find expensive and difficult.
Women suggest the effect of support they receive is considerably reduced
by this extra burden. Women's heavy involvement with HIV may thus
contribute, paradoxically, to their minimizing HIV in their own lives.

At the same time, women's increasing involvement with HIV services
has produced improvements in testing, treatment and service provision.
For example, pressure from HIV positive women's advocacy groups, initially in the U.S., led to a redefinition of AIDS to include invasive cervical
cancer. Criticisms by HIV positive African women in Britain have rendered testing and treatment less prescriptive and more consultative. Like
gay men's groups, women with HIV have also been responsible for the
targeting of HIV services, first by campaigning for women's services, later
by developing more specialized services, particularly for African women.
Indeed, British African HIV organizations and women's HIV organizations, in both of which African women play a leading role, have become a
form of activism parallel to that initiated earlier by gay men.

Clearly, it is insufficient to analyse women's lives with HIV simply in
gendered terms. An African woman like Rose, who arrived in Britain during the last decade, for instance, encountered problems any woman might
face, such as disclosing to a male partner and her family and friends, her
partner getting tested, deciding whether to have children, making deci-

sions about medical treatment and other services, and trying to work without making yourself ill. In addition, though, Rose had more specific concerns: the British African community's experiences of AZT as a poisonous drug for which they felt they were 'guinea pigs', and consequent doubts about HAART; problems of citizenship status; and her dependence for support on an African community that could be distinctly unsupportive to 'out' HIV positive women. Rose began her interview, indeed, by describing a betrayal by those closest to her: *'when my community, everyone, did not understand, that disturbed my mind'*. Lives are lived through gender, but that gendering is interwoven with experiences of sexuality and family, class and employment, racism, migration and war, that cut across gender. Such interactions can sound like a truism, but they leap out at researchers and policymakers with inescapable force in the case of HIV.

SUMMARY: WHAT WOMEN WANT

From considerations like those above, indications emerge of the kind of policies, services and support that women require in order to live with HIV with some psychological equanimity and effectiveness. Such help should be directed at empowerment and self-efficacy, as O'Leary and Jemmot (1995a) put it in their discussion of HIV prevention activities, but it must pursue this aim structurally as well as interpersonally, as Rao Gupta and her colleagues (1996) emphasize. Where possible, it must provide resources for geographical and other communities to organize their own provision (Babuma, 2000; Mukasa, 1997). Services need to address HIV through programmes focussed on women's education, employment, safety and general health. In Britain, for instance, women living with HIV would be helped by flexible employment policies, an immigration service sensitive to HIV issues, continuing prevention work for African women and all younger women, educational and advocacy work in African communities in general, and HIV services integrated with drug treatment, legal advice and counseling around abuse (Sparkes, 1998: 225–228). In medicine, women want the HIV antibody test available routinely but not compulsorily before and during pregnancy, alongside culturally sensitive counseling and balanced information (Boyd *et al.*, 1999; Mukasa, 1997; Sherr *et al.*, 1996) – requirements that, it is to be hoped, current government policy on voluntary but recommended testing will meet. They want medical providers that genuinely consult with them, and cooperation between medicine and alternative therapies. They want social services that do not stereotype them, or interfere with their parenting, or encourage them into premature disclosure or inappropriate, health-threatening work. They want services that are flexible, that do not insist on professional divisions between for instance 'counseling' and advice, or on service termination after a fixed time. They like a mix of accessible local services and confidentially assuring centralized services, out-of-work-hours services and daytime services. They want community-based services that manage the difficult synthesis between empathizing with their clients, confidentiality, and expertise (Babuma, 2000). They appreciate practical services like meals, transport and laundry, and services for children that go beyond crèche provision; they would be helped greatly by effective services for heterosexual men. Social support from other people affected and more particularly infected by HIV, especially women, is valued, but HIV status and gender rarely define the limits of HIV positive women's communities; other social and kinship networks are important too. To live with HIV is not, especially for women, to be defined by it (O'Sullivan and Thomson, 1996). But HIV will always be at times a crucial, gendered determinant of HIV positive women's lives, and they will continue to need formal and informal support that is sensitive to this impact, and to how HIV is lived differently by different women.

REFERENCES

Aggleton, Peter and Warwick, Ian (1997) Young people, sexuality and AIDS education. In Lorraine Sherr (Ed.) *AIDS and Adolescents* (pp. 79–90). Amsterdam: Harwood

Amaro, Hortensia (1988) Considerations for prevention of HIV infection among Hispanic women. *Psychology of Women Quarterly*, 12, 429–43

del Amo, Julia, Pekkuckevich, A., Phillips, Andrew *et al.* (1998) Disease projection and survival in HIV-1 infected Africans in London. *AIDS*, 12 (10), 1203–1209

Babuma, William (2000) The way forward. *Positive Nation*, March, 55

Bennett, G., Velleman, R., Barter, G. and Bradbury, C. (2000) Gender differences in sharing injecting equipment by drug users in England. *AIDS Care*, 12 (1), 77–87

Boffin, Tessa (1990) Fairy tales, 'facts' and gossip. In Tessa Boffin and Sunil Gupta (Eds.) *Ecstatic Antibodies* (pp. 156–192). London: Rivers' Oram Press

Boyd, F., Simpson, W., Hart, G., Johnstone, F. and Goldberg, D. (1999) What do pregnant women think about the HIV test? A qualitative study. *AIDS Care*, 11 (1), 21–29

Brown, Michael P. (Ed.) (1997) *RePlacing Citizenship: AIDS: Activism and Radical Democracy,.* London: Guilford Press

Catalan, Jose, Sherr, Lorraine and Hodge, Barbara (Eds.) (1997) *The Impact of AIDS: Psychological and Social Aspects of HIV Infection.* Amsterdam: Harwood

Crimp, Douglas (Ed.) (1988) *AIDS: Cultural Analysis/Cultural Activism.* Cambridge, MA: MIT Press

Ezzy, D. (2000) Illness narrative: time, hope and HIV. *Social Science and Medicine*, 50, 605–617

Feldman, Rayah and Crowley, Colm. (1997) HIV services for women in East London: the match between provision and needs. In Peter Aggleton, Peter Davis and Graham Hart (Eds.) *AIDS: Activism and Alliances* (pp. 122–141). Sussex: Falmer Press

Freitas, Rose de (2000) Treasures: African family values and HIV. *Positive Nation*, January 51, 16–20

Friedman, Samuel, Negus, Alan, Jose, Benny, Curtis, Richard, McGrady, Gene, Vera, Mildred, Lovely, Richard, Zenilmar, Jonathan, Johnson, Valerie, White, Helene, Paone, Denise and Des Jarlais, Don (1997) Adolescents and HIV risk due to drug injection or sex with drug injectors in the United States. In Lorraine Sherr (Ed.) *AIDS and Adolescents* (pp. 107–31). Amsterdam: Harwood

Friedman, Samuel, Friedmann, Patricia, Telles, Paulo, Bastos, Fransisco, Bueno, Regina, Mesquita, Fabio and Des Jarlais, Don (1998) New injectors and HIV-1 risk. In Gerry Stimson *et al.* (Eds.) *Drug Injecting and HIV Infection* (pp. 76–90). Geneva: World Health Organisation

Gorna, Robin (1997) Dangerous vessels: Feminism and the AIDS crisis. In Joshua Oppenheimer and Helena Reckitt (Eds.) *Acting on AIDS* (pp. 146–165). London: Serpent's Tail

Houveling, H., Hamers, F., Termiorshuizen, F. *et al.* (1998) A birth cohort analysis of AIDS in Europe: High incidence among young people at risk. *AIDS*, 12 (1), 85–93

Hedge, Barbara (1996) Counselling people with AIDS, their partners, families and friends. In John Green and Alana McCreaner (Eds.) *Counselling in HIV Infection and AIDS* (pp. 66–82) (2nd edn). Oxford: Blackwell

Herek, Gregory (1990) Illness, stigma and AIDS. In Paul Costa and Gary VandenBos (Eds.) *Psychological Aspects of Serious Illness*, (pp. 107–49). Washington, D.C.: American Psychological Association

Herek, Gregory, and Greene, Beverley (Eds.) (1995) *AIDS, Identity and Community*. London: Sage

Hoffman, Neal and Futterman, Donna (1996) Youth and HIV/AIDS. In Jonathan Mann and Daniel Taratola (Eds.) *AIDS in the World* (pp. 236–251). London: Oxford University Press

Hunt, Kate and Annendale, Ellen (1999) Relocating gender and morbidity: Examining men's and women's health in contemporary Western societies – Introduction. *Social Science and Medicine*, 48: 1–5

Joffe, Helen (1997) Intimacy and love in late modern conditions: implications for unsafe sexual practices. In Jane Ussher (Ed.) *Body Talk* (pp. 159–176). London: Routledge

Kippax, Susan and Crawford, Jane (1997) Facts and fictions of adolescent risk. In Lorraine Sherr (Ed.) *AIDS and Adolescents* (pp. 63–77). Amsterdam: Harwood

Kwesigabo, Z.G., Killewo, J., Sandstrom, A., Winani, S., Mhalu, F., Biberfeld, G. and Wall, S. (1999) Prevalence of HIV infection among hospital patients in North West Tanzania. *AIDS Care*, 11 (1), 87–93

Lawrence, James and Kanabus, Annabel (1999) *Women, HIV and AIDS*. Horsham, West Sussex: Avert

Lear, Dana (1997) *Sex and Sexuality: Risk and Relationships in the Age of AIDS*. London: Sage

London, A., LeBlanc, A. and Aneshensel, C. (1998) The integration of informal care, case management, and community-based services for persons with HIV/AIDS. *AIDS Care*, 10 (4), 481–504

Lucas, Ian (1995) *Growing Up Positive*. London: Cassell

McKeganey, Neil, Friedman, Samuel and Mesquita, Fabio (1998) The social context of injectors' risk behavior. In Gerry Stimson *et al.* (Eds.) *Drug Injecting and HIV Infection* (pp. 42–57). Geneva: World Health Organisation

Malliori, Meni, Zunzunegui, Maria Victoria, Rodrigues-Arenas, Angeles and Goldberg, David (1998) Drug injecting and HIV-1 infection: Major findings from the multi-city study. In Gerry Stimson *et al.* (Eds.) *Drug Injecting and HIV Infection* (pp. 42–57). Geneva: World Health Organisation

Maman, S., Campbell, J., Sweat, M. and Gieleen, A. (2000) The intersections of HIV and violence: directions for future research and interventions. *Social Science and Medicine*, 50, 459–478

Manderson, Lenore, Ty, Lee Chang and Rajanayagam, Kiruba (1997) Condom use in heterosexual sex: a review of research. In Jose Catalan, Lorraine Sherr and Barbara Hodge (Eds.) *The Impact of AIDS: Psychological and Social Aspects of HIV Infection* (pp. 1–26). Amsterdam: Harwood

Mann, Jonathan and Taratola, Daniel (Eds.) *AIDS in the World*. London: Oxford University Press

Mhereza, Hope (1998) Being boring. *Positive Nation*, June, 51

Miller, Maureen (1999) A model to explain the relationship between sexual abuse and HIV risk among women. *AIDS Care*, 11 (1), 3–20

Mukasa, Dorothy (1997) African communities living with HIV in Britain: Inequality and justice. In Joshua Oppenheimer and Helena Reckitt (Eds.) *Acting On AIDS: Sex, Drugs and Politics* (pp. 181–197). London: Serpents Tail

Mulleady, Geraldine (1992) *Counselling Drug Users about HIV and AIDS*. Oxford: Blackwell

O'Leary, Ann and Sweet Jemmott, Loretta (1995) General issues in the prevention of HIV with women. In Ann O'Leary and Loretta Sweet Jemmott (Eds.) *Women At Risk* (pp. 1–12). London: Plenum

Oppenheimer, Joshua, and Reckitt, Helena (Eds.) (1997) *Acting on AIDS: Sex, Drugs and Politics*. London: Serpent's Tail

O'Sullivan, Sue and Thomson, Kate (Eds.) (1996) *Positively Women: Living with AIDS*, London: Harper Collins

Oscamp, Stuart (Ed.) (1996) *Safer Sex and Drug Use*. New York: Sage

Patton, Cindy (1994) *Last Served? Gendering the HIV Pandemic*. London: Taylor & Francis

Patton, Cindy (1990) *Inventing AIDS*. London: Routledge

Pierret, Jeannine (2000) Everyday life with HIV/AIDS: Surveys in the social sciences. *Social Science and Medicine*, 50, 1589–1598

PHLS (1998) AIDS and STD Centre, Communicable Disease Surveillance Centre and Scottish Centre for Infection and Environmental Health. Unpublished Quarterly Surveillances

Table Number 41, 98/3

PHLS (1999a) *Communicable Diseases Report*, 25 December, 9 (52)

PHLS (1999b) *Communicable Diseases Report*, 29 October, 9 (44)

Rao Gupta, Geeta, Weiss, Ellen and Whelan, Daniel (1996) HIV/AIDS among women. In Jonathan Mann and Daniel Taratola (Eds.) *AIDS in the World* (pp. 215–228). London: Oxford University Press

Ravas, V., Siegel, K. and Gorey, E. (1998) Factors associated with HIV-infected women's delay in seeking medical care. *AIDS Care*, 10 (5), 49–62

Rhodes, Fen and Malotte, C. Kevin (1996) HIV risk interventions for active drug users: Experience and prospects. In Stuart Oscamp (Ed.) *Safer Sex and Drug Use* (pp. 207–236). New York: Sage

Rhodes, Tim, Myers, Ted, Bueno, Regina, Millson, Peggy and Hunter, Gillian (1998) Drug injecting and sexual safety: Cross-national comparisons among cocaine and opioid injectors. In G. Stimson, D. Des Jarlais and D. Ball (Eds.) *Drug Injecting and HIV Infection* (pp. 130–148). Geneva: World Health Organisation

Rhodes, Tim and Cusick, Linda (2000) Love and intimacy in relationship risk management: HIV positive people and their sexual partners. *Sociology of Health and Illness*, 22 (2), 1–26

Rieder, Ines and Ruppelt, Patricia (Eds.) (1989) *Matters of Life and Death: Women speak about AIDS*. London: Virago

Saalfield, Catharine and Navarro, Ray (1991) Shocking Pink Praxis: Race and Gender on the ACT UP Frontlines. In Diana Fuss (Ed.) *Inside/Out* (pp. 341–372). London: Routledge

Salter Goldie, Robyn, Dimatteo, Dale and King, Susan (1997) Children born to mothers with HIV/AIDS: Family psycho-social issues. In J. Catalan, L. Sherr and B. Hodge (Eds.) *The Impact of AIDS: Psychological and Social Aspects of HIV Infection* (pp. 149–158). Amsterdam: Harwood

Schwartzberg, Stephen (1993) Struggling for meaning: How HIV positive gay men make sense of AIDS. *Professional Psychology: Research and Practice*, 24, 483–490

Sherr, Lorraine (1997a) Adolescents and HIV in our midst. In Lorraine Sherr (Ed.) *AIDS and Adolescents* (pp. 5–23). Amsterdam: Harwood

Sherr, Lorraine (Ed.) (1997b) *AIDS and Adolescents*. Amsterdam: Harwood

Sherr, Lorraine, Jeffries, S., Victor, C. and Chase, J. (1996) Antenatal HIV testing: which way forward? *Psychology Health and Medicine*, 1, 99–112

Smith, Jonathan, Flowers, Paul and Osborn, Mike (1997) Interpretative phenomenological analysis and the psychology of health and illness. In Lucy Yardley (Ed.) *Material Discourses of Health and Illness* (pp. 68–91). London: Routledge

Sparks, Caroline (1998) Women and HIV. In Michael Knox and Caroline Sparks (Eds.) *HIV and Community Mental Healthcare* (pp. 211–230). Baltimore, MD: Johns Hopkins University Press

Squire, Corinne (1999) 'Neighbor who might become friends': Selves, genres and citizenship in narratives of HIV. *Sociological Quarterly*, February, 40(1), 109–38

Squire, Corinne (1997) AIDS Panic. In Jane Ussher (Ed.) *Body Talk*. London: Routledge

Ssanyu-Sueruma, Winnie (1999) Don't mess with Winnie. *Positive Nation*, March, 20–22

Ssanyu-Sueruma, Winnie (2000) The West awaits. *Positive Nation*, December/January, 31–32

Stein, Zena and Kuhn, Louise (1996) HIV in women: What are the gaps in knowledge? In Jonathan Mann and Daniel Taratola (Eds.) *AIDS in the World* (pp. 229–235). London: Oxford University Press

Stimson, Gerry, Des Jarlais, Don and Ball, Don (Eds.) (1998) *Drug Injecting and HIV Infection*. Geneva: World Health Organisation

Treichler, Paula (1988) AIDS, homophobia and biomedical discourse: An epidemic of signification. In Douglas Crimp (Ed.) *AIDS: Cultural Analysis/Cultural Activism*. Cambridge, MA: MIT Press

Weissman, Gloria and Brown, Vivien (1995) Drug-using women and HIV. In Ann O'Leary and Loretta Sweet Jemmott (Eds.) *Women At Risk* (pp. 175–193). London: Plenum

van der Straten, A., Vernon, K., Knight, K., Gomez, C. and Padian, N. (1998) Managing HIV among serodiscordant heterosexual couples: Serostatus, stigma and risk. *AIDS Care*, 20 (5), 533–548

Vuylsteke, Bea, Sunkutu, Rose and Laga, Marie (1996) Epidemiology of HIV and sexually transmitted infections in women. In J. Mann and D. Taratola (Eds.) *AIDS in the World* (pp. 97–109). London: Oxford University

Ward, Paul (1997) Sisters doing it for themselves. *Positive Nation*, February: 22–24

Wellings, Kaye and Field, Becky (1996) *Stopping AIDS: AIDS/HIV Public Education and the Mass Media in Europe*. London: Addison Wesley

Wilton, Tamsin (1997) *EnGendering AIDS: Deconstructing Sex, Text and Epidemic*. London: Sage

Watney, Simon (1994) *Practices of Freedom*. London: Rivers Oram

Weeks, Jeffrey (1995) *Invented Moralities: Sexual Values in an Age of Uncertainty*. London: Polity

World Bank (1997) *Confronting AIDS: Public Priorities in a Global Epidemic*. Oxford: Oxford University Press

---

CHAPTER 21

GYNAECOLOGICAL CANCER

Marian Pitts and Eleanor Bradley

INTRODUCTION

Gynaecological cancer includes ovarian, endometrial, uterine, cervical and vulval cancer. Together these account for 16 percent of new cancer cases in American women (Rieger *et al.*, 1998); U.K. estimates suggest that ovarian, cervical and uterine cancers account for 10 percent of new cancer cases in British women (McPherson and Waller, 1997). The prognosis for women with gynaecological cancer is good. The Cancer Research Campaign (1994–1995) produced five-year relative survival percentages for all stages of gynaecological cancer. It is estimated that 28 percent of women with ovarian cancer, 58 percent of women with cervical cancer and 70 percent of women with uterine cancer survive for five years after treatment (in Pitts and Phillips, 1998).

Women who are diagnosed with early stage gynaecological cancer have particularly good survival and low recurrence rates. Only 1 percent of women with stage IB cervical cancer suffer any recurrent illness, this is compared with over 30 percent of women with stages IIIB and IV (Van Nagell *et al.*, 1979). Eighty-nine percent of women diagnosed with stage I ovarian cancer survive for three years, yet only 10 percent of women with stage IV ovarian cancer survive for that time (Woodman *et al.*, 1997). These estimates demonstrate the importance of early diagnosis to ensure effective treatment and long-term survival. It is clear that as both screening and treatment for gynaecological cancer improve, there will be increasing numbers of women surviving gynaecological cancer (Pistrang and Winchurst, 1997).

PSYCHOLOGICAL ASPECTS OF GYNAECOLOGICAL CANCER

There are a number of issues within the experience of gynaecological cancer that warrant psychological study (see Wilkinson, in this volume). Cervical cancer screening is one of the best established screening programs available in the U.K. Within the U.K., women between the ages of 20 and 64 are routinely invited to attend screening at least once every five years. Non-attendance at screening is an important area for study since 80 percent of women dying from cervical cancer have never received cervical screening (Day, 1989 in Pitts, 1996). Health research has associated non-attendance at screening with such psychological factors as optimism, self-efficacy and anxiety as well as constituents of the Health Belief Model and the Theory of Planned Behavior). However, these models account for only around 30 percent of the variance associated with non-attendance (Pitts, 1996). Clearly, screening attendance is reliant on more than psychological factors alone. It has been suggested that socio-demographic, situational and psychological factors are all involved in the prediction of preventive health behaviors (Sheeran and Abraham, 1996).

Cancer is a stigmatized illness whereby the person with cancer becomes a 'target for others' responses to cancer' (Auchinsloss, 1995). Gynaecological cancers, perhaps because of the site of the disease, particularly evoke shame and embarrassment. This may, in part, be an outcome of the 'menstrual taboo' which has been in existence in most part of the world at some time (Hunter, 1994). Risk factors commonly associated with some gynaecological cancers are also likely to be a cause of negative response:

Risk factors cited for cervical cancer include cigarette smoking, sexually transmitted diseases such as venereal warts, multiple sexual partners, and early and frequent sexual activity. (Hofer, 1992 in Ott and Levy, 1994)

The linking of sexual activity with gynaecological cancer has been shown to be responsible for both self-blame and stigma (Crowther *et al.*, 1994; Cull *et al.*, 1993, in Pistrang and Winchurst, 1997). The continued emotional and social unacceptability of gynaecological cancer within our society has important implications for women suffering from, or learning to live with it. In particular, it may reduce the availability of social support (Auchinsloss, 1995). Emotional support has been identified as the most helpful type of support during recovery from cancer (Helgeson and Cohen, 1996). Yet, reticence to discuss gynaecological cancer may deprive women of this valuable support. Not all research has stressed the role and effectiveness of social support. Some studies have found social support to be a valuable resource for women (Glanz and Lerman, 1992; Reynolds and Kaplan, 1990 in Helgeson and Cohen, 1996); while other studies suggest social support increases dependency whilst undermining self-efficacy (Wortman and Dunkel-Schetter, 1987 in Helgeson and Cohen, 1996).

Unsurprisingly, gynaecological cancer has been associated with psychological distress. Depression and anxiety are reported with particular frequency (Anderson, 1995), with difficulties in sexual functioning, body image and self-esteem also commonly described (Pistrang and Winchurst, 1997). In investigating the psychological factors involved with gynaecological cancer it is useful to look at the follow-up process. The low recurrence rate of early stage gynaecological cancer has already been outlined; this has important implications for follow-up and monitoring of women who are 'recovered' from gynaecological cancer. It is now confirmed that attending follow-up appointments after three years is clinically ineffective and does not improve survival rates (Shumsky et al., 1994). Despite this, some women are reluctant to be discharged from routine follow-up appointments with 20 percent of them attending such follow-up for more than 10 years (Glynne Jones et al., 1997). In the absence of any clinical benefit, it seems likely that psychological needs are being fulfilled by these appointments. Glynne Jones et al. (1998) found length of attendance and high anxiety levels to be factors associated with willingness or otherwise to accept discharge.

Lampic et al. (1994) found anxiety does not differ significantly between those patients with active disease and those in remission. As many as 12 percent of patients diagnosed with cancer more than 10 years ago were found to be suffering with clinical levels of anxiety (Glynne Jones et al., 1997). It is unclear whether women attend follow-up to alleviate anxiety, or whether follow-up attendance itself elevates anxiety levels. Some women describe becoming anxious as early as two weeks prior to a follow-up appointment; this phenomenon has been labelled 'check up anxiety' (Auchinsloss, 1995). However, it may be that anxiety about health itself initiates help-seeking behaviors (such as follow-up attendance) and as such is used as a coping response (Hadjistavropoulos et al., 1998). This account has similarities with the monitoring (attending to information) and blunting (avoiding information) coping strategies described by Miller (1995).

Although it is uncertain whether hospital appointments alleviate or elevate anxiety levels during the follow-up process, it is clear that some women experience continued psychological distress during their recovery from gynaecological cancer. It may be that pre-diagnostic factors predict which women will experience adjustment difficulties after treatment for cancer (Stanton and Gallant, 1995). However, it is important that individual needs are addressed and for that effective medical communication is essential.

LACK OF CURRENT RESEARCH

Despite the psychological impact of gynaecological cancer, and the increasing number of survivors, there has been relatively little research interest. A recent survey of literature demonstrates that women with breast cancer are the major focus of much psychological research (Stanton and Gallant, 1995). Breast cancer incidence is high, accounting for 25 percent of cancer incidence in the U.K., with a five-year survival rate of 62 percent. It has been suggested that it is these high incidence and survival rates that attract research attention because there are many breast cancer survivors available for research participation (Meyerowitz and Hart in Stanton and Gallant, 1995). This does not explain, however, the current paucity of gynaecological cancer research. Although gynaecological cancer incidence is marginally lower than breast cancer, survival rates for gynaecological cancers are higher (with a survival rate of 70 percent for uterine cancer).

The early detection of breast cancer contributes to good survival. There are specific preventive measures that assist in early breast cancer detection. The success of breast self-examination (BSE) has been illustrated, with more than 90 percent of breast cancers being found by women themselves (McPherson and Waller, 1997). This introduces specific differences in psychological reactions between breast and gynaecological cancers. With BSE, a woman identifies and consequently reports a breast lump to a medical professional. In this way, she has already identified herself as potentially 'ill' and may be prepared for 'becoming sick' prior to cancer diagnosis. Alternatively, a woman presenting for routine cervical screening may feel 'healthy' prior to testing and be attending screening to 'receive reassurance that [she does] not have cancer' (McKie, 1993 in Rafferty and Williams, 1996). If cervical screening reveals an abnormality, expectations are confounded and women are unprepared for the 'sick role'. This is a good illustration of the potential difficulties between the 'healthy' and 'ill' continuum; it is possible for a woman to feel 'healthy' despite a diagnosis of serious 'illness'. The woman may not recall any pre-diagnostic symptomatology, and consequently develop a distrust of her own ability to interpret her bodily symptoms. This is problematic if the medical professional attempts to educate the woman in the identification of symptomatology indicative of recurrent illness. Instead, the woman may feel she needs to rely on the medical profession and the technological 'fix' for assurance of 'wellness' and absence of recurrence.

PSYCHOSEXUAL RESEARCH

Despite the lack of research into gynaecological cancer, there has been a focus on the psychosexual recovery of women after gynaecological cancer treatment. The reported prevalence of sexual difficulties after treatment for gynaecological cancer ranges from 30 percent to 90 percent with the extent of difficulty thought to be associated with disease site and treatment type (Auchinsloss, 1995). Radical treatments such as vulvectomy and pelvic exenteration are thought, unsurprisingly, to be particularly predictive of sexual difficulties (Ott and Levy in Adesso et al., 1994). Indeed many sexual 'difficulties' may be organic in origin, but perpetuated by psychological responses. If pain is experienced during the first attempts at sex after treatment, there may be difficulties in relaxing and eliminating pain anticipation upon future attempts (Auchinsloss, 1995). It has been suggested that after hysterectomy some women have difficulty adjusting to the loss of what they perceive to be the source of their 'femaleness' (Polivy, 1974, in Ott and Levy, 1994). It may be necessary for women to adjust to a new sexual identity after treatment for gynaecological cancer, with a consequent change in sexual needs and desire. Women treated for gynaecological cancer may 'struggle with what the cancer treatment has meant to them as women in an effort to regain a vision of themselves as complete, feminine, worthy, vital, responsive sexual partners' (Auchinsloss, 1995).

It should not be assumed, however, that sexual difficulties are universal for women with gynaecological cancer. The definition of sexual 'difficulties' is problematic as 'by defining a particular phenomenon as dysfunctional, or as sign of illness, we are implicity stating what we see as the normal boundaries of sexuality' (Ussher, 1996). For this reason, it is appropriate to treat only those 'difficulties' that are defined as such by women themselves. It may be that it is these definition difficulties which account for inconsistencies between the reporting of sexual 'problems' after gynaecological procedures. For example, although the procedure of hysterectomy has been widely connected with a high incidence of sexual problems, other research has shown no detrimental effect on women's sexuality (Gath et al., 1982 in McPherson and Waller, 1997).

In particular, we need to guard against assumptions such as that resumption of sexual activity is indicative of full recovery from gynaecological cancer. Psychosexual recovery can only be investigated directly with the woman concerned. Again, effective medical communication is vital. For those women who do identify psychosexual difficulties, counseling is a possibility. Behavioral sex therapy techniques have been suggested for the treatment of sexual difficulties after gynaecological treatment (Anderson, 1985 in Adesso, et al., 1994). However, it may be that heightened anxiety levels during gynaecological cancer recovery exacerbate sexual difficulties. Derogatis (1980) found 'patients with sexual difficulties reported higher levels of anxiety, depression and general symptomatic distress'. By focussing on all aspects of the process of recovery from cancer, and enabling effective medical communication, both psychological and medical needs will be addressed. This will require the teaching of counseling skills to health care workers involved in cancer care (Hunter, 1994).

SUMMARY

Gynaecological cancer is an illness that warrants further psychological research. In furthering our understanding about the processes involved it may be possible to develop individual interventions to help women cope with diagnosis, treatment and recovery from cancer (Rieger et al., 1998). Clinically, it is important that women are successfully supported in their understanding of those symptoms that may indicate recurrent disease.

REFERENCES

Adesso, V.J., Reddy, D.M. and Fleming, R. (1994) *Psychological perspectives on women's health.* London: Taylor & Francis

Anderson, B. (1995) Quality of life for women with gynaecological cancer. *Obstetrics and Gynaecology*, 7, 69–71

Auchinsloss, S.S. (1995) After Treatment: Psychosocial Issues in Gynaecological Cancer Survivorship. *Cancer*, 15, Nov., 76 (10), 2117–2124

Glynne Jones, H., Thomas, S., Chait, I. and Marks, D. (1997) The acceptability of planned discharge from follow-up. *Psycho-oncology*, 6, 190–196

Glynne Jones, H., Chait, I. and Marks, D. (1998) A pilot study exploring the effect of discharging cancer survivors from hospital follow-up on the work load of general practitioners. *British Journal of General Practice*, 48, 1241–1248

Hadjistavropoulos, H., Craig, K.D. and Hadjistavropoulos, T. (1998) Cognitive and behavioural responses to illness information: the role of health anxiety. *Behaviour Research and Therapy*, 36, 149–164

Helgeson, V. and Cohen, S. (1996) Social support and adjustment to cancer: reconciling descriptive, correlational and intervention research. *Health Psychology*, 13 (2), 135–148

Hunter, M. (1994) *Counselling in Obstetrics and Gynaecology.* Leicester: BPS Books

Kelly, B., Smithers, M., Swanson, C., McLeod, R., Thomson, D. and Walpole, E. (1995) Psychological responses to malignant melanoma: an investigation of traumatic stress reactions to life threatening illness. *General Hospital Psychiatry*, 17, 126–134

Lampic, C., Wennberg, A., Schill, J.E., Brodin, O., Glimelius, B. and Sjoden, P. (1994) Anxiety and cancer related worry of cancer patients at routine follow up visits. *Acta Oncologica*, 33 (2), 119–125

McPherson, A. and Waller, D. (1997) *Women's Health.* Oxford: Oxford Medical Publications.

Miller, S.M. (1995) Monitoring versus blunting styles of coping with cancer influence the information patients want and need about their disease: implications for cancer screening and management. *Cancer*, 16 July, 76 (2), 167–177

Ott, P.J. and Levy, S.M. (1994) In Adesso, V.J., Reddy, D.M. and Fleming, R. *Psychological Perspectives on Women's Health*, (Chapter 5). London: Taylor & Francis

Pistrang, N. and Winchurst (1997) Gynaecological cancer patients' attitudes towards psychological services. *Psychology, Health and Medicine*, 2 (2), 135–147

Pitts, M. (1996) *The Psychology of Preventive Health.* London: Routledge

Pitts, M. and Phillips, K. (1998) (2nd edn.) *The Psychology of Health.* London: Routledge

Rafferty, P. and Williams, S. (1996) Psychological aspects of gynaecological procedures. In C.A. Niven and A. Walker (Eds.) *Reproductive potential and fertility control.* Oxford: Butterworth-Heinemann Ltd

Rieger, E., Touyz, S.W. and Wain, G.V. (1998) The Role of the Clinical Psychologist in Gynecological Cancer. *Journal of Psychosomatic Research*, 45 (3), 201–214

Sheeran, P. and Abraham, C. (1996) The Health Belief Model. In M. Conner and P. Norman (Eds.) *Predicting Health Behaviour.* Buckingham: Open University Press.

Shumsky, A.G., Stuart, G.C.E., Brasher, P.M., Nation, J. *et al.* (1994) An evaluation of routine follow up of patients treated for endometrial carcinoma. *Gynaecologic Oncology*, 35, 229–233

Stanton and Gallant (1995) *The Psychology of Women's Health: Progress and Challenges in Research and Application.* London: American Psychologist Association

Ussher, J. (1996). Female sexuality and reproduction. In C.A. Niven and A. Walker (Eds.) *Reproductive Potential and Fertility Control.* Oxford: Butterworth-Heinemann

Van Nagell, J.R., Rayburn. W., Donaldson, F.S., Hanson, M., Guy, E.C., Yoneda, J., Marayuma, Y. and Powell, D.F. (1979) Therapeutic implications of patterns of recurrence in cancer of the uterine cervix. *Cancer*, 44, 2354–2361

Woodman, C., Baghdady, A., Collins, S. and Clyme, J.A. (1997) What changes in the organisation of cancer services will improve the outcome for women with ovarian cancer. *British Journal of Obstetrics and Gynaecology*, 104, 135–139

CHAPTER 22

CERVICAL SCREENING

Julie Fish and Sue Wilkinson

INTRODUCTION

Worldwide, cervical cancer is the eighth commonest cancer in women and in the U.K., where around 4000 women a year develop the disease (Szarewski, 1994; see Pitts and Bradley, in this volume) – a national screening program is in operation. Cervical cancer is unusual among cancers in that it has a 'warning' stage, in which abnormal, pre-cancerous cells are present for several years before cancer develops: this makes it a good candidate for screening, the aim of which is early detection of pre-cancerous cells. The screening procedure (also known as the 'smear test' or 'pap test') involves microscopic examination of a sample of cells from the cervix, in order to check for abnormalities. In order to obtain the sample, the vagina is held open using a speculum, and a spatula is passed across the surface of the cervix to remove loose cells – a procedure which many women find invasive, uncomfortable, painful or frightening (Szarewski, 1994). Difficulties often arise in interpreting the smear (Chomet and Chomet, 1989), and frequently reported errors include 'false positives' (i.e. reported abnormalities, which on rechecking do not exist) and the more common – and potentially fatal – 'false negatives' (i.e. failure to detect existing abnormalities). The 1997 screening 'scandal' in the Kent and Canterbury Health Authority in which 80,000 smears were re-screened (Wells, 1997) involved the reporting of 2194 'false negatives' over a five-year period.

The causes of cervical cancer are not known; nor is it clear how the disease is contracted (Singleton and Michael, 1993). However, cervical cancer does appear to be associated with sexual activity – and the biggest risk factor for women seems to be having penetrative sex with men. Genital wart virus (strongly linked to cervical cancer) can be passed on through semen; sperm bonding to cervical cells can interfere with their function; and smegma (the substance which collects under the foreskin of an uncircumcized penis) has also been implicated in the development of cervical cancer (Szarewski, 1994). It has long been reported that nuns (i.e. women assumed not to have had sex with men) have lower rates of cervical cancer (Cancer Research Campaign, 1990; Coney, 1995; Hulka, 1982; Walsh, 1995), and lesbians (equated with nuns and/or virgins) have also typically been assumed to be at lower risk than heterosexual women (Bailey, 1996; Dunker, 1994; Haas, 1994; Harvey *et al.*, 1988; Rosser, 1993; Simkin,

1993). But lesbians are not a unitary group (i.e. some will previously have had sex with men and some will continue to do so (Rankow and Tessaro, 1998)), and any woman who has had sex with men is potentially at risk. In addition, any woman (lesbian or heterosexual) may be subject to the other suggested risk factors for cervical cancer, e.g. smoking, childbirth, exposure to DES, and the possible hazards of a dirty workplace (Chomet and Chomet, 1989; Hulka, 1982).

Approximately 17 percent of women (in the U.K.) do not attend for screening and it is a government priority to investigate the reasons for non-attendance (Department of Health, 1993: 65). There have been a number of studies of the reasons (presumed) heterosexual women give for not attending for cervical smears, with the intention of increasing their participation (e.g. Beardow, Oerton and Victor, 1989; Burak and Meyer, 1997; Elkind et al., 1989; Majeed, Cook and Anderson, 1994). Among these reasons are: imputed personal characteristics (Harvey et al., 1988; McKie, 1993; Singleton, 1995; Naish et al., 1994; Lee, 1988); lack of knowledge (Schwarz et al., 1990); inconvenient clinic times (Edwards and McKie, 1995); lack of symptoms (Gregory and McKie); failure to prioritize own health (Saffron, 1997); and 'invalid beliefs' about the need for smears (Elkind et al., 1989; Gillam, 1991). Working class women are said to be least likely to attend for screening (Bowling and Jacobson, 1989).

LESBIANS AND CERVICAL SCREENING

Lesbians' non-attendance for cervical smears has largely been ignored. One study which compared the screening attendance of lesbians, bisexuals and heterosexuals found that lesbians were only a third as likely as heterosexual women to be told they were at risk for cervical cancer (Price et al., 1996); other studies have found that lesbians are explicitly told by health care workers that they do not need smear tests (Das and Farquhar, 1996; Rankow, 1995).

We are conducting a U.K. national survey of lesbian health care – partly modeled on the U.S. national survey of lesbian health care (e.g. Bradford and Ryan, 1988) – which includes questions about lesbians' perceptions and experiences of cervical screening. The survey entails a multidimensional sampling strategy, in order to achieve a socially and geographically diverse sample. Approximately 3600 questionnaires have been distributed through lesbian and gay social and political groups, women's health organizations, cancer organizations, a trade union for health workers, alternative bookshops and women's centers, and lesbian and gay events. To date 1065 of these – representing 116 of the 122 postal districts in the U.K. – have been returned: i.e. a response rate of approximately 30 percent (broadly comparable with other surveys of lesbian communities: Morris and Rothblum, in press). This is the largest sample of a single study conducted among lesbians in the U.K. to date.

The survey asks respondents whether they currently have cervical smears on a regular basis, and/or whether they have ever had them in the past. In addition, lesbians who have never attended for a smear are asked to explain why this is. Over half of the total sample (54 percent; n=573) say they currently have smear tests on a regular basis; 31 percent (n=327) report having had at least one smear test in the past; and 15 percent (n=165) report never having had a smear test. Excluding the 37 women who are too young to be called for screening (i.e. under 20), this represents 12 percent (n=128) of those lesbians eligible for a smear test who say they have never attended for screening. This compares with a non-attendance rate of 5 percent (of those eligible for screening) in the U.S. survey (Bradford and Ryan, 1998).

In our survey, excluding the 20 percent of women (n=25, of 128) who raised issues of time management (e.g. *'I'm hopelessly disorganized!'* – P291;[1] *'horribly busy'* – P562; *'too busy'* – P643), lesbians' explanations of why they have never attended for a smear test fell into two broad categories: 'Because I don't need one'; and 'Because of negative aspects of the procedure'.

Because I don't need one

The most frequent explanation given by lesbians for never having had a smear test was some variant of 'Because I don't need one': 40 percent (n=51, of 128) of the explanations given were classified under this category. Most frequently, lesbians mentioned not having sex with men as (self-evidently) the reason for not needing a smear test, e.g. *'I have never had sexual contact with a man'; 'Because I've never had sex with a man'; 'I have not had Intercorse [sic] with a Man'; 'never been penetrated by a man'; 'Have never had heterosexual penetrative sex'; 'I've never had sex with a man'; 'Never slept with men'; 'I've not had sexual intercourse with a man'.*

Underlying these responses is an implicit theory of a link between penetrative heterosex and cervical cancer – a link which is sometimes spelled out, as in the following response:

I do believe that lesbians are at low risk because it is via heterosexual contact that infections/ abnormalities of cells occur i.e. unprotected sex also bacteria from a man's penis has been shown to be a proven factor in the development of cervical cancer.

Occasionally, explicit comparisons were made between lesbians' and heterosexual women's risk of cervical cancer. For example, one woman said: *'I think I don't need one (as much as het. women) because I'm a lesbian who has never had penetrative sex with men';* while another commented *'sexually active heterosexual women are at greater risk at least, those who engage in unprotected penetrative heterosexual sex'.*

It was very common for lesbians to report that they had received unequivocal advice from health professionals that they did not need a smear, e.g.

1.This data tag indicates that the quotation is from participant number 291's response; participants were numbered sequentially in the order their survey responses were received.

'*the doctor has decided I do not require one as I am a lesbian and have never had a sexual relationship with a man*'; '*I didn't think I needed one because my doctor said I didn't*'; '*the nurse informed me that it was virtually unheard of for a lesbian to get cervical cancer*'; '*the nurse said as I was a lesbian I didn't need one*'; '*My doctor took me off the computer as she felt I was not at risk*'; '*My doctor seems to think that lesbians don't need a test*'. Two women reported – adding exclamation points – that their doctors apparently equated lesbianism with virginity: '*The GP said I was technically a virgin (!)*'; '*According to the heterosexist way they classify things I'm technically classed as a virgin!*'.

In the few cases where women reported discussions about risk with medical professionals, they generally indicated agreement with, and/or acceptance of, the advice not to have a smear, e.g. '*Having discussed this extensively with my GP, we agreed that I would probably find the procedure far more traumatic than the risk warrants*'. Only occasionally did women report any disagreement or uncertainty among health professionals about the need for lesbians to have smear tests, as in the following responses: '*When I talked to the doctor about smear tests, she was very unsure about whether I needed one being a lesbian*'; '*My doctor said I had to have one – then the female nurse said as I hadn't had sex with men I didn't need one*'.

In sum, then, many lesbians who had never had a smear test said that this was because they did not need one, never having had penetrative sex with men. They also attributed this view, overwhelmingly, to their health advisors.

Because of negative aspects of the procedure

Explanations of never having had a smear test were also frequently couched in terms of negative aspects of the procedure itself: some 38 percent (n=49, of 128) of the responses were classified under this category. Lesbians invoked their own previous health care experiences, the 'horror stories' of partners and friends, and 'general hearsay' in presenting a picture of cervical screening as something to be avoided.

Many women expressed worry about, or fear of, the procedure, without specifying what exactly they were worried about, or frightened of: these responses ranged from '*slightly apprehensive*' and '*do not relish the thought*' (P762); through '*scared*' and '*terrified*'; to saying the procedure '*freaks me out*' or '*scares me to death*'. However, a few women referred to past experiences of rape or child abuse to explain their anxieties or fears.

Of those who did specify negative aspects of the procedure, one of the most common expectations was that it would hurt or be painful, e.g. '*PAIN!!!*'; '*too painful*'; '*I'd rather face something a little less painful*'; '*I've heard about other people's bad and painful experiences!*'. Equally common was the expectation that the procedure would be embarrassing or humiliating, e.g. '*no chance I am going to put myself in an embarrassing situation*'; '*Embarassed to go and get one done*'; '*I've always been too embarrassed*'; '*I would feel very embarrassed*'. A few women indicated that they anticipated experiencing both pain and embarrassment, e.g. '*I'm scared it will hurt and be embarrassing*'; '*I *just panic at the thought of a huge metal croccodile being inserted into my vagina in public'.*

Other concerns expressed centered around the perceived invasiveness or intrusiveness of the procedure. One woman said:

I find the thought of some strange doctor inserting a piece of cold steel (referred to my friends as 'the apple corer') into my most private areas repulsive. A procedure I would rather avoid myself.

Others spoke of *'invasion of privacy'* and *'the intrusion or stress of the test'* (P764); saying *'the procedure is very invasive'*, or more specifically, *'I don't want to be tampered with'* and *'I don't want a man poking around in my body'*. Finally, a few of the women raised anxieties related to expectations of heterosexism in medical encounters. One said: *'I was worried that my sexuality would be questioned ... coupled with feeling uneasy about their response to lesbianism'*, while another reported: *'I'm worried about all the questions that they are going to ask, concerning hetro-sex [sic] – which I've never had'*. Occasionally the attitudes of particular medical professionals are elaborated, e.g. *'my doctor is very religious + doesn't believe in sex before marriage, never mind lesbianism'*.

In sum, then, many lesbians who had never had a smear test said that this was because they were anxious or afraid of the procedure. The negative aspects of the procedure most frequently mentioned were anticipated pain, embarrassment, and intrusiveness. Heterosexism in the health profession was also a concern.

SUMMARY

Our survey findings suggest that slightly fewer lesbians attend for cervical screening than do women in general; and indicate that lesbian non-attendees typically explain this with reference to 'not needing' a smear, and/or to seeing the procedure itself as likely to be unpleasant. We suggest that future health education campaigns could usefully address these perceptions and fears – indeed, should do so, if they are targeted specifically at lesbians; we also suggest that medical professionals need to be more aware of the particular needs of their lesbian clients.

More generally, we would wish to raise both pragmatic and logistic concerns about the efficacy and value of the (U.K.) national cervical screening program. Pragmatically, it appears that women in particular social groups are not being reached (cf also Bowling and Jacobson, 1989; Naish *et al.*, 1994); that program management is generally poor (Ross, 1989); and that errors are rife (Wells, 1997). Further questions arise both about the value of this particular program – especially as, thirty years after its inception, there has apparently been no reduction in the overall incidence of invasive cervical cancer (Austoker, 1994); and about the practice of mass screening in general as an effective way of promoting and maintaining health.

NOTE

This chapter is based on the Ph.D. conducted by Julie Fish. Her Ph.D. supervisor was Sue Wilkinson, co-author of the chapter.

REFERENCES

Austoker, J. (1994) Screening for cervical cancer. *British Medical Journal*, 309: 241–248

Bailey, J. (1996) Screening for cervical cancer: do lesbians need smear tests? *Women And Health Newsletter*: 'Lesbian Health' June. Available from: 52, Featherstone St., London EC1Y 8RT

Beardow, R., Oerton, J. and Victor, C. (1989) Evaluation of the cervical cytology screening programme in an inner city health district. *British Medical Journal*, 299, 98–100

Bowling, A. and Jacobson, B. (1989) Screening: the inadequacy of population registers. *British Medical Journal*, 298: 545–546

Bradford, J. and Ryan, C. (1988) *The National Lesbian Health Care Survey*. Washington D.C.: National Gay and Lesbian Health Foundation

Burak, L. and Meyer, M. (1997) Using the health belief model to examine and predict college women's cervical cancer screening beliefs and behavior. *Health Care for Women International*, 18 (3): 251–262

Cancer Research Campaign Factsheet (1990) *Cancer of the Cervix Uteri*. Factsheet 12

Chomet, J. and Chomet, J. (1989) *Smear Tests: Cervical Cancer its Prevention and Treatment*. London: Thorsons

Coney, S. (1995) *The Menopause Industry*. London: The Women's Press

Das, R. and Farqhuar, C. (1996) Lesbians conceptualisations of health and well-being. Paper presented to Teaching to Promote Women's Health Conference (June) Women's College Hospital,University of Toronto, Canada

DoH (1993) *Health of the Nation One Year On*. Department of Health (November)

Dunker, P. (1996) The Blue Book. In P. Dunker, and V. Wilson. (Eds.) *Cancer Through the Eyes of Ten Women*. London: Pandora

Edwards, J. and McKie, L. (1995) The potential for feminist political practice to empower the unrepresented consumer: the case of cervical screening services. *Journal of Consumer Policy*, 18, 135–156

Elkind, A., Eardley, A., Haran, D., Spencer, B. and Smith, A. (1989) Computer managed call and recall for cervical screening: a typology of reasons for non-attendance. *Community Medicine*, 11 (2), 157–162

Gillam, S. (1991) Understanding the uptake of cervical cancer screening: the contribution of the health belief model. *British Journal of General Practice*, 41, 510–513

Gregory, S. and McKie, L. (1992) Researching cervical cancer: compromises, practices and beliefs. *Journal of Advances in Health and Nursing Care*, 2 (1), 73–84

Haas, A. (1994) Lesbian health issues: an overview. In A. Dan (Ed.) *Reframing Women's Health*. Thousand Oaks, CA: Sage Publications

Harvey, J., Mack, S. and Woolfson, J. (1988) *Cervical Cancer and How to stop Worrying About It*. London: Faber & Faber

Hulka, B. (1982) Risk factors for cervical cancer. *Journal of Chronic Diseases*, 35, 3–11

Lee, L. (1998) Women – don't fear the smear. *Guardian*, 31 March

Majeed, F., Cook, D., Anderson, H., Hilton, S., Bunn, S. and Stones, C. (1994) Using patient and general practice characteristics to explain variations in cervical smear uptake rates. *British Medical Journal*, 308, 1272–1276

McKie, L. (1993) Women's views of the cervical smear test: implications for nursing practice – women who have not had a smear test. *Journal of Advanced Nursing*, 18, 972–979

Morris, J. and Rothblum, E. (in press) Who fills out a lesbian questionnaire? the interrelationship of sexual orientation, sexual experience with women and participation in the lesbian community. *Psychology of Women Quarterly*

Nathoo, V. (1988) Investigation of non-responders at a cervical screening clinic in Manchester. *British Medical Journal*, 296, 1041–1042

Naish, J., Brown, J. and Denton, B. (1994) Intercultural consultations: investigation of factors that deter non-English speaking women from attending their general practitioners for cervical screening. *British Medical Journal*, 309, 1126–1128

Price, J., Easton, A., Telljohan, S. and Wallace, P. (1996) Perceptions of cervical cancer and pap smear screening behavior by women's sexual orientation. *Journal of Community Health*, 21

(2), 89–105

Rankow, E. (1995) Lesbian health issues for the primary care provider. *Journal of Family Practice*, 40 (5), 486–496

Rankow, E. and Tessaro, I. (1998) Cervical cancer risk and papanicolaou screening in a sample of lesbian and bisexual women. *Journal of Family Practice*, 47 (2), 139–143

Ross, S. (1989) Cervical cytology and government policy. *British Medical Journal*, 299, 101–103

Rosser, S. (1993) Ignored, overlooked or subsumed: research on lesbian health and health care. *NWSA Journal*, 5 (2), 183–203

Saffron, L. (1987) Cervical Cancer: The politics of prevention. In S. O'Sullivan (Ed.) *Women's Health: A Spare Rib Reader*. London: Pandora

Schwarz, M., Savage, W., George, J. and Emohare, L. (1990) Women's knowledge and experience of cervical screening: a failure of health education and medical organization. *Community Medicine*, 11 (4), 279–289

Simkin, R. (1993) Unique health care concerns of lesbians. *Canadian Journal of Ob/Gyn and Women's Health Care*, 5, 516–522

Singleton, V. and Michael, M. (1993) Actor-networks and ambivalence: general practitioners in the U.K. cervical screening programme. *Social Studies of Science*, 23, 227–264

Singleton, V. (1995) Networking constructions of gender and constructing gender networks: considering definitions of woman in the British cervical screening programme. In K. Grint, and R. Gill (Eds.) *The Gender Technology Relation Contemporary Theory and Research*. London: Taylor & Francis

Szarewski, A. (1994) *A Woman's Guide to the Cervical Smear Test*. London: Optima

Walsh, C., Kay, E. and Leader, M. (1995) The pathology of cervical cancer. *Clinical Obstetrics and Gynaecology*, 38 (3), 653–661

Wells, W. (1997) Review of Cervical Screening Services at Kent and Canterbury Hospitals NHS Trust, NHS Executive South Thames. Report available from Department of Health, 40 Eastbourne Terrace, London W2 3QR

CHAPTER 23

BREAST CANCER: A FEMINIST PERSPECTIVE

Sue Wilkinson

INTRODUCTION

Breast cancer is the most common cancer among women, with highest incidence in the industrialized West: one woman in eight in the U.S.A., and one in 12 in the U.K., will develop breast cancer at some point in her life. It is the leading cause of death for middle-aged women in both countries, and second only to cardiovascular disease for older women (Royak-Schaler, 1994; see Pitts and Bradley, in this volume).

Despite the publicity surrounding 'the breast cancer genes' (BRCA1 and BRCA2), only 5 to 10 percent of breast cancers have an identifiable genetic component (Love, 1995). Age is the most important risk factor: fewer than a third of breast cancers occur in pre-menopausal women, and risk increases steadily with age (Royak-Schaler, 1994). Other risk factors relate to reproductive history (not having children; a 'late' first pregnancy; and a greater than average number of menstrual cycles); 'lifestyle' factors (e.g. high-fat diet, being overweight, excessive drinking); and the presence of environmental carcinogens (Rosenthal, 1997). Recent reports suggesting that lesbians have a three times higher risk of breast cancer than hetero-sexual women are not well founded (c.f. Yadlon, 1997): they are based pri-marily on a 10-year-old U.S.A. survey of lesbian health, and lesbians' risk of breast cancer is extrapolated from the finding that lesbians are less like-ly to have children, and more likely to be overweight and to abuse alco-hol.

Breast cancer has been central to feminist campaigns around women's health and in the rest of this chapter I draw on my own research, as well as other published work within the field, to explore women's experience of breast cancer and the political activism it has generated.

THE EXPERIENCE OF BREAST CANCER

Eighty-one women with breast cancer have talked with me, and with each other, in focus group discussions about their feelings on diagnosis, their relationships, their experiences of treatment, and the changes cancer had created in their lives (Wilkinson 1998a, b, 1999; Wilkinson and Kitzinger, 1999; see Pistrang, in this volume). Their experiences differ widely. The 'meaning' of breast cancer for each woman depends on its context in her life as a whole.

Diagnosis

The diagnosis of breast cancer was described by one participant as *'every woman's nightmare'*: other women said they were *'devastated'*, *'gutted'*, or *'poleaxed'* by the news. Many described feelings of fear (*'terrified'*, *'panic stricken'*, *'fear stricken'*, *'frightened'*, *'paralysed in me head with fear'*), some-times accompanied by physical reactions: such as crying, shaking uncon-trollably, or collapsing. Some women recalled their feelings of shock and disbelief (*'you don't believe it'*, *'I couldn't believe that it could happen to me'*, *'you don't think it's ever going to happen to you, and when it does you just can't believe it'*). Others described an inability to take in the information or to react to it (*'it didn't register properly'*, *'I was in a stupor and I never spoke'*, *'I just went numb'*). Feelings of detachment were common: one woman said, *'when I was told, it was someone else – it was a long while before I realised it was me'*; others described being *'on another planet'* or *'in a different world'*.

Relationships

Women often worried about other people's reactions and sometimes with-held the news of their diagnosis from aged parents, young children, or rel-atives abroad. Telling others was carefully 'managed': they waited until children had finished examinations, or sick colleagues had returned to work. *'I really did deliberately play it down'* said one woman (talking about her son), *'I thought he's far away – it would worry him sick'*. In order to protect others – especially family members – perceived as vulnerable, women may also hide or minimize their own pain, distress and anxiety: *'I daren't say too much to me husband and family for fear of distressing them'*; *'you don't want to put your worries on them do you, all the time?'*; *'you end up being strong for your friends, your family, because they don't know how to handle it'*. Expressing the views of many others, one participant commented: *'We become very good at behaving ourselves, especially as women – we're very good at hiding what we feel and just putting on a brave face for everybody else'*.

As with cancer generally (Sontag, 1979), breast cancer patients may find that people seem to avoid and fear them (almost three-quarters of Peters-Golden's (1982) respondents reported this experience). *'My neighbours seem to think I'm a leper'*, one of my research participants said, *'there's one lady in particular and she always crosses the road ... as though if she touches me she's going to get something'*. Another told how her sister (also diagnosed with breast cancer) returning unexpectedly to a friend's house, found the friend *'cleaning the cushion of the settee that she'd been sitting on ... as if she thought she could catch the cancer'*. Women are often aware of silences around cancer: people around them *'are embarrassed'*, *'don't know what to say'*, or *'just don't want to know'*:

I've found people at my work don't mention it at all ... nobody's ever approached the subject in a direct way, nobody's ever asked what my experience of it was, or what happened to me, or how I felt about it.

They also refer, usually disparagingly, to other people's use of euphemisms like *'the big C'*.

While many women spoke of colleagues, friends and family members who *'didn't want to know'*, *'just couldn't handle it'*, or *'couldn't accept it'*, others characterized the support they had received – from various sources – as *'brilliant'*: *'I had marvellous support from my husband'*; *'I've no family but my friends were absolutely wonderful'*; *'I could paper me walls with get well cards'*. A number spoke highly of the local breast care nurse and of the value of talking to other women with breast cancer: *'it's not the sympathy you want, I don't think ... it's the reassurance ... you all know because you've been there and you've had the fear'*. However, not infrequently others' attempts to offer support were experienced as excessive: women said of their partners, *'there was a sort of startling protectiveness'* or *'my husband won't let me out of his sight'*; while work colleagues were described as *'a bit suffocating at times'* or as having to be reminded *'I'm not an invalid'*. Women also disliked being called *'brave'*, or *'positive'*, feeling that this minimized their fear and pain (*'they don't know what you've gone through'*) and made it difficult for them ever to break down.

Treatment

Most of my research participants had undergone surgery for their breast cancer (35 percent lumpectomy; 63 percent mastectomy), typically backed up by radiotherapy, plus (for 64 percent) a course of tamoxifen – a synthetic anti-oestrogen drug. A further 21 percent had taken tamoxifen alone. Relatively few had been prescribed chemotherapy, or had chosen 'alternative' treatments. Women exchanged experiences of treatments and symptoms: the awfulness of not being able to wash for several weeks once 'marked up' for radiotherapy (*'the smell was horrid'*; *'I felt I ponged from here to here'*); the radiotherapy burns and skin irritation (*'bright red, I was like a tomato'*; *'as if I was on fire. … I was sort of burning'*); and the weight gain, night sweats and vaginal itching produced by tamoxifen (*'it was really driving me crazy'*; *'all inside was really raw'*).

However, they focussed most extensively on their feelings about surgery, and its consequences for their physical appearance. The psychosocial and popular literatures alike (e.g. Maguire, 1982; Kahane, 1995) suggest that a woman who has lost a breast is 'less a woman', and – like Kasper's (1995) interviewees – my research participants often spoke as if this were so: *'you're not sort of normal any more … only half a woman'*; *'I just felt like all my womanhood was being taken away and I wasn't going to be a she any more, I was going to be an it'*. They commonly expressed fears that without breasts, or with less than perfect breasts, they would be unattractive to, or rejected by, men: *'I'm very aware that there are marriages that break down under the stress … and what your body looks like'*; *'part of it was to do with me husband, I didn't know whether he was going to reject me'*; *'I was single and I thought, "Oh well, nobody's ever going to be interested in me"'*; *'nobody would want anybody who'd had their breast removed'*. Some women sought reassurances from the men around them that they were still attractive and desirable; one woman embarked upon a new love affair within days of surgery.

Of the 50 women who had had mastectomies, 48 wore (or had worn) a prosthesis – eight of these women had gone on to have breast 'reconstruction' (i.e. silicon implants). Women reported, or were attributed, as having reconstructions 'for' their husbands (even when they themselves would have preferred not to undergo further surgery). There was much swapping of information about the varieties – and general management – of prostheses: *'you can be fitted with an adhesive one'*; *'you can get stick on nipples to match your nipple'*; *'never forget your safety pins'*; *'you've got to be careful not to stick a pin in'*; *'I've got a puncture repair kit on it now'*; *'put a sponge in your swimsuit'*; *'you'll swim to one side'*. In one particularly boisterous focus group, a prosthesis was removed and passed from hand to hand; the participants from another group reconvened in the ladies' lavatory to compare prostheses.

Meyerowitz *et al* (1988) has argued that dying is more of a concern for women with breast cancer than is their appearance – and sometimes my participants suggested this too. However, statements such as *'your life's more important than a boob, isn't it?'* were relatively rare; more often women appeared to be engaged in juggling concerns about appearance and mortality, prioritizing one or the other at different times, for different reasons, and in response to others around them.

Life changes

It was common for women to claim that the experience of breast cancer had completely changed their outlook on life: heightened awareness of mortality and uncertainty about the future made them *'appreciate life'*, *'enjoy life'*, and *'live for the moment'*. One woman said:

I used to be a person who used to always look into the future. We'd got to save up for when we get older and we ought not to have a big holiday because really, you know, we might need the roof mending. I was that sort of person, but I'm not so much that now. I think to myself, 'Oh to heck with it, I might not be here next year'.

Many emphasized *'an urgency about life'*, a need to *'live life to the full'*, to *'do more with your life'*, and to *'do it today'*. One declared *'if you wanna do it, I think you've got to go for it'* – and they did: new experiences (since cancer) ranged from long-distance travel to scuba diving to flying an aeroplane. Others said *'my priorities in life have changed'* or *'I'm having to reassess what I want to do now'* – they decided to spend money, rather than save it; to take a job and become independent for the first time; or to exploit a new-found ability to leave housework undone. Several women described themselves as *'more selfish'*, saying *'You've got to think about yourself'*; *'I'm number one now'*; *'I feel I have a stronger responsibility to myself'*; *'I'm entitled to be able to do something for myself'*; and *'I want to do even more now of the things that I want to do'*.

Surprisingly few women dwelt on the lasting negative consequences of their breast cancer – most commonly mentioned was the worry that any ache or pain might signal a recurrence of the cancer. Others highlighted increased tiredness, loss of confidence, and social withdrawal.

Such experiences are documented further both in the huge popular literature on breast cancer – which includes autobiographies (e.g. Butler and Rosenblum, 1991; Lorde, 1980; Picardie, 1998; Seagrave, 1995; Wadler, 1992) and anthologies (e.g. Brady, 1991; Gross and Ito, 1991; Stocker, 1991, 1993; Ward, 1996) – and in the extensive psychosocial oncology literature (useful reviews include Meyerowitz, 1980; Meyerowitz *et al.*, 1988; Morris, 1983; Rosser, 1981 and Royak-Schaler, 1991).

THE POLITICS OF BREAST CANCER

Feminist work on breast cancer has not only made women's *own* experiences (rather than medical and psychiatric perspectives) central, but has also sought to locate these experiences within their broader social and political context. Additionally, feminist activists have campaigned for increased research funding and improved health care facilities; have set

up resource centers and support services; and have exposed commercial-
ly driven, and potentially harmful, procedures and practices in the detection and treatment of breast cancer.

Feminists (e.g. Spence, 1986; Kasper, 1995) have argued that the experience of breast cancer is profoundly shaped by the cultural emphasis on
breasts as objects of male sexual interest. They have decried the pervasive
sexualization of breasts and breast cancer both by medical professionals
and in the literature; and have deplored the associated – and largely unacknowledged – heterosexism (Wilkinson and Kitzinger, 1993). They have
spoken out against the pressure on women to 'look feminine' as quickly as
possible post-mastectomy (Meyerowitz, 1988), by being fitted immediately with prostheses, and encouraged to consider breast 'reconstruction'
(Lorde, 1980; Datan, 1989). Many feminists have objected to the dismissal
or trivialization of women's concerns: feminist psychologist Nancy Datan
(who has since died of breast cancer) suggested the implied identity for
which the breast cancer patient should strive is that of 'perpetual would-
be cheerleader', adding, with characteristic humour: 'I've never been a
cheerleader, and I couldn't see trying out for the part with falsies' (Datan,
quoted by Crawford, 1995: 168).

The feminist breast cancer movement started in the U.S.A. in the 1970s
with a few strong individuals who (like Nancy Datan) not only refused to
hide their breast cancer, but who spoke out against medical orthodoxies.
Rose Kushner (1975) was instrumental in changing surgical procedures
and Nancy Brinker (cited in Love, 1995) was an early pioneer in fund raising. Audre Lorde (1980) became visible as a black lesbian feminist with
breast cancer, passionately refusing a 'victim' identity, and speaking out
against environmental carcinogens. In the 1980s several grass-roots, community cancer projects were founded by feminist and lesbian activists,
including the Women's Cancer Resource Center in Berkeley (Jackie
Winnow), Breast Cancer Action in San Francisco (Eleanor Pred), the
Women's Community Cancer Project in Boston (Susan Shapiro), the
Mautner Project for Lesbians with Cancer in Washington, D.C. (Susan
Hester), and the Lesbian Community Cancer Project in Chicago. These
organizations campaigned for, and offered, better resources and services
for women with breast – and other – cancers, often appropriating success-
ful AIDS advocacy tactics for the breast cancer cause (Winnow, 1992).
There is a similar – although much smaller – movement in Canada.

Feminist journalists have offered some powerful exposés of the breast
cancer 'industry': highlighting the profiteering of drug companies and
cosmetic surgeons, and questioning the safety of tamoxifen trials and silicone implants, and the efficacy of mammography and genetic screening
programmes (Batt, 1994; Clorfene-Casten, 1996). Other feminist activists
continue to work (largely) *within* the medical profession and the political
establishment. Lesbian oncologist Susan Love – famously quoted for characterizing breast cancer treatments as 'slash, burn and poison' (Stabiner,
1997) – established a state-of-the-art treatment program at a leading (U.S.)
Medical-Surgical Oncology Center, and co-founded (with Susan Hester

and Amy Langer) the National Breast Cancer Coalition – an umbrella organization which co-ordinates the campaigning activities of several hundred (mainstream and radical) breast cancer groups (Love, 1995). The Coalition has achieved some spectacular successes, building a network of breast cancer advocates across the U.S.A., and obtaining a fivefold increase in federal funds for breast cancer research – including the diversion of funds from the U.S. Department of Defense (Kaufert, 1998).

Together, feminists have made the experience of breast cancer more visible; interrogated its social and cultural meanings; campaigned for – and provided – improved support and resources; and challenged the medical, scientific, and political establishments. It is an impressive record of activism – and one which, urgently, continues.

REFERENCES

Batt, S. (1994) *Patient No More: The Politics of Breast Cancer*. London: Scarlet Press

Brady, J. (Ed.) (1991) *1 in 3: Women With Cancer Confront an Epidemic*. Pittsburgh, PA: Cleis Press

Butler, S. and Rosenblum, B. (1991) *Cancer in Two Voices*. London: The Women's Press

Clorfene-Casten, L. (1996) *Breast Cancer: Poisons, Profits and Prevention*. Monroe, ME: Common Courage Press

Crawford, M. (1995) *Talking Difference: On Gender and Language*. London: Sage

Datan, N. (1989) Illness and imagery: Feminist cognition, socialization and gender identity. In M. Crawford and M. Gentry (Eds.) *Gender and Thought: Psychological Perspectives*. New York: Springer-Verlag

Gross, A. and Ito, D. (1991) *Women Talk About Breast Surgery: From Diagnosis to Recovery*. New York: HarperPerennial

Kahane, D.H. (1995) *No Less a Woman: Femininity, Sexuality and Breast Cancer* (2nd edn). Alameda, CA: Hunter House

Kasper, A.S. (1995) The social construction of breast loss and reconstruction. *Women's Health: Research on Gender, Behavior and Policy*, 1 (3), 197–219

Kaufert, P.A. (1998) Women, resistance and the breast cancer movement. In M. Lock and P.A. Kaufert (Eds.) *Pragmatic Women and Body Politics*. Cambridge: Cambridge University Press

Kushner, R. (1975) *Breast Cancer: A Personal History and Investigative Report*. New York: Harcourt Brace

Lorde, A. (1980) *The Cancer Journals*. London: Sheba Feminist Publishers

Love, S.M. with Lindsey, K. (1995) *Dr Susan Love's Breast Book* (2nd edn). Reading, MA: Addison-Wesley

Maguire, P. (1982) Psychiatric morbidity associated with mastectomy. *Experientia*, 41, 373–380

Meyerowitz, B.E. (1980) Psychosocial correlates of breast cancer and its treatment. *Psychological Bulletin*, 87 (1), 108–131

Meyerowitz, B.E., Chaiken, S. and Clark, L.A. (1988) Sex roles and culture: Social and personal reactions to breast cancer. In M. Fine and A. Asch (Eds.) *Women With Disabilities: Essays in Psychology, Culture and Politics*. Philadelphia, PA: Temple University Press

Morris, T. (1983) Psychosocial aspects of breast cancer. *European Journal of Cancer and Clinical Oncology*, 19 (12), 1725–1735

Peters-Golden, H. (1982) Breast cancer: Varied perceptions of social support in the illness experience. *Social Science and Medicine*, 16, 482–491

Picardie, R. (1998) *Before I Say Goodbye*. London: Penguin

Rosenthal, M.S. (1997) *The Breast Sourcebook*. Los Angeles, CA: Lowell House

Rosser, J.E. (1981) The interpretation of women's experience: A critical appraisal of the literature on breast cancer. *Social Science and Medicine*, 15E, 257–265

Royak-Schaler, R. (1991) Psychological processes in breast cancer: A review of selected research. *Journal of Psychosocial Oncology*, 9 (4), 71–89

Royak-Schaler, R. (1994) Health policy and breast cancer screening: The politics of research and intervention. In A.J. Dan (Ed.) *Reframing Women's Health: Multidisciplinary Research and*

Practice. Thousand Oaks, CA: Sage

Seagrave, E. (1995) *The Diary of a Breast.* London: Faber and Faber

Sontag, S. (1979) *Illness as Metaphor.* London: Allen Lane

Spence, J. (1986) *Putting Myself in the Picture: A Political, Personal and Photographic Autobiography.* London: Camden Press

Stabiner, K. (1997) *To Dance With the Devil: The New War on Breast Cancer,* New York: Delta

Stocker, M. (Ed.) (1991) *Cancer as a Women's Issue: Scratching the Surface.* Chicago: Third Side Press

Stocker, M. (Ed.) (1993) *Confronting Cancer, Constructing Change: New Perspectives on Women and Cancer,* Chicago: Third Side Press

Wadler, J. (1992) *My Breast: One Woman's Cancer Story.* London: The Women's Press

Ward, D. (1996) *One in Ten: Women Living With Breast Cancer.* St Leonards, NSW: Allen & Unwin

Wilkinson, S. (1998a) Focus groups in health research: Exploring the meanings of health and illness. *Journal of Health Psychology,* 3 (3), 329–348

Wilkinson, S. (1998b) Focus group methodology: A review. *International Journal of Social Research Methodology,* (3), 181–203

Wilkinson, S. (1999) Women talking causes: Content, biographical and discursive analyses. (Under submission)

Wilkinson, S. and Kitzinger, C. (1993) Whose breast is it anyway? A feminist consideration of advice and 'treatment' for breast cancer. *Women's Studies International Forum,* 16 (3), 229–238

Wilkinson, S. and Kitzinger, C. (1999) Thinking differently about thinking positive: A discursive approach to cancer patients' talk. (Under submission)

Winnow, J. (1992) Lesbians evolving health care: Cancer and AIDS. *Feminist Review,* 41, 68–76

Yadlon, S. (1997) Skinny women and good mothers: The rhetoric of risk, control and culpability in the production of knowledge about breast cancer. *Feminist Studies,* 23 (3), 645–677

CHAPTER 24

PARTNER SUPPORT FOR WOMEN WITH BREAST CANCER: A PROCESS ANALYSIS APPROACH

Nancy Pistrang

INTRODUCTION

Our relationships with other people can make a difference in how we adapt to serious illness. For example, cancer patients seem to adapt better – both psychologically and physically – when they have good 'social support' (for a review see Helgeson and Cohen, 1996; see Wilkinson, in this volume). Although there is now a large body of research pointing to the importance of social support in adaptation to illness, we know very little about what social support actually consists of. Precisely what happens in relationships with others that may help or hinder one's efforts to cope with an illness such as cancer?

This chapter presents some of my research on women who have been treated for breast cancer, focussing on the relationship between these women and their male partners. In particular, I will describe a new approach to studying social support and illustrate this with excerpts of a conversation between a breast cancer patient and her husband. My aim is both to demonstrate a methodological approach, as well as to provide some insight into how support is communicated (and sometimes fails to be communicated) within the partner relationship.

WHY STUDY THE PARTNER RELATIONSHIP?

The partner is one important source of emotional support for women coping with cancer (for a review see Manne, 1998). Studies of breast cancer indicate that women usually want to talk about their cancer-related concerns with their partner and often perceive poor communication with him as a problem (Lichtman *et al.*, 1987; Pistrang and Barker, 1992). In an interview study of 113 breast cancer patients (Pistrang and Barker, 1995), we found that satisfaction with the partner's 'informal helping' (that is, communication where one person is attempting to alleviate the emotional distress of another) was associated with women's psychological well-being. Furthermore, even though most women reported having good informal help from at least one other person, this did not compensate for problematic helping from the partner. Our data suggested that communication problems with the partner are a risk factor in women's psychological response to breast cancer.

A few studies have pointed to the kinds of communication problems that sometimes arise when one member of the couple has a serious illness. For example, partners may minimize or maximize the seriousness of the illness, or may refrain from talking about the illness altogether (Coyne *et al.*, 1990; Dakof and Taylor, 1990; Vess *et al.*, 1988). Because the partner has an emotional stake in the woman's recovery, he may find it too painful to talk about the seriousness of the illness. Furthermore, each member of the couple may want to protect the other from emotional distress, making it difficult to discuss their feelings or concerns, such as the fear that breast cancer may recur or spread (Pistrang and Barker, 1992).

Examining how partners attempt to provide support can contribute to our understanding of women's experiences of breast cancer, and can also provide an empirical basis for interventions to maximize support. Of course, not all women have partners and not all partners are men. I am not suggesting that the absence of a partner leaves women without support or that other sources of support are unimportant (for example, Pistrang and Barker (1998) found that support from other women who had been treated for breast cancer can be extremely helpful). Nor am I implying that only heterosexual relationships should be studied. The work that I will describe focusses on support in the context of heterosexual relationships, but the paradigm can be applied to a range of other relationships.

A NEW METHOD FOR STUDYING SOCIAL SUPPORT

Most studies of social support rely on retrospective, self-report methods and tell us how people feel, on average, about the support they get from others. As a result, we know very little about the interactive – the 'social' – nature of social support. What makes for a supportive interaction between two people? And how do both members of the dyad view such interactions? Over recent years, researchers have called for a change of methodological emphasis in order to address these questions (e.g. Burleson *et al.*, 1994; Coyne and Bolger, 1990; Sarason *et al.*, 1994).

My colleagues and I (Pistrang *et al.*, 1997) have proposed an approach which involves examining actual conversations where one member of a dyad is attempting to provide support to the other, and obtaining participants' perceptions of those conversations, i.e. how the participants make sense of the interaction in the context of their relationship. This approach integrates observational and self-report methods, with the aim of obtaining a fuller description of the complexities of communication. Our methods are conducive to intensive, idiographic studies that look in detail at communication within a dyad.

We conceptualize social support as a form of 'help-intended communication' (Goodman and Dooley, 1976), which ranges on a continuum from formal helping (that given by trained professionals such as therapists) to informal helping (that given in everyday interactions by friends, family, etc.). It seems plausible that formal and informal helping share some common properties; that is, similar principles may operate in effective helping of whatever type (Rogers, 1957; Stiles, 1992; Winefield, 1987). This conceptualization leads to a focus on the process of helping, rather than the content of helping. We are interested in process variables such as the helper's empathy, the degree to which she or he tries to explore the helpee's concern or to find a solution, and how the helper's own concerns may get in the way of listening.

As part of this process framework, we emphasize the distinction between intention and impact: the helper's intention in saying something does not always correspond to the impact it has on the helpee. The traditional content categories of social support (e.g. 'esteem support') fail to make this distinction and obscure potentially important process variables, such as empathy, which may play a central role in good helping.

Our approach to process analysis aims to make sense of conversations by utilizing multiple sources of data (the conversation itself as well as the participants' self-report about their experience of it) and multiple perspectives (from each member of the couple as well as from 'experts' or trained raters). We take a 'methodological pluralist' approach, using both quantitative and qualitative methods as appropriate (Barker *et al.*, 1994).

The case example below illustrates this approach to studying social support. It is taken from an intensive study of four married couples in which the woman had been treated for breast cancer within the previous year (Pistrang *et al.*, 1997; Rutter, 1993). The couple first participated in a semi-structured communication task. This consisted of a 15–minute, audio-taped conversation, in which the woman (the Discloser) was asked to talk about a personal concern to do with her illness and the man (the Helper) was asked to try to be helpful in whatever way seemed natural to him. After the conversation, the couple participated in separate, parallel tape-assisted recall sessions. This procedure consisted of playing back the audio-tape of the conversation and stopping after each 'talking turn' to ask a standard series of questions. The questions focussed on two key dimensions: the impact of the Helper's response on the Discloser, and the intention behind the Helper's response.

A CASE EXAMPLE

Mr. and Mrs. B were in their late 30s, had been married for 14 years and had three school-aged children. Mr. B worked as an administrator in a sales department and Mrs. B worked as a part-time secretary. Mrs. B had been diagnosed with breast cancer 16 months ago and had been treated by lumpectomy, radiotherapy and chemotherapy. Mrs. B had an extensive family history of breast cancer.

In the first part of the conversation, Mrs. B talks about her fear of the cancer recurring. The following episode begins approximately 30 seconds into the conversation. (Numbers refer to the talking turn and the letters D or H indicate whether the Discloser (woman) or the Helper (partner) is speaking.)

5 D: *I think probably if it came back then I'd have to have more, even if it was still very small, that they would give me more treatment ... [H: More radium?] [D: Yeah.] [H: I think so, yeah.] ... to try and stop it coming back again and uh, also the chemotherapy. I don't really like injections and things anyway, so, it's not particularly nice. It's quite lucky I wasn't sick or anything the first time but ...*

6 H: *Yeah, with a bit of good luck and good fortune smiling upon you, you hopefully won't have a recurrence ... [D: No, but ...] ... I mean your mum, well your mum's had a mastectomy, but your mum hasn't had any problems at all has she?*

7 D: *I think the mastectomy is different, I mean ... [H: Yeah.] ... and she had such extensive treatment, her treatment was for a year that they probably just killed off anything and everything anyway ...*

In the tape-assisted recall, Mrs. B said that she felt her husband meant well, but that there was a clash between their styles of coping:

Because I know [partner], I know he's being as supportive and as helpful as he sees that he can, but often he is very flip about life, it's just the way he is. He doesn't allow for anything to worry him, until it happens, and then he worries about it. I sometimes get a bit angry with him, I know he means well, but it's not exactly what you want. You know it's not purposeful, it's just his character.' She also felt irritated with his comparison of her mother with herself: 'You can't liken what my mother had and me. Our diagnostics and operations were miles apart, also years apart ... It [his response] didn't seem to have any real input to the particular prob-

lem, the thing I was talking about – recurrence in myself. It was the wrong response.

She felt his intention was *'to try to lighten it up, make it less serious'*. She would have liked him to:

make more positive sounds, like 'Yes, it may come back, but we're here, we'll get through it'. Something more supportive than just 'No, we won't worry about that 'til it happens' – because sometimes you do need to worry about it, so that you're prepared. It's doing that 'brushing it under the carpet' thing, 'just ignore it and it'll go away' – I don't think you can.

Mr. B said his intention was to *'try to put her thoughts onto a positive line, always look on the bright side of things, always be optimistic rather than pessimistic'*. He did not feel that anything got in the way of his being helpful at this point. He noted that *he* felt better for reassuring his wife that things were going to be OK.

This brief interchange (turns 5–7) encapsulates a discrepancy between the partners' styles of coping with emotional distress and their beliefs about how to be helpful. Mr. B attempts to reassure and be upbeat: his message is 'look on the bright side'. Although Mrs. B recognizes her husband's good intentions, his response fails to acknowledge her fears of recurrence. This does not get addressed directly in the conversation, but emerges clearly in the tape-assisted recall.

This same theme, and variants of it, recur throughout much of the conversation. In the excerpt below, Mrs. B has begun to talk about how to deal with the fear and her need to express her distress.

15D: *Yeah, um, it's just difficult. It's difficult to even know what it is that does frighten you sometimes. And sometimes you just want to sit down and have a real good cry. And, you're not really sure why it is that you want to have a real good cry. I think I've had lots more bouts of lows since the diagnostics and the operation, etc, than I ever had before. I mean I was usually quite uppy, quite often get low and depressed and …*

16H: *Well I think that it's natural, I mean you're pretty bouncy most of the time. It's rare you get a real downer, very rare.*

17D: *That's because I feel that I have to be. Sometimes you're sort of pressurising yourself into behaviour that maybe you don't, you don't really feel like you want to be at this party but here you are anyway so you just make the best time of it. I mean you're treating life in the same fashion; 'I'm here, let's just get on and enjoy it', but inside, you're thinking 'this is just … '*

18H: *Yeah, but if you let the inside take over, it's a downward spiral, isn't it? You've got to keep on top of it, you've got to. I mean you've done well up until now, keeping on top of it.*

19D: *Sometimes you just want to let go. I mean you help me to stay up on top, but I don't know, sometimes maybe it's not a bad thing to kind of let go and…*

20H: *Oh it's always a good thing to have a good howl and a cry and tell someone how you feel, but um ...*

21D: *It's embarrassing too. I mean, you feel that you're upsetting the people around you and somehow letting them down. I mean, I couldn't howl in front of the children.*

Mr. B's responses at turns 16 and 18 again illustrate his attitude of being 'positive': he emphasizes the importance of keeping 'negative' emotions at bay. In turn 20, he does acknowledge that expressing feelings may be helpful. However, he ends this acknowledgement with a 'but ... ', which seems to express an ambivalence about the usefulness of expressing feelings: the 'but' seems to partially retract the acknowledgment. Following this, in turn 21, Mrs. B then hints at her own ambivalence about expressing painful feelings. This is more explicit in the tape-assisted recall, where she described both wanting her husband to give her 'permission to let go', as well as her own reluctance to do this (and her envy of others who do): *'I've built up a wall where I don't allow emotions out, so it annoys me when others dare to'.*

Examining the conversation as it evolved over time, we identified a cyclical process in the interaction, with a periodicity of about 10 talking turns, that revolved around the couple's ambivalences about disclosing painful emotions. In each cycle, Mrs. B expresses her need to 'let feelings out' and Mr. B focusses on being positive and the hazards of letting feelings out; Mrs. B then concurs with this view, but soon afterwards comes back to her need to 'let go'. The conversation seems like a dance around the core issue – the fear of expressing painful feelings – which never gets talked about directly or resolved.

SUMMARY

I hope to have illustrated how a process analysis approach can shed some light on social support in close relationships for women with serious illness. By examining an actual conversation as well as the participants' moment-by-moment perceptions of it, we can begin to understand the complexities of help-intended interactions. In the particular conversation illustrated above, Mr. B's attempts to provide support were clearly well-intentioned, but they often did not match up with Mrs. B's needs and therefore did not have a helpful impact. Interestingly, this intention-impact discrepancy was not explicitly discussed in the conversation itself, nor was it apparent from quantitative measures which we also included in the study (Mrs. B tended to rate Mr. B as very supportive and understanding). It was only in the tape-assisted recall sessions, which asked detailed questions about each participant's experience, that the personal meanings of the interaction, in the context of the couple's relationship, became clear.

Further research utilizing a process analysis approach is needed in order to identify commonalities or patterns of helping that occur across dyads. Such data can then be used to provide the building blocks for interventions to maximize the support that occurs within close relationships. Serious illnesses such as breast cancer pose challenges to couples, and if the intricacies of the support process can be better understood, we may be able to help couples to support each other more effectively. Ultimately, this may help women (and men) in their adaptation to serious illness.

REFERENCES

Barker, C., Pistrang, N. and Elliott, R. (1994) *Research Methods in Clinical and Counselling Psychology*. Chichester: John Wiley and Sons Ltd

Burleson, B.R., Albrecht,T.L., Goldsmith, D.J. and Sarason, I.G. (1994) Introduction: The communication of social support. In B.R. Burleson, T.L. Albrecht and I.G. Sarason (Eds.) *Communication of Social Support: Messages, Interactions, Relationships, and Community* (pp. xi–xxx). Thousand Oaks, CA: Sage

Coyne, J.C. and Bolger, N. (1990) Doing without social support as an explanatory concept. *Journal of Social and Clinical Psychology*, 9, 148–158

Coyne J.C., Ellard J.H. and Smith, D.A.F. (1990) Social support, interdependence, and the dilemmas of helping. In B.R. Sarason, I.G. Sarason and G.P. Pierce (Eds.), *Social Support: An Interactional View* (pp. 129–149). New York: Wiley

Dakof, G.A. and Taylor, S.E. (1990) Victims' perceptions of social support: What is helpful from whom? *Journal of Personality and Social Psychology*, 58, 80–89

Goodman, G. and Dooley, D. (1976) A framework for help-intended communication. *Psychotherapy: Theory, Research and Practice*, 13, 106–117

Helgeson, V.S. and Cohen, S. (1996) Social support and adjustment to cancer: Reconciling descriptive, correlational, and intervention research. *Health Psychology*, 15, 135–148

Lichtman, R.R., Taylor, S.E. and Wood, J.V. (1987) Social support and marital adjustment after breast cancer. *Journal of Psychosocial Oncology*, 5, 47–74

Manne, S. (1998) Cancer in the marital context: A review of the literature. *Cancer Investigation*, 16, 188–202

Pistrang, N. and Barker, C. (1992) Disclosure of concerns in breast cancer. *Psycho-Oncology*, 1, 183–192

Pistrang, N. and Barker, C. (1995) The partner relationship in psychological response to breast cancer. *Social Science and Medicine*, 40, 789–797

Pistrang, N. and Barker, C. (1998) Partners and fellow patients: Two sources of emotional support for women with breast cancer. *American Journal of Community Psychology*, 26, 439–456

Pistrang, N., Barker, C. and Rutter, C. (1997) Social support as conversation: Analysing breast cancer patients' interactions with their partners. *Social Science and Medicine*, 45, 773–782

Rogers, C.R. (1957) The necessary and sufficient conditions for therapeutic personality change. *Journal of Consulting Psychology*, 21, 95–103

Rutter, C. (1993) How breast cancer patients and their partners talk about their concerns. Unpublished M.Sc. dissertation, University College London

Sarason, I.G., Sarason, B.R. and Pierce, G.R. (1994) Relationship-specific social support: Toward a model for the analysis of supportive interactions. In B.R. Burleson, T.L. Albrecht and I.G. Sarason (Eds.) *Communication of Social Support: Messages, Interactions, Relationships, and Community* (pp. 91–112). Thousand Oaks, CA: Sage

Stiles, W.B. (1992) *Describing talk: A taxonomy of verbal response modes*. Newbury Park, CA: Sage

Vess, J.D., Moreland. J.R., Schwebel, A.I. and Kraut, E. (1988) Psychosocial needs of cancer patients: Learning from patients and their spouses. *Journal of Psychosocial Oncology*, 6, 31–51

Winefield, H.R. (1987) Psychotherapy and social support: Parallels and differences in the helping process. *Clinical Psychology Review*, 7, 631–644

CHAPTER 25

CHRONIC PELVIC PAIN

Marian Pitts, Linda McGowan and David Clark Carter

INTRODUCTION

The woman who bitterly complains of persistent, bizarre pelvic pain is the bête noir of the gynaecologist. (Benson et al., 1959)

Forty years later this statement still holds true. Chronic pelvic pain (CPP) is one of the most common gynaecological complaints. It can be defined as lower abdominal pain located in the pelvis, which is not specifically related to the menstrual cycle, and which has a duration of longer than six months. In a high proportion of such cases, no identifiable pathology can be found. A telephone Gallup poll in the U.S. found that, among women between 18 and 50 years of age, 14 percent had suffered with pelvic pain in the past three months (Mathias *et al.*, 1996). An estimate of prevalence among a clinical population found that nearly 40 percent report CPP (Zondervan *et al.*, 1998).

A curious aspect of CPP is that it is defined in gender-specific terms. A man has a pelvis and yet pain in that region would not be classified as CPP; which has been defined and treated as a gynaecological condition. This classification of CPP has dominated the nature of research into the condition.

EARLY STUDIES

Since the 1950s, CPP has been associated with psychiatric morbidity. In an influential study Duncan and Taylor (1952) carried out clinical interviews with women suffering from CPP whilst measuring the conductance of blood through the vaginal wall. They concluded that many of the women interviewed in this manner showed repressed hostility, anxiety and neuroses. The fact that hostility remained repressed under these circumstances is a testimony to what women will tolerate from gynaecologists. This study, however, was seen as seminal in demonstrating a link between underlying psychological mechanisms and the occurrence of CPP. Studies throughout the 1960s continued to search for the particular psychological characteristics associated with women suffering from CPP (Gido-Frank *et al.*, 1960, Castelnuovo-Tedesco and Krout, 1970).

The emergence of laparoscopy in the late 1970s as a diagnostic tool was greeted enthusiastically by researchers in CPP. Laparoscopy allows the pelvic and abdominal viscera to be viewed via a fibre-optic instrument. It then became possible to identify definite pathology in some cases of CPP. However, it still left a large proportion of CPP sufferers without a clear diagnosis. The earlier work, which had characterized all women suffering from CPP as neurotic, now became refined to apply such characteristics mainly to those women who could not been shown to have obvious pathology following laparoscopy (Beard et al., 1977). Many studies now reported higher rates of neuroticism, sexual problems, depression, somatization, disease conviction, and disturbed family relationships in CPP women without obvious pathology (Bak et al., 1990; Grandi et al., 1988; Magni et al., 1986). Not all studies, however, found these differences and we decided to address the area by carrying out a meta-analysis of 22 articles reporting work on women with CPP (McGowan et al., 1988).

METHODOLOGICAL CONSIDERATIONS

Our analysis showed that the absence of appropriate comparison and control groups jeopardized the validity of many studies. At least two comparison groups are needed when considering CPP: one should be a group of women also suffering from a gynaecological condition which requires hospitalization, but who are not experiencing CPP, e.g. women attending hospital for investigations of infertility; the second should be a comparison group of women who are suffering from a painful chronic condition, but not in the pelvic region (e.g. headaches or myofacial pain). By comparing across these groups it is possible to disentangle those personal characteristics (if any) which are specific to CPP. Within the group of CPP women it is also possible to distinguish between those for whom an organic cause is subsequently found, and those whose condition remains apparently non-organic following laparoscopy. Meta-analysis of these studies found that women with CPP were very like women suffering from other kinds of pain in their levels of anxiety, depression and neuroticism; and that both groups of women suffering from painful conditions, not surprisingly, showed higher levels of psychological morbidity than women who were free of pain (McGowan et al., 1998). In a subsequent empirical study, we have confirmed the meta-analytic findings (McGowan et al., in press). No study examined in the meta-analysis reliably confirmed the suggestion that women with CPP who subsequently are found to have an organic problem can be distinguished psychologically from those who are not.

THE ROLE OF ABUSE

Almost the only characteristic which seems to set apart women with CPP from those suffering from other painful conditions is the experience of abuse, usually childhood sexual abuse. Recent studies (Walker et al., 1995; Walling et al., 1994; Collett et al., 1998) have found higher rates of abuse, both in childhood and, in some cases, during adulthood. However, Rapkin (1990) interpreted his own mixed results by questioning a specific link between CPP and sexual abuse. The incidence of sexual and physical abuse has also been found to be elevated in other chronic pain groups (Karol *et al.*, 1992; Domino and Haber, 1987). As abuse histories are more prevalent in chronic pain populations, a higher proportion of women with CPP might be expected to report some abuse than pain-free groups. Given the site of the pain, a relationship between pelvic pain and abuse has an intuitive appeal. However, we need to be cautious about the role of abuse in the aetiology of CPP. Indeed others, e.g. Fry *et al.* (1993) also question the specificity hypothesis but acknowledge that abuse history may be a relevant factor in a certain subgroup of women with CPP.

MEDICAL CONSULTATIONS

Several studies now confirm that women with CPP are regarded negatively by both their general practitioners and by gynaecologists. This is evident from guides in publications for GPs which allude to possible psychosomatic elements involved with CPP:

Gynaecological symptoms predominate when women attend their general practitioner. This does not always mean that gynaecological pathology is present, for symptoms often reflect a state of mind in which the pelvic organs represent the milieu interieur just as the businessman's stomach and the anxious person's large bowel do. (Chamberlain, 1987)

In a telephone survey of 145 GPs, we found that the majority of doctors regarded women with CPP negatively, with a clear view of the role of psychosomatic factors. One GP commented: '*I think it's more common in women who are depressed, they tend to be introverted, they are miserable people*'; whilst another said: '*I'm talking anecdotally here, they're usually on the big side, quite overweight, they are usually suffering from other pathologies, they are anxious types, worriers, they can be inadequate and they are not the best copers*' (McGowan *et al.*, 1999).

Surprisingly, we found a fair degree of confidence among GPs that they could reliably distinguish between those women who would be found to have an organic basis for their pain following laparoscopy, and those who would remain 'non-organic'. Forty-three percent of our sample were confident they could distinguish at the first consultation, with a further 11 percent feeling that they would be able to distinguish on further consultation. The basis for making the distinction was illuminating, illustrating the negative perceptions afforded to women whose pain turns out to be 'non-organic': '*I think you can tell from the thickness of the medical record*', said one; whilst another suggested: '*If they are young and have thin notes it tends to be organic, if they have fat notes it's probably non-organic*'.

A study of gynaecologists by Selfe *et al.* (1998) showed that a favorable rating of the quality of the consultation by the patient was associated with good recovery at six months follow-up. The authors emphasized the importance of good communication as a basis for successful treatment for these patients. Kamm (1997) notes that women with CPP form a substantial part of the workload of gynaecologists, gastroenterologists and surgeons and fears that the patient's physical and social disability can become compounded by diagnostic confusion and ineffective treatments. He comments *'The end result is often a sense of helplessness in both the patient and the physician'*. An important focus for future research would examine ways of improving the consultation experience for women with CPP.

MISSING VOICES

Very recently, there has begun to emerge a literature which considers CPP from the point of view of those women who suffer from it. We interviewed 19 women suffering from CPP pre-laparoscopy. We found that many women battle daily with their pain, yet continue to fulfil their multiple roles. This is not to say that CPP does not affect women's quality of life, but the effects are often subtle. Grace (1995) in a study of CPP women with mixed pathology, found their first priority was to understand what was wrong, and then to gain access to the appropriate treatment. The lack of validation from a diagnosis increases feelings of uncertainty about the cause and course of their condition. This, in turn, heightens the focus on the investigative laparoscopy as being able to provide the definitive answer. The technique is viewed as 'an all seeing camera', a powerful tool that provides answers. Unfortunately, around two-thirds of laparoscopies fail to detect any obvious pathology; from the 19 women in our study, only four had pathology confirmed at laparoscopy. What emerges from both our and Grace's interviews is a very different picture from the biomedical literature; in contrast to the negative medical discourse, the women's discourses reveal strengths and the development of coping strategies which reduce the negative impact of their condition. CPP pervades most aspects of women's lives, especially their identities and sexualities, yet remain what might be expected with the presence of chronic pain. The high incidence of psychopathology and overt sexual problems reported in the previous medical and psychiatric literature was not confirmed in our studies. Perhaps it is time to redefine chronic pelvic pain as a painful condition related only indirectly to gynaecological concerns.

REFERENCES

Bak, A.P., Verhage, F., Drogendijk, A.C., Voitus van Hamme, J.W.E. and Duivenoorden, A. (1990) Chronic pelvic pain and neurotic behaviour. *Journal of Psychosomatic Obstetrics and Gynaecology*, 11, 29–35

Beard R.W., Belsey, E.M., Lieberman, B.A. and Wilkinson, J.C.M. (1977) Pelvic pain in women. *American Journal of Obstetrics and Gynecology*, 128, 566

Benson, R.C., Hanson, K. and Matarazzo, J. (1959) Atypical pelvic pain in women: gynecologic and psychiatric considerations. *American Journal of Obstetrics and Gynecology*, 77, 806–823

Castelnuovo-Tedesco, P. and Krout, B.M. (1970) Psychosomatic aspects of chronic pelvic pain. *International Journal of Psychiatry in Medicine*, 1, 109–126

Chamberlain, G. (1987) Gynaecology in 1987. *The Practitioner,* 231, 8 January

Collett, B.J., Cordle, C.J., Stewart, C.R. and Jagger, C. (1998) A comparative study of women with chronic pelvic pain, chronic nonpelvic pain and those with no history of pain attending general practitioners. *British Journal of Obstetrics and Gynaecology,* 105 (1) 87–92

Domino, J.V. and Haber, J.D. (1987) Prior physical and sexual abuse in women with chronic headache: clinical correlates. *Headache,* 27, 310–314

Duncan, C.H. and Taylor, H.C. (1952) A psychosomatic study of pelvic congestion. *American Journal of Obstetrics and Gynecology,* 64, 1–12

Fry, R.P.W., Crisp, A.H., Beard, R.W. and McGuigan, S. (1993) Psychosocial aspects of chronic pelvic pain. *Postgraduate Medical Journal,* 69, 566–574

Gido-Frank, L., Gordon, T. and Taylor, H.C. (1960) Pelvic pain and female identity. *American Journal of Obstetrics and Gynecology,* 79, 1184–1202

Grace, V.M. (1995) Problems women patients experience in the medical encounter for chronic pelvic pain: A New Zealand study. *Health Care for Women International,* 16, 509–519

Grandi, S., Fava, G.A., Trombini, G., Orlandi, C., Bernardi, M., Gubbini, G. and Michelacci, L. (1988) Depression and anxiety in patients with chronic pelvic pain. *Psychiatric Medicine* 1 (4), 1–7

Kamm, M.A. (1997) Chronic pelvic pain in women: gastroenterological, gynaecological or psychological? *International Journal of Colectoral Disorders,* 12 (2), 57–62

Karol, R., Micka, R.G. and Kuskowski, M. (1992) Physical, emotional and sexual abuse among pain patients and health care providers: Implications for psychologists in multidisciplinary pain treatment centers. *Professional Psychology: Research and Practice,* 23 (6), 480–485

Magni, G., Andreoli, C., DeLeo, D., Martinotti, G. and Rossi, C. (1986) Psychological profile of women with chronic pelvic pain. *Archives of Gynecology,* 237, 165–168

Mathias, S.D., Kupperman, M., Liberman, R.F., Lipshutz, R.C. and Steege, J.F. (1996) Chronic pelvic pain: prevalence, health-related quality of life, and economic correlates. *Obstetrics and Gynaecology,* 87 (3), 321–327

McGowan, L., Clark Carter, D. and Pitts, M.K. (1998) Chronic Pelvic Pain: A meta-analysis. *Psychology and Health,* 13, 937–951

McGowan, L., Pitts, M.K. and Clark Carter, D. Women with chronic pelvic pain: A comparative study (submitted for publication)

McGowan, L., Pitts, M.K. and Clark Carter, D. (1999) Chronic Pelvic Pain: The General Practitioner's Perspective. *Psychology, Health and Medicine,* 4 (3), 303–317.

Rapkin, A.J. (1990) History of physical and sexual abuse in women with chronic pelvic pain. *Obstetrics and Gyecology,* 68 (1), 13–15

Selfe, S.A. Matthews, Z. and Stones, R.W. (1998) Factors influencing outcome in consultations for chronic pelvic pain. *Journal of Women's Health,* 7 (8), 1041–1048

Walker, E.A., Katon, W., Harrop-Griffiths, J., Holm, L., Russo, J. and Hickok, L.R. (1988) Relationship of chronic pelvic pain to psychiatric diagnoses and childhood sexual abuse. *American Journal of Psychiatry,* 145 (1), 75–79

Walling, M.K., O'Hara, M.W., Reiter, R.C., Milburn, A., Lilly, G. and Vincent, S.D. (1994) Abuse history and chronic pain in women: I: Prevalences of sexual abuse and physical abuse. *Obstetrics and Gynecology,* 84 (2), 193–199

Zondervan, K.T., Yudkin, P.L., Vessey, M.P., Dawes, M.G., Barlow, D.H. and Kennedy, S.H (1998) The prevalence of chronic pelvic pain in women in the United Kingdom: a systematic review. *British Journal of Obstetrics and Gynaecology,* 105 (1), 93–99

CHAPTER 26

WOMEN AND SOMATIC DISTRESS

Annemarie Kolk

INTRODUCTION

Somatic distress is highly prevalent in women. They suffer from a range of sex-specific conditions regarding reproduction and, compared to men, they endure more acute as well as mild chronic diseases (see contributions by Pitts *et al.*, and Wilkinson, Squire and Reilly, in this volume). In addition, they experience more medically unexplained physical symptoms, that is physical symptoms that can not be accounted for by a medical diagnosis. Because of their ill-health, they have a higher medical care use. Health differences between women and men – though modest – have been consistently found (Gijsbers van Wijk and Kolk, 1997; Verbrugge, 1989). This chapter first questions the validity of sex differences in medically unexplained symptoms and somatization by discussing the gender bias in research and practice, the distinction between the experience and the report of symptoms, and the association of somatic and emotional distress. Secondly, it addresses the development of a comprehensive model for research into women's somatic distress.

THE VALIDITY OF GENDER DIFFERENCES IN PHYSICAL SYMPTOMS

The perception of bodily changes is an everyday experience. However, most of these physical sensations are not experienced as symptoms of disease. Being mild and transient, they are ignored, or acted upon by self-medication, bed rest and diet. A small proportion of these physical sensations are experienced as symptoms that deserve medical attention, and result in a medical consultation. An even smaller proportion ends in a diagnosis of organic disease or in a psychiatric diagnosis. Thus the symptoms covered by diagnoses of organic disease and by diagnoses of somatoform, anxiety and depressive disorders, or even the symptoms presented in primary care, are out of proportion to those experienced in the community (e.g. Mayou *et al.*, 1995).

Within the realm of psychiatry, medically unexplained symptoms are classified as a somatoform disorder or as an element of an affective or an anxiety disorder. The somatoform disorders: somatization disorder, undifferentiated somatoform disorder (including fibromyalgia, irritable bowel,

and chronic fatigue), conversion disorder, pain disorder are more prevalent in women, whereas hypochondriasis and body dismorphic disorder
are equally common in women and men (APA, 1994; Toner, 1995). The criteria for somatoform disorders are often not fully met; consequently, the
prevalence rates of these disorders are relatively low. In primary care studies (e.g. Kroenke and Spitzer, 1998) and in community studies (e.g.
Kroenke and Price, 1993), women are found to experience more medically unexplained symptoms as well.

As these differences are observed repeatedly, irrespective of sample
and instrument, they seem to be robust. However, gender biases in these
studies are well documented. There is gender bias in sampling, i.e. no use
of probability sampling of the population, no proportionate representation of the sexes within studies, and no analysis of findings by gender.
There is gender bias within diagnostic criteria as well, i.e. criteria are
themselves biased in favor of one sex relative to the other (Hartung and
Widiger, 1998). Moreover, the diagnostic process is liable to gender bias in
applying diagnostic criteria because of bias within assessment instru-
ments and within the clinician (Garb, 1997; Worrell and Robinson, 1995).

As it is difficult to distinguish between the experience of symptoms and
the reporting of symptoms, it is possible that differences between women
and men represent differences in the reporting, not in the experience of
symptoms. The findings may be due to variations in the willingness to
report, women being more likely to disclose their distress, especially to
female interviewers (Verbrugge, 1985). Different processes and factors
underlie experience and reporting. What is presented is as much determined by social context as it is by the experienced problem. The presentation of somatic symptoms can be understood as cultural idioms of distress, as metaphors for experience, as social positioning, and as social commentary or contestation (Kirmayer and Young, 1998).

Medically unexplained physical symptoms determine far less of the sex
difference in health and medical care utilization than gynaecological and
obstetrical diagnoses, and preventive health care (especially concerning
contraception). Still, these symptoms are often over-emphasized when it
comes to the characterization of women's health. Today, people refrain
from depicting women as hysterical. Hysteria has been replaced by somatization disorder in psychiatric nosology, and women are now stereotyped as somatizers. The prototypic somatizing patient is 'a lower socio-
economic status woman with a history of multiple functional symptoms,
presenting with physical complaints suspected of having a basis in
depression or anxiety, who exaggerates the significance of her distress'
(Kirmayer and Robbins, 1991: 654).

On the one hand, women are supposed to be the true somatizers in the
traditional sense, i.e. expressing their emotional problems as somatic distress; on the other hand, they are found more ready to acknowledge negative emotions and a need for mental health care (e.g. Wool and Barsky,
1994). The primary care studies of Kirmayer and Robbins (1991, 1996)
seem to remove this paradox. They distinguish between three dimensions

of somatization: level of medically unexplained symptoms, hypochondriacal worry, and somatic presentation of a psychiatric disorder. Patients with high levels of medically unexplained symptoms were more likely to be female, and this gender effect is independent of anxiety and depressive disorders (Kroenke and Spitzer, 1998). Women were not over-represented among individuals with hypochondriacal worry. Contrary to expectations, the majority of the somatic presenters, women as much as men, offered psychosocial origins for their distress, the initial somatizers readily, and the facultative somatizers when the possibility was explicitly raised. In this respect, they were not different from the first two groups. However, a small group of somatic presenters persistently rejected psychosocial explanations. These true somatizers were more likely to be men.

The belief that somatization, in the sense of the persistent expression of emotional problems as somatic distress, is a widespread phenomenon, especially in women, proved to be false. Somatic distress is inextricably bound up with emotional distress. Somatic symptoms in general and medically unexplained symptoms in particular are found to be strongly and consistently associated with emotional distress (Simon *et al.*, 1996), in women as well as in men (Piccinelli and Simon, 1997). This highlights the constructive side of the concept of somatization.

As somatic distress without emotional distress is rare, the concept of somatization is best considered a product of mind-body dualism and thus a social construction.

The concept of somatization reproduces two fundamental dualism's that are deeply embedded in Western medicine, health psychology, and indeed, in the everyday concept of the person. The first is that mind and body are distinct realms, so that there is something noteworthy or even exceptional about people who express in somatic terms problems that a professional would situate in the psychological realm. The second is that what is physical is somehow more real, substantial, and ultimately, more legitimate as illness than what is psychological. (Kirmayer and Taillefer, 1997: 333)

A COMPREHENSIVE MODEL OF SOMATIC DISTRESS

Sex in itself offers no sufficient explanation for the variability in symptom experience. Nor can differences be simply or directly reduced to any single factor, be it biological, psychological or sociological. Several integrative theories have been proposed to account for the biological, psychological or sociological factors in somatic distress (e.g. Pennebaker, 1982; Kirmayer and Young, 1998). The model discussed here is largely based upon these theories (Gijsbers van Wijk and Kolk, 1997).

Intra-individual as well as inter-individual differences in the experience of physical symptoms are primarily the products of differences in symptom perception, i.e. in the awareness and interpretation of physical sensations. Symptom perception is a concept within an information-processing model that incorporates physiological, cognitive, emotional, social and cultural factors. This information-processing model represents an adaptive, dynamic model in which attention regulation and interpretation are central concepts. This means that except for extreme conditions there is an ever-changing contribution of physiological, cognitive, emotional, social and cultural factors to the perception of physical sensations and the experience of symptoms.

Differences between women and men, but also among women and among men can be explained by differences with respect to these factors, their interaction, and their differential impact. For example, the perception of physical sensations in women seems to be guided by top-down processes, by the appraisal of signals from the body in relation to situational cues. In contrast, men's perception appears to be controlled by bottom-up processes, by signals from their body only. It shows that both top-down (the Schachter and Singer model) and bottom-up (the William James model) explanations can be valid (Pennebaker and Roberts, 1992).

Somatic factors

Physical sensations arise from fluctuations in normal bodily processes (e.g. a drop in blood glucose level when hungry); from emotions (e.g. an increase in heart rate when angry); from environmental conditions (e.g. a drop in skin temperature due to cold); and from organic disease (e.g. an increase in body temperature due to infectious disease). Women probably have more, and more fluctuating, somatic input than men due to reproductive processes such as the menstrual cycle, pregnancy and delivery, and menopause. However, the awareness of a change in bodily state is not only necessarily primarily determined by physical processes but depends on the attention we pay to it or can pay to it.

Social factors

Given a limited attention capacity, there is a continuous competition between the amount and salience of internal information on the one hand and the amount and salience of external information on the other. The more our attention is absorbed by daily hassles or work the less our awareness of bodily sensations, even more so when these sensations are mild or ambiguous – that is, unless they act as stressors (overload) and contribute to a negative mood/emotional state, and the physical sensations that go with it. In contrast, when life and work are repetitious and boring (underload) attention to and awareness of somatic sensations will increase. Applied to the life of women, the constrictions of their gender role and their low social position, this competition of cues hypothesis is consistent with negative health effects resulting from isolation, unemployment, or undemanding, low-status jobs, as well as from conflicts due to multiple roles, not the multiple roles in themselves.

Cognitive and emotional factors

Attention to bodily sensations not only depends on internal and external information, but also on a tendency to selective attention to the body. Once attention is focussed on the body, physical sensations can even be amplified, i.e. even mild sensations can be experienced as noxious and intense. Due to socialization processes and the increasing medicalization of normal bodily processes, women are assumed to be more sensitive to physical sensations – to selectively attend to their body – whereas somatic amplification has been found to be unrelated to gender.

Given the awareness of physical sensations, their meanings are not yet clear. The same sensation (e.g. sweating) can result in multiple interpretations. First, the sensation can be attributed to a somatic disease (e.g. a fever or infection). The interpretation of a sensation as a symptom of disease is guided by illness schemes, cognitive structures that are based upon earlier experiences with and ideas about illness and disease. Secondly, the sensation can be attributed to emotions or emotional distress (e.g. anxious or nervous). Thirdly, a situational interpretation can be the most plausible (e.g. a warm room). The attribution of sensations along these dimensions has not been found to be related to gender.

The interpretation of a sensation can be obvious but often it is complicated to disentangle its origin, especially when it is relatively mild and ambiguous. Women have to choose not only between diseases, emotions and situations, but also between relatively normal bodily changes related to the menstrual cycle, pregnancy/delivery, and menopause. It takes time to decide upon what is going on, valuable time in the case of a serious physical disease. The denial of the symptoms of a serious disease because its meaning is too threatening, can further prolong the decision process. Conversely, the experience of emotional distress can be too threatening and become dissociated from the experienced somatic distress, as seems to occur as a consequence of physical and/or sexual abuse.

SUMMARY

Women's somatic distress must be understood and explained, not discarded as vague, complaining or just a form of somatizing. Therefore, research on sex differences in medically unexplained symptoms and related clinical practice should make an effort to dispose of gender bias. Moreover, somatic distress should not be studied apart from emotional distress. It is of paramount importance to study separately the factors underlying the experience and the report of symptoms.

A symptom perception model as described here brings together somatic, emotional, cognitive and social factors as well as mechanisms known to affect the experience of symptoms. It can stimulate and integrate research that emphasizes a multidimensional approach to somatic and emotional distress.

REFERENCES

American Psychiatric Association (1994) *Diagnostic and Statistical Manual of Mental Disorders* (4th edn). Washington, D.C.: American Psychiatric Press

Garb, H.N. (1997) Race bias, social class bias, and gender bias in clinical judgement. *Clinical Psychology: Science and Practice*, 4, 99–120

Gijsbers van Wijk, C.M.T. and Kolk, A.M.M. (1997) Sex differences in physical symptoms: The contribution of symptom perception theory. *Social Science and Medicine*, 45, 231–246

Hartung, C.M. and Widiger, T.A. (1998) Gender differences in the diagnosis of mental disorders: Conclusions and controversies of the DSM-IV. *Psychological Bulletin*, 123, 260–278

Kirmayer, L.J. and Robbins, J.M. (1991) Three forms of somatization in primary care: Prevalence, co-occurrence and sociodemographic characteristics. *Journal of Nervous and Mental Disease*, 179, 647–655

Kirmayer, L.J. and Robbins, J.M. (1996) Patients who somatize in primary care: A longitudinal study of cognitive and social characteristics. *Psychological Medicine*, 26, 937–951

Kirmayer, L.J. and Young, A. (1998) Culture and somatization: Clinical, epidemiological, and ethnographic perspectives. *Psychosomatic Medicine*, 60, 420–430

Kroenke, K. and Price, R.K. (1993) Symptoms in the community. Prevalence, classification, and psychiatric comorbidity. *Archives of Internal Medicine*, 153, 1474–1480

Kroenke, K. and Spitzer, R.L. (1998) Gender differences in the reporting of physical and somatoform symptoms. *Psychosomatic Medicine*, 60, 150–155

Mayou, R., Bass, C. and Sharpe, M. (1995) Overview of epidemiology, classification, and aetiology. In R. Mayou, C. Bass and M. Sharpe (Eds.) *Treatment of Funtional Somatic Symptoms* (pp. 42–65). New York: Oxford University Press

Pennebaker, J.W. (1982) *The Psychology of Physical Symptoms*. New York: Springer Verlag.

Pennebaker, J.W. and Roberts, T. (1992) Toward a his and her theory of emotion: Gender differences in visceral perception. *Journal of Social and Clinical Psychology*, 11, 199–212

Piccinelli, M. and Simon, G. (1997) Gender and cross-cultural differences in somatic symptoms associated with emotional distress. An international study in primary care. *Psychological Medicine*, 27, 433–444

Simon, G., Gater, R., Kisely, S. and Picinelli, M. (1996) Somatic symptoms of distress: An international primary care study. *Psychosomatic Medicine*, 58, 481–488

Toner, B.B. (1995) Gender differences in somatoform disorders. In M.V. Seeman (Ed.) *Gender and Psychopathology* (pp. 287–309). Washington, D.C.: American Psychiatric Press

Verbrugge, L.M. (1985) gender and health: An update on hypotheses and evidence. *Journal of Health and Social Behavior*, 26, 156–182

Verbrugge, L.M. (1989) The twain meet: Empirical explanations of sex differences in health and mortality. *Journal of Health and Social Behavior*, 30, 282–304

Wool, C.A. and Barsky, A.J. (1994) Do women somatize more than men? Gender differences in somatization. *Psychosomatics*, 35, 445–452

Worrell, J. and Robinson, D. (1995) Issues in clinical assessment with women. In J. Butcher (Ed.) *Clinical Personality Assessment. Practical Approaches* (pp. 158–171). New York: Oxford University Press

CHAPTER 27

PMS RESEARCH: BALANCING THE PERSONAL WITH THE POLITICAL

Jacqueline Reilly

INTRODUCTION

This chapter begins with a consideration of empirical research into pre-menstrual syndrome which, it is argued, has become bifurcated along broadly political lines (see also Vanselow, in this volume). One strand of research adopts a perspective which constructs the psychosocial context of women's subjective experiences as either irrelevant to, or at best a medi-ating factor in, a pathophysiologic process. The other strand adopts a broadly feminist approach which attributes women's negative premen-strual experiences to psychosocial factors. However, if women who expe-rience PMS are to gain maximum benefit, their subjective experiences must be central to the research process. This chapter concludes by consid-ering what this may entail for both qualitative and quantitative researchers seeking to understand PMS.

BACKGROUND

Premenstrual syndrome was first noted in the research literature as pre-menstrual tension in 1931, when Frank described it as an 'indescribable tension' appearing premenstrually and accompanied by 'a desire to find relief by foolish and ill-considered actions' (p. 1054), which he attributed to hormonal causes. PMS has since become established as a medical con-dition, and is included, for example, in the *Diagnostic and Statistical Manual of Mental Disorders* (DSM). Moreover, PMS as a term has also entered com-mon parlance and is frequently featured in the media, mostly in ways which either suggest that it is an almost universal part of women's expe-rience or which sensationalize the problem by associating it with violence by women (Hey, 1985; Chrisler and Levy, 1990). The term PMS itself is a hotly disputed one, and various researchers have preferred other names for the condition, such as molimina (Prior *et al.*, 1986) or premenstrual changes (Choi, 1992), or have distinguished between PMS and premenstrual symptoms (Ussher, 1996) or have proposed not one but several syndromes (e.g. Halbreich and Endicott, 1982; Abraham and Rumley, 1987). PMS was also controversially included in the DSM (see Figert, 1995 for analysis of this controversy) first as Late Luteal Phase Dysphoric disorder and later as Premenstrual Dysphoric Disorder, to add to the list of available labels. However, the term most commonly used for the condition remains PMS, which will be used throughout this chapter.

TAKING STOCK

It is a cliché to state that empirical research into PMS has produced a confusing array of results which are difficult to assimilate into a coherent account of the problem. It is equally a cliché to state that these results have been heavily influenced by the methodological preferences of those conducting the research, and that failure to achieve consensus even on the definition of the problem has severely hampered efforts to synthesize the body of research evidence into a coherent account of women's premenstrual experiences. Nevertheless, these observations have been the basis of several attempts to revitalize research in this area, by describing how the existing body of evidence may be categorized. Such analyses hope to provide a sensible basis for further research which is informed by a thorough consideration of previous findings in relation to important theoretical and methodological issues. Several commentators, including Walker (1995) and Ussher (1992) have provided useful and insightful typologies of research to date, Walker in terms of the meta-theoretical approaches guiding research in the area and Ussher in terms more explicitly relating these to the perspectives adopted by the researchers themselves, which she categorizes into those advocating a bio-medical theoretical and treatment approach and those preferring psychosocial theories and treatments.

Both Walker and Ussher provided a thoughtful, detailed and fine-grained analysis, but another dichotomous characterization of the research to date may be an appropriate perspective to adopt at this juncture. A useful way to categorize research in this area may be simply to divide it in terms of the assumptions and beliefs of the researchers. That is, research can be divided into that which is conducted by those who believe that PMS is a 'real' condition, whether physiological or psychological in origin, and that which is conducted by researchers who do not. Note that this characterization, in common with Ussher (1992) is based on the beliefs of the researchers and thus indirectly on their understanding of what the existing literature means, rather than on any aspect of the research itself. This understanding is not achieved solely on the basis of the objective characteristics of the research evidence available to them, but also on the basis of their assessment of that research evidence in the light of their own pre-existing knowledge and understanding, and their preferred explanatory frameworks. The use of the word 'belief' in relation to this understanding is deliberate, as it makes explicit the often hidden sub-jective contribution to the research process. Thus, the political nature of empirical research into PMS is both explicitly acknowledged and directly attributed to the people who conduct it; it is the researchers who either believe or do not believe that PMS is a 'real' condition.

Doubtless many researchers would be reluctant to acknowledge their own position with regard to this dichotomy and would argue that (regard-less of their beliefs) they are trained to assess research evidence in an objective and value-free manner. This, after all, is a basic aspiration of (social) scientists. It is not, however, the purpose of this chapter to reiter-ate the ongoing debate about whether research can ever be truly objective and value-free, which has been conducted at length in the feminist litera-ture (e.g. Harding, 1987; Hollway, 1989). Suffice it to state that, given the proposed dichotomous categorization of the perspectives evident in most PMS research, it is inevitable that most researchers will, at the very least, appear to their readers as 'either one or the other'. By adopting this dichotomous categorization and relating it directly to the politics of the researchers themselves, it is possible to render visible not only the defi-ciencies in the research to date but also the reasons for them, and to pro-pose that these deficiencies may only be satisfactorily addressed by the adoption of a new political approach to the subject.

THE BIOPSYCHOSOCIAL APPROACH TO PMS

There have been many exhortations to the research community to adopt a biopsychosocial approach to the empirical study of PMS (e.g. Miota *et al.*, 1991; Ussher and Wilding, 1992; Walker, 1995). If these suggestions had generated a body of biopsychosocial evidence, it is possible that under-standing of the problem would have been enhanced, and that a third option in terms of available perspectives on the nature of PMS would have become readily available to researchers. However, the number of studies undertaken which could be said to have fully embraced this approach as a research philosophy is very small. In the main, the manifestation of the biopsychosocial approach in the research literature has been a superficial one, with research being routinely conducted according to either a med-ical or a psychosocial model, with the addition in most cases of only a cur-sory nod in the direction of the elements of the biopsychosocial approach which have been neglected in the design.

This amounts to the virtual maintenance of the status quo which has pertained since PMS was first critically examined in the feminist literature. As Ussher (1996) notes, professional boundaries and the increased risk of Type I errors as a result of the large number of variables examined are sig-nificant factors militating against biopsychosocial research approaches. However, the illusion that a consensus has been achieved as to the biopsy-chosocial nature of the PMS phenomenon is counterproductive. It gives the impression, for example, that researchers are able to adopt an objective (and apolitical) approach in their quest for understanding of what is undoubtedly a complex phenomenon. As Ussher (1996) points out, more-over, the biopsychosocial approach has the same epistemological basis as the models used by the majority of those involved in empirical research into PMS.

Thus, the medical literature continues to generate studies which indi-cate a fundamental set of assumptions on the part of the researchers as to the aetiology of PMS, the optimum research methodology for studying the disorder, and the interpretations which best account for findings (e.g. Steiner, 1997; Schmidt *et al.*, 1998). The medical model may be 'softened' by the inclusion of a few psychosocial variables in the research design, but the fundamental assumptions remain: that PMS has a physiological basis; that scientific research methods derived from the natural sciences are the most appropriate means of investigating the problem; and that results should be interpreted primarily in terms of the physiological processes and/or effects observed, with psychosocial variables relegated to the sta-tus of possible mediating factors.

The other strand of empirical research on PMS, in contrast, is feminist influenced and almost universally based on the idea that menstrual cycles are normal, that they have no inevitable consequences or correlates in terms of performance or mood changes, and that to acknowledge that they may have any such consequences or correlates is to pathologize nor-mal female biological function and thus to further disadvantage women as a class (e.g. Laws, 1985; Nash and Chrisler, 1997). PMS has also been portrayed as a strategy used by some women in order that they may behave contrary to female sex-role stereotypes without risk of sanction, a strategy which then results in these women feeling guilt over their own counterstereotypical behavior (Gottlieb, 1988). Clearly, this strand of the feminist perspective on PMS is one which privileges the accounts and experiences of some women over the accounts and experiences of other women.

Given the power relationship inherent in the research context, this priv-ileging of one perspective at the expense of another results in a line of argument which is difficult, if not impossible, to refute. Any counterargu-ments put forward by women who report PMS are easily dismissed as merely a result of their false consciousness. This perspective is usually put forward accompanied by solemn disclaimers that women who report PMS are *intentionally* using their biology as a ploy. This type of research, however, is very unlikely to take biological factors into account in the research design, and while researchers may acknowledge that biological cycles may have mood or behavioral effects, they are unwilling to concede that these are sufficiently severe to cause distress. If distress is being expe-rienced, the patriarchal system has duped the woman concerned into believing that she should be distressed (Caplan *et al.*, 1992a).

By inference, however, it is the individual who is as much at fault as the system, as those women who are affected must be unable to appreciate the influences which are making them distressed, while those who are not duped are able not only to appreciate, but also to resist, these influences.

Some commentators (e.g. Laws, 1985; Caplan *et al.*, 1992b; Parlee, 1992) have acknowledged that they feel uncomfortable with this logic, and moreover that it simply does not 'fit' some women's experience. Women who are highly educated and aware of sociocultural influences, who have stable and positive personal relationships and are under no particular stress, may still report that they experience negative changes premenstrually and that they believe them to be a result of the menstrual cycle itself.

A glance at the psychological literature reveals a mixture of political stances and research designs, with some researchers continuing to conduct research which is based on the medical model of the aetiology of the problem, and others adopting the alternative political position, one which could be loosely termed feminist, but with very few adopting a genuinely biopsychosocial approach. As Ussher (1996) notes, all of the major strands of existing evidence are a result of research conducted within the positivist/realist epistemology which prescribes a particular methodology and a set of acceptable research methods which must be followed if the evidence produced is to be considered legitimate knowledge.

CONSEQUENCES OF THE STATUS QUO

Given that only two political positions within the same epistemological framework have been available from which to conduct research into PMS, the possibility for the biopsychosocial approach to be genuinely espoused by a majority of PMS researchers was greatly reduced. Moreover, the necessity to provide evidence in regard to each available political position has resulted in the categorization of women's experiences by researchers as normal or abnormal, clinical or sub-clinical, mental health problem or not, for the purposes of empirical research. Thus, women may find themselves labeled false or true positive or false or true negative for PMS (e.g. Hamilton and Gallant, 1990) or stoic, healthy or hypervigilant (Blechman and Clay, 1987) or find that while they experience a 29 percent change in negative affect prior to menstruation, they are labeled normal or subclinical or false positive, while their peer who manifests a 30 percent change is labeled as experiencing 'true' PMS, or having a clinical condition, or as abnormal. Moreover, as Warner and Walker (1992) point out, 30 percent is an arbitrary figure which Steege (1989) acknowledged to be the product of a consensus of expert opinion rather than of a systematic evaluation of the empirical evidence.

However, this is not the only consequence of the bifurcation of PMS research along political lines. It is also the case that such treatments as are currently available are also linked to these positions. Two articles (Yonkers and Brown, 1996; Pearlstein, 1996) sum up the treatment options available, which fall under the headings of pharmacological and non-pharmacological. Thus, if a woman reports to a GP complaining of PMS, she may be offered a sympathetic ear and general lifestyle advice on diet and exercise, or she may be medicated, according to the GP's own preferred explanation of the problem. Moreover, treatment tends to be offered on a trial and error basis, an enterprise complicated by the relatively large placebo effects known to be prevalent in the condition (Walker, 1995). While some of the recent evidence on the successful use of SSRIs in the treatment of PMS is encouraging in terms of providing relief for women who complain of severe disruption of their lives premenstrually, the finding that a drug which regulates serotonin produces symptomatic relief does not indicate that the aetiology of the problem must necessarily lie within the serotonergic system. Moreover, these drugs may have unpleasant side effects and many women may prefer to avoid drug treatments if possible. Indeed, Eagan (1985) has noted that many pharmacological treatments which have been offered to women reporting PMS over the years have been of dubious efficacy and even potentially harmful. Conversely, but less often noted in the literature, if a woman believes herself to have a medical condition related to her menstrual cycle, well-meaning advice alone from a GP may be construed as trivializing what is perceived as a severe problem.

Thus far, the term 'medical condition' has been used in this chapter as though it were unproblematic, but that is not the case. In fact, there has been considerable debate among feminists as to whether constructions of PMS as a psychiatric disorder (LLPDD and later PMDD in DSM, for example) or indeed as a medical condition at all (see Caplan *et al.*, 1992; Parlee, 1992) should be challenged. However, Parlee's point – that it is examination of the multiple constructions of PMS by different groups such as doctors, psychiatrists and women who report the problem which are likely to be productive in terms of understanding the problem its effects and practical interventions – is a crucial one if we are to change, rather than perpetuate, the status quo in PMS research.

CHANGING THE STATUS QUO

Clearly, ideology has played a central role in producing the bifurcated body of PMS research. In order to propose a means of changing this status quo, it is useful to consider the course of research since Frank first described the condition in 1931.

Looking at the early literature, one is struck by the vague use of the term premenstrual tension from the outset. Indeed, there was remarkably little concern about the precise operational definition of the condition, and it could be surmised that there was little need for serious consideration of this matter, as the notion of female instability related to the menstrual cycle was a well-established one, as was the notion that this instability was best managed by medical means (Showalter, 1985; Ussher, 1996). Thus, from the outset, the condition was, for the purposes of research, whatever the researcher defined it to be in terms of symptoms examined, timing of the symptoms and other potentially confounding factors. Hence, when early second-wave feminists began to deconstruct the concept of PMS, the fact that it was not a clearly defined and unitary concept made its deconstruction a relatively simple matter.

However, the accurate and precise operational definition of variables is integral to the success of any scientific investigation. Poorly defined variables result in findings which are open to a variety of interpretations. This proved to be the case with regard to PMS; a plethora of definitions of the syndrome and an equally bewildering number of variations in methodology were soon to render the body of empirical evidence almost uninterpretable. This situation has been compounded over the years, with each new statistical technique, each more sophisticated design only adding to the layers of confusion surrounding the problem.

However, there has been a relatively recent trend towards menstrual cycle research of a different sort, which is conducted using qualitative methods (e.g. Choi and McKeown, 1997; Kissling, 1996; Oxley, 1997; Lovering, 1995; Reilly, 1997; Swann and Ussher, 1995). This has been an interesting development for several reasons. First, applying a qualitative methodology to the study of women's menstrual experiences, including PMS, entails both an epistemological and a practical shift in emphasis. Epistemologically, the use of qualitative methods is associated with an acceptance that there is no one objective truth to be uncovered by investigation, rather there are a multitude of perspectives on any given problem, none of which should be privileged over the others as all accounts are equally valid. Thus, a qualitative perspective takes participants' accounts of their own experiences as a starting point from which investigation should proceed, instead of imposing the researcher's own perceptions of what those experiences are from the outset. Second, a qualitative investigation is not designed a priori by the researcher but instead the design emerges as the research itself progresses, and is guided by this process. Thus, sampling procedures tend to be purposeful or theoretical as opposed to representative or random (Lincoln and Guba, 1985). In effect, early sampling produces data which when analysed may be used to guide later sampling. Third, concerns over sample size and composition and their relationship to the reliability and validity of the data are replaced by the need to achieve saturation of the categories generated by the data (Morse, 1995) and by concerns that the data be adequately triangulated (Lincoln and Guba, 1985).

A qualitative approach also has more practical implications. The researcher is required to disclose relevant personal information to increase the credibility of the analysis, thus allowing the reader access to possible biases in interpretation of results. This obligation to disclose, when adequately addressed, allows access to precisely the type of information which is, ideally, irrelevant to scientific investigation. Nevertheless, this information is usually inferable in the quantitative literature from the interpretation of results, which is nevertheless presented as objective.

Ussher (1996) has argued persuasively that an epistemological shift towards a material-discursive approach is indicated if the commonly cited impasse in PMS research is to be ended. However, such an epistemological shift has implications beyond these.

QUALITATIVE RESEARCH AND A NEW POLITICAL POSITION

Adoption of a qualitative research methodology has both practical and epistemological correlates which, when applied to the problem of PMS, are conducive to the development of a third possible political position on the topic. For example, the general tendency of qualitative methods to entail open approaches such as coding all data and deriving categories or themes from the data themselves rather than imposing categories which have been determined a priori, in effect place the research participants at the center of both the research and the analysis (which are typically not separated in the way they are in quantitative investigations). In fact, it could be claimed that the conscious locating of participants at the center of the research process by the researcher, who then discloses pertinent personal information when writing up his or her findings for publication, constitutes a new political position for PMS researchers, and one which is equally available to all researchers, whether they adopt quantitative or qualitative methodologies and regardless of their beliefs as to the aetiology of PMS.

For a qualitative researcher, putting women at the center of the analysis is not a radical departure. Recent qualitative studies have concentrated on the accounts of participants, and have provided a useful perspective on women's menstrual experiences. By avoiding arbitrary *a priori* decisions (such as selecting who should participate on the grounds of a score on a questionnaire, or a medical diagnosis, or endocrine status), they have been able, for example, to provide detailed descriptions of women's experiences around menstruation and PMS which is contextualized and therefore implicitly biopsychosocial.

For the quantitative researcher, putting women at the center of the analysis may entail some adjustment in terms of relinquishing what Burman has called the 'methodological fetishism so prevalent in scientistic (i.e. aspiring to "natural" scientific status) disciplines such as psychology' (1997: 785), and for example interpreting results more cautiously given that acknowledgment of the contextualized nature of the research and the participants' experience would be required. However, it has been suggested that quantitative research would be greatly enhanced by the adoption of practices such as reflexivity (Stevenson and Cooper, 1997).

However, adopting a political approach which is woman-centered has implications over and above the epistemological. A woman-centered political approach to PMS would not privilege concern for women as a class over concern for individual women's experiences. Feminist objections to the term PMS inevitably center on the argument that only women are affected by PMS, and thus any acknowledgment that biological processes are involved in the production of negative premenstrual changes would perpetuate notions of women as the weaker sex. This may be the case, but if so, from a woman-centered perspective it is nevertheless up to researchers and feminists alike to fully investigate the problem and to interpret and publicize their findings as carefully as possible. Markens

(1996), for example, has noted the lack of consideration of issues such as class and race in PMS research, and calls for feminists to 'problematize women's biological as well as social experiences' (p. 42). PMS is a long-standing and widely used term, and looks set to remain so. Any research which furthers understanding of the problem, and may even provide useful avenues for addressing it to the benefit of those women who complain that it impacts on their lives, must reduce the prejudice against women as a class, rather than perpetuate it.

DEVELOPING A WOMAN-CENTERED APPROACH

In my own research into PMS (Reilly, 1997; Reilly and Kremer, 1999), I used a mainly qualitative methodology, which facilitated consideration of all factors the participants chose to raise in relation to their own experiences surrounding PMS and menstruation. In so doing, I was also able to delve into political issues as they arose from the analysis, and developed a strong sense as this process unfolded that research conducted within a positivist/realist epistemological framework has to date missed the point about PMS. PMS is a label used by women to describe a variety of experiences, which do not remain constant but vary over time and circumstance within the same woman as well as between women. Some participants reported similar experiences every cycle, others noted that external stress could impact on their experience, others stated that they never knew what to expect in terms of both PMS and menstruation. Moreover, some participants explicitly stated that they felt that PMS was used to 'put women down' but nevertheless believed that, if a woman was severely affected by the problem, allowances should be made for it, both at home and in the workplace. There was a great deal of ambivalence and sometimes contradiction in what participants said about PMS and menstruation. They seemed to view PMS and menstruation as intertwined concepts within the same 'package', often seeming unable to talk exclusively about one without referring to the other.

These observations, and numerous others, suggest that when women say they have PMS, they may mean a variety of things and they frequently mean something different to the definitions in the research literature. Thus when they consult a GP for advice, they may feel that their problem is trivialized or alternatively that it is overly medicalized. In either case, the problem is that they are being offered treatment on the basis of evidence which has been gathered within a particular epistemological framework and which does not necessarily map onto their own experiences. A positivist/realist framework as noted by Ussher (1996) has little hope of adequately addressing all of the experiences women describe as PMS within a single model; such models are too complex, and depend for their predictive value on the assumption that if women have similar antecedents, these must necessarily have similar consequences. Moreover, such an approach does not acknowledge the subjective nature of women's menstrual experiences, an issue which is of paramount importance if this phenomenon is to be understood. It is clearly valuable to contextualize women's experiences by considering both internal (physiological and psychological) factors and external (psychosocial and cultural) factors, but in the final analysis, a woman who calls her own experience PMS has sole access to the meanings she attaches to that label.

I have thus concluded that it would be helpful to develop a new political approach to the study of PMS, one which is compatible with qualitative methods but which can also be employed in quantitative research. A woman-centered approach, which considers as its starting point that women's accounts of their own experiences are as valid as any interpretations put on those accounts by researchers, could begin to address the deficiencies in our understanding of the problem in several ways. First, we need much more research into women's experiences in order to provide a comprehensive description of both menstruation and PMS, including a description of the various meanings and emotions related to them. Second, we need to recognize that we do not have to choose between biological and psychosocial explanations. Women's experiences which they may call PMS are a product of a multiplicity of internal and external influences interacting in complex ways. We need to consider macro and micro levels of analysis in order to begin to understand these relationships, but should not privilege the reproductive and biological aspects over others (Ussher, 1992). Ussher (1996) has shown how the adoption of a materialist/discursive approach may be a useful step in reconciling disciplinary divides and furthering understanding of PMS. It is the contention of this chapter that a woman-centered approach, as an available political position which makes no assumptions about the aetiology of PMS and which places the experience of the individual at the center of analysis, would be an obvious extension to Ussher's suggestion.

REFERENCES

Abraham, G.E. and Rumley, R.E. (1987) Role of nutrition in managing the premenstrual tension syndromes. *Journal of Reproductive Medicine*, 32, 405–422

Blechman, E.A. and Clay, C.J. (1987). The scientific method and ethical treatment of premenstrual complaints. In B.E. Ginsberg and B.F. Carter (Eds.) *Premenstrual Syndrome: Ethical and Legal Implications in a Biomedical Perspective* (pp. 223–236). New York: Plenum Press

Burman, E. (1997) Minding the gap: Positivism, psychology and the politics of qualitative methods. *Journal of Social Issues*, 53 (4),785–802

Caplan, P.J., McCurdy-Myers, J. and Gans, M. (1992a) Should 'Premenstrual Syndrome' Be Called a Psychiatric Abnormality? *Feminism and Psychology*, 2 (1), 27–44

Caplan, P.J., McCurdy-Myers, J. and Gans, M. (1992b) Reply to Mary Brown Parlee's Commentary on PMS and psychiatric anomaly. *Feminism and Psychology*, 2 (1), 109

Choi, P.Y.L. (1992) The psychological benefits of physical exercise: Implications for women and the menstrual cycle. *Journal of Reproductive and Infant Psychology*, 10, 111–11

Choi, P.Y.L. and McKeown, S. (1997) What are young undergraduate women's qualitative experiences of the menstrual cycle? *Journal of Psychosomatic Obstetrics and Gynecology*, 18, 259–265

Chrisler, J.C. and Levy, K.B. (1990) The media construct a menstrual monster: a content analysis of PMS articles in the popular press. *Women and Health*, 16, 89–104

Eagan, A. (1985) The selling of premenstrual syndrome: who profits from making PMS 'the disease of the 1980s'? In S. Laws, V. Hey and A. Eagan (Eds.) *'Seeing Red': The Politics of Premenstrual Tension* (pp. 80–89). London: Hutchinson

Figert, A.E. (1995) The three faces of PMS: The professional, gendered and scientific structuring of a psychiatric disorder. *Social Problems*, 42, 56–73

Frank, R.T. (1931) The hormonal causes of premenstrual syndrome. *Archives of Neurology and Psychiatry*, 26, 1053–1057

Hamilton, J.A. and Gallant, S.J. (1990) Problematic aspects of diagnosing premenstrual phase dysphoria: Recommendations for psychological research and practice. *Professional Psychology: Research and Practice*, 21 (1), 60–68

Gottlieb, A. (1988) American Premenstrual Syndrome. A mute voice. *Anthropology Today*, 4 (6), 10–13

Halbreich, U. and Endicott, J. (1982) Classification of premenstrual syndromes. In R.C. Friedman (Ed.) *Behaviour and the Menstrual Cycle* (pp. 243–265). New York: Marcel Dekker

Harding, S. (1987). *Feminism and methodology*. Indianapolis: Indiana University Press

Hey, V. (1985) Getting away with murder: PMT and the press. In S. Laws, V. Hey and A. Eagan (Eds.) *'Seeing Red': The Politics of Pre-menstrual Tension* (pp. 65–79). London: Hutchinson

Hollway, W. (1989) *Subjectivity and Method in Psychology: Gender, Meaning and Science*. London: Sage

Kissling, E.A. (1996) Bleeding out loud: communication about menstruation. *Feminism and Psychology*, 6 (4), 481–504

Laws, S. (1985) Who needs PMT? A feminist approach to the politics of premenstrual tension. In S. Laws, V. Hey and A. Eagan (Eds.) *'Seeing Red': The Politics of Premenstrual Tension* (pp. 17–64). London: Hutchinson

Lincoln, Y.S. and Guba, E.G. (1985) *Naturalistic Enquiry*. Beverly Hills, CA: Sage

Lovering, K. (1995) '... but nobody said, nobody noticed at all': young adolescent girls and menarche. Paper presented to the Psychology of Women Section of the British Psychological Society, Annual Conference, Bristol, 5–7 July

Markens, S. (1996) The problematic of 'experience'. A political and cultural critique of PMS. *Gender and Society*, 10 (1), 42–58

Miota, P., Yahle, M. and Bartz, C. (1991) Premenstrual syndrome: A bio-psycho-social approach to treatment. In Taylor, D.L. and Woods, N.F. (Eds.) *Menstruation, Health and Illness* (pp. 17–64). New York: Hemisphere Publishing

Morse, J.M. (1995) The significance of saturation. *Qualitative Health Research*, 5 (2), 147–149

Nash, H.C. and Chrisler, J.C. (1997) Is a little (psychiatric) knowledge a dangerous thing? the impact of premenstrual dysphoric disorder on perceptions of premenstrual women. *Psychology of Women Quarterly*, 21, 315–322

Oxley, T. (1997) Menstrual management: An exploratory study. *Feminism and Psychology*, 8 (2), 185–191

Parlee, M.B. (1992). On PMS and psychiatric abnormality. *Feminism and Psychology*, 2 (1), 105–108

Pearlstein, T. (1996) Nonpharmacologic treatment of premenstrual syndrome. *Psychiatric Annals*, 26 (9), 590–594

Prior, J.C., Vigna, Y. and Alojada, N. (1986). Conditioning exercise decreases premenstrual symptoms. A prospective, controlled three month trial. *European Journal of Applied Physiology*, 55, 349–355

Reilly, J. (1997) The psychology of premenstrual syndrome: A grounded perspective. Unpublished Ph.D. dissertation, School of Psychology, The Queen's University of Belfast

Reilly, J. and Kremer, J. (1999) A qualitative study of women's perceptions of premenstrual syndrome: implications for general practitioners. *British Journal of General Practice*, 49, 783–78

Schmidt, P.J., Nieman, L.K., Danaceau, M.A., Adams, L.F. and Rubinow, D.R. (1998). Differential behavioral effects of gonadal steroids in women with and in those without premenstrual syndrome. *New England Journal of Medicine*, 338 (4), 209–216

Showalter, E. (1985) *The Female Malady: Women, Madness and English Culture*. London: Virago

Steege, J.F. (1989) Symptom measurement in premenstrual syndrome. In L.M. Demer, J.L. McGuire, A. Phillips and D.R. Rubinow (Eds.) *Premenstrual, Postpartum and Menopausal Mood Disorders* (pp. 53–63). Baltimore: Urban and Schwarzenberg

Steiner, M. (1997) Premenstrual syndromes. *Annual Review of Medicine*, 48, 447–455

Stevenson, C. and Cooper, N. (1997). Qualitative and quantitative research. *The Psychologist*, 10 (4), 159–160

Swann, C.J. and Ussher, J.M. (1995) A discourse analytic approach to women's experience of premenstrual syndrome. *Journal of Mental Health*, 4, 359–367

Ussher, J.M. (1992). The Demise of Dissent and the Rise of Cognition in Menstrual-Cycle Research. In J.T.E. Richardson (Ed.) *Cognition and the Menstrual Cycle* (pp. 132–173). New York: Springer-Verlag

Ussher, J.M. (1996) Premenstrual syndrome: Reconciling disciplinary divides through the adoption of a material-discursive epistemological standpoint. *Annual Review of Sex Research*, 7, 218–251

Ussher, J.M. and Wilding, J.M. (1992) Interactions between stress and performance during the menstrual cycle in relation to the premenstrual syndrome. *Journal of Reproductive and Infant Psychology*, 10, 83–101

Walker, A. (1995) Theory and methodology in premenstrual syndrome research. *Social Science and Medicine*, 41 (6), 793–800

Warner, P. and Walker, A. (1992) Editorial: Menstrual cycle research: time to take stock. *Journal of Reproductive and Infant Psychology*, 10 (2), 63–66

Yonkers, K.A. and Brown, W.A. (1996) Pharmacologic treatment of premenstrual syndrome. *Psychiatric Annals*, 26 (9), 586–589

CHAPTER 28

WHAT DOES SYSTEMS THEORY HAVE TO DO WITH PREMENSTRUAL COMPLAINTS?

Wendy Vanselow

INTRODUCTION

Making sense of the considerable research literature on premenstrual syndrome (PMS) can be a daunting task (see Reilly, in this volume). One can approach the subject from biomedical, psychological, sociological, anthropological and feminist viewpoints and arrive at totally different conclusions. Like the four blind men examining the elephant, we may never see the whole picture unless we can incorporate these multiple perspectives. Systems theory provides a framework for integrating these diverse approaches in a biopsychosocial model. Not only can this improve our understanding of the literature about this complex problem but also it provides more options for helping women with premenstrual complaints.

Engel's biopsychosocial model is the application of systems theory to human health and explains how illness exists on several interacting levels at the same time. Systems theory recognizes that there are multiple levels of existence with each level in the hierarchy having features and laws that are unique to that level. For instance, molecular chemistry cannot explain the organization of cells or organ systems and physiology cannot explain human behavior.

Nothing exists in isolation. Whether a cell or a person, every system is influenced by the configuration of the systems of which each is a part, that is, by its envi-

ronment ... Neither the cell nor the person can be fully characterized as a dynamic system without characterizing the larger system ... of which it is part. (Engel, 1977)

The biopsychosocial model is not reductionist in that, for instance, the effects of environment on the individual are not merely translated into chemical changes, but it recognizes that human beings interpret their experience and operate within systems of meaning. Thus illness has behavioral as well as biological aspects.

For the purposes of women with premenstrual complaints, relevant systems might include the reproductive, endocrine, and central nervous systems, the psychological disposition of the individual and the way they interpret their world, the dynamics of the couple relationship, the family system, the work environment, the social system and the culture. Different disciplines have an interest in these various systems and may have highly individual ways of knowing, developing particular arguments and research techniques to explore their area of expertise. A greater flexibility in moving between paradigms may be required if we are to expand our understanding of this complex phenomenon.

The following is a brief overview of the literature pertaining to PMS.

BIOMEDICAL

Biomedical research has been characterized by a constant search for a cure with treatments ranging from nutritional supplements, to various hormones and psychotropic medications, and all the way to medical or surgical castration. Controlled trials of PMS treatments invariably report very high placebo response rates; few substances have shown consistent significant benefit compared with placebo.

Exhaustive testing of menstrual cycle hormones has yielded no significant or consistent abnormality (Rubinow *et al.*, 1988). At the same time there have been attempts to clarify a definition of premenstrual disorder that is scientifically acceptable for research purposes. This is difficult in a condition where there are no objective markers. Double-blind placebo-controlled trials, which are the gold standard of biomedical research, ideally require a clearly defined and measurable condition with homogenous samples free of confounding comorbid conditions. Rigorous application of research criteria inevitably results in very high exclusion rates; what is gained in precision may be lost in generalizability.

Of note also is the fact that in this highly subjective area of research, intercurrent physical and psychiatric illnesses are regarded as grounds for exclusion from clinical trials, but scant attention is paid to the social circumstances surrounding the premenstrual complaint. Relationship breakdown and marital discord have been shown to be common in women presenting with PMS (Clare, 1983). Yet in this condition where the major treatment outcome is a self-assessment of mood, little significance is attached to these issues. The tacit assumption is that any such discord results from the woman's (hormonal) problem rather than it being a contributing factor to her complaint.

Most recent treatment options supported by research appear to be the serotonin-enhancing antidepressant medications but these have been assessed in a highly selective population of women with severe mood disorder. These women represent only a small fraction of the women who have premenstrual complaints and this reflects the great difficulty in obtaining scientifically appropriate samples from what is an essentially heterogenous condition. The DSM IV (American Psychiatric Association, 1994) clearly recognizes that psychiatric comorbidity is high in women with 'PMS' and that premenstrual exacerbation of intercurrent depressive disorder is far more common than an isolated premenstrual dysphoric disorder.

Other comorbid conditions are important also. The premenstrual pain and lowered mood of endometriosis may result in a premenstrual complaint but not be regarded as PMS because the primary condition is gynaecological. Menstrual migraine has been shown to be a separate condition from PMS. Other medical problems such as epilepsy, arthritis and irritable bowel syndrome, which can be exacerbated in the premenstrual phase, may easily be confused with PMS.

Thus it may be more appropriate to investigate the effects of hormonal cyclicity on pathological conditions such as depression rather than pathologizing the hormone cycle itself.

DOES A HORMONE-SENSITIVE DISORDER EXIST?

Surprisingly little evidence has accumulated in this regard. Arguments supporting the existence of a hormone-sensitive mood disorder include the cited increased incidence of psychological disturbance at times of hormone withdrawal such as postpartum and at menopause. Cross-sectional studies do not show any significant hormonal difference between women suffering psychiatric disorders at these times and non-sufferers. Similarly women complaining of PMS are no different hormonally to non-sufferers. It is likely therefore that expression of such disorders represents a vulnerability in the central nervous system. Some psychiatric disorders are reported to vary with the menstrual cycle, most prominently depressive and bipolar disorders. Oestrogen has been purported to be an effective antidepressant in women (Klaiber et al., 1979).

In the treatment of premenstrual syndrome, hysterectomy without oophorectomy has been associated with persistence of symptoms (Backstrom et al., 1981), suggesting that hormonal effects are important beyond the possible placebo effect of removing menstruation. More recently a highly sophisticated study by Schmidt and colleagues (1998) demonstrated that only women with a history of premenstrual dysphoria responded negatively to the reintroduction of menstrual cycle hormones following complete cycle suppression.

SOCIOCULTURAL

Considerable controversy surrounds the notion of a premenstrual syndrome. Whilst the 1980s saw PMS finally acknowledged as a disease entity in the U.S.A., historical and anthropological studies suggest that no such disorder was described prior to the twentieth century, even though mythology about menstruation abounded. PMS is clearly a culturally specific condition of urbanized Western societies (Richardson, 1995). Cyclical change may be regarded as normative but varies according to culture. In developed Western nations the most prominent premenstrual complaints are psychological and to some extent the emergence of PMS parallels the increasing rates of psychological ill-health in these countries. In addition, women in these countries experience more menstrual cycles than ever before because of earlier menarche, fewer pregnancies and less time lactating. It has been suggested that an increasing number of uninterrupted cycles may be associated with an increased risk of PMS (Bancroft, 1995).

PSYCHOSOCIAL

Menstrual cycles are for many women a regular part of life by which to mark time. This coupled with repeated messages from the media that the premenstrual phase is a negative experience has generated a climate where attribution of all manner of complaints to PMS is rife. Up to 50 percent of women reporting premenstrual complaints do not demonstrate cyclical symptoms when assessed prospectively (Rubinow and Roy-Byrne, 1984). In one study of healthy women, 30 percent reported PMS and about the same number did show some cyclical variability in mood. However there was no correlation between those claiming to suffer from PMS and those demonstrating cyclical change. The clearest determinant of premenstrual complaint related to psychosocial distress (Hardie, 1997).

FEMINIST PERSPECTIVE

The connection between psychological ill-health and women's bodies has for a long time occupied so-called objective science. Historically based on the male body as the norm, women by definition are regarded as inherently deviant. Female behavior perplexing to the male view has been attributed to her physiology rather than her position in society. Comparisons have been drawn between the nineteenth-century diagnosis of hysteria and the contemporary reproductive syndromes of PMS, postnatal depression and menopause as expressions of social powerlessness rather than illness (Ussher, 1992).

Socially, women in Western cultures are emerging from their role as second-class citizens. They are more educated, less vulnerable to their reproductive capacities and potentially more in control of their own lives than ever before. Their education is primarily directed towards career fulfilment in the workplace. At the same time the prevailing cultural stereotype of women as passive nurturers remains firmly embedded. In moulding themselves to be the perfect wife, mother or support person for others, the phenomenon of self-silencing ensues (Jack, 1991). Western society has changed rapidly with increasing rates of divorce, often resulting in complex family structures. Employment is less stable and more women are entering the paid work force. The consequence of attempting to resolve the many demands made upon her may be the eruption of seemingly uncharacteristic rage. This may or may not coincide with a tendency for premenstrual irritability. Labelling the behaviour as PMS creates an acceptable medicalization which contains the situation without threat to the status quo. Women are the victims of their raging hormones and not to be taken seriously.

Thus several possible explanations for the phenomenon are worthy of study. These include the following:

- the existence of a hormone-sensitive mood disorder
- the contribution of comorbid conditions be they gynaecological, medical or psychological
- the self-silencing of women in a male-dominated culture undergoing major changes to family structure and employment
- a culturally determined attribution of negative experience to the premenstrual phase.

These explanations are not mutually exclusive. A systems theory approach allows for any combination of these issues to be at play in the individual presenting with premenstrual complaints.

For the practitioner attempting to help women with premenstrual complaints a comprehensive history is essential. This should include medical, gynaecological and psychiatric details as well as information about the current family and family of origin. Family relationships discussed during the construction of a genogram can be as helpful in diagnosis as the prospective symptom charts so widely advocated. Another useful instrument is a brief depression inventory administered in the follicular (pre-ovulatory) phase of the cycle to detect the existence of an underlying depressive illness so common in cases of severe premenstrual complaints.

Finally the presentation of premenstrual complaints provides an opportunity for positive change. Frequently the expectation of taking a tablet that will make it all better needs to be challenged and women are often ready for major adjustments both in their life circumstances and in their perception. Assisting women to regain control of their lives can be the most rewarding aspect of working with women with premenstrual complaints.

REFERENCES

American Psychiatric Association (1994) *Diagnostic and Statistical Manual of Mental Disorders*. (4th edn). Washington D.C.: APA

Backstrom,T., Boyle, H. and Baird, D.T. (1981) Persistence of symptoms of premenstrual tension in hysterectomized women. *British Journal of Obstetrics and Gynaecology*, 88, 530–536

Bancroft, J. (1995) The menstrual cycle and the well-being of women. *Social Science and Medicine*, 41 (6), 785–791

Clare, A.W. (1983) Psychiatric and social aspects of premenstrual complaints. *Psychological Medicine*, 4, 1–58

Engel, G.L. (1977) The need for a new medical model: a challenge for biomedicine. *Science*, 196, 129–136

Hardie, E.A. (1997) Prevalence and predictors of cyclic and noncyclic affective change. *Psychology of Women Quarterly*, 21, 299–314

Jack, D.C. (1991) *Silencing the Self: Women and Depression*. Cambridge, MA: Harvard University Press

Klaiber, E.L., Broverman, D.M., Vogel, W. and Kobayashi, Y. (1979) Estrogen therapy for severe persistent depressions in women. *Archives of General Psychiatry*, 35, 550–554

Richardson, J.T.E. (1995) The premenstrual syndrome: a brief history. *Social Science and Medicine*, 35, 45–56

Rubinow, D.R., Roy-Byrne, P., Hoban, C., Gold, P. and Post, R. (1984) Prospective assessment of menstrually related mood disorders. *American Journal of Psychiatry*, 141 (5), 684–686

Rubinow, D.R., Hoban, M.C., Grover, G.N., *et al.* (1988) Changes in plasma hormones across the menstrual cycle in patients with menstrually related mood disorders and in control subjects. *American Journal of Obstetrics and Gynecology*, 158: 5–11

Schmidt, P., Neiman, L., Danaceau, M., Adams, L. and Rubinow, D. (1998) Differential behavioural effects of gonadal steroids in women with and in those without premenstrual syndrome. *New England Journal of Medicine*, 338 (4), 209–216

Ussher, J. (1992) Reproductive rhetoric and blaming the body. In P. Nicolson and J. Ussher (Eds.) *The Psychology of Women's Health and Health Care* (pp. 31–61). London: Macmillan

CHAPTER 29

MENSTRUAL CYCLE AND EATING BEHAVIOR

Louise Dye

INTRODUCTION

This chapter examines the effect of the menstrual cycle on food intake and the effect that patterns of food intake, most notably dieting, can have on the menstrual cycle. The hormonal fluctuations of the menstrual cycle clearly affect the amount of energy ingested. This chapter suggests that macronutrient selection is less clearly influenced but that mood state and cravings can partly determine the foods consumed by women premenstrually. The effect of restrictive food intake and dieting practices is reviewed and recent evidence suggests that the effects of these on the menstrual cycle and fertility, although sometimes subtle, may be a cause for concern. Dieting therefore appears to have adverse physical as well as psychological effects.

The relationship between the hormonal fluctuations of the reproductive cycle is bi-directional (see Richardson, in this volume). The menstrual cycle affects food intake, via changes in total energy consumed, macronutrient selection, food preferences and food cravings. Conversely, recent research is demonstrating that our eating behavior may influence the hormonal fluctuations which regulate the reproductive cycle.

The aim of this chapter is to review the bi-directional nature of the relationship between the menstrual cycle and eating behavior. The effect of the menstrual cycle on appetite control has recently been reviewed (Buffenstein *et al.*, 1995; Dye and Blundell, 1997). Changes in food intake, preferences and cravings have also been linked to mood (Bancroft *et al.*, 1988; Brzezinski *et al.*, 1990; Dye *et al.*, 1995) and serotonin has been suggested to be one mediator of this relationship (Wurtman, 1993; Dye and Blundell, 1997). There has been less research on the second position but the high prevalence of dieting in young women – 40 to 50 percent of women are believed to be on a diet at any one time (Polivy and Herman, 1987) – suggests that the menstrual cycle can be influenced by eating behavior with important implications for the reproductive health of women.

APPETITE CONTROL: FOOD INTAKE, EATING BEHAVIOR AND FOOD CRAVING

Human food intake can be assessed by means of quantitative aspects of food consumption such as the energetic value of food and its macronutrient composition (proportion of fat, protein and carbohydrate). Appetite is also represented by qualitative aspects such as food choice, food preferences and appreciation of the sensory aspects of food (taste, palatability, mouth-feel, etc.). Subjective phenomena such as the perception of hunger, fullness and hedonic sensations which accompany eating are also important (Hill *et al.*, 1995). Food cravings and urges to eat specific food products are an additional facet of eating behavior. Changes induced by the hormonal fluctuations of the menstrual cycle may be detected in various aspects of eating including changes in hunger, cravings for certain foods, alteration in meal size or snacking, adjustments in consumption of fat or carbohydrate, and an overall change in energy intake. The factors which affect food intake are shown in Figure 1.

MENSTRUAL CYCLE CHANGES IN FOOD INTAKE

Studies of food intake in primates and other mammals during the oestrus cycle indicate consistently lower food intake around the time of ovulation in rats (Herberg *et al.*, 1972), pigs (Friend, 1969), goats (Forbes, 1971), sheep (Tarttelin, 1968) and rhesus monkeys (Rosenblatt *et al.*, 1980).

Studies in a number of primate species indicate that highest food intake occurs consistently in the luteal phase with the nadir of food intake around the time of ovulation (Rosenblatt *et al.*, 1980).

Initially, elevated food intake in the luteal phase was attributed to increased levels of progesterone (Gilbert and Gillman, 1956). Later, the ovulatory decrease in intake was attributed to the appetite suppressant effects of oestrogen (Czaja, 1978), the luteal phase increase being thus due to the inhibitory action of progesterone on oestrogenic activity.

In humans, a distinct pattern of fluctuation in food intake has also been observed. Generally, energy intake is higher in the postovulatory or premenstrual/luteal phase of the cycle than in the preovulatory or follicular phase. Of 30 studies, reviewed by Dye and Blundell (1997), 25 studies reported significantly higher luteal energy intake than follicular intake. The remainder showed no significant effects of menstrual cycle phase. Two exceptions are Wurtman et al., (1989) and Krakow (1992) who show follicular energy intake to be non-significantly greater than luteal intake in subjects with no premenstrual symptoms and women not taking oral contraceptives respectively. In conditions where cyclic fluctuations in hormones are absent or minimized, no effects on food intake are apparent, e.g. in women using oral contraceptives (Anantharaman-Barr et al., 1988; Krakow, 1992), or women with anovulatory cycles (Barr et al., 1995). The time of ovulation represents the nadir of food intake during the menstrual cycle (Johnson et al., 1994).

MACRONUTRIENT INTAKE

In contrast to cyclic effects on total energy intake, reports about the patterns of macronutrient intake during the menstrual cycle are less consistent.

There has been some suggestion of significantly increased carbohy-

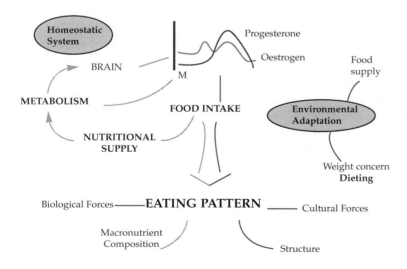

Figure 1. Direct and indirect effects of hormonal fluctuations on the Homeostatic System

drate consumption premenstrually (Brzezinski *et al.*, 1990; Dalvit-McPhillips, 1983); reductions in protein and carbohydrate intake at ovulation (Lyons *et al.*, 1989); and premenstrual increases in fat intake (Anantharaman-Barr *et al.*, 1988; Johnson *et al.*, 1994) or fat and protein intake (Gallant *et al.*, 1987).

There are, however, inconsistencies both between and within studies. Results may differ depending on whether actual intake of a macronutrient (in grammes) or the relative proportion that a macronutrient contributes to total energy intake (in percentage) is considered. While absolute intake of a macronutrient may increase significantly from the follicular to luteal phase (e.g. Barr *et al.*, 1995), the percentage of energy intake, for instance fat or carbohydrate, may fail to be differentiated. The predominant view has been that it is carbohydrate intake which increases in the luteal phase (Wurtman *et al.*, 1989). However, there is an equal number of studies which document significant increases in fat intake at this stage of the cycle (Dye and Blundell, 1997). Such results may represent general increases in appetite rather than specific increases in preferences for a particular macronutrient.

FOOD CRAVINGS AND MOOD: A ROLE FOR SEROTONIN?

Studies of food craving during the menstrual cycle have produced a range of findings about both the pattern and nature of food cravings. The predominant trend however, seems to be an increase in both the frequency and severity of food craving in the premenstruum (Dye *et al.*, 1995; Hill and Heaton-Brown, 1994). This tendency has been observed in varied samples of women (e.g. with and without PMS and/or premenstrual depression), suggesting that the experience of PMS sufferers is more severe but not necessarily qualitatively different from that of 'normal' women.

There are indications that depression and food cravings may coexist premenstrually (Bancroft *et al.*, 1988) and that this relationship may result in the selection of foods that might ameliorate poor mood (Wurtman, 1993). Serotonin (5–Hydroxytryptamine) is involved in the regulation of mood and appetite (Spring *et al.*, 1987). Levels of serotonin can be modulated by ovarian (Severino, 1994) and have been shown to be lower in the luteal phase in animals and humans (Ashby *et al.*, 1988,1992). Carbohydrate (CHO) consumption can produce increased uptake of tryptophan, a precursor of serotonin, by the brain and consequently increase the synthesis of serotonin (Fernstrom and Wurtman, 1971). Thus it has been argued that eating CHO can serve as a form of self-medication to raise mood.

Indeed, Wurtman *et al.* (1989) have demonstrated that the deliberate administration of carbohydrate can relieve premenstrual depression. The consumption of a CHO-rich, protein-poor evening meal improved mood in PMS sufferers in the late luteal phase but had no effect on mood in the follicular phase or in non-symptomatic control subjects. This is consistent with a carbohydrate-induced increase in serotonin occurring during the premenstruum.

However, there is little evidence for a selective craving for carbohydrate foods premenstrually or for a preferential intake of carbohydrate (Buffenstein *et al.*, 1995; Dye and Blundell, 1997). Consequently, the idea that individuals attempt to medicate themselves by eating carbohydrate is not yet substantiated. However, Dye and Blundell (1997) suggest that there is a role for serotonin in premenstrual food craving and increased energy intake, although this need not necessarily result in the consumption of CHO. If levels of serotonin are lower premenstrually, there will be relatively weaker control over appetite (Blundell, 1992) making individuals more susceptible to internal and environmental stimuli that facilitate eating and elicit food craving. Hence premenstrually some women may be vulnerable to overconsumption and craving and also to lowered mood.

THE EFFECTS OF FOOD INTAKE ON THE MENSTRUAL CYCLE

The discussion so far has focussed on the effects of hormonal changes on food intake. The second element of this chapter concerns the idea that food intake also affects hormones, which in turn affect the rhythm of the menstrual cycle. One major issue here is the concept of dieting, which may involve about 40 percent or more of the female population. Dieting can be defined as self-induced attempts to restrict food consumption and to control the pattern of eating. Therefore dieting is likely to influence measured food consumption, food choice and other aspects of eating. Pirke *et al.* (1989) have shown that dieting causes menstrual irregularities and three major factors which influence this relationship have been identified. Firstly, age – younger women are more susceptible to diet-induced menstrual irregularities. Secondly, the amount of weight loss – the greater the weight loss the higher the likelihood of menstrual irregularities. Thirdly, the nature of the diet – vegetarian diets affect the cycle more than a non-vegetarian diet, even when both cause the same amount of weight loss (Barr *et al.*, 1994; Dye, 1996; Pirke *et al.*, 1986). It is also well accepted that eating disorders such as anorexia nervosa and bulimia nervosa as well as excessive exercise are associated with disturbances of the hypothalamic-pituitary-gonadal axis (Pirke *et al.*, 1986; 1989).

However, it appears that restrained eating without active dieting can also produce disruption of the ovarian cycle. It is well known that amenorrhea occurs when body weight falls substantially. There is evidence that the ovarian cycle can be affected when body weight falls below 13 percent of ideal body weight (Frisch and Revelle, 1970, 1974). In some cases there is no absence of menstruation and little to indicate that hormones are inadequate. However, fertility is compromised (Schweiger *et al.*, 1992).

Highly restrained women can show a disturbance of follicle development or luteal phase hormonal disruption even when there is no loss of weight and no secondary amenorrhea. The usual pattern of food intake across the menstrual cycle is not seen in women with highly restrained eating patterns (Schweiger *et al.*, 1992). This could be due to the effects of low energy intake on hormonal cycles, or because of a tonic inhibition over eating which obscures any underlying physiological influence.

We also are becoming increasing aware of the effects of certain nutritional regimes on hormones which can be immediate, such as alteration of follicular phase length. Long-term changes such as the increase in hormone-dependent cancers observed in migrants to the U.S.A. are related to adoption of a Western style diet (Adlercreutz, 1991). Low fat and high fibre diets appear to be associated with increased follicular phase length (Goldin *et al.*, 1994). However, it is unclear whether the effects observed are due to the reduction in fat or the concomitant increase in fibre. One suggestion has been that diets containing phytoestrogens (such as soya diets) reduce circulating ovarian steroids and adrenal androgens and thereby increase menstrual cycle length (Lu *et al.*, 1996).

The regulation of reproduction appears to rely upon an optimal level of nutrition and body weight. The ob-protein, leptin (Halaas *et al.*, 1995) serves as a signal linking adipose tissue to central neural pathways. Plasma levels of leptin correlate well with BMI and percentage body fat and are reduced in eating disordered patients (e.g. Hebebrand *et al.*, 1997). The relationship between leptin and reproduction and neuroendocrine regulation has recently been reviewed (Hoggard *et al.*, 1998; Mantzoros and Cogswell, 1999). Leptin may be one signal of metabolic state which is recognized by the brain and involved in the weight and diet-mediated regulation of reproduction. For example, injections of leptin can restore fertility in mutant mice which have difficulty reproducing (Chehab *et al.*, 1996) and cause early onset of reproductive function in normal female mice (Chehab *et al.*, 1997). The role of leptin in human reproduction is likely to be become clearer in the near future.

In conclusion, there are clearly cyclical fluctuations in energy intake associated with the menstrual cycle. Although changes in macronutrient selection are less well defined, it is apparent that both energy intake and macronutrient selection have implications for the reproductive health of women. Serotonin is involved in this mediation of appetite during the menstrual cycle and leptin may be a further signal of reproductive state. As well as extremes of under and overweight, dieting may have important, sometimes unseen, effects on the menstrual cycle.

REFERENCES

Adlercreutz, H. (1991) Diet and sex hormone metabolism. In I. R. Rowland, (Ed.) *Nutrition, Toxicity and Cancer* (pp. 137–195). London: CRC Press

Anantharaman-Barr, H.G., Clavien, H., Gmunder, B. and Pollett, P.E. (1988) Nutrient intake and the menstrual cycle. *Int. J. Obesity*, 143

Ashby, C.R. Jr., Carr, L.A, Cook, C.L., Steptoe, M. and Franks, D.D. (1988) Alteration of platelet serotonergic mechanism and monoamine oxidase activity in premenstrual sundrome. *Biol. Psychiatry*, 24, 225–233

Ashby, C.R. Jr., Carr, L.A, Cook, C.L., Steptoe, M. and Franks, D.D. (1992) Inhibition of serotonin uptake in rat brain synaptosomes by plasma from patients with premenstrual syndrome. *Biol Psychiatry*, 31, 1169–1171

Bancroft, J., Cook, A., Davidson, D., Bennie, J. and Goodwin, G. (1991) Blunting of neuroendocrine responses to infusion of L-tryptophan in women with perimenstrual mood change. *Psychol. Med.*, 21, 305–312

Bancroft, J., Cook, A. and Williamson, L. (1988) Food craving, mood and the menstrual cycle. *Psychol. Med.*, 18, 855–860

Barr, S. I., Janelle, K.C. and Prior, J.C. (1995) Energy intakes are higher during the luteal phase of ovulatory menstrual cycles. *Am. J. Clin. Nutr.* 61, 39–43

Blundell, J.E. (1992) Serotonin and the biology of feeding. *Am. J. Clin. Nutr.*, 55, 1555–1595

Brzezinski, A. A., Wurtman, J. J., Wurtman, R. J., Gleason, R., Greenfield, J. and Nader, T. (1990) d-Fenfluramine suppresses the increased calorie and carbohydrate intakes and improves the mood of women with premenstrual depression. *Obstet. Gynecol.*, 76, 296–301

Buffenstein, R., Poppitt, S.D., McDevitt, R.M. and Prentice, A.M. (1995) Food intake and the menstrual cycle: a retrospective analysis with implications for appetite research. *Physiology and Behaviour*, 58(6), 1067–1077

Chehab, F.F., Lim, M.E. and Lu, R.H. (1996) Correction of the sterility defect in homozygous obese female mice by treatment with the human recombinant leptin. *Nature Genetics* 12, 318–320

Chehab, F.F., Mounzih, K., Lu, R.H. and Lim, M.E. (1997) Early onset of reproductive function in normal female mice treated with leptin. *Science,* 275, 88–90

Czaja, J.A. (1978) Ovarian influences on primate food intake: Assessment of progesterone actions. *Physiol. Behav.*, 21, 923–928

Dalvit-McPhillips, S.P. (1983) The effect of the human menstrual cycle on nutrient intake. *Physiol. Behav.*, 31 (2), 209–212

Dye, L. (1996) Dietary Intake, restraint and vegetarianism. Paper presented at the Annual Conference of the Psychobiology Section September 1995. *Proceedings of the British Psychological Society*, 4 (2), 92

Dye, L. and Blundell, J.E. (1997) Menstrual cycle and appetite control: implications for weight regulation. *Human Reproduction*, 12 (6), 1142–1151

Dye, L., Warner, P. and Bancroft, J. (1995) Food craving during the menstrual cycle and its relationship to stress, happiness of relationship and depression. *J. Aff. Dis.*, 34, 157–164

Fernstrom, J. D. and Wurtman, R. J. (1971) Brain serotonin content: Increase following ingestion of carbohydrate diet. *Science*, 174, 1023–1025

Forbes, J.M. (1971) Physiological changes affecting voluntary food intake in ruminants. *Proc. Nutr. Soc.*, 30, 135–142

Friend, D.W. (1969) Self-selection of feeds and water by swine during pregnancy and lactation. *J. Amin. Sci.*, 32, 658–666

Frisch, R.E. (1994) Height and weight at menarche and a hypothesis of menarche. *Archives of Diseases in Childhood,* 46, 695–701

Frisch, R.E. and Revelle, R. (1970) The right weight: body fat, menarche and fertility. *Proc. Nutr. Soc.*, 53, 113–129

Gallant, M.P., Bowering, J., Short, S.H., Turkki, P.R. and Badawy, S. (1987) Pyridoxine and magnesium status of women with premenstrual syndrome. *Nutr. Res.* 7, 243–252

Gilbert, C., and Gillman, J. (1956) Changing pattern of food intake and appetite during the menstrual cycle of the baboon *(Papio ursinus)* with a consideration of some of the controlling endocrine factors. *S. Afr. J. Med. Sci.*, 21, 75–88

Goldin, B.R., Adlercreutz, H., Dwyer, J.T., Swenson, L., Warram, J.H. and Gorbach, S.L. (1994) The effect of dietary fat and fiber on serum estrogen concentrations in premenopausal women under controlled dietary conditions. *Cancer*, 74 (3), 1125–1131

Halaas, J.J., Gajiwala, K.S., Maffei, M. *et al.* (1995) Weight-reducing effects of the plasma protein encoded by the obese gene. *Science*, 269, 543–546

Hebebrandt, J., Blum, W., Barth, N., Coners, H., Englaro, P., Juul, A., Ziegler, A., Warnke, A., Rascher, W. and Remschmidt, H. (1997) Leptin levels in patients with anorexia nervosa are reduced in the acute stage and elevated upon short-term weight restoration. *Molecular Psychiatry*, 2 (4), 330–334

Herberg, L.J., Pye, J.G and Blundell, J.E. (1972) Sex differences in the hypothalamic regulation of food hoarding: hormones versus calories. *Animal Behav.*, 20, 186–191

Hill, A.J. and Heaton-Brown, L (1994) The experience of food craving: a prospective investigation in healthy women. *Journal of Psychosomatic Research*, 38, 801–814

Hill, A.J., Rogers, P.J. and Blundell, J.E. (1995) Techniques for the experimental measurement of human eating behavior and food intake: a practical guide. *Int. J. Obesity*, 19, 361–375

Hoggard, N., Hunter, L., Trayburn, P., Williams, L.M. and Mercer, J.G. (1998) Leptin and reproduction. *Proc. Nutr. Soc.* 57, 421–427

Johnson, W.G., Corrigan, S.A., Lemmon, C.R. *et al.* (1994) Energy regulation over the menstrual cycle. *Physiology and Behaviour*, 56, 523–527

Krakow, K. (1992) Gibt es ein Zyklusabhängiges Ernährungsverhalten? Unpublished dissertation, Fachhochschule Münster

Lu, L.J., Anderson, K.E., Grady, J.J. and Nagamani, M. (1996) Effects of soya consumption for one month on steroid hormones in premenopausal women: implications for breast cancer risk reduction. *Cancer Epidemiology, Biomarkers and Prevention*, 5 (1), 63–70

Lyons, P.M., Truswell, A.S., Mira, M., Oizzard, J. and Abraham, S.F. (1989) Reduction of food intake in the ovulatory phase of the menstrual cycle. *Am. J. Clin. Nutr.*, 49, 1164–1168

Mantzoros, C.S. and Cogswell, R.J. (1999) Leptin's role in regulation of neuroendocrine function. *Molecular Psychiatry*, 4 (1), 6

Pirke, K.M., Laessle, R.G., Schweiger, U., Broocks, A., Strowitzki, T., Huber, B., Tuschl, R.J. and Middendorf, R. (1989) Dieting causes menstrual irregularities in normal weight young women through impairment of episodic luteinizing hormone secretion. *Fertil. Steril.*, 51 (2), 263–268

Pirke, K.M., Schweiger, U., Laessle, R.G., Dickhaut, B., Schweiger, M. and Waechtler, M. (1986) Dieting influences the menstrual cycle; vegetarian versus nonvegetarian diet. *Fertil. Steril.*, 46, 1083–1088

Polivy, J. and Herman, C.P. (1987) Diagnosis and treatment of normal eating. *J. Consult. Clin. Psychol.*, 55, 635–644

Rosenblatt, H., Dyrenfurth, I., Ferin, M. and Vande-Wiele, R.L. (1980) Food intake and the menstrual cycle in rhesus monkeys. *Physiol. Behav.*, 24, 447–449

Schweiger, U., Tuschl, R.J., Platte, P., Broocks, A., Laessle, R.G. and Pirke, K.M. (1992) Everyday eating behaviour and menstrual function in young women. *Fertil. Steril.*, 57, 771–775

Severino, S. K. (1994) A focus on 5–Hydroxytryptamine (serotonin) and psychopathology. In J.H. Gold and S.K. Severino (Eds.) *Pre-menstrual Dysphorias: Myths and Realities.* New York: American Psychiatric Association

Spring, B., Chiodo, J. and Bowen, D.J. (1987) Carbohydrates, tryptophan, and behaviour: a methodological review. *Psychological Bulletin*, 102,234–256

Tarrtelin, M.F. (1968) Cyclical variations in food and water intake in ewes. *J. Physiol.*, 195, 29–30

Wurtman, J.J., Brzezinski, A., Wurtman, R.J. and Laferrere, B. (1989) Effect of nutrient intake on premenstrual depression. *Am. J. Obstet. Gynecol.*, 161, 1228–1234

Wurtman, J.J. (1993) Nutritional intervention in premenstrual syndrome. In S. Smith and I. Schiff (Eds.) *Modern Management of Premenstrual Syndrome.* New York: W.W. Norton

CHAPTER 30

HORMONES AND BEHAVIOR: COGNITION, MENSTRUATION AND MENOPAUSE

John T. E. Richardson

INTRODUCTION

Most women between the ages of 15 and 50 are regularly affected by the hormonal and physiological changes that are associated with the cyclical process of ovulation and menstruation. Research with animals has shown that the hormones oestrogen and progesterone alter the electrical and chemical features of nerve cells (Pfaff and McEwen, 1983), and in humans there is evidence of systematic fluctuations during the normal menstrual cycle in the electrical potential and activity of the brain (Abramowitz and Dubrovsky, 1980; Becker *et al.*, 1982). These findings suggest that there might be corresponding fluctuations in women's behavior and particularly in their intellectual performance.

This suggestion accords with the view commonly held by both women and men in Western cultures, that the premenstrual and menstrual phases of the menstrual cycle (in other words, the few days before and after the onset of bleeding) are characterized by intellectual debilitation (Brooks-Gunn and Ruble, 1986). Menstruation is widely thought to impair thinking, decision making, reasoning and remembering in both girls and women and to disrupt their performance in educational contexts. This expectation is, in turn, apparently borne out by women's own accounts of the symptoms which they typically experience during the premenstrual and menstrual phases, both in daily activities and in formal academic studying (see Richardson, 1992).

In short, the menstrual cycle appears to have major implications for women's health, both in terms of their own expectations and perceptions of their cognitive abilities and in terms of the expectations and perceptions of other people. Nevertheless, personal reports and cultural stereotypes simply do not constitute adequate evidence of objective debilitation. In general, people are very poor at assessing their own cognitive abilities, and their subjective reports may have little objective validity (Herrmann, 1984; Martin and Jones, 1984). I want to consider the research evidence on, first, the impact of menstruation on women's intellectual performance and, second, the impact of the menopause on women's intellectual performance.

COGNITION AND THE MENSTRUAL CYCLE

There is in fact a considerable research literature on intellectual performance over the menstrual cycle. Sommer (1992) provided a critical examination of this literature and she concluded that, in a wide range of cognitive tasks, there was simply no good evidence to support the idea of premenstrual or menstrual debilitation. This conclusion even encompassed research on the academic performance of female students assessed by means of examinations or class tests (see also Richardson, 1991). Contrary to the reports of women, and the expectations of women and men, menstruation does not appear to impair women's intellectual capabilities at all.

One possibility, of course, is that menstruation affects some women but not others. However, there is no good evidence for any intellectual debilitation in women who report more premenstrual symptoms or menstrual discomfort, in women who produce high scores on measures of extraversion, neuroticism or anxiety, nor even in women who believe in the debilitating effects of menstruation (Richardson, 1991; Sommer, 1983, 1992).

Instead, both women and men seem to ascribe women's cognitive failures during the premenstrual and menstrual phases to the process of menstruation, but to ascribe similar failures at other times to external, situational factors.

The overwhelming lack of evidence for any intellectual debilitation around the time of menstruation does not appear to discourage researchers from looking for it. Boyle (1997) obtained reports of menstrual symptoms from 427 girls in Years 10 to 12 at several Australian secondary schools and found that these tended to be negatively correlated with their end-of-year grades six months earlier. Although Boyle concluded that menstrual symptoms affected academic performance, his results are equally consistent with the notion that academic failure exacerbates menstrual symptoms. Moreover, the effects which he obtained were most pronounced for symptoms experienced in the middle of the menstrual cycle, and it is (to say the least) rather odd to describe these as 'menstrual' symptoms.

COGNITION AND THE MENOPAUSE

If fluctuations in oestrogen and progesterone give rise to variations in intellectual performance, then this should also be evident around the time of the menopause. Strictly speaking, 'menopause' refers to the point of total cessation of the menstrual cycle, usually defined in terms of an absence of periods for one year. This can occur at any age between 40 and 60, but the most common age is 51 years (Treloar, 1982). The more general term, 'climacteric', refers to the gradual changes associated with the end of reproductive capability which occur over a period of several years as a result of decreasing ovarian function.

Menopausal symptoms vary in their nature and their prevalence between different cultures (Lock, 1986, 1993). What is interesting in the present context is that problems of memory or concentration are reported only very rarely. Indeed, many surveys either omit cognitive symptoms altogether or else view them simply as a consequence of physical or emotional symptoms (e.g. Kaufert and Syrotuik, 1981). In a survey of women drawn from an urban population in the United States, 25 percent reported 'forgetfulness' as a symptom experienced because of the menopause (Polit and LaRocco, 1980), but a more recent study in the United Kingdom found that the proportion of women who reported an 'inability to concentrate' was roughly 25 percent across an age range between 37 years and 58 years (Quine and Rubin, 1997; Rubin and Quine, 1996).

The latter survey found that more than a third of the women believed that hormone replacement therapy (HRT) was likely to relieve an inability to concentrate, regardless of whether they were receiving or had received HRT themselves. There is consistent evidence from clinical trials that HRT tends to enhance moods and cognition, but its effects in both respects are fairly modest (see Halbreich, 1997; Sherwin, 1997). Some researchers have claimed that the menopause tends to accelerate the cognitive decline that is associated with aging and that HRT protects women against this process (e.g. Halbreich *et al.*, 1995; Kimura, 1995; Resnick *et al.*, 1997).

If the menopause disrupts intellectual performance, then this should become apparent as an interaction between the effects of age and gender in results obtained from representative samples of men and women of different ages. Schaie (1996) presented test results obtained from several thousand participants tested over the previous 40 years. Both cross-sectional and longitudinal comparisons showed similar patterns of performance in men and women across a wide variety of cognitive tasks up to the age of 67. There were no significant interactions between the effects of age and gender and no suggestion of any dip in the performance of women in their early 50s.

Nilsson *et al.* (1997) administered a battery of tests concerned with various aspects of memory function to a total of 3,000 participants drawn from the general population of a Swedish city (see also Herlitz *et al.*, 1997). There was just one significant interaction between the effects of age and gender: this occurred on a measure of semantic memory based upon tests of word comprehension and general knowledge. Indeed, men and women showed similar patterns of performance up to the age of 70, and there was no suggestion on any of the measures of a reduction in the performance of women around the age of 50 (L.-G. Nilsson, personal communication).

SUMMARY

The notion that women's intellectual capabilities might be influenced by the hormonal processes associated with the menstrual cycle is supported both by neurophysiological evidence and by cultural expectations. However, the research literature indicates that there are no consistent variations in women's cognitive performance during the normal menstrual cycle, either in everyday activities or in the more cognitively demanding tasks that are encountered in educational settings. Equally, there is no evidence for any intellectual impairment associated with the menopause. In short, then, the menstrual cycle appears to have little or no impact upon the efficiency of women's intellectual functioning. This is clearly an important message for women in resisting discriminatory policies and practices in the workplace or daily life based upon mistaken assumptions concerning their ability to perform reliably and consistently throughout the normal working lifetime.

REFERENCES

Abramowitz, M. and Dubrovsky, B. (1980) CNV characteristics throughout the normal menstrual cycle. In H.H. Kornhuber and L. Deecke (Eds.) *Progress in Brain Research: Vol. 54. Motivation, Motor and Sensory Processes of the Brain: Electrical Potentials, Behaviour and Clinical Use* (pp. 441–446). Amsterdam: Elsevier

Becker, D., Creutzfeldt, O.D., Schwibbe, M. and Wuttke, W. (1982) Changes in physiological, EEG and psychological parameters in women during the spontaneous menstrual cycle and following oral contraceptives. *Psychoneuroendocrinology*, 7, 75–90

Boyle, G.J. (1997) Effects of menstrual cycle moods and symptoms on academic performance:

A study of senior secondary school students. *British Journal of Educational Psychology, 67,* 37–49

Brooks-Gunn, J. and Ruble, D.N. (1986) Men's and women's attitudes and beliefs about the menstrual cycle. *Sex Roles, 14,* 287–299

Halbreich, U. (1997) Role of estrogen in postmenopausal depression. *Neurology, 48,* (5, Suppl. 7), S16–S20

Halbreich, U., Lumley, L.A., Palter, S., Manning, C., Gengo, F. and Joe, S.H. (1995) Possible acceleration of age effects on cognition. *Journal of Psychiatric Research, 29,* 153–163

Herlitz, A., Nilsson, L.-G. and Bäckman, L. (1997) Gender differences in episodic memory. *Memory and Cognition, 25,* 801–811

Herrmann, D.J. (1984) Questionnaires about memory. In J.E. Harris and P.E. Morris (Eds.) *Everyday Memory, Actions and Absent-Mindedness* (pp. 133–151). London: Academic Press

Kaufert, P. and Syrotuik, J. (1981) Symptom reporting at the menopause. *Social Science and Medicine,* 15E, 173–184

Kimura, D. (1995) Estrogen replacement therapy may protect against intellectual decline in postmenopausal women. *Hormones and Behavior, 29,* 312–321

Lock, M. (Ed.) (1986) *Anthropological Approaches to Menopause (Culture, Medicine and Psychiatry,* Vol. 10, No. 1). Dordrecht, The Netherlands: Reidel.

Lock, M. (1993) *Encounters With Aging: Mythologies Of Menopause in Japan and North American.* Berkeley, CA: University of California Press

Martin, M. and Jones, G.V. (1984) Cognitive failures in everyday life. In J. E. Harris and P. E. Morris (Eds.) *Everyday Memory, Actions and Absent-Mindedness* (pp. 173–190). London: Academic Press

Nilsson. L.-G., Bäckman, L., Erngrund, K., Nyberg, L., Adolfsson, R., Bucht, G., Karlsson, S., Widing, M. and Winblad, B. (1997) The Betula prospective cohort study: Memory, health, and aging. *Aging, Neuropsychology, and Cognition, 4,* 1–32

Pfaff, D.W. and McEwen, B.S. (1983) Actions of estrogens and progestins on nerve cells. *Science,* 219, 808–814

Polit, D.F. and LaRocco, S.A. (1980) Social and psychological correlates of menopausal symptoms. *Psychosomatic Medicine, 42,* 335–345

Quine, L. and Rubin, R. (1997) Attitude, subjective norm and perceived behavioural control as predictors of women's intentions to take hormone replacement therapy. *British Journal of Health Psychology, 2,* 199–216

Resnick, S.M., Metter, E.J. and Zonderman, A.B. (1997) Estrogen replacement therapy and longitudinal decline in visual memory: A possible protective effect? *Neurology, 49,* 1491–1497

Richardson, J.T.E. (1991) The menstrual cycle and student learning. *Journal of Higher Education, 62,* 317–340

Richardson, J.T.E. (1992) The menstrual cycle, cognition, and paramenstrual symptomatology. In J.T.E. Richardson (Ed.) *Cognition and the Menstrual Cycle* (pp. 1–38). New York: Springer-Verlag.

Rubin, R. and Quine, L. (1996) *Women's attitudes to the menopause and the use of Hormone Replacement Therapy.* Paper presented at the London conference of the British Psychological Society, December

Schaie, K.W. (1996) *Intellectual Development in Adulthood: The Seattle Longitudinal Study.* Cambridge: Cambridge University Press.

Sherwin, B.B. (1997) Estrogen effects on cognition in menopausal women. *Neurology, 48* (5, Suppl. 7), S21–S26

Sommer, B. (1983) How does menstruation affect cognitive competence and psychophysiological response? In S. Golub (Ed.) *Women and Health: Vol. 8. Lifting the Curse of Menstruation* (pp. 53–90). New York: Haworth Press

Sommer, B. (1992) Cognitive performance and the menstrual cycle. In J.T.E. Richardson (Ed.), *Cognition and the Menstrual Cycle* (pp. 39–66). New York: Springer-Verlag

Treloar, A.E. (1982) Predicting the close of menstrual life. In A.M. Voda, M. Dinnerstein and S.R. O'Donnell (Eds.) *Changing Perspectives on Menopause* (pp. 289–304). Austin: University of Texas Press

SEX HORMONES AS BIOCULTURAL ACTORS: RETHINKING BIOLOGY, SEXUAL DIFFERENCE AND HEALTH

Celia Roberts

INTRODUCTION

In everyday experience in the West, women put a range of negative experiences down to sex hormones. Hormones are used to explain the edginess of PMT, the tearfulness of a new mother, the weariness of an aging woman (see Dye, Dinnerstein, and Richardson, in this volume). Men too are sometimes – although less often – described as hormonal. Aggressiveness, unfaithfulness, the love of violent sport, are popularly understood as testosterone-driven.

Within Western biomedical and technoscientific thought, similar forms of biological explanation are used. Differences between men and women, physically, behaviorally and psychologically, are held, at least in part, to be biologically produced. Again, the sex hormones (oestrogen, progesterone and testosterone) are thought to be especially potent here. It is held by physiologists, for example, that the absence or presence of 'male' sex hormones (androgens) in foetuses determines the development of male or female reproductive systems in utero. Whilst genetic factors are also important, the absence of 'appropriate' amounts of sex hormones will result in a mismatch between a child's genetic and phenotypic sex (Sherwood, 1997; Wolpert, 1993; Baker, 1980). Other scientists, those working in the field of behavioral endocrinology for example, make further claims for the role of sex hormones in the production of sexual differences. They argue that beyond producing sexually differentiated bodies (reproductive systems, general morphologies – breasts, hair patterns, voice depth, etc.), sex hormones are also active in the production of sexually differentiated behaviors. So-called 'typical' male and female behaviors in children (boys' preference for rough-and-tumble play, girls' preference for playing with dolls) are held to be caused by brain differences produced in utero by sex hormones (Ehrhardt, 1984; Ehrhardt and Meyer-Bahlburg, 1981; Donovan, 1988; Reinisch *et al.*, 1991). Adult behaviors are also explained by some in this way, although most such explanations favor 'interactive' or 'multiplier' models in which social effects (such as the rewarding of certain behaviors over a lifetime) are thought to interact with hormones to produce sexual differences (Reinisch *et al.*, 1991; Witelson, 1991). Within scientific discourse, sex hormones are also held to be involved in sexual drive, and aggression, and of course with aging in both men and women. Aging in fact, is now often described as an endocrinopathy, that is, as a hormonal disorder which can be remedied with hormone replacement therapies. Issues of sexual difference are important here too – menopausal women have long been described as losing their femininity, and now aging men are understood to be less masculine. Once more, hormones are seen to be responsible for sexual difference.

SEX VS GENDER

For feminists interested in the body, and particularly in women's health, these assertions regarding the role of sex hormones are both difficult to ignore and troubling to accept. Claims that differences between men and women are the result of biological forces have a long history of association with oppressive and limiting views of women's capabilities and functions. In nineteenth-century England, for example, doctors argued that women's reproductive systems made them unsuited to advanced education. Menstruation and ovulation required so much energy, it was argued, it would be dangerous to divert any effort into study (Russett, 1989; Bland, 1995). Feminists have had a long history of refuting such biological claims (Bland, 1995; Caine, 1992). For over two centuries, they have argued that women's biological differences from men cannot be seen as static or inevitable, and should not be used to deny women access to any aspect of life. In most cases feminists have not argued that differences between the sexes do not exist, but rather have questioned either the causes of, or the significance attributed to, these differences. In the nineteenth century, feminists argued that women's physical weakness and lack of energy was not caused by biological differences, but rather was a product of inactive lives, poor diet, and restrictive clothing. Such differences, as was pointed out at the time and has been convincingly argued since, were also highly class specific – working-class women were expected and able to undertake hard physical work (Russett, 1989; Bland, 1995).

In more recent years, feminist arguments against biological reductionism have become increasingly sophisticated in their attempts to rethink the interrelation of biology and culture. Since the 1970s, such arguments have been focussed largely around the meaning of two concepts – 'sex' and 'gender'.

The term 'gender' comes from a particular Anglo-American psychobiological/sexological view which positions biological sex as a structuring materiality which interacts with culture to produce gender. Gender, in this view, is connected directly, although not without cultural effort, to sex. Gender is the social interpretation of sexed biology.

This view of gender has been strongly criticized by feminists in recent decades. Originally, following the work of Simone de Beauvoir (1988 [1949]), feminists argued for a clearer distinction to be made between sex and gender. They rejected the naturalized intertwining of the two produced particularly by American psychology and sexology. This clearer sex/gender distinction acknowledged biological differences between men and women, but argued that the significance of these was social. There was no necessary link between sex and gender.

This was a ground-breaking view and remains the inspiration of much feminist and other thinking about the significant role of social interpretations of biological differences. In the 1980s, however, a compelling criticism of this position arose, informed by radical rethinkings of psychoanalysis and by post-structuralist theories. The critique, made in Australia by such theorists as Moira Gatens and Elizabeth Grosz, was basically that the body remains strongly significant in the production of gender. As Gatens argued, it matters what sort of body experiences or displays gender (Gatens, 1983). Masculinity lived by a male body has very different meanings and effects to masculinity lived by a female body. The significant part of this position, however, which distinguished it from the psychological/sexological view of the intertwining of sex and gender, was its understanding of the body as itself socially produced or inscribed. This understanding of the body, informed by rereadings of psychoanalysis in particular, rejected a view of biology as fixed and static, and instead posited terms such as 'morphology', 'the lived body', and 'the imaginary body', to emphasize that although the body was important in theorizing experience, it did not dictate the content of gender (Grosz, 1989, 1990, 1994; Gatens, 1993, 1996). Gatens, for example, argued that imaginary bodies are formed both by the particular culture in which they live and by their individual history of psychical experience:

The imaginary body is socially and historically specific in that it is constructed by: a shared language; the shared psychical significance and privileging of various zones of the body (e.g. the mouth, anus, the genitals); and the common institutional practices and discourses (e.g. medical, juridical, and educational) on and through the body. (Gatens, 1983: 152)

In a broader way, this understanding was part of a flourishing of writing – which continues today – analysing the body as culturally produced. All types of historical texts about the body, especially medical and scientific ones, were examined in order to discover and reveal the social nature of their descriptions (Laqueur, 1992; Scheibinger, 1989, 1993). Phenomenological accounts of bodily experience also emphasized the plastic and historically located nature of embodiment (Duden, 1991; Young, 1990). Michel Foucault's work on the history of sexuality received enormous attention, as he was read to show the production of bodies by power/knowledge regimes (Foucault, 1987). Psychoanalytic theorists wrote at length about the role of language and the unconscious in the production of bodies (Kristeva, 1982; Irigaray, 1985, 1993; Grosz, 1989).

Into the 1990s, however, difficulties arose in relation to these theories of the social nature of the body. Questions were asked about the extent of the cultural construction of the body and the nature of the process of construction. Although the social nature of a scientific description of the reproductive organs may be demonstrated (Laqueur, 1992), is it possible to say how this construction constructs the flesh and blood of individual bodies? While it may be clear that phenomena such as hysterical paralysis or phantom limb indicate a cultural experience of the body (Gatens, 1983; Grosz, 1994), or that diet and exercise regimes produce different types of bodies (Gatens, 1996: 68–69), what of smaller things such as chromosomes, and indeed hormones? Are they culturally constructed? Do they exist outside of representations of them and if so, how can we gain any access to this? If descriptions are always social, does this necessarily mean that bodies are entirely social too?

In feminist theory these questions coalesced in the early 1990s around the issue of essentialism and how to understand differences between the sexes. Questions about the cultural construction of the body led theorists to ask what the nature of difference actually was. If some difference was to be claimed between men and women in terms of embodiment, what did this rely on? Was some sort of biological claim being made, thereby making the argument essentialist, or on the other hand, was an impossibly flexible body being posited in which all differences were social and changeable? These debates caused a crisis in feminist theory. They led to the questioning of the status of the category 'women' itself – if there was no essential (biological or otherwise) commonality between women, how could they be considered a group? These debates were also fuelled by the interventions of women of color, anti-racist feminists, and lesbian and queer theorists who criticized the racist and heterosexist understandings of the term 'women' prevalent in feminist theories.

THEORIZING SEX HORMONES

The problem of how to theorize biology remains contentious. Whilst feminist theorists have clearly demonstrated that biological forces such as sex hormones cannot be seen to operate in isolation from culture – that there is no simple 'biological body' which can be isolated from 'social gender' – there is resistance also to any suggestion that 'everything is social', or that biology has no productive role at all in regards to sexual differences. For the field of women's health, in which sex hormones feature prominently as both contributors to, and treatments of, discomfort and illness, such a view would, I suggest, be untenable. The question then arises, how can feminists think about sex hormones (and, by extension, biology in general) in ways which neither deny their activity, nor grant them excessive potency in the production of femaleness and maleness, femininity and masculinity?

My suggestion in relation to this perplexing and important question is to understand hormones as biocultural actors. This notion comes from a stream of thinking in contemporary science studies which attempts to understand non-human and non-living objects as active participants in the construction of worlds. Traditionally in science, the objects studied by scientists (bodies, hormones, molecules, plants, etc.) are considered to be passive. The only active participant in science is the scientist (Keller, 1995; Haraway, 1991: 183–201; 1997). The rethinking of science which takes place within this field of science studies attempts to problematize this active/passive distinction. Theorists such as Bruno Latour, Donna Haraway, John Law and others argue that science is better understood if its objects are seen as both active and cultural. By this they mean that scientific objects are not 'natural' entities 'discovered' by science, but rather are active participants in the scientific process. Thus they are also cultural, as science is a cultural practice. The analyses of science that these theorists undertake, then, are examinations of the multiple interactions between actors (human and non-human) which constitute scientific practice.

My suggestion to view hormones as biocultural actors is inspired by Donna Haraway's conceptualization of bodies, which comes out of this view of scientific practice. Haraway rejects both biological determinist arguments *and* understandings of bodies as entirely cultural ideological productions. She believes that there can be no access to bodies outside of language or discourse, but argues that this does not mean that language forms bodies. Her formulation of bodies as 'material semiotic actors' (Haraway, 1991: 183–201) stresses the importance of the object of knowledge in the production of bodies, 'without *ever* implying the immediate presence of such objects or, what is the same thing their final or unique determination of what can count as objective knowledge of a biological body at a particular historical juncture' (Haraway, 1992: 298). Thus Haraway argues that bodies, like all scientific 'objects', materialize in social interaction between human and non-human actors. These materializations occur within structures of power/knowledge including scientific journals, cultural images and texts, visual technologies, and all types of research. Entities such as hormones, then, are constructs of elaborate systems of power/knowledge, but are also active, and can have significant effects on bodies and lives.

This understanding of hormones as biocultural actors is useful in that it disrupts the active/passive distinction used in traditional understandings of science and allows for the activity of hormones within bodies without granting them excessive potency (the ability to *create* sexual difference). Sex hormones as biocultural actors can be seen to play an active, *although not determining* role in the production of historically and culturally specific bodies. This view of hormones is useful for thinking about women's health because hormones become entities which, whilst potent, are not separate from the cultural instantiation of sexual difference in any particular culture. In this view, clear distinctions cannot be made between biology (hormones) and culture (women's lives, culturally constructed embodiments). Women's health then becomes negotiable across the interwoven and productive fields of biology and culture.

HORMONE REPLACEMENT THERAPY

The case of hormone replacement therapy (HRT) provides a good example. As mentioned earlier, within contemporary Western medical discourse aging is figured as an endocrinopathy – a pathological disruption to levels of sex hormones within the body. This disruption is held not only to cause symptoms such as hot flushes in women, but to increase their risk of osteoporosis and heart disease. HRT is currently widely prescribed as a treatment of this condition. It has been argued by numerous writers (Coney, 1991; Greer, 1991; Klein and Dumble, 1994), however, that HRT should be rejected by feminists on the basis that it interferes with 'natural' aging. The prescription of HRT is seen by Coney, Greer and others as part of a misogynous medicalization of women's lives. It is suggested that women should refuse HRT and instead age 'naturally'. What is problematic about these arguments is the contrast made between HRT-taking and 'natural' aging. In appealing to the natural, these arguments make a claim for a body that exists outside of culture, suggesting that a body which does not consume HRT experiences a non-cultural process of senescence. Changes in sex hormones within aging bodies, in this view, are figured as biological. Distinctions between endogenous hormones and hormonal medications are also affirmed here: hormones within the body are positioned as natural, whilst those given in medical treatment are unnatural.

Thinking of hormones as biocultural actors, rather than natural entities, means that feminist analyses of HRT would change. Instead of regarding HRT as a cultural imposition on 'natural' bodies, we would think about the move of hormones into the body via HRT medication as part of a set of interactions between many actors: between entities within the body (hormones, blood, cell walls, organs, etc.); scientists; laboratory entities used in experiments; historical and cultural understandings of sexual differences; pharmaceutical companies; advertising agencies; general practitioners; the embodied experiences of individuals taking HRT; pregnant mares (whose urine is used to provide estrogens for HRT); technologies used in the production and packaging of medications; scientific studies of the effects of HRT; and stories circulated about HRT in the media and between friends. The analysis of HRT would require detailed tracing of the interplay of these factors, and an examination of the ramifications of this interaction of actors. Within this view, HRT could not be adequately understood outside these interactions, for they are what produces its functioning within bodies (Roberts, 1998). The complexities of these interactions demonstrate that the biological and the cultural cannot be separated in the analysis of hormones and their production of sexual differences in humans through medications such as HRT.

SUMMARY

Rather than seeing hormones as simply 'biological', and women's health as a 'natural' state to which we can be returned (a view that leads either to the rejection of Western medicine as unnatural, or to the shoring up of its claims to authority in knowing the biological and thus health), thinking of hormones as biocultural actors means that women's health becomes negotiable across the interwoven and productive fields of biology and culture. Sex hormones can be viewed as playing an interactive role in the production of what are deemed healthy and unhealthy sexed bodies, but this role is not fixed. Women's health remains a political question of negotiation among biocultural actors of both human and non-human kinds.

REFERENCES

Baker, Susan J. (1980) Biological influences on human sex and gender. *Signs: Journal of Women in Culture and Society*, 6 (1), 80–96

Bland, Lucy (1995) *Banishing the Beast: English Feminism and Sexual Morality 1885–1914*. London: Penguin Books

Caine, Barbara (1992) *Victorian Feminists*. Oxford: Oxford University Press

Coney, Sandra (1991) *The Menopause Industry: A Guide to Medicine's 'Discovery' of the Mid-life Woman*. Melbourne: Spinifex Press

de Beauvoir, Simone (1988) [1949] *The Second Sex*, H.M. Parshley (Trans. and Ed.). London: Picador

Donovan, Bernard. T (1988) *Humors, Hormones and the Mind: An Approach to the Understanding of Behavior*. New York: Stockton Press

Duden, Barbara (1991) *The Woman Beneath the Skin: A Doctor's Patients in Eigthteenth-Century Germany*, T. Dunlap (Trans.). Cambridge: Harvard University Press

Ehrhardt, Anke A. and Meyer-Bahlburg, Heino F.L. (1981) Effects of prenatal sex hormones on gender-related behavior. *Science*, 211, 20 March, 1312–1318

Ehrhardt, Anke A. (1984) Gender differences: a biosocial perspective. *Nebraska Symposium on Motivation*, 33, 37–57

Foucault, Michel (1987) *A History of Sexuality: An Introduction*, R. Hurley (Trans.). London: Penguin Books

Gatens, Moira (1983) A critique of the sex/gender distinction. In J. Allen and P. Patton (Eds.) *Beyond Marxism: Interventions After Marx* (pp. 143–160). Sydney: Intervention Press

Gatens, Moira (1996) *Imaginary Bodies: Ethics, Power and Corporeality*. London: Routledge

Greer, Germaine (1991) *The Change: Women, Aging and the Menopause*. London: Hamish Hamilton

Grosz, Elizabeth (1989) *Sexual Subversions: Three French Feminists*. Sydney: Allen and Unwin

Grosz, Elizabeth (1990) A note on essentialism and difference. In Sneja Gunew (Ed.) *Feminist Knowledge: Critique and Construct* (pp. 332–344). New York: Routledge

Grosz, Elizabeth (1994) *Volatile Bodies: Toward a Corporeal Feminism*. Sydney: Allen and Unwin

Haraway, Donna J. (1991) *Simians, Cyborgs and Women: The Reinvention of Nature*. New York: Routledge

Haraway, Donna J. (1992) The promises of monsters: a regenerative politics for inappropriate/d others. In L. Grossberg, C. Nelson and P. Treichler (Eds.) *Cultural Studies*. New York: Routledge

Haraway, Donna J. (1997) *Modest_Witness@Second_Millennium. FemaleMan©_Meets_Onco Mouse™: Feminism and Technoscience*. London: Routledge

Irigaray, Luce (1985) *This Sex Which is Not One*, C. Porter and C. Burke (Trans.). Ithaca: Cornell University Press

Irigaray, Luce (1993) *An Ethics of Sexual Difference*, C. Burke and G. C. Gill (Trans.). Ithaca: Cornell University Press

Keller, Evelyn Fox (1995) *Reflections on Gender and Science* (Tenth Anniversary Edition). New Haven: Yale University Press

Klein, Renate and Dumble, Lynette J. (1994) Disempowering midlife women: the science and politics of hormone replacement therapy (HRT). *Women's Studies International Forum*, 17 (4), 327–343

Kristeva, Julia (1982) *The Power of Horror: An Essay on Abjection*, L. S. Roudiez (Trans.). New York: Columbia University Press

Laqueur, Thomas (1992) *Making Sex: Body and Gender From the Greeks to Freud*. Cambridge: Harvard University Press

Reinisch, June Macover, Ziemba-Davis, Mary and Sanders, Stephanie A. (1991) Hormonal contributions to sexually dimorphic behavioral development in humans. *Psychoneuroendocrinology*, 16 (1–3), 213–278

Roberts, Celia (1998) *Messengers of Sex: Hormones, Science and Feminism*. Unpublished Ph.D. thesis. University of Sydney

Russett, Cynthia (1989) *Sexual Science: The Victorian Construction of Womanhood*. Cambridge: Harvard University Press

Scheibinger, Londa (1989) *The Mind has No Sex? Women in the Origins of Modern Science*. Cambridge: Harvard University Press

Scheibinger, Londa (1993) *Nature's Body: Sexual Politics and the Making of Modern Science*. Cambridge: Harvard University Press

Sherwood, Lauralee (1997) *Human Physiology: From Cells to Systems* (3rd edn). St. Paul: West Publishing Company

Witelson, Sandra. F. (1991) Neural sexual mosaicism: sexual differentiation of the human temporo-parietal region for functional asymmetry. *Psychoneuroendocrinology*, 16 (1–3), 131–153

Wolpert, Lewis (1993) *The Triumph of the Embryo*. Oxford: Oxford University Press

Young, Iris Marion (1990) *Throwing Like a Girl and Other Essays in Feminist Philosophy and Social Theory*. Bloomington: Indiana University Press

CHAPTER 32

REPRODUCTION: A CRITICAL ANALYSIS

Carol A. Morse

INTRODUCTION

Reproductive ability in most women lasts for around 40 years from the onset of menstruation to its final point of cessation at menopause. Within these four decades a majority of women seek at least one pregnancy and childbirth, followed by up to a quarter of a century or more of active parenting. Conversely, up to 15–20 percent of women who want and seek pregnancy unexpectedly find themselves unable to achieve it, or to carry a fertilized gamete to term and produce a live birth. There are also around 9 percent of women who never seek or want a pregnancy, preferring instead to pursue a career and commit to a relationship without producing a child.

MOTHERHOOD: TO BE OR NOT TO BE IN AN ERA OF REPRODUCTIVE CONTROL

Pregnancy and birth are widely regarded as peak experiences in a woman's life by society at large yet there is also considerable ambiguity in attitudes towards a pregnant woman's status (Williams, 1987). She may be regarded as fragile and vulnerable yet also strong; she may be stigmatized, particularly in relation to occupational opportunities where women in general, and pregnant women and mothers of children in particular, may be considered 'problematic' as employees, or 'selfish' compared to other employees who are not pregnant nor mothers of young children with particular needs.

During the last 25 years there has been a growing global concern regarding the burgeoning worldwide population. Simultaneously, increasingly effective means of fertility self-regulation have allowed many women in industrialized countries in particular, to exercise their own timing when their reproductive choices may be made and to reduce the number of their pregnancies. Alternatively, in developing countries, the apparent population crisis provides enormous concern necessitating the state to step in and exert legislated control policies to enforce limitations to family size. The intention is to deal with the present strain of unstable economies trying to balance national debts and feed their over-large societies. In the medium to longer term, enforced reductions in family size will mean that while both women and men can be available to seek work and contribute to the national economy, there will be fewer children available to contribute to the family's own income, and, in the longer term, that fewer adults will be available to take care of the aged of the future. Conversely, in industrialized countries, the spectre of the aged sector 'blowout', also produces fears that, due to the very low birth rates, increasing numbers of aged people will have no younger relatives available to care for them, nor to contribute taxes that will provide for social services, so that the state will face an unprecedented economic burden of care and provision. To prevent this occurrence, subtle and increasing pressures exist for young adult women to relinquish their employed work status and return to the home to produce more babies, so that family members and the older generation can be cared for in times of sickness, disability and old age. Thus, in both societies, these movements are driven by sociopolitical forces that continually center on the role and activities of women, which traditionally are exemplified by and regarded as primarily reproductive. These attempts at political solutions were identified at least 25 years ago (see Brewster-Smith, 1973), and can be characterized as 'mutual coercion, mutually agreed on'. Educated women anywhere will seek freedom to choose their sexual relationships, timing and numbers of pregnancies and births. The less educated will suffer from low individual fertility control unless ensured by governmental policies with the simultaneous threats to women's health brought about by unsafe practices and lack of opportunity to access affordable professional health services. In times of economic depression in both developing and industrialized societies, birth rates may lower but abortions soar (Brody, 1983).

DESIRES FOR A CHILD

It is commonly believed that everyone expects and wants to produce at least one child. This is not actually true (see Woollett and Marshall, in this volume). According to research in the U.S. up to 4 percent of adults opt to remain childfree (Williams, 1987) and in Australia this figure is around 9 percent (Callan, 1989). This still leaves a large percentage who do expect and desire to produce a child. There are several identified motivating factors that contribute to this drive. These are reported to include: achieving a sense of some importance and recognized adult status; being truly needed by another human being which affords the opportunity for exercising power and influence; providing a bridge to the future; diminishing the fear of one's own death; and providing an opportunity for the expansion of oneself (Neal *et al.*, 1989).

There are also several perceived advantages to becoming a parent, of which foremost is the notion that a child makes a 'true' family if it is accepted that no other relationship configuration should be accorded that characterization. Even though in contemporary society other types of groupings are also regarded and accepted as a family beyond the traditional notion of two heterosexual adults and one or more children living together (Sarantakos, 1996). Disadvantages include the return to traditional roles that seems to be inevitable for many new families, due to the domestic division of labor where the woman manages the home and cares for the children while the man is the primary or only breadwinner; the real or perceived reduction in income, with accompanying financial hardships and the usual curtailing of leisure pursuits; and obstruction to the full expression and experience of the adult partnership that a child's presence brings. An Australian study (Callan, 1987) that compared childfree adults and parents found that the list of disadvantages was reported by both groups but there were also gender-based differences between the groups. Mothers were less aware or less likely to admit negative aspects of being a parent, although they also reported greater fatigue and admitted to a lack of personal time and space within their daily lives; childfree men and the fathers were equally aware of the negatives. The childfree men and women, compared to the parents, reported perceptions of lack of personal time, disruptions to their lifestyle and expressed concern that being a parent would afford few opportunities for adult development and learning. Thus, the so-called 'lure' of parenthood (Gerson, 1980) seems to be decided on early in a relationship and is positively influenced by memories of either a warm and caring family of origin that must be repeated (reproduced), or else memories of hostility that impel one to do better and compensate for one's own remembered disadvantages.

INFERTILITY

In industrialized societies the prevalence of infertility is estimated at around 15 to 19 percent. Approximately 20 to 25 percent is attributed to male organic factors alone (Glover *et al.*, 1996), 5 percent to female organic factors only, around 10 percent to unexplained factors, and the remainder to combined factors affecting both partners. The commonsense view would predict that the discovery of an inability to conceive and/or to carry a fertilized gamete to viability would trigger considerable distress in the individual and their partner. Research indicates that more emotional distress is reported by women than by men, although men may experience a range of negative feelings for their female partner, when either they themselves are the infertile partner, or the female partner is the one accorded the diagnosis. In a pronatalist society that values sexual prowess in the male and fecundity in the female, infertility would pose a greater crisis especially where alternative social roles other than parenthood are limited. In Western societies there clearly are other options for adult fulfilment and personal development, yet the prevailing family-based culture, the emphasis on coupledom leading to parenthood at some point, places significant pressures on childless individuals and couples that accentuate their 'deviance' and exclusion from the mainstream.

Earlier studies have emphasized the 'crisis' that infertility poses, with unexplained causes in particular being linked to psychodynamic theories of 'psychogenic conflicts' operating against conception. More recent studies have found little support for pre-existing psychopathology in couples presenting for investigation and treatment (e.g. Connolly et al., 1992). Studies carried out in the 1970s and early 1980s tended to focus almost exclusively on the woman, suggesting implicitly or explicitly that infertility was a 'woman's problem'. Over time, research identified particular male factors, and gradually fertility difficulties became recognized as a problem affecting the couple.

Regardless of the source or rationale for the inability to conceive, the obstructed fulfilment of a desire and loss of expectations for a usual human function, produce an inevitable negative impact on each partner and trigger psychological needs that require attention. An important aspect to bear in mind is that studies have been carried out on those couples who present for treatment and thereby express their desire for assistance and hopeful rescue from their predicament. Large-scale population-based studies have yet to be carried out examining the exact impacts of finding oneself or one's partner infertile, comparing those individuals who choose not to seek ways of overcoming the problem with others who do seek help through treatment or other means such as fostering or adopting a child. It is commonly assumed by the fertile that all adults have similar desires. Yet a considerable proportion actively do not want or intend to conceive (Callan, 1987). Obviously, the need for psychological adjustment is paramount when a desire is thwarted involuntarily (e.g. infertility), rather than when the choice to remain childfree is made in the full knowledge and acceptance of that situation.

Research on infertility can be criticized on several counts of which perhaps the most important one is the assumption that it is the woman's problem alone. There is also assumed homogeneity in infertile couples who present for assistance to health and medical professionals. As well, the nature of the process of reacting to infertility and its treatment has been found to constitute a two-stage stress model of response and adaptation over time (e.g. Berg and Wilson, 1991), rather than one type of reaction termed 'adaptive or maladaptive'. Psychological distress is reduced when couples set their own boundaries for the number and type of inter-ventions they would undergo, and over what time frame. As well, the individual and interactive effects on each partner need to be taken into account (e.g. Glover *et al.*, 1996).

Clearly, taking charge of one's problem and remaining in decisional control assist in managing the stress emanating from diagnosis, consider-ations of alternative treatments and their success or failure, and making determinations for their future life with infertility. The important psycho-logical task is for couples to accept themselves and each other with the 'flaw' of infertility even within a seemingly free yet subtly pronatalist soci-ety where parenting dominates the collective consciousness.

EARLY PARENTING

Parenting, the outcome of motivational factors and desires for a child, is recognized as a labor intensive activity that absorbs enormous energy, time and effort continuously for up to two to three decades. The period of transition from pregnancy to parenting has been viewed as a crisis, a chal-lenge and a normative stage in adult development that requires significant changes in lifestyle and roles for all new parents (Goldberg, 1988). Though recent studies indicate that the majority of adults achieve parenthood with very few lasting or serious difficulties, many reports over the past 15 years or more have focussed on the negative experiences of achieving parent-hood characterized by significant mood disorders and marital disharmo-ny (Terry, 1991; Wheatley, 1996). Negative experiences and influences impact on the postnatal quality of interpersonal life, which in turn leads to long-lasting adverse effects on the child's optimal emotional and social development, contributing to high divorce rates and compromised men-tal health of men, women and their children (Cowan and Cowan, 1988; Terry *et al.*, 1991).

One of the most recognized issues linked to childbirth is postnatal mood disorder in women, or postnatal depression (PND) of varying severity and complexity, from transient 'blues' to clinically significant depression and occasional psychosis in predisposed mentally ill women (see Nicolson, in this volume). Medical research has focussed on identify-ing hormonal explanations for the apparent sudden onset of persistent depressed mood which may be severe enough to benefit from hospital-ization and medication of the woman. While no empirical support for a hormonal source of causation has been identified, health science profes-sionals have proposed social explanatory theories that identify low sup-port and role strains, or explanations stemming from medicalization of pregnancy and birthing (Short *et al.*, 1992).

PND tends to remit after a time-limited period either spontaneously or following medical and/or psychotherapy treatment. Unfortunately, a sig-nificant proportion of women are likely to experience a further episode of depression with subsequent births. This indicates a continued need for different methods of problem identification, proactive management for those at risk and better treatment strategies for those already suffering.

Again, the woman has been regarded as the first target for examination when seeking an explanatory cause for the condition. Recent research is undertaking longitudinal studies of the path and process to birthing of couples and seeking to identify similarities and differences between those who experience depressed mood and those who do not. As well, the differential experiences of each partner in the couple is being investigated (e.g. Morse et al., 1998), revealing that distress/depressed mood starts early on in the pregnancy, persists into the early postnatal phase, and a proportion of expectant fathers also experience similar mood problems that follow the same course and emanate from very similar sources of vulnerability. Thus a psychosocial model may explain why some individuals or couples who start a pregnancy may find themselves experiencing significant levels of negative moods that persist to the early postnatal phase at least and which may continue on to adversely affect the mental health and well-being of each family member. Until competent procedures are in place to identify those most at risk as early as possible, with appropriate provisions of help, individual distress and marital breakdown will continue and the socio-emotional development and well-being of the infant and its parents will remain unsupported, with possible long-term adverse sequelae for all concerned. Importantly, peri-natal depression/distress needs to be considered as a difficulty of the couple and not only perceived as a 'woman's problem'.

REFERENCES

Berg, B.J. and Wilson, J.F. (1991) Psychological functioning across stages of treatment for infertility. *Journal of Behavioral Medicine*, 14, 1, 11–26

Brewster-Smith, M. (1973) A social psychological view of fertility. In J. Fawcett (Ed.) *Psychological Perspectives on Population* (pp. 3–18). New York: Basic Books

Brody, E.B. (1983) The context of desire: reproductive choice in an era of coercion and freedom. In L. Dennerstein and M. DeSenarclens (Eds.) *The Young Woman* (pp. 229–235). Amsterdam: Elsevier

Callan, V.J. (1987) The personal and marital adjustment of mothers, voluntary and involuntary childless wives. *Journal of Marriage and the Family*, 48, 849–856

Connolly, K.J., Edelmann, R.J., Cooke, I. and Robson, J. (1992) The impact of infertility on psychological functioning. *Journal of Psychosomatic Research*, 36, 5, 459–468

Cowan, P.A. and Cowan, C.P. (1988) Changes in marriage during the transition to parenthood: must we blame the baby? In: G.Y. Michaels and W.A. Goldberg (Eds.) *The Transitions to Parenthood: Current Theory and Research* (pp. 114–154). Cambridge: Cambridge University Press.

Gerson, M.J. (1980) The lure of motherhood. *Psychology of Women Quarterly*, 5 (2), 207–218

Glover, L., Gannon, K., Sherr, L. and Abel, P.D. (1996) Distress in sub-fertile men: a longitudinal study. *Journal of Reproductive and Infant Psychology*, 14, 23–36

Goldberg, W.A. (1988) Perspectives on the transition to parenthood. In G.Y. Michaels and W.A. Goldberg (Eds.) *Transition to Parenthood: Current Theory and Research* (pp. 1–20). Cambridge: Cambridge University Press

King, C.R. (1992) The ideological and technological shaping of motherhood. *Women and Health*, 19 (2/3), 1–12

Morse, C.A., Buist, A. and Durkin, S. (1998) Fathers' influences on adjustment in new mothers. Paper presented to the Annual Conference of the Australian Psychological Society

Neal, A.G., Groat, H.T. and Wicks, J.W. (1989) Attitudes about having children: a study of 600 couples in the early years of marriage. *Journal of Marriage and the Family*, 51, 313–328

Saranatakos, S. (1996) *Modern Families: An Australian Text*. Melbourne: Macmillan
Short, S. and Lumley, J. (1992) *Having a baby in Victoria*. Report to the Department of Human Services, Victoria
Terry, D.J. (1991) Predictors of subjective stress in a sample of new parents. *Australian Journal of Psychology*, 43, 1, 29–36
Terry, D.J., McHugh, T.A. and Noller, P. (1991) Role dissatisfaction and the decline in marital quality across the transition to parenthood. *Australian Journal of Psychology*, 43 (3), 129–132
Wheatley, S. (1996) Prepartum sources of social support as predictors of early postpartum depression, positive affect and negative affect: partners in parenthood: who needs them? Paper presented to the Annual Conference of the British Psychological Society
Williams, J.H. (1987) *Psychology Of Women: Behavior In A Biosocial Context*. New York: Norton

CHAPTER 33

PREGNANCY: A HEALTHY STATE?

Harriet Gross

INTRODUCTION

Pregnancy is considered to be a normal, healthy experience. Like other reproductive events, pregnancy is also a time when otherwise healthy women have significant contact with health professionals. The public management of this personal event is centered on women to ensure safe delivery of a healthy baby.

During pregnancy, women are experiencing considerable changes, both physically and psychologically, which have implications for women's health in pregnancy and beyond, for how women feel about their pregnancy, and for their well-being, as well as how they are viewed by others. In this chapter I will look briefly at pregnancy and how women's experience is characterized within the context of women's health.

THE DISCOURSE OF PREGNANCY

The predominant discourse of pregnancy and childbirth positions them as biological and medical events (Woollett and Marshall, 1997) and this discourse links directly to pregnancy as a health state. As with many other 'health' conditions, the effect is to present pregnancy as inherently problematic. At the same time, locating pregnancy as a healthy, natural/biological state can include representing even the most problematic pregnancies and deliveries as 'normal' (e.g. Linell and Bredmar, 1996). Natural and medical discourses both imply and permit a removal of control, but loss of control contrasts with a further discourse of pregnancy, one of rights and responsibilities. The effect of these discourses of pregnancy appears to be that women are simultaneously assigned to a passive role, as recipients of care and containers for their infants, and to an instrumental role, whereby their actions will determine their child's future health, intelligence and success. Failure to act accordingly (for example, attend antenatal appointments) may engender personal guilt and permit public criticism. This paradoxical positioning of pregnancy continues when considering the women's psychological health in pregnancy. The major psychological discourse of pregnancy is of transition (Raphael-Leff, 1991) and this too identifies both a passive/responsive role and an active problem-solving role in a woman's personal engagement with her pregnancy.

The discourse of pregnancy as a biological and medical event focusses on a metaphor of containment, where the woman is regarded as a vessel for the foetus, an essential but secondary role. This metaphor also places women as being at the mercy of elemental forces (Smith, 1992) which may endanger the contents of the vessel. The metaphor runs through all areas of pregnancy and surfaces in medical advice and popular literature. Containment is also the dominant theme in research investigating pregnancy and health, where the emphasis is on the effect of various individual factors or situational variables on the outcome of pregnancy (the baby), rather than on the nature of women's experience or interpretation of their situation. For instance, Hickey *et al.* (1995) report on the effects of stress on preterm delivery, and in similar studies Hatch *et al.* (1997) and Homer *et al.* (1990) investigated whether particular activities, such as standing and lifting at work, were linked to rates of foetal growth or preterm delivery. The pathologizing of female functioning in pregnancy is replayed in the equation of pregnancy with sickness, in employment legislation for example (Hanlon, 1995). As well as being at the mercy of their biology, women must act responsibly: Taylor Myers and Grasmick (1990), when investigating the social context in which pregnancy is embedded, indicate that expectations of pregnant women are that they will take responsibility for their own health and that of their baby, that is, they will behave appropriately in order to reduce any risks.

THE MEDICALIZATION OF PREGNANCY

The attention on women's health in pregnancy is managed through the provision of antenatal and obstetric care, which emphasizes the need to monitor health in order to reduce problems and minimize risk. When a woman is in good physical condition during pregnancy, for example, the probability of complications during labor and delivery may be lowered (e.g. Dewey and McRory, 1994; Simpson, 1996). The justification for medical involvement in pregnancy is the need to reduce any such complications and to identify and treat serious conditions of pregnancy which can significantly affect women's health, as well as that of their baby directly or indirectly, for instance through preterm labor or low birthweight. These conditions include those associated with high blood pressure and hypertension, such as pre-eclampsia, which are some of the most important causes of maternal and foetal morbidity and mortality in Western countries. Other serious conditions include toxemia, obstetric cholestasis, and gestational diabetes among others. The medicalization of pregnancy and childbirth has been ongoing throughout this century both in the West and more recently in developing countries, and is well documented elsewhere (see, for example, Barker, 1998; Garcia, Kilpatrick and Richards, 1990; Murphy Lawless, 1998; Oakley, 1984; Tew, 1990). The desire to reduce adverse outcomes for a few impacts on all pregnancies by over-emphasizing the health problems of pregnancy, rather than validating women's experience as mothers and carers.

Technological developments, such as antenatal screening procedures (e.g. ultrasound scanning) may emphasize the involvement of medical professionals, particularly in the early weeks of pregnancy, drawing on the medical and biological discourse to confirm pregnancy status and to reassure women that all is normal, and incidentally confirming in a very practical way, women's role as vessel (see Ennis, in this volume). Such technological activity may give women greater peace of mind about their baby's health or may create greater anxiety (Clements *et al.*, 1998; Fearn *et al.*, 1982; Hyde, 1986). The same medical procedures also emphasize women's instrumental role in a successful, problem-free pregnancy; the identification of the foetus as a potentially healthy baby could be interpreted as a means by which women are encouraged to adopt responsible behaviors. Increased understanding of factors affecting birth outcome has made it possible to advise women what they should do to ensure their own and their infant's well-being. This involves careful monitoring of their own behaviors, for example eating properly and watching their weight, giving up smoking, taking exercise, avoiding certain substances and foods, as well as attending to the physical changes occurring in the baby and themselves. The health-monitoring activities sustain the medical/biological discourse and contribute to the construction of a discourse of rights and responsibilities surrounding women's health behaviors in pregnancy.

THE PSYCHOLOGY OF PREGNANCY

The psychology of pregnancy has reflected the medical/biological discourse and tended to see pregnancy as a problematic event. Pregnancy is represented as a potentially stressful life event (it scores 40 on the Holmes and Rahe Social Readjustment Scale, 1967), which, consistent with the metaphor of containment, may have negative consequences for foetal health. In this respect, discourses of transition represent pregnancy, and particularly first pregnancy, as a stressful experience with possible negative impact on women's psychological well-being; as a potential crisis state, involving shifts in identity and the move from non-motherhood to motherhood, and possible confrontations with unresolved issues (Breen, 1975; Deutsch, 1947; Raphael-Leff, 1991). In this view pregnancy may be associated with feelings of loss as well as gain. Consistent with the focus on problems, there is less reporting of positive emotions (Green, 1990; Paarlberg *et al.*, 1996) though pregnancy is often a desired and planned-for state and there are likely to be feelings of excitement and delight as well as anxiety.

Research indicates that levels of depression and anxiety are reported during pregnancy but do not remain static. Rather, they change over the period of pregnancy, in line with what women are experiencing (e.g. Gross and Pattison, 1995; Wolkind and Zajicek, 1981). Thus levels of reported anxiety are higher at the beginning and towards the end of pregnancy, which can be regarded as normal and appropriate reactions to the situation, for example, awaiting test results or impending labor and delivery, or leaving work. In addition, previous reproductive history may contribute to high levels of anxiety (van den Akker *et al.*, 1990). There is some evidence that some women's depressed mood states during pregnancy may be associated with post-natal depression (Elliot *et al.*, 1983; Nicolson, 1998) and while some women report feelings of emotional well-being, some report depression and anxiety at levels that could be associated with psychiatric conditions (Bibring, 1959; Brockington, 1996; Condon, 1987a).

Despite the legitimacy of any distress, women may not always interpret it as such. For example, some symptoms of anxiety and depression are somatic and overlap with minor physical concomitants of pregnancy, such as nausea, tiredness, sleeping problems. Awareness of such symptoms may permit women to account for their feelings, using the biological discourse, as a normal part of pregnancy – 'just my hormones'. Women may account for other psychological changes in a similar way: cognitive failure or memory lapses are reported by women anecdotally and have been investigated by various researchers (e.g. Brindle *et al.*, 1991; Gross and Pattison, 1995; Jarrahi-Zahed, 1969; Poser *et al.*, 1987; Sharp *et al.*, 1993). The occurrence of such lapses contributes to public representations of pregnant women as at the mercy of their hormones and has even led to suggestions that women's brains may shrink during pregnancy (Holdcroft, 1997) and thus that in pregnancy women might be unreliable or less intelligent. Explanations for changes in cognitive functioning in pregnancy attribute them to physiological/biological effects, either hormonal or neurological, or to psychological effects, related to cognitive overload and attentional deficits resulting from stress, or to a re-positioning of self towards inner functioning (Condon, 1987b). We have previously suggested (Gross and Pattison, 1995) that increased health monitoring integral to pregnancy care may increase awareness of all aspects of functioning and the likelihood of reporting or noticing minor lapses, particularly for some women. Because these incidents are identified during pregnancy, they become associated with it as part of the checklist of its possible effects. The health context of pregnancy therefore offers the opportunity to increase the range of behaviors that can be accounted for within a normal/natural process, and responsibility for any failures may be relinquished.

Any realignment of identities associated with transition occurs in a personal and social context and a further significant aspect of pregnancy is its

public visibility. The visibility of pregnancy as an embodiment of reproductive fertility and sexuality can transgress boundaries between the personal or private and the public domains and affect both personal and public beliefs about pregnancy. As women re-conceptualize themselves as
members of a particular 'club', they become public property, which in turn
will determine what they are interested in, who they will turn to for
advice or information (Baker, 1989). Both the medical discourse and the
discourse of rights and responsibilities permits others to comment upon
the pregnancy itself and women's response to it. Pregnant women and
their bodies become the focus for comments and advice from all and
sundry.

Pregnancy may offer women the opportunity to present themselves differently; some women report feeling less attractive (Oakley, 1980; Slade,
1977) while for others the period of being pregnant can be positive; pregnancy can provide an opportunity for fat women to feel 'normal' (Wiles,
1987). Instead of being viewed as 'ornament' or 'seducer' (Price, 1988),
pregnant women's bodies shift towards being viewed as 'functional'
(Charles and Kerr, 1986), and thus personal remarks about appearance or
behaviors are countenanced under a banner of biology not sexuality, and
invited by the discourse of responsibility.

SUMMARY

Thus, to conclude, pregnancy is a private usually joyous event, concerned
with personal transitions, hopes and aspirations. At the same time pregnancy is also a highly visible, even public event, a rite of passage, and a
natural process. In health terms, it can be placed alongside women's other
reproductive experiences, such as menstruation or menopause. It is associated with a specific range of health concerns, where women's health is
largely viewed in terms of their infant's well-being. The focus on foetal
health maintains a paradoxical discourse regarding women's health in
pregnancy, whereby a rhetoric of loss of control (the bio-medical discourse) and of responsibility are integral to the way that pregnancy is represented to, and by, women.

REFERENCES

Baker, D. (1989) Social identity in the transition to motherhood. In S. Skevington and D.
  Baker (Eds.)*The Social Identity of Women*. London: Sage
Barker, K.K. (1998) A ship upon a stormy sea: the medicalization of pregnancy. *Social Science
  and Medicine*, 47 (8), 1067–1076
Bibring, G.L. (1959) Some considerations on the psychological processes in pregnancy.
  Psychoanalytic Study of the Child, 14, 113–121
Breen, D. (1975) *The Birth of a First Child*. London: Tavistock
Brindle, P.M., Brown, M.W., Brown, J., Griffith, H.B. and Turner, G.M. (1991) Objective and
  subjective memory impairment in pregnancy. *Physiological Medicine*, 21: 647–653
Brockington, I. (1996) *Motherhood and Mental Health*. Oxford: Oxford University Press
Charles, N. and Kerr, M. (1986) Food for feminist thought. *Sociological Review*, 34, 537–572
Clements, S., Wilson, J. and Sikorski, J. (1998) Women's experience of ultrasound scans. In S.

Clements (Ed.) *Psychological Perspectives on Pregnancy and Childbirth*. Edinburgh: Churchill Livingstone

Condon, J.T. (1987a) Psychological and physical symptoms during pregnancy. a comparison of male and female expectant parents. *Journal of Reproductive and Infant Psychology*, 5, 207–213

Condon, J.T. (1987b) Altered cognitive functioning in pregnant women: a shift towards primary process thinking. *British Journal of Medical Psychology*, 60, 329–334

Deutsch, H. (1947) *The Psychology of Women*. New York: Grune and Stratton

Dewey, K.G. and McCrory, M.A. (1994) Effects of dieting and physical activity on pregnancy and lactation. *American Journal of Clinical Nutrition*, 59 (suppl), 446S-53S

Elliott, S., Rugg, A.J., Watson, J.P. and Brough, D.I. (1983) Mood changes during pregnancy and after the birth of a child. *British Journal of Clinical Psychology*, 22, 295–308

Fearn, J., Hibberd, B.M., Laurence, K.M., Roberts, A. and Robinson, J.D. (1982) Screening for neural tube defects and maternal anxiety. *British Journal of Obstetrics and Gynaecology*, 89, 218–221

Garcia, J., Kilpatrick, R. and Richards, M. (1990) *The Politics of Maternity Care*. Oxford: Clarendon

Green, J. (1990) Is the baby alright and other worries. Paper presented at the Tenth Anniversary Conference of the Society for Reproductive and Infant Psychology, Cambridge, England

Gross, H. and Pattison, H. (1995) Cognitive failure during pregnancy. *Journal of Reproductive and Infant Psychology*, 13: 17–32

Hanlon, J. (1995) The 'sick' woman: pregnancy discrimination in employment. *Journal of Gender Studies*, 4, 315–323

Hatch, M., Ji, B.T., Shu, X.O. and Susser, M. (1997) Do standing, lifting, climbing, or long hours of work during pregnancy have an effect on fetal growth? *Epidemiology*, 8 (5), 530–536

Hickey, C.A., Cliver, S.P., Mulvihill, F.X., McNeal, S.F., Hoffman, H.J. and Goldenberg, R.L. (1995) Employment related stress and preterm delivery: a contextual examination. *Public Health Reports*, 110 (4), 410–418

Holdcroft, A. (1997) Reported in *New Scientist*, 11 January 1997

Holmes, T.H. and Rahe, R.H. (1967) The Social Readjustment Rating Scale. *Journal of Psychosomatic Research*, 11, 213–218

Homer, C.J., James, S.A. and Siegel, E. (1990) Work-related psychosocial stress and risk of preterm, low birthweight delivery. *American Journal of Public Health*, 80, 173–177

Hyde, B. (1986) An interview study of pregnant women's attitudes to ultasound scanning. *Social Science and Medicine*, 22, 587–592

Lee, C. (1998) *Women's Health*. London: Sage

Linell, P. and Bredmar, M. (1996) Reconstructing topical sensitivity: aspects of face-work in talks between midwives and expectant mothers. *Research on Language and Social Interaction*, 29 (4), 347–379

Murphy Lawless, J. (1998) *Reading Birth and Death: A History of Obstetric Thinking*. Cork: Cork University Press

Nicolson, P. (1998) *Postnatal Depression*. London: Routledge

Oakley, A. (1980) *Women Confined*. Oxford: Martin Robertson

Oakley, A. (1984) *The Captured Womb: A History of the Medical Care of Pregnant Women*. Oxford: Blackwell

Paarlberg, K.M., Vingerhoets, A.J.J.M., Passchier, J., Heiner, A.G.J.J., Dekker, G.A. and Vangeijn, H.R. (1996) Psychosocial factors as predictors of maternal well-being and pregnancy related complaints. *Journal of Psychosomatic Obstetrics and Gynaecology*, 17 (2) 93–102

Poser, C.M., Kassirer, M.R. and Peyser, J.M. (1986) Benign encephalopathy of pregnancy. *Acta Neurologica Scandinavica*, 73, 39–43

Price, J. (1988) *Motherhood: What It Does to Your Mind*. London: Pandora

Raphael Leff, J. (1991) *Psychological Processes Of Childbearing*. London: Chapman and Hall

Reading, A. (1983) *Psychological Aspects of Pregnancy*. London: Longman

Scott, G. and Niven, C.A. (1996) Pregnancy: a bio-psycho-social event. In C.A. Niven and A. Walker (Eds.) *Conception, Pregnancy and Birth*. London: Butterworth/Heinemann

Sharp, K., Brindle, P.M., Brown, M.W. and Turner, G.M. (1993) Memory loss during pregnancy. *British Journal of Obstetrics and Gynaecology*, 100, 209–215

Simpson, J.L. (1993) Are physical activity and employment related to preterm birth and low birth weight? *American Journal of Obstetrics and Gynaecology*, 168: 1231–8

Slade, P. (1977) Awareness of body dimensions during pregnancy: analogue study.

Psychological Medicine, 7, 245–252

Smith, J.A. (1992) Pregnancy and transition to motherhood. In P. Nicolson and J. Ussher (Eds.) *Psychology of Women's Health and Healthcare.* London: Macmillan

Taylor Myers, S. and Grasmick, H.G. (1990) The social rights and responsibilities of pregnant women: an application of Parson's Sick Role model. *Journal of Applied Behavioural Science,* 26 (2), 157–172

Taylor, S.E. and Langer, E.J. (1977) Pregnancy: a social stigma? *Sex Roles,* 3, 27–35

Tew, M. (1990) *Safer Childbirth.* London: Chapman & Hall

van den Akker, O., Sweeny, V. and Rosenblatt, D. (1990) Psychological factors associated with pregnancy and the postnatal period in women at risk for preterm labour/delivery. Paper presented at the 10th Anniversay Conference of the Society for Reproductive and Infant Psychology, Cambridge, England

Wiles, R. (1990) I'm not fat, I'm pregnant. In S. Wilkinson and C. Kitzinger (Eds.) *Women and Health: Feminist Perspectives.* London, Taylor & Francis

Wolkind, S. and Zajicek, E. (1981) *Pregnancy: A Psychological and Social Study.* Academic Press, London

Woollett, A. and Marshall, H. (1997) Discourses of pregnancy and childbirth. In L. Yardley (Ed.) *Psychology of Women's Health: Material Discourses of Health and Illness.* London: Routledge

CHAPTER 34

SCREENING: A CRITIQUE

Maeve Ennis

INTRODUCTION

Some forms of predictive testing and health screening have been available in a limited way for many years, and screening is now an intregal part of our health service.

However, in pregnancy and during childbirth women are asked to make decisions about tests and screening which can have serious consequences for themselves and the foetus. It would appear that in many areas women are not given adequate information to make informed choices and little consideration is given to the psychological effects of these choices. This chapter looks at the role of some forms of biomedical technology in pregnancy and childbirth.

With the advances in technology and particularly biogenetics more and more patients, for a variety of reasons, are being offered the option of screening. In many cases this is offered not as an option but as part of the diagnostic procedure. Many of these patients are ambivalent about the value of technology, however few reject it out of hand. Scientific information marshals a great deal of respect, even when its use may not be entirely apparent to the recipient of the test or it has no apparent use. In prenatal diagnostic testing, doctors recommendations usually carry the force of command and even suggestions by nurses and other health care workers carry a great deal of power. Browner and Press report that in many parts of the United States doctors routinely recommend AFP (alpha fetoprotein) testing for Down's syndrome and neural tube defects (anencephaly and spina bifida) There are few effective treatments for either of these conditions and no hope of cure – aborting the pregnancy is the only means of prevention. Yet few rejected the test even though most said they would not agree to abortion in the event they tested positive (Browner and Press 1996).

For some time now, during pregnancy and childbirth, women have been offered, either for themselves or their baby, a variety of tests and screening. The most routine of these is ultrasound scanning and biochemical tests during pregnancy and electronic foetal monitoring and foetal blood sampling during labor. These are known by the medical profession as tests of maternal and foetal well-being and the results of these tests impact heavily on decisions about patient care. The questions I am asking here are: what are these tests and what are they for?

ANTENATAL SCREENING

In the United Kingdom and the Republic of Ireland the first test offered is an ultrasound scan. This is to confirm the age of the foetus. This scan involves measure of the baby's head and possible length. However, because the size of babies varies in mid-pregnancy, the age estimate is not precise. At about 12–16 weeks women are offered biochemical screening which involves taking a maternal blood sample. This is to test for Down's syndrome and neural tube defects. This test is offered to all women over the age of 35–38 and in some centers to younger mothers also. This permits the estimation of the risks of Down's syndrome for each individual pregnancy. The incidence of the syndrome is 1.3 per 1000, with the incidence increasing with maternal age. Until recently screening was confined to women over the age of 35–38, and a positive result was generally followed by amniocentesis which carries with it a 1 in 100 chance of miscarriage as it involves insertion of a needle into the amniotic sac surrounding the foetus to draw off fluid. According to Vyas (1994), on this basis one in 20 women would be offered screening and the risk of giving birth to a baby with Down's syndrome would be comparable to the risk of miscarriage due to the procedure. He suggests that the screening program was based on questionable arguments relating to the provision of service and the assumption that the impact of giving birth to a Down's baby equated to losing a baby (Vyas, 1994).

This method of screening did not reduce the incidence of Down's syndrome in the community by very much. Only 30 percent of babies with Down's syndrome are born to mothers over 35, the remaining 70 percent being born to younger women who individually are at less risk but who form 95 percent of the pregnant population. This risk was seldom if ever discussed with these younger women at antenatal visits with doctors or midwives.

Biochemical screening, which is much less invasive as it involves only a blood test, is now offered to most pregnant women regardless of age in the U.K. and Ireland. Called the Barts, the Leeds, or the triple test, it measures the level of two, three or four markers in the mother's blood. This permits estimation of the risk of Down's syndrome for each pregnancy, and those deemed to be at high risk are advised to have an amniocentesis to confirm whether or not their baby has a syndrome, so they can be offered a termination of the pregnancy. Vyas has reported that several prospective analyses have shown detection rates of 48–91 percent with false positive rates of 3.7 percent to 5.7 percent. This means that younger women are made aware of their individual risk and older women who are negative are spared the risk of amniocentesis (Vyas, 1994). In practice, in a screening program, about 3 percent of tests will throw up a positive result, which can induce anxiety, at least for a short while, in quite a large number of women. This would suggest that it is an area where there is a need for good communication between medical staff and patients.

However, some studies have questioned the adequacy of information given to women about the tests before they undergo them (e.g. Smith *et al.*, 1994). They suggest that the implication of false positive and false negative results are not fully understood by most women, and that they are improperly prepared for the possible adverse outcomes of screening. Although the Royal College of Obstetricians and Gynaecologists has laid down standards for counseling both before and after the test, a study by Green in which she surveyed all practicing obstetricians in England and Wales, found that nearly half her sample did not have adequate resources for this counseling (Green, 1994). Stratham and Green note that while all screening tests produce a proportion of false positive results women were often pressurized to have amniocenteses quickly without full information on the test itself or on the implications of a positive diagnosis. Their study found that while women were told that screening had apparently revealed something sufficiently worrying to warrant an invasive procedure with a risk of miscarriage, they were told to go away and not worry about it. This lack of acknowledgment of women's feelings meant there was no discussion of what would happen if Down's syndrome was diagnosed. They suggest that medical services at a local level are unprepared for an abnormal result, and believe the tests will bring comfort to pregnant women; this, despite the fact that screening tests have been a part of routine antenatal care for many years and a literature exists documenting women's negative experience of these (Stratham and Green, 1994; see Weaver, in this volume).

SCREENING DURING LABOR

Foetal monitoring was developed to help health workers assess foetal well-being during the birth process. Mothers and babies are screened during labor for identification of foetal compromise, maternal risk and confirmation of normal progression of that labor. The mother's condition is checked by repeated blood pressure measurement, temperature checks and urine sampling for hydration. There is a variety of ways in which the foetus can be monitored, and a variety of reasons why it is done. The most widely used method of assessment of well-being in the foetus is a monitoring of the foetal heart rate. Because maternal blood flow to the placenta can be severely diminished during contractions, labor has the potential to damage the foetus. Asphyxiation in babies during labor and at birth has been linked to abnormally fast or slow heart rates (James, 1993), so this assessment is crucial.

However, the method of this assessment is controversial. The foetal heart can be monitored by Pinard stethoscope, or electronically using a cardiotocograph (CTG) which is worn by the mother across her abdomen and gives a paper, and sometimes audible, trace of the foetal heart rate. It can be used continuously or intermittently. It can be reassuring for mothers as they can see how the foetus is withstanding the contractions of labor. But if it is carried out continuously it can severely restrict the mother's mobility, and, unless time is taken to explain exactly what the trace or sound means, it can also cause as much distress as reassurance in some mothers.

An even more thought-provoking finding is that with the advent of continuos electronic foetal monitoring have come higher rates of surgical intervention – Caesarean delivery of the foetus during the early stages of labor and forceps delivery during the later stages. When compared to intermittent use of a Pinard stethoscope, continuous electronic monitoring doubled the rate of Caesarean section for 'foetal distress' (James, 1993). It could be argued that anything that results in more live births and less genuinely compromised babies can not be bad even when it involves more surgical intervention. Sadly this does not appear to be the case. Outcomes have been examined using randomized control trials and these have shown that continuous foetal monitoring appears to have no benefit in terms of neonatal outcome in the vast majority of births (Neilson, 1995). It has, however, been proven effective in high-risk labors (Steer, 1999). A further drawback to continuous foetal monitoring is that the interpretation of the trace can be difficult for less experienced junior doctors (the doctors most likely to be on duty in the labor ward), who despite their lack of experience are often overconfident. An error rate of 35 percent was found in one study (Ennis, 1992). The most recent Confidential Inquiry into Perinatal Deaths suggests that in 60 percent of labor cases there were possibly avoidable errors related to incorrect monitoring of foetal heart rate (Steer, 1999). It would appear that poor training of junior doctors in this procedure was implicated in many of these cases.

Despite its bad press, continuous foetal monitoring is still routine in most obstetric units. Doctors will argue that it may not be perfect but it is the best there is to date, and that it is better 'to be safe than sorry'. This may be true, but it may not be the only reason that extensive monitoring, both in pregnancy and labor, is being carried out. There is an increasing tendency for patients to seek redress when thing go wrong; this has had the repercussion that some doctors are now practicing defensive medicine for medico-legal reasons. A survey of obstetricians in the U.K. and Ireland (N=1192) found that more than 20 percent perceived foetal heart rate monitors to be inaccurate, but despite that, 80 percent of them continued to use them, generally for medico-legal reasons (Ennis *et al.*, 1991). When this leads to unnecessary Caesarean sections and instrumental deliveries then it is clearly doctors' interest and not the mothers that is being served.

SUMMARY

During pregnancy and labor women have to make several decisions, sometimes in a very short space of time. In pregnancy they have to decide whether to participate in screening; if they have a negative result, whether to have a diagnostic test; and finally what to do if an abnormality is detected. During labor and birth they must decide whether or not to have the foetus continuously monitored, and sometimes, whether to have an instrument or even a Caesarean delivery. However, as Stratham and Green (1993) and James (1993) have pointed out, women are not always given enough information to make informed choices and little consideration is given to the psychological consequences of these decisions. Refusal can be construed as lack of responsibility on the part of the pregnant woman (Browner and Press, 1993).

Women should be given all the available information about the tests, including the fact that there may be a degree of uncertainty about the results. They have the right to expect adequate counseling before making their choices, including the right to refuse a test or procedure. The reasons for and risks of screening and testing must be explained by health care workers and the assumptions that they are 'routine' and 'safe' explored.

REFERENCES

Browner, C.H. and Press, Nancy (1996) The production of authoritative knowledge. *American Prenatal Care. Medical Anthropology Quarterly*, 10 (2), 141–156

Ennis, M. (1992) The mismatch between confidence and competence in reading foetal heart traces. Paper given at the BPS conference, London

Ennis, M., Clark, A. and Grudzinskas, J.G. (1991) Change in obstetric practice in response to fear of litigation in the British Isles. *Lancet*, 338, 616–621

Green, Josephine M. (1994) Serum screening for Down's syndrome: Experiences of obstetricians in England and Wales. *British Medical Journal*, 309, 769–772

James P. (1993) Cardiotocography during labour. *British Medical Journal*, 306, 347–348

Neilson JP. (1995) EFM vs. intermittent auscultation in labour. In M.J.N.C. Keirse, M.J. Renfrew, C. Crowther (Eds.) *Cochrane Collaboration*. Cochrane Library. Issue 2. Oxford: Update Software

Smith, Deana K., Shaw, Robert W. and Marteau, Theresa (1994) Informed consent to undergo serum screening for Down's syndrome: The gap between theory and practice. *British Medical Journal*, 309, 776

Steer, P. (1999) Assessment of mother and foetus in labour: ABC of labour care. *British Medical Journal*, 318; 18, 858–861

Vyas, Sanjay. (1994) Screening for Down's syndrome: ignorance abounds. *British Medical Journal*, 309, 753–754

Stratham, Helen and Green, Josephine (1993) Serum screening for Down's syndrome: Some women's experience. *British Medical Journal*, 307, 174–176

Wald, N.J. (1988) Maternal serum screening for Down's syndrome in early pregnancy *British Medical Journal*, 297, 883–887

CHAPTER 35

CHILDBIRTH

Jane J. Weaver

INTRODUCTION

In my contribution to this book I would like highlight some of the arguments that have been made to refute the medical model of childbirth care, and discuss the possibility of control over the birth process for childbearing women. The medical model has been dealt with in considerable depth elsewhere (for example, Arms, 1994; Wagner, 1994; Tew, 1995), so I will only summarize some of the key points here. Maternal control will be explored in the light of the legacy this medical model has left for both childbearing women and for those who care for them.

THE MEDICAL MODEL OF CARE

There has been a marked fall in maternal and perinatal mortality rates over the past 60 years. Childbirth is safer than ever before. Doctors, in particular, have used this as justification for the concomitant increase in medical intervention in the birth process (see Morse, and Ennis, in this volume).

However, there is no real evidence that intervention and reduced mortality are causally related (Savage, 1986). Better maternal health due to improved living standards and easier access to contraception and abortion also correlate with the decrease in the mortality figures (Wagner, 1994; Tew, 1995). Moreover, it is argued, medical intervention has the potential to be harmful in itself. It can create as many childbirth complications as it solves. Sometimes the use of one intervention can trigger the necessity for a series of others (Wagner, 1994). As Maeve Ennis has demonstrated in Chapter 34, pregnancy screening tests can have a high false positive rate. Under certain circumstances this can then lead to an (unnecessary in many cases) increase in induction of labor to deliver a baby who is perceived to be at risk. When induction involves the use of drugs to stimulate contractions women often report increased levels of pain. Thus they are more likely to require epidural anaesthesia. This results in a lack of sensation. Combined with the slower progress caused by the immobility of continuous electronic monitoring (now necessary because of the woman's inability to feel contractions and concern about the well-being of the foetus) this increases the likelihood of instrumental or surgical delivery. This in its turn will require an abdominal incision or an episiotomy, thus increasing both maternal and foetal trauma. As Maeve Ennis has pointed out, a second cause of instrumental delivery can be misinterpretation of the monitor's trace.

Equally worrying is the realization that many of the interventions (both technological and otherwise) in everyday use in childbirth care were introduced very soon after their development without any in-depth evaluation of their benefits and disadvantages (Donnison, 1988; Campbell, 1990). It is only in more recent years that sound evidence has been sought to support already established obstetric practices and, it must be conceded, this evidence has often been found to be lacking (Enkin *et al.*, 1995).

All of this is not to denigrate the obstetric profession – most, if not all, of whom have the well-being of their childbearing clients genuinely at heart. Instead my aim is to show that this medical model of care, directed at processes which are purely physical – maternal and foetal well-being – nevertheless has an implicit psychological agenda which is all the more damaging because of its hidden nature. Misuse of technology, such as that described above, can be, and is being, addressed. But in the very way it functions, obstetric technology also carries messages about the hazardous nature of birth and about the unique expertise of the obstetric or midwifery professional. These messages live on, infiltrating the rhetoric of the new childbirth paradigm.

THE NEW PARADIGM

One of the more noticeable trends in midwifery care, or at least in the rhetoric surrounding midwifery care, in Britain in the past 10 years has been a move to acknowledge psychological aspects of childbirth. No longer, it is argued, is it sufficient to strive only for the physical well-being of mother and baby during pregnancy, labor and birth, as it has been in the recent past. It is now recognized that the care of the parturient woman must be extended to enable her to make the social and emotional adaptation necessary for successful postnatal functioning as both a woman and a mother (Page, 1998).

Such a paradigm shift has taken many guises. For example, it is evident in government-sponsored documents such as the *Changing Childbirth Report* (Department of Health, 1993), which recommends, among other things, that the childbearing woman should be fully involved in choosing her care, and thus enabled to feel involved and empowered. It is also evident in recent legal moves which ensure the right of childbearing women not to be subjected to forced intervention (Hewson, 1999), and in current interest in the psychological effects of traumatic childbirth experiences (Allen, 1998). This shift implicitly, sometimes explicitly, challenges widespread belief in the efficacy of the medical model of childbirth care – the assumption that birth is a pathological state, to be managed by experts who know what is best for the woman – and explicates the potential control of the childbearing woman.

THE RHETORIC OF CONTROL

As mentioned above, part of the shift towards an acknowledgment of the psychology of childbirth has been a move towards involving childbearing women in the planning of their care. This is in recognition that a negative perception of the care given during labor and birth can have adverse effects on postnatal psychological well-being. As an aside, it should be noted that there has been less interest in positive postnatal mood (Green and Kafetsios, 1997). Neither has the embeddedness of labor and birth in the rest of the woman's life been acknowledged. Life experiences might color the way pregnancy is perceived, for example, and empowerment or its lack during pregnancy might take women into labor and birth with powerful preconceived expectations of the amount of control they are going to achieve (Weaver, 1999). Notwithstanding these issues if, as I am arguing, childbirth itself continues to be represented as something hazardous then the involvement of childbearing women in their own care is liable to be limited.

So where are these representations of hazardous childbirth? As indicated earlier, there is a huge literature addressing the questionable nature of the medical model, and either implicitly or explicitly reconstructing birth as a natural process. Maternity units all over Britain, and indeed across much of the world, are moving to embrace the new paradigm (Page, 1991), which pressure groups such as the National Childbirth Trust have advocated for many years. Many, although not all, individual midwives and obstetricians speak highly of the concept of childbearing women's involvement in their care (Green *et al.*, 1994). Nevertheless birth *is* still often positioned as hazardous by what midwives both say and do.

This becomes particularly apparent when the birth process threatens to move beyond the medical model of conventional hospital delivery. For example, it has recently been reported that, despite the moves to give British childbearing women more autonomy, home birth is often still discouraged by midwives because of their personal attitudes and views (Hosein, 1998). Midwives who do offer the choice of delivery at home often find themselves criticized by their colleagues (Hobbs, 1997). One of the main debates around home birth has always been its safety, despite evidence that home birth is recognized as a safe option for women with low-risk pregnancies (Stewart, 1998). It is highly probable that not a few of the midwives who find objections are afraid of adverse consequences. Similarly, in my own research I found that some midwives were caught between their desire to give their clients choice and their personal opinion that the choice was a dangerous one. For example, one midwife said:

I'm not going to go into the um birthing pool with the mother because I don't want to be accountable for whatever happens to the baby, you know ... I'm not sure I'd be happy (short pause) to deliver a live baby in the bath. But um if she insists, 'That's what I want to do', God help me (laughs). I don't know. Really. (Weaver, 1999)

This midwife's problem was that she did not, personally, feel that water-births were safe, despite working on a unit with a policy which said they were. Since the recommendations of the *Changing Childbirth Report* (Department of Health, 1993) have begun to be implemented, carers are meant to give women all the available options. In theory at least, after the correct training, she should have been willing to discuss the possibility of waterbirth with any client who asked for it, whilst taking into account any clear obstetric contraindications. However, initially this midwife stated categorically that she was not willing to help with a water birth. Later she modified her position to some extent by saying that she did not know what she would do if the woman insisted. It was clear from her conversation that her fears threatened to limit the amount of freedom her clients would have to choose this option.

However, in the aforementioned study, it was not only the midwives who implied that they would be restricted by the potential hazards of childbirth. Childbearing women expressed similar fears:

Interviewer: *Did you think about home birth?*

Woman: *Oh I think that's selfish personally. Because my fear would be something would go wrong, and you're too far from the hospital. The hospital have the equipment. I can't see that it's [hesitates] it's a responsible thing to do for your baby. I mean, for yourself, it's up to you. But there's another living being involved.*

This woman positioned herself as opposed to home birth, but not because of her own distaste. In fact she did not express her personal opinion of home delivery (*'for yourself, it's up to you'*). Personal opinion was positioned as unimportant against the greater issue of safety for the baby, and the problem of maintaining this safety when separated from the technology of the hospital (the 'equipment'). The implications are therefore twofold: that birth is a process where things can go wrong; and that only in a technological hospital environment will these emergencies be dealt with successfully. Both implications can be traced back to the medical model, which reifies technology, and which positions childbirth as something which can only be defined as normal in retrospect (Booth, 1981).

In my research I noted that three themes featured particularly strongly in the talk of primiparous women: that a first birth was an unknown situation for them; that their paramount concern was for the safety of the baby; and that as a result of these two themes, they felt they should trust the 'experts' – the midwives and doctors. Thus the women often positioned professional recommendations as more important than their own wishes for the birth (Weaver, 1999).

As has been shown in this chapter and Chapter 34, safety concerns and the reification of the experts arise directly out of the medical model. However, it is partly because of medicalization that childbirth has been removed from the public domain into hospital. At one time birth would have been a much more visible process, taking place within the family. It would not have been an unknown situation to young women who would have seen (or at least been nearby) when mothers, sisters and other relatives gave birth. In other words, the unfamiliar nature of birth can also be traced, to some extent, to medicalization.

When young women do see birth these days, it is often as a representation on television, frequently as part of a fictional programme, but sometimes as a documentary. A recent study showed that the majority of these representations depicted birth as something dramatic and unpredictable, requiring a rush to hospital with the baby being delivered by a doctor dressed in gown and mask (Clement, 1997). When home birth was portrayed, it was usually unplanned or resulted in the death of the baby. Thus the medical model has also infiltrated media representations and as such has the potential to reinforce the images planted by medicalized childbirth.

In other words, pregnant women, particularly those expecting their first babies, are bound by the psychological consequences of the medical model on many sides. They are restricted by the fears it has created in their minds (when, it must be reiterated, birth is safer than ever before); by the limited and medicalized images to which they have access; by the point of view of the midwives who care for them; and by the continued representation of medical and midwifery personnel as experts. It is forgotten that women have their own expertise in their ownership and knowledge of their own bodies, in the knowledge they have sought and gained and from their past experiences (Hunt and Symonds, 1995).

SUMMARY

Clearly, giving women choices and control over their own births can include making every technological aid available to women who are frightened. Similarly, giving control must include encouraging women to take control of *when* they take control – that is, to relinquish control when they choose and take it up again when they wish to. Nevertheless it seems that, although the new paradigm has done much to change procedures and practices within obstetrics and midwifery, the much slower process of changing professional attitudes, and of changing images of childbirth within society and women's minds, will take much longer.

REFERENCES

Allen, S. (1998) A qualitative analysis of the process, mediating variables and impact of traumatic childbirth. *Journal of Reproductive and Infant Psychology*, 16 (2/3), 107–131
Arms, S. (1994) *Immaculate Deception II: A Fresh Look at Childbirth*. Berkeley, California: Celestial Arts

Booth, R.T. (1981) Never at home. *Maternal and Child Health*, 6, 228–232

Campbell, R. (1990) The place of birth. In J. Alexander, V. Levy and S. Roch (Eds.) *Intrapartum Care. A Research Based Approach*. Basingstoke: Macmillan

Clement, S. (1997) Childbirth on television. *British Journal of Midwifery*, 5 (1), 37–42

Department of Health (1993) *Changing Childbirth: The Report of the Expert Maternity Group*. London: HMSO

Donnison, J. (1988) *Midwives and Medical Men. A History of the Struggle for Control of Childbirth* (2nd edn). New Barnet, Hertfordshire: Historical Publications Ltd

Enkin, M., Keirse, M.J.N.C., Renfrew, M. and Neilson, J. (1995) *A Guide to Effective Care in Pregnancy and Childbirth*. Oxford: Oxford University Press

Green, J. and Kafetsios, K. (1997) Positive experiences of early motherhood: predictive variables from a longitudinal study. *Journal of Reproductive and Infant Psychology*, 15 (2), 141–157

Green, J., Kitzinger, J.V. and Coupland, V.A. (1994) Midwives' responsibilities: medical staffing structures and women's choice in childbirth. In S. Robinson and A.M. Thompson (Eds.) *Midwives, Research and Childbirth* (Vol. 3). London: Chapman and Hall

Hewson, B. (1999) Midwifery and the law: a legal round-up of 1998. *RCM Midwives Journal*, 2 (2), 54–56

Hobbs, L. (1997) Transferring the risk. *MIDIRS Midwifery Digest*, 7 (3), 381–382

Hosein, M.C. (1998) Home birth: is it a real option? *MIDIRS Midwifery Digest*, 8 (4), 518

Hunt, S. and Symonds, A. (1995) *The Social Meaning of Midwifery*. Basingstoke: Macmillan

Page, L. (1998) Preface. In S. Clement (Ed.) *Psychological Perspectives on Pregnancy and Childbirth*. Edinburgh: Churchill Livingstone

Page, L. (1991) The midwife's role in modern health care. In S. Kitzinger (Ed.) *The Midwife Challenge*. London: Pandora

Savage, W. (1986) *A Savage Enquiry: Who Controls Childbirth?* London: Virago

Stewart, M. (1998) Homebirth: safe or not? Commentary. *MIDIRS Midwifery Digest*, 8 (4), 479

Tew, M. (1995) *Safer Childbirth. A Critical History of Maternity Care* (2nd edn). London: Chapman and Hall

Wagner, M. (1994) *Pursuing the Birth Machine: The Search for Appropriate Birth Technology*. Camperdown, New South Wales, Australia: ACE Graphics

Weaver, J.J. (1999) Control in childbirth. A material-discursive evaluation with primiparous women and their midwives. Unpublished Ph.D. dissertation, University of London

CHAPTER 36

MOTHERHOOD AND MOTHERING

Anne Woollett and Harriette Marshall

INTRODUCTION

In this chapter we examine some issues raised for women's health and well-being as they become or do not become mothers, focussing on the diversity of ways in which women experience the transition to motherhood. We position these within dominant discourses which construe motherhood as 'natural' and 'normal' and as providing women with key identities.

Note: The extracts are from interviews conducted as part of Woollett's research by Natasha Gray (postgraduate student) and Patsy Fuller (research assistant).

NOT BECOMING MOTHERS: CHILDLESS WOMEN

Even though motherhood is construed as a 'natural' and 'normal' role, a substantial minority of women do not become mothers (e.g. Graham, 1993; see Morse, in this volume). The reasons for women's childlessness and responses to it vary. Childlessness is considered normative for women such as lesbians and women who are disabled, although this is increasingly challenged (Parks, 1998; Thomas, 1997). The childlessness of able-bodied women in heterosexual relationships is more visible and women are likely to be asked why they are not mothers. Women who choose not to become mothers resist constructions of motherhood as compulsory in contrast to women who are childless because of infertility (Franklin, 1996; Morrell, 1994; Woollett, 1991).

Developments in medical treatments have increased the visibility of infertility. They also encourage women to consider infertility as a biological problem for which medical solutions are most appropriate, even though treatments are costly and stressful and the success rates are low (Stanworth, 1987; Jones and Hunter, 1996). Rendering infertility as a medical problem means there is comparatively little discussion of the experiences of childless women: when motherhood is the natural condition for women, the identities and activities of non-mothers are 'interpreted through the lens of this deficiency' (Morrell, 1994: 89). Women who are not mothers negotiate their identities within discourses which privilege motherhood and deny women identities and selfhood outside motherhood (Glenn, 1994; Ireland, 1993).

Theorizing/experiencing motherhood

Becoming and not becoming mothers are often conceptualized as 'individual' decisions, although these decisions are made within a narrow framework. Women are free to choose how many children to have – as long as they do not opt for 'no' children, 'only' one child, or 'too many' children; and when to have children – but preferably when they are not 'too young' or 'too old' (Woollett, 1996).

Motherhood is positioned as 'normal' and 'natural' and compulsory for ALL women, and this is reiterated often in women's accounts: becoming a mother constitutes 'a natural progression' for women which is emotionally satisfying and 'ultimately fulfilling' (Weaver and Ussher, 1997; Woollett and Nicolson, 1998a). The diversity of situations in which women bring up children is considered predominantly in terms of problems and pathology (Woodward, 1997). Motherhood is construed as problematic for those women who do not bring up children in the 'right' circumstances and at the 'right' time. These 'other' mothers include single women (Silva,

1996); young women (Phoenix, 1991); older women (Berryman, 1991); lesbians (Parks, 1998); disabled women (Thomas, 1997); women in prison (Garcia Coll *et al.*, 1998) and women who are mentally ill (Croghan and Miell, 1998). The representation of these 'other' mothers is further problematized by arguments that their mothering lacks 'quality' and their children do not do as well as children brought up in traditional families (Garcia Coll *et al.*, 1998; Phoenix and Woollett, 1991; Woollett and Phoenix, 1997).

SINGLE MOTHERS

The problematizing of 'other' mothers is exemplified in approaches to single mothers, especially when they are also 'young' and 'black' (Phoenix, 1991; Phoenix, 1996). However, 'single motherhood' is a complex category: while some women are on their own when they become mothers, others become single mothers as a result of death, divorce or breakdown of relationship. Many women remain 'single' for only a short time because they enter new relationships (Graham, 1993).

By focussing on the lack/absence of the child's father, there is little recognition of the range of factors which often make single motherhood difficult. Mother-headed families are more likely to be living in poverty and difficult housing circumstances than two-parent families, and single motherhood is often combined with employment outside the home, adding further to the work load of women bringing up children on their own (Garcia *et al.*, 1998; Graham, 1993; Millar, 1996).

Negative constructions of 'single mothers' are often challenged, as in the following extract:

I've had to fight and organise … that's made me a more determined person….
They've [children] got more input into their lives, haven't they? They've got more
people coming in and out. I think maybe their lives are more flexible than they
would have been … They've had to get used to things like staying at their Dad's
over night … I think that made them more adaptable.

Single mothers often argue that they are doing well under difficult circumstances (*'I've had to fight and organise'* and *'made me a more determined person'*) which can be construed as an advantage for their children's development (*'they've got more people coming in'*, *'their lives are more flexible'* *'made them more adaptable'*) and as building a case to challenge accounts of single parenting as lacking. The reference to *'people coming in and out'* indicates the ways in which single mothers may be supported by their extended families and neighborhoods (Graham, 1993; Phoenix, 1991; Silva, 1996, especially chapter by Burghes).

MOTHERHOOD AS EMBODIED EXPERIENCE: PREGNANCY AND CHILDBIRTH

Most women become mothers by giving birth to children, although this is not the case for women who adopt children or who care for children as step-mothers (Smith *et al.*, 1998). In early pregnancy women often report physical symptoms such as sickness and nausea and later problems associated with their increased size and weight (Niven, 1992; Oakley, 1979). Pregnancy and childbirth are often subjected to close medical monitoring and interventions such as induction and assisted delivery (such as Caesarean section; see Ennis, in this volume). As a result medical accounts of reproductive 'health' and 'normality' are hegemonic in Western cultures (Davis-Floyd, 1994; Ussher, 1989; Woollett and Marshall, 1997).

However, these medical models and constructions of 'health' are challenged by consumer groups, and feminist and critical research which argues that pregnancy and childbirth are primarily 'normal' and healthy processes (see Gross, in this volume). Similarly models of pregnancy and childbirth expressed primarily in biological and depersonalized terms (such as 'the uterus' and the 'foetus') are challenged by accounts which emphasize their psychological and social significance for women's identities, relations with partner and family members (Davis-Floyd, 1994; Woollett and Marshall, 1997).

Women's experiences of pregnancy and childbirth vary considerably as do their ways of coping with the disparate ideas about pregnancy and childbirth. While some women subscribe to interventionist approaches to pregnancy and childbirth, others (and groups campaigning for more woman-centered childbirth) argue for the recognition of the social and psychological significance of pregnancy and childbirth (Davis-Floyd, 1994; Niven, 1992; Woollett and Marshall, 1997; Woollett and Nicolson, 1998b).

POST PARTUM

In contrast with constructions of women's health in pregnancy and childbirth, it is assumed that women recover rapidly after delivery, require little in the way of postnatal care and are immediately able to take care of their infants. This also contrasts with the care of women and babies in the past and in other cultures based on ideas that women need to rest and recover from childbirth (Niven, 1992; Woollett and Marshall, 1997; Woollett and Nicolson, 1998b).

While many women do recover quickly after childbirth and are pleased to care for their babies, others recover more slowly, especially when their deliveries involved major interventions. A significant proportion of women are still experiencing physical and psychological problems months after delivery (Woollett and Parr, 1997). When women's physical recovery after childbirth is slow, women report more problems in breast feeding and with their sexual relations (Alder, 1994).

MOTHERING: WOMEN'S EXPERIENCES AND FEELINGS

Women often express satisfaction with motherhood and their relations with their babies, in line with Western ideas about attachment, are often described in terms of intense emotionality (Lewis and Nicolson, 1998). However, there is also considerable variability in women's feelings, with some women enjoying looking after children more than others, in ways which often relate to the quality of their support from family, friends and community (Das Gupta, 1995; Levitt *et al.*, 1996; Llewelyn and Osborne, 1990; Nicolson, 1998).

Constructions of motherhood as 'natural' and as ultimate satisfaction often means that the psychological and social costs of motherhood are underestimated. In Western cultures the provision of 'good' mothering requires women to subordinate their own needs and identities to those of their children, and to be continuously available and sensitive (Brown *et al.*, 1997; Wearing, 1984; Woollett and Phoenix, 1996).

Women acknowledge the costs of motherhood which they characterize as 'responsibility' and 'tying you down' in opposition to 'enjoying life' and having 'time to ourselves' (Weaver and Ussher, 1997; Woollett, 1996). Motherhood is often experienced as hard and tiring work, and for many Western women as isolation (Weaver and Ussher, 1997; Lewis and Nicolson, 1998). These dominant constructions of motherhood as 'ultimate fulfilment' and as 'natural' for women make difficult women's articulation of negative feelings such as anger and guilt without seeming to be 'bad mothers' (Parker, 1995). In their use of phrases such as 'but I wouldn't be without them' women neutralize the costs of motherhood and obscure the difficulties they experience, reproducing notions that motherhood is easy (see Weaver and Ussher, 1997; Graham, 1993).

Women's ambivalent feelings are explained as both 'natural' and 'unnatural'. Constructions of motherhood as 'natural' means that women may experience their feelings as 'unnatural' and as difficult to talk about, further increasing their guilt and sense of failure as 'good/normal' mothers (Llewelyn and Osborne, 1990; Wetherell, 1995). But women's negative feelings are also explained as 'natural' responses to hormonal changes in the post partum. This alerts women and those around them to negative as well as positive feelings, but normalizing women's negative feelings can result in their being dismissed as 'only their hormones' rather than being taken seriously (Nicolson, 1998; Nicolson, this volume).

These explanations are challenged by those which contextualize women's feelings in terms of the hard physical and emotional work of mothering and the changes motherhood brings to women's lives, relationships and identities. The work of motherhood is both endless and invisible, often coming to notice only when things go 'wrong' (Wetherell, 1995). By concentrating on one-to-one relations between mothers and young children, psychological models often do not relate well to the experiences of women bringing up two or more children and to diversity among children, for example in terms of their gender, health and disability (Munn, 1991; Gregory, 1991). Psychological models also fail to acknowledge children's agency and the ways in which motherhood changes as children get older (Brannen *et al.*, 1994; Moore *et al.*, 1996; Woollett and Phoenix, 1996).

For many women motherhood involves withdrawal from the world of work which is experienced as loss – financial loss as well as loss of social contacts and identities (Llewelyn and Osborne, 1990; Wetherell, 1995; Woollett and Nicolson, 1998a; Nicolson, in this volume). A mother of young children describes her loss of identity in the following extract:

You do tend to feel as if you're not there... both jobs that I done, I was very independent.... And so I'm used to being in charge. I know I'm in charge now, but when you have children, specially when they start nursery or toddler groups, it's 'Richard's mum' and 'David's mum', you've lost your identity.... You're not yourself.... You do feel as if you lose your identity.

'*I know I'm in charge*' suggests that mothers are powerful figures in children's lives, giving them a valued position and role, although this is often experienced by mothers as blame when/if children do not '*turn out right*' (Wetherell, 1995; Woollett and Phoenix, 1996; Glenn, 1994).

WOMEN'S OTHER IDENTITIES AND RELATIONS

Motherhood and becoming a mother impact on women's other roles and identities, and their social relations, including those with fathers/partners, the wider family and neighborhood, and through employment (Burman, 1994; Woollett and Phoenix, 1996; Das Gupta, 1995).

Motherhood often brings changes in women's family roles. In spite of the commitment of many men and women to 'equality' and 'sharing the caring', when they become mothers, family roles become more highly gendered and women take greater responsibility for child care and household tasks than they and their partners had expected (Backett, 1987; Croghan, 1991). These changes are explained in terms of 'rationality': it 'makes sense' for women to take responsibility for children and household tasks in the majority of households where they earn less than male partners (Dryden, 1998). The discrepancy between expectations of 'equality' and 'sharing' and the gendered nature of family roles is a source of considerable dissatisfaction for women, and especially for women who are highly committed to 'sharing the caring' (e.g. Croghan, 1991; Ruble *et al.*, 1988).

MOTHERHOOD AND EMPLOYMENT

In Western cultures, motherhood is also positioned in terms of women's employment outside the home. Many women with children are in paid employment and combine motherhood with employment (Lewis, 1991). Their employment often provides women with some financial independence, although because women fit employment around children and child care, often their jobs are casual, unskilled and badly paid. When women have greater financial independence, men are more involved in child care and household tasks (Wetherell, 1995). However, even women in full-time employment take greater responsibility than fathers for family roles including arrangements for child care. The impact of employment for many women, therefore, is to increase their power within families, but also their workloads (Brannon and Moss, 1988; Easterbrooks and Goldberg, 1985).

SUMMARY

In this chapter we argue that women become pregnant, give birth, bring up children and experience motherhood in a diversity of situations. However, within psychological theorizing some approaches and discourses (e.g. medical approaches and attachment models) dominate and are used to define what are 'normal' responses and strategies for coping with motherhood and mothering. As a result the contradictions between approaches and their implications for women's coping are less often considered – e.g. between 'risk' in pregnancy and 'well-being' in post partum, between motherhood as 'natural/instinct' and the costs of motherhood for women, motherhood as central and dominant identity for women and as one of many identities and relationships in which women engage – and less frequently addressed. The implications for practice and policy are that the meanings of motherhood for women and the situations in which they are mothering need to be taken into account in evaluating how 'well' women are adjusting or fulfilling their roles as mothers.

REFERENCES

Alder, B. (1994) Postnatal sexuality. In P.Y.L. Choi and P. Nicolson (Eds.) *Female Sexuality: Psychology, Biology and Social Context*. Hemel Hempstead: Harvester Wheatsheaf

Backett (1987) The negotiation of fatherhood. In C. Lewis and M. O'Brien (Eds.) *Reassessing Fatherhood: New Observations on Fathers and the Modern Family*. London: Sage

Berryman, J. (1991) Perspectives on later motherhood. In A. Phoenix, A. Woollett and E. Lloyd (Eds.) *Motherhood: Meanings, Practices and Ideologies*. London: Sage

Brannen, J. and Moss, P. (1991) *Managing Mothers: Dual Earner Household After Maternity Leave*. London: Unwin

Brannen, J., Dodd, K., Oakley, A. and Storey, P. (1994) *Young People, Health and Family Life*. Milton Keynes: Open University Press

Brown, S., Small, R. and Lumley, J. (1997) Being a 'good mother'. *Journal of Reproductive and Infant Psychology*, 15, 185–200

Burman, E. (1994) *Deconstructing Developmental Psychology*. London: Routledge

Croghan, R. (1991) First-time mothers' accounts of inequality in the division of labour. *Feminism and Psychology*, 1, 221–246

Croghan, R. and Miell, D. (1998) Strategies of resistance: 'bad' mothers dispute the evidence. *Feminism and Psychology*, 8, 445–466

Das Gupta, P. (1995) Growing up in families. In P. Barnes (Ed.) *Personal, Social and Emotional Development in Children*. Buckingham: Open University Press

Davis-Floyd, R.E. (1994) The technocratic body: American childbirth as cultural expression. *Social Science and Medicine*, 38, 1125–1140

Dryden, C. (1998) *Being Married, Doing Gender: A Critical Analysis of Gender Relationships in Marriage*. London: Routledge

Easterbrooks, M.A. and Goldberg, W.A. (1985) Maternal employment and mothers, fathers and toddlers. *Developmental Psychology*, 29, 774–78

Franklin, S. (1997) *Embodied Progress: A Cultural Account of Assisted Conception*. London: Routledge

Garcia Coll, C., Surrey, J.L. and Weingarten, K. (1997) (Eds.) *Mothering Against the Odds: Diverse Voices of Contemporary Mothers*. New York: Guilford Press

Glenn, E.N. (1994) Social constructions of mothering: a thematic overview. In E.N. Glenn, G Chang and L.R. Forcey (Eds.) *Motherhood: Ideology, Experience and Agency*. New York: Routledge

Graham, H. (1993) *Health and Hardship in Women's Lives*. Hemel Hempstead: Harvester Wheatsheaf

Gregory, S. (1991) Challenging motherhood: mothers and their deaf children. In A. Phoenix, A. Woollett and E. Lloyd (Eds.) *Motherhood: Meanings, Practices and Ideologies*. London: Sage

Ireland, M.S. (1993) *Reconceiving Motherhood: Separating Motherhood from Female Identity*. New York: Guilford Press

Jones, S.C. and Hunter, M. (1996) The influence of context and discourse on infertility experience. *Journal of Reproductive and Infant Psychology*, 14, 93–111

Lewis, S.E. and Nicolson, P. (1998) Talking about early motherhood: recognizing loss and reconstructing depression. *Journal of Reproductive and Infant Psychology*, 16, 177–198

Levitt, M.J. Weber, R.A. and Clark, M.C. (1986) Social network relationships as sources of maternal support and well-being. *Developmental Psychology*, 22, 310–316

Lewis, S. (1991) Motherhood and employment: the impact of social and organisational values. In A. Phoenix, A. Woollett and E. Lloyd (Eds.) *Motherhood: Meanings, Practices and Ideologies*. London: Sage

Llewelyn, S. and Osborne, K. (1990) *Women's Lives*. London: Routledge

Millar, J. (1996) Mothers, workers, wives: Comparing policy approaches to supporting single mothers. In E.B. Silva (Ed.) *Good Morning Mothering: Feminist Perspectives on Lone Motherhood*. London: Routledge

Moore, M., Sixsmith, J. and Knowles, K. (1996) *Children's Reflections on Family Life*. London: Falmer

Morrell, C.M. (1994) *Unwomanly Conduct: The Challenges of Intentional Childlessness*. London: Routledge

Munn, P. (1991) Mothering more than one child. In A. Phoenix, A. Woollett and E. Lloyd (Eds.) *Motherhood: Meanings, Practices And Ideologies*. London: Sage

Nicolson, P. (1998) *Post Natal Depression: Psychology, Science and the Transition to Motherhood*. London: Routledge

Niven, C. (1992) *Psychological Care For Families: Before, During and After Birth*. Oxford: Butterworth/Heineman

Oakley, A. (1979) *Becoming a Mother*. Harmondsworth: Penguin

Parker, R. (1995) *Torn in Two: The Experience of Maternal Ambivalence*. London: Virago

Parks, C.A. (1998) Lesbian parenthood: a review of the literature. *American Journal of Orthopsychiatry*, 68, 376–389

Phoenix, A. (1991) *Young Mothers?* Cambridge: Polity

Phoenix, A. and Woollett, A. (1991) Motherhood: social construction, politics and psychology. In A. Phoenix, A. Woollett and E. Lloyd (Eds.) *Motherhood: Meanings, Practices and Ideologies*. London: Sage

Ruble, D.N., Fleming, A.S., Hackel, L.S. and Stangor, C. (1988) Changes in the marital relationship during the transition to first time motherhood: effects of violated expectations concerning division of household labor. *Journal of Personality and Social Psychology*, 55, 78–87

Silva, E.B. (1996) *Good Enough Mothering? Feminist Perspectives on Lone Motherhood*. London: Routledge

Stanworth, M. (1987) *Reproductive Technologies: Gender, Motherhood and Medicine*. Cambridge: Polity

Thomas, C. (1997) The baby and the bath water: disabled women and motherhood in social context. *Sociology of Health and Illness*, 19, 622–643

Ussher, J. (1989) *The Psychology of the Female Body*. London: Routledge

Wearing, B. (1984) *The Ideology of Motherhood*. Sydney: Allen and Unwin

Weaver, J.J. and Ussher, J. (1997) How motherhood changes life: a discourse analytic study with mothers of young children. *Journal of Reproductive and Infant Psychology*, 15, 51–68

Wetherell, M. (1995) Social structure, ideology and family dynamics: the case of parenting. In J. Muncie, M. Wetherell, R. Dallos and A. Cochrane (Eds.) *Understanding the Family*. Sage: London

Woodward, K. (1997) Motherhood: identities, meanings and myths. In K. Woodward (Ed.)

Identity and Difference: Culture, Media and Identities. London: Sage

Woollett, A. (1991) Having children: accounts of childless women and women with reproductive problems. In A. Phoenix, A. Woollett and E. Lloyd (Eds.) *Motherhood: Meanings,
Practices and Ideologies*. London: Sage

Woollett, A. (1996) Reproductive decisions. In A. Walker and K. Niven (Eds.) *Psychology of
Reproduction: Volume 2: Conception, Pregnancy and Birth*. Oxford: Butterworth/Heinemann

Woollett, A. and Phoenix, A. (1996) Motherhood as pedagogy: developmental psychology
and the accounts of mothers of young children. In C. Luke (Ed.) *Feminisms and Pedagogies
of Everyday Life*. New York: SUNY Press

Woollett, A. and Marshall, H. (1997) Accounts of pregnancy and childbirth. In L. Yardley
(Ed.) *Material Discourses of Health and Illness*. London: Routledge

Woollett, A. and Parr, M. (1997) Psychological tasks for women and men in the post-partum.
Journal of Reproductive and Infant Psychology, 15, 159–183

Woollett, A. and Phoenix, A. (1997) Deconstructing developmental psychology accounts of
mothering. *Feminism and Psychology*, 7, 2, 275–282

Woollett, A. and Nicolson, P. (1998a) The social construction of motherhood and fatherhood.
In A. Walker and C. Niven (Eds.) *The Psychology of Reproduction. Vol 3: Infancy and
Parenthood*. Oxford: Butterworth/Heinemann

Woollett, A. and Nicolson, P. (1998b) Post-partum Experiences. In A. Walker and C. Niven
(Eds.) *The Psychology of Reproduction. Vol 3: Infancy and Parenthood*. Oxford:
Butterworth/Heineman

CHAPTER 37

COMPETING EXPLANATIONS OF POSTPARTUM DEPRESSION: WHAT ARE THE BENEFITS TO WOMEN?

Paula Nicolson

INTRODUCTION

It is widely believed by health care professionals, clinical researchers and thus 'consumers'/mothers, who rely on those experts for information, that depression after childbirth is a distinct entity. It is explained as different from depression at any other time of life, or depression that men, or women who are not mothers, might suffer. Postpartum depression is frequently attributed to hormone changes at the time of birth and subsequent hormonal imbalance or to pre-existing psychiatric disturbance. Close examination of the quality of evidence to support this position, however, suggests that there are more likely to be logical explanations for low mood, depressed episodes or clinical depression during the postnatal months. Many women experience new motherhood as a disruptive life event; they may be subject to physical pain, extra stress, deteriorating domestic and social relationships. This may be for a number of reasons but crucially resonates with the low status, expectations and resources available for the motherhood role.

Explanations presented in this chapter range from medical accounts, which focus upon biological explanations, to feminist accounts, which emphasize the inherent difficulties that the traditional social context places upon the lives of mothers.

WHAT IS POSTNATAL DEPRESSION? THE 'SCIENTIFIC' PERSPECTIVE

Between 1980 and 1990 more than 100 studies on PND were published (Whiffen, 1992). Despite increasingly abundant data, it remains difficult to identify any advances in explanations of why women get depressed after childbirth. There are rational reasons why (particularly) medical research has reached this impasse. Contemporary medical research is characterized by large-scale randomized control trials (RCT), frequently sponsored by government agencies or multi-national drug companies, seeking to identify the effectiveness of one treatment over another (see Oakley, 1990). While not all clinical research is funded this way, the model of the RCT is the standard from which other forms of research are seen to *deviate* and have to justify their designs. In order to operate within this framework, it is standard practice to take for granted an objective means of identifying an 'illness'.

A major characteristic of the traditional research literature is that almost none of the scientific papers sets out a clear operational definition of PND. This point has not escaped notice. Almost 20 years ago commentators argued that the literature has 'failed to distinguish among the maternity blues, post partum affective psychoses, and mild to moderate post partum depression' (Hopkins *et al.*, 1984: 498). And studies of PND 'are beset by methodological problems such as problems in the definition of depression itself' (Pollock *et al.*, 1980: 1).

Despite the absence of operational definitions, an implicit model of PND has emerged. PND is characterized by scientists through its *temporal location*, as occurring during the first 12 months following childbirth; the *variety of its form*, which varies according to when during the postnatal period and how long depressive episodes occur; whether it is in fact an 'illness' with a physical cause, or a *response* to 'stress' or a 'life event'; how far it actually is *linked to childbirth itself* or simply connected to being a new mother; and finally there is interest in the *incidence* (Nicolson, 1998).

When does postnatal depression develop?

Postnatal depression is defined, somewhat tautologically, as depression that occurs during the first 12 months following childbirth (see Nicolson, 1998). Within the time span of 12 postnatal months, however, there is a relative deficiency in the information about duration and course (Hopkins *et al.*, 1984). Some evidence suggests PND lasts from six to eight weeks (O'Hara *et al.*, 1983) whereas other studies suggest that problems may persist throughout the first year (Pitt, 1968; Ballinger *et al.*, 1979). Pollock and colleagues indicate that PND has an influence on the mother for at least three years. Moreover, Brown and Harris (1978) and Lewis (1995) have shown that women with young children up to school age often report being depressed.

The symptoms and signs of PND

Whether or not a woman is displaying the signs and symptoms of PND is of primary importance to clinicians from all disciplinary backgrounds. These are not always clear from the research literature. The term PND loosely appears to embrace a variety of 'conditions'. Oakley (1979) identified these as:

a) the blues which was a weepiness and anxiety that occurred between two and ten days following the birth which is usually seen to be transitory (Pitt, 1968; Harris, 1981; Kendell *et al.*, 1984; York, 1990);
b) depression and anxiety on arriving home with the baby which lasts as week or two (Cox *et al.*, 1983);
c) depressed 'moods' with good and bad days around three months after delivery (Oakley, 1980);
d) clinical depression which is enduring and includes other symptoms such as loss of appetite and sleep disturbance, (Hopkins *et al.*, 1984; Dalton, 1989).

PND, it appears, is used non-specifically as a 'catch-all' diagnosis for emotional and psychiatric problems after childbirth.

Is PND an 'illness' or a logical response to 'stress'?

Characteristic of much traditional research on postnatal depression is that it is unproblematically perceived as a psychiatric condition. Despite almost 30 years of research there is still a lack of clarity about the similarities and differences between postnatal mental illness, depression and psychosis. Several authors who set out to describe one kind of 'disorder' (as listed in the section above) are prone to 'concept slippage' thereby referring to a broadly located 'postpartum mental illness' or 'psychiatric disorders associated with childbearing' (e.g. Margison, 1990). Moreover, this conceptual framework is used time and again to embrace 'conditions' that are not taken to be psychiatric in any practical sense, and are not typically referred for psychiatric treatment.

The debate concerning the relationship between puerperal psychosis and other postpartum 'disorders' – whether they are mutually exclusive or form part of a continuum – also, has not been resolved (Sneddon, 1982). Neither has the debate on how far, if at all, postnatal 'illnesses' differ qualitatively from non-puerperal conditions (Katona, 1982). As Appleby (1990) asserts: 'Little progress has been made towards an understanding of the aetiology of postpartum psychosis, despite the long-standing assumption that it is precipitated by biological factors' (Appleby, 1990: 109). Researchers interested in PND as a response to childbirth as a life event, focus on depression as a reaction to stress and the lack of social support (Oakley, 1980; Elliot, 1990) and on the whole tend to be social scientists rather than medically oriented researchers.

IS PND LINKED TO CHILDBIRTH?

Brockington and Kumar (1982) suggested that the 'precise' definition of the links between motherhood and mental illness is 'elusive', which potentially raises doubts about the special and unique relationship (Brockington and Kumar, 1982: 2). They declare though that they themselves are convinced of the link – although they are going with their instincts rather than the evidence. Steiner (1979), reviewing the psychobiology of mental disorders associated with childbearing, argued that postpartum mental illness is not a unitary phenomenon and neither is the physiology of the puerperium a cause in itself of any of the symptoms (Steiner, 1979: 449). Therefore clinical problems that occur during this period are either triggered by non-biological factors or are attributable to other causes. Cox (1994) found that it was not until 1992 that the World Health Organisation accorded puerperal mental disorders the status of a separate category. 'The new version of their International Classification of Diseases (ICD-10; WHO, 1992) does, however, go some way towards addressing this issue. Mental disorders occurring at this time may now be categorized as puerperal, but only if they cannot otherwise be classified' (Cox, 1994: 4).

Incidence of PND

There is little consensus on the incidence of PND (Hopkins et al., 1984). There are claims that 7 percent (Dalton, 1971), between 10 and 20 percent (York, 1990), 24 percent (Frate et al., 1979), and 30 percent (Gordon et al., 1965) of women have depression severe enough to need treatment; 50–80 percent experience the 'blues' (Pitt, 1973; Harris, 1981; York, 1990) and 33 percent experience depressed moods (Oakley, 1979). Hopkins and colleagues (1984) argue that these disparities are due to the lack of comparable criteria for measurement. Oates (1994) indicates that it is also likely that many 'cases' lie undetected.

COMPETING MODELS OF PND

The literature on postnatal depression divides roughly into two approaches or models: the 'medical' which emphasizes individual characteristics that *predispose women to becoming depressed* after childbirth, and the 'social science' which stresses external, *psycho social factors which act as stressors.*

The medical perspective

Discussion of problematic histories or congenital vulnerabilities overlaps into the debate about the unity of PND (Barzilai and Davies, 1972). Some researchers argue that depression at any stage of the life cycle is due to hormonal imbalances and attempts have been made to link postnatal depression and pre-menstrual tension (e.g. Anzalone, 1978; Dalton, 1971). Some studies have proposed that an episode of the 'blues' predisposes women to subsequent PND (e.g. Cox *et al.*, 1982) although Kumar and Robson (1978) did not find this link. Holden (1994) argues that PND may be the precursor for depression later in life. Others have linked anxiety and depression in pregnancy to PND (Tod, 1964; Dalton, 1971) although Cox *et al.* (1982) could not confirm that women free of symptoms during pregnancy could become depressed postnatally. Davidson (1972) and Pitt (1973) have linked ambivalent and hostile feelings in early pregnancy with the 'blues'. Frommer and O'Shea (1973) have also linked attitudes towards pregnancy and subsequent depression. A family history of emotional disorder also has been connected to PND (Nilsson *et al.*, 1970; Gordon *et al.*, 1959; Ballinger *et al.*, 1979).

The social science perspective

Social scientists take more account of the context of early motherhood and the experience of birth in order to develop their theoretical positions. Hopkins *et al.* (1984) see research on postpartum depression as offering a 'unique opportunity to clarify the relationship between a specific stressor (the birth of a child) and the development of psychiatric illness' (1984: 498). They are persuaded by evidence suggesting stressful life events are a significant influence in the development of depression (Brown and Harris, 1978) and that because childbirth is a significant stressor in its own right (Grossman *et al.*, 1980) additional stresses in this period contribute towards depression. This concurs with the early findings of Elliot (1985) who further proposed that 'Postnatal depression is ... a realistic response to the life event of birth and to the stress of the maternal role, in combination with other life stresses' (Elliot, 1985: 3).

The stressors documented include unsatisfactory marriages (Kumar and Robson, 1978; Paykel *et al.*, 1980; Cox *et al.*, 1982; Rossan, 1987), loneliness and lack of adult company (Sharpe, 1994) as well as the role changes that might be involved for some women during the transition to motherhood such as leaving paid employment, running a home and taking responsibility for infant care (Elliot, 1985). Lack of social support has been documented as leading to depression (Henderson, 1981; Mueller, 1980) although until recently only a few studies (O'Hara *et al.*, 1983; Paykel *et al.*, 1980) have related social support specifically to PND.

Hopkins and colleagues (1984) argued that cause and effect in relation to stressors and PND had not been explored effectively. However, much effort has gone into investigating the relationship between childbirth as a life event since the mid-1980s and there is evidence that depression can be alleviated through providing practical and social support (Elliot, 1990).

Finally there is evidence that an unsatisfactory birth experience may be related to subsequent depression either because of technological intervention (Oakley, 1980; Day, 1982) including induction or poor quality medical care, and suggested that women are more prepared to endure pain than to loose control over labor and delivery (Cartwright, 1979). Tew (1978) and Kitzinger (1978) both argue that hospital rather than home births are more likely to make women depressed.

The 'social science' position embraces a more liberal, broader view of the individual in context, conceptualizing her as a potential victim of social stress. Although this model proposes the view that PND is an understandable reaction to stress, it fails to identify how the *experience itself* varies between individuals.

WOMEN'S EXPERIENCES OF POSTNATAL DEPRESSION: DIFFERING WITH THE EXPERTS?

Since the mid-1970s feminist psychologists in the U.S. and Europe have identified the clear influence of gender-bias in favor of a male perspective on psychological research and knowledge (Bem, 1993), re-focussing attention upon the role of science in constructing a knowledge base that makes women and female perspectives invisible (e.g. Crawford and Maracek, 1989; Wilkinson, 1996). As Gilligan (1993) makes clear, it does not matter how well a scientist believes that their methodology is objective, when it comes to the crunch, they interpret their findings through their own, gendered eyes. A man (and most scientists are either men or are involved in teams where a man is the leader) exploring data on PND, will see it as a discrete episode in the mother's life which is irrational and related in some way to the biology of birth. There has been a long tradition through which this view has taken shape (see Ehrenreich and English, 1978; Ussher, 1989; Moscucci, 1993). The acknowledgment that lack of social support and the stress of early motherhood are important has only recently been taken seriously, but as argued above, this has been treated simply as a means of *adding* the social context to the biology and does not represent a feminist perspective in which women's experiences are the focal point

Women talking about postnatal depression implicitly make connections between the fact that the infant enters their life in a dynamic, developing context and that there is no consistent or objective experience of 'becoming a mother'. They apply this to different occasions when they have had children and between themselves and other women (Nicolson, 1998). They frequently explain their experiences in terms which relate more closely to accounts of depression following hospitalization (Revans, 1968), psychosocial transitions (Murray Parkes, 1971) and disruption and loss (Marris, 1986) than they do to those encapsulated in the clinical/medical discourse. In Western societies childbirth usually takes place in hospital which means that women's experience of pregnancy and the first hours and days of motherhood are circumscribed within a medically managed framework (Niven, 1992). Consequently, an unease evolves between the competing requirements of mothers and attending clinicians, in that for the majority of women, pregnancy and birth are about having a baby and becoming a mother; for the doctors, successful action is the delivery of a healthy baby and (as far as possible) mother (Graham and Oakley, 1981).

Women depressed following childbirth do not see themselves primarily as ill. They explain their experiences as related to the context and circumstances of their particular stage of motherhood. However, they also take on the clinically acknowledged identity of a patient suffering from a recognized 'condition' for a range of complex reasons which link all of us to the dominant culture and belief systems in which we account for ourselves. The priority Western society attributes to clinical science is more problematic at the end of the twentieth century than ever before. Clinical science has changed life-expectations both because of substantive developments and because of the relationship of science to the media which influences human beliefs, understanding and socialization.

Most adults thus expect a baby to enhance their lives; with the *arrival* of the baby itself as a happy and fulfilling event. This was an important issue in my research (Nicolson, 1998). A critical theme in all the women's accounts was that of *loss* which is taboo in the expert literature on birth and motherhood. The linking of 'loss' with childbirth also conflicts with everyday understanding of the transition to motherhood. Loss and motherhood appear paradoxical. Of course they are not. Women who become mothers (each time) lose at least their autonomy, sense of identity, work, time, friends, relationship pattern, sexuality, sense of their own body, and health and comfort. These losses occur (like all such losses) in a complex way as part of biographical experience and in the context of subjective understanding.

Conducting qualitative research focusses on and gives maximum credibility to the respondents' perspectives. It further enables the complex nature of the relationship between individuals (including the respondent and researcher) and the individual and their social and cultural network to be exposed. PND is not an objective diagnostic category but a term that is easily and loosely used to explain or mask the multitude of experiences that surround the conditions that impact on the experience of childbirth and motherhood. These are most effectively identified through taking respondents' accounts seriously.

SUMMARY

The scientific understanding of PND has developed over the last 20 years in terms of explaining how often and under what circumstances some women experience it. However the diversity of explanations that remain current in the scientific literature appear to be treading parallel paths with little concession to understanding women's own accounts of why they feel how they do. What is missing it seems is a means and willingness to explore the complexities in the lives of the women when they have babies.

The transition to motherhood can never be a standardized event. Everyone's life is different. Nevertheless researchers in this area appear daunted by the challenge of explaining PND in its everyday context.

REFERENCES

Anzlaone, M. K. (1977) Postpartum depression and prementrual tensions; Life stress and marital adjustment, Boston: Ph.D. Thesis

Appleby, L. (1990) The aetiology of post partum psychosis: Why are there no answers? *Journal of Reproductive and Infant Psychology*, 8 (2), 109–118

Ballinger, B., Buckley, D.E., Naylor, G.J. and Stansfield, D.A. (1979) Emotional disturbance following childbirth: Clinical findings and urinary excretion of cyclic AMP. *Psychological Medicine*, 9, 293–300

Barzilai, S. and Davies, A.M. (1973) Postpartum mental disorders in Jerusalem: Survey of hospitalised cases 1964–1967. *British Journal of Social Psychiatry and Community Health*, 6 (2) 80–89

Bem, S. (1993) *The Lenses of Gender*. New Haven: Yale University Press

Brockington, I.F. and Kumar, R. (1982) *Motherhood and Mental Illness*. London:Academic Press

Brown, G and Harris, T. (1978) *The Social Origins Of Depression*. London: Tavistock

Cartwright, A. (1979) *The Dignity of Labour*. London: Tavistock

Cox, J.L. and Holden, J. (1994) (Eds.) *Perinatal Psychiatry: Use and Misuse of the Edinburgh Postnatal Depression Scale*. London: Gaskell/Royal College of Psychiatrists

Cox, J. L., Connor, Y.M. and Kendell, R.E. (1982) Prospective study of the psychiatric disorders of childbirth. *British Journal of Psychiatry*, 140, 111–117

Cox, J.L., Connor, Y.M., Henderson, I., McGuire, R.J. and Kendell, R.E. (1983) Prospective study of the psychiatric disorders of childbirth by self-report questionnaire. *Journal of Affective Disorders*, 5, 1–7

Crawford, M. and Maracek, J. (1989) Psychology reconstructs the female: 1968–1988. *Psychology of Women Quarterly*, 13, 147–166

Dalton, K. (1971) Prospective study into puerperal depression. *British Journal of Psychiatry*, 118, 689–692

Dalton, K. (1980/1989 revised edition) *Depression After Childbirth*. Oxford: Oxford University Press

Davidson, J.R.T. (1972) Postpartum mood change in Jamaican women: A description and discussion of its significance. *British Journal of Psychiatry*, 121, 659–663

Day, S. (1982) Is obstetric technology depressing? Radical Science Journal, 12, 659–663

Ehrenreich, B. and English, D. (1979) *For Her Own Good: 150 Years of the Experts' Advice to Women*, London: Pluto

Elliot, S.A. (1985) A rationale for psychosocial intervention in the prevention of postnatal depression. Paper presented at the first Women in Psychology Conference, Cardiff, S. Wales

Elliot, S.A. (1990) Commentary on 'Childbirth as a life event'. *Journal of Reproductive and Infant Psychology*, 8, 147–159

Frommer, E.A. and O'Shea, G. (1973) Antenatal identification of women liable to have problems in managing their infants. *British Journal of Psychiatry*, 123, 149–156

Gilligan, C. (1993) *In a Different Voice: Psychological theory and Women's Development*. London: Harvard University Press

Gordon, R.E., Kapostins, E.E. and Gordon, K.K. (1965) Factors in postpartum emotional adjustment. *Obstetrics and Gynaecology*, 25, 158–166

Graham, H. and Oakey, A. (1981) Competing ideologies of reproduction. In H. Roberts (Ed.) *Women, Health and Reproduction*. London: RKP

Harris, B. (1981) Maternity Blues In East African Clinic Attenders. *Archives Of General Psychiatry*, 38, 1293–1295

Henderson, S. (1981) Social relationships, adversity and neurosis: An analysis of prospective observations. *British Journal of Psychiatry*, 138, 391–398

Holden, J. (1994) Can non-psychotic depression be prevented? In J. Cox and J. Holden (Eds.) *Perinatal Psychiatry: Use and Misuse of the Edinburgh Postnatal Depression Scale*. London Gaskell/Royal College of Psychiatrists

Hopkins, J., Marcus, M. and Campbell, S.B. (1984) Postpartum depression: A critical review. *Psychological Bulletin*, 95, 498–515

Katona, C.L. (1982) Puerperal mental illness: Comparisons with non-puerperal controls. *British Journal of Psychiatry*, 141, 447–452

Kendell, R.E., MacKenzie, W.E., West, C., McGuire, R.J. and Cox, J.L. (1984) Day to day mood changes after childbirth: Further data. *British Journal of Psychiatry*, 145, 620–625

Ketai, R.M. and Brandwin, M.A. (1979) Childbirth related psychosis and familial symbiotic conflict. *American Journal of Psychiatry*, 136, 190–193.

Kitzinger, S. (1978) *Women as Mothers*. Glasgow: William Collins

Kumar, R. and Robson, K. (1978) Neurotic disturbance during pregnancy and the puerperium: Preliminary report of a prospective survey of 119 primiparae. In M. Sandler (Ed.) *Mental Illness in Pregnancy and the Puerperium*. Oxford: Oxford Medical Publications

Lewis, S. E. (1995) A search for meaning: Making sense of depression. *Journal of Mental Health*, 4, 369–n382

Margison, F. (1990) Editorial: Special Issue on psychiatric disorders associated with childbearing. *Journal of Reproductive and Infant Psychology*, 8 (2), 63–66

Marris, P. (1986) *Loss and Change*. London: Tavistock

Moscucci, O. (1993) *The Science of Woman: Gynaecology and Gender in England 1800–1929*. Cambridge: Cambridge University Press

Mueller, D. (1980) Social networks: A promising direction for research on the relationship of the social environment to psychiatric disorder. *Social Science and Medicine*, 14, 147–161

Murray-Parkes, C. (1971) Psychosocial transitions: A field for study. *Social Science and Medicine*, 5, 101–115

Nicolson, P. (1998) *Postnatal Depression: Psychology, Science and the Transition To Motherhood*. London: Routledge

Nilsson, A. (1970) Para-natal emotional adjustment: A prospective study of 165 women, Part 1. *Acta Psychiatrica Scandanavica*, 47 (supp 220), 1–61

Niven, C. (1992) *Psychological Care for Families: Before, During and After Birth*. Oxford: Butterworth Heinemann

O'Hara, M.W., Rehm, L.P. and Campbell, S.B. (1983) Postpartum depression: A role for social network and life stress variables. *Journal of Nervous and Mental Diseases*, 171, 336–341

Oakley, A. (1979) The baby blues. *New Society*, 5 April, 11–12

Oakley, A. (1980) *Women Confined: Towards a Sociology of Childbirth*. Oxford: Martin Robertson

Oakley, A. (1990) Who's afraid of the randomised control trial? Some dilemmas of the scientific method and 'good' research practice. In H. Roberts (Ed.) *Women's Health Counts*. London: Routledge

Oates, M. (1994) Postnatal mental illness: organisation and function of services. In J. Cox and J. Holden (Eds.) *Perinatal Psychiatry: Use and Misuse of the Edinburgh Postnatal Depression Scale*. London Gaskell/Royal College of Psychiatrists

OPCS (1995) *1993 Birth Statistics England and Wales*, HMSO: London

Pitt, B. (1968) 'Atypical' depression following childbirth. *British Journal of Psychiatry*, 122, 431–433

Pitt, B. (1978) Introduction. In M. Sandler (Ed.) *Mental Illness in Pregnancy and the Puerperium*. Oxford: Oxford Medical Publications

Pollock, S., Blurton Jones, N., Evans, M. and Woodson, E. (1980) Continuities in post natal depression. Paper presented at the British Psychological Society's special conference on childbirth, University of Leicester

Revans, R.W. (1968) *Standards for Morale: Cause and Effect in Hospital*. Oxford: Nuffield Provisional Hospital Trust

Rosenwald, G C. and Stonehill, M.W. (1972) Early and late post partum illnesses. *Psychosomatic Medicine*, 34, 129–137

Rossan, S. (1987) Changes in the marital relationship during pregnancy and early motherhood. Paper presented at the second Women and Psychology Conference, Brunel University

Sharpe, S. (1994) *Just Like a Girl: From the Seventies to the Nineties*. Harmondsworth: Penguin

Sneddon, J. (1982) Is puerperal psychosis an entity after all? Paper presented at the Marce Society Conference, Institute of Psychiatry, London

Steiner, M. (1979) Psychobiology of mental disorders associated with childbearing: An overview. *Acta Psychiatrica Scandinavica*, 60, 449–464

Tew, M. (1978) The case against hospital deliveries. In S. Kitzinger and J. Davis (Eds.) *The Place of Birth*. Oxford: Oxford University Press

Tod, E.D.M. (1964) Puerperal depression: A prospective epidemiological study. *Lancet*, 2, 1264–1266

Ussher, J. M. (1989) *The Psychology of the Female Body*. London: Routledge & Kegan Paul

Whiffen, V.E. (1992) Is postnatal depression a distinct diagnosis? *Clinical Psychology Review*, 12, 485–508

World Health Organisation (1992) *The ICD-10 Classification of Mental and Behavioural Disorder*. Geneva: WHO

Wilkinson, S.J. (Ed.) (1996) *Feminist Social Psychologies: International Perspectives*. Milton Keynes: Open University Press

York, R. (1990) Pattern of postpartum blues. *Journal of Reproductive and Infant Psychology*, 8 (2), 67–74

CHAPTER 38

DECONSTRUCTING 'HYSTERECTOMIZED WOMAN': A MATERIO-DISCURSIVE APPROACH[1]

Pippa Dell

INTRODUCTION

In this chapter it will be argued that contemporary (biomedical) research into women's experience of hysterectomy, as with research on the naturally occurring menopause (Hunter and O'Dea, 1997; Gannon, 1998), reproduces the classical constructions of non-reproductive women as pathological without considering the complex ways in which these more modern (biomedical) discourses act as 'social practices that systematically form the object of which they speak' (Foucault, 1972: 49). In particular, it will be shown that biomedical (and other) discourses routinely problematize the 'hysterectomized woman's' post-operative experience(s) in terms of, for example, loss of femininity, sexuality and mental health, without exploring the diverse range of possible (and potentially positive) meanings such surgery might have for the women concerned. Adopting a materio-discursive approach (see Ussher, 1997; Malson, 1997, 1998), the 'hysterectomized woman' is re-theorized here as a complex site, constituted and regulated by historically specific *gendered* socio-cultural contexts that have consequences for 'her' embodied experience. The discussion will draw on an analysis of a series of interviews with hysterectomized women to illustrate the materio-discursive production(s) of hysterectomized bodies and embodied subjectivities by focussing on the construction(s) of women's bodies prior to surgery, and finally, suggest some new directions for both feminist research and clinical practice.

Historically, the uterus and its attendant menstrual capability has been a potent signifier of women's emotional well-being and sexuality (Ussher, 1989, 1991, 1997). As far back as Roman times, menstrual blood was deemed toxic, its apparent retention within the body after menopause construed both as poisonous to the woman and as causing 'physical, sexual and emotional decline' (Hunter and O'Dea, 1997: 200). This link between women's reproductive organs and mental health is also evident in the ancient Greek use of the term *hysteria*, literally wandering of the womb, to describe the nervous disorders associated with infertility. As Plato's Timaeus stated 'the womb of women ... when remaining unfruitful long beyond its proper time gets discontented and angry, and wandering in every direction through the body ... drives them to extremity causing all varieties of disease' (Raphael, 1972: 106). Underlying both of these classical viewpoints is an understanding of woman as potentially pathological but for the successful workings of her reproductive system, a 'normalization' of the female body based entirely on its fecundity. Women's sexuality thus becomes constructed as 'an instinct for reproduction' (Weeks, 1990: 143) clearly located within a heterosexual discourse. Further, the end of a woman's fertility is patently a dangerous time both physiologically and psychologically, signifying dis-ease and asexuality[2]. These early cultural constructions of the materiality of women's bodies serve to illustrate how discourses can 'engender particular social practices and regulate (embodied) ways of being' (Malson, 1997: 228). Whilst none would now consider the 'wandering womb' as *the* cause of sexual and emotional distress in women (Ussher, 1993), this function is now relegated to the ovary and its circulating hormones (see, Hunter and O'Dea 1997; Walker, 1997; Gannon, 1997). As will become clear in this chapter, biomedical discourses of the womb that has 'wandered from the body altogether' (Raphael, 1972: 106) continue to problematize the hysterectomized woman by locating her experience in terms of this socio-historic construction of 'woman' as 'reproductive body'.

THE BIOMEDICAL CONSTRUCTION OF 'HYSTERECTOMIZED WOMAN'

After the last planned pregnancy the uterus becomes a useless, bleeding, symptom producing, potentially cancer-bearing organ and therefore should be removed. (Wright, 1969: 560)

The patient suffers with endogenous depression characterized by agitation, somatic symptoms, depressive mood and insomnia. The depression is severe and is more refractory to treatment than other depressions. (Kinch and Steinberg, 1982: 200)

Hysterectomy is now the most common type of major surgery performed on women in Western Europe, Australia and America (Poettgen, 1993; Kinnick and Leners, 1995; Haller *et al.*, 1998)[3]. Estimates of numbers of women undergoing such surgery range from 20 percent in Britain (Chaplle, 1995) to between 33 and 50 percent of women in America, depending on the geographical region (Greer, 1999)[4]. Some 90 percent of these operations will occur for benign reasons. Indications for simple hysterectomy include endometriosis, menorrhagia, prolapse, myoma, dyspareunia, pelvic inflammatory disease and birth control, as well as a prophylaxis for infiltrative carcinoma (Wijma *et al.*, 1984; Cohen *et al.*, 1989; Treloar *et al.* 1999). Whilst there is no reason for women to suffer these gynaecological problems unnecessarily, and indeed reported increases in numbers of operations have been attributed to changes in the attitudes of patients who are simply less willing to live with gynaecological symptoms as well as to improved surgical techniques (Wright, 1969; Ananth, 1978; Selwood and Wood, 1978; Bukovic *et al.*, 1995; Westhoff, 1996), the iatrogenic nature of the surgery and the consequences for early onset of menopause and infertility have become a matter of concern (Kinnick and Leners, 1995)[5].

Firmly embedded within a positivist research agenda, over the last 60 years mainstream psychological and medical perspectives have conceptualized the hysterectomized woman as a distinct clinical entity, a 'syndrome' (Richards, 1974) whose organic and psychological *causes* (Everson *et al.*, 1995) can be delimited objectively and appropriately treated. Research in this field has focussed on the scientific measurement of women's endocrine levels, physiology and psychiatric profiles posthysterectomy (e.g. Ryan, 1997; Rako, 1998; Khastgir and Studd, 1998; Galyer *et al.*, 1999), these variables in turn being used to corroborate the existence of the syndrome (e.g. Richards; 1974, Kinch and Steinberg, 1982). Research has also been concerned with identifying those symptoms that are typical of the post-hysterectomy syndrome and which distinguish these women from the 'normal' population (Ananth, 1978). Further, in line with the modern emphasis on preventative medicine, studies have also tried to isolate the psychophysiological and social variables prior to surgery that help *individual* women to cope with its aftermath. Failure to find differences between hysterectomized and non-hysterectomized women (e.g. Gould, 1986; Humphries, 1980; Gath *et al.*, 1995; Alexander *et al.*, 1996), which incidentally characterizes much of the research since the late 1960s (Cohen *et al.*, 1989), has been attributed to the hysterectomized woman having, for example, appropriate 'hysterectomy attitudes', locus of control and social support (Schulze *et al.*, 1988) or particular and positive perceptions of 'the feminine role' in society today (Cohen *et al.*, 1989). These are seen as acting as 'mediating variables' in the individual woman's response to surgery.[6]

Within this biomedical context hysterectomy has been primarily constructed as a problem for women, the material event discursively produced as a potentially pathologizing experience, the woman herself stereotypically conceptualized as 'depressed with poor self image and decreased sexual functioning' (Cohen *et al.*, 1989: 53) *and* as inhabiting an always-already diseased body requiring continuing medical intervention (Whitlock *et al.*, 1998). However, it should be noted that the hysterectomized body is also a body freed from disease, no longer 'useless, bleeding, symptom producing, [and] potentially cancer bearing' (Wright, 1969: 560). That is, for many women hysterectomy can be seen as a positive experience liberating them from the fear of cancer and the discomfort of menorrhagia and dyspareunia (Dell and Papagiannidou, 1999). So why is it that research in this field is set up, almost by default, to problematize this experience? For example, despite a growing number of studies that report falling rates of morbidity, researchers (and the medical profession) continue to define women's experiences in terms of negative variables (e.g. Galyer et al.,1999; Gath et al., 1995). As Foucault (1972) has argued, discourses and thus discursively produced bodies are only made possible by a variety of socio-cultural (material and discursive) conditions, that is they do not emerge in a vacuum (Malson, 1997). It is my contention that the hysterectomized body, as with other pathologized (infertile) women's bodies (Hunter and O'Dea, 1997; Woollett, 1996; Malson, 1998) is also always-already caught up in patriarchal discourses that constitute 'woman's body' and thereby 'woman' in terms of her reproductive organs and functions (e.g. Veith, 1965; Foucault, 1972; Micale, 1990; Gannon, 1998). That is, biomedical (and other) understandings of the possible experiences of hysterectomy are limited by the patriarchal conflation of 'woman' with her (apparently) biologically determined 'feminine role' (see McNay, 1992) such that post-surgery loss of the uterus *signifies* loss of 'femininity' and 'womanhood'.[7] To fully appreciate women's experience(s) of hysterectomy then, researchers and women alike should take note of recent critiques of the modernist concept of the (essential) 'woman' as guaranteed by her (reproductive) body (e.g. Weedon, 1987; Poovey, 1988; Butler, 1990; 1993) and *both* explore the range of potential meanings the 'hysterectomized body' might sustain (what Foucault calls 'a surface of emergence') *and* explicate their materio-discursive construction (Ussher, 1997; Malson, 1997, 1998).

ILLUSTRATING A MATERIO-DISCURSIVE APPROACH

To question reductive and predominantly negative biomedical explanations of the hysterectomized body is not, of course, to deny the coporeality of this body (see Malson, 1997), or indeed, the physical consequences of surgery. Indeed, despite the improvements in surgical techniques[8] and post-operative care in recent years, hysterectomy is still a serious and potentially life-threatening operation, with high rates of post-operative infection (36 to 58 percent) and incidence of complications (25 to 43 percent) reported in the literature (Greer, 1999). Given that there is now a range of alternative non-surgical and (less invasive) surgical techniques[8] to treat most of the benign indicators for hysterectomy and indeed there is mounting concern about the necessity of many of these operations (Geller et al., 1996; Minkin and Wright, 1996; Greer, 1999), an important question to address is why are considerable numbers of women still undergoing such surgery and indeed *requesting* it (Marchant-Haycox and Salmon, 1997; Marchant-Haycox et al., 1998)? Or, more particularly, *how* are women's bodies being constructed prior to surgery, such that hysterectomy appears inevitable? In order to address this question I want to draw on some previously unpublished research based on interviews with Greek women who had had hysterectomies accompanied by oophorectomy.[9] Amongst other issues, the women were asked to discuss their experiences of and ideas about surgery and its aftermath. Transcripts of these parts of the interviews have provided the basis for the present analysis.

As is clear from the following extracts, both the(se) women and their gynaecologists constructed the women's bodies firmly within a biomedical model of anatomical cause requiring a surgical intervention (c.f. Marchant-Haycox and Salmon, 1997): the women's presenting symptoms of heavy bleeding being construed as a signifier of disease by both parties rather than, for example, part of the natural process of aging (Gannon, 1998).

Interviewer: *What were your thoughts and feelings before the operation?*

Participant 2: *I was completely unprepared about this fact. I didn't know something was wrong with me and that I had to have an operation...I visited the doctor because I had a lot of bleeding during my period and that was the only sign ... Because I had all that blood I had to have the operation. Of course this was very sudden for me and I was completely unprepared and of course I wanted a second opinion. I went to another doctor who was also a friend. The second one said that it wasn't necessary and that fibroids sometimes disappear with menopause. But I got obsessed with the whole situation and decided to get it done and over with.*

Participant 10: *Of course I was afraid that something might happen. It could be different from those that the doctors had told me. Two years ago another doctor who was curing me had told me that it wasn't anything but the operation had to be done. So I decided it after great consideration. I was bleeding every day.*

Interviewer: *When you went to the doctor and he told you had to have the operation how did you react?*

Participant 10: *I was scared. What was very sudden was when I went to the hospital and the professor told me 'you can stay now, you are ready for the operation'. I checked in on Friday and was operated on on Tuesday. It came like that, very fast. That was good from the point that I didn't have time to think about it very seriously. Fortunately, everything went fine.*

This construction of the gendered body as diseased by reason of its bleeding has several consequences. Firstly, the experience of illness calls attention to the body: something has gone wrong, the taken-for granted body has become what Toombs (1992: 134) has called an 'inescapable embodiment', the subject of considerable conscious attention (*'I got obsessed with the whole situation'*; *'I decided it after great consideration'*). Secondly, this body changes the sense of self. Foregrounding heavy bleeding as a fact of one's own (problematic) embodiment has produced a self which is simultaneously empowered to act – deciding to have the operation – and powerless (c.f. Martin, 1994) – making this decision hands over control of one's body to the medical specialists who then exercise their authority to act (*'It wasn't anything but the operation had to be done'*; *'You can stay now, you are ready for the operation'*). Thirdly, this construction of body as diseased comes as a shock to the 'unprepared self' provoking fear and anxiety. (*'I didn't know something was wrong with me'*; *'Of course I was afraid that something might happen; I was scared'*) precipitating the decision to have surgery. This response (which was common to many of the women interviewed) reiterates socio-culturally prevalent and derisive constructions of 'woman' as 'emotional' and 'vulnerable' and 'at the mercy of her unruly body' (Malson and Ussher, 1996: 515). It simultaneously positions them as needing medical help which as Gannon (1998: 294) has argued ensures 'the continued inferior status of women because they *require* concern and attention'.

Participant 1: *The first and dominating feeling was fear. I didn't want the whole situation to finish. I was very afraid of what they would find. The doctor explained everything but I was afraid. After discussing it with the doctor I decided to have the operation. The doctor told me I was very young and I had to have the operation in order to avoid more serious problems later.*

Participant 4: *The first reaction was panic, but I also had problems in the past. I had a test and the doctor told me if I wanted I could have a hysterectomy and there was going to be close attendance for years afterwards.*

As the above extracts indicate, the consequences of 'labelling and treating life's experiences and variabilities as illnesses' (Gannon, 1998: 295) are not confined just to the treatment of heavy bleeding and fibroids with hysterectomy. Whilst surgery may obviate *'more serious problems later'* the intrusion of medical surveillance continues *'for years afterwards'* as presumably does the paternalistic view that these women are inherently dependent and in need of appropriate advice and guidance (*'The doctor told me I was very young and I had to have the operation'*; *'the doctor told me if I wanted I could have a hysterectomy'*). For these women then deciding to have a hysterectomy is not so much about exercising informed choice but rather is seen as a necessity to regain control over a body discursively constructed as diseased by reason of its bleeding. Whilst the inconvenience of menstruation which cannot easily be managed (*'I was bleeding every day'*) and which positions women as 'other' in post-industrial society (e.g. Martin, 1989) may indeed require treatment, it should also be noted that none of these women described feeling ill before going to see their doctors, only bloody (cf. Ussher, 1989; 1991).

SUMMARY

The value of this type of analysis is that it allows an explication of how socio-cultural and medical discourses constitute women's bodies as diseased – in these extracts by reason of their bleeding (*'I had a lot of bleeding ... and that was the only sign'*) – and how these discourses regulate embodied subjectivity, in these women both as empowered and powerless, *and* as emotional and vulnerable. These constructions have consequences for the material regulation of women's bodies, in this case resulting in (the apparent inevitability of) hysterectomy to 'cure' both the body and the embodied subject. However, these discourses are not 'the truth' about the body, but 'regimes of truth' in relationship with the body that is purported to be known (c.f. Malson, 1997: 230). As Foucault has argued, we must:

imagine a world of discourse ... as a multiplicity of discursive elements that can come into play ... Discourses are not once and for all subservient to power or raised up against it, any more than silences are. We must make allowance for the complex and unstable process whereby discourse can be both an instrument and an effect of power, but also ... a point of resistance and a starting point for an opposing strategy. (1979: 100–101)

Adopting a materio-discursive approach to understanding women's experiences of hysterectomy is useful then as it can show how certain discursive elements do come into play and how at the level of the body (Foucault, 1980) they can be used as point(s) of resistance. For example, for those women who require (or have already had) surgery, within biomedical discourses there is always-already the possibility of constructing the hysterectomized body as a healthy body, freed from the symptom-producing and potentially cancerous womb. This more positive discursive construction of the hysterectomized body as a liberated body contains within it the 'conditions of possibility' (Foucault, 1980) to construe women's experiences post-hysterectomy as health giving and life enhancing. It is my contention that researchers should be encouraged to focus on elucidating these more positive aspects of women's experiences, a recognition of which may also empower women to resist those explanations of their experience(s) which are unhelpful and to regain control over what happens to their bodies, for example when discussing the possibility of surgery with their doctors. Further, the tendency of both the medical profession and society 'to pathologize normal and healthy behavior ... and to interpret [women's] health issues related to age and lifestyle as medical problems requiring medical treatment' (Gannon, 1998: 294) needs to be countered (see also Swann, 1997; Hunter and O'Dea, 1997). For example, whilst heavy bleeding may be construed as a problem for some women, it is also part of the natural process of aging and will stop with the menopause. To view menorrhagia as predominantly a medical problem, when for two-thirds of women such blood loss is within the 'normal' range (Greer, 1999), says more about society's regulation of the female body (c.f. Ussher, 1989) than it does about its concern for 'her' health. Efforts to reduce unnecessary hysterectomies then should be directed at *identifying* 'appropriate' clinical indications for such surgery (Geller, Burns and Brailer, 1996), and disseminating this information to both patients and physicians through continuing clinical and public education (Fox-Young *et al.*, 1995; Geller *et al.*,1996; Scriven and Tucker, 1997). In brief, adopting a materio-discursive approach allows the hysterectomized body to be placed within its gender-specific socio-historical context whilst simultaneously implicating this context in the production of embodied experience(s). That is, 'by theorising and researching the body as a complex interface of the discursive and extra-discursive, as a product *and* a precondition of the micro-physics of power that function in discourse' (Malson, 1997: 231, emphasis in original) these 'micro-physics of power' can be resisted, *and* social and political change (in both the treatment and researching of hysterectomized women) imple-mented.

NOTES

1. I would like to dedicate this chapter to the memory of my father, Major H.E.Dell, who died peacefully in his sleep during its preparation. I would also like to extend my sincere grat-itude to the editor, Dr Jane Ussher, for her support and understanding during this difficult time. Thanks also to Dr Helen Malson and Dr Irina Anderson for their insightful com-ments on an earlier draft, and to Sophia Papagiannidou for conducting the interviews.
2. For the 'Roman matron', medical intervention to 'preserve well-being, physical and sex-ual attractiveness' (Hunter and O'Dea, 1997: 200) involved bloodletting to purge the cir-culatory system of toxins. More modern day medicalization involves hormone replace-ment therapy to preserve femininity (see Wilson, 1966).
3. Three types of operation are currently available; abdominal, vaginal, or laparoscopically assisted vaginal, and may be accompanied by oophorectomy (removal of the ovaries) and partial vaginectomy.
4. Differences in numbers of women from different socio-economic backgrounds who are referred for surgery have also been noted. There is evidence, for example, that for 'benign' diagnoses such as heavy menorrhagia and myomas, Danish and American woman with lower levels of education, occupational status and 'family net worth' are more likely to undergo surgery than those from better educated backgrounds and social status (Settnes and Jorgensen, 1996; Brett, Marsh and Madans, 1997; Marks and Shinberg, 1997). However, a very different picture has emerged in Finland, where socio-economic dispar-ities in access to private health services have been linked to the positive correlations found between income and hysterectomy rates (Keskimaki, Salinto and Aro, 1996; Luoto, Keskamaki and Reunanen, 1997).
5. Moreover, in America, where highest rates of surgery prevail, hysterectomy has recently come under the scrutiny of women's health advocates who believe that at least 25 percent of hysterectomies carried out are unnecessary (Minkin and Wright, 1996). Additionally, the American medical insurers, Medicare and Medicaid, have tried to reduce the number of operations by insisting on second opinions. This has resulted in half the scheduled operations being cancelled (Greer, 1999).
6. Additionally, it is also worth noting that earlier studies were cross-sectional, and later studies prospective, which may also have contributed to differences in findings over the years.
7. Indeed, in those patriarchal cultures where women are primarily defined in terms of their sexual functioning, fertility and child-rearing capabilities, women's reactions to hysterec-tomy have been found to be particularly negative (Steiner and Aleksandrowicz, 1970; Williams, 1973; 1976; Lalinec-Michaud and Engelsmann, 1989)
8. Non-surgical techniques for menorrhagia (heavy bleeding) include tranexamic acid and mefenamic acid (Fraser, Pearse, Shearman et al, 1981) which reduce blood flow by 45 to 60 and 30 to 45 percent respectively (Greer, 1999). The simplest non-surgical way to deal with myomas (fibroids), as they are oestrogen dependent, is to wait for the menopause. Alternatively, gonadotropic-releasing hormone (GnRH) agonists (e.g. Lupron) can be used to control oestrogen levels, as can the contraceptive pill. Lupron can also be used to

control endometriosis. Surgical techniques to deal with menorrhagia include dilatation and curettage (scraping out the endometrium) and endometrial ablation (cauterising the womb lining with lasers), whilst fibroids can be removed individually (myomectomy) leaving the uterus intact (Minkin and Wright, 1996).

9. These were ten middle-class women, aged between 40 and 52, all of whom had had surgery for benign conditions. All were well educated and lived in traditional families in Thessaloniki, the second largest city in Greece after Athens. The interviews were carried out in Greek following a semi-structured interview schedule and transcribed verbatim.

REFERENCES

Alexander, D., Naji, A., Pinion, S., Mollison, J., Kitchner, H., Parkin, D., Abramovich, D. and Russell, I. (1996) Randomized trial comparing hysterectomy with endometrial ablation for dysfunctional uterine bleeding: psychiatric and psychosocial aspects. *British Medical Journal,* 312 (7026)**,** 280–284

Ananth, J. (1978) Hysterectomy and depression. *Obstetrics and Gynecology,* 2 (6), 724–733

Brett, K., Marsh, J. and Madans, J. (1997) Epidemiology of hysterectomy in the United States: Demographic and reproductive factors in a nationally representative sample. *Journal of Women's Health,* 6(3), 309–316

Bukovic, D., Delmis, J., Rudan, I. and Eljuga, D. (1995) A proposal of ovarian cancer prevention program in Croatia. *Collegium Antropologicum,* 19(2), 373–380

Butler, J. (1990) *Gender Trouble: Feminism and the Subversion of Identity.* London: Routledge

Butler, J. (1993) *Bodies that Matter: On the Discursive Limits of 'Sex'.* London: Routledge

Chaplle, A. (1995) Hysterectomy: British National Health Service and private patients have very different experiences. *Journal of Advanced Nursing* 22**,** 900–906

Cohen, S., Hollingsworth, A. and Rubin, M. (1989) Another look at psychologic complications of hysterectomy. *Journal of Nursing Scholarship,* 21**,** 51–53

Dell, P. and Papagiannidou, S. (1999) Hysterical talk? A discourse analysis of Greek women's accounts of their experiences following hysterectomy with oophorectomy. *Journal of Reproductive and Infant Psychology,* 17 (4)**,** 391–404

Everson, S., Matthews, K., Guzick, D., Wing, R. and Kuller, L. (1995) effects of surgical menopause on psychological characteristics and lipid levels: The healthy woman study. *Health Psychology,* 14 (5), 435–443

Foucault, M. (1972) *The Archaeology of Knowledge and the Discourse on Language,* A. Sheridan (Trans.) New York: Pantheon Books

Foucault, M. (1979) *The History of Sexuality, vol 1. An Introduction,* R. Hurley (Trans.) London: Penguin,

Foucault, M. (1980) *Power/knowledge: Selected Interviews and Other Writings, 1972–1977.* G. Gordon (Ed.) Brighton: Harvester

Fox-Young S., Sheehan, M., O'Connor, V., Cragg, C. and DelMar, C. (1995) Women's perceptions and experience of menopause: A focus group study. *Journal of Psychosomatic Obstetrics and Gynecology,* 16 (4), 215–221

Fraser, I., Pearse, C., Shearman, R., Elliot, P., McIlveen, J. and Markham, R. (1981) Efficacy of mefenamic acid in patients with a complaint of menorrhagia. *Obstetrics and Gynaecology,* 58**,** 543–551

Galyer, K., Conaglen, H., Hare, A. and Conaglen, J. (1999) The effect of gynecological surgery on sexual desire. *Journal of Sex and Marital Therapy,* 25 (2), 81–88

Gannon, L. (1998) The impact of medical and sexual politics on women's health. *Feminism and Psychology,* 8 (3), 285–302

Gath, D., Rose, N., Bond, A., Day, A., Garrod, A. and Hodges, S. (1995) Hysterectomy and psychiatric disorder: Are the levels of psychiatric morbidity falling? *Psychological Medicine,* 25 (2), 277–283

Geller, S., Burns, L. and Brailer, D. (1996) The impact of nonclinical factors on practice variations: the case of hysterectomies. *Health Services Research,* 30 (6), 729–750

Gould, D. (1986) Recovery from hysterectomy. *The Practitioner,* 30**,** 756–757

Greer, G. (1999) *The Whole Woman.* London: Doubleday

Haller, U., Wyss, P., Schilling, J. and Gutzwiller, F. (1998) Quality assessment in gynecology and obstetrics projects and experience in Switzerland. *European Journal of Obstetrics, Gynecology and Reproductive Biology,* 76 (1), 75–79

Humphries, P. (1980) Sexual adjustment after hysterectomy. *Issues in Health Care of Women,* 2

(2), 1–14

Hunter, M. and O'Dea, I. (1997) Menopause: Bodily changes and multiple meanings. In J. Ussher (Ed.) *Body Talk: The Material and Discursive Regulation of Sexuality, Madness and Reproduction.* London: Routledge

Keskimaki, I., Salinto, M. and Aro, S. (1996) Private medicine and socio-economic differences in the rates of common surgical procedures in Finland. *Health Policy,* 36 (3), 245–259

Khastgir, G. and Studd, J (1998) Hysterectomy, ovarian failure and depression. *Menopause,* 5 (2), 113–122

Kinch, R. and Steinberg, S. (1982) Counselling in obstetrics and gynecology. In D. Danforth (Ed.) *Obstetrics and Gynecology.* Philadelphia: Harper and Row

Kinnick, V. and Leners, D. (1995) Impact of hysterectomies on women's lives: A prospective study. *Journal of Women and Ageing,* 7(1/2), 133–144

Lalinec-Michaud, M. and Engelsmann, F. (1989) Cultural factors and reaction to hysterectomy. *Social Psychiatry and Psychiatric Epidemiology,* 24, 165–171

Luoto, R., Keskimaki, I. and Reunanen, A. (1997) Socioeconomic variations in hysterectomy: evidence from a linkage study of the Finnish hospital discharge register and population census. *Journal of Epidemiology and Community Health,* 5(1), 67–73

McNay, L. (1992) *Foucault and Feminism.* Cambridge: Polity Press

Malson, H. (1997) Anorexic bodies and the discursive production of feminine excess. In J. Ussher (Ed.) *Body Talk: The Material And Discursive Production of Sexuality, Madness and Reproduction.* London: Routledge

Malson, H. (1998) *The Thin Women: Feminism, Post-Structuralism and The Social Psychology of Anorexia Nervosa.* London: Routledge

Malson, H. and Ussher, J. (1996) Bloody women: A discourse analysis of amenorrhea as a symptom of anorexia nervosa. *Feminism and Psychology,* 6 (4), 505–521

Martin, E. (1989) *The Woman in The Body: A Cultural Analysis of Reproduction.* Milton Keynes: Open University Press

Martin, E. (1994) *Flexible Bodies: Tracking Immunity in American Culture: From the Days of Polio to The Age of AIDS.* Boston, MA: Beacon

Marks, N. and Shinberg, D. (1997) Socioeconomic differences in hysterectomy: The Wisconsin longitudinal study. *American Journal of Public Health,* 87 (9), 1507–1514

Marchant-Haycox, S., Liu, D, Nicholas, N. and Salmon, P. (1998) Patients' expectations of outcome of hysterectomy and alternative treatments for menstrual problems. *Journal of Behavioral Medicine,* 21 (3), 283–297

Marchant-Haycox, S. and Salmon, P. (1997) Patients' and doctors' strategies in consultations with unexplained symptoms: Interactions of gynecologists with women presenting menstrual problems. *Psychosomatics,* 38 (5), 440–450

Micale, M. (1990) Hysteria and its historiography: The future perspective. *History of Psychiatry,* 1 (1), 33–124

Minkin, M. and Wright, C. (1996) *What Every Woman Needs To Know About Menopause: The Years Before, During and After.* New Haven: Yale University Press

Poettgen, H. (1993) Clinical contribution to the crisis of female identity after the loss of uterus. *Psychotherapie Psychsomatik Medizinische Psychologie,* 43 (12), 428–431

Poovey, M. (1988) Feminism and deconstruction. *Feminist Studies,* 14 (1), 51–65

Rako, S. (1998) Testosterone deficiency: A key factor in the increased cardiovascular risk to women following hysterectomy or with natural ageing? *Journal of Women's Health,* 7 (7), 825–829

Raphael, B. (1972) The crisis of hysterectomy. *Australian and New Zealand Journal of Psychiatry,* 6, 106–115

Richards, D. (1974) A post-hysterectomy syndrome. *Lancet,* 26 October, 983–985

Ryan, M (1997) Hysterectomy: Social and psychosexual aspects. *Baillieres Clinical Obstetrics and Gynaecology,* 11 (1), 23–36

Scriven, A. and Tucker, C. (1997) The quality and management of written information presented to women undergoing hysterectomy. *Journal of Clinical Nursing,* 6 (2), 107–113

Schulze, C., Florin, I., Matschin, E., Souglioti, C. and Schulze, H-H. (1988) Psychological distress after hysterectomy: A predictive study. *Psychology and Health,* 2, 1–12

Selwood, T. and Wood, C. (1978) Incidence of hysterectomy in Australia. *Medical Journal of Australia,* 65, 201–204

Settnes, A. and Jorgensen, T. (1996) Hysterectomy in a Danish cohort. prevalence, incidence and socio-demographic characteristics. *Acta Obstetricia et Gynecologica Scandanavia,* 75 (3), 274–280

Steiner, M. and Aleksandrowicz, D. (1970) Psychiatric sequelae to gynecological operations. *Israel Annals Psychiatry*, 8, 186–192

Swann, C. (1997) Reading the bleeding body: Discourses of premenstrual syndrome. In J. Ussher (Ed.), *Body Talk: The Material and Discursive Regulation of Sexuality, Madness and Reproduction*. London: Routledge

Toombs, S (1992) The body in multiple sclerosis: A patient's perspective. In D. Leder (Ed.) *The Body in Medical Thought and Practice*. Dordrecht: Kluwer Academic

Treloar, S., Do, K., O'Connor, V., O'Connor, T., Yeo, M. and Martin, N (1999) Predictors of hysterectomy: An Australian study. *American Journal of Obstetrics and Gynecology*, 180 (4), 945–954

Ussher, J. (1989) *The Psychology Of The Female Body*. London: Routledge

Ussher, J. (1991) *Women's Madness: Misogyny or Mental Illness?* London: Harvester Wheatsheaf

Ussher, J. (1993) The construction of female sexual problems: Regulating sex, regulating women. In J. Ussher and C. Baker (Eds.) *Psychological Perspectives On Sexual Problems: New Directions In Theory And Research*. London: Routledge

Ussher, J. (1997) Introduction: Towards a material-discursive analysis of madness, sexuality and reproduction. In J. Ussher (Ed.) *Body Talk: The Material and Discursive Regulation of Sexuality, Madness and Reproduction*. London: Routledge

Veith, I. (1965) *Hysteria: The History of a Disease*. Chicago: University of Chicago Press

Walker, A. (1997) *The Menstrual Cycle*. London: Routledge

Weeks, J. (1990) *Sex, Politics And Society: The Regulation of Sexuality Since 1800*. London: Longman

Weedon, C. (1987) *Feminist Practice And Post-Structuralist Theory*. Oxford: Blackwell

Westhoff, C. (1996) Ovarian cancer. *Annual Review of Public Health*, 17, 85–96

Whitlock, E., Johnson, R. and Vogt, T. (1998) Recent patterns of hormone replacement therapy use in a large managed care organization. *Journal of Women's Health*, 7 (8), 1017–1026

Wijma, K., Jauer, F. and Janssens, J. (1984) Indications for, prevalence and implications of hysterectomy: A discussion. *Journal of Psychosomatic Obstetrics and Gynaecology*, 3, 69–77

Williams, M. (1973) Cultural patterning of the feminine role. *Nurse Forum*, 12, 378–387

Williams, M. (1976) Easier convalescence from hysterectomy. *American Journal of Nursing*, 76, 438–440

Wilson, R. (1966) *Forever Feminine* New York: Evans

Woollett, A. (1996) Infertility: from inside/out and outside/in. In S. Wilkinson and C. Kitzinger (Eds.) *Representing The Other: A Feminism and Psychology Reader*. London: Sage

Wright, R. (1969) Hysterectomy: Past, present and future. *Obstetrics and Gynecology*, 33, 560–563

CHAPTER 39

THE EXPERIENCE OF ABORTION: A CONTEXTUALIST VIEW

Mary Boyle

INTRODUCTION

Including a chapter on abortion in a psychology text on women's health might seem unremarkable. Abortion is, after all, a health issue in the sense that it is a medical procedure usually performed by doctors on women's bodies. It is also a procedure which may have consequences for women's physical and psychological well-being. Equally, when women do not have access to safe, legal abortion they do not simply accept unwanted pregnancies. Many resort to illegal abortion often at significant cost to life and health. But abortion is not just a health issue. It is a procedure which brings together medical, social, psychological, moral, legal and political issues in what is often an extremely controversial way. This difficult mix is reflected in abortion's unusual position as a medical procedure specifically controlled by law; in many countries, including the United Kingdom, it is controlled by criminal law. Psychological research on abortion has tended to distance itself from these aspects and has often treated abortion as predominantly a health issue for individual women (Boyle, 1997). My aim in this chapter is to provide a more comprehensive account of women's experience of abortion which acknowledges abortion's status as a contentious social issue (see Denious and Russo, in this volume, for an analysis of abortion and women's mental health).

It is not, however, simply a matter of adding on social or legal aspects to what is basically a health issue in order to provide a more rounded picture. This is because the relative neglect of social and political aspects of abortion in psychological research is not an accidental oversight, to be remedied by the addition of more variables; it is a strategic decision which reflects both psychology's traditional focus on the individual and an attempt to present psychological research on abortion as objective and value-free. Abortion research is thus not only aligned to psychology's overall project as an objective science of the individual, it is also made more palatable to policy makers (see e.g. Adler, 1992; Adler *et al.*, 1992). Thus, research on women's psychological responses to abortion has been successfully used in the U.S. to argue against restricting women's choices in abortion (Adler *et al.*, 1992). And, although this may be seen as a positive use of the research, I shall argue that focussing on individual women's health and well-being in relation to abortion is potentially detrimental to women and to public debate; I shall also argue that we need to develop alternative theoretical frameworks to increase understanding of how women's experience of abortion is constructed through the controversial social, legal and moral contexts in which abortion takes place. The first part of the chapter will examine this context by discussing the ways in which abortion, and women in relation to abortion, are represented in abortion legislation and legislative debates. This will be followed by discussion of the role of psychological research in producing and supporting particular representations of women in relation to abortion. The second part of the chapter will look at possible relationships between these representations and women's experience of abortion.

THE CONTEXT OF ABORTION: THE LEGAL CONTEXT

Legislation on particular topics does not just tell us what we may or may not do; it reflects social concerns and preoccupations; it seeks to bring about specific states of affairs and it constructs, or makes psychological subjects of, those whom it seeks to regulate (Smart, 1989). For example, the construction of the 'provocative woman' and the 'untrustworthy woman' are fundamental to aspects of legal procedure on rape. The process of developing particular laws can also tell us a great deal about why some states of affairs or psychological constructions of people are seen as more desirable than others and about the arguments which are used to try and bring these about. A key feature of abortion law, and one which is usually neglected in psychological literature, is that it regulates *women*. I will focus here on the ways in which abortion law and legislative debates construct particular types of women.

Abortion Law Constructs 'Woman'

In Great Britain, access to abortion is regulated by the 1967 Abortion Act and the 1990 Human Fertilisation and Embryology Act. Women may obtain abortions on two main grounds: if the risks to their or their existing children's physical or mental health of continuing the pregnancy is greater than the risks of termination OR if there is a substantial risk that the child will be seriously handicapped. Two doctors must agree that one of these applies, although there are exceptions for emergencies. Abortions are allowed up to 24 weeks although, again, there are exceptions for grave risks to life or health.

The situation in the United States is more complex because individual states may regulate abortion. Overall, however, abortion is regulated by the 1973 Supreme Court ruling *Roe v Wade*, which states that the constitutional right to privacy is broad enough to encompass a woman's decision to terminate her pregnancy, at least in the first trimester. The Court ruled that in the first trimester, 'the attending physician, in consultation with his [sic] patient, is free to determine without regulation by the state, that in his medical judgement the patient's pregnancy should be terminated'. The ruling is surprisingly vague about the grounds on which a doctor might grant or refuse abortion (presumably seeing that as not the business of the state) and on what kind of state regulation would be appropriate in the second or third trimesters. This lack of specificity has led to extensive attempts by individual states to regulate abortion, often in a restrictive way (see Goggin, 1993 for a detailed account of U.S. legislation).

In a few, mainly European, countries, abortion is available on request in the first three months although as for example in Germany, this may involve mandatory counseling and/or a waiting period (Richardson, 1999). In other countries, abortion is subject to health grounds similar to, or more restricted than, those of British legislation; in some countries, abortion is largely illegal, with doctors exercising more or less discretion in carrying out abortions, often in the guise of other medical procedures (see Boyle and McEvoy, 1998, for a discussion of this situation in Northern Ireland; see Eggert and Rolston, 1994; Furedi, 1995 and Hadley, 1996 for further details of the law worldwide).

Overall, then, abortion is strongly regulated by the state, either throughout pregnancy or for the greater part of it. In line with the idea that legislation constructs 'legal subjects' of those it seeks to regulate, an analysis of both the development and content of abortion law suggests three images of 'woman' which both lie behind and are reproduced by legislation: the weak and vulnerable woman; the indecisive woman and the immoral woman.

THE WEAK AND VULNERABLE WOMAN

Abortion legislation which relies on health grounds inevitably constructs women as weak and vulnerable in the face of unwanted pregnancy. In Britain, for example, the large majority of abortions are carried out because the woman is said to be suffering from, or vulnerable to psychiatric disorder, usually neurotic disorder (Office of National Statistics). Similarly, those who support less restrictive abortion legislation tend to rely heavily on justificatory accounts of female vulnerability in the face of unwanted pregnancy (Boyle, 1997). For example, the U.S. Supreme Court ruling *Roe v Wade* justified access to abortion partly on the grounds that:

The detriment that the state would impose upon the pregnant woman by denying this choice altogether is apparent ... Maternity or additional offspring, may force upon the woman a distressful life or future. Psychological harm may be imminent. Mental and physical health may be taxed by childcare.

Abortion is thus presented as a form of therapy for existing or impending psychological disorder, hence the term 'therapeutic abortion'.

THE INDECISIVE WOMAN

Legislation which requires the abortion decision to be made by doctors depends more or less explicitly on representations of women who do not know their own minds. Remarks made in the U.K. abortion debates on the 1967 Abortion Act, illustrate this point:

The phase of rejection is short-lived and is hardly in evidence after the fourth month and many have written to express their gratitude to us for our refusal to terminate. This has some bearing on recommending abortion ... for the state of not wanting is generally a temporary one, while to abort is a permanent and final act. (Official Record Commons, 22 July 1966: 102; MP quoting correspondence from a doctor)

That brings me to the point doctors have made to me, that in the first three months many women are feeling perfectly 'seasick' the whole time and will do anything. But after that their maternal instinct takes over and they do not want to be aborted. (Official Record Lords, 12 July 1967, quotation marks in original)

Although these speakers supported restrictive legislation, in Britain at least, those who support more liberal abortion laws have consistently rejected proposals that women themselves should make the abortion decision.

That women may initially make the 'wrong' decision in requesting an abortion, and may change their minds, is also implied by legislation which requires counseling or waiting periods:

In most civilized countries, there is a requirement before an abortion is permitted that the woman – who in such circumstances will obviously be in a state of great distress – is counselled by a doctor. There is a pause during which she is given the opportunity to consider the situation. (ORC, 24 April 1990: 219)

There have been many attempts – more or less successful – to introduce counseling and waiting period provisions in U.S. law; in Germany, the compromise reached on abortion law following the reunification of Germany requires that the woman receive counseling before being issued with a certificate permitting the abortion (Richardson, 1999; see also Hadley, 1996 for a discussion of this issue in Australian legislation). To query the provision of counseling before abortion, to see it as a potential problem, is not to suggest that women be deprived of the opportunity to discuss their decision. It is, however, to emphasize that the mandatory or even routine provision of counseling – rather than asking the woman if she feels discussion would be helpful to her – carries with it assumptions about women's ability to make firm and 'correct' decisions about reproduction.

THE IMMORAL WOMAN

Woman's morality in relation to abortion is called into question most explicitly by the frequently made claim that women have abortions for 'trivial' reasons or for 'convenience'. Indeed, it is difficult to overemphasize the strength and pervasiveness of these claims throughout abortion debates, from the British Medical Journal's claim in 1929 that abortion had become 'a fashion' to the claim made in the U.K. parliament that 'the *de facto* grounds for abortion in the great mass of cases is now that of serious inconvenience to the mother' (ORC, 24 April 1990: 252). A Northern Ireland politician also claimed that 'most abortions are the result of fornication and lust and not of conception within marriage ... these girls have been committing fornication and have had to have abortions to get rid of the resulting problems' (NIALRA, 1989: 27). Although arguments like these are usually put forward by those who support restrictive legislation, it is notable that they are not often directly challenged by supporters of more liberal laws. Instead, claims about women's immorality tend to be countered by accounts of weak and vulnerable women, who need abortion as therapy. In other words, it is only by presenting women as weak, as in need of help, that accusations of immorality can be circumvented.

I have argued (Boyle, 1997) that these diverse constructions of women – as vulnerable, as indecisive, as immoral – are actually part of a complex unified system of thought about women's nature which legislators have drawn on to support both liberal and restrictive legislation and which has allowed both sides to avoid presenting women as rational individuals capable of making important life decisions.

But these negative constructions of women in relation to abortion are only possible in the face of equally negative constructions of abortion itself. It has been claimed, for example, that 'abortion destroys women psychologically and physically' (ORC, 24 April 1990: 224) and that '[abortion] is a disaster for everybody involved' (ORC 21 June, 1990: 1148). It has also been claimed that abortion has socially damaging effects, that liberal laws would 'brutalise our country in the eyes of the world' (ORC, 13 July 1967: 1357) and that '[there is] great concern in society in general at the way in which freely available abortion has changed the nature of society (ORC, 22 January 1988: 1261).

Just as negative constructions of women in relation to abortion depend on negative constructions of abortion, these in turn depend on obscuring the potentially negative aspects of alternatives to abortion – motherhood and adoption. In British abortion debates, those who support restrictive legislation are almost totally silent on the potential problems of motherhood and adoption, in spite of evidence of the negative outcomes for women of either option (Cates *et al.*, 1982; Tew, 1990; David, 1992; Russo *et al.*, 1992; Sobol and Daly, 1992; Nicolson, 1998). Those who support liberal legislation are more likely to acknowledge the potential problems of motherhood but at the center of these arguments lies the idea that women should be allowed abortions so as better to serve their existing families:

Does the Hon. Gentleman agree that it is because mothers are concerned about the quality of life for their whole families that they have abortions? ... They risked their lives and the freedom of those who helped them [have illegal abortions] because of their desire to maintain the quality of life for their families. (ORC, 24 April 1990: 209)

[under adverse conditions] it becomes quite impossible for [a woman] to fulfil her real function, her worthwhile function as a mother of holding together the family unit. (ORC, 22 July 1966: 1098)

The U.S. Supreme Court ruling *HL v Matheson*, which allowed judicial veto of an abortion decision made by an 'immature minor', also presented motherhood as the 'easy option':

If the pregnant girl elects to carry her child to term the medical decisions to be made entail few – perhaps none – of the potentially grave emotional and psychological consequences of the decision to abort. (cited in Melton and Russo, 1987: 70)

THE CONTEXT OF ABORTION: PSYCHOLOGICAL RESEARCH

We have seen that abortion legislation implies constructions of women which are limited and often negative. These representations, however, exist in a complex relationship to 'scientific' theory within psychology and psychiatry. This section will briefly examine this relationship in two ways: first in terms of psychological research on abortion and, second, in terms of research not directly on abortion but which may have influenced debates on abortion.

Psychological Research on Abortion

As I mentioned in the introduction, researchers have tried to distance psychological research from the contentious social and moral issues which surround abortion. Adler et al. (1992), for example, claimed that 'it was recognized that differing moral, ethical and religious perspectives impinge on how abortion is perceived. Our mission, however, was not to assess values, but to consider the best available scientific evidence on psychological responses to abortion' (1194). This attempt to 'purify' psychological research on abortion, however, is unlikely to be successful. Instead, it has been strongly argued (e.g. Albee, 1986; Prilleltensky, 1994; Fox and Prilleltensky, 1997) that psychological research and theory is inextricably linked to social values which influence what is questioned and what taken for granted, how a subject area is conceptualized, what is seen as evidence, and so on. To deny these values is not to be objective or neutral but to reinforce them, not least by allowing their operation to remain obscure.

With this is mind, it is notable that one of the most striking aspects of abortion research is its persistent preoccupation with the potentially negative effects of abortion on individual women. Wilmoth (1992), for example, reviewed 15 studies of the psychological effects of abortion which, overall, measured 52 outcome variables. Forty-two of these were wholly negative (e.g. depression, shame, guilt, anxiety); five referred to 'relief'; three could have been positive or negative. Only one clearly positive variable – happiness – was mentioned in two studies. Similarly, Miller (1992) reviewed seven theoretical models of 'possible long-term consequences of abortion'. The contents of five of these were wholly negative and did not seem to allow for other than negative responses to abortion; one, the crisis model, allowed both negative responses and 'relief', while the learning model allowed both positive and negative change following abortion. The only positive change mentioned by Miller, however, was increased use of contraception.

It can't be argued that this preoccupation with the negative effects of abortion has been necessary as a result of legislators' demands for evidence on the effects of abortion. Psychiatry and psychology were focussing on abortion's potential to harm women for decades before U.S. psychologists' official involvement in the legislative process; and even if researchers often failed to find much evidence of harm (see Adler et al., 1992 and Clare and Tyrrell, 1994 for reviews), the very act of looking so assiduously reveals a strong belief that such effects were to be expected.

Psychology and 'Woman'

I suggested earlier that the varied representation of 'woman' in abortion debates and legislation – as vulnerable, as indecisive, as immoral – were part of a unified picture of 'woman' which has been strongly constructed during the late nineteenth and twentieth centuries (Boyle, 1997). Psychological and psychiatric research has played a crucial role in this process, while claims to professional and scientific authority have lent credibility to arguments which have drawn on these constructions.

The idea of woman as vulnerable is central to abortion legislation and this idea, in turn, has been strongly reinforced by theory and research which position women as weak, as subject to mental disorder, in relation to their reproductive processes (e.g. Showalter, 1987; Ussher, 1989, 1991; Nicolson, 1998). Research which focusses on abortion's potential to harm women can be seen as part of this tradition. Similarly, arguments about women's moral deficiencies in relation to abortion are reflected in psychological theory which positions women as morally inferior through their supposed concern for contingent or relational moral reasoning rather than through a male concern with abstract and universal moral principles (Piaget, 1932/1965; Kohlberg, 1976; Freud, 1977; Gilligan, 1982). Finally, abortion's position as a deviant and potentially harmful option is reinforced by research which makes central women's role as mothers (Phoenix and Woollett, 1991; Morell, 1994) and which pathologizes women who find motherhood problematic (Nicolson, 1998).

Of course, the relationship between psychological theory and arguments made in abortion debates is not one-way. Psychological theory not only constructs certain images of women which are claimed to rest on scientific authority; it draws on, reflects and reproduces representations of women, particularly in relation to their moral and psychic weakness, which have far more ancient roots than modern psychology (Boyle, 1997). The combination of cultural tradition and claims to scientific authority, however, is formidable. One of its most important effects is to leave women with a very limited range of what might be called publicly sanctioned positions from which to understand or deal with their experience of abortion. As we have seen, these include being weak and vulnerable, being indecisive and being immoral. The persistent search for negative consequences, and the absence of an equally persistent search for positive effects, also places women in the unenviable position of being subject to mental disorder if they do not have an abortion – and thus the abortion is allowed – or subject at least to mental distress if they do. What neither legislation nor legislative debates in most countries of the world allows to women is to approach abortion from a position of strength. The exception to this, of course, is the claim that the woman is exercising her 'right to choose'. As Smart (1989) has pointed out, however, rights-based arguments are problematic in that every right may be countered by its opposite. Thus the 'right to choose' is countered by the 'right to life', which positions women who have abortions as baby killers. Behaviors such as crying, expressing guilt, fear of the future and concerns about coping are thus more consonant with these positions than behaviors such as assertively stating that you have decided that you do not want to be pregnant, are going to terminate it, are happy with the decision and do not anticipate any negative effects.

It is not a matter here of saying that women should behave in one way or another in relation to their abortion decision, but of emphasizing that discourses surrounding abortion provide women with both limited and predominately negative options. The next section will consider how these constructions of abortion, and of women in relation to abortion, might conflict with, but also structure, women's experience.

WOMEN'S EXPERIENCE OF ABORTION

Contrary to the image of the indecisive woman who needs help to reach the 'right' decision about abortion, research suggests that the large majority of women do not find the abortion decision difficult and that the decision is often made before the pregnancy is confirmed. For example, only 12 percent of women surveyed by Osofsky *et al.* (1973) said that they found the decision to have a first trimester abortion difficult. However, 51 percent of women who had abortions after the first three months said that the decision was difficult. This higher figure is not surprising as women having later abortions include those aborting abnormal foetuses (and, possibly, much-wanted pregnancies) and those who have delayed the decision precisely because they found it difficult. As might be expected from Osofsky *et al.*'s results, Smetana and Adler (1979) found that 92 percent of the variance in the abortion decision (i.e. whether the pregnant women in their sample did or did not have abortions) was accounted for by the woman's intention to have, or not have, an abortion, stated before they knew the results of a pregnancy test. Holmgren (1994) similarly found that 70 percent of the women in her sample had made the decision to have an abortion before the pregnancy was confirmed. Again in conflict with the image of the indecisive woman who may change her mind in a 'waiting period', Miller (1992) reported that 71 percent of his sample were 'very certain' about their decision and 90 percent either 'very' or 'mostly' certain.

This is not to suggest that the abortion decision is stress-free. Women, however, may retain the conviction that they are 'doing the right thing' in the face of distress related to circumstances surrounding the abortion or even positive feelings about the pregnancy:

[I felt] alone, very much alone. I felt like turning on my heels and going back but not because of the abortion but because I was on my own.

As we were about to take off [to travel to the clinic in London] I was going to start to cry and I don't know why. I was confused if you know what I mean. But I wasn't confused about what I was coming to do, confused because I was going into a foreign country and thinking what was ahead of me and I was scared. (Boyle and McEvoy, 1998: 300)

I have three children and I felt sure I didn't want more, but when I got pregnant something inside me was making me feel good about it. I think it was the memory of the fact that whenever I was pregnant before it had been the right thing, we'd been thrilled. But ... it really did seem to me that this pregnancy was a choice between me and the baby. (Neustatter, 1986: 16–17)

Similarly, women studied by Kolker and Burke (1993), who had had abortions for foetal abnormality, stressed that although the experience had been worse than expected, they would make the same choice again in similar circumstances.

Women may be convinced that their decision is appropriate but their experience of making and implementing their decision may still be very negative in so far as it reflects negative constructions of abortion and women who have abortions:

You really do think you are walking into a murder house [the abortion clinic] you know, like the man who killed all the people and buried them under the floor boards. (Boyle and McEvoy, 1998: 295)

[If] it's found out that I've been over here and had an abortion, I think I'd have to move home, probably lose a lot of friends, maybe not be able to go to work. (ibid: 298)

I wanted to ask the gynaecologist what was going to happen but I couldn't do anything but weep after he'd called me a silly child who would have to suffer for my mistake. (Neustatter, 1986: 51)

He told me I was trying to fix the law to suit myself and that all these women killing babies was a sign of the times ... I began to feel very upset and uneasy. (ibid: 34)

I had the abortion but felt extremely guilty for my actions ... I often wonder what other people would think of me if they knew what I had done. (Wasielewski, 1992: 116)

The relationship between the social construction of abortion and women's experience of it can also be highlighted by examining the reasons women give for having abortions. Torres and Forrest's (1988) survey of almost two thousand women suggests that their stated reasons for having abortions can be grouped into those involving personal characteristics (e.g. not old enough; not ready for the responsibility; health problems) and those involving the woman's circumstances, such as relationships with her partner, financial worries and desire to continue education. In a re-analysis of these data, Russo *et al.* (1992) showed that different groups of women tended to give different reasons for deciding to have an abortion. For example, women who were already mothers were less likely to give education and job-related reasons and more likely to cite responsibilities to others and their partner's unemployment; adolescents were more likely than adult women to say that they were not ready for child rearing. It is notable, however, that 23 percent of the women in Torres and Forrest's study reported that their partner's desire for the abortion had contributed to their decision.

The reasons for choosing abortion given by some of the women in Boyle and McEvoy's (1998) study reflect these categories:

I never had any doubt I would go through with it. It's not because of the shame from being a single parent, I could cope with that, but I was not ready for the commitment. (293)

The most important thing in my life had happened in that I got to university. I'm only starting my career and I'm not going to put it on the line. Not everybody gets to university and I want to make the most of it (pause) As well as that, I'm not ready to bring up a child yet ... if I had a child I wouldn't be able to look after it properly. (293)

I have a son at seventeen and I'm having a bad time with him, I couldn't cope with another baby at this time [pause] I'm highly strung plus I'm used to my freedom [pause] My boyfriend ... there is a chance that he will leave me and I'll be on my own again and that would scare me. (293)

As would be expected, these reasons are grounded in women's experience: they involve relationships with others, assessments of capabilities and personal aspirations. They are, in a word, contextual. The women do not, as Hadley (1996) has put it, act out a law court in their heads, based on universal principles of morality or justice. Yet it is precisely this contextual reasoning which has been denigrated in both lay and scientific accounts of morality (Gilligan, 1982). It is this conflict between women's experience and the lower status accorded contextual reasoning – except in the most extreme circumstances – which leaves women open to accusations that they are having abortions for trivial or specious reasons, or for 'mere convenience'.

A woman's claimed certainty about her abortion decision may therefore mask a complex process of reaching and implementing her decision against what Wasielewski (1992: 119) has called a 'backdrop of contradictory definitions of abortion'. This relationship between social constructions of abortion and women's experience will be examined further in the next section.

Psychological Responses to Abortion

Studies of women's reactions to abortion suggest that the large majority do not suffer significant negative effects (Adler *et al.*, 1992; Clare and Tyrrell, 1994). So consistent is this research that even a U.S. Government official in the Reagan administration, who did not support liberal abortion legislation, testified to Congress that the problem of the development of significant psychological problems after abortion was 'minuscule from a public health perspective' (Koop, 1989; cited in Adler *et al.*, 1992: 1202). This research, however, is problematic for a number of reasons.

First, as I mentioned earlier, it is based on a persistent search for negative effects of abortion and this emphasis, even if it is through claims about their absence, reveals an assumption that such effects are to be expected. At the very least, this research ensures that women's potential suffering through abortion is kept at the forefront of our minds. A second, and closely related problem is that the research is highly individualistic. It often involves the use of questionnaires or rating scales which purport to detect the presence of psychological attributes such as anxiety, depression, guilt or relief. Such research provides a very limited and one-dimensional picture of women's responses, not only because these attributes are often chosen in advance by the researcher, thus limiting what can be 'discovered' about women's responses but also because the research often fails to consider the relationship between the experience of abortion and its social context. A number of studies *have* examined what are often called 'risk factors' for negative reactions to abortion. These include allegiance to religious and cultural groups which do not support abortion and lack of social support for the woman's decision (Congleton and Calhoun, 1993; Clare and Tyrrell, 1994). This research, however, tends to treat both social context and women's reactions as a series of discrete variables which are statistically related. It also fails to consider the possible role of legal and professional constructions of abortion in mediating women's responses, as researchers tend not to include these factors in their list of 'risk variables'. The research therefore provides a rather limited picture of the relationship between context and psychological response. Finally, research on the psychological effects of abortion is paradoxically problematic in that the absence of negative effects has been used, particularly by U.S. psychologists, as an argument against attempts to restrict access to abortion. This can, of course, be seen as a positive use of the research. The problem is that researchers can then find it difficult to focus on the full range of women's reactions to abortion, both positive and negative; indeed, women themselves have expressed reluctance to talk frankly about the variety of emotions they experience about abortion, for fear that these will be used as an argument to refuse the abortion or to restrict access for other women (Fletcher, 1994; Hadley, 1996). What is needed is an approach which integrates experience and context and which rejects the idea that psychological reactions to abortion can somehow tell us whether it should be allowed or restricted.

INTEGRATING CONTEXT AND EXPERIENCE

Shotter (1993) has argued that individual responses to particular situations should be thought of as the 'marking off' of aspects of collective debate and communal thinking, but which in our society are redefined psychologically as individual attributes or possessions. Similarly, Henriques *et al.* (1984) and Hollway (1989) have criticised the idea of the 'unitary rational subject' which has so influenced psychological theory, and have argued instead that each of us is simultaneously positioned in relation to multiple and often contradictory discourses and the social practices produced by them.

This suggests that our psychological experience is inseparable from our social world of language, assumptions and meanings, or, as Henriques *et al.* (1984) have put it, we are 'always already social'. And, to the extent that multiple meanings surround an event, our experience will be potentially fragmented: we will have available to us a number of subject positions which will provide us with particular images and concepts, ways of thinking and speaking and ways of representing ourselves in relation to particular events. Women's responses to abortion, then, are unlikely to be adequately conveyed by scores on a scale of, say, depression or anxiety or by terms such as 'relief' or 'guilt', especially if these are taken to represent free-standing psychic attributes.

In line with the idea that women's responses to abortion are inseparable from the social meanings which surround it, Wasielewski (1992) has suggested that whether a woman has 'the power to ideologically define the abortion context' will be an important factor in her response to abortion. In other words, a positive response to abortion may depend on the woman's being able to reach and maintain a secure and positive personal definition of her situation. Yet one of the most striking aspects of abortion is the extent to which women are told what they *ought* to think or feel about their decision; indeed, it is difficult to think of any other decision, taken by millions each year, about which such forceful, extreme and often contradictory statements are made in the public arena. It is perhaps not surprising, then, that having support from others for their decision consistently emerges as a factor predicting a more positive response to abortion.

But 'support' is not a unitary concept. A woman may have support from her partner or friends, but her experience is still structured by the conflicting and often negative discourses which surround abortion. Women's own accounts of their experience show clearly the difficulties of reaching a secure definition of their experience:

[Having the abortion] would be an acknowledgement to me that I am an ambitious person ... it means that my family would necessarily come second. There would be an incredible conflict about which is tops and I don't want that for myself. (Gilligan, 1982: 97)

I had never actually resolved that I was doing it for me. Actually, I had to sit down and admit ... 'I honestly don't feel that I want to be a mother' ... [i]t was just a horrible way to feel. (ibid: 86)

I didn't like the idea of abortion, it does seem like murder to me, but even so, it was preferable to destroying two grown people's lives. (Neustatter, 1989: 20)

The consultant suggested I was killing a baby because I wanted to go on having a comfortable life. In fact we have no money and little space for another child ... I had felt quite confident that ... I was making the right decisions ... Suddenly I saw him expressing the way the world would judge me. I just wanted to hide myself away feeling everyone would see me as selfish and evil. (ibid: 65)

Some of the women in Boyle and McEvoy's sample experienced such conflict between their own definition of abortion as right for them at that time, and their culture's very negative construction of it, that they simply 'blanked out':

It's wrong [pause] inherently wrong [pause] to wilfully make a decision to end a potential life [pause] That's morally wrong ... I think you just go into automatic, don't let yourself think about it too much. (1998: 295)

To tell you the truth, I just blanked it all out ... you feel that if you do think about it too much you'll not be able to cope. (ibid)

Women's own definition of their situation may also be challenged by what they have been told they ought to feel after the abortion:

It's just that I don't feel any sorrow or anything for the baby, I don't, just relief ... I feel as if I should be having some feelings after it. I feel absolutely heartless, I don't feel as if I have killed a baby, I don't feel that at all. I feel as if I've had a tooth out and that's terrible. (Boyle and McEvoy, 1998: 296).

You know you hear about these stages after death, stages of mourning. I wouldn't know with a baby what stages there would be, what stage would be the next and so on. Maybe this is natural what I'm doing now, but I'll be waiting on the next stage. Maybe it won't come but I'll be waiting on it. And if it does come, waiting to see if there is another one.(ibid: 297)

[After the abortion] I felt I had no right to just be happy; I felt I had failed in getting pregnant and not wanting it and that I had to be punished for that. (Neustatter, 1986; 92)

I realised after about six weeks that I just hadn't thought about the abortion. But that made me feel dreadful. I went into an awful depressed guilty state and I made myself think about it.(ibid: 96–7)

These accounts highlight some of the ways in which negative constructions of abortion may mediate women's experience. The persistent focus on negative aspects of abortion has also obscured its potentially positive effects on women. Indeed, as we have seen, many studies and theoretical models do not even allow such effects to be described. Although no-one would recommend abortion as a growth experience, it is important to acknowledge that in making the abortion decision a woman is taking control of her life and, for perhaps the first time, making important decisions about whether and when to have children. Lazarus (1985) noted that some women saw the experience as showing that they had the strength to deal with a crisis; one woman described it as 'a very liberating experience'. In other studies, women describe themselves as more independent and less passive or as seeing moral judgements as more complex than before:

I felt a confidence in myself I hadn't before. I found too that I didn't need to play the 'little girl', the helpless female to my partner so much. (Neustatter, 1986: 112)

Emotionally, I'm a much stronger person now. The experience has made me take more control over my life. (ibid: 114)

I have always disagreed with it. My friend had it done ... and I thought, it's killing a baby, a wee innocent baby but when it comes to yourself, you realise. (Boyle and McEvoy, 1998: 298)

SUMMARY

I am not suggesting here that in the absence of negative social definitions of abortion, women's 'real' or 'true' experiences could be discovered. On the contrary, the psychological experience of abortion, like other experiences such as childbirth or divorce, is inevitably mediated and constructed by its social context. I have argued that this context provides women with a limited and often negative set of constructions about themselves and their decision. I have also argued that traditional psychological research has done little to challenge these limitations. Yet acknowledgment of the context in which women experience abortion is crucial for at least three reasons. First, women's accounts of abortion can sound confused, uncertain and contradictory. Within the framework of the unitary rational subject, this may be seen as undesirable, as indicating 'ambivalence' or indecisiveness or a need for professional guidance over the decision. From a constructionist view, however, such varied or fragmented accounts are inevitable, given the conflicting subject positions offered by the abortion debates *and* the potential conflict between the negative constructions of abortion and women offered by debates and legislation, and the woman's own definition of abortion as necessary for her at that time. Second, claims about psychological reactions have been central to abortion debates but have often been simplified as 'negative' and 'not negative' by different sides in the debate. Such arguments can make it look as if women's' reactions are intrinsic to abortion (it is either harmful or benign). A contextual approach not only challenges this but highlights the problems of assuming that research on women's reactions to abortion can somehow tell us whether access should be restricted. Finally, acknowledgment of context means acknowledging that psychological research on abortion is part of the context which structures women's experience and not an objective and neutral discovery of that experience. Providing as comprehensive as possible account of women's experience, and acknowledging the values which inform research practice, can therefore be seen as not simply a scientific but also a social responsibility.

REFERENCES

Adler, N.E. (1992) Unwanted pregnancy and abortion: Definitional and research issues. *Journal of Social Issues*, 48, 19–35

Adler, N.E. David, H.P., Major, B.N., Roth, S.H., Russo, N.F. and Wyatt, G.E. (1992) Psychological factors in abortion: a review. *American Psychologist*, 47, 1194–1204

Albee, G.W. (1986) Towards a just society: lessons from observations on the primary prevention of psychopathology. *American Psychologist*, 41, 891–898

Boyle, M. (1997) *Re-thinking Abortion: Psychology, Gender, Power and the Law*. London: Routledge

Boyle, M. and McEvoy, J. (1998) Putting abortion in its social context: Northern Irish women's experience of abortion in England. *Health*, 2, 283–304

Cates, W., Smith, T.C., Rochat, R.W. and Grimes, D.A. (1982) Mortality from abortion and childbirth. Are the statistics biased? *Journal of the American Medical Association*, 9 July, 192–195

Clare, A.W. and Tyrrell, J. (1994) Psychiatric aspects of abortion. *Irish Journal of Psychological Medicine*, 11, 92–98

Congleton, G.K. and Calhoun, L.G. (1993) Post-abortion perceptions: A comparison of self-identified distressed and non-distressed populations. *International Journal of Social Psychiatry*, 39, 255–265

David, H.P. (1992) Born unwanted: long-term developmental effects of denied abortion, *Journal of Social Issues*, 48, 163–181

Eggert, A. and Rolston, B. (Eds.) (1994) *Abortion in the New Europe*. London: Greenwood

Fletcher, R. (1994) Women speak out against the great unmentionable. *Irish News*, 8 April

Fox, D. and Prilleltensky, I. (1997) *Critical Psychology*. London: Sage

Freud, S. (1977) Some psychical consequences of the anatomical distinction between the sexes. In J. Strachey (Ed. and Trans.) *On Sexuality: Three Essays on the Theory of Sexuality*, vol 7, The Pelican Freud Library. First Published 1925

Furedi, A. (1995) (Ed.) *The Abortion Law in Northern Ireland*. Belfast: The Family Planning Association Northern Ireland

Gilligan, C. (1982) *In a Different Voice: Psychological Theory and Women's Development*. Cambridge: Harvard University Press

Goggin, M.L. (Ed.) (1993) *Understanding the New Politics of Abortion*. Newbury Park, CA: Sage

Hadley, J. (1996) *Abortion: Between Freedom and Necessity*. London: Virago

Henriques, J., Hollway, W., Urwin, C., Venn, C. and Walkerdine, V. (1984) *Changing the Subject*. London: Methuen

H.L. v Matheson 450 U.S. 398 (1981)

Hollway, W. (1989) *Subjectivity and Method in Psychology: Gender, Meaning and Science*. London: Sage

Holmgren, K. (1994) Repeat abortion and contraceptive use: report from an interview study in Stockholm. *Gynecological and Obstetric Investigations*, 37, 254–259

Kohlberg, L. (1976) Moral Stages and moralization: the cognitive developmental approach. In T. Lickona (Ed.) *Moral Development and Behaviour Theory: Research and Social Issues*. New York: Holt, Rinehart and Winston

Kolker, A. and Burke, B.M. (1993) Grieving the wanted child: ramifications of abortion after prenatal diagnosis of abnormality. *Health Care for Women International*, 14, 513–526

Lazarus, A. (1985) Psychiatric sequelae of legalized elective first trimester abortion, *Journal of Psychosomatic Obstetrics and Gynaecology*. 4, 141–150

Melton, G.B. and Russo, N.F. (1987) Adolescent abortion: psychological perspectives on public policy. *American Psychologist*, 42, 69–72

Miller, W.B. (1992) An empirical study of the psychological antecedents and consequences of induced abortion. *Journal of Social Issues*, 48, 67–93

Morell, C. M. (1994) *Unwomanly Conduct: The Challenges of Intentional Childlessness*. New York: Routledge

Neustatter, A. (with Newson, G.)(1986) *Mixed Feelings: The Experience of Abortion*. London: Pluto Press

Nicolson, P. (1998) *Post-Natal Depression: Science and the Construction of Motherhood.* London: Routledge

The Northern Ireland Abortion Law Reform Association (1989) *Abortion in Northern Ireland: The Report of an International Tribunal.* Belfast: Beyond the Pale Publications

Osofsky, J.D., Osofsky, H.J. and Rajan, R. (1973) Psychological effects of abortion: with emphasis upon immediate reactions and follow-up. In H.J. Osofsky and J.D. Osofsky (Eds.) *The Abortion Experience.* Hagerstown, MD: Harper and Row

Phoenix, A., Woollett, A. and Lloyd, E. (Eds.) (1991) *Motherhood: Meanings, Practices and Ideologies.* London: Sage

Piaget, J. (1932/1965) *The Moral Judgement of the Child.* New York: The Free Press

Prilleltensky, I. (1994) Psychology and social ethics. *American Psychologist,* 49, 966–967

Richardson, T. (1999) An Examination of the Political Controversy Surrounding Abortion Reform in Germany. Social Politics Paper No. 6 University of East London

Roe v Wade (1973) 410 U.S. 113. Reproduced in Doerr, E. and Prescott, J.W. (Eds.) (1989) *Abortion Rights and Fetal Personhood.* Long Beach, CA: Centerline Press

Russo, N.F., Horn, J.D. and Schwartz, R. (1992) US abortion in context: selected characteristics and motivations of women seeking abortions. *Journal of Social Issues,* 48, 183–202

Showalter, E. (1987) *The Female Malady: Women, Madness and English Culture.* London: Virago Press

Shotter, J. (1993) *Cultural Politics of Everyday Life.* Milton Keynes: Open University Press

Smart, C. (1989) *Feminism and the Power of Law.* London: Routledge

Smetana, J.G. and Adler, N.E. (1979) Decision-making regarding abortion: a value x expectancy analysis. *Journal of Population,* 2, 338–357

Sobol, M. P. and David, K.J. (1992) The adoption alternative for pregnant adolescents: decision making, consequences and policy implications. *Journal of Social Issues,* 48, 143–161

Tew, M. (1990) *Safer Childbirth?* London: Chapman and Hall

Torres, A. and Forrest, J.D. (1988) Why do women have abortions? *Family Planning Perspectives,* 20, 169–176

Ussher, J.M. (1991) *Women's Madness: Misogyny or Mental Illness?* London: Routledge

Ussher, J.M. (1989) *The Psychology of the Female Body.* London: Routledge

Wasielewski, P.L. (1992) Post-abortion syndrome: Emotional battles over interaction and ideology. *Humboldt Journal of Social Relations,* 18, 101–129

Wilmoth, G.H. (1992) Abortion, public health policy, and informed consent. *Journal of Social Issues,* 48, 1–17

CHAPTER 40

BODY IMAGE

Sarah Grogan

INTRODUCTION

Body image relates to a woman's perceptions, feelings and thoughts about her body, and incorporates body size estimation, evaluation of body attractiveness, and emotions associated with body shape and size (Grogan, 1999). Body image is socially constructed. To fully understand women's body image we need to look at the cultural milieu in which women operate. This is a summary of recent work on social pressure to be slim, and the ways that age, sexuality and ethnicity impact on body image; including an evaluation of how body dissatisfaction can impact on women's health through cosmetic surgery, dieting, 'eating disorders', and exercise (including bodybuilding). It is concluded that cultural acceptance of diversity in body types is likely to lead to a reduction in body dissatisfaction, and improved health for women.

SOCIAL PRESSURE TO BE SLIM

In Western societies, slimness is a valued attribute for women, and is associated with attractiveness, self-control, social skill, occupational success, and youth (Bordo, 1993). The idealization of slenderness is a relatively recent phenomenon. Plumpness in women was considered fashionable and erotic until relatively recently (Fallon, 1990), and it is possible to trace an historical evolution from the plump body types preferred until the start of the twentieth century to the thin types preferred today (Grogan, 1999).

Studies of body satisfaction in Britain, the United States and Australia have reliably found that women of all ages tend to be dissatisfied with their bodies, mostly wishing to be thinner. When women have been asked to pick silhouette figures representing their current and ideal body size, American, Australian, and British women and girls reliably pick thinner sizes for their ideal than their current size (Lamb *et al.*, 1993; Tiggemann and Pennington, 1990; Wardle *et al.*, 1993), and interview work substantiates these findings, showing that women and girls would mostly like to be slimmer. They express dissatisfaction to the extent that they believe that they differ from the slender ideal (Charles and Kerr, 1986; Grogan and Wainwright, 1996).

Several authors in the 1980s and 1990s have suggested that Western beauty norms set up impossible ideals for women, and that these unrealistic ideals keep women in a subordinate position by ensuring that we put our energies into vigilance over our bodies. In the 1980s, Susan Brownmiller in her book *Femininity* (1984) shows how women's bodies have been controlled and restricted throughout history to conform to prevailing aesthetics (through corsetry and more recently through dieting), and how these practices serve to weaken women physically. Wendy Chapkis (1986) also argues that women are oppressed by a 'global culture machine' (made up of the advertising industry, communications media and the cosmetic industry) which promotes a narrow Westernized beauty ideal to women all over the world. In the 1990s Susan Bordo (1993) has argued that preoccupation with fat, diet, and slenderness in women is normative. She suggests that the Western feminine ideal is a body completely under control, tight and contained, and that Western women are submerged in a culture where slimness in women is associated with a specific (positive) set of cultural meanings. Sandra Bartky (1990) argues that every aspect of women's bodies is objectified, so that women feel estranged from their bodies. These analyses are useful in contextualizing women's body dissatisfaction within a culture where women are expected to conform to an unrealistically slim ideal.

Body image is socially constructed and depends to a certain extent on the values placed on particular body types in that culture. Studies that have looked at body dissatisfaction in different cultural and sub-cultural groups have reliably found that women tend to be more satisfied with their bodies, and are less likely to want to be thinner, in groups where there is less pressure to be thin. For instance, British and American studies have suggested that Afro-Caribbean, Asian, and Hispanic women and girls are likely to report higher desired body weights, larger desired body shapes, and fewer weight concerns than white girls and women (Abrams et al., 1993; Harris, 1994, Neff et al., 1997; Tsai et al., 1998; Wardle and Marsland, 1990; Wardle et al., 1993). It seems likely that these differences in ideals and body concern relate to sub-cultural differences in pressures on women to be slender.

Sexuality may also impact on body satisfaction. There is some evidence that heterosexual women may (on average) have lower body satisfaction than lesbians.

Susan Beren and colleagues (1997), in interviews with young adult lesbians found that sexual relationships with women encouraged acceptance of one's body. Michael Siever (1994) found that lesbians were more satisfied with their bodies than were heterosexual women, and some of the lesbian group indicated that they had suffered with body dissatisfaction and disordered eating before they came out. These authors suggest that lesbian sub-cultures may have a protective function in relation to body dissatisfaction, because they place less emphasis on youth and beauty, and do not promote the unrealistic ideals seen in mainstream heterosexual culture. Studies of body image in heterosexual women have tended to find that women experience pressure from male partners to be slender (Charles and Kerr, 1986), and studies of men's preferences for women's bodies show a tendency to prefer slender body types (Fallon and Rozin, 1985; Huon et al., 1990). Naomi Wolf (1991) predicted that a woman-loving philosophy (among heterosexual women and lesbians) would promote more positive and accepting images of the female body.

Studies of body satisfaction across the life span have tended to find that women of all ages report similar levels of dissatisfaction. Girls as young as nine reliably choose (age relevant) body silhouettes that are thinner than their current size as their ideal (Tiggemann and Pennington,1990), and girls from the age of eight imitate the discourse of older girls, and women, expressing body dissatisfaction and concern over weight gain (Chernin, 1993; Grogan and Wainwright, 1996). Patricia Pliner and colleagues (1990) found that women were more concerned about eating, body weight, and physical appearance, and had lower appearance self-esteem than men at all ages from 10 to 79. More recently, Sue Lamb and colleagues (1993) have found that younger (aged about 20) and older (about 50) women presented body ideals that were much thinner than their perceived size. These findings are also borne out by interview work, where women from 16 to 63 have similar levels of dissatisfaction. Women reliably report dissatisfaction with stomach, hips and thighs, are motivated to lose weight, and represent an ideal that is tall and slim with firm breasts, irrespective of age (Grogan, 1999).

HEALTH IMPLICATIONS OF BODY DISSATISFACTION

Women's body dissatisfaction impacts on health in a variety of ways. Women who are dissatisfied with their body may opt for cosmetic surgery to correct perceived inadequacies, may diet, may develop 'eating disorders', and may exercise to try to change body shape and weight.

Cosmetic Surgery

The 1990s have seen a significant increase in the numbers of women receiving cosmetic surgery in the U.K. and the U.S., especially liposuction and breast augmentation procedures, despite publicity about health risks associated with the 'surgical fix' (Allen and Oberle, 1996; Gillespie, 1996; Viner, 1997). This branch of medicine is the most 'gendered' of medical specialities; with the interaction usually involving a male health care professional and a female patient (Davis, 1998). Researchers have tried to understand why some women feel that they need cosmetic surgery, in spite of known health risks and complications. Kathy Davis (1995) argues that understanding why women engage in a practice that is painful and dangerous must take women's explanations as a starting point. Davis sees women as active and knowledgable agents. The women she interviewed reported that they had made free choices, and felt that they were 'taking control' over the look of their body. Kathryn Morgan (1991) argues that although women may feel that they are making a free choice, such freedom is not really possible in a culture where women's bodies are objectified, and where the cultural ideal is set by men. Collusion with restricted models of femininity may seem to be a rational choice for some women at the individual level, in a context where women are judged by their appearance. Health professionals who are concerned about the high uptake of cosmetic surgery and its potential health risks need to take into account social pressures on women to conform to the slender, full-breasted ideal, to understand women's motivations for engaging in this health-damaging behavior, rather than pathologizing them as having Body Dysmorphic Disorder (Davis, 1995; Philips and Diaz, 1997).

Dieting

Another potentially health-damaging behavior that can result from body dissatisfaction is the reduction of eating (dieting). Most women have attempted to change weight and shape at some time in their lives by reducing their eating. Estimates of the frequency of dieting in American and British women show that about 95 percent of women have dieted at some stage in their lives (Ogden, 1992); and about 40 percent of women are dieting at any one time (Horm and Anderson, 1993).

In a study of British women aged 18 to 35, Adrian Furnham and Nicola Greaves (1994) found that 48 out of 55 (87 percent) had dieted or were currently dieting. When asked reasons for dieting, women were more likely than men to cite 'to be slim' and 'to increase confidence and self-esteem'. However, research suggests that dieting is unlikely to lead to long-term weight loss, and may in fact lead to lowered self-esteem in the long term. Most researchers find that diets lead to a range of negative health effects (including 'dieter's hypertension'), and result in long-term weight loss in only about 5 percent of non-obese dieters (Brownell and Rodin, 1994). The other 95 percent of women are likely to feel that they have failed, leading to guilt and self-recrimination. Nickie Charles and Marion Kerr (1986) found that most of the women they interviewed had dieted as a way to lose weight, and most felt that they had failed because they had been unable to keep to the diet plan due to feelings of hunger. This led to lowered self-esteem. Clearly, dieting is damaging to women's health for a variety of reasons (Charles and Kerr, 1986; Ogden, 1992).

'Eating Disorders'

Body dissatisfaction has also been linked to the development of 'eating disorders'. The term 'eating disorder' is generally used to describe eating patterns that fall outside the normal range, usually involving severe restriction of food intake (anorexia nervosa), and regular binge eating and 'purging' (bulimia nervosa; usually vomiting but sometimes using laxatives or vigorous exercise). Culture plays an important role in the development of 'eating disorders' (Benveniste *et al.*, 1999). It is generally accepted that anorexia and bulimia are more common in countries that value slimness, and that when people move from cultures that value plumpness to those where slenderness is valued, they become more likely to develop problematic relationships with food (Rosen, 1990; Orbach, 1993). However, many women are exposed to the 'culture of slenderness' and only a few become anorexic or bulimic, so clearly other factors are involved (see Malson, and Nasser, in this volume).

Studies that have looked at the relationship between body dissatisfaction and eating attitudes in the general population of college women and high school students have reliably found a significant relationship between body dissatisfaction and problematic relationships with food (Rosen, 1990). Those with most problematic relationships with food are likely to be most dissatisfied with their bodies, usually perceiving them to be too heavy. However, studies that have specifically looked at body dissatisfaction in women classified as having 'eating disorders' have tended to find that women with anorexia or bulimia do not differ significantly on body satisfaction scales from other women (Garner *et al.*, 1983; Wilson and Smith, 1989). This probably reflects the generally high levels of food preoccupation and low body esteem in women in the general population (Charles and Kerr, 1986; Chesters, 1994; Zellner Harner and Adler, 1989). Body dissatisfaction may be a necessary condition, but is certainly not a sufficient condition for the development of 'eating disorders'. Many other factors have been implicated in the development and maintenance of 'eating disorders' including perceptions of lack of control (Orbach, 1993) and low self-esteem (Button *et al.*, 1996). Clearly an understanding of 'eating disorders' needs to be informed by an investigation of cultural pressures on women, as suggested by Jodie Benveniste *et al.* (1999), and also needs to take into account individual pressures on particular women, to understand why some women develop 'eating disorders' and others do not.

Exercise

One of the few positive health implications of body dissatisfaction is that it may lead to increased exercise in women. Furnham and Greaves (1994) found that women were likely to say that they exercised primarily for weight control, to alter body shape. Most estimates suggest that about 50 percent of women under 40 engage in some form of exercise (Cox *et al.*, 1993; Ingledrew *et al.*, 1998). Positive effects are not limited to changes in muscle tone and fitness (although this might be what motivates in the first place), but extend to body image and self-concept.

Adrian Furnham and colleagues (1994) found that exercising women tended to perceive thin shapes more negatively, and more muscular shapes more positively, than non-exercising women, and had a more positive perception of their own bodies than those who did not exercise. This may be because exercise contributes to a slimmer, more toned body. It is also likely that physical mastery increases self-esteem. Clearly, promotion of moderate exercise could have a variety of positive effects on women's body satisfaction and health.

Sports that build muscle are seen as inappropriate for women in mainstream Western culture (Mansfield and McGinn, 1993), although body building in women in Britain and the United States is increasing (Korkia, 1994). Sandra Bartky (1990) sees bodybuilding as an empowering practice that challenges the cultural association of muscularity (and strength) with masculinity. Leena St Martin and Nicola Gavey (1996) also argue that bodybuilding is a way to challenge dominant ideologies that represent women as physically weak (but see also Bordo, 1990). Bodybuilding may represent a health risk if women take anabolic steroids to maximize the effects of weight training (Korkia, 1994). However, for many women it could be an effective way to increase strength and to develop a more positive body image, with all the attendant positive effects on health (St Martin and Gavey, 1996).

SUMMARY

Women's body image is socially constructed, and body dissatisfaction and dieting are normative in cultures where slenderness is the ideal. Women in particular social groups in Western cultures (white, and heterosexual) may be at particular risk for body dissatisfaction. There are no noticeable differences in women of different ages. Women present similar discourses around body image, and make similar body shape choices from childhood into their seventies. In order to understand why women may engage in health-damaging behaviors such as cosmetic surgery, dieting, starvation and 'purging', health care professionals need to take account of social pressures on women to conform to the slender ideal. Only through an understanding of the meanings attached to slenderness for women in Western culture will those involved in health promotion be able to challenge these health-damaging behaviors. Moderate exercise may (for some women) be a useful way to develop a more positive body image, and bodybuilding may also promote alternative versions of beauty for women. Cultural acceptance of diversity in body types is likely to lead to a reduction in body dissatisfaction and an improved quality of life for women.

REFERENCES

Abrams, K., Allen, L. and Gray, J. (1993) Disordered eating attitudes and behaviors, psychological adjustment, and ethnic identity: a comparison of black and white female college students. *International Journal of Eating Disorders*, 14, 49–57

Allen, M. and Oberle, K. (1996). Augmentation mammoplasty: a complex choice. *Health Care for Women International*, 17 (1), 81–90

Benveniste, J., LeCouteur, A. and Hepworth, J. (1999). Lay theories of anorexia nervosa: a discourse analytic study. *Journal of Health Psychology*, 4 (1), 59–70

Bartky, S. (1990) *Femininity and Domination: Studies in the Phenomenology of Oppression*. New York: Routledge

Beren, S., Hayden, H., Wilfley, D.E. and Striegel-Moore, R.H. (1997). Body dissatisfaction among lesbian college students. The conflict of straddling mainstream and lesbian cultures. *Psychology of Women Quarterly*, 21 (3), 431–445

Bordo, S. (1990) Reading the slender body. In M. Jacobus, E. Fox Keller and S. Shuttleworth (Eds.) *Body Politics*. New York: Routledge

Bordo, S. (1993) *Unbearable Weight: Feminism, Western Culture, and the Body*. Berkeley: University of California Press

Brownell, K.D. and Rodin, J.R. (1994) The dieting maelstrom: is it possible and advisable to lose weight? *American Psychologist*, 49, 781–791

Brownmiller, S. (1984) *Femininity*. New York: Linden Press

Button, E., Sonuga-Barke, E., Davies, J. and Thompson, M. (1996) A prospective study of self-esteem in the prediction of eating problems in adolescent schoolgirls: questionnaire findings. *British Journal of Clinical Psychology*, 35, 193–203

Chapkis, W. (1986) *Beauty Secrets*. London: The Women's Press

Charles, N., and Kerr, M. (1986) Food for feminist thought. *Sociological Review*, 34, 537–572

Chernin, K. (1983) *Womansize: The Tyranny of Slenderness*. London: The Women's Press

Chesters, L. (1994) Women's talk: food, weight and body image. *Feminism and Psychology*, 4 (3), 449–457

Cox, B.D., Huppert, F.A. and Whichelow, M.J. (Eds.) (1993) *The Health and Lifestyle Survey: Seven Years On*. Aldershot: Dartmouth

Davis, K. (1995) *Reshaping the Female Body: The Dilemma of Cosmetic Surgery*, London: Routledge

Davis, K. (1998) Pygmalion's in plastic surgery. *Health*, 2 (1), 23–40

Fallon, A. (1990) Culture in the mirror: sociocultural determinants of body image. In T. Cash and T. Pruzinsky (Eds.) *Body Images: Development, Deviance and Change*. New York: Guilford Press

Fallon, A. and Rozin, P. (1985) Sex differences in perceptions of desirable body shape. *Journal of Abnormal Psychology*, 94 (1), 102–105

Furnham, A. and Greaves, N. (1994) Gender and locus of control correlates of body image dissatisfaction. *European Journal of Personality*, 8, 183–200

Furnham, A., Titman, P. and Sleeman, E. (1994) Perception of female body shapes as a function of exercise. *Journal of Social Behaviour and Personality*, 9, 335–352

Garner, D. and Garfinkel, P. (1981) Body image in anorexia nervosa: measurement, theory, and clinical implications. *International Journal of Psychiatry in Medicine*, 11, 263–284

Garner, D., Olmsted, M. and Garfinkel, P. (1983) Does anorexia nervosa occur on a continuum? *International Journal of Eating Disorders*, 2, 11–20

Gillespie, R. (1996) Women, the body, and brand extension of medicine: cosmetic surgery and the paradox of choice. *Women and Health*, 24, 69–85

Grogan, S. and Wainwright, N. (1996) Growing up in the culture of slenderness: girls' experiences of body dissatisfaction. *Women's Studies International Forum*, 19, 665–673

Grogan, S. (1999) *Body Image: Understanding Body Dissatisfaction in Men, Women and Children*. London: Routledge

Harris, S. (1994) Racial differences in predictors of college womens body image attitudes. *Women and Health*, 21, 89–104

Horm, J. and Anderson, K. (1993) Who in America is trying to lose weight? *Annals of Internal Medicine*, 119, 672–676

Huon, G., Morris, S. and Brown, L. (1990) Differences between male and female preferences for female body size. *Australian Psychologist*, 25, 314–317

Ingledrew, D.K., Markland, D. and Medley, A.R. (1998) Exercise motives and stages of change. *Journal of Health Psychology*, 3 (4), 477–490

Korkia, P. (1994) Anabolic steroid use in Britain. *International Journal of Drug Policy*, 5, 6–9

Lamb, C.S., Jackson, L., Cassiday, P. and Priest, D. (1993) Body figure preferences of men and women: A comparison of two generations. *Sex Roles*, 28, 345–358

Mansfield, A. and McGinn, B. (1993) Pumping irony: the muscular and the feminine. In S. Scott and D. Morgan (Eds.) *Body Matters* (pp. 49–68). London: Falmer

Morgan, K. (1991) Women and the knife: cosmetic surgery and the colonization of womens bodies. *Hypatia*, 6, 25–53

Neff, L., Sargent, R., McKeown, R., Jackson, K. and Valois, R. (1997) Black-white differences in body size perceptions and weight management practices among adolescent females. *Journal of Adolescent Health*, 20, 459–465

Ogden, J. (1992) *Fat Chance: The Myth of Dieting Explained*. London: Routledge

Orbach, S. (1993) *Hunger Strike: The Anorectic's Struggle as a Metaphor for Our Age*. London: Penguin

Phillips, K.A. and Diaz, S.F. (1997). Gender differences in body dysmorphic disorder. *Journal of Nervous and Mental Disease*, 185 (9), 570–577

Pliner, P., Chaiken, S. and Flett, G. (1990) Gender differences in concern with body weight and physical appearance over the life span. *Personality and Social Psychology Bulletin*, 16, 263–273

Rosen, J. (1990) Body image disturbances in eating disorders. In T. Cash and T. Pruzinsky (Eds.) *Body Images: Development, Deviance and Change*. (pp. 190–214). New York: Guilford Press

Siever, M. (1994) Sexual orientation and gender as factors in socioculturally acquired vulnerability to body dissatisfaction and eating disorders. *Journal of Consulting and Clinical Psychology*, 62, 252–260

St Martin, L. and Gavey, N. (1996) Women's bodybuilding: feminist resistance and/or femininitys recuperation. *Body and Society*, 2, 45–57

Tiggemann, M. and Pennington, B. (1990) The development of gender differences in body-size dissatisfaction. *Australian Psychologist*, 25, 306–313

Tsai, C.Y., Hoerr, S.L. and Song, W.O. (1998) Dieting behaviour of Asian college women attending a US University. *Journal of American College Health*, 46, 4, 163–168

Viner, K. (1997) The new plastic feminism. *Guardian*, 4, July, 5

Wardle, J. and Marsland, L. (1990) Adolescent concerns about weight and eating; a social-developmental perspective. *Journal of Psychosomatic Research*, 34, 377–391

Wardle, J., Bindra, R., Fairclough, B. and Westcombe, A. (1993) Culture and body image: body perception and weight concern in young Asian and Caucasian British women. *Journal of Community and Applied Social Psychology*, 3, 173–181

Wilson, G.T. and Smith, D. (1989) Assessment of bulimia nervosa: an evaluation of the eating disorders examination. *International Journal of Eating Disorders*, 8, 173–179

Wolf, N. (1991) *The Beauty Myth: How Images of Beauty Are Used Against Women*. New York: William Morrow

Zellner, D., Harner, D. and Adler, R. (1989) Effects of eating abnormalities and gender on perceptions of desirable body shape. *Journal of Abnormal Psychology*, 98, 93–96

CHAPTER 41

ANOREXIA NERVOSA

Helen Malson

INTRODUCTION

This chapter sets out to explore how gender and gender ideologies are implicated in the concept of 'anorexia nervosa' and in the lived experiences and subjectivities of girls and women diagnosed as 'anorexic'. In doing this it also seeks to question the commonplace distinctions made between normal and pathological body-management practices and embodied subjectivities; a distinction which forms the basis of scientific and clinical conceptions as well as of public understandings of 'anorexia'. However, by exploring some of the resonances between women's normalized and pathologized eating practices and embodied subjectivities and by highlighting recent feminist work in this field, the chapter seeks to suggest that this distinction between normal/healthy and patholo-gized/unhealthy is neither a valid nor useful way of understanding women's un/healthy relationships to their/our bodies and selves and food.

WOMEN, BODIES AND EATING IN HISTORICAL AND CULTURAL CONTEXTS

The term 'Anorexia nervosa' first emerged in Western medical discourse at the end of the nineteenth century (Lasegue, 1873; Gull, 1874) and was initially conceptualized as a particular manifestation of 'hysteria' (Malson, 1998; Hepworth and Griffin, 1995) which was, as Showalter (1985) among others notes, *the* female malady *par excellence* of Victorian society. 'Gender' thus featured significantly in science's first attempts to understand women's self-starvation. Not only were the majority of those first 'anorex-ic patients' young women but 'femininity' also figured strongly in Victorian medical discourse as an aetiological explanation of anorexia. Like hysteria (Showalter, 1985; Douglas-Wood, 1973; Sayers, 1982; Foucault, 1979), anorexia was presented as a manifestation of a 'feminine nature' which was simultaneously normal (for women) and intrinsically pathological (Malson, 1992, 1998; Hepworth and Griffin, 1995).

Today gender features no less strongly in both popular and clinical understandings of 'anorexia'. Diagnoses of 'anorexia' have risen sharply in Western countries since the 1960s and an estimated 95 percent of those diagnosed as 'anorexic' are girls and women (Hughes, 1991). Thus, as Wooley *et al.* (1994: ix) note, 'one may speculate about the role of gender in many conditions, but in the case of eating disorders, where nearly all the sufferers are female, the importance of gender is beyond debate'. Moreover, for many feminist clinicians working in this field there is 'an obvious resonance between the acute anguish of eating disorder sufferers and the troubles of ordinary women'. The mental and physical health of 'anorexic' and 'ordinary' women is in some way related via our contem-porary gender ideologies and practices. 'Anorexia' is undoubtedly 'say-ing something about what it means to be a woman in late twentieth cen-tury culture' (Malson, 1998: 6). What 'it' *is* saying though is perhaps rather less clear. And the difficulty lies as much in the problems of defin-ing what we mean by 'anorexia nervosa' as it does in defining what we mean by 'ordinary women'.

'Anorexia nervosa' is currently defined as a mental and behavioral dis-order (WHO, 1992) characterized by a reduction in food intake, resulting in a body weight of at least 15 percent below 'normal'; accompanied by an intense fear of gaining weight, an over-valuation of thinness, and by body image distortion (APA, 1987, WHO, 1992). As such, 'anorexia' seems to represent an intensified manifestation of the behaviors, pre-occupations and concerns of many girls and women in contemporary Western soci-eties. Survey after survey indicates that the majority of girls and women in the West today habitually restrict their/our food intake (Grunewald, 1985; Unsworth and Shattock, 1993); wish to be thinner than they/we are (Huon and Brown, 1983; Rothblum, 1994); fear becoming fatter (Chernin, 1983; Wolf, 1994); and report body image distortions such that they/we frequently over-estimate their actual body size (Heilbrun and Friedberg, 1990). It is hard to exaggerate either the prevalence or the intensity of women's pre-occupations with and distress surrounding their/our food intake and body weight/shape, or the actual and potential detrimental (mental and physical) health consequences of this. Indeed 'dieting' and body dissatisfaction are so widespread that they have been described as both descriptively and prescriptively normative (Polivy and Herman, 1985) and so intense that, for example, women responding to a survey by *Glamour* in 1984 'chose losing 10–15 lbs above success in work or in love as their most desired goal' in life (Wooley and Wooley, 1984, cited in Wolf, 1994: 96). Indeed, a desire to lose weight may outweigh a desire to be healthy (Rothblum, 1994) or even to live: I recently read the transcript of an interview conducted by an undergraduate student researching women's experiences of attending diet clubs (Passmore, 1999). The interviewee, a woman who was also currently undergoing treatment for cancer, related how distressing it was for her that, unlike the other patients receiving similar cancer treatments, she had not lost weight. Even in the face of her own potential death, the importance of achieving the thinness required for physical 'feminine perfection' had not, it seemed, diminished.

There is, then, an arena of obvious resonance between 'anorexia' and 'the troubles of ordinary women' (see Wooley *et al.*, 1994: ix) to be found in their/our pre-occupation and distress surrounding eating and body weight/shape. And, as numerous feminists and others have already argued, the body dissatisfaction and associated body management practices of 'ordinary' *and* 'anorexic' women can only be adequately understood within the context of a societal idealization of thinness as a central criterion of feminine perfection. Societal denigrations of fatness and prejudice against 'fat' people, particularly women, have been well-documented (Rothblum, 1994; Agell and Rothblum, 1991; Rothblum *et al.*, 1990; Bordo, 1990) as has a societal preference for thinness, again, particularly in women (Dejong and Kleck, 1986; Silverstein et al., 1986; Garner and Garfinkel, 1980). Indeed, it might be argued that, despite (or, perhaps more precisely, because of) women's increased economic and political 'emancipation', the pressures on women to conform to an ever-thinner ideal have increased over recent decades (Wolf, 1990; Hesse-Biber, 1991). The number of diet-related articles in the popular media has continued to rise steeply since the 1960s whilst the average size and weight of women models portrayed in the popular media has progressively decreased (Silverstein *et al.*, 1986; Garner *et al.*, 1980). And research indicates that media portrayals of thin 'feminine perfection' are not without some effect. Looking at pictures of (thin) women fashion models and media stars seems to result in both women (Shaw, 1995; see also Grogan, 1999) and men (Kenrick and Gutierres, 1980; see also Wooley, 1994) becoming even more critical of women's bodies.

UN/HEALTHY EATING AND THE POLITICS OF PATHOLOGIZATION

Whether the media is responsible for our cultural idealization of the thin female body or whether it is 'merely' re-articulating and promulgating already-existing societal norms (see Grogan, 1999, and in this volume), it is abundantly clear that we inhabit a cultural context which places enormous emphasis on women's physical appearance; which prescribes ever-thinner 'ideals' of 'feminine perfection', and which thereby imposes ever-more stringent requirements on girls and women to engage in 'dieting' and other body management practices such as exercise (see Rothblum, 1994) and even surgery (see Bordo, 1990), often to the detriment of their physical as well as mental health (Rothblum, 1994), in order to achieve this 'ideal'. It is a cultural context which can be understood as producing and promoting not only 'ordinary' women's body dissatisfaction and dieting behavior but one that has become increasingly acknowledged as playing some role in the aetiology of eating disorders (e.g. Garner *et al.*, 1983; Hsu, 1989; Fallon *et al.*, 1994; Shaw, 1995; Malson, 1996). The effects of this cultural context, and perhaps of the diet and fashion industries in particular, cannot be underestimated (Malson, 1997; see also Nasser, in this volume).

Yet, as Susie Orbach (1993: xxiii; see also Wolf, 1994; Bordo, 1993) has noted, the prevalence of 'dieting' and body image pre-occupations and dissatisfaction among Western girls and women is often seen as an inevitable, quasi-natural state of affairs rather than as a cause for concern. 'No one', she suggests,

is much concerned by statistics that show that 80 percent of women in countries like the USA, the U.K., New Zealand and Australia are dieting at any given moment. The anguish and distress behind these figures are concealed behind an attitude that accepts this as the norm and sees no further need for questions. Women like to diet. Women expect to diet. Women are accustomed to diet. Women have a tendency to fat. Women are vain. Women are always so self-involved.

By promulgating a representation of 'women' as 'naturally' preoccupied with our bodily appearance and as 'naturally' predisposed to restricting our food intake, contemporary gender ideologies often succeed in normalizing women's dieting and body dissatisfaction. The distress that many 'ordinary' girls and women experience in relation to their/our bodies and the accompanying dieting and other body management practices in which they/we engage are naturalized and thereby rendered inevitable, inconsequential, trivial, invisible (Wolf, 1994).

At the same time, however, 'eating disorders' have become an increasingly prominent topic in the popular media as well as the academic and clinical literatures. And, whilst 'ordinary' women's dieting and body dissatisfaction is frequently viewed as 'normal', eating disorder sufferers are more often considered to be 'abnormal' and a matter of serious concern. Images of emaciated young 'anorexic' women are shocking. As Susan Bordo (1990: 84) has argued, the way in which eating disorders are portrayed often encourages 'a side show experience' between the 'normal' viewer and the 'freakish' anorexic. 'Anorexia' is thus presented to us as beyond the pale of 'normal' femininity.

This production of a seemingly categorical divide between 'ordinary' women and 'eating disordered' women works in tandem with the divisions made in clinical discourse and practice between 'normal' and pathologically disordered eating. Within medical, psychiatric and psychological discourses and practices 'anorexia' is conceptualized as an *individual* pathology, a quasi-natural clinical entity located within the pathologized individual woman (Malson, 1998). Its medical status as a diagnostic category undoubtedly indicates a gravity which is clearly appropriate. For it would be ethically indefensible not to view 'anorexia' as a very serious predicament. Problematically, however, the medicalization of women's 'disordered' eating and distress about their/our bodies also individualizes the problem. Whether 'anorexia' is conceptualized in terms of physiological dysfunction, cognitive bias, psychological predisposition, unresolved psychodynamic conflict or whatever, the problem tends to be located within the individual 'anorexic' girl or woman rather than her surroundings, such that 'she' is also presented as categorically different from 'normal' women.

Yet, as outlined above, in contemporary Western societies vast numbers of girls and women experience considerable body dissatisfaction and regularly restrict their food intake in attempts to achieve an ever-thinner 'ideal' of physical 'feminine perfection'. To make any categorical distinction between 'anorexia nervosa' (or other eating disorders such as 'bulimia') and the widespread food restriction and body weight/shape preoccupations of 'ordinary' girls and women thus seems problematic. It is not that 'anorexia' is not an extremely serious issue: 'it' is expressive of considerable psychological distress and often has devastating consequences for women's physical health. It may be, however, that to view 'anorexia' as an *individual* pathology is not the best way of understanding 'the problem'. It may be 'that our very notion of "pathology" might be usefully abandoned' (Littlewood, 1991) so that we can then explore the complex and multiple meanings of 'anorexic' experiences and practices and thereby more fully comprehend their 'resonances' with the experiences and body management practices of 'ordinary' women (see Wooley *et al.*, 1994).

From this perspective we can begin to see 'anorexia' *not* as an individual pathology lying beyond the pale of 'normal femininity' but rather as an intensified collectivity of experiences and damaging body management practices located precisely *within* the parameters of 'normality'; produced by the same complex matrix of discursive and material practices which produce and regulate 'normal' 'feminine' subjectivities in contemporary Western(ized) cultures. Thus, if we dispense with the concept of pathology (see Littlewood, 1991), which both individualizes 'anorexic' predicaments and separates them from those of 'ordinary' women, then we may be better able to understand both 'dieting' and 'anorexia'. We may be better able to de-trivialize 'the beauty myth' (see Wolf, 1991) as an aspect of contemporary culture which produces and regulates women and women's (mental and physical) health in often very negative ways *and* to comprehend 'anorexia' not as an individual pathology, not as a bizarre aberration from allegedly healthy 'normality', but as a complex and highly distressing collectivity of experiences and body management practices constituted and regulated by our contemporary gender-specific cultural contexts (Eckermann, 1997; Malson, 1996).

RECENT FEMINIST PERSPECTIVES AND THE CATEGORY OF 'WOMÆN'

Such a move is already apparent in various ways in some feminists' and others' writings on 'anorexia' (e.g. Orbach, 1986; Fallon *et al.*, 1994; Bordo, 1993; Eckermann, 1997; Malson, 1998). In *Four Generations of Women: Our Bodies and Lives,* for example, Brigman (1994) offers a poignant autobiographical account of the bodies and lives of her grandmother, her mother, herself and her daughter, which illustrates how cultural prescriptions of feminine beauty can be seen to construct, regulate and devastate the lives and health of 'ordinary women' (in this case particularly of her mother). That the piece forms part of the edited collection *Feminist Perspectives on Eating Disorders* (Fallon *et al.*, 1994). highlights the necessity of understanding 'anorexia' and other 'eating disorders' within the context of the discursive and material practices which produce and regulate 'normal' 'feminine' subjectivities (and women's health) in contemporary Western(ized) cultures.

Moreover, a serious attention to and analysis of the discursive and material contexts in which 'women', women's bodies and women's health are constituted and regulated enables us to comprehend the socio-historical specificities, and the complex and multiple meanings of the various terms with which we are attempting to grapple. 'Beauty', for example, has already been repeatedly shown to be an 'empty' term whose meaning and strictures vary considerably from one cultural context and historical era to the next (e.g. Seid, 1994). It has, moreover, as numerous feminists (e.g. Boskind-Lodahl, 1976; Chernin, 1983; Lawrence, 1984; Wolf, 1991; Ussher, 1991; Orbach, 1993; Fallon *et al.*, 1994) have often argued, functioned as both a vehicle for and an expression of women's subjection in heteropartiarchal societies. Cultural imaginings of 'feminine beauty' cannot then be adequately understood as 'simply' reflecting what is 'naturally' attractive in women but are, rather, part of the complex expressions of cultural productions and regulations of gender and gender inequalities which are then further cross-cut by issues of, for example, ethnicity, class, dis/ability, sexual orientation and age (Smith, 1982; Bordo, 1993; Grogan, 1999; Malson, 1999). The hegemonic ideal of 'beauty' in contemporary Western culture is not only gender-specific since a variety of other inequality issues are equally profoundly articulates within this 'ideal'. 'Feminine perfection' is young, white, middle-class, thin, toned, blonde and blue-eyed (see Smith, 1982; Bordo, 1993). As Bordo (1993: 254–255) has argued:

The general tyranny of fashion – perpetual, elusive, and instructing the female body in a pedagogy of personal inadequacy and lack – is a powerful discipline for the normalization of all women in this culture. But even as we are all normalized to the requirements of appropriate feminine insecurity and preoccupation with appearance, more specific requirements emerge in different cultural and historical contexts ... when Oprah Winfrey admitted on her show that she had desperately longed to have 'hair that swings from side to side' when she shakes her head, she revealed the power of racial as well as gender normalization, normalization not only to 'femininity', but to the Caucasian standards of beauty that still dominate on television, in movies, in popular magazines.

Bordo's example (see also Smith, 1982) thus illustrates some of the complexities embedded in the concept of 'beauty' and thereby also illustrates the complexities of gender. It illustrates the necessity of conceptualizing 'woman' not as a unitary quasi-natural category but as a multiple fiction (see Walkerdine, 1986, 1990; Wetherell, 1986) 'written', regulated and lived in articulation with other (discursively constructed) categories such as sexual orientation, ethnicity, dis/ability and socio-economic status. And, if we thus re-theorize 'womæn' (see Malson, 1999) as a heterogeneous, fragmented, multiple and always socio-historically contingent 'volatile collectivity' (Riley, 1988: 1) in this way then it becomes apparent that 'female persons can be very differently positioned [in relation to "woman" and in relation to normalizing standards of "feminine beauty"] so that the apparent continuity of the subject of "woman" [and of "her" relationship(s) with regimes of "feminine beauty"] is not to be relied on' (Riley, 1988 1–2). And, as a central aspect of hegemonic 'feminine beauty', thinness, and the body management practices through which it is sought, will inevitably impact on (different) women in a variety of complex ways (see Bordo, 1993; Grogan, 1999).

SUMMARY

To seek to understand the relationships between 'anorexia', 'dieting', 'women' and women's health requires therefore that we engage with the diversity existing within the category of 'women' *and* with the complexities of the discursive and material contexts in which 'women', 'bodies', 'feminine beauty' and power inequalities are constituted and regulated. It thereby urgently requires that we further interrogate the *multiple* meanings of 'anorexia' and of self-starvation and thinness generally. For the meanings of thinness and of not eating go beyond a concern 'only' with attempts to achieve a heterosexually attractive 'feminine' appearance (Bordo, 1990, 1993; Malson and Ussher, 1996a, 1997; Malson 1998;

Katzman and Sing, 1997). The thin female body and the associated body management practices in which women engage sustain a variety of often conflicting meanings including a rejection of, resistance to or ambivalence about patriarchally prescribed femininities (Orbach, 1983, Bordo, 1990, Malson and Ussher, 1996b) or it may signify a protest against a proscribed 'vocational motherhood' (Katzman and Sing, 1997). Likewise, thinness and self-starvation may express an assertion of independence, autonomy and (self) control (Bruch, 1973; Bordo, 1990; Malson and Ussher 1996b) and, as such, 'anorexia' has been interpreted as expressive of the cultural dilemma created by the requirement that we inhabit the antithetical identities of self-controlled, disciplined worker and of self-indulgent consumer (Bordo, 1990; see also Turner, 1982; Malson, 1999). 'It' might, differently again, express both an anti-consumption ethic, an antipathy towards the late capitalist culture of mass-consumption whilst, 'it' simultaneously produces (and destroys) a body which in being hyper-thin is also 'hyper-cool' (Turner, 1992: 221; Brumberg, 1988; Malson, 1999). Self-starvation may be a culturally constructed way of producing an otherwise lacking identity whilst at the same time being an expression of self-hatred and a form of self-annihilation (Malson, 1998; see also Bruch, 1973). In short, 'anorexia' and women's 'anorexic' bodies may be expressive of a *multiplicity* of societal concerns and dilemmas that are particular to and constituted in the socio-economic, cultural, political and often gender-specific dynamics of contemporary Western cultures.

REFERENCES

Agell, G. and Rothblum, E.D. (1991) Effects of clients' obesity and gender on the therapy judgements of psychologists, *Professional Psychology: Theory, Research and Practice*, 22, 223–229

American Psychiatric Association (1987) *Diagnostic and Statistical Manual of Mental Disorder* (rev. 3rd edn). Washington, D.C.: APA

Bordo, S. (1990) Reading the slender body. In M. Jacobus, E. Fox Keller and S. Shuttleworth (Eds.) *Body/politics: Women and the Discourses of Science*. London: Routledge

Bordo, S. (1992) Anorexia nervosa: Psychopathology as the crystallization of culture. In H. Crowley and S. Himmelweit (Eds.) *Knowing Women: Feminism and Knowledge*. Cambridge: Polity Press in association with Open University Press

Bordo, S. (1993) *Unbearable Weight: Feminism, Western Culture and the Body*. Berkeley: University of California Press

Boskind-Lodahl, M. (1976) Cinderella's step-sisters: A feminist perspective on anorexia nervosa and bulimia. *Signs*, 2 (2), 342–356

Bruch, H. (1973) *Eating Disorders*. New York: Basic Books

Brumberg, J. (1988) *Fasting Girls: The Emergence Of Anorexia Nervosa as a Modern Disease*. Cambridge, MA: Harvard University Press

Chernin, K. (1983) *Womansize: The Tyranny of Slenderness*. London: Women's Press

Dejong, W. and Kleck, R.E. (1986) The social psychological effects of overweight. In C.P. Herman, M.P. Zanna and E.T. Higgins (Eds.) *Physical Appearance, Stigma and Social Behaviour: Third Ontario Symposium in Personality and Social Psychology* (pp. 65–88). Hilllsdale: Erlbaum

Douglas-Wood, A. (1973) The fashionable disease: Women's and their treatment in nineteenth century America. *Journal of Interdisciplinary History*, 4 (1), 25–52

Eckermann, L. (1997) Foucault, embodiment and gendered subjectivities: The case of voluntary self-starvation. In A. Peterson and R. Bunton (Eds.) *Foucault, Health and Medicine*. London: Routledge

Fairburn, C.G. and Cooper, P.J. (1982) Self-induced vomiting and bulimia nervosa: an undetected problem. *British Medical Journal*, 284, 1153–1155

Fallon, P., Katzman, M.A. and Wooley, S.C. (Eds.) (1994) *Feminist Perspectives on Eating Disorders*. London: Guilford

Foucault, M. (1979) *The History of Sexuality, Volume 1* (1990 edn). London: Penguin

Garner, D.M. and Garfinkel, P.E. (1980) Socio-cultural factors in the development of anorexia nervosa. *Psychological Medicine*, 10, 647–656

Garner, D.M., Garfinkel, P.E., Schwartz, D. and Thompson, M. (1980) Cultural expectations of thinness in women. *Psychological Report*, 47, 483–491

Garner, D.M., Garfinkel, P.E. and Olmsted, M.P. (1983) An over-view of socio-cultural factors in the development of anorexia nervosa. In P. Darby, P.E. Garfinkel, D.M. Garner and M.P. Olmsted (Eds.) *Anorexia Nervosa: Recent Developments in Research*. New York: Alan Liss

Grogan, S. (1999) *Body Image*, London: Routledge

Grunewald, K.K. (1985) Weight control in young college women: who are the dieters? *Journal of the American Dietetic Association*, 85 (11), 1445–1450

Gull, W.W. (1874) Anorexia nervosa (apepsia hysterica, anorexia hysterica). *Transactions of the Clinical Society*, 7 (2), 22–28

Heilbrun, A.B. and Friedberg, L. (1990) Distorted body image in normal college women: possible implications for the development of anorexia nervosa. *Journal of Clinical Psychology*, 46 (4), 398–401

Hepworth, J. and Griffin, C.(1995) Conflicting opinions? 'Anorexia nervosa', medicine and feminism. In S. Wilkinson and C. Kitzinger (Eds.) *Feminism and Discourse*. London: Sage

Hesse-Biber, S. (1991). Women, weight and eating disorders: a socio-cultural and political analysis. *Women's Studies International Forum*, 14, 173–191

Hoek, H.W. (1991) The incidence and prevalence of anorexia nervosa and bulimia nervosa in primary care. *Psychological Medicine*, 21 (2), 455–46

Hsu, L.K.G. (1989) The gender gap in eating disorders: why are the eating disorders more common amongst women? *Clinical Psychology Review*, 9, 393–407

Hughes, J. (1991) *An Outline of Modern Psychiatry* (3rd edn). Chichester: Wiley

Huon, G. and Brown, B. (1983) Psychological correlates of weight control amongst anorexia nervosa patients and normal girls. *British Journal of Medical Psychology*, 57, 61–66

Katzman, M.A. and Sing, L. (1997) Beyond body image: The integration of feminist and transcultural theories in the understanding of self-starvation. *International Journal of Eating Disorders*, 22 (4), 385–394

Kenrick, D.T. and Gutierres, S.E. (1980) Contrast effects and judgements of physical attractiveness: When beauty becomes a social problem. *Journal of Personality and Social Psychology*, 38, 131–140

Lasegue, C. (1873) On hysterical anorexia. *Medical Times and Gazette*, 2, 6/27 September, 265–266, 367–369

Lawrence, M. (1984) *The Anorexic Experience*. London: The Women's Press

Littlewood, R. (1991) Against pathology. *British Journal of Psychiatry*, 159, 696–702

Malson, H. (1998) *The Thin Woman: Feminism, Post-Structuralism and the Social Psychology of Anorexia Nervosa*. Routledge, London

Malson, H. (1999). Womæn under erasure: Anorexic bodies in postmodern context. *Journal of Community and Applied Social Psychology*, 9, 137–153

Malson, H. and Ussher, J.M. (1996a) Body poly-texts: discourses of the anorexic body. *Journal of Community and Applied Social Psychology*, 6, 267–280

Malson, H. and Ussher, J.M. (1996b). Bloody women: A discourse analysis of amenorrhea as a symptom of anorexia nervosa. *Feminism and Psychology*, 6 (4), 505–521

Malson, H. and Ussher, J.M. (1997) Beyond this mortal coil: Femininity, death and discursive constructions of the anorexic body. *Mortality*, 2 (1), 43–61

Morrison, T. (1999) *The bluest eye*. London: Vintage

Orbach, S. (1993) *Hunger Strike*. London: Penguin

Passmore, E. (1999) Project. Unpublished manuscript, University of East London

Polivy, J. and Herman, C.P. (1985) Diagnosis and treatment of normal eating. Special Issue: eating disorders, *Journal of Consulting and Clinical Psychology*, 55, 635–644

Riley, D. (1988) *Am I That Name? Feminism and the Category of 'Women' In History*. Basingstoke: Macmillan

Rothblum, E.D. (1994) 'I'll die for the revolution but don't ask me not to diet': Feminism and the continuing stigmatization of obesity. In P. Fallon, M.A. Katzman and S.C Wooley (Eds.) *Feminist Perspectives on Eating Disorders*. New York: Guilford Press

Rothblum, E.D., Brand, P.A., Miller, C.T. and Oetjen, H. (1990) The relationship between obesity, employment discrimination and employment victimization. *Journal of Vocational*

Behaviour, 37, 251–266

Russell, G.F.M. (1979) Bulimia nervosa: an ominous variant of anorexia nervosa. *Psychological Medicine*, 9, 429–448

Sayers, J. (1982) *Biological Politics: Feminist and Anti-Feminist Perspectives*. London: Tavistock

Seid, R.P. (1994) Too 'close to the bone': The historical context for women's obsession with slenderness. In P. Fallon, M.A. Katzman and S.C. Wooley (Eds.) *Feminist Perspectives on Eating Disorders*. London: Guilford

Shaw, J. (1995) Effects of fashion magazines on body dissatisfaction and eating psychopathology in adolescent and adult females. *Eating Disorders Review*, 3 (1) 15–23

Showalter, E. (1985) *The Female Malady: Women, Madness and English Culture, 1830–1980*.London: Virago

Silverstein, B., Peterson, B. and Perdue, L. (1986) Some correlates of the thin standard of bodily attractiveness for women. *International Journal of Eating Disorders*, 5, 895–905

Smith, D.E. (1982) *Texts, Facts and Femininity*

Turner, B.S. (1982) The discourse of diet. In M. Featherstone, M. Hepworth and B.S. Turner (Eds.) (1991) *The Body: Social Process and Cultural Theory*. London: Sage

Turner, B.S. (1992) *Regulating Bodies: Essays in Medical Sociology*. London: Routledge

Unsworth, T and Shattock, R. (1993) Cosmo survey results: your love and hate relationship with food. *Cosmopolitan* (March) 90–95

Ussher, J.M. (1991) *Womens Madness: Misogyny or Mental Illness*. Hemel Hempstead: Harvester Wheatsheaf

Walkerdine, V. (1986) Post-structuralist theory and everyday social practice: The family and the school. In S. Wilkinson (Ed.) *Feminist Social Psychology*. Open University Press, Milton Keynes

Walkerdine, V. (1990) Paper presented at the Discourse and Gender Conference, Birkbeck College, London

Wetherell, M. (1986) Linguistic repertoires and literary criticism: New directions for a social psychology of gender. In S. Wilkinson (Ed.) *Feminist Social Psychology: Developing Theory And Practice*. Milton Keynes: Open University Press

Wolf, N. (1991) *The Beauty Myth: How Images of Beauty Are Used Against Women*. London: Chatto and Windus

Wolf, N. (1994) Hunger. In P. Fallon, M.A. Katzman and S.C. Wooley (Eds.) *Feminist Perspectives On Eating Disorders*. New York: Guilford Press

Wooley, O.W. (1994) And man created 'woman': Representations of women's bodies in Western culture. In P. Fallon, M.A. Katzman and S.C. Wooley (Eds.) *Feminist Perspectives On Eating Disorders*. London: Guilford

Wooley, S.C. and Wooley, O.W. (1984) Feeling fat in a thin society. *Glamour*, February

Wooley, S.C., Fallon, P. and Katzman, M.A. (1994) Introduction. In P. Fallon, M.A. Katzman and S.C Wooley (Eds.) *Feminist Perspectives on Eating Disorders*. New York: Guilford Press

World Health Organisation (1992) *ICD-10*. Geneva: WHO

CHAPTER 42

LOOKING GOOD AND FEELING GOOD: WHY DO FEWER WOMEN THAN MEN EXERCISE?

Precilla Y. L. Choi

INTRODUCTION

In order to answer the question of why fewer women than men participate in physical activity, this chapter critically examines how recreational exercise is promoted to women. It argues that in being promoted as a beauty activity instead of a healthy activity, patriarchal notions of femininity are perpetuated. This can serve to discourage women from taking up and maintaining an exercise program and therefore deny them the physical and psychological benefits that can be attained.

Current consensus indicates that appropriate levels of physical activity can reduce depression and anxiety and increase psychological well-being, and that physically active lifestyles are associated with decreased risk of all-cause mortality, incidence of coronary heart disease, colon cancer and diabetes (Pate *et al.*, 1995). In addition, Choi and Mutrie (1997) concluded from their review that there are particular ways (associated with reproductive function) in which involvement in physical exercise could be particularly beneficial for women. Higher levels of physical activity are associated with less negative mood premenstrually; women who continue to be physically active during pregnancy report more positive body image; and both pre- and post-menopausal women who engage in physical activity report higher levels of psychological well-being and self-esteem compared to those who do not. However, in spite of the physical and psychological benefits of exercise and active health promotion over the last two decades, it is still the case that the majority of the population do not take part in sufficient physical exercise to afford significant health benefits (Allied Dunbar National Fitness Survey (ADNFS), 1992). What is even more worrying are the findings from British (ADNFS, 1992; Office of Population Census and Surveys, 1996), American and Canadian studies (Vertinsky, 1997) that show this to be a greater problem for women than men. Why do fewer women than men take part in regular physical exercise?

PHYSICAL EXERCISE AS A BEAUTY ACTIVITY

Cultural analyses have revealed that nearly every civilization has sought to impose a uniform shape upon the female form (Fallon, 1994) and for the nineties, usually white, woman the social pressures in relation to her body are not just to be slim (see Grogan, Malson and Nasser, in this volume). Her body must also be firm and well toned, reflecting the cultural and societal acceptance of physical exercise that has permeated notions of the ideal body over the last two decades in Western societies (Bordo, 1990). There is significant potential, therefore, for a woman's participation in physical activity to be influenced by this social pressure concerning her body and indeed this is borne out in the considerable psychological research that has examined motivational factors implicated in participating in physical exercise (see Biddle, 1995). One consistent finding from this research, is that significantly more women than men report weight control and physical appearance as reasons for exercising (e.g. Canada Fitness Survey, 1983; ADNFS, 1992; Markland and Hardy, 1993; Davis, *et al.* 1995). This suggests that physical exercise is seen as a beauty activity as well as or instead of a health activity. Consider this quote from one of Drew's

(1996) research participants in her qualitative study of motivations to exercise:

I exercise if I need it at the time – depending on whether I am dieting or not ... if I was lovely and slim I wouldn't be obliged to go and do any [exercise] and that is it really. Partly the health benefit that I could improve my figure. (Drew, 1996a: 63)

Here the research participant sees an 'improved figure' as an indicator of health. If her figure was better she would be healthier ('lovely') and would not need to exercise. This has also been very apparent to me in my discussions with women at sports centres, gyms and other exercise settings. 'Why are you here when you are not fat?' is a question that I am frequently asked. (Incidentally, many of the women who ask me this are not fat either but seem to be implying that they are.)

Morse (1988) has argued that physical exercise has become the latest commodity in the highly commercialized beauty culture. Instead of being promoted to women as a way of improving physical and psychological health, it is promoted as a way of losing weight and improving muscle tone and appearance. Furthermore, this weight loss and improved appearance are equated with health. An example of how this occurs is illustrated in Duncan's (1994) qualitative analysis of the American health and fitness magazine *Shape*. In the 1992 September and October issues of the magazine success stories of women who had improved their bodies were featured. Instead of reporting resting heart rate, cholesterol levels and blood pressure – the true indicators of health and fitness – measurements of bust size, hips, waist, pounds and percentage of body fat lost were given. As changes in some of these measurements have little to do with fitness or health, Duncan (1994) suggests that the aim of the magazine is to deceive the reader into believing that it is inch loss that will lead to improved health. She argues:

Why else would Shape document these measurements? Furthermore, these charts invite the reader to compare her measurements to those of the model. The implicit message: How well do YOU measure up, compared to our healthy, lovely model? (55–56)

Moreover, Duncan points out the assumption of *Shape* magazine that women's bodies are flawed and that every woman should try to improve. An invitation to reshape their bodies is extended to all readers, not just those who are overweight or unshapely.

Not only will inch loss improve health, it will also lead to an improved life! Consider this extract from *Shape*, analysed as part of Markula's (1995) ethnographic study of the aerobics sub-culture:

If you balk at pool-party invitations; if you lie awake at night wondering how to cover your thighs while keeping cool and looking great; if you seriously consider moving to Antarctica as soon as the hot weather sets in – this workout is for you. (434)

This voice of liberation – endless pool parties without worry – masks a control of women by a patriarchal society where the body is always imperfect.

WOMEN'S IMPERFECT BODIES

To perfect the body it is fragmented into problem parts such as stomach, thighs, bottoms and under-arms and special exercises in order to tone them are recommended (Markula, 1995). Whole exercise classes devoted to these such as the 'Tums, Bums and Thighs' classes appear to be hugely popular in Britain. Advertising of exercise videos also emphasize that the exercises will address these problem areas. Consider the promotional text of two exercise videos produced by *Cosmopolitan* magazine which I saw advertised in the March 1994 U.K. issue:

The latest fat-burning cardiovascular step challenge! Plus a fantastic toning section for a flatter stomach and a trimmer waist. (Cosmopolitan Step Workout video)

The ultimate body toning workout to firm your stomach, tone your thighs and shape up your bustline. (Cosmopolitan Tonetics video)

These so-called problem areas happen to be some of those that biologically distinguish women from men. Optimum female reproductive function requires sufficient levels of body fat and women are biologically predisposed to store this fat in the breast, hip, thigh and stomach areas. Consistently being told that these areas are problematic leads to dissatisfaction with the female form.

Of course, participation in physical exercise can provide true health benefits irrespective of the primary motive, being beauty. As one exercise guru says of aerobics: 'they [women] go to the program to improve their looks and get fitness and health as fringe benefits' (Cooper, 1970: 134). It could, therefore, be asked why it matters if women are motivated to exercise for beauty when they will still attain health benefits through participation regardless.

One reason why it matters is that in a beauty-related exercise subculture, alongside the belief that beauty will result from exercise, this can also translate into a belief that one has to be beautiful in order to exercise.

I love doing aerobics but since I changed jobs I've put on weight so I've stopped going. I wouldn't be seen dead in a leotard. (Drew, 1996a: 63)

Swimming here is a nightmare, there is definitely a negative loop in my motivation. There's a wonderful pool in Northern California where the women are all at least fourteen stone and it's heaven for me. It's wonderful to feel almost thin. (Drew, 1996a: 63)

Women, therefore, might be discouraged from taking part in some forms of exercise because the emphasis on appearance fosters finding fault with their bodies (Davis, 1997). Thus, instead of having a positive effect on body image, a negative body image may be reinforced.

A second reason why it matters is that the physiological evidence indicates that it is not possible to lose fat in a very specific area by working the underlying group of muscles (Sharkey, 1990). A goal of inch loss in the above-mentioned problem areas as a result of exercise is, therefore, unrealistic so, analogous with the diet industry, women are being sold a false premise by the fitness industry. Furthermore, motivation to exercise which begins with unrealistic goals is more likely to lead to drop-out (Biddle and Mutrie, 1991). This is important because it is only through long-term adherence to physical exercise that health benefits are realized.

A third reason is that in an environment of beauty-related exercise, there is little opportunity to take pride in attaining the real health benefits of exercise. For example, one woman in Markula's (1995) ethnographic study felt pride and shame simultaneously in her increased physical strength:

It is really contradictory, because the very things that I do in aerobics, like my class always has this long session of push-ups, I'm strong and I feel uncomfortable with that, but at the same time I'm proud of that, not proud, that makes me feel good about myself to be strong, but I don't know. (439)

This sense of contradiction stems from the current ideal body that is slim and toned, not strong, and the traditional notions of gender that equate strength with masculinity, not femininity. Empowerment, a term often associated with sport and physical exercise, refers to 'the confident sense of self that comes from being skilled in the use of one's body' (Whitson, 1994: 354). The above quote from Markula (1995) illustrates how, in an environment where exercise is undertaken to improve the imperfect body in order to look more beautiful, not to strengthen it in order to be more physically able, there is little pride to be had in the increased strength that inevitably occurs. This is not empowering.

EMPOWERING WOMEN THROUGH EXERCISE

Sport and physical exercise are key areas (previously reserved for men) which have allowed women access to success and expression of bodily strength and skill. Through physical activity many women can be, and are, empowered by the reinforcement of positive attitudes towards their bodies and a sense of power from their physical abilities (Theberge, 1987). For example, a number of women in Markula's (1995) study did not exercise for beauty reasons but to be strong and independent:

because if I am physically strong, I can do things that I want to do: I can unscrew jam jars – I don't have to ask some guys to do it for me – I can put the trash out;

I can lift things. I don't like feeling weak and helpless and end up asking people to do things for me. (438)

SUMMARY

It is certainly not the case that all women who exercise or take part in sport do so for beauty reasons or that all *Shape* readers believe their bodies to be flawed. However, in attempting to answer the question: 'Why do fewer women than men exercise?', I propose that the construction of physical exercise as a beauty product is a way of controlling women's bodies. Beauty-related exercise limits perceptions of the female body and perpetuates patriarchal notions of femininity (Hargreaves, 1994) and thus results in fewer women than men exercising in (at least) two ways. Firstly, many women resist patriarchal notions of the ideal body and therefore shun the 'exercise for beauty' discourse, but in the absence of an alternative exercise discourse they are not motivated to take part. Secondly, as I have already argued, for those women who are motivated to take part for beauty reasons the unrealistic goals and/or increased body disatisfaction may lead them to drop out.

A whole host of other factors specific to women may also influence their non-involvement in physical exercise. Examples from sociological research include barriers such as inadequate street lighting, poor public transport, lack of childcare facilities as well as ethnic and religious factors such as strict codes of dress (Women's Sports Foundation, 1995). Moreover, even in this age of greater equality households, caring responsibilities continue to be a barrier for women but not for men (ADNFS, 1992; Drew, 1996b). In encouraging more women to exercise, health promotion must change from an androcentric approach within a patriarchal framework to a more woman-centered approach. Social barriers must continue to be addressed in order to move towards greater equality of opportunity. The potential for true physical and psychological health, as opposed to beauty, must be emphasized and the exercise subculture must facilitate empowerment by emphasizing mastery over outcomes, by celebrating the physical achievements of all participants, and by including all participants whatever their body shape and size.

REFERENCES

Allied Dunbar National Fitness Survey (1992). London: Sports Council and Health Education Authority

Biddle, S. (1995) Exercise motivation across the lifespan. In S.J.H. Biddle (Ed.) *European Perspectives on Exercise and Sport Psychology*. Champaign: Human Kinetics

Biddle, S. and Mutrie, N. (1991) *The Psychology of Physical Activity*. Berlin: Springer-Verlag

Bordo, S. (1990) Reading the slender body. In M. Jacobus, E. Fox Keller, and S. Shuttleworth (Eds.) *Body/Politics: Women and the Discourse of Science* (pp. 83–112). New York: Routledge

Canada Fitness Survey (1983) *Fitness and Lifestyle in Canada*. Ottawa: Canada Fitness Survey

Choi, P.Y.L. and Mutrie, N. (1997) The psychological benefits of physical exercise for women: improving employee quality of life. In J. Kerr, A. Griffiths and T. Cox (Eds.) *Workplace Health: Employee Fitness and Exercise*. London: Taylor & Francis

Cooper, K.H.(1970) *New Aerobics*. Philadelphia: Lippincott

Davis, C. (1997) Body image, exercise and eating behaviours. In K.R. Fox (Ed.) *The Physical Self: From Motivation To Well Being* (pp. 143–174). Champaign: Human Kinetics

Davis, C., Fox, J., Brewer, H. and Ratusny, D. (1995) Motivations to exercise as a function of personality characteristics, age and gender. *Personality and Individual Differences*, 19 (2), 165–174

Drew, S. (1996a) Subjectivity and contextuality in understanding and changing inactivity. In C. Robson, B. Cripps and H. Steinberg (Eds.) *Quality and Quantity: Research Methods in Sport and Exercise Psychology* (pp. 60–66). London: British Psychological Society

Drew, S. (1996b) Moving towards active living: understanding the contextual nature of barriers to physical activity. *Health Psychology Update*, 23, 10–14

Duncan, M.C. (1994) The politics of women's body images and practices: Foucault, the panopticon and *Shape* magazine. *Journal of Sport and Social Issues*, 18, 48–65

Fallon, A.E. (1994) Body image and the regulation of weight. In V.J. Adesso, D.M. Reddy and R. Fleming (Eds.) *Psychological Perspectives on Women's Health* (pp. 127–180). London: Taylor & Francis

Hargreaves, J. (1994) *Sporting Females*. London: Routledge

Markland, D. and Hardy, L. (1993) The exercise motivations inventory: preliminary development and validity of a measure of individuals reasons for participation in regular exercise. *Personality and Individual Differences*, 15 (3), 289–296

Markula, P. (1995) Firm but shapely, fit but sexy, strong but thin: postmodern aerobicizing female bodies. *Sociology of Sport Journal*, 12, 424–453

Morse, M. (1988) Artemis ageing: exercise and the female body on video. *Discourse*, 10, 20–53

Mutrie, N. (1995), Sport and exercise psychology. In G. McLatchie, M. Harries, C. Williams and J.B. King (Eds.) *A.B.C. of Sports Medicine* (pp. 88–91). London: BMJ Publishing Group

Office of Population Census and Surveys (1996) *Living in Britain: Results from the 1993 General Household Survey*. London: HMSO

Pate, R.R., Pratt, M., Blair, S.N., Haskell, W.L., Macera, C.A., Bouchard, C., Buchner, D., Ettinger, W., Heath, G.W., King, A.C., Kriska, A., Leon, A.S., Marcus, B.H., Morris, J., Paffenbarger, R.S., Patrick, K., Pollock, M.L., Rippe, J.M., Sallis, J. and Wilmore, J.H. (1995) Physical activity and public health. *Journal of the American Medical Association*, 273, 402–407

Sharkey, B.J. (1990). *Physiology of fitness* (3rd edn). Champaign: Human Kinetics

Theberge, N. (1987) Sport and women's empowerment. *Women's Studies International Forum*, 10 (4), 387–393

Vertinsky, P. (1997) Physical activity, sport and health for girls and women: issues and perspectives. Paper presented at the Pre-Olympic Scientific Congress, Dallas, July 1996 and reprinted in the *Bulletin of the International Association of Physical Education and Sport for Girls and Women*, 7 (1), 1–15

Whitson, D. (1994) The embodiment of gender: discipline, domination and empowerment. In S. Birrel and C. Cole (Eds.) *Women, Sport and Culture*. Champaign, IL: Human Kinetics

Women's Sports Foundation (1995) *Women and Sport: A Syllabus Guide for Teachers and Lecturers*. London: Women's Sports Foundation

CHAPTER 43

GENDER, CULTURE AND EATING DISORDERS

Mervat Nasser

INTRODUCTION

Feminist theories suggest that conflicts over gender definition could be at the heart of the vulnerability of modern Western women to eating pathology. These gender-specific issues of eating disorders have commonly been discussed in connection with the position of women in the Western industrialized world. In so doing the feminist argument failed to address these issues in their wider cultural context. Women in other cultures were thought to be immune from such conflicts by virtue of well-defined sex roles as well as adherence to traditional family structures. These factors were thought to afford them protective mechanisms against developing such disorders. However recent epidemiological data showed the emergence of eating disorders in many of the societies that were initially thought to be free of such problems.

The emergence of eating disorders in other cultures/ societies was commonly attributed to 'Westernization', arguably mediated by homogenized media icons. However the use of Westernization as a concept proved to be rather simplistic as it failed again to address the true societal forces that shape 'bodies' and 'genders'. There was a need therefore to attempt to connect 'gender' with 'culture' and particularly examine the issue of *gender imbalance at times of culture change*. This necessitated a shift in our thinking from the traditional 'weight focussed' approach to 'identity'. Within this new framework other possible anorexic equivalents could also emerge which share with the main anorexic syndrome the same underlying sociocultural dynamics There are a number of pressures that are now placed upon women globally which convey conflicting cultural messages. Hence eating disorders and other possible anorexic equivalents need to be seen as adaptation strategies or problem-solving tactics, helping women worldwide in their pursuit of self-definition within the progressive differentiation of societies under change.

THE EVOLUTION OF BODY REGULATION AS SYMBOLIC OF GENDER AND CULTURAL IDENTITY

Starvation, vomiting and purging following bingeing, are all self-inflicted body regulatory mechanisms that collectively came to be known as eating disorders. This is a term that encompasses between its two extremes, anorexia and bulimia, a spectrum of weight/shape focussed behaviors of varying degrees of morbidity (see chapters by Malson and by Grogan, in this volume).

The weight and menstrual loss characteristic of the anorexic syndrome initially suggested the presence of a biological substrate (Russell, 1970). However anorexia nervosa was soon to change its identity from a rare hypothalamic disorder to a 'disorder of identity' within a pathological framework of familial interactions. The anorexic behavior began to be seen as resulting from a failure of individuality or incomplete identity within the domestic circle (Selvini-Pallazoli, 1974, Bruch, 1978). Inherent in the theory of identity, is the significance of the body as a 'locus for control'.

Ego psychologists made inferences as to the possible association between environmental/ societal changes and these disorders, namely the emergence of the middle class, the bourgeois values, the move towards a nuclear family and the creation of adolescence. However the thrust of their argument was by and large gender neutral and individual focussed. The questions of Why women? and Why now? remained largely unanswered.

In an attempt to address this issue, the 'identity hypothesis' was further extended and the notion of external demands, advanced by Bruch (1978), was carried further to embrace all the societal demands put on women. The pursuit of thinness became metaphorical of woman's striving to formulate a new identity in the face of changing societal roles (Orbach, 1986; Wolf, 1990; Gordon, 1990). The issue of gender and eating disorders became the subject of extensive analysis; it was posited that anorexia nervosa could indeed be saying something about 'what it means to be a woman in the Western culture' (Malson, 1998). The anorexic syndrome changed from being an obscure morbidity to a public predicament, a metaphor for, and a manifestation of a multiplicity of socio-cultural concerns of the late twentieth century (Turner, 1992; Malson and Ussher,1996; see chapters by Helen Malson and Sarah Grogan, in this volume).

FROM 'WESTERN TO WESTERNIZED': THE FEMINIST/CULTURAL SPLIT

This feminist perspective, while offering individual and varying analyses that made a notable contribution to the understanding of the anorexic phenomenon, was nonetheless limited by not addressing its full sociological scope. The focus has always been on the demands of one specific cultural setting, namely the Western culture. The social mandate of feminine thinness is firmly rooted in Western cultural values and beliefs. The morbid pursuit of thinness thus evolved into a 'culture-bound ' psychopathology. The link between gender and culture was referred to in transcultural research, where it was suggested that women run a higher risk of developing culture-bound psychopathology more than men (Littlewood, 1986).

However, in research on eating disorders, this link has been absent.

Arguably, the gender-specific conflicts that were considered the basis for eating disorders were seen as belonging exclusively to Western women. Other women remained immune. Many feminist theories were influenced by a stereotyped view and a fixed notion of other cultures, often seeing non-Western societies as static and lacking the potential for change. Non-Western women were assumed to be protected from the turmoil facing women in the West through different aesthetic values, maintained traditional family structures and clear-cut gender definitions.

However in an analysis of 'feminism across cultures', Nasser (1997) pointed to the fact that feminist movements similar to those in the West also arose in other non-Western societies, resulting in questions and debates around traditional gender roles. The majority of non-Western women have significantly changed their position over recent years, with increasing numbers being highly educated and working outside the family. It is clear therefore that the pressures that are hypothesized to increase Western women's propensity to eating disorders are now shared by all other women, hence there are no convincing grounds to continue with the assumed immunity of the *other* women.

Another dimension to the argument of the 'culture specificity' of eating psychopathology was derived from the apparent absence of these morbid behaviors in other cultures. This notion of rarity was supported by the scarcity of published epidemiological material on the subject at that time. However, a review of recently published research in this field challenged this assumption and pointed to the emergence of these disorders in societies and cultures that were for a long time presumed immune to this pathology. This research included case reports of eating disorders among different ethnic groups in the U.S.A. and the U.K. as well as community studies of disordered eating behaviors in Japan, the Middle East, China, South America and Africa. Contrary to original thought, the results of these investigations showed eating disorders to be occurring in these societies with similar or even higher rates than those reported in the West (Nasser, 1997).

The culprit for this apparent global emergence of eating pathology was largely explained in terms of 'Westernization'. Once they had surpassed their specific geographical sites of culture-boundedness, eating disorders became 'Western induced phenomenon'. This meant that the phenomenon continued to be seen within the limited remit of the concept of one culture, i.e. the 'West' – if it is not exclusively 'Western' it had to be 'Westernized'. This concept of Westernization was often restricted to the process of identification with Western values in relation to weight and shape preferences for women. This is commonly attributed to the power of 'the global media' in disseminating these values and its role in shaping and homogenizing public perceptions in this respect. The pressure to 'remake the body' to match this newly unified cultural aesthetic ideal is now seen to be universally propagated through international commercial advertising and worldwide satellite networks.

The argument that women identify with 'unified media', informed by a central Western cultural value system, is rather simplistic. This concept clearly fails to explain the intra-Western variations, such as the higher rates of this morbidity in the American society compared to central Europe (Neumarker *et al.*, 1992) or intra-European variations. Also the concept of 'Westernization' does not offer a sufficient reason for the emergence of eating pathology in Eastern Europe following the recent economic and political changes (Rathner *et al.*, 1995), or the observed increase in prevalence after the fall of the Apartheid regime among black South Africans girls, who were previously exposed to white/Western values (Le Grange *et al.*, 1998).

Westernization does not tell us either why eating disorders morbidity has increased in the kibbutzim by 800 percent in the past 25 years (Kaffman and Sadeh, 1989) or the reasons behind the differences in eating disorders rates between the 'north' and the 'south' of Italy, (Ruggiero *et al.*, in press). It would not provide us with a plausible explanation as to the differences in the rates between urban and rural Japan, or give reasons for the 100 percent increase in incidence of anorexia nervosa reported there over a five-year period (Ohezeki *et al.*, 1990; Suematsu *et al.*, 1985).

The most problematic aspect of the concept of 'Westernization', however, is the fact that it is reductionist. It simply does not tell us how the 'outside' gets 'inside'. It merely deals with the body as a passive template over which cultural discourses are written, disconnecting it from the internal processes of the individual (Lester, 1997). The concept of Westernization is therefore limited; it does not go far enough in exploring the constituent forces that truly shape bodies and genders. There is a need to look into these forces in more depth and to understand the processes through which they impact on the individual's sense of identity and the presentation of distress. These societal forces include increasing levels of urbanization, the worldwide adoption of markets as an economic strategy, the disappearance of traditional family structures and the imminent threat to national identity. All of these forces are no longer a predicament of one particular culture but a worldwide concern.

BODY POLITICS AND CULTURAL ANOREXIC EQUIVALENTS

Foucault (1977) saw individuals as the vehicles of power and the body as the site where dissent is articulated. The notion of 'rebellion through the body' is integral to the feminist analysis of the anorexic position, where anorexia is seen as a form of body control assumed by women in the absence of real control or power in other areas of their lives (Orbach, 1986). However, the weight-focussed approach to body control in eating pathology and its limited application to one culture hindered the full definition of the cultural meaning of the body as dependent on the existing social structure and subsequently a platform for various forms of interpretation and regulation.

This myopic view, which tended to see culture as a mere geographic or national entity, has been instrumental in creating a split between the individual and the culture, leading to the marginalization of the body as a medium for negotiating social change. From this vantage point, eating disorders can not mean 'media induced pathology', simply encouraged by women's susceptibility to 'media image identification' and promoted by the prevailing Western cultural ideal of thinness with its current global perspective.

Arguably, the body pathology (or body control), encountered in eating disorders is more likely to be reflective of self-control and self-definition and therefore needs to be seen as a social coping strategy (albeit morbid) used by women in an attempt to negotiate power within societies undergoing change. This view should encourage us to look deeply into the issue of power imbalance, rather than focus solely on gender (Katzman, 1997). Perhaps the study of peculiarities in the presentation of the anorexic phenomenon in other societies and the other variants of body control could widen our horizons in this respect. Such analysis is likely to give us an idea of the scale of worldwide societal change and the kind of pressures that are now placed upon women globally.

The following three situations provide a window on the impact of societal changes on women's sense of their self and body, and hint at the reservoir of knowledge that remains largely untapped.

SELF-STARVATION AS A LOST VOICE

Katzman and Lee (1997) argued that the over-reliance on the dread of fatness as a diagnostic criterion in eating psychopathology has led to an overall underestimation of the magnitude of these problems in societies where women are normally underweight even by Western standards, such as China, Japan and India. They added that the weight/thinness-focussed approach to the anorexic phenomenon has also failed to address the true meaning of 'self starvation' in cultures like China. In an investigation of a group of anorexic females in Hong Kong, more than half of the population studied displayed no conscious fear of becoming fat (Lee *et al.*, 1993). In another study, carried out on a similar population in Singapore, none of the participants reported symptoms that can be connected with fat phobia (Kok and Tian, 1994).

Historically, self-starvation in the absence of weight obsessions can be traced back to ascetic forms of food denial, where the power of food refusal was seen as a metaphor for individual power and a pursuit of individual freedom. Bell (1985) argued that the fasting of the medieval Italian female saint is not dissimilar to the anorexic pursuit of thinness; each pursues her externally different but psychologically analogous objective with compulsive devotion. The style of presentation of the female saint was obviously rooted in the religious framework of the medieval era. Curiously, this ascetic denial of food also appeared to correspond to periods in history where individual opportunities for overt recognition were generally curtailed (Vanderycken and Van Deth, 1993).

In this way, Lee (1995) explained self-starvation in China as symbolic of loss of voice in a social world perceived to be oppressive. He derived support for his interpretation of 'food refusal and food phobia' in Chinese society from Littlewood's (1995) assertion that South Asian women have the tendency to use self-starvation as a means of achieving a kind of self-determination in the face of conflicting social demands.

TYRANNY OF SLENDERNESS OR TYRANNY OF MARKETS

If self-starvation in China is voicing women's struggle to cope with an ambivalent social environment, the emergence of eating pathology in East Europe after the major politico-economic changes also seems to be conveying the same message. The worldwide adoption of free markets has created a major social and cultural upheaval, particularly for those countries that previously had a state-controlled economy. The undermining of the socialist collectivist structure in former communist Europe, the kibbutzim, China and other countries that experimented with socialist regimes contributed towards increased women's ambiguity and confusion over their position in society and their gender roles.

In countries where socialist policies prevailed for a time, women's sense of value appeared to derive from taking part in an overall social policy with no link being made between their sense of inner worth and their external appearance. Women were also protected in their education, employment and child care. There was full acceptance of women's work and over-employment to ensure full employment was the rule in these countries. With economic reform, market forces are now pushing the unproductive labor out and women are more likely than men to be casualties of this exercise. It has been said that the dictatorship of the party has been replaced by the dictatorship of the market.

In an analysis of the new definitions of gender in the post-socialist era, I have previously argued (Nasser, 1997) that the political changes following the decline of communism have led to reformulations of the position and the role of women in these societies. Greater disparity began to emerge between what women expected of themselves and what they thought society expected of them. The higher the degree of societal ambivalence about the expectations of women, the greater the ambiguity that women experience of their role and the more likely to resort to 'body' as a milieu for expressing this confusion and distress.

THE NEW VEILING PHENOMENON

Perhaps my biggest contention here is to consider the new veiling phenomenon as an anorexic equivalent. The act of veiling – not different from subjecting the body to anorexic transformation – entails the extinguishing of the three-dimensionality of the body and the editing out of any diversity, leading to a false homogenization of the body (Becker and Hamburg,

1996). The new veiling initially began two decades ago in countries like Egypt and was taken up in increasing numbers by young educated and working women. This is no longer restricted to the Middle East. Veiling is currently being adopted by many young Moslem women of various national backgrounds all over the world. The phenomenon clearly invites special analysis that go beyond the generalized reactivation of tradition or the simple notion of Islamic resurgence. The adoption of the veil by women in those societies is a deliberate act of choice that makes a personal statement in response to conflicting pressures and competing cultural values.

Macleod (1991) asked why women would now reduplicate conditions which seem to represent their subordination less than a century ago. She saw these women as caught between a drive towards modernity and ambitious economic goals, and traditional female identity. Under the circumstances the act of veiling can be seen as 'accommodating protest', a peculiar way of resolving the conflicting struggle of the woman as wife/mother and the woman as worker. This analysis is again not distant from the feminist analysis of the Western anorexic position.

The contradictory intentions signaled by adopting the veil seem to reflect the contradictory messages that face women today. Both the anorexic and the young veiled woman internalize their own struggle for true autonomy into one with their own body – though disguised as a struggle to achieve a socially valued goal. (I have referred to this as 'rebellion through conformity' (Nasser, 1997).) It is important nonetheless to point to the fact that this covering the body is not associated with seclusion. It is purely a woman's desire to hide while remaining firmly present in the public domain. These cloths are subject to women's control but also symbolic of women's constraints which clearly reflect their ambiguous position.

Chernin (1986) argues that the anorexic position adopted by women signifies a hidden struggle for self-development at a turning point in both the individual woman's life and women's history as a whole, which may paradoxically lead to a collective refusal of this self-development and a rejection of the freedom opportunities that seem available to her in response to an inner historical voice constantly questioning the legitimacy of female development. The 'dietary ritual' or the 'dress ritual' may therefore be seen as unspoken rites of passage, in the absence of cultural reference for women to express themselves in the process of self-development; a peculiar choice that is taken up by a sizeable group, as if it is an attempt towards performing a collective ritual that may eventually succeed in enabling identity creation and ultimately female social development.

Both anorexia and the veil form systems of messages conveyed through the body. In their gestures of self-discipline/control they lead to a sense of distinction, superiority and moral elevation. Both are forms of veiled resistance adopted by women who are torn between tradition and modernity; they represent both women's and society's ambivalence about women's progress and development. However the reasons why a young woman would choose the veil or the anorexic look is open to speculation and bound by a set of circumstances, namely class and economic structures. In contrast to anorexia, the veil was commonly associated with women from lower middle-class backgrounds, a mode of protest that is perhaps used by a subordinate group in response to inequalities of both class and gender (Nasser, in press).

SUMMARY

In the past two decades the whole world has faced global changes. It has become clear that human distress is now being shaped by the same universal forces – social, political and economic. In this analysis I have attempted to explain the use of the body as a medium for expressing distress, through an integrated cultural and feminist model. The ultrathinness of the Western anorexic position, the self-starvation without weight phobia in China, or the adoption of the veil by educated and working young women in the Middle East, are all symbolic gestures of women's pursuit of self-definition within societies undergoing change. These are coping mechanisms adopted by women in response to paradoxical cultural pressures and contradictory sets of social conditions. They are social actions disguised as morbidity; their purpose is to help women cope with forces of transition and bridge the gap between nostalgia and futurism.

REFERENCES

Becker, A. and Hamburg, P. (1996) Culture, the media and eating disorders. *Harvard Rev. Psychiatry*, 4, 163–167
Bell, I. R. (1985) *Holy Anorexia*. Chicago: University of Chicago Press
Bruch, H.(1978) *The Golden Cage: The Enigma of Anorexia Nervosa*. London: Open University Books
Chernin, K. (1986) *The Hungry Self: Women Eating and Identity*. London: Virago
Foucault, M. (1977) *Discipline and Punish: The Birth of the Prison* (1987 edn). London: Penguin
Gordon, R. (1990) *Anorexia and Bulimia: Anatomy of a Social Epidemic*. Cambridge, MA: Basil Blackwell
Kaffman, M. and Sadeh, T. (1989) Anorexia nervosa in the Kibbutz: factors influencing the development of monoideistic fixation. *Int. J. Eating. Disord.*, 8 (1), 33–53
Katzman, M.A. (1997) Getting the difference right: It is power not gender that matters. *Euro. Eat. Dis. Review*, 5 (20), 71–74
Katzman, M.A. and Lee, S. (1997) Beyond body image: The integration of feminist and transcultural theories in understanding self starvation. *Int. J. Eat. Dis.*, 22, 385–394
Kok, I.P. and Tian, C.S. (1994) Susceptibility of Singapore Chinese schoolgirls to anorexia nervosa: Part 1(psychological factors). *Singapore Medical Journal*, 35, 481–485
Lee, S. (1995) Self starvation in context: towards a culturally sensitive understanding of anorexia nervosa. *Soc. Sci. Med.*, 41, 25–36
Lee, S., Ho, T.P. and Hsu, L.K.G. (1993) Fat phobic and non-fat phobic anorexia nervosa: A comparative study of 70 Chinese patients. *Hong Kong. Psychological Medicine*, 23, 999–1017
Lester, R.J. (1997) The(dis)embodied self in anorexia nervosa. *Soc. Sci. Med.*, 44 (4); 479–489
Le Grange, D., Telch, C.F. and Tibbs, J. (1998) Eating attitudes and behaviours in 1,435 South African Caucasian and non-Caucasian College Students. *Am. J. Psychiatry*, 155 (2), 250–254
Littlewood, R. (1986) Russian dolls and chinese boxes: an anthropological approach to the implicit models of comparative psychiatry. In J. Cox (Ed.) *Transcultural Psychiatry*. London: Croom Helm
Littlewood, R. (1995) Psychopathology and personal agency: Modernity, culture change and eating disorders in South Asian societies. *British Journal of Medical Psychology*, 68, 45–63

Macleod, A. (1991) *Accomodating Protest: Working Women, the New Veiling and Change in Cairo*. New York: Columbia University Press

Malson, H. (1998) *The Thin Woman: Feminism, Post-Structuralism and the Social Psychology of Anorexia Nervosa*. London: Routledge

Malson, H. and Ussher, J. (1996) Body poly-texts discourses of the anorexic body. *Journal of Community and Applied Psychology*, 6, 267–280

Nasser, M. (1997) *Culture and Weight Consciousness*. London: Routledge

Nasser, M. (1999) The new veiling phenomenon: is it an anorexic equivalent? A polemic. *Journal of Community and Applied Psychology*, 9, 407–412

Neumarker, U., Dudeck, U., Voltrath, M., Neumarker, K. and Steinhausen, H. (1992) Eating attitudes among adolescent anorexia nervosa patients and normal subjects in former West and East Berlin: a transcultural comparison. *Int.J. Eating Disord.*, 12 (3), 281–289

Ohzeki, T., Haanaki, K., Motozumi, H., Ishitani, N., Maatsuda-Ohatahra, H., Sunaguchi, M. and Shiraki, K. (1990) Prevalence of obesity, leanness and anorexia nervosa in Japanese boys and girls aged 12–14 years. *Ann. Nutrition and Metabolism*, 34, 208–212

Orbach, S. (1986) *Hunger Strike: The Anorexic Struggle as a Metaphor For Our Age*. New York: Norton

Rathner, G., Tury, F., Szabo, P., Geyer, M., Rumpold, G., Forgaces, A., Sollner, W. and Plottner, N. (1995) Prevalence of eating disorders and minor psychiatric morbidity in central Europe before the political changes of 1989: A cross-cultural study. *Psychological Medicine*, 25, 1027–1035

Rugggiero, G.M., Hanover, W., Mantero, M., Feerari, N., Papa, R. and Cavagnini, X. (in press) Body disatisfaction and acceptance of mass media appearance ideals in northern and southern Italian non clinical girls and in underweight and non underweight eating disorders girls. *Eating and Weight Disorders*

Russell, G.F.M. (1970) Anorexia nervosa: its identity as an illness and its treatment. In J. Harding-Price (Ed.) *Modern Psychological Medicine*, Vol. 2 (pp. 131–164). London: Butterworths

Selvini-Pallazoli, M. (1974) *Self Starvation: From the Individual to Family Therapy in the Treatment of Anorexia Nervosa* (trans. by A. Pomerans) (2nd edn). New York: Jason Aronson

Suematsu, H., Ishikawa, H., Kuboki, T. and Ito, T. (1985) Statistical studies of anorexia nervosa in Japan, detailed clinical data on 1,011 patients. *Psychotherapy and Psychosomatics*, 43, 96–103

Turner, B.S. (1992) *Regulating Bodies: Essays in Medical Sociology*. London: Routledge

Vandereycken, W. and van Deth, R. (1993) *The History of Self Starvation: From Fasting to Anorexic Girls*. London: Athlone Press

Wolf, N. (1990) *The Beauty Myth*. London: Chatto & Windus

CHAPTER 44

WOMEN WITH ANDROGEN INSENSITIVITY SYNDROME (AIS)

Celia Kitzinger

INTRODUCTION

Androgen insensitivity syndrome (AIS) in women is a form of intersexuality – an unusual but naturally occurring combination of chromosomes, gonads and genitals which does not fit into the culturally constructed two-sex system. Although this diagnostic category has only been developed in the past 50 years (with the advent of chromosomal testing), AIS women have always existed (see Dreger, 1998) and there is speculation that both Queen Elizabeth I and Joan of Arc may have been androgen insensitive.

All AIS women are conceived with XY chromosomes – the usual male pattern. As with ordinary XY embryos, differentiation in the early stage of foetal life is as a male. The testes form and produce a hormone which suppresses the development of the internal female organs (the fallopian tubes, uterus, cervix, and the upper third of the vagina) and they also produce androgen which, in most XY foetuses leads to the development of the penis. About one in every 20,000 XY foetuses is completely insensitive to androgen (CAIS) and instead develops external genitalia which at birth are generally indistinguishable from those of ordinary XX baby girls. About half of these are diagnosed as CAIS in infancy because they have a swelling (hernia) in the groin area, which upon investigation turns out to be undescended testes. Some other XY foetuses are only partially insensitive to androgen (PAIS) and they develop larger clitorises and labial fusion, sometimes – depending on the degree of androgen insensitivity (see Quigley *et al.*, 1995 for a grading scheme) – to the extent of having 'ambiguous' genitals (i.e. not clearly 'male' or 'female') or a small penis and scrotum (some PAIS babies are reared as males). For a clear and straightforward explanation of AIS, see Warne, 1997.

Many of the difficulties faced by women with AIS, as for other intersex people, are caused not by their biology, but by the society in which they live (see Newman, in this volume). Doctors are often confused, dismayed or appalled by AIS and do not give truthful and accurate information either to women with AIS or to their parents. The mother of a 10-month-old baby was told by the surgeon who discovered testicles: 'basically you've got a little boy with a girl's genitals; take it home and bring it up as a girl' (this was in 1993!); another was advised to put her AIS daughter up for adoption and try again for a 'real' girl. Doctors have lied to parents (and, later, to the daughters), with stories of 'twisted' or 'cancerous' ovaries, or a 'diseased uterus', leaving women to grapple with, as one woman expressed it, 'the sense of being an outsider without knowing just what kind of outsider I was'. The hushed conversations, the embarrassment of doctors, the explanations which don't add up, lead women and girls with AIS to the belief that they have a defect so monstrous that nobody is willing to discuss it.

Many CAIS girls are diagnosed at puberty when they fail to start their periods, but are often given misleading information (or told downright lies) about their bodies. One woman had exploratory surgery at age 18 to determine why her periods hadn't begun. The doctor told her that investigations:

revealed no uterus and that my 'ovaries' had herniated. My 'ovaries' were removed because they were 'abnormal'. I was not told the full truth about my diagnosis. I overheard some nursing staff discussing me and saying 'but she seems so female' and I thought this was strange.

Another woman was 19 when a gynaecologist marched into her hospital room and, in front of several other patients and some nurses:

rattled off the diagnosis that I was born without a uterus, had 'bad ovaries' that needed to be removed, and had a short vagina that could be lengthened with a skin graft from my thigh once I'd found someone willing to marry me. Then he walked out. (Flora, 1996)

The blundering paternalism of medical practitioners like these, who seek to protect young women from the knowledge of their own diagnoses, causes a great deal of unnecessary suffering. The 18-year-old finally worked out her diagnosis from a newspaper article, and realized that 'there were other sufferers and that I was not just a one-off "freak of nature" after all'. The 19-year-old explicitly asked for a diagnosis five years later (it was then the mid 1970s) and was told that 'the details of my condition could not be disclosed to me because they were so awful' – leading to suicidal despair as she searched in vain through medical books, expecting to die young or to contract a horrible disease (Flora, 1996). In circumstances like these, learning the truth is often an enormous relief.

In their dealings with AIS women and their families, doctors commonly try to deflect attention away from genetics (their Y chromosome) and gonads (their testes) towards their 'female' hormone (oestrogen), female body shape and external genitals. The medical literature focusses on the external appearance of CAIS girls as 'entirely female' and sometimes claims that the inability of CAIS women to respond to their 'male' hormone (androgen) makes them *more* female than XX women whose bodies do respond to androgens. The older medical books, in particular, wax lyrical about the supposed femininity of AIS women, and doctors seem sometimes to be overcompensating for their discomfort and anxiety about AIS with glib and sweeping statements about these women's super-female qualities – their 'luxuriant' breast development, their tall slim build, clear skin, and suitability as fashion models. Doctors – and sometimes parents, too – may manage their concern about AIS with an optimistic dismissal of the difficulties involved as little more than the relatively common problem of infertility, faced by many XX women as well. Some women with AIS suggest that this emphasis on their essential femaleness works as a coping mechanism for people who are horrified and dismayed by 'failed maleness', the Y chromosome in a female body.

Strategies like these may serve to reassure others but they do little to help girls and women with AIS. A girl growing up with AIS has to cope with lack of menstruation as a rite of passage into adulthood, with lack of pubic and underarm hair, and with what the literature describes as 'infantile' (pale, under-developed) nipples, as well as with their knowledge that they are infertile. As a result, they often feel they miss out on all the 'girlie' conversations of adolescence, and they also often avoid contact with potential sexual partners (of either sex). They know that they are different from other women, and it is not helpful to pretend otherwise.

For example, medical textbooks often simply do not mention that AIS women typically have short vaginas – rarely more than 6 cm and often much shorter, compared with an average of 9 cm in XX women. Women are often not given this information by their doctors, but are left to discover it for themselves. One woman with CAIS says that doctors reassured her parents, after her hernia repair, that (apart from her infertility) she would be able to live 'as a perfectly normal woman':

So when my parents told me, aged 10 or so, that I probably wouldn't menstruate or be able to have babies, they had no reason to suspect that I might have other problems too. Whilst I discovered for myself very soon thereafter that my vagina was only about 1 cm long, the family doctor, and hence my parents, seemed oblivious to this problem ... I had spent my teenage years in petrified shame and isolation with my terrible unspeakable discoveries. I didn't know of the existence of vaginoplasty surgery and felt I was a loathsome freak with no prospect whatsoever of forming any adult relationships.

The AIS Support Group reports that 'several women have told us that they actually had to be admitted to hospital with internal haemorrhage following their first attempts at intercourse'. In response to the concerns of many women, the group's newsletter regularly features information about vaginal dilation and different surgical techniques for lengthening the vagina. For many women with AIS, as for women (and men) more generally, 'real' sex, 'going all the way', is culturally understood as heterosexual intercourse, and is an important marker both of adulthood and of true womanhood. Given this heterosexist social context, the paucity of discussion of other ways in which women with AIS might give and receive sexual pleasure is unsurprising.

The key AIS-related surgeries are orchidectomy (removal of the testes), vaginoplasty (extension or construction of a vagina) and, for women with PAIS, clitoridectomy, clitoral reduction, or clitoral recession. These latter operations are often performed in infancy: infants with clitorises larger than 0.9 cm are routinely subjected to cosmetic genital surgery, not because their genitals endanger their health, but because they endanger their culture's dichotomous sex system (Kessler, 1998). Morgan Holmes (n.d.) considers her 'clitoral recession' (a procedure in which the midsection is removed and the glans reattached to the base) to be 'a serious amputation in which a perfectly functioning body part is stolen'. Angela Moreno, now in her late twenties, describes how her PAIS went undetected until puberty, when the increased androgen production from her testes caused her to 'masculinize' – resulting in a clitoridectomy without her informed consent in a Chicago hospital in the 1980s:

One day when I was 12, I climbed out of the bath and was dancing around the bathroom as I dried myself. Mum was walking by, and glanced in at me through the open door. She looked so shocked at what she saw that I was afraid. Mum was reacting to the sight of my clitoris. I'd been aware for a few months that my cli-

toris was growing longer, but I'd thought that it was normal – just puberty. From Mum's alarmed reaction, though, it wasn't. She called the doctor, who told her to bring me in the next day ... I was now told I had ovarian cancer and needed a hysterectomy, but the doctors said that if anyone asked, I was to say I was having hernia surgery. My parents gave me a card which read, 'Nothing has changed. You are still our sweet little girl'. I wondered what they meant ... After my 'secret' operation, I woke up screaming with pain ... I felt a crusty blanket of dried blood in my genital region – what had they done to me? I didn't know that I'd actually just undergone a clitoridectomy – female genital mutilation. (Moreno, 1998)

Women with AIS and PAIS, along with other intersex people and their allies, are beginning to speak out about the abuse and neglect they have suffered from the health care system and are making demands for better health care. Organizations like the Intersex Society of North America (ISNA) and the AIS Support Group (UK) highlight the following issues:

1. *The right to know one's own diagnosis.*
   This is a fundamental right (the diagnosis belongs to the patient, not to the doctor) and should be upheld by the (U.K.) General Medical Council 1998 guidelines requiring doctors to be open with their patients. Doctors should provide information in an emotionally supportive environment and should accurately describe the patient's diagnosis. Women who suspect they have AIS (or a related diagnosis) have the right to expect doctors to be willing to accurately answer specific questions such as: 'Do I have XY chromosomes?'; 'Do I have XX chromosomes?'; 'Do I have testicular tissue?', 'Do I have ovarian tissue?', 'What surgery did I receive as a child?' One of the strongest messages from intersex people is that the conspiracy of silence which surrounds them causes far more anguish and distress than does intersex itself. The foremost researchers in this area now emphasize that 'full and honest disclosure is best' (Diamond and Sigmundson, 1997), and that even very young children can gradually be given accurate information (Goodall, 1991).

2. *The availability of information, counseling and support, both at the time of diagnosis and subsequently, for the girl/woman with AIS and her family.*
   This should include the opportunity to explore such issues as: grief about one's own diagnosis, lack of menstruation, infertility, and concern about sex and gender issues, including those related to surgically altered genitalia, unusual genital appearance, short vagina, and absent pubic hair. 'Preparing the youngster for intimate personal relationships as an adult should be a priority, tempting as it may be to divert attention away from sexuality issues and towards substitute goals' (AIS Support Group, 1999). ISNA recommends that such discussions should always address issues of heterosexism and homophobia, and researchers emphasize the need for counseling to cover 'the full gamut of heterosexual, homosexual, bisexual, and even celibate options'

(Diamond and Sigmundson, 1997: 1048). Intersexuality affects the whole family: parents may feel angry, sad and fearful for their child's future, and mothers (the 'carriers' of AIS) may feel guilty for passing on a genetic condition to their child. Although an estimated one-third of cases result from spontaneous mutation, AIS is often an inherited (recessive) condition and many women have sisters, aunts and nieces with AIS. The stigma and taboo attached to AIS means, however, that it may never be discussed within the family. Other women in the same family may be 'carriers' and it is helpful for them to be informed about AIS and to have the opportunity to work through the options available (e.g. testing for carrier status, prenatal diagnosis) and their feelings about this *before* they become pregnant. Health professionals should always offer women with AIS information about support groups: for many AIS women, meeting others is 'like waking up from a bad dream,' 'like a mist clearing', 'like finding the door to the world'.

3. *The right to consent to, or to refuse, surgery based on accurate information.*
ISNA is campaigning against all forms of cosmetic genital surgery on infants, including vaginoplasty, clitoral reduction or recession, and clitoridectomy. Instead the option of surgical and hormonal intervention should be offered when the intersex child is older and undertaken only at the request and with the fully informed consent of the child, including the possibility of discussing sexual function with adults who have undergone similar surgeries, and validation of the child's right to delay or to choose no surgery at all. Some leading intersex researchers (e.g. Diamond and Sigmundson, 1997) support this position and advise against cosmetic genital surgery or orchidectomy for AIS infants. In the U.K., some parents of CAIS girls diagnosed in infancy are refusing permission to remove the child's testicles allowing her to make her own informed decision about this at puberty (Broks, 1999), and the young teenager, Joella Holliday, (who has a different intersex condition) has successfully exercised her right to refuse vaginoplasty, with the support of her mother (*Q.E.D*, 1998). Informed consent to genital operations such as vaginoplasty should be based on an accurate understanding of non-surgical alternatives (such as pressure dilation), of the various different surgeries available, and of their varying success rates and associated complications. It is also, of course, important for everyone – AIS and non-AIS – to understand that vaginal penetrative sex with a man is not the only possible means of sexual expression.

4. *The development of better research which addresses women's concerns.*
Research on intersex reflects the male bias of health research more generally. The medical profession treats women with AIS as 'failed males'. As one PAIS woman says, there 'seems to be an attitude on the part of doctors that female assignment is sort of an inferior second choice that they are forced to fall back on if their masculinizing therapies are not good enough'. Other suggestions for future research which have been

discussed in the newsletter of the AIS Support Group include: the use of female orgasm instead of penile penetration as a criterion for 'successful' genital surgery; research on improving surgical and non-surgical techniques for producing greater vaginal depth; better understanding of hormone supplement/replacement therapies for AIS women; the effects of early orchidectomy on bone density and the problem of osteoporosis; and the breast cancer risk of AIS women. Finally, according to Chase (1998: 198) there is currently 'no research effort to improve erotic functioning for adult intersexuals whose genitals have been altered, nor are there psychotherapists specializing in working with adult intersex clients trying to heal from the trauma of medical intervention'.

5. More sensitive and better informed health care.
Genital inspections and photography (intersex people are often used as teaching material) should be kept to a minimum and should require permission. General practitioners need to be much better informed: some of the crassest responses to children with AIS come from doctors with no specialist knowledge ('bring him, her or it in then', said one GP after a mother explained that her daughter had AIS). Adult women with AIS report being repeatedly asked about their last period and their contraceptive use: some are even being given 'cervical' smears (though they don't have a cervix!). It should not be the responsibility of AIS women or their parents to educate doctors. Health professionals should actively seek out information such as that provided by the AIS Support Group, and by ISNA, and thereby educate themselves.

Psychology of women and health psychology have barely begun to address issues relevant to intersexuality in general or to women with AIS in particular (Kitzinger, 1999). On the contrary, there is often a bland assumption that all women (by definition) have XX chromosomes and (with rare exceptions) a vagina, uterus, and ovaries. The experience of women with AIS offers an important challenge to feminism and to psychology.

REFERENCES

AIS support group (1999) *Fact sheet*, 25 February. Available from P.O. Box 269, Banbury, OX15 6YT, U.K.

Broks, P. (1999) Trust me – I'm a patient. *Wavelength: Science, Society, the Media*, 23, 8–10

Chase, C. (1998) Hermaphrodites with attitude: Mapping the emergence of intersex political activism. *GLQ*, 4, 189–211

Diamond, M. and Sigmundson, H.K. (1997) Management of intersexuality: Guidelines for dealing with persons with ambiguous genitalia. *Archives of Pediatric and Adolescent Medicine*, 151, 1046–1045

Dreger, A.D. (1998) *Hermaphrodites and the Medical Invention of Sex*. Cambridge, MA: Harvard University Press

Flora, P. (1996) Canadian representative of the AIS Support Group. *ALIAS*, 1 (5), 11–12

Goodall, J. (1991) Helping a child to understand her own testicular feminisation. *The Lancet*, 337, 33–35

Holmes, M. (n.d.) Re-membering a queer body. Leaflet available from ISNA-Canada, Box 1076, Haliburton Ontario, Canada, KOM 1SO

Kessler, S.J. (1998) *Lessons from the Intersexed*. New Brunswick, NJ: Rutgers University Press
Kitzinger, C. (1999, in press) Intersexuality: Deconstructing the sex/gender binary. *Feminism and Psychology*, 9 (4)
Moreno, A. (1998) Am I a man or a woman? *19 Magazine* (September), 16–18. (See also, Moreno, A.(n.d) In Amerika they call us hermaphrodites. Leaflet published by the Intersex Society of North America, PO Box 31791, San Francisco CA 94131, USA
Q.E.D. (1998) British Broadcasting Corporation TV programme, 9 December
Quigley, C. *et. al.* (1995) Androgen receptor defects: Historical, clinical and molecular perspectives. *Endocrine Reviews*, 16, 271–321
Warne, G.L. (1997) *Complete Androgen Insensitivity Syndrome*. Available from the AIS Support Group, P.O. Box 269, Banbury, OX15 6YT, U.K.

CHAPTER 45

TRANSGENDER ISSUES

Louise K. Newman

INTRODUCTION: TRANSGENDER EXPERIENCE AND MENTAL HEALTH

It is a relatively new development to include transgender issues in a text on women's health. This is despite the fact that most analyses of women's health focus on the risk/vulnerability and protective factors inherent in the category 'woman' as the subject of women's health and adopt a social-construction model of gender which sees 'gender' as distinct from 'sex' (see Kitzinger, in this volume).

Feminist theories in particular have worked to maintain the distinction between biology and culture while, at the same time, maintaining a place for difference – the different experiences of male and female bodies. These debates over biologism, essentialism and cultural construction of gender categories are also played out in the responses to, and theories of, individuals who challenge gender stereotypes and categories and identify as transgendered, transsexual or transvestite. Transgendered individuals (used here to refer to those individuals who challenge existing gender categories) face the dilemma of feeling uncomfortable with their socially assigned gender role, or the feeling that their subjective gender-identity is at variance with their anatomical sex. Within these simplified descriptions are a variety of experiences of gender and sexuality which raise issues about the generally held models of gender-identity and about the nature of subjectivity itself (Butler, 1990).

In some feminist debates, the male to female transsexual who identifies as 'woman' and sometimes as 'lesbian' is seen as invalid, 'not real', and therefore denied access to 'women's' services and resources. Similarly, female to male transgendered individuals have been mistrusted and seen as identifying with the oppressor. These views do little to advance understanding of the issues involved and reflect a categorical model of gender difference. It is clear that there are varieties of transgender experience which, by their very existence, raise questions about the models of gender-identity inherent in the psychiatric and mental health discourses which equate fixed gender-identity (and sexuality) with normality. The transgender experience with the medical and mental health professions in some ways recapitulates the experience of gay, lesbian and bisexual communities and the protracted debates over the pathologizing of homosexuality per se.

Currently, there are significant criticisms of the system of conventions (Benjamin Standards) requiring psychiatric/mental health professional assessment of individuals seeking sex-modifying procedures (hormones, surgical intervention). This often adversarial encounter is seen to work against meeting the legitimate mental health needs of individuals with gender issues and to operate to reinforce rigidly defined gender categories. Transgender communities argue that various gender and social identities are possible – that there is a continuum of masculinity/femininity and that gender is not logically or necessarily aligned with the body, genitals or social role. The development of new gender options, options which can be non-surgical or non-hormonal, has emerged as a transgender politics which rejects traditional mental health models and demands cultural change (Califia, 1997).

There are, however, individuals who are significantly distressed by their gender issues who come into contact with psychiatrists and mental health professionals and those who are pursuing SMPs who are required to obtain mental health assessments. It is important not to minimize the difficulties faced by transgendered individuals in dealing with gender issues compounded by social misunderstanding, stigma and discrimination. These issues also apply to the lack of specific health and community services and relative scarcity of mental health professionals working in this area.

This chapter examines the models of gender identity, development and disorder in current practice and looks at the varying experiences of transgendered individuals.

GENDER IDENTITY AND GENDER VARIATION

Gender identity has several components:

- biological sex
- core gender identity
- gender role
- sexual orientation.

Current theoretical models distinguish 'sex' from 'gender'. Gender refers to the social performance indicative of an internal sexed identity – the outward trappings of masculinity or femininity as socially defined. Gender is a social category and/or an interpretation of anatomical difference. Sex refers to biological sex and anatomy, but even biology is complex and subject to interpretation. In nature, there may well be more than two sexes, or at least a variability in sexual characteristics. Biological sex may be defined on many levels – sex-determining genes, sex chromosomes, HY sex-determining antigen, gonads, hormones, internal reproductive structures, or external genitalia. In some individuals, sex cannot be determined as exclusively 'male' or 'female' and is something else altogether – the 'third' gender. Psychoanalytic theories describe the development of gender-identity in infancy. Core Gender Identity is defined by Stoller as the fundamental sense of belonging to one sex. This is an emotionally valued sense of identity and develops between the ages of 18 months and three years. (Stoller, 1968; Fast, 1984). The first stage of gender identity, gender labeling, begins around the age of 18 months when the child learns to discriminate between the sexes. Most children of three or four have gender stability, that is, they recognize that they will stay the same over time. Gender constancy is an understanding that one cannot change sex and develops by age five years. According to psychoanalytic theorists, the acquisition of gender-identity occurs as a component of separation and individuation, and the development of self-identity. The attachment relationship is the context in which identity and sexual identity develop. Gender role is incorporated in the self as a set of behaviors, attitudes and personality traits designated socioculturally as masculine or feminine. In children, this is measured by such variables as affiliative preference for same-sex peers, fantasy and play roles, and type of play. There is an ongoing controversy over the influence of biological variables such as prenatal sex hormones on observable gender-role behavior. Sexual orientation is defined by response to sexual stimuli. Sexual identity refers to the definitions of oneself in terms of sexual preference. Sexual orientation emerges after puberty but is not necessarily congruent with sexual identity. For example, it is possible for an individual to be primarily aroused by homosexual stimuli but to identify himself as a heterosexual.

These components of gender identity were not theorized and identified in this way until the 1950s when technology became available to treat intersexed individuals. The problem then became one of how to decide what sex the intersexed infant should be assigned to. Money and Erhardt, studying the rearing of these children, decided that sex of rearing – upbringing – was the most important factor in producing a 'successful' outcome as male or female. They also stated that attempting to change a child's gender after the age of two years was not likely to be successful (Fast, 1984). The diagnostic category of Gender Identity Disorder emerges in a particular historical context after the development of the model of sex and gender and with biological advances for use in 'treatment' of these conditions.

Transsexualism is a relatively recent phenomenon. In the twentieth century, it has become possible with medicine and technology for an individual to 'change' sex. Transsexualism emerged in the mid-twentieth century and is defined, as in the DSM, by the demand for sex change. This is not to say that individuals have not crossed gender for centuries but that what we have come to call a disorder is only possible with developments in plastic surgery and endocrinology. In a sense, we have produced a particular form of transsexual with a particular life story that needs to be told for admission to surgical treatment.

The arguments that circulate around the body of the transsexual are the very same arguments that reveal the tensions in the Sex-Gender model: how much is biology, how much is culture, what is sexed subjectivity, what are the ethical issues surrounding the individual's ownership of and right to change their own body (Lewis, 1995)?

The same tensions were present when homosexuality was still a 'Disorder' in the DSM. Interestingly, when homosexuality was removed from the DSM in 1980, Transsexualism made it in as Gender Identity Disorder. We are currently seeing some strong lobbying to have it removed.

Gender Identity Disorder in the DSM IV refers to a strong identification with and preference for the gender role characteristics of the other sex. This is expressed through play, behavior and verbal statements of a desire to be the other sex. Some children have gender dysphoria, or unease about their sex.

Diagnostic Criteria for Gender Identity Disorder

- A strong and persistent cross-gender identification (not merely a desire for any perceived cultural advantages of being the other sex).
- In adolescents and adults, the disturbance is manifested by symptoms such as a stated desire to live or be treated as the other sex, or the conviction that he or she has the typical feelings and reactions of the other sex.
- Persistent discomfort with his or her sex or sense of inappropriateness in the gender role of that sex.
- In adolescents and adults, the disturbance is manifested by symptoms such as preoccupation with getting rid of primary and secondary sex characteristics (e.g. request for hormones, surgery or other procedures to physically alter sexual characteristics to simulate the other sex) or belief that he or she was born the wrong sex.
- The disturbance is not concurrent with a physical intersex condition.
- The disturbance causes clinically significant distress or impairment in social, occupational or other important areas of functioning.

In the 1950's Harry Benjamin had found in his work with adult transsexuals that many gave a history of early cross-gender behavior. Overall, it appears that these early cross-gender behaviors are a strong developmental predictor of adult homosexuality rather than transsexuality.

Most young children receiving this diagnosis correctly label their own sex but have a desire to be the other sex. This desire may be articulated as early as two or three years of age.

Stoller (1968), from a psychoanalytic point of view, comments on an overly close relationship with the mother – an excessively symbiotic physical relationship – and the absence of a psychological father in boys with GID. Mothers, Stoller thought, had their own conflicts over femininity, suffered penis envy, were excessively masculine in their own childhoods, and bisexual. The transsexual-to-be little boy cannot separate from his mother or identify with his father so he 'becomes' his mother (Blanchard and Steiner, 1990).

Biological theories have looked at possible genetic influences and the effects of prenatal sex hormones. Studies of children for evidence of possible sex-related differences in cognitive abilities noted that, as a group, GID boys are considered physically attractive (Walters and Buss, 1986; Zucker and Bradley, 1995). It is unclear, of course, whether any of these factors tell us anything about biology or nature. Intersex children are known to their parents as being ambiguously sexed. Parents go through the decision-making process about which sex their child will be and this clearly influences their relationship with the child. The focus on genitals, and the often protracted multiple operations needed to correct them, must mean that parents are sensitized to possible gender deviance. Ambiguity about gender is not very well tolerated in our culture, by parents or surgeons, and the demand is to operate to fix the body as a medical/surgical emergency in infancy. Normality is defined as congruence between sexual anatomy and gender identity. To be gendered in opposition to sex is to have a disorder – despite the fact that sex and gender are analytically distinct.

What can we learn from the study of non-Western cultures and their systems of sex and gender? In the West, gender is used to distinguish socially constructed roles and cultural representations from biological sex. What we call gender is seen as social; biological sex is seen as its point of origin and natural limit. In this model, gender should conform to sex.

The study of non-Western cultures reveals great variability on the sociocultural features of sex roles and also wide variation in beliefs concerning the body and what constitutes sex. Anatomy is interpreted differently in different cultures and not necessarily seen as fixed. Amongst the Zuni tribe of North American Indians, for example, sex is not allocated immediately on birth as there is a belief it may change. Complex beliefs and rituals are used to discover the sex of the infant which has surprisingly little to do with genitals. The activity and concern around the intersex infant in our culture may be seen as acting our similar rituals and a particular form of cultural anxiety. The study of non-Western cultures shows that gender can be multiple and autonomous from sex. Gender categories use perceptions and interpretations of anatomical and physiological difference between bodies but these perceptions are always mediated by cultural categories and meaning. In other words, there may be no such thing as nature or biology as the real of existence but only a gender system that produces sex (Heldt, 1996).

In Western psychology, gender identity is generated primarily by sex assignment as male or female at birth. Mixed gender role, ambivalent gender identity, or a gender identity that fluctuates over the life span are seen as problematic if not pathological. In other cultures, ambivalent and non-stable gender roles and identities are not necessarily pathological. In some cultures, ambiguous gender socialization of children does occur and results in ambivalent gender identity or a gender identity that can be transformed at some stage and new roles adopted. The well-known 'penis at 12' syndrome in the Dominican Republic and equivalents in Papua New Guinea and the South Pacific is culturally known and accepted. Children with ambiguous genitalia and a 5 alpha reductase deficiency virilize at puberty, essentially 'changing' from girls to boys. Even those raised as girls successfully become men. Social position and cultural intelligibility appear to be important. Amongst North American Indians, cross-gendered individuals known as Berdaches have been documented in many groups. The Berdaches have a supernaturally sanctioned social position of some privilege and constitute a 'new' gender, neither male nor female. The Hijras of India also pose a challenge to Western ideas of sex and gender. This diverse group of hermaphrodites, ceremonially castrated males and 'effeminate' men worship the Mother Goddess and perform at births and marriages. They exist within the Hindu tradition where deities are frequently sexually ambiguous or change sex. In the Tantric sect, the Supreme Being is a hermaphrodite and male transvestism is used in religious devotions. Hinduism appears to allow for many sexual contradictions and ambiguities.

In Western culture, the situation is somewhat different. Sexual ambiguity is not well tolerated and this has contributed to the emergence of an adversarial system in which the psychiatrist becomes the gatekeeper and is seen by the transsexual as a barrier to surgical treatment. Many transsexuals do not want to discuss psychological issues – for them, the problem is hormonal, biological and surgical and the psychiatrist is an unwelcome intruder (Brown and Maunsley, 1996). Children with aberrant gender-role behaviors distress their families, schools, peers and certainly are distressed by this themselves. And yet, there is little evidence on the effectiveness of interventions and there are serious questions about the ethics of the intervention. Those who believe that the therapeutic interventions should focus on eliminating the cross-gender behavior argue that this is the ethical choice for several reasons – reduction of social ostracism, treatment of underlying psychopathology, prevention of transsexualism and, more controversially, the prevention of homosexuality. Others argue that attempting to change the behavior will not eliminate the 'disorder' and will further damage the individual. In this view, the strategy becomes one of increasing social acceptance and helping the child live in a culture which is stigmatizing and punitive to those who cross gender categories.

There is no way of understanding the transsexual phenomenon without situating it historically and socioculturally. Individuals who have a sense of discomfort with their allocated gender face a difficult predicament with major implications for psychosocial functioning. Societies with restrictive and rigid gender categories are more likely to produce individuals who do not 'fit'. In a gender polarized society, the alternative given to these individuals is to shift from one pole to the other and adopt the 'opposite' gender (Bullogh and Bullogh, 1993). This is, of course, impossible – there is no easy magic for changing sex; surgery is complex and often unsatisfactory.

In some ways, the genitals have become a metaphor for the 'self'. The transsexual seeks a coherent and fixed gender identity as the core organizing structure of sexed subjectivity – an endless quest for authenticity. Some have multiple revision operations, endless plastic surgery and yet remain unsatisfied. This raises questions about the functioning of mental health services and the need to provide services and supports which can help individuals find reasonable solutions to their gender predicament (Israel and Tarver, 1997).

TRANSGENDER EXPERIENCES

There have been numerous attempts to classify the varieties of transgender experience and issues of biological males. Both the major psychiatric classification systems include categories of transsexualism and transvestism but also recognize that an individual may experience 'gender dysphoria' without meeting criteria for either of these diagnoses. Gender identity disorder is defined in DSM-IV as a broad grouping including transsexualism, gender identity disorder of childhood, and gender identity disorder of adolescence or adulthood (non transsexual type).

For the mental health clinician who is often the gatekeeper controlling access to surgery and other sex-modifying interventions, the task is to distinguish the 'true transsexual' (or primary transsexual) from others with lesser degrees of gender dysphoria or other gender issues for which surgery is not considered appropriate treatment. This system has, in practice, encouraged the 'patient' to produce a particular gender narrative and the clinician to 'put' the story into a particular classification system. Both these attempts preclude more meaningful discussion of the individual's gender issues and make working collaboratively towards individual self-acceptance and self-development extremely difficult.

As for biological men, it is clear that women have varying experiences of gender issues and gender dysphoria. There has been more open discussion of female to male transgender issues and acknowledgment of a long, if hidden, history of biological women 'living as men' in several societies.

Similar attempts at classification exist. Blanchard and Steiner (1990) describes both homosexual and heterosexual gender dysphoria in women but allude to other possible positions. Homosexual gender dysphoric women are sexually attracted to women and represent a spectrum of cross-gendered behaviors. The boundaries between masculine lesbianism ('bull dyke') and transsexualism are unclear and controversial but the development of more effective sex reassignment surgery may see greater numbers seeking gender transition. The supposed rarity of female to male transsexualism may reflect the limitations of surgical intervention as well as the lesser visibility of the individuals in some societies (Stryker, 1998).

ASSESSMENT ISSUES

Understanding the individual's transgender experiences should be seen as part of an overall assessment of mental health issues.

Understanding the Presentation

An individual with gender issues may present with unrelated or related mental health problems or a focus on gender identity itself. There may be a direct request for SMPs or a more general wish to clarify gender identity or explore cross-gender behavior. Some individual's present in crisis or distress and may have experienced interpersonal, family and social problems.

Children and adolescents are usually a cause of anxiety for others around them. Anxiety and depression may be significant and any individual in crisis should be assessed for the presence of suicidal ideation and risk of self-harm.

Understanding the Gender Issues

An exploration of gender identity and wishes and the history of gender development helps clarify these issues which may be important in ongoing psychological support. This aims at facilitating self-knowledge and self-acceptance and resolving underlying trauma rather than providing a 'diagnosis' for its own sake.

CASE EXAMPLE
Adam, a 37-year-old biological female living as a male, has a background of sexual and emotional abuse and the experience of having been abandoned by his mother who failed to protect him. He has been depressed and suicidal and sees being male as the only position of safety. Major therapeutic issues for Adam are to explore the unresolved sexual abuse and the effects that emotional abandonment have had on the development of his sense of identity.

Assessing the Role of SMPs

Part of the process of formulating an individual's mental health needs is understanding the role of SMPs as a component of gender transition. For some individuals, these are seen as the 'final solution' to problems of gender identity and there is considerable emotional over-investment in the results of surgery/hormones. Traditional gender clinics have been criticised for enforcing a rigid gender model by focussing on the likelihood that the individual seeking treatment will 'pass' as an 'acceptable' female but it is also clear that for some clients, this is the desired result. Issues of informed consent and providing adequate support for exploration of non-medical interventions are important in clinical practice.

CASE EXAMPLE:
Nicole, a 15-year-old biological female, presents with the desire to commence testosterone and have a bilateral mastectomy. She adopts a male appearance and identifies with male interests and a male peer-group. She sees herself as a heterosexual male and is adamant that she is not a lesbian.

She does not want to discuss the emotional aspects of her decision and says she 'has always been a boy' and that there is nothing to discuss.

Coordination of Ongoing Support

The level and type of support needed should be classified as part of general assessment. Where the transgender community has organized support and counseling services, these should be used to help with issues such as housing and employment needs, and referral to other services such as speech pathology as required.

Longer term psychotherapy has several roles:

- exploring issues of identity and understanding of gender issues
- improving self-esteem and interpersonal functioning
- supporting social process of disclosure
- assisting with the emotional trauma of gender change.

These roles are best kept independent of the referral process for sex modifying procedures.

TREATMENT ISSUES

Gender clinics and clinicians referring individuals for sex modifying procedures are guided by the Benjamin Standards of Care. These suggest a comprehensive assessment and diagnosis, a period of 12 months living in the desired gender role (the 'real life test') and ongoing psychotherapeutic support.

The role of the clinician is to decide which individuals will benefit from SMPs and achieve a sense of desired gender identity and subjective relief. Candidates considered inappropriate for surgical intervention include those with ambivalence and confusion regarding subjective gender, acute major psychiatric illness or substance abuse, and lack of success in living in the new gender role (Ratnam, 1987).

It is important to maintain a supportive and therapeutic involvement with candidates not accepted for surgery and explore other varieties of gender expression.

A series of follow-up studies of sex reassignment surgery found that the majority of appropriately selected individuals benefit from the procedure in terms of personal satisfaction and functioning. Lack of personal and social supports, difficulties in interpersonal functioning and social disadvantage have been implicated in post-surgical dissatisfaction and distress (Ross, 1989). Clinicians need to coordinate support and work towards improving post-surgical adjustment and minimize the individual's preoccupation with excessive surgical intervention.

TRANSGENDER SERVICES

The provision of appropriate health services for transgender communities remains a relatively neglected issue. Service planning involves both assessing the health needs of the community and providing education and training for professionals in gender issues. Education and training needs to address issues of specific groups such as youth, HIV positive individuals, and older persons with gender concerns, and the needs of families and children of transgendered clients.

There is continuing concern that general or mainstream health service providers do not adequately meet the needs of transgender clients and that as a group the transgendered community has elevated rates of health problems, particularly mental health problems. The care of transgendered individuals in mental health, hospital and correctional institutions has also been criticised. Several institutions and organizations now have as policy the rights of the transgendered individual to safety and protection and to receive hormone treatment while in custody/care (Steiner, 1985).

SUMMARY

There are complex issues involved in the understanding of and intervention in transgender conditions. To date, there has been little in the way of open dialogue with transgender communities and only recently have there been more collaborative attempts to look at new models of care and service provision.

The implications of listening to the varieties of transgender experience are significant as they involve a rethinking of models of sex, gender, subjectivity and their pathologies.

REFERENCES

Blanchard, R. and Steiner, B (Eds.) (1990) *Clinical Management of Gender Identity Disorders in Children and Adults.* Washington: American Psychiatric Press

Brown, M. and Maunsley, C. (1996) *True Selves: Understanding Transsexualism.* San Francisco: Jersey-Bass

Bullogh, V. and Bullogh, B. (1993) *Crossdressing, Sex and Gender.* Philadelphia: University of Pennsylvania Press

Butler, J. (1990) *Gender Trouble. Feminism and the Subversion of Identity.* New York: Routledge

Califia, P. (1997) *Sex Changes. The Politics of Transgenderism.* San Francisco: Cleis Press

Fast, I. (1984) *Gender Identity: A Differentiation Model.* New Jersey: Analytic Press

Heldt, G. (Ed.) (1996) *Third Sex Third Gender: Beyond Sexual Dimorphism in Culture and History.* New York: Zone Books

Israel, G. and Tarver, D. (1997) *Transgender Care*. Philadelphia: Temple University Press

Lewis, F. (1995) *Transsexualism in Society*. Melbourne: MacMillan

Money, J. and Ehrhartd, A.A. (1972) Man and Woman, Boy and Girl. Baltimore, MD: Johns Hopkins University Press.

Ratnam, S. (1987) SMS in the male transsexual. *British Journal of Hospital Medicine*, 38, 204–213

Ross, M. (1989) Effects of adequacy of GRS on psychological adjustment. *Archives of Sex Behaviour*, 18, 145–153

Steiner, B.W. (1985) *Gender Dysphoria: Development, Research, Management*. New York: Plenum

Stoller, R. (1968) *Sex and Gender*, Vol. 1. New York: Science House

Stryker, S. (Ed.) (1998) The transgender issue. *GLQ A Journal of Lesbian and Gay Studies*, 4 (2), 145–159.

Walters, W. and Buss, M. (Eds.) (1986) *Transsexualism and Sex Reassignment*. New York: Oxford University Press

Zucker, K. and Bradley, S. (1995) *Gender Identity Disorder and Psychosexual Problems in Children and Adolescents*. New York: Guilford

CHAPTER 46

UNDERSTANDING WOMEN'S DEPRESSION: LIMITATIONS OF MAINSTREAM APPROACHES AND A MATERIAL-DISCURSIVE ALTERNATIVE[1]

Janet M. Stoppard

INTRODUCTION

This chapter begins with an overview of knowledge about women's depression from the currently dominant viewpoint in which depression is defined as a form of mental disorder that afflicts individual women. Explanations for women's depression which have addressed biological, psychological and social influences, either singly or in combination, are analysed to reveal their limitations, particularly their neglect of women's lived experience and the social-cultural context of women's lives. Development of knowledge from a feminist perspective is identified as a more useful strategy for exploring women's experiences of being depressed. The chapter concludes by outlining a material-discursive framework for understanding women's depression that encompasses both women's embodiment and the socio-cultural conditions that shape their lived experiences.

I was at work one day and I felt I couldn't stay there and I couldn't function. Mainly because of my concentration and I just felt that I couldn't stay there. But I don't know what was leading up to all of that. I was feeling kind of down, but I didn't really know why. And I was feeling blue and I didn't know really why. (Sarah)

I was depressed for years before it occurred to me that that was what it was. Um, like off and on....I thought of myself as [messed] up, but not really as depressed ... I'd been really, just really upset all the time ... (Tracy)

In these brief excerpts, Sarah and Tracy (not their real names) describe their experience of being depressed. They were interviewed as part of a study on women's experiences of their treatment for depression (see Gammell and Stoppard, 1999). Along with the other women who participated in this study, they had been diagnosed by a physician (either a family doctor or psychiatrist) as suffering from depression.

In Western countries, depression has been described as the 'common cold' of mental health problems (Burns, 1992). Among those who receive treatment for a psychiatric illness in hospital, a high proportion are likely to be diagnosed with depression (Bebbington, 1996; Busfield, 1996; Ussher, 1991). Epidemiological studies provide information on the prevalence of depression among people living in the community; findings from such studies have indicated that depression is one of the more prevalent forms of mental disorder (Regier *et al.*, 1988; Weissman *et al.*, 1993). A distinctive pattern of findings has emerged in research on depression – whether studies involve patients or surveys with people living in the community, rates of depression generally are found to be at least twice as high for women as for men. In an article published in 1977, Weissman and Klerman documented a 2 to 1 ratio of women to men among the depressed and since that time, numerous studies have confirmed this observation (Culbertson, 1997; Nolen-Hoeksema, 1990; Weissman and Olfson, 1995).

There is now general recognition among researchers and mental health professionals that depression is a mental health problem which afflicts women more than men (McGrath *et al.*, 1990; Nolen-Hoeksema, 1990; Ussher, 1991). Women are also the major recipients of antidepressant drugs, the principal form of medical treatment for depression (Hamilton and Jensvold, 1995; Olfson and Klerman, 1993). While there is a consensus that women are particularly prone to depression, there is less agreement about the causes of this gender-related pattern and a range of explanations has been proposed.

EXPLAINING WOMEN'S DEPRESSION

... plus I went through ah, started menopause when I was 40 so I'm on hormone replacement therapy. I think it's a combination of everything. (Jane) (Gammell and Stoppard, 1999: 118)

Because the kids are going to be the kids. They are at the age where they are going to make you depressed ... they are at the age where they are never going to be satisfied anyway, so of course, I'm the one that's gonna end up depressed or upset ... (Mary) (Scattolon and Stoppard, 1999: 212)

These two excerpts illustrate common strategies used by women in their attempts to explain depressive experiences. These explanatory strategies have been referred to as the 'women's bodies' and 'women's lives' approaches (Stoppard, 1997). When women try to make sense of their depressive experiences, they are likely to draw upon one or other of these explanations.

In some respects, women's accounts reflect popularized versions of experts' theories of depression. The 'women's bodies' form of explanation parallels biological theories and the 'women's lives' approach corresponds to social theories. Contemporary biological theories of depression highlight female reproductive physiology, particularly hormonal influences associated with menstruation, pregnancy, childbirth and menopause as underlying women's vulnerability to depression (Gallant and Derry, 1995; Lock, 1993; Stanton and Danoff-Burg, 1995). The example above in which 'Jane' attributes her depression to menopause reflects this explanatory approach. In contrast, 'Mary' explains her depression in terms of stress involved in being a mother and coping with the demands of child-raising. In this social approach, depression is attributed to sources of stress arising in the course of women's everyday lives (Doyal, 1995; McGrath *et al.*, 1990). One of the best known of the social approaches to explaining depression is the theory developed by Brown and Harris (1978, 1989) based on their research with women. According to this social theory, depression in women is linked to the experience of adversity, especially events and conditions with negative implications for the ongoing quality of women's everyday lives. Stresses inherent in childcare have been identified by Brown and Harris as likely to increase women's chances of becoming depressed if they also experience a negative event, such as the break up of an intimate relationship, death of a close relative, or loss of income through unemployment.

In addition to biological and social explanations for women's depression, it has been proposed that women already are more vulnerable than men to this form of disorder because of their 'feminine' psychology. According to psychological theories, the particular configuration of personality characteristics which women tend to develop are ones which also increase their susceptibility to depression. Thus, the tendency of women to be more oriented than men towards relationships with others (Jack, 1991), to be less assertive and competitive than men in their interpersonal interactions (McGrath *et al.*, 1990), and to respond in more emotional and less active ways to negative events (Nolen-Hoeksema, 1990) has been identified by some theorists as predisposing women to depressive experiences.

Currently, biological, social and psychological theories, either singly or in combination (e.g. psychosocial and biopsychosocial models), represent the dominant or 'mainstream' approaches to understanding women's depression. In research based on these theories, findings in support of one or other approach have been reported, but no clear consensus has emerged among researchers about how best to explain women's depression and new theories continue to be proposed. A satisfactory answer to the question 'Why is depression more prevalent among women than men?' still eludes researchers (Bebbington, 1996). Part of the reason for this situation, as I have argued elsewhere (Stoppard, 2000), lies in assumptions about knowledge and how research should be conducted, which underpin mainstream approaches and have the effect of excluding or distorting women's experiences.

LIMITATIONS OF MAINSTREAM APPROACHES TO RESEARCH ON WOMEN'S DEPRESSION

When women's experiences are neglected or reinterpreted to fit experts' theories, the explanations for depression generated are not only likely to be less helpful for women's attempts to understand their own depressive experiences, they also foster treatment strategies with a restricted focus on individual women and their bodies. Similar limitations can be identified across the range of mainstream approaches to explaining women's depression. First, each of the theories outlined in the previous section incorporates a medical-psychiatric conception of depression as a disorder within an individual which is characterized by specific symptoms. Depression is defined by a set of symptoms which include sad or apathetic mood, negative or pessimistic thoughts, lack of energy to engage in every-day activities, and disrupted sleep (e.g. insomnia) and appetite (e.g. weight loss). In much of the research on depression, especially in North America, researchers define depression in terms of the criteria for 'depressive disorder' specified in the *Diagnostic and Statistical Manual of Mental Disorders* (DSM) published by the American Psychiatric Association (APA, 1994). Although discussion about how depression should be defined for research and diagnostic purposes continues (Coyne, 1994; Culbertson, 1997), the starting point for these definitional debates is experts' conceptions, rather than women's accounts of their depressive experiences. As pointed out however by Hamilton (1995), the form of depression designated by experts as the modal variant of this disorder may be more typical of men's than women's experience.

A second limitation common to mainstream approaches derives from their grounding in positivist assumptions about how knowledge is developed (see Lee, in this volume). A key positivist tenet concerns objectivity – the requirement that research be conducted in accord with methods which eliminate subjective influences. In practice, this means that investigators pursue topics which allow measurement of 'variables', so that the resulting data can be analysed using statistical procedures. One consequence of this positivist viewpoint is that people's accounts of their experiences are ruled out as too subjective to be an appropriate source of knowledge. Such knowledge, it is claimed, will inevitably be biased and therefore both unreliable and invalid. The preferred strategy in mainstream research is to collect people's responses on standardized questionnaires designed by researchers. Apart from foregoing the richness of information yielded by individuals' accounts in their own words, the effect of these positivist methods is to substitute researchers' interpretations for knowledge developed from the standpoint of research participants.

A third limitation of mainstream approaches is that the scope of inquiry is focussed narrowly on the area each field defines as its particular domain. For instance, psychological research on depression addresses the behavior, thoughts and feelings of depressed individuals, whereas medical research focusses on the biological body, particularly the role of genetics and brain biochemistry, while neither field is concerned with the social and cultural contexts within which people live their lives and become depressed. Sociologists and anthropologists, on the other hand, take society and culture as their special concern, but have tended not to investigate topics such as depression. One result of these disciplinary divides is that much of the available knowledge about depression is 'decontextualized' – devoid of social context. The requirements of positivist research methods make invisible, through exclusion, the social, cultural, economic, and political influences that both shape, and form the background to, women's everyday lives.

Finally, in mainstream approaches, gender-related influences are addressed superficially because gender is defined in a narrow way as sex of assignment, i.e. based on the biological sex categories of female and male. This restricted conceptualization of gender means that links between women's depression and the gendered division of labour within society (e.g. women have primary responsibility for childcare but are under-represented in public decision-making positions) and between women's depressive experiences and symbolic aspects of gender (e.g. cultural beliefs about femininity and masculinity) remain unexplored.

RESEARCH FROM A FEMINIST STANDPOINT PERSPECTIVE

An alternative to the positivist methods of mainstream approaches is provided by research from a feminist standpoint perspective (Harding, 1991; Henwood and Pidgeon, 1995; Smith, 1987). Adopting a feminist standpoint means beginning research with women's experiences rather than experts' concepts and theories (see Lapsley, Waimarie Nikora and Black, in this volume). Conducting research from a feminist standpoint also involves a shift in understanding of what constitutes a legitimate source of knowledge. Positivist notions of objectivity give way to the recognition that all knowledge is socially constructed. In research informed by a social constructionist epistemology, human values and sociocultural influences are acknowledged as prestructuring all knowledge about the world and as integral to the research process (Harding, 1996). From this epistemological stance, women's experiences are viewed as a legitimate source of knowledge and the scope of research methods is broadened to include those that address meaning and subjective experience, methods which collectively have been referred to as 'discursive' (Harre and Stearns, 1995; Parker, 1997).

Research based in discursive methods may appear to have a limited focus on language and talk to the neglect of more material or 'real' aspects of lived experience. One such reality is the human body and another is the physical and social environment in which we live. A research strategy which begins with women's experiences, however, does not mean that material aspects of the world are necessarily excluded from consideration. In mainstream research on depression, because of existing separations between fields of study, for instance between psychology and medicine, embodied experiences are rarely explored simultaneously with subjective experiences, so these two aspects of experience remain unconnected, investigated by different researchers. When research starts from women's accounts, a rather different picture of the experience of depression emerges. Instead of separate symptoms, some primarily subjective and others involving bodily functions, women's accounts reflect the inter-twined embodied and subjective character of their depressive experiences, as illustrated by the following excerpts:[2]

Well, I've sat and cried and cried, most of the time I was laying in the bed, and stuff over nothing. A thought would just come, and I don't know, I'd just break down and cry.

That's how I describe it I guess, night and day. Then when you're better you wonder why you were sick … Your self-esteem is very low, um, you withdraw … You know, like it's not just the emotional part of it, but, but it affects you physically.

When research on women's depression is conducted from a feminist standpoint, women's accounts are viewed as a valid source of knowledge about their lived experiences. A social constructionist epistemology opens up avenues for re-visioning the body in ways that escape the reductionist assumptions of mainstream theories in which the body is conceptualized solely as a biological entity. An alternative theoretical framework within which to understand embodiment and women's embodied experiences is one that has been termed 'material-discursive' (Stoppard, 1998; Ussher, 1997a; Yardley, 1997).

A MATERIAL-DISCURSIVE ALTERNATIVE FOR UNDERSTANDING WOMEN'S DEPRESSION

The guiding assumptions of a material-discursive approach have been summarized by Yardley (1997: 15):

Because we are intrinsically social and embodied beings, the material dimension of human lives is always socialised – mediated by language and consciousness and modified by social activity – while the discursive dimension is inevitably physically manifested, in our speech and behaviour, institutions and technology. (emphasis in original)

A material-discursive perspective provides a framework for understanding women's depressive experiences which can encompass both material aspects of women's lives (including embodiment) and the discursive conditions which shape their lived experiences (see Mooney-Somers and Ussher, in this volume).

The material conditions of women's lives are linked to the gendered organization of everyday activities. For instance, women are primarily involved in providing care within the home for children and other family members, whereas their work outside the home is undervalued compared to men's. Such arrangements are maintained by structural conditions and social institutions which create and control the allocation of material (e.g. economic) resources along gendered lines. These gendered patterns are buttressed by discursive conditions which are mediated through language and everyday social interactions between people. The phrase 'discursive conditions' here refers to the range of linguistically mediated constructions embedded in local cultural knowledge and those transmitted through materials produced by the various media (TV, newspapers, magazines, movies, advertising, etc.). These discursive resources form the cultural background to people's everyday lives and include shared ideas about what it means to be and act as a woman – how to be a 'good' woman. Being a 'good' woman is signified by a woman's appearance (appropriately feminine and attractive to men) and also by the quality of the caring work she performs on behalf of family members. The ideas circulating within a culture which have women as their focus have been referred to as 'discourses of femininity' (Bordo, 1993; Ussher, 1997b).

Discourses of femininity do more than reflect beliefs about women shared by people living within a particular socio-cultural context. They also shape the contours of women's everyday lives and regulate how women explain and understand their lived experiences. In turn, women's bodies provide the means for engaging in practices of femininity, whether maintaining an attractive appearance or caring for family members. Thus, the lived experiences of women are always both embodied and subjective, both material and discursive (Stoppard, 1998, 2000). The following extracts from women's accounts about coping with being depressed show how female bodies are an aspect of the material resources which women draw upon as they engage in everyday practices of femininity. A woman's body not only expresses her gender; it also provides a means for performing activities deemed womanly responsibilities.

so I get up at 5:30, use the bathroom, make [school] lunches [for children], make breakfast ... supper time comes, they eat, leave the dishes in the sink and go and they listen to music, on the phone or in bed ... I get stuck with the dishes, then cleaning up ...[3]

I looked after my family, plus my husband's family. Whenever anybody got sick, they always called [Jane] ... She ... could never say no.[4]

Accounts like these are typical of those given by women we have interviewed. It is hardly surprising, then, that fatigue and tiredness are among the more common health problems reported by women, problems which women attribute to the burdensome nature of their work inside and outside the home (Popay, 1992; Walters 1993). Women's talk about their everyday activities reflects the taken-for-granted character of the work they do on behalf of family members, as something they do as a matter of course.

and I still made their supper, and I would still do their laundry, and I would still do whatever I feel is my duty to do for them. (Scattolon and Stoppard, 1999: 210)

I still did my daily activities ... You know, had supper ready, had dinner ready, had their lunches ready. Did the wash. But none of that had ceased, you know. But I did it because ... well you do it. (Gammell and Stoppard, 1999: 120)

According to discourses of femininity, women can feel satisfied with themselves when they engage in activities signifying that they are good women. From a material-discursive perspective, a woman is likely to feel good when her everyday practices are in keeping with cultural ideals of the good woman. Meeting these culturally defined standards may be manifested concretely by having well-behaved and healthy children, a harmonious marital relationship, and a well-kept home. What happens, however, when a woman's caring work becomes, or already is, routinized and taken-for-granted, or children misbehave, or a partner is unappreciative, neglectful or abusive? At the same time, a woman may be locked into a double day of work inside and outside the home because of financial necessity. Lack of financial resources has a direct impact on a woman's capacity to fulfil the requirements of a good woman, as illustrated in the following excerpt:

With these children ... you try and tell them you got your food, take it easy on the food ... and then when there's nothing left, of course they sit and cry and of course, we get depressed ... because it's not there. We don't have the money to get more ... I just go in the room and cry. (Scattolon and Stoppard, 1999: 210)

Under conditions in which a woman's efforts do not lead to the personal sense of satisfaction that cultural discourses promise, she may redouble her efforts, working harder, with the hope that she will achieve the illusive sense of fulfilment and good feelings that are supposed to accompany the practices of the good woman. This strategy is limited, however, by the human body as a finite material resource. In this process, a woman may eventually come to realize that although she strives to engage in activities signifying that she is a good woman, the sense of well-being she achieves is hardly commensurate with her efforts. Instead, a woman's everyday activities are more likely to lead to exhaustion of her body and depletion of her morale. Such embodied and subjective experiences can be understood as part of what is called depression. This analysis leads to the conclusion that an approach encompassing both material and discursive dimensions of women's lives can provide a framework for understanding women's depression that not only has specific implications for women coping with being depressed, as well as for practitioners (counselors, therapists, etc.) who work with depressed women. It also has implications more generally for women's well-being and emancipation.

NOTES

1. The author acknowledges the support of a grant from the Social Science and Humanities Research Council of Canada (#410–97–0127) to carry out the research on women's depression drawn upon in this chapter.
2. The first of these excerpts is taken from an interview conducted as part of the author's research and the second is from an interview carried out by Yvette Scattolon as part of the research for her doctoral dissertation (Scattolon, 1999), supervised by the author.
3. This excerpt is from Scattolon (1999).
4. This excerpt is from the author's research.

REFERENCES

American Psychiatric Association (1994) *Diagnostic and Statistical Manual of Mental Disorders: DSM-IV*. Washington, D.C.: American Psychiatric Association

Bebbington, P. (1996) The origins of sex-differences in depressive disorder: bridging the gap. *International Review of Psychiatry*, 8, 295–332

Bordo, S. (1993) *Unbearable Weight: Feminism, Western Culture and the Body*. Berkeley, CA: University of California Press

Brown, G.W. and Harris, T.O. (1978) *Social Origins of Depression: A Study of Psychiatric Disorder in Women*. London: Tavistock

Brown, G.W., and Harris, T.O. (1989) Depression. In G.W. Brown and T.O. Harris (Eds.) *Life events and Illness* (pp. 49–93). London: Unwin Hyman

Burns, D.D. (1992) *Feeling Good: The New Mood Therapy*. New York: Avon

Busfield, J. (1996) *Men, Women and Madness*. London: Macmillan

Coyne, J.C. (1994) Self-reported distress: Analog or ersatz depression? *Psychological Bulletin*, 116, 29–45

Culbertson, F.M. (1997) Depression and gender: An international review. *American Psychologist*, 52, 25–31

Doyal, L. (1995) *What Makes Women Sick? Gender and the Political Economy of Health*. New Brunswick, NJ: Rutgers University Press

Gallant, S.J. and Derry, P.S. (1995) Menarche, menstruation, and menopause: Psychosocial research and future directions. In A.L. Stanton and S.J. Gallant (Eds.) *Psychology and Women's Health: Progress and Challenges in Research and Application* (pp. 199–259). Washington, D.C.: American Psychological Association

Gammell, D.J. and Stoppard, J.M. (1999) Women's experiences of treatment of depression: Medicalization or empowerment? *Canadian Psychology*, 40, 112–128

Hamilton, J.A. (1995) Sex and gender as critical variables in psychotropic drug research. In C.V. Willies, P.P. Rieker, M.M. Kramer and B.S. Brown (Eds.) *Mental Health, Racism, and Sexism* (pp. 297–349). Pittsburgh, PA: University of Pittsburgh Press

Hamilton, J.A. and Jensvold, M.F. (1995) Sex and gender as critical variables in feminist psychopharmacology research and pharmacology. *Women and Therapy*, 16, 9–30

Harding, S. (1991) *Whose Science? Whose Knowledge? Thinking from Women's Lives*. Ithaca, NY: Cornell University Press

Harding, S. (1996) Gendered ways of knowing and the 'epistemological crisis' of the west. In N.B. Goldberger, J.M. Tarule, B.M. Clinchy and M.F. Belenky (Eds.) *Knowledge, Difference and Power: Essays Inspired By Women's Ways Of Knowing* (pp. 431–451). New York: Basic Books

Harre, R. and Stearns, P. (Eds.) (1995) *Disursive Psychology in Practice*. London: Sage

Henwood, K. and Pidgeon, N. (1995) Remaking the link: Qualitative research and feminist standpoint theory. *Feminism and Psychology*, 5, 7–30

Jack, D.C. (1991) *Silencing the Self: Women and Depression*. Cambridge, MA: Harvard University Press

Lock, M. (1993) *Encounters With Aging: Mythologies of menopause in Japan and North America*. Berkeley, CA: University of California Press

McGrath, E., Keita, G.P., Strickland, B.R. and Russo, N.F. (1990) *Women and Depression: Risk Factors and Treatment Issues*. Washington, D.C.: American Psychological Association

Nolen-Hoeksema, S. (1990) *Sex Differences in Depression*. Stanford, CA: Stanford University Press

Olfson, M.D. and Klerman, G.L. (1993) Trends in prescription of antidepressants by office-based psychiatrists. *American Journal of Psychiatry*, 150, 571–577

Parker, I. (1997) Discursive psychology. In D. Fox and I. Prilleltensky (Eds.) *Critical Psychology: An Introduction* (pp. 284–298). London: Sage

Popay, J. (1992) 'My health is all right, but I'm just tired all the time': Women's experience of ill health. In H. Roberts (Ed.) *Women's Health Matters* (pp. 99–120). London: Routledge

Regier, D.A., Boyd, J.H., Burke, J.D., Rae, D.S., Myers, J.K., Kramer, M., Robins, L.N., George, L.K., Karno, M. and Locke, B.Z. (1988) One-month prevalence of mental disorders in the United States: Based on five epidemiologic catchment area sites. *Archives of General Psychiatry*, 45, 977–986

Scattolon, Y. (1999) Perceptions of depression and coping with depressive experiences among rural women in New Brunswick. Unpublished doctoral dissertation, University of New Brunswick, Canada

Scattolon, Y. and Stoppard, J.M. (1999) 'Getting on with life': Women's experiences and ways of coping with depression. *Canadian Psychology*, 40, 205–219

Smith, D.E. (1987) *The Everyday World as Problematic: A Feminist Sociology*. Toronto: University of Toronto Press

Stanton, A.L. and Danoff-Burg, S. (1995) Selected issues in women's reproductive health: Psychological perspectives. In A.L. Stanton and S.J. Gallant (Eds.) *Psychology and Women's Health: Progress and Challenges in Research and Application* (pp. 261–305). Washington, D.C.: American Psychological Association

Stoppard, J.M. (1997) Women's bodies, women's lives and depression: Towards a reconciliation of material and discursive accounts. In J.M. Ussher (Ed.) *Body Talk: The Material and Discursive Regulation of Sexuality, Madness and Reproduction* (pp. 10–32 London: Routledge

Stoppard, J.M. (1998) Dis-ordering depression in women: Toward a materialist-discursive account. *Theory and Psychology*, 8, 79–99

Stoppard, J.M. (2000) *Understanding Depression: Feminist Social Constructionist Approaches*, London: Routledge

Ussher, J.M. (1991) *Women's Madness: Misogyny Or Mental Illness*. Hemel Hempstead: Harvester Wheatsheaf

Ussher, J.M. (Ed.) (1997a) *Body Talk: The Material and Discursive Regulation of Sexuality, Madness and Reproduction*. London: Routledge

Ussher, J.M. (1997b) *Fantasies of Femininity: Reframing the Boundaries of Sex*. London: Penguin

Walters, V. (1993) Stress, anxiety and depression: Women's accounts of their health problems. *Social Science and Medicine*, 36, 393–402

Weissman, M.M., Bland, R., Joyce, P.R., Newman, S., Wells J.E. and Wittchen, H. (1993) Sex differences in rates of depression: Cross-national perspectives. *Journal of Affective Disorders*, 29, 77–84

Weissman, M.M. and Klerman, G. (1977) Sex differences and the epidemiology of depression. *Archives of General Psychiatry*, 34, 98–111

Weissman, M.M. and Olfson, M. (1995) Depression in women: Implications for health care research. *Science*, 269, 799–801

Yardley, L. (Ed.) (1997) *Material Discourses of Health and Illness*. London: Routledge

Women's Narratives of Recovery from Disabling Mental Health Problems: A Bicultural Project from Aotearoa/New Zealand[1]

Hilary Lapsley, Linda Waimarie Nikora and Rosanne Black

INTRODUCTION

This chapter describes three women's accounts of recovery from depression experienced as mothers. The women's narratives are part of a larger bicultural study, carried out in Aotearoa/New Zealand, of recovery from disabling mental health problems. In examining the women's stories, we emphasize gender and ethnicity, as well as identity and agency, in texts of illness and recovery.

A central task of feminist psychology today is to theorize and investigate how women's experience is gendered, through the material conditions and the symbolic discursive processes of social life (Ussher, 1997). Women's experiences of mental ill-health in Western cultures are gendered and regulated through such processes. Social inequalities foster psychological distress and, in the symbolic realm, this distress is naturalized in discourses on femininity and women's bodies (Busfield, 1996; Chesler, 1972; Showalter, 1987; Ussher, 1991, 1997).

Stoppard (1997, and Chapter 46), in discussing depression, advocates the use of feminist standpoint epistemologies in research, with their emphasis on 'the perspectives of those whose lives are shaped and constrained (or marginalized) by the dominant social order' (p. 26). She argues that we need to research women's accounts of mental ill-health, which have the potential to provide alternative discourses and to 'offer the individual more affirming, more empowering and less stigmatizing, self-blaming ways of interpreting their experiences' (p. 28).

THE AOTEAROA/NEW ZEALAND CONTEXT

In Aotearoa/New Zealand, Maori are providing counter-discourses to that of the mainstream. Their context is a legacy of colonization which involved repetitive breaches of the Treaty of Waitangi, the founding document of our nation, which lays out the basis for partnership between Maori, as the indigenous people of Aotearoa, and settler (Pakeha) populations (Thomas and Nikora, 1997). For psychologists in this country, the challenge is to honour the Treaty through the development of Maori and local psychologies, and through mutually beneficial partnerships, as well as stand-alone initiatives in research and practice (Nikora, 1993).

There has been recognition that Maori experiences of health and illness differ, both culturally and materially, from non-Maori experiences (Durie, 1988). Health statistics portray an alarming deficit in Maori health which, it is argued, results from poverty, social exclusion and cultural disempowerment (Durie, 1998; Te Puni Kokiri, 1998). Maori health initiatives have begun to deliver innovative services, incorporating indigenous holistic health practices with Western biomedical approaches. In the mental health area, there is usually a commitment to enhancing Maori identity, through cultural renewal, to strengthen individuals, enabling them to draw more fully on resources to deal with ill-health (Hirini, 1997; Durie, 1986).

A BICULTURAL PROJECT

The bicultural research project described in this paper investigates narratives of recovery from disabling mental health problems. Our team has two principal investigators, one Maori and one Pakeha, and a Pakeha project researcher. We have worked with a group of interviewers, Maori and Pakeha of both sexes. In our work we seek to examine the gendered and cultured experience of developing a mental health problem, recovering from it, and continuing with life afterwards.

Forty stories from Maori and non-Maori men and women have now been recorded and transcribed, after a lengthy process of selecting appropriate individuals to interview. This involved widespread consultation with consumer and community groups and health services. We chose to interview people who felt that they had experienced a mental health problem which was disabling, and from which they had now recovered. We suggested that people would not currently be using psychiatric medication and would not have had contact with mental health services over the last two years; most of the people we interviewed met these criteria. Selection for diversity was also a goal. We achieved a range of ages, occupations, educational backgrounds and illness experiences. We interviewed people whose experiences ranged from extensive periods of hospitalization to those who had never used mental health services; and people who had experienced different forms of mental health problems and a variety of diagnoses.

The narrative emphasis of the project provides an innovative edge. Instead of investigating causes or cures, we take for granted that experiences of mental ill-health occur in the lifetime of many individuals. We asked people to tell us their stories of ill-health and recovery. In examining their transcripts, we inquire into the ways in which gender and culture shape these experiences, with a particular interest in how such experiences might transform identity.

At present, we are in the early stages of a systematic analysis of the narratives. We will be identifying, using qualitative data analysis procedures, themes in recovery and life change. As well, we will analyse the discursive constructions of gender, ethnicity and mental health in the texts. Here we introduce our work on texts of recovery through an analysis of three narratives of depression in mothers of young children.

Pare

Pare is a Maori woman in her mid-thirties. During her tertiary studies, undertaken as an adult student, she heard a talk about postnatal depression, and realized that the symptoms described were exactly what she had experienced after the birth of each of her five children.

She had first become pregnant at age 19. Pare was unable to tell her mother, who was ashamed of her, that the pregnancy had resulted from rape. After the child was born, she began a long-term relationship with a man who already had children of his own. Together, they had four more children, and after each birth she often had trouble sleeping, becoming exhausted, depressed and unable to manage. In her words, 'I was a zombie… a real mess and I couldn't cope'. Her partner was often unhelpful, though on one occasion when she walked out and left him with the children, he acknowledged how hard she worked.

Pare's mother often helped out during these periods of 'breakdown', taking the children, or taking her daughter home for a few days so she could sleep. She often criticised or blamed Pare, which made their relationship difficult. Her mother and sister also made sure Pare got outside help, taking her to the doctor or getting a Plunket (early childhood) nurse to call. What usually happened was that after a period of rest, attempts to lighten the load at home, and getting together better support structures, Pare would take charge of her family again.

The years she spent raising small children were hardworking and productive. Pare became deeply involved in community affairs, as well as doing paid work, getting a tertiary education and a professional qualification. She also supported her husband's career and contributed to a family business.

With repeated experiences of not coping, she began to learn some useful ways of restoring herself and of understanding her depression. She told us, for example, of a tohunga (healer) who helped her lay to rest the spirit of a friend, which had disturbed her after his untimely death. A chance to carry out a research project on postnatal depression, as part of her studies, helped her put her experience into context. A doctor gave her anti-depressants, which she found very helpful, wishing that she had used them earlier.

Pare began to see her depressions as not only postnatal, but tied into other aspects of her life and her body. Her sister encouraged her to identify a relationship between depression and her monthly cycle. An elderly uncle felt moved to visit her after a dream. He told her of his experience of sexual abuse, provided a *karakia* (prayer) and a cleansing ritual. This led to two years of counseling for sexual abuse in her childhood, as well as over the rape which led to her first pregnancy. One unhelpful contact was with a parent help agency, where she felt the Maori counselors 'knew post-natal depression in a negative way' and she was anxious that they might take her children away.

Although depression is still a risk, Pare is far removed from the young woman who did not know what was going on; now she knows 'it isn't just me'. She recently separated from her partner and moved to another city to continue her studies, resulting in financial difficulties. She felt low and thought of joining a 'depression group' but told herself, 'I'm sick of being depressed and I don't ever want to be there again'. Instead, she joined a group with Maori women because she wanted to be around them, and 'I knew one of the areas, my last area, really, to look at was oppression and how it's affected my life'.

Kim

Kim is a middle-aged Pakeha woman who has worked in secretarial and administrative roles, usually with community organizations. She has been married for 25 years and has three children. She was brought up with seven brothers and sisters in a very sheltered Catholic family. At 19 she had a breakdown after finishing a relationship with an older man, who had violated her moral standards, causing her to lose respect for herself.

Later she married and after her second child was born, she began to get depressed and lose confidence, though she managed to get herself over 'that little hump'. But when she and her husband moved away from the city she had lived in all her life, and a third child was born, she became very depressed, compared herself unfavourably to the other mothers she knew, and began to stay in bed most of the day, crying. The doctor gave her anti-depressants, which made things worse, and alternative healers could not provide anything useful, either. She spent three brief periods in a psychiatric hospital over the next two years, where she received shock treatment and anti-psychotic medications.

It was just so incredibly devastating to end up in a mental hospital... I always thought there was a 'them' and an 'us'. There was a type of person that became mentally ill and there was another type, which was me and my family, but there I was, locked in the day room.

She had lots of support from her husband and her parents, and a 'wonderful' friend was very supportive, too. But when she made no improvement they became discouraged. Kim's husband wrote a letter to her parents where he said, 'I can't do anything more for her. I think she needs to come and live with you'. He did not send the letter, and to Kim it was an indication of 'how desperate he became'. Instead, she was hospitalized again and her husband soldiered on with his paid work, looking after the children and coming to visit her as well. 'I had a lovely family. Three beautiful children, lovely husband. But I was depressed.'

No one in the hospital talked to her about her feelings; instead, they provided confinement, humiliation, a 'chemical strait jacket', the opportunity to make Muppets and macramé baskets, and torture in the form of ECT. In desperation she ran away, leaving the children on the corner of her sister-in-law's street as she felt unable to ask her sister-in-law to look after them. She considered suicide, but 'because of my upbringing I couldn't do myself in because I'd go to hell'. She was returned to face another spell in Lake Alice, a psychiatric hospital.

What helped Kim recover from depression was joining GROW, a self-help mental health organization modelled along the lines of Alcoholics Anonymous. A cousin suggested it, and there she found acceptance and love, and was helped to develop the personal resources she needed to overcome depression. Looking back, she believes that she never had a chance to grow up and learn to take responsibility for her own life. The practical techniques taught by GROW encouraged her to overcome her moods and take charge of her situation.

When she was asked to become a group leader, Kim began to read and re-educate herself, and to advocate for GROW in the community, eventually taking on a national role in the organization. In her eyes this was her true 'rehabilitation'. Recently she recalled her hospital files, where she found she had been labelled variously as schizophrenic and schizoaffective. She has also recognized that sexual abuse from a baby-sitter, which she never told her parents about, profoundly affected her later relationships.

Fiona

Fiona, a Maori woman in her late thirties, went into a 'deep depression' after the break-up of her marriage, where she had experienced violence from her partner and acute jealousy at his unfaithfulness. Her sister and a close friend had died in a car accident a year earlier, and she was grieving for that loss as well. She lost weight, could not sleep and stayed in bed all day, 'like a zombie'. Her family was very concerned, and her parents took the two children to stay with them. Fiona began drinking a lot and taking drugs. She quit her well-paying job, left her nice home and left town.

I think I must have looked like a normal person, but inside, it was like this shattered person walking around ... It was an ugly time, it was a big black hole.

For nearly two years she lived the life of 'lost people', drinking and 'getting wasted' and during this time gained a criminal conviction, which she felt was an affront to her 'goody-two shoes' family who were very respectable.

The turning point came when her family asked her to take the children back. They felt that she had been given her grieving time, and now she should resume with normal life. She felt she had to make a choice then, between being the local 'drunkard, druggie ... all spaced out person', which was a 'safe place', or returning to her responsibilities. It was hard for her to come back from what she calls the

Cop out zone ... It was a zone that I needed. Time out ... By the same token, it takes a hell of a lot to come out of that place.

One person who helped during this period was her grandmother, who was 'into whakapapa' (genealogy/lineage) and who taught Fiona that she was responsible not only to herself, but to her whole extended family, past and future. Her grandmother told her 'all the reasons that I needed to love me, 'cause there's more to me than just myself'.

Throughout her recovery, though Fiona saw a doctor, she had no contact with mental health services. She wanted to avoid being labeled, even though she thought therapy might have been useful. And if any of her children ever suffered in the same way,

I would rather they go through the cycle I did than go through some sort of western thing.

Working in a Maori health organization has strengthened her understanding of Maori health practice, which emphasizes the interdependence of the individual in relation to their *whanau* (family), and community, across time.

If I look at my whakapapa and I look back, my great grandchildren will be looking at their whakapapa and seeing me in there, and I hold that so dear to me. That's awesome. That's why I love it where I'm at. It's very Maori.

ACHIEVING RECOVERY

What do we hear in the stories of these three women? All experienced forms of depression, which led to an inability to cope with mothering. All describe the anguish and disconnectedness of the experience of depression, and the guilt and feelings of inadequacy associated with not being able to keep going.

Each woman had concerned and caring relatives, though only in the Maori families was there a belief that it was the right thing to do to step in and take care of the children, or to provide a refuge, in the case of Pare. Maori households are more flexible, and it has been the norm for children to live for extended periods of time with *whanau*/relatives, especially the first-born who are sometimes claimed with delight by their grandparents. Both Fiona's and Pare's eldest children had already spent time living with grandparents.

Transferring oneself or one's children back to the family of origin was unthinkable for Kim, in a Pakeha context. She did not wish to bear the stigma of failure and reproduce the relations of childhood by being sent back to her parents as if she were faulty goods. When she ran off she was too ashamed to make arrangements for childcare; Pare and Fiona also took off suddenly, but there was far less sense of shame about others stepping in. Their context emphasized interdependence, not dependency.

Recovery texts for all three echo the same themes, but with culturally different resonances. Western resources were used by both Fiona and Pare. Pare wished she had discovered antidepressants earlier on, whereas Fiona refused to take hers as prescribed, but using the sleeping pills the doctor gave her encouraged a drug habit. Pare's relative, the psychiatric nurse, told her that she wasn't in a bad enough state to go to a psychiatric hospital, and even though Pare herself once insisted to the doctor that she *was* bad enough, a short rest in a nursing home was provided instead. Fiona avoided the stigma of mental health care, preferring the streets, and Kim, of course, had the full complement of interventions, which proved traumatic.

The Maori resources drawn on by Fiona and Pare strengthened them and did not come with the stigma attached to Western services. Pare's uncle prayed for her, conducted a healing ceremony and encouraged her to come to terms with her sexual abuse for the sake of her *whanau* (family). For this process she used a Maori sexual abuse service; she also had traditional help with the disturbing 'sucking' feeling of being haunted. When she felt ready to step beyond depression, she took her low feelings to a Maori women's group, where she could share an analysis of colonization. Fiona's chief healing resource was her grandmother's love, and cultural wisdom, in turn reflecting the most primary relationship in Maori culture, grandparent to grandchild.

The healing resource for Kim was her connection with GROW, where she came to understand wider support, love without dependency, the importance of a healthy relationship to both herself and the community; she was able to access a sustaining spiritual dimension.

As women, mental illness did not serve to threaten their femininity (whereas some of the men in the study certainly experienced their masculinity as threatened). Each was aware of the difficulties arising from their responsibilities as mothers, but each felt strongly committed to, competent in, and drew pride from that role, except when undermined by illness. Work outside the home was also important, and taking on community responsibilities strengthened Pare and Kim. Fiona emphasized the loss of her well-paying job as strongly as the fact of her children being taken by her parents.

Fiona and Pare experienced lack of support, and abuse in Fiona's case, from their male partners and both were clear in their decision to move on, despite the pain caused, which for Fiona was the trigger for depression. Each woman needed to deal with trauma arising from violence, in the form of either sexual abuse as children or partner violence.

Though the women's experiences were culturally embedded, for each the recovery process involved fully experiencing the anguish, sadness and life-threatening nature of depression; seeking their own individual solutions at a time when they felt especially cut off from others, despite family support; and undergoing substantial change in their understanding of themselves in relation to their cultural and social worlds. As they dealt with personal issues, gained more experience with what healed and what harmed, they became more ready to advocate for their own needs and at the same time, participate fully in their own communities. They clearly recognized that depression, while very real and embodied, was not inherent to them and not their fault; and that in dealing with it they had proved their strength.

As with many of our other participants, these stories of recovery emphasize their own agency and help from their own support systems, rather than the health system. More often than not, participants in the larger study were critical of mental health interventions, especially psychiatric and inpatient settings. Participants' taking of responsibility for recovery, however, did not mean that they blamed themselves for their disorder; on the contrary, it was when they were most unwell that they tended to blame themselves, often making futile efforts to restore the status quo. Mostly there was a sense of the illness as a real, bodily experience arising from within themselves, yet recovery involved a struggle against being overwhelmed by their illness, at the same time not rejecting it; and a struggle not to be defined by the illness and its resultant stigma. Discourses on recovery often placed mental ill-health as the outcome of their life situation and mental health as involving strengthening or alteration in identities, leading to social and personal insights, a sense of their own needs and a sense of connectedness. Their texts of illness are social texts, gendered and raced, and so are their recovery texts, yet the latter drew on the more empowering cultural resources available to them as women and men, Maori and non-Maori, rather than disempowering stereotypes which had once defined them more fully.

NOTE

1.This research was supported by the Health Research Council of New Zealand and the University of Waikato Faculty of Arts and Social Sciences. Many other individuals and organizations gave us their assistance, and we are deeply grateful to those who gave their time to be interviewed.

REFERENCES

Busfield, J. (1996) *Men, Women and Madness: Understanding Gender and Mental Disorder.* New York: New York University Press
Chesler, P. (1972) *Women and Madness.* New York: Avon Books
Durie, M.H. (1986) Te taha hinengaro: an integrated approach to mental health. *Community Mental Health in New Zealand*, 1 (1), 4–11
Durie, M. (1998) *Whaiora: Maori Health Development* (2nd edn). Auckland: Oxford University Press
Hirini, P. (1997) Counselling Maori clients. *New Zealand Journal of Psychology*, 26, 13–18
Nikora, L.W. (Ed.) (1993) *Cultural Justice and Ethics*. Hamilton: University of Waikato
Showalter, E. (1987) *The Female Malady: Women, Madness and English Culture, 1830–1980.* London: Virago
Stoppard, J.M. (1997) Women's bodies, women's lives and depression: towards a reconcilia-

tion of material and discursive accounts. In J.M. Ussher (Ed.) *Body Talk: The Material and Discursive Regulation of Sexuality, Madness, and Reproduction*. London: Routledge

Te Puni Kokiri (1998) *Progress Towards Closing Social and Economic Gaps Between Maori and Non-Maori*. Wellington: Te Puni Kokiri. Ministry of Maori Development

Thomas, D.R. and Nikora, L.W. (1996) From assimilation to biculturalism: Changing patterns in Maori-Pakeha relationships. In D. Thomas and A. Veno (Eds.) *Community Psychology and Social Change: Australia and New Zealand Perspectives* (2nd edn). Palmerston North: The Dunmore Press

Ussher, J.M. (1991) *Women's Madness: Misogyny or Mental Illness*. Amherst: University of Massachusetts Press

Ussher, J.M. (1997) (Ed.) *Body Talk: The Material and Discursive Regulation of Sexuality, Madness, And Reproduction*. London: Routledge.

CHAPTER 48

WOMEN, STRESS AND WORK: EXPLORING THE BOUNDARIES

Rebecca Lawthom

INTRODUCTION

This chapter uses a fictional narrative device to explore the ways in which women may experience stress across the work-family interface. First, it explores the context in which work undertaken by women is understood. The nature of the work-family 'boundary' is examined in terms of both positive and negative impacts upon women. Particular attention is given to the narrow way in which 'work' is conceptualized and women are perceived as a homogenous grouping. Harassment at work is used as an illustration of ways in which women's sexed bodies can be threatening in the workplace, providing a further source of stress. The need for feminist understandings of women's complex positions within domestic and paid arenas is identified, through a critical appraisal of diverse literatures.

LIZ'S NARRATIVE

Liz is a 40-year-old secretary working in a research team at a university. She is contracted to work 37.5 hours a week but as her boss is a busy academic who also undertakes private consultancy work, her hours are often considerably longer, extending into the evenings and weekends. Liz is keen to move up the administration pay scale and achieve promotion, but is not confident about her ability. Her time management skills are constantly called into question by unrealistic demands placed upon her by the research team. In addition to work pressures, her other tasks on behalf of the team include buying presents (relational tasks), organizing birthday teas, picking up dry cleaning and on occasions walking dogs and baby-sitting (for the boss). She is in a long term lesbian relationship and her partner is not out at work. This sometimes presents problems as she is invited to functions with her partner and sometimes experiences harassment (which is difficult to name given her short-term contract). She experiences the stress of working full time, managing a family and caring for aging parents. Her absence from work is often understood in terms of gender (women's problems).

This narrative is woven from diverse experiences and is a 'fiction' (Banks and Banks, 1998). The aim of this research device is to illustrate how working women often straddle the boundary between home and work, experiencing guilt and stress within the family domain and work pressure (which can be harassment) within the work domain. Is also fits in with Hunt's (1998) work on the use of storytelling to generate critical thinking about women's mental health and emotional health care. The narrative can be read in diverse ways. From a mainstream perspective, we may turn to the literature on occupation stress, clerical work and home work boundaries, and speculate on ways in which Liz might improve her context. Using a feminist reading (recognizing the plurality of feminisms) I am using in particular the literature on stress at work and the notion of sexuality and harassment with which to understand the narrative.

THE CONTEXT OF WOMEN'S WORK AND WOMEN'S HEALTH

The overlapping concerns of research into women's health and women at work share a number of underpinning issues. First, that theory, research and practice focus on men in health contexts (e.g. Stanton, 1995; Lee, 1998) and in work contexts (Lawthom, 1999; Marshall, 1995). Second, the addition of women to the research agenda in both health and work domains has been restricted in focus. In health arenas, women's health has been conceptualized narrowly as the ability to reproduce (Ussher, 1992). In work contexts, the focus is restricted primarily to paid work, privileging societal definitions of what constitutes work (Pahl, 1988). Moreover, within the paid work arena, research on working women has been overly preoccupied with women at the higher echelons of organization (Hartley and Mackenzie-Davey, 1997) with some notable exceptions (Cavendish, 1992; Pringle, 1989).

These starting points are the foundation for a feminist analysis which deconstructs and reconstructs the ways in which gendered ideas, practices and institutions position women's health in work contexts both at the hearth (Doyal, 1995) and at work. From a feminist perspective, I recognize the plurality of feminisms (Mama, 1995) but use the term 'women' to refer to a diverse collective of females, differentiated by ethnicity, class, disability and sexuality. Feminisms while still 'other' to the dominant discourses need to retain a collective identity if transformation of dominant power relations in society is a common goal (Yuval-Davis, 1993).

The concerns of the present chapter are explorations of women at work. Where are women in work? Despite the increasing feminization of work, women are concentrated in certain sectors and particular occupations (e.g. Doyal, 1995). Work for women is more likely to be service-type work or homework, without trade union protection. Trends suggest paid work is much more common for women but economic forces restructuring the traditional workplace form the impetus, rather than feminist attitudes. Inequity exists within the clearly segregated workplace and undermines the egalitarian ideology. In the U.K., one-third of all female workers are employed on a part-time basis and 75 percent of women are found in clerical, cleaning, catering, sales or ancillary professions (Social Trends, 1995), thus extending women's domesticity into the paid arena. The U.S. Bureau of Labor Statistics (1991) indicated that 45 percent of employed women worked in clerical and service occupations and 22 percent in sales. Whilst the participation of women in the labor force has increased considerably (e.g. Davidson, 1996), the challenge of managing the home-work interface is increasingly difficult (Lewis and Cooper, 1996). Work-family conflict is significantly and positively related to depression, poor physical health and heavy alcohol use (Frone *et al.*, 1996).

STRESS AT WORK AND HOME

The effects of waged work upon well-being suggests both positive and negative effects. Large scale American studies indicate that employed women enjoy better mental health than those outside the labor market (e.g. Repetti *et al.*, 1989). However, the psychosocial work environment is an important determinant of health status among working women. High strain work is associated with lower vitality, mental health, higher pain and overall lower health status (Amick, Kawachi *et al.*, 1998). Lombardi and Ulrich (1997) explore the ways in which the contexts of paid work and unpaid housework are related to women's sense of mastery, depressed mood and anxiety. In a large-scale study, this research found that the physical demands of work were related to depressed mood but were felt more strongly among employed women (as opposed to home makers).

Stress at work is often explored through psychological job demands, in particular decision latitude (the scope to make decisions) and psychological demands. Studies have found that high psychological demands, low decision latitude and low social support significantly predict depression (e.g. Niedhammer *et al.*, 1998). A large U.K. study explored gender differences in occupational stress and strain in 1,000 civil servants, identifying sources of job-related stress which may be predictive of negative stress outcome (Bogg and Cooper, 1998). Females within the service reported significantly more job dissatisfaction and suffered poorer mental and physical health. In addition women reported more concern about their work roles, factors associated with the particular job and the constraints of the job.

One of the major stressors women face is the home-work interface. The assumption is that women do paid work in addition to the responsibility of the domestic arena, including childcare, caring generally and house-work. Not only does this assumptive framework affect women's health and status but undermines 'both the possibility of a renegotiation of social roles at a personal level, and the possibility of radical reorganisation or social structures which might facilitate such renegotiation' (Lee, 1998: 93). The permeability of the home-work boundary for women is well demon-strated by Matthews *et al.* (1998). The study explored psychosocial work characteristics for those in and outside of paid employment using 11,407 participants from a British birth cohort sample. The psychosocial factors explored were learning opportunities, monotony, pace of work and flexi-bility of breaks. Overall, women reported more negative work character-istics than men, due to differences in monotonous work and learning opportunities. Women in full-time employment reported fewer negative characteristics than part-time or home workers. The latter group reported fewer learning opportunities and greater monotony than paid workers.

The relevance of work to diverse groups of women is relatively unex-plored in the literature. Roberts and Friend (1998) explored career momen-tum in mid-life women, classifying them as increasing, maintaining or decreasing momentum in their career and exploring work and family pat-terns, importance of work to their identity, personality characteristics and psychological well-being. Women with high career momentum tended to be in higher status jobs, viewed work as more central to identity, and scored higher on measures of self-acceptance, independence and effective functioning.

There is clearly an ongoing tension between etiologically oriented research – particularly those that focus on the demand control model and the need to expand the work stress field to include gender and class spe-cific exposure contexts. Other important variables such as work-related social support, exploring the gendered nature of the work process by including measures of the emotional, and invisible labor performed by women (Johnson and Hall, 1996).

HARASSMENT AT WORK

Sexual harassment within the workplace is widespread (see Thomas, in this volume). A plethora of surveys indicate that around 50 percent of women report experiencing sexual harassment at work (e.g. Industrial Society, 1993). Whilst women can correctly label harassment they are often unwilling to take action against employers or use policies to assist, believ-ing that they will suffer negative consequences. Kitzinger and Thomas (1994) show how sexual harassment can be erased through discourse. Their work suggested that the pervasiveness of sexual harassment, women's refusal to position themselves as 'victims', and positioning harassment in terms of sexual interest all assist in contesting the existence of harassment or disputing the intentions behind 'it'. Thomas (in this vol-ume) observes that the focus on incidence rates and definitions of the concept divert attention away from the effects upon women. Moreover, the ways in which harassment is handled seem linked to the representations that women have about harassment. The issue is further clouded by the relationship between gender, sexuality and appropriate work behaviors.

McDowell (1995) explores the links between power relations, hetero-sexuality, identity and the body in the workplace. The body in this analysis is (hetero)sexed and is significant in shaping power relations at work. Moreover, work (paid employment) *is* performance, often undertaken (within a service-based economy) by embodied, gendered and sexed individuals. Personal attributes, indeed sexuality, are an intrinsic part of the product termed jobs which depend upon a 'managed heart' (Hochschild, 1983). Harassment here is less visible and more an implicit part of the job.

Leidner (1991, 1993) defines service sector employment as 'interactive' work where 'distinctions among product, work process and worker are blurred or non-existent, since the quality of the interaction may itself be part of the service offered' (Leidner, 1991: 115). Here, workers need to conform to a conventional, heterosexual image of masculinity and femininity – the gaze of employer, clients and customers ensuring 'normalization'. Women discipline themselves to conform to idealized notions of feminine beauty, or compulsory (hetero)sexual attractiveness (e.g. Bordo, 1993, Coward, 1984). Social anthropologists point out that bodies receive the imprint of cultural norms: 'mutilated or forced into unnatural positions, the body presents a vivid image of "construction"' (Strathern, 1989: 51). Ramazanoglu and Holland (1993: 260) point out that 'there is a complex interaction between grounded embodiment, the discourses of sexuality and institutionalized power' which varies across location and time.

Women's sexed bodies are threatening in the workplace for the very reason that they are not meant to be there. Much workplace behavior – jokes, comments (harassment) – draw attention to this embodiment and construct them as 'other' to a disembodied masculine norm. Young (1990) terms these oppressive behaviors 'cultural imperialism' – a key structure in enforcing dominant oppressive social relations. The dominant group's perspective and its establishment becomes the norm. This process of 'othering' is heightened in macho cultures such as merchant banking where male embodiment is valorized through sexual discourses emphasizing the possession of 'iron balls' or 'big dicks' (Lewis, 1989; McDowell and Court, 1994) by traders who 'consummate' deals. A hegemonic idealized notion of heterosexual masculinity is the dominant image.

The *politics of appearance* are evidenced through dress codes where adherence to corporate norms is important. Looking professional yet minimizing sexual allure is important for younger women. More senior women use dress as performance to create or subvert. Bordo observes that 'feminine' decorativeness may function 'subversively' in professional contexts dominated by highly masculinist norms (such as academia) (Bordo, 1993).

The purpose of the body and self-presentation (in service arenas) is to create an acceptable image which conforms to the selling script. Women are often encouraged to flirt with clients (making them 'special') or to involving themselves in social and semi-social activities, blurring pleasure and business boundaries. Rugby, golf, opera, dinner are all arenas where single women are expected to entertain clients. Women talked about their different feminized strategies to win sales within merchant banking. The latter, like service jobs in general, involves 'emotional work'. Client/banker interactions depend on what Stinchombe (1990) termed 'ethnomethodological competence' – the capacity to make use of unspoken norms of behavior (here norms of heterosexual attraction).

Selling products involves selling oneself and Hochschild (1983) argues that this has consequences for subjectivity where workers become alienated from their feelings and have difficulty in feeling authentic. Workplace selves are constructed as other persona. Junior women are more likely to adopt a masculinist version of self in the workplace – Acker (1990) terms this the 'honorary male' strategy. Dellinger and Williams (1997) explore women's use of makeup in the workplace. Appropriate makeup use is strongly associated with assumptions of health, heterosexuality and credibility in the workplace. Women can transform the meanings of wearing make up and occasionally subvert institutional norms.

The arenas focussed on here – stress and harassment – shed some light on Liz's narrative. First, the stress of home/work pressures which forms a continuum rather than isolated 'work' stress (paid) and domestic gender-roled related stress. Second, the idea that stress is an individualized construct which can be 'managed'. Third, the idea of the lesbian body at work (which can both be feminine but not heterosexed). These all demonstrate the way in which women's bodies, and hence psychological reactions such as stress, are understood in workplace and domestic settings.

Whilst there is mixed evidence about the benefits and disadvantages of waged work on well-being, research has concentrated upon 'developed' countries while work on formal and informal sectors continues to go unresearched. Moreover, in 'developed' countries, a further body of research links working women to harmful effects upon children. Here, the focus on child emotional development and behavior puts the child's needs before the mother's (the absent working father is rarely considered). Within paid work, there is little tightly controlled research to examine the effect of harassment upon health (Thomas, in this volume) or to explore the impact of hidden sexuality. The complexity of women's home/work experiences are not mirrored in research. Lee (1998) points out that research on women's health within empiricist traditions often partializes women's experiences and is biologically reductionist in focus. Similarly, research on women at work more often constitutes narrow definitions of work and within that often confines experiences to measurement variables such as stress. Work outside the paid domain (more often explored by feminists) should focus on the boundary between paid and unpaid forms of work. An extensive consideration of the method, aims and ways forward for feminist approaches to research on women's psychological health is given in Lee (1998, chapter 13).

SUMMARY

How can feminism make sense of and challenge the status quo? Working women (within paid or domestic spheres), many of whom would not identify themselves as feminists, need the kind of analysis and gendered lens which feminism can provide. From a community psychological perspective, Prilleltensky (1989) has criticised psychology's focus on the individual and on cognitive adjustment, rather than practical change, by advocating a world order in which 'solutions for human predicaments are to be found within the self, leaving the social order unaffected' (p. 796). It is too simple to engage women in stress management programs or 'development' activities which encourage women to change (i.e. become assertive in order to avoid harassment). Feminism needs to embrace this potential complexity. A feminist analysis should problematize health and work-related issues as simple individual constructs and explore the wider context within which health, gender and work are understood. Understanding women as people in context will allow research to generate legislative and practical change.

REFERENCES

Acker, J. (1990) Hierarchies, jobs, bodies: A theory of gendered organisations. *Gender and Society*, 4, 139–158

Amick, B.C., Kawachi, I., Coakley, E.H., Lerner, D., Levine, S. and Colditz, G.A. (1998) Relationship of job strain to health status in a cohort of women in the United States. *Scandinavian Journal of Work, Environment and Health*, 24 (1), 54–61

Bogg, J. and Cooper, C.L. (1998) An examination of gender differences for job satisfaction, mental health and occupational stress among senior UK civil servants. *International Journal of Stress Management*, 1 (2), 159–172

Bordo, S. (1993) *Unbearable Weight: Feminism, Western Culture and the Body.* London: University of California Press

Cavendish, R. (1982) *On the Line.* London: Virago

Coward, R. (1984) *Female Desire: Women's Sexuality Today,* London: Granada

Davidson, M. (1996) Women and Employment. In P. Warr (Ed.) *Psychology at Work.* Harmondsworth: Penguin

Dellinger, K. and Williams, C.L. (1997) Make up at work: Negotiating appearance rules in the workplace. *Gender and Society*, 11 (2), 151–177

Doyal, L. (1995) *What Makes Women Sick? Gender and the Political Economy of Health.* London: Macmillan

Frone, M.R., Russell, M. and Barnes, G.A. (1996) Work-family conflict, gender and health related outcomes: A study of employed parents in two community samples. *Journal of Occupational Health Psychology*, 1 (1), 57–69

Hartley, J. and Mackenzie-Davey, K. (1997) Organizational psychology: theory. The gender agenda in organizations: a review of research about women and organizational psychology. *Feminism and Psychology*, 7 (2), 214–223

Hochschild, A. (1983) *The Managed Heart: Commercialisation of Human Feeling.* Berkeley: University of California Press

Hunt, L. (1998) Woman to women support: lessons from an Australian case story. *Patient Education and Counselling*, 33 (3), 257–265

Industrial Society (1993) *No Offence.* London: Industrial Society

Johnson, J.V. and Hall, E.M. (1996) Dialectic between conceptual and causal inquiry in psychosocial work environment research. *Journal of Occupational Health Psychology*, 1 (4), 362–374

Kitzinger, C. and Thomas, A. (1995) Sexual harassment: a discursive approach. In S. Wilkinson and C. Kitzinger (Eds.) *Feminism and Discourse: Psychological Perspectives.* London: Sage

Lawthom, R. (1999) Using the 'f' word in organizational psychology: foundations for critical feminist research. *Annual Review of Critical Psychology*, 1, 65–78

Lee, C. (1998) *Women's Health: Psychological and Social Perspectives*. London: Sage

Leidner, R. (1991) Serving hamburgers and selling insurance. *Gender and Society*, 5, 154–177

Lewis, M. (1989) *Liar's Poker: Two Cities: True Greed*. London: Hodder and Stoughton

Lewis, S. and Cooper, C.L. (1996) *The Work-Family Challenge: Rethinking Employment*. London: Sage

Lombardi, E.L., Ulrich., P.M. (1997) Work condition, mastery and psychological distress: Are housework and paid work contexts conceptually similar? *Women and Health*, 26 (2), 17–39

Mama, A. (1994) *Beyond the Masks: Race, Gender and Subjectivity*. London: Routledge

Matthews, S., Hertzman, C., Ostry, A. and Power, C. (1998) Gender. work roles and psychosocial work characteristics as determinants of health. *Social Science and Medicine*, 46 (11), 1417–1424

McDowell, L. (1995) Body work: heterosexual performances in city workplaces. In M.D. Bell and G. Valentine (Eds.) *Mapping Desire: Geographies of Sexualities*. London: Routledge

McDowell, L. and Court, G. (1994) Missing subjects: Gender, power and sexuality in merchant banking: *Economic Geography*, 70, 229–251

Niedhammer, I., Goldberg, M., Leclerc, A., Bugel, I. and David, S. (1998) Psychosocial factors at work and subsequent depressive symptoms in the Gazel cohort. *Scandinavian Journal of Work, Environment and Health*, 24, 197–205

Pahl, R. (Ed.) (1988) *On Work: Historical, Comparative and Theoretical Approaches*. Oxford: Blackwell

Prilleltensky, I. (1989) Psychology and the status quo. *American Psychologist*, 44, 795–802

Pringle, R. (1989) Bureaucracy, rationality and sexuality: the case of secretaries. In J. Hearn, D.L. Sheppard, P. Tancred-Sheriff and G. Burrell (Eds.) *The Sexuality of Organizations*. London: Sage

Ramazanoglu, C., and Holland, J. (1993) Women's sexuality and men's appropriation of desire. In C. Ramazanoglu (Ed.) *Up Against Foucault: Explorations of Some Tensions Between Foucault and Feminism*. London: Routledge

Repetti. R., Matthews, K. and Waldron, I. (1989) Employment and women's health: effects of paid employment on women's mental and physical health. *American Psychologist*, 44 (11), 1394–1401

Roberts, B.W. and Friend, W. (1998) Career momentum in mid-life women: Life context, identity and personality correlates. *Journal of Occupational Health Psychology*, 3 (3), 195–208

Stanton, A.L. (1995) Psychology of women's health: Barriers and pathways to knowledge. In A.L. Stanton and S.J. Gallant (Eds.) *The Psychology of Women's Health: Progress and Challenges in Research and Application*. Washington, D.C.: American Psychological Association

Stinchombe, A.L. (1990) 'Work institutions and the sociology of everyday life. In K. Erikson and S.P. Vallas (Eds.) *The Nature of Work: Sociological Perspectives*. New Haven: Yale University Press

Strathern, M. (1989) Between a melanesianist and a deconstructive feminist. *Australian Feminist Studies*, 10, 49–69

Ussher, J. (1992) Reproductive rhetoric and the blaming of the body. In P. Nicolson and J.Ussher (Eds.) *The Psychology of Women's Health and Health Care*. Basingstoke: Macmillan

Young, I. M. (1990) *Justice and the Politics of Difference*. Princeton: Princeton University Press

Yuval-Davis, N. (1993) Beyond difference: women and coalition politics. In M. Kennedy, C. Lubelska and V. Walsh (Eds.) *Making Connections: Women's Studies, Women's Movements, Women's Lives*. London: Taylor & Francis

THE SOCIO-POLITICAL CONTEXT OF ABORTION AND ITS RELATIONSHIP TO WOMEN'S MENTAL HEALTH

Jean Denious and Nancy Felipe Russo

Good health is essential to leading a productive and fulfilling life, and the right of all women to control all aspects of their health, in particular their own fertility, is basic to their empowerment. ...

The human rights of women include their right to have control over and decide freely and responsibly on matters related to their sexuality, including sexual and reproductive health, free of coercion, discrimination and violence. ...

Platform for Action: Fourth World Conference on Women, Beijing China, sections C.93; C.96.

INTRODUCTION

These words, contained in the national platform for action of the United Nations Fourth World Conference on Women, recognize a basic reality: good health is a necessary condition for women's full participation in social, political and economic life, and women's ability to control their fertility – that is, to be able to both time, space, and limit their childbearing – is a necessary condition for good health. Reproductive rights are thus crucial for women's physical and psychological health; and addressing political attempts to restrict these rights becomes a key element in any global health agenda for women.

An estimated 22 percent of all pregnancies worldwide are terminated by abortion. Most women around the world have more children than they desire, and wish to halt or delay future births (Alan Guttmacher Institute (AGI), 1999), and abortion plays a major role in enabling many of them to meet their reproductive goals. Nevertheless, one in four women live in countries where abortion is severely restricted or prohibited by law. Even within countries where abortion is legal, fierce political controversy threatens women's access to abortion services, effectively limiting their reproductive rights (AGI, 1999).

Here, we take a brief look at abortion worldwide. We consider how political controversy shapes our understanding of abortion, and discuss how political strategies and tactics to deny women access to abortion have implications for women's physical and psychological health (see also Boyle, in this volume).

ABORTION WORLDWIDE

Abortion rates differ widely across cultures and continents (see AGI, 1999). Although legal status is a major factor in accessibility to abortion and often reflects the culture's attitude toward abortion, it does not adequately explain the variation in rates across countries. For example, abortion is generally legal in Europe, but the rate varies widely across that region. In Eastern Europe, the rate of abortion is four times higher (approximately 80 abortions per 1,000 women aged 15–44) than in Western Europe. Western Europe's abortion rate also is lower than that of Latin America, despite the fact that abortion is highly restricted in Latin American countries. Such differences reflect a multitude of sociocultural and economic factors, but they underscore an important fact – legal and social sanctions do not stop women from seeking to control their reproduction.

Legal status *is* a large determinant of how safely abortion is practiced and the conditions under which women can obtain it. At 0.6 to 1.2 deaths per 100,000 abortions (depending on length of gestation – earlier abortions are safer), mortality rates are negligible in countries where abortion is legal on broad grounds and is performed by licensed physicians. The risk of dying from an abortion is substantially lower than the risk of childbirth, which ranges between six to 25 per 100,000 live births in developed countries (AGI, 1999).

In developing countries, where laws tend to be more often restrictive and abortions must therefore be performed clandestinely (e.g. by the woman herself or an unqualified practitioner), the mortality rate is much higher (e.g. in Latin America, the death rate is 119 per 100,000 abortions; in Africa the figure is 680 per 100,000 abortions). The World Health Organization estimates that 13 percent of pregnancy-related deaths around the world result from unsafe abortion (AGI, 1999). Socioeconomic status can play a large role in women's ability to obtain safe abortions, however. More affluent women can afford to pay qualified doctors to perform illegal abortions, whereas poor women are more likely to attempt the abortion themselves or to have it performed by someone who is not medically trained.

The differences across nations of how abortion is handled legally, construed culturally, and obtained individually appear somewhat associated with levels of socio-economic development. Although there is variation within equally developed countries, overall, developing countries are much more likely to have restrictive abortion laws than developed countries. In some countries, such as Chile and Nepal, for example, women have been and continue to be jailed for having abortions. But it is important not to stereotype developing countries as anti-abortion. Among the 55 countries with liberal laws, the five countries with no restrictions are Canada, China, North Korea, Vietnam and Zambia. Further, three of the developing countries with the largest populations – China, India, and Vietnam – have generally liberal laws (AGI, 1999).

Abortion is a socially constructed issue. It holds multiple meanings (e.g. feminist/moral/health/population issues) and these meanings are malleable (see Boyle, in this volume, for additional discussion). We emphasize the importance of considering abortion's meaning in its political context, but always remembering that whatever the context, how abortion is practiced has profound health implications.

ABORTION IN POLITICAL CONTEXT

Romania's history of liberalization, restriction, and re-liberalization of abortion laws provides a natural stark demonstration of the impact that abortion laws can have on women's health (see Baban, 1999, for a more in-depth description of these events). In 1957 Romania passed the most liberal abortion law in Europe and for nearly a decade Romanian woman had access to legal abortion to control their childbearing. In October of 1966, however, under the repressive pro-natalist regime of Nicolae Ceausescu, the liberal abortion policy was abruptly reversed without warning. A number of other legal changes, including a revision of the penal code to punish abortion providers, buttressed the abortion restrictions. Legal and political machinery was established to ensure that pro-natalist policies were enforced. These included mandatory reproductive health examinations by factory physicians who had to monitor women's pregnancies for the state and who received their full salary only if the plant workers met their birth quota.

What happened? As might be expected, the birth rate rose abruptly from 14.3 per 1,000 women aged 15 to 44 in 1966 to 27.4 in 1967. Most relevant here, however, is the abrupt rise in maternal death rates. In 1966 the maternal mortality rate was 85.9 per 100,000 live births; in 1967 it jumped to 96.8. It continued to rise as the pro-natalist policies became more stringently enforced, hitting a high of 174.8 in 1983. Abortion-related maternal mortality went from 23.4 in 1966 to 32.8 in 1967, rising to a high of 151.3 in 1982 (Baban, 1999).

In December of 1989, Ceausescu was overthrown. On its first day in power, the new government reversed the restrictive legislation. The health effects were dramatic. Maternal mortality dropped from 169.6 in 1989 to 83.6 in 1990. It has continued to drop, and was 41.4 in 1997. Abortion-related maternal mortality dropped from 147.4 in 1989 to 57.5 in 1990 and was 21.1 in 1997 (Baban, 1999).

This case is perhaps extreme in the abruptness of the legal restriction and in the lengths the state went to enforce its pro-natalist policies. In countries with access to modern contraception, the impact of abortion restrictions would be expected to be less dramatic. Not all countries have such access, however; and other evidence of the health effects of restrictive abortions policies is not difficult to find. For example, about one out of five maternal deaths in Latin America result from unsafe abortion (AGI, 1999).

Nonetheless, Romania's case is a real life demonstration of the impact of abortion policies on women's health. It reminds us that although abortion debates are multidimensional, involving feminist, social, political, economic, and religious stakeholders (among others), health issues must never be forgotten.

In considering health effects, we must also remember that mistimed childbearing (e.g. teenage pregnancies, closely spaced births) has negative physical, psychological, and social effects on mothers and children as well. Abortion currently plays a substantial role in enabling women to time and space their childbearing. In the United States, for example, nearly one-half of abortion patients in 1987 were mothers, and nearly one in four of those mothers had a child under two years of age (Russo, Horn and Schwartz, 1992). The health implications of these facts are revealed in the findings that spacing births more than two years apart would reduce the risk of low birth weight and neonatal death in the United States by an estimated 5 to 10 percent below current levels (Miller, 1991). Further, when children are born less than two years apart, the health of both children is affected. The younger child is two-and-a-half times more likely to die than a child who is born more than two years after an older sibling. For the older child the increased risk is less, but still substantial: 63 percent (Potts and Thapa, 1991).

Although concerns for women's physical safety are the primary focus of health agendas in countries where abortion remains illegal and thus unsafe, arguments against abortion on grounds of physical health have become baseless in places where abortion is legal and can be performed safely. A survey of the political history of abortion in the U.S. reveals an interesting trend in the construction of arguments and strategies against reproductive rights. For some time (and still today), those who believed that abortion should be illegal focussed on the moral question of whether an abortion was murder, and whether a mother's rights could supersede those of a foetus. *Roe v Wade*, the U.S. Supreme Court decision that made abortion legal, did little to settle the issue politically. Its framing of the issue set the stage for psychological status of the mother to assume a larger status in what has been called the 'abortion wars' (Solinger, 1998). Part of the rationale behind the landmark ruling was based on recognition of the negative effects of unwanted childbearing on women's physical and mental health, and indeed, unwanted childbearing is correlated with a host of negative psychological and social factors for both the mother and child, including poverty, single parenthood, abuse and neglect, lower educational achievement for mother and child, and juvenile delinquency (David, 1992; Russo, 1992).

Political forces opposing abortion have used this emphasis on the psychological well-being of the mother to construct new arguments for restricting access to abortion. The claim is that the Court failed to balance its concern for the negative effects of abortion with the 'fact' that abortion is detrimental to women's mental health. This argument, typically based on anecdotal reports and uncontrolled studies, is increasingly raised in other areas of the world as well, and has been found in areas as diverse as New Zealand and Central and Eastern Europe (David, 1999).

Certain pro-life forces have developed a new legal strategy called the Jericho Plan that is based on belief in a 'post-abortion syndrome'. The goal is to make abortion inaccessible despite its legal status by making physicians 'fully liable for all the physical, psychological, and spiritual injuries they inflict on women' (Elliot Institute, 1997). They advertise for women who are depressed or feeling sad and guilty after having an abortion, and under the guise of 'healing' they tell them that they did not receive full, informed consent about the procedure. They encourage women to translate their sadness into anger at their abortion providers, and then refer them to pro-life attorneys who will sue for damages on their behalf. For example, a website sponsored by Priests for Life asks supporters to 'encourage mothers who have been harmed by abortion to bring suits against the abortion industry', and provides a list of telephone numbers of organizations that will help women sue their doctors. Life Dynamics, one of the organizations listed, is said to have a nation-wide network of 600 lawyers ready to file such suits (Farley, 1995). Meanwhile, others attempt to pass legislation to make physicians civilly and criminally liable for such damages (liabilities not covered by malpractice insurance).

This threatens women's health directly, by creating justifications for legislative proposals to decrease women's access to safe abortion. In addition to damaging women's confidence in their ability to cope after an abortion, prejudging the cause of women's mental health problems and attributing their problems to having an abortion, may undermine their efforts to seek appropriate mental health treatment. This is of particular concern if the women become distracted from exploring the effects of negative life events that precede or run concurrently with the unwanted pregnancy, such as sexual abuse and intimate violence. Finally, a construction of abortion which increases its social stigma can encourage women to feel shame and guilt at their decision to terminate pregnancy. This can then be used as further evidence of abortion's 'harmful' mental health effects. We discuss the physical, psychological, and social implications of this construction below.

THE INFLUENCE OF ABORTION POLITICS ON WOMEN'S PHYSICAL HEALTH

Safe abortions have been made less obtainable through several avenues: by systematically lowering the number of abortion clinics and licensed abortion practitioners (e.g. through the threat of violence), pro-lifers have decreased access, particularly for poor and rural women, to adequate abortion facilities. Other restrictions reduce the safety of abortion by thwarting women's ability to have the procedure performed early in pregnancy (in the first eight weeks), when it is safest and most protected by law. Parental and spousal consent requirements can make it more difficult for minors and women married to unsupportive partners to obtain first-trimester abortions. Unforunately, many young women would rather risk having an unsafe abortion than tell their parents they are pregnant.

Research indicates that women married to supportive partners usually include them in the decision (Russo and Pope, 1993). Women in unhappy, conflicted, and/or violent marriages are most likely to make the decision to have an abortion on their own, and for good reason. Lack of social support, high interpersonal conflict, and experience of abuse all decrease women's ability to cope with stressful life events (Koss *et al.*, 1994; Major *et al.*, 1997). The choice not to include others in one's reproductive decisions can thus be seen as a positive coping strategy. Combating policies which undermine women's ability to make autonomous decisions is an important component of any reproductive rights agenda.

Informed consent scripts and mandatory waiting periods may also delay abortions by misleading women into fearing the psychological consequences of their decision to terminate their pregnancy. This, too, increases the likelihood of unwanted childbearing or late-term abortion, circumstances that are undeniably negative, no matter what side of the debate one falls on.

UNDERSTANDING THE LINKS OF PSYCHOLOGICAL HEALTH TO UNWANTED PREGNANCY AND ABORTION

In characterizing abortion as an experience that inevitably incurs psychological damage, the pro-life agenda can justify its attempts to outlaw the procedure under a guise of concern for women's well-being. Negative mental health indicators in women having abortions are deliberately mislabeled as psychological sequelae, rather than correlates, and are attributed to the woman's experience of abortion, rather than the factors surrounding her unwanted pregnancy.

It is not surprising that women reporting having an abortion report higher levels of anxiety and depression, suicidal ideation, and lower life satisfaction (Russo and Denious, 2000). These are risk factors for unwanted pregnancy, and are common outcomes of partner violence, and of childhood physical and sexual abuse. In a secondary analysis of data from a national survey, we found that women who reported having an abortion were much more likely to report experiencing both childhood abuse and partner abuse (Russo and Denious, 2000). Almost half of the women who said they had had an abortion reported that they felt verbally or emotionally, physically or sexually abused as a child. They were more than three times as likely to report experiencing all of these three types of abuse than the women who did not report having an abortion (15.8 percent vs. 4.4 percent). With respect to intimate abuse, women who reported abortions were significantly more likely to report experiencing both non-physical (62.2 percent vs. 43.2 percent) and physical (20 percent vs. 11.4 percent) violence in their relationships.

The abortion group also expressed more depressive symptoms than the non-abortion group, showing a correlation between abortion and negative mental health indicators. Research suggests that early victimization sets the stage for future abuse and is also linked to engagement in high-risk sexual behaviors (Koss, Heise and Russo, 1994). Thus, women with a history of abuse are both more likely to display negative psychological symptoms and to have unintended pregnancies. When we separated out the contributions of childhood and partner abuse, however, abortion no longer made a significant contribution to level of depression. Other studies have repeatedly shown this pattern, as well. The relationships of psychological and social factors to abortion (e.g. self-esteem, depression, income, and education) are no longer significant when factors prior to the pregnancy are taken into account. That is not to say that no individual woman is ever troubled or distressed by having an abortion. But being upset and feeling guilty is not the same has having a mental disorder worthy of the label 'post-abortion syndrome'. Severe negative reactions happen rarely and for the general population overall, the abortion experience itself has no significant *independent* association with mental health (Russo and Dabul, 1997; Russo and Denious, 1998b; Russo and Zierk, 1992).

Undeniably, abortion occurs in a stressful context; it can be difficult to disentangle psychological effects of pregnancy – wanted and unwanted – from an abortion experience. The controversy surrounding abortion rights threatens women's health by clouding and dismissing the effects that negative life events that are correlated with unwanted pregnancy may have on women's mental health status. Negative mental health indicators in women having abortions are deliberately mislabeled as psychological sequelae, and are attributed to the woman's experience of abortion. Experiences of childhood abuse, partner violence, and other predictive risk factors for unwanted pregnancy so integral to women's health, are ignored in these attempts to link abortion to psychological health. When such a large proportion of women experiencing unwanted pregnancy are victims of childhood abuse and have partners who are abusive, violent, and/or uncooperative in using contraception, misattribution of the mental health effects of such experiences to having an abortion both distracts women from working on the sources of their problems and undermines their confidence in their ability to cope with the stress of their unwanted pregnancy.

It is important to remember that the meaning of abortion is socially constructed. This common experience in women's lives can be made to seem wrong and shameful, and women in turn can suffer from this social construction. Increasing women's confidence in their ability to cope with an abortion has been found to lower their depressive symptoms after an abortion (Major *et al.*, 1990). Conversely, constructions of abortion which increase its social stigma can affect women's psychological well-being by encouraging them to feel shame and guilt at their decision to terminate pregnancy.

For example, the Elliot Institute (1998) provides a list of 'Steps Toward Healing', including telling women to 'admit your personal responsibility', 'Pray for God's forgiveness', and to forgive others, recognizing that '[t]hey too acted out of ignorance, fear, or petty human selfishness'. A 'post-abortion syndrome' whereby women purportedly experience a variety of negative psychological symptoms, such as depression, anxiety, guilt, and other manifestations common to PTSD, is constructed and used with the goal of restricting and eventually eradicating access to abortion. Portraying abortion as a mentally damaging experience does a great disservice to women who have a multitude of reasons for choosing to terminate their pregnancy. For example, about half of the adult women who have abortions in the U.S. are already mothers; concern for the welfare of the children they already have is often a primary motivation in their decision.

Other tactics, such as anti-abortion demonstrations and harassment at abortion clinics, are also designed to create guilt and shame in women obtaining abortions. Cozzarelli and Major (1998) conducted a study of women's psychological responses to anti-abortion activities, and found that women experiencing shame and guilt in response to anti-abortion activities such as picketing and blocked entrances to clinics reported greater levels of post-abortion distress. Women who possessed more negative pre-pregnancy attitudes were more depressed overall and were more strongly affected by anti-abortion activities. In other words, these strategies are most effective when used on women who already express negative mental health indicators.

SUMMARY

Abortion is a complex, multidimensional issue, but we argue that health concerns must have a central place in any abortion debate. Efforts to restrict access to safe abortion are a severe health threat to women, and are a critical and integral part of any women's health agenda. Ironically, recent pro-life strategies claiming that abortion damages women's mental health are being used to argue for restrictive legislation. We do not deny that a woman may experience negative post-abortion emotional responses; each individual case is unique, and should be treated as such. For most women, however, abortion is a resolution of a stressful situation. Although women may have some negative emotions about the experience, typically their positive emotions are stronger than their negative feelings and most are satisfied that they have made the right decision for themselves (Adler, 1979; Adler et al., 1990, 1992; Russo 1992, 1999). Misrepresenting the health risks and projecting baseless concerns for women's physical and psychological well-being as a means to restrict access to safe abortion undermines women's social progress and threatens their access to adequate health care. In the context of women's health, it is important to understand how women's diverse life circumstances affect their ability to cope with difficult decisions and situations. We will be better able to address reproductive health issues, such as abortion, when we consider them both in the context of women's lives (e.g. coping resources, social support, partner violence, early experiences of abuse, incidence of depression), and in the context of socio-political agendas which seek to undermine women's rights.

REFERENCES

Adler, N. (1979) Emotional responses of women following therapeutic abortion. *American Journal of Orthopsychiatry*, 45, 446–454

Adler, N.F., David, H. P., Major, B. N., Roth, S. H., Russo, N. F. and Wyatt, G. E. (1990) Psychological responses after abortion. *Science*, 248 (April 6), 41–44

Adler, N.F., David, H. P., Major, B. N., Roth, S. H., Russo, N. F. and Wyatt, G. E. (1992) Psychological factors in abortion: A review. *American Psychologist*, 47, 1194–1204

Alan Guttmacher Institute (1999) *Sharing Responsibility: Women, Society, and Abortion Worldwide*. New York: Alan Guttmacher Institute

Baban, A. (1999) Romania. In H. P. David (Ed.) *From Abortion to Contraception: A Resource to Public Policies and Reproductive Behavior in Central and Eastern Europe from 1917 to The Present* (pp. 191–221). Westport, CN: Greenwood Press

Cozzarelli, C., and Major, B. (1998) The impact of antiabortion activities on women seeking abortions. In L. J. Beckman and S. M. Harvey (Eds.) *The New Civil War: The Psychology, Culture, and Politics of Abortion* (pp. 81–104). Washington, D.C.: American Psychological Association

David, H.P. (1999) Overview. In H. P. David (Ed.) *From Abortion to Contraception: A Resource to Public Policies and Reproductive Behavior in Central And Eastern Europe from 1917 to the Present* (pp. 3–22). Westport, CN: Greenwood Press

David, H.P. (1992) Born unwanted: Long-term developmental effects of denied abortion. *Journal of Social Issues*, 48, 163–181

Elliott Institute (1997) Let Us Show You How We Will STOP ABORTION. Advertising flyer, Elliot Institute, P. O. Box 7348, Springfield, IL., U.S.A.

Farley, C. (1995) Malpractice as a weapon. *Time*, 145 (10), 65

Koss, M.P., Goodman, L.A., Browne, A., Fitzgerald, L., Keita, G.P. and Russo, N.F. (1994) *No Safe Haven: Male Violence Against Women at Home, at Work, and in the Community*. Washington, D.C.: American Psychological Association.

Koss, M.P., Heise, L. and Russo, N.F. (1994) the global health burden of rape. *Psychology of Women Quarterly*, 18, 509–530

Major, B., Zubek, J. M., Cooper, M. L., Cozzarelli, C. and Richards, C. (1997) Mixed messages: Implications of social conflict and social support within close relationships for adjustment to a stressful life event. *Journal of Personality and Social Psychology*, 72, 1349–1363

Major, B., Cozzarelli, C., Sciacchitano, A.M., Cooper, M.L., Testa, M. and Mueller, P.M. (1990) Perceived social support, self-efficacy, and adjustment to abortion. *Journal of Personality and Social Psychology*, 59, 452–463

Miller, J.E. (1991) The birth intervals and perinatal health: An investigation of three hypotheses. *Family Planning Perspectives*, 23, (2), 62–70

Potts, M. and Thapa, S. (1991) Child survival: The role of family planning. *Populi*, 17, 12–23

Russo, N.F. (1992) Psychological aspects of unwanted pregnancy and its resolution. In J.D. Butler and D.F. Walbert (Eds.) *Abortion, Medicine, and the Law* (4th edn) (pp. 593–626). New York: Facts on File

Russo, N.F. (1999) Understanding emotional responses after abortion. In J.C. Chrisler, C. Golden, and P. Rozee (Eds.) *Lectures on the Psychology of Women* (2nd edn) (pp. 260–273). New York: McGraw-Hill

Russo, N.F., and Dabul, A. (1997) The relationship of abortion to well-being: Do race and religion make a difference? *Professional Psychology: Research and Practice*, 28, 23–31

Russo, N.F., and Denious, J.E. (1998a) Why is abortion such a controversial issue in the United States? In L.J. Beckman and S. M. Harvey (Eds.) *The New Civil War: The Psychology, Culture, and Politics of Abortion* (pp. 25–60). Washington, D.C.: American Psychological Association

Russo, N.F., and Denious, J.E. (1998b) Understanding the relationship of violence against women to unwanted pregnancy and its resolutions. In L.J. Beckman and S.M. Harvey (Eds.) *The New Civil War: The Psychology, Culture, and Politics of Abortion* (pp. 211–234). Washington, D.C.: American Psychological Association

Russo, N.F., and Denious, J.E. (1999) Violence in the lives of women having abortions:

Implications for public policy practice. *Professional Psychology: Research and Practice* (in press)

Russo, N. F., Horn, J. and Schwartz, R. (1992) Abortion in context: Characteristics and motivations of women who seek abortions. *Journal of Social Issues*, 48, 128–201

Russo, N.F. and Pope, L. (1994) Implications of violence against women for reproductive health: Focus on abortion services. APA conference, 'Psychological and Behavioural Factors in Women's Health: Creting an Agenda for the 21st Century. Washington, D.C. May

Russo, N.F., and Zierk, K. (1992) Abortion, unwanted childbearing, and women's well-being. *Professional Psychology: Research and Practice*, 23, 269–280

Solinger, R. (Ed.) *Abortion Wars: A Half Century of Struggle, 1950–2000.* Berkeley, CA: University of California Press

United Nations (1996) *The Beijing Declaration and the Platform for Action: Fourth World Conference on Women: Beijing, China: 4–15 September 1995. New York: UN/DPI/1766/Wom*

CHAPTER 50

WOMEN AND PSYCHOSIS

Emmanuelle Peters

INTRODUCTION

Much has been written about sex differences in the epidemiology and aetiology of schizophrenia and other psychoses. However, most of this work is biological in nature, concentrating on genetic, brain and diagnostic differences. Much less has been written on the social and environmental challenges faced by women with psychosis, with services appearing to regard the chronically mentally ill as almost genderless. This chapter will review the literature on sex differences and gender-specific needs of women with severe mental illness, and will address the implications of these findings for service delivery issues.

BIOLOGICAL DIFFERENCES

Accumulated evidence suggests a consistent pattern of observed differences in the course and expression of schizophrenia[1] between men and women. Differences have been reported in a plethora of areas, including age of onset, incidence, course, premorbid adjustment, symptomatology and clinical presentation. There are also well-established differences in aetiology, for instance in familial loading, structural brain abnormalities, and history of obstetric complications in their mothers (for reviews see: Andia and Zisook, 1991; Castle *et al.*, 1995; Harding and Hall, 1997; Goldstein, 1997; Salem and Kring, 1998).

Community-based studies suggest that the incidence of schizophrenia ranges from approximately twice as high in men than in women (Iacono and Beiser, 1992) to equal rates (Meltzer *et al.*, 1995). However, women tend to show more affective and depressive symptoms (McGlashan and Bardenstein, 1990), and are more often given the diagnosis of 'schizoaffective disorder', mirroring the finding that neurotic disorders (especially depression) are more common in women (Kessler *et al.*, 1994). Men have an earlier age of onset, with a mean difference of approximately three to five years (Szymanski *et al.*, 1995), and a second peak in illness onset occurs in women during their mid- to late forties which is absent in men (Castle *et al.*, 1995). Overall, women have a more benign course of illness, with better premorbid adjustment and intellectual functioning (Shtasel *et al.*, 1992), fewer hospitalizations (Test *et al.*, 1990), better response to neuroleptics (Andia *et al.*, 1995), and more likelihood of sustaining relationships and having community support networks (Walker *et al.*, 1985). Biological studies indicate that women have higher rates of psychoses in their first-degree relatives (Murray *et al.*, 1992), but lower rates of obstetric complications and early brain injury (O'Callaghan *et al.*, 1992). The literature concerning brain abnormalities is rather mixed (Goldstein, 1997), and the differences found may interact with family history (Salem and Kring, 1998). There is some evidence that men have more overall evidence of structural brain abnormalities, although the specific abnormalities are variable (Lewine *et al.*, 1990).

While the differences in illness course and expression are fairly well established, the reasons behind those differences are highly disputed. Nevertheless, the available explanations in the literature tend to be almost exclusively biological in origin. For instance, several researchers have suggested that oestrogen has a protective effect in women with schizophrenia (e.g. Castle *et al.*, 1995). It has also been argued that the male form of schizophrenia is characteristic of a neurodevelopmental disorder, whereas the predominantly female form may be genetically related to the 'affective disorders' (Castle and Murray, 1991; Castle *et al.*, 1995). There is also the possibility that gender differences in schizophrenia reflect an overlay of gender differences in normal personality, although gender differences found in other types of mental health problems, such as depression and bipolar illness, tend to be in the opposite direction (Bardenstein and McGlashan, 1990).

SOCIAL DIFFERENCES

At the other extreme of the biological models, some feminist writers (Chesler, 1989), and some proponents of 'normalization' (Wolfensberger and Tullman, 1982), have argued that women diagnosed with mental illness are victims of a psychiatric system which is patriarchal and oppressive, and need to be liberated from a traditionally 'devalued' patient role and deleterious associations with mental health professionals and services. However, Perkins (1991) argues that these sets of ideas confuse the idea of 'sickness' with 'disability', and deny the very real existence of serious and long-term social disabilities in women with enduring psychiatric problems. She makes the analogy with physical disability: 'there is little to be gained from construing the physically disabled as "sick" and trying to cure them, but much to be gained from acknowledging their disability and providing the necessary specialist supports and aids' (p. 133). She further points out that denying social and psychiatric disabilities, and refusing to exercise our power as professionals under the guise of promoting user-empowerment, will guarantee that women's needs will not be met.

Already women are less likely to be referred to specialist services, even though they are twice as likely to be identified by their GP to be suffering from mental illness (Goldberg and Huxley, 1992; see Stoppard, in this volume). This is true even of services from which they are, potentially, more likely to benefit than men: for instance, they are less often referred to psychological therapies such as cognitive behavior therapy for psychosis (Garety et al., 1994; Garety, 1995), despite the fact that they are better at forming relationships than men with similar levels of disability (Cook, 1998). Bachrach (1984) also concludes that the originally progressive movement of deinstitutionalization into programmes of community care has had specific detrimental effects on severely disabled women, in such areas as sexual exploitation and violence, homelessness, diversion into the criminal justice system, and stigmatization. Furthermore, community programmes have typically generated lower expectations and lower input of services for women than men despite equal levels of disability, both in the United States (Bachrach, 1985) and in the U.K. (Perkins and Rowland, 1986). In some ways both the medical and feminist/normalization models have ignored the complex interrelationships between biological vulnerabilities and consequences of environmental events on women's lives. Mental health services in general have failed to acknowledge the social differences experienced by women with schizophrenia, despite substantial evidence that attending to environmental factors is critical to the recovery of people diagnosed with severe mental illness (Anthony and Blanch, 1989).

For instance, women are particularly likely to have low-status employment or no employment, and to experience poverty, which itself is associated with an increased risk and exacerbation of mental illness (Warner, R., 1994). Although overall there are more homeless men than women, homeless women are more likely than men to have a mental illness (Cook and Marshall, 1996), but there are less homeless shelters available to women, both in the United States (Baxter and Hopper, 1982) and in the U.K. (Weller et al., 1987). The situation is similar with respect to jail detainees: they are less numerous than men, but are more likely to have a serious mental illness, and less likely to receive help (Veysey, 1998). Women with schizophrenia are more likely than men to be married or cohabiting or to have young children, and they often experience difficulties in sustaining these roles, although they are not even routinely asked if they are parents, let alone what help they may need to fulfill this role (Rouse, 1995). They also tend to be more sexually active (Test et al., 1990), and are therefore more at risk of unwanted pregnancies and sexually transmitted diseases such as AIDS (Katz et al., 1994), although few psychiatric services see sexual counseling and family planning as part of their remit. On the positive side, women with severe mental illness appear to be better than men at forming and sustaining relationships, staying in contact with their families, forming networks of friends, living independently, and being engaged in activities outside the home with others, both in the United States (Grusky *et al.*, 1985) and in the U.K. (Conning and Rowland, 1991). Despite this, lower levels of independence and achievement are expected from women, and this is reflected in their community programme placements (Bachrach, 1984; Perkins and Rowland, 1991).

Despite the extensive literature on sex differences in schizophrenia, there is a dearth of literature on the implications of these differences for the specific needs of women with psychosis and for service delivery issues (Levin-Lubotsky *et al.*, 1998). Studies have indicated that there is only a small amount of overlap between indicators of diagnosis, distress and disability (Ciarlo *et al.*, 1992), and the emphasis on diagnosis and the medical model of treatment in psychiatry has underscored the importance of considering multiple dimensions when assessing need and planning services. To address this issue, Cook (1998) has proposed a multivariate model of 'enablement' and 'disablement' on psychiatric and social outcomes which comprises women's societal status, role expectations, illness course, and service use. Variables which may act as social enablements include the later age of illness onset, better premorbid functioning, fewer hospitalizations, greater community participation, greater likelihood of being in a cohabiting relationship and of living independently. Variables representing disablements would include lower income, extra burden of childcare responsibility, less referral to and use of specialist services, and reduced expectations of functioning. Some variables can also act as both enablements and disablements. For instance, on the one hand relationships with a significant other and with children may provide protective social support, represent fulfilling and 'normative' social roles, and be important in providing a sense of worth and competence. On the other hand, married women of low socioeconomic status with young children and no employment are at increased risk of developing depression (Brown and Harris, 1978). In addition, women with a mental illness are more likely to marry a spouse who also has a psychiatric disorder, thus increasing the risk of marital discord and exacerbation of their own psychiatric symptoms. In turn, the stress of parenting under conditions of poverty, social isolation, and marital discord increases the risk of childhood disorders (Hammen *et al.*, 1987), thus increasing the difficulties associated with parenting. This model illustrates that women with psychotic illnesses experience a different set of risks than men, and that service providers should start to acknowledge that the chronically mentally ill are gender-differentiated persons (Test and Berlin, 1981).

VIOLENCE AND SEXUAL ABUSE

One important variable already alluded to is violence and sexual abuse.

Violence is very gender specific (Mezey and Stanko, 1996): overall, men are more likely to experience interpersonal aggression, but certain types of trauma are more prevalent among women, such as domestic violence and sexual assaults (Kessler *et al.*, 1995). Although physical and sexual abuse survivors do not seem to have higher than normal rates of schizophrenia (Hanson, 1990), women who have been subjected to severe abuse tend to experience psychotic-like symptoms, such as dissociative symptoms, auditory hallucinations, and paranoid ideation (Mollon, 1996). Furthermore, patients with psychotic disorders who have been abused are more likely to have a poor outcome than their non-abused counterparts (with more severe symptoms, more suicidal symptoms, and less response to psychopharmacological and psychosocial interventions; Beck and van der Kolk, 1987). Moreover, disproportionately more women than men with severe mental illness report physical and sexual assault in adulthood (Jacobson and Richardson, 1987), leaving them in pernicious, continuing cycles of experiences of trauma, mental illness and retraumatization.

It is now becoming increasingly clear that women may even be subjected to assault when going into hospital for 'treatment', and that fear of or actual sexual abuse (predominantly by male patients, but sexual harassment from staff has also been reported) can make the experience more damaging than therapeutic (Plumb, 1993; Sayce, 1996). Sharing a restricted environment, such as a psychiatric ward, with disturbed male patients can be extremely threatening and distressing for all women, but especially if they have been abused in the past. This can be further exacerbated if they are detained on a section of the Mental Health Act, and therefore unable to escape. A recent survey of 309 wards in England and Wales revealed that 94 percent of the wards were mixed, with approximately two-thirds of women patients not having access to women-only sleeping areas and bath/shower and toilet facilities (Warner, L. and Ford, 1998). This is despite the fact that women patients report the availability of women only areas and facilities as one of their main priorities (Subotsky, 1991); one particular local survey indicated that only 3 percent of over 100 women users wanted to be on a mixed ward (Sayce, 1996). Staff on over half of the mixed wards sampled by Warner and Ford reported problems of sexual harassment of women patients, ranging in severity from disinhibited behavior and remarks (43 percent) to actual sexual assault (4 percent). A further difficult issue concerns the exploitation of vulnerable women, for instance women who may be sexually disinhibited because of their illness (e.g. hypomania), which can then lead to sexual intercourse or relationships which might not be regarded as consensual. The incidence of this problem was reported as the second highest (37 percent), and was regarded as especially worrying by many staff. Overall, the Mental Health Act Commission report for the years 1995–97 is frighteningly accurate: 'It is an unacceptable irony that many women patients, detained in the interest of their health or their safety, find themselves in hospital conditions that not only feel threatening but, in fact, offer inadequate safety and privacy' (HMSO, 1997).

SUMMARY

Individuals with a severe mental illness have traditionally been understood primarily in terms of the course of their illness and their response to biological treatments. This has led to much of the literature focussing on diagnostic and biological differences between the sexes, while the effects of gender on individuals' social and interpersonal histories, their problems, their use of services, and service effectiveness have been largely ignored. The narrow medical focus has meant that women's goals, motivations, and life tasks are seen as subsumed by their psychotic illness, while the significance of gendered roles and needs and their interaction with psychiatric problems and cultural context has been missed. This has led to services which are, more often than not, 'gender-blind', and inadequate to meet the specific needs of women with psychosis. Hopefully, recent concerns regarding sexual harassment and violence in mixed wards, and the growing involvement of user-groups in the planning of services (Subotsky, 1991; Plumb, 1993), will lead to more women-only wards and services which are sensitive to the needs of the largely invisible group of chronically mentally ill women (Perkins, 1991).

NOTE

1.There is much debate concerning the validity and reliability of the diagnosis of 'schizophrenia' which has led some researchers to question its very exsistence (e.g. Bentall *et al.*, 1988). Although models which emphasize the continuity of mental illness are likely to be more accurate representations of psychotic experiences (e.g. Claridge, 1994), the terms 'schizophrenia', 'psychosis' and 'severe/chronic mental illness' will be used in this chapter for the sake of brevity.

REFERENCES

Andia, A.M. and. Zisook, S. (1991) Gender differences in schizophrenia: A literature review. *Annals of Clinical Psychiatry*, 3, 333–340

Andia, A.M., Zisook, S., Heaton, R.K. *et al.* (1995) Gender differences in schizophrenia. *Journal of Nervous and Mental Disease*, 183, 522–528

Anthony, W.A. and Blanch, A.K. (1989) Community support programs: What have we learned? *Psychosocial Rehabilitation Journal*, 12, 55–81

Bachrach, L. (1984) Deinstitutionalization and women. *American Psychologist*, 39, 1171–1177

Bachrach, L. (1985) Chronically mentally ill women: Emergence and legitimation of programme issues. *Hospital and Community Psychiatry*, 36, 1063–1069

Bardenstein, K.K. and McGlashan, T.H. (1990) Gender differences in affective, schizoaffective, and schizophrenic disorders: A review. *Schizophrenia Research*, 3, 159–172

Baxter, E. and Hopper, K. (1982) The new mendicancy: Homeless in New York City. *American Journal of Orthopsychiatry*, 52, 393–408

Beck, J.C. and van der Kolk, B. (1987) Reports of childhood incest and current behavior of chronically hospitalised psychotic women. *American Journal of Psychiatry*, 144, 1474–1476

Bentall, R.P., Jackson, H.F. and Pilgrim, D. (1988) Abandoning the concept of schizophrenia: Some implications of validity arguments for psychological research into psychotic phenomena. *British Journal of Clinical Psychology*, 27, 303–324

Brown, G.W. and Harris, T.O. (1978) *The Social Origins of Depression.* London: Tavistock

Castle, D.J. and Murray, R.M. (1991) The neurodevelopmental basis of sex differences in schizophrenia. *Psychological Medicine*, 21, 565–575

Castle, D., Abel, K., Takei, N. and Murray, R. (1995) Gender differences in schizophrenia: Hormonal effect or subtypes? *Schizophrenia Bulletin*, 21, 1–12

Chesler, P. (1989) *Women and Madness* (2nd edn). New York: Harcourt Brace Jovanovich

Ciarlo, J. A., Shern, D.L., Tweed, D.L. *et al.* (1992) The Colorado Social Health Survey of Mental Health Service Needs: Sampling, instrumentation and major findings. *Evaluation and Program Planning,* 15, 133–148

Claridge, G. (1994) Single indicator of risk for schizophrenia: Probable fact or likely myth? *Schizophrenia Bulletin,* 20, 151–168

Conning, A.M. and Rowland, L.A. (1991) Where do people with long-term mental health problems live? *British Journal of Psychiatry,* 158 (Suppl. 10), 80–84

Cook, J.A. (1998) Independent community living among women with severe mental illness: A comparison with outcomes among men. In B. Levin-Lubotsky, A. Blanch, and A. Jennings (Eds.) *Women's Mental Health Services. A Public Health Perspective* (pp. 99–121). Thousand Oaks, CA: Sage Publications

Cook, J. and Marshall, J. (1996) Homeless women. In K. Abel, M. Buszewicz, S. Davison, S. Johnson and E. Staples (Eds.) *Planning Community Mental Health Services for Women* (pp. 112–128). London: Routledge

Garety, P.A., Kuipers, L., Fowler, D., Chamberlain, F. and Dunn, G. (1994) Cognitive-behavioural therapy for drug-resistant psychosis. *British Journal of Medical Psychology,* 67, 259–271

Garety, P.A. (1995) Review of *Cognitive-Behavior Therapy of Schizophrenia,* by D.G. Kingdon and Turkington, D. *Psychological Medicine,* 25, 652–653

Goldberg, D. and Huxley, P. (1992) *Common Mental Disorders.* London: Routledge

Goldstein, J.M. (1997) Sex differences in schizophrenia: Epidemiology, genetics and the brain. *International Review of Psychiatry,* 9, 399–408

Grusky, O., Tierney, K. Manderscheid, R.W. *et al.* (1985) Social bonding and community adjustment of chronically mentally ill adults. *Journal of Health and Social Behavior,* 26, 49–63

Hammen, C.L., Gordon, D., Burge, D. *et al.* (1987) Maternal affective disorders, illness and stress: Risks for child psychopathology. *American Journal of Psychiatry,* 144, 736–741

Hanson, R.K. (1990) The psychological impact of sexual abuse on women and children. *Annals of Sex Research,* 3, 187–223

Harding, C.M. and Hall, G.M. (1997) Long-term outcome studies of schizophrenia: Do females continue to display better outcomes as expected? *International Review of Psychiatry,* 9, 409–418

HMSO (1997) *The Mental Health Act Commission Seventh Biennial Report 1995–1997.* London

Iacono, W.G. and Beiser, M. (1992) Where are the women in first-episode studies of schizophrenia? *Schizophrenia Bulletin,* 18, 471–480

Jacobson, A. and Richardson, B. (1987) Assault experiences of 100 psychiatric inpatients: Evidence of the need for routine enquiry. *American Journal of Psychiatry,* 144, 908–913

Katz, R.C., Watts, C. and Santman, J. (1994) AIDS knowledge and high risk behaviors in the chronic mentally ill. *Community Mental Health Journal,* 30, 395–402

Kessler, R.C., McGonagle, K.A., Zhaos, S. *et al.* (1994) Lifetime and 12–month prevalence of DSM-III-R psychiatric disorders in the United States: Results from the national comorbidity survey. *Archives of General Psychiatry,* 51, 8–19

Kessler, R.C., Sonnega, A., Bromet, E., Hughes, M. and Nelson, C.B. (1995) Post-traumatic stress disorder in the National Comorbidity Survey. *Archives of General Psychiatry,* 52, 1048–1060

Levin-Lubotsky, B., Blanch, A. and Jennings, A. (1998) *Women's Mental Health Services. A Public Health Perspective.* Thousand Oaks, CA: Sage Publications

Lewine, R.J., Gulley, L.R., Risch, C.S., Jewart, R. and Houpt, J.L. (1990) Sexual dimorphism, brain morphology, and schizophrenia. *Schizophrenia bulletin,* 16, 195–203

McGlashan, T.H. and Bardenstein, K.K. (1990) Gender differences in affective, schizoaffective, and schizophrenic disorders. *Schizophrenia Bulletin,* 16, 319–329

Meltzer, H., Gill, B. Petticrew, M. et al. (1995) *The Prevalence of Psychiatric Morbidity among Adults Living in Private Households.* London: HMSO

Mezey, G. and Stanko, E. (1996) Women and violence. In K. Abel, M. Buszewicz, S. Davison, S. Johnson and E. Staples (Eds.), *Planning Community Mental Health Services for Women* (pp. 160–176). London: Routledge

Mollon, P. (1996) *Multiple Selves, Multiple Voices: Working with Trauma, Violation, and Dissociation.* Chichester: John Wiley & Sons

Murray, R.M., Jones, P., O'Callaghan, E., Takei, N. and Sham, P. (1992) Genes, viruses and neurodevelopmental schizophrenia. *Journal of Psychiatric Research,* 26, 225–235

O'Callaghan, E., Sham, P., Takei, N., Glover, G. and Murray, R.M. (1191) Schizophrenia after prenatal exposure to 1958 A2 influenza epidemic. *Lancet,* 337, 1248–1250

Perkins, R. (1991) Women with long-term mental health problems: Issues of power and powerlessness. *Feminism and Psychology,* 1, 131–139

Perkins, R. and Rowland, L. (1986) Sex differences in service usage in long-term psychiatric care: Are women adequately served? *British Journal of Psychiatry,* 158 (Suppl. 10), 75–79

Plumb, A. (1993) The challenge of self-advocacy. *Feminism and Psychology,* 3, 169–187

Rouse, B.A. (1995) *Substance Abuse and Mental Health Statistics Sourcebook.* Washington, D.C.: Superintendent of Documents, U.S. Government Printing Office

Salem, J. and Kring, A. (1998) The role of gender differences in the reduction of etiologic heterogeneity in schizophrenia. *Clinical Psychology Review,* 18, 795–819

Sayce, L. (1996) Campaigning for change. In K. Abel, M. Buszewicz, S. Davison, S. Johnson. and E. Staples (Eds.) *Planning Community Mental Health Services for Women* (pp. 231–247). London: Routledge

Shtasel, D.L., Gur, R.E., Gallacher, F. *et al.* (1992) Gender differences in the clinical expression of schizophrenia. *Schizophrenia Research,* 7, 225–231

Subotsky, F. (1991) Issues for women in the development of mental health services. *British Journal of Psychiatry,* 158 (Suppl. 10), 17–21

Szymanski, S., Lieberman, J.A., Alvir, J.M. *et al.* (1995) Gender differences in onset of illness, treatment response, course, and biologic indexes in first-episode schizophrenic patients. *American Journal of Psychiatry, 152,* 698–703

Test, M.A. and Berlin, S.B. (1981) Issues of special concern to chronically mentally ill women. *Professional Psychology,* 12, 136–145

Test, M.A., Burke, S.S. and Wallisch, L.S. (1990) Gender differences of young adults with schizophrenic disorders in community care. *Schizophrenia Bulletin,* 16, 331–344

Veysey, B.M. (1998) Specific needs of women diagnosed with mental illnesses in U.S. jails. In B. Levin-Lubotsky, A. Blanch and A. Jennings (Eds.) *Women's Mental Health Services. A Public Health Perspective* (pp. 368–390). Thousand Oaks, CA: Sage Publications

Walker, E.F., Bettes, B.A., Kain, E.L. and Harvey, P. (1985) Relationship of gender and marital status with symptomatology in psychotic patients. *Journal of Abnormal Psychology,* 94, 42–50

Warner, L. and Ford, R. (1998) Women in hospital: Conditions for women in inpatient psychiatric units: The Mental Health Act Commission 1996 national visit. *Mental Health Care,* 11, 225–228

Warner, R. (1994) *Recovery from Schizophrenia.* (2nd edn). London: Routledge

Weller, B.G., Weller, M.P., Coker, E. *et al.* (1987) Crisis at Christmas 1986. *Lancet,* 1, 553–554

Wolfensberger, W. and Tullman, S. (1982) A brief outline of the principle of normalisation. *Rehabilitation Psychology,* 27, 131–145

CHAPTER 51

WOMEN AND DEMENTIA: FROM STIGMA TOWARDS CELEBRATION

Kate Allan

INTRODUCTION

Dementia is an umbrella term for a group of neurological conditions, the most well-known of which is Alzheimer's Disease. Symptoms include memory loss, confusion, disorientation, loss of skills, behavior and personality change. Dementia has traditionally been considered to be a progressive, irreversible condition with no cure. Prevalence figures vary, but it is thought that dementia affects 8 percent of people over the age of 65. It is not caused by aging alone, but risk does increase sharply with age (Livingstone and Hinchliffe, 1993). Dementia also affects younger people with 4 percent being under the age of 65 years. Whilst Jorm *et al.* (1987) report that women are not thought to be more prone to developing dementia than men, Cheston and Bender (1999) in reviewing data on gender differences (e.g. Lindesay *et al.*, 1989) conclude that women are at greater risk. In either case, as 58 percent of the over-60 population and 66 percent of the over-85 population are women, the majority of those with dementia are female (Goddard and Savage, 1994) and, with the aging of the population, these numbers are set to rise significantly.

THE STIGMA OF DEMENTIA

Dementia is terrifying. It touches on a range of deeply held fears all at once in a way that few other conditions do. For one thing it affects mainly those in later life, and we live in a deeply agist society which denigrates and despises older people (Bytheway, 1995). In addition to the fear generated by old age itself, dementia has traditionally been considered to be a form of mental illness, and for this reason it carries another whole raft of fears and prejudices, particularly those around deviance, strangeness and dangerousness. Dementia is perhaps the most extreme instance of a condition which is believed to bring about the loss of personal responsibility, self-control, dignity and, ultimately, of human status itself.

Further to the age and mental illness stigmas, dementia is seen as entailing the progressive loss of intellectual power. We live in a 'hyper-cognitive culture' (Post, 1995: 3) which prizes and rewards intellectual ability and achievement, and marginalizes and disempowers those who are seen not to possess these qualities. Finally, dementia is an illness which leads to death. It therefore carries all the stigma, fear and superstition which death holds for us in Western culture (Aries, 1981). Images of dementia as a form of 'living death' (Woods, 1989; Sweeting, 1991) are common, with even Jonathan Miller, the President of the Alzheimer's Society, describing the person with the condition as an 'uncollected corpse' (Miller, 1990: 3). Although such a characterization is much less likely to be used now, these attitudes illustrate the depth of our revulsion towards the person who develops this disease, and explains our desire to avoid and distance ourselves from this manifestation of the frailty of the human body and mind.

In addition to all of the above sources of stigma there is also the fact that most people with dementia are women. The popular image of the 'slow, stupid, unhealthy, unattractive and dependent' older woman abounds in our society (Ginn and Arber, 1993: 60). Superimposed on the problem of generalized agism is the 'double jeopardy' suffered by older women (Rodeheaver and Datan, 1988), and the disregarding of their experience even within the feminist movement (Macdonald and Rich, 1984).

MAKING SENSE OF DEMENTIA

Until recently, dementia was viewed as a purely medical entity. Structural brain pathology was assumed to account for the progressive and irreversible decline of the intellect, self-awareness, capacity for meaningful relationships, and a coherent emotional life. The outlook in terms of treatment was hopeless, and aims of care were limited to the attending of physical needs. Abnormal behavior, and the withdrawal and deterioration observed, were regarded as evidence of the inexorable encroachment of the condition, and justified the fact that minimal resources were devoted to caring for those affected, and supporting those who cared for them.

It is difficult to describe the extent of the changes the last decade has seen in the understanding of and interest in this common condition. Whilst high-profile work – genetic studies, neuro-imaging and drug treatments – continue in the medical field, by far the most exciting developments are in the social sphere. In the context of a wider critique of the medicalization of human experience (Friedson, 1970) we have come to recognize the socially constructed element of dementia (Lyman, 1989; Sabat and Harre, 1992; Harding and Palfrey, 1997; Cheston and Bender, 1999). Thinkers like Kitwood (1997) have led the way in highlighting the role of psychosocial factors – principally the way that we, as people without dementia, think and behave – in the presentation and progression of the condition. Kitwood has championed the need to recognize and enhance the 'personhood' of the affected individual, and the possibility of 'rementia' – a reversal of the process of decline.

With the 'emergence of the person' (Downs, 1997), we now have an utterly different landscape of understanding and possibilities compared with that of just ten years ago. The 'Zeitgeist of the late nineties ... is a fascination with dementia' (Bender and Wainwright, 1998: 24). However, an agenda for addressing issues for women with dementia has hardly begun to develop.

THE NEED FOR EMPOWERMENT

Along with the recognition of personhood and subjectivity has come acknowledgment of the need to find ways of empowering people with dementia to find voices to express their thoughts, feelings and needs (Goldsmith, 1996). Work of this nature is in its infancy, and as yet we lack any kind of framework for learning about and addressing specific sources of disadvantage for women with dementia, and as users of services. Effective empowerment must recognize that most of the present generation of people with dementia are women who have grown up with a strong habit of deference to medical personnel and service providers. They have not been encouraged to question practices and assumptions, or to see themselves in a consumer role.

There is some recognition of issues for women users of mental health services generally (e.g. Williams and Watson, 1996; see Stoppard, in this volume), but in the only study of its kind so far, Proctor (1998) undertook consultation work with women with dementia about their views of services with an awareness of gender issues and power differentials to the forefront. She discusses the process of 'othering' (Wilkinson and Kitzinger, 1996) in the context of services for women with dementia.

Empowerment of service users will hasten the development of accessible and efficient services for diagnosis (Fearnley *et al.*, 1997), and for the recognition and treatment of concurrent psychiatric illness which is so common in dementia (Teri and Wagner, 1992). It is imperative that the development of services which meet the needs of ethnic minority groups is fostered (Manthorpe, 1994) and that the needs of those with both learning difficulties and dementia are addressed (Koenig, 1995). And as part of the wider raising of consciousness of the abuse of older women (Aitken and Griffin, 1996), it should be recognized that women with dementia may be especially vulnerable. Other focuses for othering include sexuality, class issues and poverty, and experience of substance abuse. There is an urgent need for work which addresses these complex issues.

Empowerment issues extend to recognizing the work of those providing support for people with dementia, in both paid and unpaid positions (Finch, 1984). Again, most of these people are women.

DEMENTIA FROM THE INSIDE

Following on from the discovery of the person within dementia, and the realization that they are much more like ourselves than different, we have begun to be able to wonder what it *feels* like to have dementia. Two people diagnosed with the condition have written books about their experiences (Davis, 1989; Friel-McGowin, 1993), and we now have theoretical and empirical work in this area (Froggat, 1988; Cohen, 1991; Cheston and Bender, 1999; Keady and Gilliard, 1999). Killick (1997a), who works with people with dementia as a Writer in Residence, provides us with a wealth of astonishing insights into the world of the person with the condition:

My mind, my whole sphere of life, is full. I was very fond of my life. It seems that I'm losing it more and more. Oh dear, it isn't fair when your heart wants to remember!

It is now up to us to learn how to better communicate with people with dementia (Crisp, 1999), and to recognize both the possibilities and the implications of doing so (Killick, 1999; Gibson, 1999).

DEMENTIA AND RELATIONSHIPS

Within the biomedical model, thinking about relationships was exclusively preoccupied with the negative effects of dementia, with the perception of burden and stress, and the risk of physical and mental morbidity which awaited the helpless 'carer'. Although caring for a person with dementia is a tremendous challenge, and does carry real risks (Zarit and Edwards, 1996), new perspectives on relationships emerge from personal accounts of caring (McKinlay, 1998; Bayley, 1998; Grant, 1998; Brough, 1998). Often a powerful spiritual element is evident in these. McKinlay (1998: 1–2), who has written about her mother, tells us that she spoke of her experience as that of a *'top layer being stripped'*. Her daughter describes dementia as *'an experience of being stripped to essences. A journey of the soul'*. Fictionalized accounts (e.g. Forster, 1989; Ignatieff, 1994) of the impact of dementia on relationships also offer powerful insights and belie the image of their exclusively destructive nature.

Another theme evident in these powerful and immediate stories is the idea that dementia challenges relationships to find new depths and channels, and new places for people to meet and share their humanity. John Bayley's (1998) account of the dementia of his novelist wife, Iris Murdoch, emphasizes the new physical intimacy they found as time went on – *'We kiss and embrace now much more than we used to'* (p. 164), and sums up their relationship thus: *'every day we move closer and closer together'* (p.183). Care assistant Laurel Rust, describing her relationship with a woman with dementia, says *'Amy and I have developed an intimacy that is hard to describe, an intimacy that makes me think of companionship differently because Amy does not know my name and has never asked'* (Rust, 1986). Gray-Davidson (1993: 169) talks of successful caring as a process of release from roles – *'mind-created pictures of what we want from a person or what we expect or how we judge'*. This has obvious implications for women whose lives can be so dominated by roles and responsibilities.

COMMUNICATION AND CREATIVITY

If the urge to create and to communicate our experiences are fundamental to our humanity, and if it is true that extremes of human experience may stimulate the creative drive, then those with dementia are surely people who have deep and important things to tell us.

The neurologist and writer, Oliver Sacks (1985: 37–38), asserts that:

in Korsakoffs or dementia or other such catastrophes, however great the organic damage and Humean dissolution, there remains the undiminished possibility of reintegration by art, by communion, by touching the human spirit: and this can be preserved in what seems at first a hopeless state of neurological devastation.

Killick (1997b: 7) argues powerfully for a recognition of the creativity that people with dementia demonstrate in their use of language – 'suddenly talk blooms with metaphor, allusion, the currents of feeling are reflected in rhythm and cadence'. From his work we find evidence of awareness, pain and loss, and also humor and playfulness, and their messages challenge us to respond to their continued – indeed developing – personhood in new and deeper ways.

Jenny and Oropeza (1993; back cover) describing the paintings of people with dementia, many of them women who had never held a brush before, say:

As we stand before their paintings they call out to us in a way that we cannot ignore. They tell us their stories in a language we all understand, transmitted-feelings and emotions trapped inside. Slipping beyond words, their paintings show us glimpses of who they were and who they still are.

Of the role of music, Bright (1992:178) writes:

Because of the capacity to respond to music ... the client has an experience of success and consequent increase in self-esteem which appears to be effective even in those who are incapable of describing their feelings or the reasons for them.

Alongside expression through the arts, and with the recognition that people with dementia continue to try to make sense of their experiences, to integrate them into a meaningful whole, we see that there are many ways we can encourage and support them. There is increasing interest in the place of reminiscence and life story work which acknowledges the lived experience of older people, and its meaning for them (Bornat, 1994; Gibson, 1997). As one woman with dementia put it *'you climb to the top of the family tree and look at the vista from there'* (Killick, 1994: 6). Work on narrative approaches is also rapidly developing (Mills, 1997; Bruce, 1999). Whilst psychotherapy remains a scarce resource for older people generally, we find that in dementia there is still the potential to use such means to achieve resolution (Cheston, 1998). Cheston and Bender (1999) have argued that opportunities for psychotherapy should be offered at all stages of dementia, and also as routinely to those with dementia as to those without.

We also recognize that many older people, and perhaps especially women, have experiences of trauma in their earlier lives which may resurface in the context of dementia (Miesen and Jones, 1997). Responding to the special needs of people in this situation is another sphere which is demanding further work. Work exploring issues of sexuality for both men and women with dementia is beginning to appear (Sherman, 1999), and more should follow.

Interest in spirituality and dementia is also burgeoning (e.g. Tibbs, 1998), and contributing to the reassessment of the nature of this mysterious condition and possibilities for positive responses. Everett (1996: 167) emphasizes how much people with dementia have to give us if we are able to overcome our shallowness and embarrassment: 'They are magic mirrors ... they show us the masks behind which we hide our authentic personhood from the world'. And since dementia is a condition which leads to death, we have a similar expanding of horizons in relation to work in the field of the care of the dying (Kovach, 1997).

In short, everywhere there is an outpouring of enthusiasm and ideas, and huge potential for greater appreciation of those who are going to such extremes of human experience. We have come a long way from the image of the 'uncollected corpse', but still have much further to go. Dare we open ourselves truly to the experience, expressiveness and vitality of these women? Dare we face and explore our fears and celebrate the potential for development in the midst of dementia, and its consequences for our systems of values? We would not only be enhancing the well-being of those who live with the condition now, and the chances for the many yet to come – and remember some of us will be women with dementia – but also finding new ways to enlarge and deepen our understanding of what it means to be human:

As we discover the person who has dementia we also discover something of ourselves, for what we ultimately have to offer is not technical expertise but ordinary faculties raised to a higher level: our power to feel, to give, to stand in the shoes (or sit in the chair) of another. (Kitwood, 1993: 17)

REFERENCES

Aitken, L. and Griffin, G. (1996) *Gender Issues in Elder Abuse.* London: Sage

Aries, P. (1981) *The Hour of Our Death.* Harmondsworth: Penguin

Bayley, J. (1998) *Iris: A Memoir of Iris Murdoch.* London: Duckworth

Bender, M. and Wainwright, A. (1998) Dementia: Reversing out of the dead end. *PSIGE Newsletter,* 66, 22–25

Bornat, J. (1994) *Reminiscence Reviewed.* Buckingham: Open University Press

Bright, R. (1992) Music therapy in the management of dementia. In B. Miesen and G. Jones (Eds.) *Care-giving in Dementia: Research and Applications.* London: Routledge

Brough, B.S. (1998) *Alzheimer's with Love.* Lismore, Australia: Southern Cross University Press

Bruce, E. (1999) Holding on to the story: older people, narrative and dementia. In G. Roberts and J. Holmes (Eds.) *Healing Stories: Narrative in Psychiatry and Psychotherapy.* Oxford: Oxford University Press

Bytheway, B. (1995) *Ageism.* Buckingham: Open University Press

Cheston, R. (1998) Psychotherapeutic work with people with dementia: A review of the literature. *British Journal of Medical Psychology,* 71, 211–231

Cheston, R. and Bender, M. (1999) *Understanding Dementia: The Man With The Worried Eyes.* London: Jessica Kingsley

Cohen, D. (1991) The subjective experience of Alzheimer's Disease: The anatomy of an illness as perceived by patients and families. *American Journal of Alzheimer's Care and Related Disorders and Research,* May/June, 6–11

Crisp, J. (1999) Towards a partnership in maintaining communication. In T. Adams and C. Clarke (Eds.) *Dementia Care: Developing Partnerships in Practice.* London: Balliere-Tindall

Davis, R. (1989) *My Journey into Alzheimer's Disease.* Amersham: Scripture Press

Downs, M. (1997) The emergence of the person in dementia research. *Ageing and Society,* 17, 597–607

Everett, D. (1996) *Forget Me Not: The Spiritual Care of People with Alzheimer's.* Edmonton: Inkwell Press Ltd

Fearnley, K., McLennan, J. and Weaks, D. (1997) *The Right to Know? Sharing the Diagnosis of Dementia.* London: ASAD

Finch, J. (1984) Community Care: Developing non-sexist alternatives. *Critical Social Policy,* 9, 6–18

Forster, M. (1989) *Have the Men Had Enough?* London: Penguin Books

Friedson, E. (1970) *Profession of Medicine.* New York: Dodd, Mead and Company

Friel-McGowin, D. (1993) *Living in the Labyrinth: A Personal Journey Through the Maze of Alzheimer's.* San Francisco: Elder Books

Froggat, A. (1988) Self-awareness in early dementia. In B. Gearing, M. Johnson and T. Heller (Eds.) *Mental Health Problems in Old Age: A Reader.* Buckingham: Open University Press

Gibson, F. (1997) Owning the past in dementia care: creative engagement with others in the present. In M. Marshall (Ed.) *State of the Art in Dementia Care.* London: CPA

Gibson, F. (1999) Can we risk person-centred communication? *Journal of Dementia Care,* 7 (5), 20–24

Ginn, J. and Arber, S. (1993) Ageing and cultural stereotypes of older women. In J. Johnson and R. Slater (Eds.) *Ageing and Later Life.* London: Sage

Goddard, E. and Savage, D. (1994) *People Aged 65 And Over: A Study Carried Out on Behalf of The Department of Health As Part of The 1991 General Household Survey.* London: HMSO

Goldsmith, M. (1996) *Hearing the Voice of People with Dementia: Opportunities and Obstacles.* London: Jessica Kingsley

Grant, L. (1998) *Remind Me Who I Am, Again.* London: Granta

Gray-Davidson, F. (1993) *Alzheimer's: A Practical Guide for Carers to Help You Through the Day.* London: Piatkus

Harding, N. and Palfrey, C. (1997) *The Social Construction of Dementia: Confused Professionals?* London: Jessica Kingsley

Ignatieff, M. (1994) *Scar Tissue.* London: Vintage

Jenny, S. and Oropeza, M. (1993) *Memories in the Making: A Program of Creative Art Expression for Alzheimer Patients.* San Francisco: Alzheimer's Association of California

Jorm, A.F., Korten, A.E. and Henderson, A.S. (1987) The prevalence of dementia: A quantitative integration of the literature. *Acta Scandinavia,* 76, 465–479

Keady, J. and Gilliard, J. (1999) The early experience of Alzheimer's disease: Implications for partnership and practice. In T. Adams and C. Clarke (Eds.) *Dementia Care: Developing Partnerships in Practice.* London: Balliere-Tindall

Killick, J. (1994) *Please Give Me Back My Personality!* Stirling: DSDC

Killick, J. (1997a) When your heart wants to remember. *Elderly Care,* 9, 38–39

Killick, J. (1997b) *You Are Words.* London: Hawker

Killick, J. (1999) Pathways through pain: A cautionary tale. *Journal of Dementia Care,* 7 (1), 22–24

Kitwood, T. (1993) Discover the person, not the disease. *Journal of Dementia Care,* 1 (6), 16–18

Kitwood, T. (1995) Positive long-term changes in dementia: Some preliminary observations. *Journal of Mental Health,* 4, 133–144

Kitwood, T. (1997) *Dementia Reconsidered: The Person Comes First.* Buckingham: Open University Press

Koenig, B.R. (1995) *Aged and Dementia Care Issues for People with an Intellectual Disability. Volume 1: Literature Review and Survey of Carers.* Brighton: Minda Inc

Kovach, C.R. (1997) *End-Stage Dementia Care: A Basic Guide.* Philadelphia: Taylor & Francis

Lindesay, J., Briggs, K. and Murphy, E. (1989) The Guy's/Age Concern Survey: Prevalence rates of cognitive impairment, depression and anxiety in an urban elderly community. *British Journal of Psychiatry,* 155, 317–329

Livingstone, G. and Hinchliffe, A.C. (1993) The epidemiology of psychiatric disorders in the elderly. *International Review of Psychiatry,* 5, 317–326

Lyman, K.A. (1989) Bringing the social back in: A critique of the biomedicalisation of dementia. *Gerontologist,* 29, 597–605

Manthorpe, J. (1994) Reading around: Dementia and ethnicity. *Journal of Dementia Care,* Sept/Oct, 22–23

Miesen, G. and Jones, G. (1997) Psychic pain resurfacing in dementia: from new to past trauma. In L. Hunt, M. Marshall and Rowlings, C. (Eds.) *Past Trauma in Late Life.* London: Jessica Kingsley

Miller, J. (1990) Goodbye to all this. *Sunday Review, Independent on Sunday,* 15 April, 3–5

Mills, M. (1997) Narrative identity and dementia: a study of emotion and narrative in older people with dementia. *Ageing and Society,* 17, 673–698

Macdonald, B. and Rich, C. (1984) *Look Me in the Eye: Old Women, Aging and Ageism.* London: The Women's Press

McKinlay, A. (1998) *inner>out: A journey with dementia.* Rothesay: Charcoal Press

Post, S. (1995) *The Moral Challenge of Alzheimer's Disease.* Baltimore: Johns Hopkins University Press

Proctor, G. (1998) User's views of services: Listening to older women with dementia. *PSIGE Newsletter,* 66, 25–27

Rodeheaver, D. and Datan, N. (1988) The challenge of double jeopardy: Toward a mental health agenda for ageing. *American Psychologist,* 43, 648–654

Rust, L. (1986) Another part of the country. In J. Alexander *et al.* (Eds.) *Women and Aging: An Anthology by Women.* Corvallis, OR: Calyx

Sabat, S. and Harre, R. (1992) The construction and deconstruction of self in Alzheimer's disease. *Ageing and Society,* 12, 443–461

Sacks, O. (1985) *The Man Who Mistook His Wife for a Hat.* London: Pan Books

Sherman, B. (1999) *Sex, Intimacy and Aged Care.* London: Jessica Kingsley

Sweeting, H. (1991) Caring for a relative with dementia: Anticipatory grief and social death. *Generations*, 16, 6

Teri, L. and Wagner, L. (1992) Alzheimer's Disease and depression. *Journal of Consulting and Clinical Psychology*, 3, 379–391

Tibbs, C. (1998) *The Heart of the Matter*. Paper given at the Alzheimer's Disease Society Conference, Northampton

Williams, J. and Watson, G. (1996) Mental health services that empower women. In T. Heller, J. Reynolds, R. Gomm, R. Muston and S. Pattison (Eds.) *Mental Health Matters*. London: Macmillan

Wilkinson, S. and Kitzinger, C. (1996) *Representing the Other*. London: Sage

Woods, R.T. (1989) *Alzheimer's Disease: Coping with a Living Death*. London: Souvenir Press

Zarit, S.H. and Edwards, A.B. (1996) Family caregiving: research and clinical intervention. In R.T. Woods (Ed.) *Handbook of the Clinical Psychology of Ageing*. Chichester: Wiley

---

CHAPTER 52

THE EXPERIENCE OF CHILDHOOD SEXUAL ABUSE: A PSYCHOLOGICAL PERSPECTIVE OF ADULT FEMALE SURVIVORS IN TERMS OF THEIR PERSONAL ACCOUNTS, THERAPY, AND GROWTH

Christine D. Baker

To the outside world I appear to be a perfectly normal and even successful young woman who has managed to 'have it all'. I am surprised at times when together with admiration I can even detect some envy in the eyes of other women and tell myself, 'if only they knew'. All my life I feel as though I have been putting on a front and it is only the very few who have known me closely that get a glimpse of my fears, my feelings of failure, and my relentless standards in an attempt to over-come a deep insecurity. You see, I was sexually abused as a child by my father, and the day he decided to 'teach me the facts of life' he destroyed my ability to trust and be close to others. It is only very recently that I have started to realise what effects this experience has had on me and I have never been able to tell anyone, not even close friends, because I feel so dirty and ashamed and even responsible for what happened ... I have also never been able to sustain a close relationship with a man and always seem to be drawn to people who are unable to consider my needs and feelings and who are ambivalent about commitment. I always get a sense of aban-donment when the relationships end and this increases my sense of failure and defectiveness. To compensate for these feelings I have thrown myself into develop-ing my career and at my age hold quite a senior position in the firm in which I work. The respect I get from my colleagues, together with my financial independ-ence, give me the illusion of success and wholeness I so much need, but now I have met a man who truly loves and understands me and wants to commit to the rela-tionship I find that more than ever I am haunted by the past and my inability to trust. (Eloise)

INTRODUCTION

The above account gives a very succinct picture of survivors' initial presentation to therapy, and while not all female survivors have the same degree of effectiveness in their public life as Eloise, the inner feelings of shame, guilt, and the need for secrecy expressed, are almost universal. In this chapter, I hope to provide the reader with further insights about the experience of female survivors, which I have myself gained, during a decade's therapeutic work with over 200 survivors who presented for treatment to the clinical psychology department of a small but cosmopolitan community in the United Kingdom (Baker, 1999; Baker, in preparation).

In my capacity as clinical psychologist, I have largely devoted the past decade to working with female survivors of sexual abuse. The interest was generated, initially, during the course of seeing women who were referred for psychosexual counselling (Baker, 1992). I became very interested in observing that frequently, the sexual difficulties which survivors of sexual abuse reported appeared to be a function of the general dynamics of the relationship rather than dysfunctional constructs per se. That is, these women did not, generally, suffer with arousal difficulties, anorgasmia, dyspareunia, and vaginismus, but rather, they had difficulties in their sexual responses and behavior within relationships due to feelings of anger, guilt, shame, low self-esteem, and lack of trust. All of this was underpinned by a strong need to be in control (see also Croghan and Meill, in this volume).

The above distinctions have not, in my view, been put to empirical scrutiny and when sexual difficulties in female survivors are mentioned, these are not specified in terms of the overall power dynamics of the relationship. This initial observation a decade ago increased the impetus to learn about the experience of having been sexually abused in general, and I began to develop a specific clinical interest in seeing female survivors for individual therapy. I have found this experience most enriching in that it has afforded me the privilege of entering the world of survivors and gaining a wealth of knowledge about the subjective impact of their abuse. Most importantly, it has had a dramatic effect in shaping my theoretical approach as well as clinical intervention when working with female survivors in particular, and other clients in general. It is this aspect of my work which I wish to focus on here. I think that it will provide important insights to other practitioners in the field and may inspire much needed empirical work. In my case, I have deliberately not subjected my involvement with survivors to the scrutiny of impersonal questionnaires and orthodox scientific methodology and thus my work so far can be argued to be a personal account of my clinical observations and experience.

I consider that there are good reasons for this: Firstly, survivors' most pressing priority is their wish for personal validation of their experience. My initial attempts at handing out questionnaires had the effect of alienating survivors and I am particularly grateful to one survivor who communicated to me by letter that she would rather see a more accessible therapist who would be more interested in listening to her. I am indebted to this woman who fortunately pointed out to me (very early on in my career) the importance of listening, coupled with congruence, empathy, and positive regard as being focal personal attributes which are necessary for successful engagement in therapy.

Secondly, it is my view that our understanding of the experience of survivors is still in its infancy due not least to the endemic secrecy within families (including the abused), but also the adoption by various studies of differential definitions of what constitutes sexual abuse (Brown and Finkelhor, 1986; Glaser and Frosh, 1993; Ferguson, 1997). Moreover, there are obvious difficulties in conducting well-controlled studies which take into account the multitude of variables involved in the impact that the sexual abuse will have on survivors. Some of these variables will be referred to later but, suffice to say, extended subjective accounts from survivors and therapists are needed in order to provide the necessary piloting for further empirical work.

Finally and most importantly, I consider that we need to take a new look at survivors and begin to move away from seeing them as victims who carry pathology. It is true that the experience of having been sexually abused can have, for some, far reaching clinical and personal implications but I was impressed, in my work, to note the degree of resilience, strength, and survival attributes which most of the women possessed.

THEORY AND PRACTICE: A THREE STAGE INTEGRATED MODEL

The three-stage integrated model which I adopt has been developmentally modulated over the course of my involvement with survivors of sexual abuse, in terms of three phases of therapy which I term: engagement, challenge and independence. This model is a very fluid one and provides both myself and the survivors with a useful sliding rule of the course of our progress, along which we can travel up or down at any given time. Implied in this approach are some key elements referring to therapeutic alliance, role of the therapist, and model integration. In the remainder of this chapter I will illustrate the terms I have just mentioned and will use Eloise's therapeutic progress as an illustrative example.

Eloise referred herself to the psychology department following a particularly upsetting argument with her current boyfriend who accused her of not showing him affection and of being ambivalent about her feelings towards him. If you remember, in Eloise's statement above, she asserted that she was finding it difficult to trust and was being 'haunted by the past'. Indeed, her presentation at our first meeting gave me the impression that she was ambivalent about becoming engaged in therapy and even more uncertain about discussing the issue of the sexual abuse which she referred to without elaboration. This presentation can be typical in the case of a survivor's first appointment and it is, therefore, crucial to be attentive to all characteristics which relate to the therapist's personal presentation as well as those of the physical environment if effective engagement on the part of the client is to take place. Issues relating to the therapist's congruence, empathy, and positive regard (Rogers, 1957; Wood, 1996; Wilkins, 1999) are particularly pertinent in imparting a feeling of acceptance, warmth, and understanding. Indeed, in this first and most crucial phase of therapy, I view my initial role as being one of creating an environment which communicates safety and therefore enhances the potential for trust and engagement. It is only when this is established that a collaborative therapeutic relationship can emerge within which to tackle the presenting problems for which survivors request help. In the case of Eloise, as with most survivors of abuse, trusting others is often an alien concept since being abused as a child can establish maladaptive schemas which the survivor uses as a template for negotiating relationships in adulthood (Young, 1994; Young and Klosko, 1993). Maintaining a good level of engagement and mutual collaboration throughout the course of therapy is crucial and it cannot be assumed that a survivor will remain engaged, particularly when difficult issues are being addressed. This brings me to the next phase of therapy, which I term challenge.

It is indeed very challenging to a survivor's sense of well-being when the specifics of the sexual abuse are addressed and also when they realize that they need to make changes in their current ways of behaving if they are to successfully deal with the past. During this phase of therapy my role extends into being a 'guide' or 'limited parent' (Young, 1994). Limited reparenting may be explained in terms of being an adopted 'relational paradigm' which affords the possibility of assuming different therapeutic postures (when necessary) and within which it becomes safe to integrate two or more treatment modalities without creating anxiety in the survivor (Rappaport, 1991). In the case of Eloise, the challenges which she aspired to resolve were: the resolution of the abuse itself; understanding the apparent lack of protection from her mother and resolving the ambivalent feelings she had about her; understanding the apparent gulf between on the one hand, her ability to manage her daily life and career and on the other hand, her inability to form satisfying relationships with men; the necessity to create a positive self-image by acknowledging the importance of establishing healthy personal boundaries and also being in tune with personal needs.

This is certainly not an exhaustive list of potential difficulties and for other survivors these may include issues such as, self-destructive behavior (e.g., eating disorders, self-harm, alcohol and substance abuse, anxiety, depression). Given this brief overview of potential difficulties it becomes clear that no one theoretical approach may be deemed adequate at addressing all of the issues for one person, let alone for each individual who presents for help. On the other hand, a sound theoretical model from which to 'borrow' from more than one school of thought is vital, coupled with a good level of practical experience. As noted earlier, the limited reparenting paradigm facilitates the use of integration and is particularly

Behavioural and Cognitive Therapies, Dresden

Baker, C.D. (in preparation) *Female Survivors of Sexual Abuse: A Practitioner's Guide.* London: Routledge

Brown, B. and Finkelhor, D. (1986) Impact of child sexual abuse: A review of the research. *Psychological Bulletin,* 1, 66–77

Ferguson, A.G. (1997) How good is the evidence relating to the frequency of childhood sexual abuse and the impact such abuse has on the lives of adult survivors? *Public Health,* 111, 387–391

Glaser, G. and Frosh, S. (1993) *Child Sexual Abuse.* London: Macmillan

Maslow, A. (1954) *Motivation and Personality.* New York: Harper & Row

Rappaport, R.L. (1991) When eclecticism is the integration of therapist postures, not theories. *Journal of Integrative and Eclectic Psychotherapy,* 10, 164–172

Rogers, C.R. (1957) The necessary and sufficient conditions of therapeutic personality change. *Journal of Consulting and Clinical Psychology* 21, 95–103

Wilkins, P. (1999) The relationship in person-centred counselling. In C. Feltham (Ed.) *Understanding the Counselling Relationship.* London: Sage

Wood, J.K. (1996) The person-centered approach: toward an understanding of its implication. In R. Hutterer, G. Pawlowsky, P.E. Schmid and R. Stipsits (Eds.) *Client-Centered and Experimental Psychotherapy: A Paradigm in Motion.* Frankfurt-am-Main: Peter Lang

Young, J.E. (1994) *Cognitive Therapy for Personality Disorders: A Schema-Focused Approach* (2nd edn). Sarasota, FL: Personal Resources Exchange

Young, J.E. and Klosko, J.S. (1993) *Reinventing Your Life.* London: Penguin

CHAPTER 53

PSYCHODYNAMIC PSYCHOTHERAPY

Janet Sayers

INTRODUCTION

Psychotherapy with women (as with men) can involve group, individual, or self-help methods. Its orientation may be cognitive behavioral, psychodynamic, or humanistic. It may involve transactional analysis, or draw on a range of other currently available 'alternative therapies'. The London Women's Therapy Centre, and similar centers in the U.K. and America often adopt a primarily psychodynamic approach. It is this approach that I will describe through case illustrations of ways in which psychotherapy with women seeks to take into account social and more immediate interpersonal issues in order to alleviate the distress for which women seek therapy (see also Baker, and Gibbs, in this volume).

RACISM AND HETEROSEXISM

Wider social factors include the historical and material contexts that determine the inequalities and abuses suffered by women by virtue of their sex, class, ethnicity, sexual orientation, physical or mental disability, maternal and marital status, age, and so on. A case illustration of therapists con-fronting these wider social factors – particularly heterosexism (see also Schwartz, 1998; Shelley, 1998) – comes from Mary Lynne Ellis (1997).

The case concerns a 29-year-old woman, Gloria, the second of four chil-dren of a white English mother and black Nigerian father who died when Gloria was 18. In once-weekly free psychotherapy with Ellis lasting just over three years, Gloria often talked of her first memory of being taunted, when she was 10 and went to a new school, with being a 'wog' and a 'chocolate drop'. It was 'like a television set with the sound turned down', she said. She could not hear or speak. Being subject to her fellow-pupils' racism compounded her desperation about her white mother rejecting her because she was black, and her father rejecting his culture in favor of ingratiating himself into white English society.

Ellis takes up ways in which this led Gloria initially to experience and violently berate her, Ellis, for rejecting her, as Gloria thought, for being black. Dreading lest rejection make her utterly empty and annihilated, Gloria frantically sought to glean an identity through joining groups for black women, lesbians, incest survivors, alcoholics, compulsive eaters, dyslexics, and so on. Confronting this in therapy, as well as Ellis refusing to allow Gloria to act out against her the violence impelled in her by feel-ing empty and rejected, led Gloria to begin to feel less destructive and warmer towards her parents and a new girlfriend, Paula, whom she met while in therapy with Ellis. Gradually she became less driven to possess and dominate others. As a result, by the end of therapy, she was more able to find intimacy with others without it being ruined by the violence pre-viously unleashed in her by being separate and different, not least in being lesbian and black.

TRANSFERENCE AND COUNTER-TRANSFERENCE

Social factors – including the history of imperialism, racism, and the pathologizing of lesbianism – affect the attitudes women transfer from outside therapy into their feelings about their therapists. Addressing these attitudes as they emerge in the 'transference' relation of women to their therapists is a means of confronting in order to find ways of alleviating the ills done by these wider social issues.

These issues also affect the 'counter-transference' attitudes of therapists to their patients. Sheila Ernst (1997) illustrates the point with an example from a disabled therapist working with a disabled patient, Isabel. In supervision the therapist described how, despite feeling angry at the dis-crimination she suffered in being patronized and treated as a child on account of her disability, she found herself doing the same to Isabel. She treated her as a child. At one session, for instance, Isabel described how she had been silenced at a job interview by a man – an 'RAF type' with sil-ver hair and handlebar moustache – reminding her of her father. At this the therapist found herself thinking of Isabel as a child she must teach and train for the next interview. Temporarily it stopped her recognizing and working with the problems that Isabel was actually bringing to this session. These included feeling she had gone far enough for the time being with therapy. They also included the repercussions, in her interview, of having been victim of her father's violence due to his irritation at her physical disability making her so slow.

OVER-IDENTIFICATION

Isabel's therapist initially over-identified with her in equating disability, as society does generally, with being child-like. Her reaction, writes Ernst, is an instance of the widespread tendency among women to over-identify with each other. The American psychoanalyst, Nancy Chodorow (1978), attributes this tendency to mothers over-identifying with infant daughters by virtue of their being the same sex. Whether or not this is the cause of women's over-identification with each other, issues of over-identification, sameness and difference often arise in therapy by and with women. An example from my own practice is the case of Eva (Sayers, 1998).

Eva was referred for NHS therapy when she was in her late twenties having spent her family's savings financing her bulimic bingeing and purging. She first became bulimic, she told me, after being sexually abused by her uncle in her early teens. Making herself sick was a means of staying home so as not to have to see him. She blamed her mother for her bulimia. She blamed her mother's 'abandonment' of her to go to work when she was five first driving her to comfort herself with food. She blamed her mother for not telling her about sex leading to her not taking sufficient precautions as a teenager against being abused by her uncle. She also blamed her mother for being so uptight and superior that she could not tell her about her uncle abusing her. Anyway, said Eva, had she told her mother she would not have believed her.

How Eva wished her mother had looked after her better. How she wished I would look after her. But she also could not bear to be with me or her mother. We were too horribly the same as her. Her mother, she said, thought she was so superior and grand. But she was common. So was Eva. Her mother was petty. So was Eva. What Eva most hated about her mother was the way she scratched her legs. But Eva too scratched. She constantly scratched at the arm of the chair in which she sat in therapy with me. I too was no good, just like her mother, just like her. (For more details on eating disorders see Dolan and Gitziner, 1994.)

SELF-OTHER AMBIVALENCE

Treating oneself and others as no good brings me to one final point, namely the way in which therapy seeks to help women discover, face and bring together their feelings of good as well as bad about themselves and others in their past and present, inner and outer lives. (For more on psychoanalysis, ambivalence and depression see Sayers, 2000; Jack, 1993.) Examples from my NHS practice include Lisa (a jazz musician in her late

40s), referred for therapy because she felt so bad about herself, and felt such lack of self-confidence following the breakdown of her marriage. She remembered her mother suffering the same lack of self-confidence when she, Lisa, was a teenager, due largely to the sexism of Lisa's father in criticising and generally doing down her mother as a way to prove his own superiority. Lisa remembered longing to get away. She remembered imagining her father saving her from the imprisoning sameness with her depressed and depressing mother by the two of them gallivanting abroad as he often talked of doing in the adventure stories with which he regaled Lisa in her teens.

Lisa felt the same with me, that I was depressing and depressed, that the only escape was to tell exciting, gallivanting stories about herself and her boyfriends, past and present. She both wanted, and did not want to be with me, just as she wanted and did not want to be with her mother as a teenager. Therapy involved confronting these divided feelings of sameness and difference, closeness and separation, as they arose in therapy with me. As a result Lisa began to feel more warmly towards her mother and less unrealistically idealizing of her father. She divided her parents and others into good and bad. She became more able to bring these and other figures together in her mind as loved as well as hated. As a result she became more confident of having loved and good figures around her with which to offset what she hated and felt was bad.

She felt better about herself. She expressed the confidence this gave her by making a present for me – a jazz composition on the theme of 'London Bridge is falling down'. It represented her increasing friendliness to her nursery rhyme childhood self. It also represented the collapse of her previous false idealization of her father as both exciting and intimidating. These feelings now gave way to more realistic, warmer feelings towards her father, mother, and others. And, with this warmth, both inside and out, she felt able to leave therapy much more self-assured than when she started.

CONCLUSION

Lack of self-confidence is a frequent but not the only problem bringing women to therapy. Lisa's case, together with others described above, nevertheless serves to illustrate some of the ways in which therapists working with women seek to address both wider social issues and more immediate interpersonal factors as they operate in the relationship between women in individual psychotherapy. I have sought to demonstrate how therapists address these factors as they arise in women's transference and counter-transference relationship with each other in therapy as a means of alleviating the impact of depression and sexual abuse, eating disorders, and violence and issues of sameness and difference involved in sexism, racism, lesbianism and disability.

REFERENCES

Chodorow, N. (1978) *The Reproduction of Mothering*. Berkeley: University of California Press

Dolan, B. and Gitzinger, J. (1994) *Why Women? Gender Issues and Eating Disorders*. London: Athlone Press

Ellis, M.L. (1997) Who speaks? Who listens? Different voices and different sexualities, *British Jornal of Psychotherapy*, 13 (3), 369–83

Ernst, S. (1997) The therapy relationship. In M. Lawrence and M. Maguire (Eds.) *Psychotherapy with Women*. London: Macmillan

Jack, D. C. (1993) *Silencing the Self: Women and Depression*. London: HarperCollins

Sayers, J. (1998) *Boy Crazy: Remembering Adolescence, Therapies and Dreams*. London: Routledge

Sayers, J. (2000) *Kleinians: Psychoanalysis Inside Out*. Cambridge: Polity Press

Schwartz, A. E. (1998) *Sexual Subjects: Lesbians, Gender and Psychoanalysis*. London: Routledge

Shelley, C. (1998) *New Perspectives on Psychotherapy and Homosexuality*, London: Free Association Books

CHAPTER 54

SELF-PSYCHOLOGY

Anna Gibbs

INTRODUCTION

This chapter looks at a relatively recent current in psychoanalytic psychotherapy, one which emphasizes the need for the therapist to understand things from the client's perspective. It explains how self-psychology differs from other psychoanalytic psychotherapies, and then takes a look at what self-psychology means by a 'self' and what sorts of problems with our experience of self-functioning might lead us to do therapy. It explains what the therapist's job might be, and discusses how the therapist will try to repair the bond with the client after a failure in therapeutic empathy (see also Sayers, in this volume).

Self-Psychology here names a very broad movement in contemporary psychoanalytic psychotherapy. It provides a way of thinking and working clinically that may be especially helpful to women because of its particular emphasis on intersubjectivity in the therapeutic situation (the way in which both the client and the therapist shape the interaction); its focus on affects (feelings) as well as insight, and its willingness to engage critiques of gender and sexuality, both at a theoretical level and as they impact directly on the therapy.

WHAT IS DIFFERENT ABOUT SELF-PSYCHOLOGY?

Self-Psychology rejects the idea that the therapist functions as a 'blank screen' on which the patient's perceptions of the therapist as they are informed by her experience of other people in the past, are projected as transference. In self-psychology by contrast, transference does not represent a distortion of an objective reality (and especially not a reality equivalent to the therapist's). Rather, the forms of transference which are the focus of Self-Psychology are seen as expressions of unfulfilled need, and a desire for the growth and development of a particular aspect of the self. While interpretations offered from within a classical or Kleinian framework may sometimes take on a persecutory feel for the client, or may simply feel too far removed from her own reality to enable her to feel sufficiently understood, Self-Psychology emphasizes the ways in which the therapist (however little he or she apparently says or does) impacts on the subjective reality of the client. Experience of and ideas about gender and sexuality (as well as other factors such as ethnicity, religion and age) may play an important part in what the client responds to in the therapist (and vice versa). Of paramount importance will be the interaction between them. Self-Psychology acknowledges that particular interactions are actively shaped by two people who each bring their own unique ways of relating and their own characteristic expectations and assumptions. It is this awareness of the intersubjective dimensions of psychic life that ultimately facilitates the in-depth exploration of the patient's subjectivity and the particular repetitive themes that form the 'organizing principles' of her self.

WHAT IS A SELF?

The 'self' in self-psychology exists at the interface of the individual and the other. Subjectively, it is what we experience as a familiar felt 'pattern of awarenesses'. Feelings of realness, authenticity and autonomy give a positive coloring to the self, while low self-esteem gives a negative coloring. Out of the intersubjective field (in the first instance, the relationship between infant and caretaker) are formed the features which are essential to the ongoing creation and maintenance of self. These are agency (the experience of oneself as a competent center of initiative, author of one's own actions); coherence (a sense of one's own embodiment, a feeling of 'wholeness' or integrity); affectivity (the experience of patterned inner qualities of feeling); and history (a sense of continuity with one's own past). Our experience in each of these areas creates a tendency toward a 'characteristic shape and enduring organization' made up of unique patterns of feelings and thoughts which shape our behavior and the choices we make. But it is affective experience, or experience of feeling states, which plays the biggest role in the organization of self-experience in creating intersubjective relatedness and an inner world which is communicable to others both verbally and non-verbally, and which may be shared with them in relationships of varying degrees of intimacy.

WHY DO THERAPY?

Therapy may be helpful when someone suffers a disturbance – of varying degrees of severity – in one or all of the four main functions of the self: cohesion, continuity, agency and affective vitality. Such disturbances might manifest as ongoing experiences of emptiness ranging from a generalized lack of purpose and enjoyment in work or relationships, to intense but 'empty' depression. Low self-esteem and feelings of worthlessness, and an inability to satisfactorily self-regulate (e.g. difficulty sleeping, organizing one's time, eating) or to modulate intense or overwhelming affect are other common signs. Or disturbances may be the result of trauma, or of a sudden change in one's circumstances (the death of someone important to us, migration, loss of a job). In any case, such disturbances produce a tendency to what is called 'fragmentation' (falling apart, not being able to 'keep it together'), which may be signalled in the therapeutic situation by momentary incoherence or sudden silence, but which may also take the more severe forms of dissociation, uncontrollable rage, overwhelming distress or shame, or panic attacks. Loss of time, as in schizophrenic 'fugue states', might be an extreme symptom. On the other hand, extreme perfectionism or reliance on intellect to the exclusion of feelings might be a way of retaining a little control in the face of an emotional world experienced (not always consciously and usually for good reason) as dangerous and unstable.

Insufficient integration of affective experience seems to lie at the heart of these disturbances of self-experience: we may not be able to experience some affects fully (as when we are unaware of our own anger); or we may feel others as too intense and such intensity may feel overwhelming. Sometimes we may not be able to give verbal form to our feelings, and when we are unable to represent them in this way we are prevented from reflecting on them as part of the process of our own ongoing organization of self-experience. Alternatively, if we feel that some affects are prohibited or are actually or potentially dangerous to ourselves or others, we come to experience our feelings as 'bad', and the self-structure that we do form may be negatively colored as a result.

WHAT DOES THE THERAPIST DO?

The role of the therapist is to facilitate the client's free, associative elaboration of her own affective experience, and to respond empathically to that experience. Empathy (as distinct from sympathy, compassion, or reassurance) means trying to understand what it feels like to be the client, and it entails a fundamental positive regard for the patient as a unique individual. Psychoanalytic empathy implies the capacity to absorb and articulate affective experience. Technically, empathy was defined by Kohut (1959) as a sustained process of 'vicarious introspection' and posited it as the main method of psychoanalytic exploration of someone's inner world, of what it feels like to be that particular person. It is a means of investigating – by the sustained feedback process of trial and error – the experience of the client (including her experience of the therapist) from the client's own standpoint, and it implies the authority of the client's experience rather than that of the therapist. It is this empathic attitude that tends to calm anxiety and which enables the client's account of her subjective experience to deepen and the therapist to begin to meet her needs for mirroring and idealizing.

Mirroring and idealizing refer to two different poles of self-experience. Mirroring refers to the need to have our own experience (especially our emotional experience) understood and accepted. Mirroring is a form of validation which builds self-esteem, helps to establish a sense of autonomy and an ability to initiate our own goal-directed behavior. In other words, it enables basic self-assertion because it establishes the authenticity of our own feelings, so that the reality of our experience can be trusted sufficiently to enable us to act on it. The idealizing pole of the self concerns the need to feel oneself part of a reliable and soothing presence who is able to provide affect-regulating functions we may not yet have if our earliest caretakers have been unresponsive to our feelings, were unable to tolerate intense emotion themselves, or needed us to take care of their own feelings.

When responding to a client's need for idealizing, the therapist is able to help the client modulate extreme negative affects (most commonly rage, fear, distress, or shame). By means of mirroring, the therapist is able to enhance the experience of positive affects such as joy and interest, and to help the client recognize feelings which are experienced but for which there are as yet no words, or affects which are only felt as physical sensations or illnesses. Needs for 'twinship', or the experience of sharing one's feelings with someone similar to oneself, as with a peer group, may also be met in therapy. So also may the need for a temporary or prolonged merging with the therapist at times of intense emotional stress. By having these needs met, often for the first time, the client gradually develops a greater capacity to restore her own emotional balance and to use her feelings as a way of determining 'what feels right' for her.

WHAT HAPPENS WHEN THE THERAPIST DOESN'T UNDERSTAND?

The need for mirroring and idealizing experiences represents a movement towards growth on the part of the client and it is the role of therapeutic empathy to facilitate this in a safe environment in the context of a strong bond with the therapist. When this is working well, we say that the therapist is affectively 'attuned' to her client. However everyone's experience is different, and there are times when a therapist's empathy will inevitably fail. When this happens, the client may actually come to experience the therapist as 'just the same as everyone else', just like all those people who have failed her in the past. Such moments of empathic failure produce a rupture of the secure bond between client and therapist. In this case, it is the job of the therapist to recognize that she has made a mistake, that she has failed to understand an important aspect of the client's experience, and to repair the therapeutic bond by acknowledging the mistake. She will then explore the client's experience of this break in empathy (or disjunction) with her, linking it to other similar experiences the client may have had in the past and coming to understand the meaning of these experiences. The forging of links between past and present experience assists the client's experience of cohesion and continuity, and her own growing understanding of the contours of her emotional world will also promote the growth of feelings of competence which in turn enable her to act as a center of initiative.

REFERENCES

Basch, Michael Franz (1988) *Understanding Psychotherapy: The Science Behind the Art*. New York: Basic Books

Brandschaft, Bernard (1994) To free the spirit from its cell. In R. Stolorow, G. Atwood and B. Brandschaft (Eds.) *The Intersubjective Perspective*. London: Jason Aronson

Demos, Virginia (1984) Empathy and affect: reflections on infant experience. In J. Lichtenberg, M. Bornstein and D. Silver (Eds.) *Empathy I*. Hillsdale: Analytic Press

Kohut, H. (1959) Introspection, empathy and psychoanalysis: An examination of the relationship between mode of observation and theory. In P. Ornstein (Ed.) *The Search for the Self: Selected Writings of Heinz Kohut: 1950–1978*, Volume 1 (pp. 205–232). New York: International Universities Press

Lee, Ronald R. and Martin, J. Colby (1991) *Psychotherapy after Kohut: A Textbook of Self-Psychology*. Hillsdale: Analytic Press

Stern, Daniel (1985) *The Interpersonal World of the Infant*. New York: Basic Books

Stolorow, Robert (1994) Subjectivity and self psychology. In R. Stolorow, G. Atwood and Brandschaft, B. (Eds.) *The Intersubjective Perspective*. London: Jason Aronson

Stolorow, Robert and Atwood, George (1992) *Contexts of Being: The Intersubjective Foundations of Psychological Life*. London: Analytic Press

Stolorow, Robert, Brandschaft, Bernard and Atwood, George (1977) *Psychoanalytic Treatment: An Intersubjective Approach*. London: Analytic Press

THE HEALTH OF OLDER WOMEN

CHAPTER 55

REPRESENTATIONS OF MENOPAUSE AND WOMEN AT MIDLIFE

Antonia C. Lyons and Christine Griffin

INTRODUCTION

Linguistic and visual representations of women's health and menopause experience at midlife are revealing of social concerns regarding the control of health care, and the construction of women's aging. They also show the extent to which a consensus exists on the nature and character of menopausal women (Kaufert and Lock, 1997). Culturally dominant perspectives on menopause and women at midlife are also important because sociolinguistic discourses are taken up by women and reproduced in their talk and action, influencing women's experiences of menopause (including choices surrounding whether or not to use hormone replacement therapy (HRT)). Further, how physicians and medical professionals think about menopause and treat women experiencing menopausal symptoms depends upon the currently accepted model of menopausal women (Kaufert and Lock, 1997). In this chapter we briefly describe some of the research on representations of menopause and midlife women, taking as a starting point our own preliminary analysis of self-help texts on menopause and HRT. We examine representations of menopause and women at midlife in these texts, and compare them with representations across other textual sites, including medical textbooks, academic writing and advertisements. We also discuss some of the implications of these representations.

We focussed on two texts on menopause as part of an ongoing research project into constructions of women and midlife in self-help books (Lyons and Griffin, in preparation). As Allwood (1996) points out, the self-help genre is one that has been mainly directed towards women, and provides a site to examine contested notions of expertise and responsibility in a specific area. The first of the books we examined was written by Dr. Robert C.D. Wilson and entitled *Understanding HRT and the Menopause* (Which? Books, 1996). This book was aimed at all woman approaching menopause who want to make 'truly informed, responsible decisions about their own health at this challenging time of life'. The second text was written by Kendra Sundquist – *Menopause made Easy: How to Turn a Change into a Change for the Better* (1992, published by Robinson). While Wilson's book is medically oriented and pro-HRT, Sundquist's is at a basic level and is relatively neutral about HRT; it is aimed at women who are 'worrying' about this stage of their lives.

In describing menopause, Wilson draws heavily on negative terms associated with decline and deficiency. For example, he discusses the hormone changes that occur in women both during puberty and during menopause, and the contrast in terms used for these descriptions clearly highlights the pejorative discourse associated with changes during menopause:

*Puberty begins when oestrogen **floods** into the bloodstream, causing early **budding** of breast tissue, **influencing** the development of fat deposits and **smoothing** body contours to produce the characteristic female outline. (p. 15, emphasis added)*

*'The vagina, uterus and cervix are areas where oestrogen is readily taken up and which consequently **suffer** when **deficiency** occurs: their lining, or surface tissue, then tends to **atrophy**. The vagina **shortens**, the skin surface **weakens** and **thins** and blood supply **diminishes**.' (p. 28, emphasis added)*

Hormones during puberty are assumed to 'flood' and cause 'budding', whereas during menopause hormone changes cause certain parts of the body to 'suffer' and become 'deficient'. Menopause is constructed as a disease, a health hazard which requires professional 'management'. This 'menopause as disease' discourse is prevalent in academic writing, the overwhelming majority of which situates this time of women's lives within a biomedical framework (see Dinnerstein, and Roberts, in this volume). Thus, it has tended to ignore social, cultural and political aspects of women's experiences of menopause and midlife (Dickson, 1990). A review of published menopause literature from 1984–1994 found that only 6 percent of all published work included any social or psychological themes; most of these studies examined the link between menopause and depression or mood (Rotosky and Travis, 1996).

Menopause has also been related to images of disease and deficiency in medical textbooks. For example, Martin (1987) has shown how the menopause is described in medical texts using the metaphor of the factory, which constructs events as failing in their purpose. Terms such as 'deprive' 'degenerate', 'decline', 'withdrawn', and 'deteriorate' are frequently used. Our own examinations of British medical texts on menopause and HRT highlight the same disease discourse. The menopause is overtly constructed as negative, and discussed as a 'deficiency disease', as the following quotes demonstrate:

The menopause can be considered as a state of hormone deficiency; HRT is, in effect, merely bringing women back up to the baseline from which they descended as a result of the deficiency. (Smith and Studd, 1993: 34)

[menopause] is the most obvious manifestation of a gradual decline in ovarian function … The ovaries fail because they run out of primordial follicles…hormone production progressively declines. (Smith and Studd, 1993: 1)

The negative, technical language of menopause that is employed in medical texts and academic literature has far-reaching consequences. The tendency for the medical profession to view menopause as a pathological state must come in part from the way it is constructed within medical texts (Martin, 1987). Rotosky and Travis (1996) have argued that the academic literature's portrayal of menopause as a deficiency disease sanctions it as such by virtue of its publication within academic journals. These negative constructions, which are also apparent in the self-help texts, inhibit the way in which we think about women's experiences at midlife, limit our understandings (Ventura, 1995), and decrease the accessibility of public debate (Conrad and Schneider, 1980, cited in Bell, 1990).

In an apparent contrast to the construction of menopause as a disease, one of the self-help texts we examined also employed a discourse of 'menopause as natural':

[menopause] is a natural process for all women, a biological change that usually occurs. (Sundquist, 1992: 1)

Remember: menopause is a natural event, not a disease. (Sundquist, 1992: 9)

The view of 'menopause as natural' is contrasted with the medical perspective:

These doctors view menopause, a natural event in a women's life, as a disease that needs to be treated and managed. (Sundquist, 1992: 51)

Despite this 'menopause as natural' discourse, terms from the 'menopause as disease' discourse are also employed in this book so that the two discourses become conflated. For example, the term 'symptoms' is used, implying illness or disease, and indicating the pervasiveness of the 'disease' discourse. This apparently contradictory juxtaposition of the 'menopause as natural' and the 'menopause as disease' discourses is not unusual, as we have found from our analyses of other self-help texts on menopause (e.g. Smith, 1996; McKenzie, 1994).

The 'menopause as natural' discourse has been widely employed by feminist writers in an attempt to resist the medicalization of menopause and the widespread use of HRT. For example, Germaine Greer's book, *The Change: Women, Ageing and the Menopause* (1991), emphasizes the positive meanings associated with menopause and aging, and argues that women at midlife should get in touch with the spiritual and 'natural' aspects of their experience. Authors argue that pharmaceutical companies dominate the menopause discourse and research, and that research into more 'natural, safer, healthier and less expensive forms of prevention and treatment' has been carried out but has not received the same degree of vigorous promotion as profit-making techniques have (Birnbaum, 1990: 250). Lupton (1996) has critically examined the way in which the 'menopause as natural' discourse functions, and she contends that it is limiting and seeks to define menopause in certain ways for women (for example, implying that women should accept the aging process gracefully or stoically endure symptoms rather than seeking medical help).

In addition to the 'disease' and 'natural' accounts of menopause, we also identified the discourses of choice and responsibility in both self-help texts. Through these discourses the menopause was represented as a period of life in which women were expected to make sensible and responsible decisions concerning their health and future well-being. These decisions were not just about using HRT and potentially reducing the risk of diseases such as osteoporosis and cardiovascular disease, but about health more generally:

Health means more than just being disease-free. It also means feeling good about yourself, about the world you live in and about the degree of control you have over your own life. Menopause is a time to look carefully at your lifestyle and how it might affect your health. (Sundquist, 1992: 51)

Sundquist goes on to discuss lifestyle choices including those concerning diet, exercise, alternative therapies, and 'vaginal vitality' (how to keep the vagina healthy). In contrast, Wilson discusses 'managing the change with or without hormone replacement therapy' (book front cover). Such a statement suggests that women have a degree of choice regarding the use of HRT; however after reading the book it seems that this choice is actually an illusion. The implication of the choice and responsibility discourses in this book is that unless there are medical reasons not to take HRT, this is the sensible and responsible thing to do. For example, in question-answer format, Wilson discusses oestrogen:

*What does oestrogen do? 1. Maintains the health and **proper** functioning of the genital organs. (p.22, emphasis added)*

Oestrogen deficiency is linked with, but not always entirely responsible for, the various symptoms and signs which occur around the menopause. (p.27)

These descriptions of oestrogen changes at the time of menopause imply that a woman's genitals will no longer function properly during and following menopause! Such notions are also apparent in Wilson's consideration of alternative therapies:

There are several hormone-free preparations which may be of benefit. They are, however, of limited assistance because none is able to compensate for the absence of oestrogen in the body. (p. 91)

In linking menopause so strongly to the (negative) hormonal changes which occur at this time, it seems that the reader is positioned in such a way that choosing not to take HRT is somehow silly, or not sensible. When the reader is asked to consider HRT, however, they are treated as rational human beings who can gain information and weigh up the risks and benefits of such a decision before going to seek medical advice. In the introduction, Wilson claims that the book 'enables women to make the right decision' (p. 14) (thus implying that there is only one), and that the book 'will put [women] in a much stronger position to take responsibility for the key decisions of their personal health management' (p. 14). In this way the two self-help texts we examined saw health as a virtue, and menopause as a time when women could demonstrate their responsibility and independence by 'managing' their menopause through gaining information, using HRT, or changing their lifestyles. However, this discourse which positions women as able to self-manage their health is contradictory with the positioning of medical professionals as the experts not only on menopause, but also on women's bodies:

It's not really surprising that so many women haven't got a clue about what they've got 'down there'. (Sundquist, 1992: 17)

Today good health, and a healthy body, are understood as signs of internal self-discipline (Lupton, 1996). Similar representations of menopause as a time of personal health management have been identified in other media, which are now major carriers of information about health and health care across the lifespan (Bury, 1997; Elliott, 1994; Nettleton, 1997). For example, a Canadian study examined visual representations of mid-age women in the pharmaceutical literature and the mass media of the 1990s, and contrasted these images with those in the 1970s (Kaufert and Lock, 1997). While the 1970s menopausal woman was shown as depressed and sickly looking, the 1990s version is shown 'glowing with fitness, with well-maintained teeth, hair and skin, far too fit to break a hip, have a heart attack [etc.]' (p. 81). Their analysis demonstrated one consistent message in the media, namely that menopause marks a critical choice point in women's lives, and the authors concluded that health is viewed as the new virtue for aging women.

An additional feature of both 'popular' and academic constructions of menopause is the cultural and social specificity of most representations. Firstly, there is a pervasive tendency to link menopause so closely to the reproductive system that textual representations refer only to women who have had children. The implication here is that 'only mothers bleed', to paraphrase the song title. Even Germaine Greer's book *The Change* (1991), which presents radical arguments concerning the over-prescription of HRT and the negative stereotyping of women in midlife, falls into this trap. Greer herself does not have children, so this is a particularly perplexing assumption for her to have made. Allied to this close association between menopause and (the end of) motherhood is the implicit focus on heterosexual women. Few academic or self-help texts indicate that lesbian or bisexual women even exist, still less that they might experience menopause in specific ways, although there are a few exceptions (MacKenzie, 1994).

Secondly, in most texts on menopause, there is a pervasive, though frequently implicit focus on the experiences of white, middle-class women living in relatively affluent industrialized societies (Komesaroff *et al.*,1997). Self-help texts frequently advise women about the mixed blessings of the 'empty nest syndrome', which relies on a model of the nuclear family norm. The experience of diminishing involvement in child care after one's children have passed puberty is unfamiliar to most women living in extended family systems, as it is to women who have not had children. In addition, many non-Western cultures operate with different, and less negative, representations of midlife and older age for women, such that the premium on youth which pervades discourses around HRT and menopause appears far less relevant (Greer, 1991). Some self-help texts do recognize the existence of such cultural difference, but without this affecting their overall representation of menopause as inevitably unpleasant and distressing (e.g. Smith, 1996). Few studies include women of color in their samples of respondents, so we still know relatively little about their accounts of living through the menopause.

SUMMARY

How women interpret bodily changes at midlife is likely to be intimately related to the social and cultural discourses surrounding menopause and women's aging. As Hunter and O'Dea (1997) have cogently argued, a woman's subjectivity exists between her perception of physical changes and the discursive constructions of the menopause, which are influenced by social, political and cultural practices and traditions. This does not deny the reality of menopause as a biological process, but emphasizes that interpretations of this process depend heavily on social and cultural beliefs and constructions.

REFERENCES

Allwood, R. (1996) 'I have depression, don't I?': Discourses of help and self-help books. In E. Burman, G. Aitken, P. Allred, R. Allwood, T. Billington, B. Goldberg, A.G. Lopez, C. Heenan, D. Marks and S. Warner (Eds.) *Psychology Discourse Practice*. London: Taylor & Francis

Bell, S.E. (1990) Changing ideas: The medicalisation of menopause. In R. Formanek (Ed.) *The Meanings Of Menopause: Historical, Medical And Clinical Perspectives*. Hillsdale NJ: Analytic Press

Birnbaum, D. (1990) Self-help for menopause: A feminist approach. *Annals of the New York Academy of Sciences*, 592, 250–252

Bury, M. (1997) *Health and Illness in a Changing Society*. London: Routledge

Dickson, G.L. (1990) A feminist post-structuralist analysis of the knowledge of menopause. *Advances in Nursing Science*, 12, 15–31

Elliott, J. (1994) A content analysis of the health information provided in women's weekly magazines. *Health Libraries Review*, 11, 96–103

Greer, G. (1991) *The Change: Women, Ageing and the Menopause*. London: Hamish Hamilton

Hunter, M. and O'Dea, I. (1997) Menopause: Bodily changes and multiple meanings. In J. Ussher (Ed.) *Body Talk: The Material and Discursive Regulation of Sexuality, Madness and Reproduction*. London: Routledge

Kaufert, P.A. and Lock, M. (1997) Medicalization of women's third age. *Journal of Psychosomatics, Obstetrics and Gynaecology*, 18, 81–86

Komesaroff, P., Rothfield, P. and Daly, J. (Eds.) (1997) *Reinterpreting menopause: Cultural and philosophical issues*. New York: Routledge

Lupton, D. (1996) Constructing the menopausal body: The discourses on hormone replacement therapy. *Body and Society*, 2, 91–97

Lyons, A.C. and Griffin, C. (In preparation) *Representations of Women and Midlife in Self-Help Texts on Menopause*

MacKenzie, R. (1994) *Menopause: A Practical Self-Help Guide for Women*. London: Sheldon Press

Martin, E. (1987) *The Woman in the Body*. Buckingham: Open University Press

Nettleton, S. (1997) Governing the risky self: How to become healthy, wealthy and wise. In A. Peterson and R. Bunton (Eds.), *Foucault, Health and Medicine*. London: Routledge

Rotosky, S.S. and Travis, B.B. (1996) Menopause research and the dominance of the biomedical model 1984–1994. *Psychology of Women Quarterly*, 20, 285–312

Smith, M. (1996) *Dr Mike Smith's Postbag: HRT*. London: Kyle Cathie Ltd

Smith, R. and Studd, J. (1993) *The Menopause and Hormone Replacement Therapy*. London: Martin Dunitz

Sundquist, K. (1992) *Menopause Made Easy: How to Turn a Change into a Change for the Better*. London: Robinson

Ventura, M. (1995) Talkin' American 2. In R. Hoelton (Ed.) *Encountering Cultures* (2nd edn). Englewood Cliffs, NJ: Prentice-Hall

Wilson, R.C.D. (1996) *Understanding HRT and the Menopause*. London: Which? Books, Consumer's Association

---

CHAPTER 56

PSYCHOLOGICAL WELL-BEING IN AGING WOMEN

Linda Gannon

INTRODUCTION

In cultures where aging is despised and feared and women are valued for fertility and beauty, the aging woman is often the target of pity and ridicule – portrayed as lonely, sick, frail, and unhappy (see Allen, and Lyons and Griffin, in this volume). While some scholars ascribe distress essentially to genetics and/or childhood trauma, I am among those who believe psychological distress to be due primarily to contextual causes such as poor working conditions, sexual and racial discrimination and oppression, poor health, hostile family environments, poverty, and inadequate social support. These potentially chronic stressors are likely to become increasingly destructive to an individual's well-being if they persist: A single incident of gender discrimination may be ignored, but 60 years of such discrimination may be devastating, rendering aging women vulnerable to both physical and psychological distress through the accumulated effects of chronic stress. While the feminist movement has been somewhat successful in changing misogynist values and improving the life circumstances of women, gender discrimination continues to limit the opportunities for physical and psychological well-being. Although a woman's approach to midddle and old age and her well-being during these later stages of life is unique and individual, certain phenomena that typically accompany the aging process – loss of social and financial status, retirement, the loss of a partner and friends to illness and death, isolation, and deteriorating functional capacity[1] and physical health – are likely to interfere with psychological well-being for most individuals.

PHYSICAL WELL-BEING

The separation of mind and body in Western culture and science is a consequence of Descartes' philosophical doctrine of dualism. While this view remains prominent today, newer research, such as that demonstrating the detrimental effects of psychological stress on the immune system, has begun to blur these boundaries. Social and biological scientists are beginning to recognize the mutually interactive and synergistic dependencies between physical and psychological well-being. Consequently, old age tends to be characterized by high individual variability but predictable consistency across domains of health – the extremes being the individual who reports poor health, few friends and family, insufficient financial resources, low energy, low self-esteem, psychological distress, poor quality food, and inadequate access to medical care, and the individual reporting excellent health, close friends and family, adequate resources, high energy, self-confidence, psychological well-being, nutritional food, and access to quality medical care. In other words, with experience and age, the interdependency between physical and psychological well-being strengthens – one cannot be studied without considering the other.

Physical health status has a major impact on the adjustment of older adults. Regardless of how it is measured (self-rated, functional status, number of chronic conditions, number of physician visits or number of prescribed medications), health has been consistently related to depression in virtually all studies on community-dwelling elders. Although true for both sexes, the relationship may be particularly strong in women. (Koenig and Blazer, 1992: 240)

This interdependence between physical and psychological well-being was assessed in a cross-national study conducted by the World Health Organization (Simon *et al.*, 1996) at 15 intervention sites. At all sites, the number of current physical complaints (medically explained or not) was significantly correlated with psychological distress regardless of the geography or economic development of the country.

The medical profession has devoted most of its resources to the study and successful treatment of acute illnesses. Relatively ignored have been chronic illnesses which typically have an insidious onset, are difficult to diagnose, and are, by definition, not curable. Many, if not most, chronic diseases develop in the context of chronic causes and, many, if not most of these are injurious life conditions. Thus, the accumulated effects over decades of a poor diet, a sedentary activity level, substance abuse, and environmental pollution are expressed as chronic, progressive physical illnesses, such as hypertension, obesity, asthma and osteoporosis. The vast majority of elderly have some form of chronic disease. The clear parallelism between the physical and psychological realms leads us to the conclusion that those factors crucial to physical well-being – diet, exercise, environment – are highly salient to psychological well-being as well.

The questions remain as to why physical health seems to cause, or at least be associated with, psychological well-being, and why this relationship increases with age. Although a variety of explanations present themselves, the most parsimonious is, perhaps, that physical illness reduces one's control in everyday life. As one ages, the probability of suffering from an illness or chronic condition that results in disability, reduced functional capacity, or chronic pain increases. These outcomes result in a reduced ability to exert control over everyday and future events.

CONTROL

The sense of control has been identified repeatedly as an important ingredient for successful aging. (Lachman and Weaver, 1998: 553)

The salience of control over important life events and experiences is a crucial component of all major theoretical models of psychological well-being. The learned helplessness model, emerging from conceptual innovations and empirical research by Seligman (1975), is, perhaps, the impetus for the current generation of scholarly work on the association between control and psychological well-being. According to Seligman, persons who are exposed to situations in which their behavior does not impact their environment, their responses do not effect outcomes, and/or the environment appears to be not contingent upon their efforts, will feel useless and helpless. Persons learn to be helpless (and, therefore, depressed) if they are exposed to repeated evidence that they have little control over their environment.

As persons age, they are increasingly likely to experience a loss of control due to disability, chronic disease, poverty, and/or threats to personal safety (Lachman and Weaver, 1998). Perceiving important events to be beyond one's control tends to reduce motivation and increase depression – both of which, in turn, may result in acquiescing to life styles that further reduce the opportunity for control (see Baty, in this volume). In traditional Western societies, gender is a strong predictor of control. Most of the governing, financial and commercial aspects of society are controlled by men; men are viewed as 'head' of their families. The masculine sex role (decisive, self-confident) implies control whereas the feminine sex role (unassertive, dependent) implies helplessness. As a consequence of these social, political, and economic conditions, women tend to have less control throughout life than do men. For these reasons, women might be expected to be particularly vulnerable to helplessness and depression when faced with the prospect of aging and the loss of what little control they did have. Yet, women are not increasingly likely to report depression as they progress through middle and old age.

Interestingly, the stereotype of the depressed and lonely old lady is apparently just that – a stereotype: women do not get more depressed with age, aged women have considerably lower suicide rates than do aged men, and, importantly, women live longer. In discussing these data, Schlossberg (1980) has suggested that women do not miss the control they never had. An alternative or additional explanation, however, is that the changes in control that occur after middle age are somewhat different for women and men. Among men who have followed relatively traditional paths, the focus was work, characterized by paid employment and much influence in the social, political, and family spheres – roles typified by considerable control. In this same traditional context, women's lives were essentially nurturing their children and dependence on their husbands – roles with little opportunity for control. With age, men tend to lose control when they retire and their children leave home, but I would argue that changes accompanying middle and old age in women are often associated with *increased* control. When children grow up and leave home, women's control over their everyday schedule increases. If a woman is newly divorced or widowed, although the loss is distressing, the ultimate result is likely to be an increase in control. For some women, this is the first time they have lived alone and been responsible for their own personal care. They may, of necessity, learn about finances and how to fix the plumbing and, while these experiences may be approached with fear and foreboding, meeting the challenges increases self-esteem, self-efficacy, and feelings of being in control.[2] Indeed, the salience of physical well-being to psychological well-being may be grounded in the commonsense notion that the better one's physical health, the greater one's ability to exert control over important arenas of life.

Situations that are particularly characteristic of the elderly include residence in a nursing home or other similar institution, disability, and chronic pain – all of which are associated with diminished control (Logue, 1991). Nursing homes severely restrict individual choice in most life activities (such as diet, schedule, and leisure activities) resulting in extremely low levels of control. This may result in a downward spiral of health since lack of control is associated with diminished competency of the immune system, rendering the individual vulnerable to illness; illness, in turn, acts to decrease control further which, in turn, increases vulnerability to illness (Rodin, 1989).

Emerging theoretical frameworks of control include that of

Heckhausen and Schulz (1995) who proposed a dichotomous schema in which primary control refers to achieving impact on the environment external to the individual whereas secondary control designates an impact on the self: 'primary control is usually characterized in terms of active behavior engaging the external world, whereas secondary control is predominantly characterized in terms of cognitive processes localized within the individual (p. 297). The elderly are commonly faced with age-related health declines that preclude primary control. Faced with these restrictions, they may increasingly depend on secondary control strategies including adherence to religious beliefs, adjusting downward their concepts of ideal self, contrasting their own situation with that of others who have less control, and increasing the value of available activities while decreasing the value of activities no longer possible.

Heckhausen and Schulz (1995) claim the high salience of personal control to be universal: 'primary control is invariant across cultures and historical time' (p. 286). Yet, their model was developed and tested only in the United States – a society in which control, influence, and power are highly valued. In contrast, cultures in which the values of cooperation and non-violence, rather than achievement and competition, form the basis of beliefs and values may place little value on controlling others and the environment. Indeed, I would argue that the research literature on personal control does not apply, even within the Western cultures, to those who are or have been politically and economically oppressed for reasons of race, ethnicity, gender or age. These individuals do not have access to 'control over others' and, instead, develop in a context in which 'control over self' is emphasized. This latter form of control according to Gergen (1989) is, in essence, the freedom to act, the ability to plan and pursue one's own goals, and a recognition of the consequences of one's actions; it proceeds from the wise incorporation of experience into one's life schemas.

In Western societies, men who adhere to traditional values seek power and control over other people and the environment, whereas the roles of women do not include the domination or control of others. Rather, women are socialized to follow the 'cooperative' path and achieve psychological and physical well-being through self-awareness, social understanding, and control over their own lives. If this is the case, then the transition into old age may be an easier course for women than for men. Instead of a time of loneliness and despair, old age for women might be viewed as a natural culmination of their earlier years; their life experiences may provide considerable wisdom and ever greater development.

DEPRESSION

The most common expression of psychological distress in women of any age is depression (see Stoppard, in this volume). Intuition and logic predict both an increase and a decrease in depression with age. As women grow older, they may experience less depression as they learn to cope with or avoid situations likely to cause distress. Or, they may experience more depression as chronic stressors (poverty, racial and gender discrimination) continue and the destructive effects accumulate. Still others predict increased depression with loss of fertility due to either the hormonal environment associated with menopause or to the psychological 'loss'. The considerable empirical data indicate that the incidence of depression in women tends to *decrease* in middle and old age; the life stage during which women are most likely to report depression is when at home with young children (Gannon, 1999; Pearlin, 1975; Radloff, 1975). This is not to say that depression is a trivial or non-existent concern for aging women. In spite of the absence of a particular vulnerability to depression in mid- and old-age women, many do experience depression. Furthermore, the sources of depression in aging women and the resources available to maintain psychological well-being undoubtedly differ in some respects from those of younger women.

Aging women often face the loss of a partner to death; the ensuing loneliness and isolation are considered precursors to depression. Nevertheless, in spite of the fact that widowhood is an almost expected life event for heterosexual elderly women, the resulting depression tends to be time-limited, unless the loss is accompanied by financial hardship or physical illness (Nolen-Hoeksema *et al.*, 1994; Thompson *et al.*, 1991). In the U.S., over half of the widows live alone, yet the social consequences of living alone do not appear to be highly stressful for women. In the U.S., 31 percent of elders live alone and expressed the wish to do so as long as they could (Howie, 1992). Furthermore, while living alone or with someone other than a spouse was associated with a higher mortality risk for men, there was no detrimental influence on survival for women (Davis *et al.*, 1997). Living alone, however, is, for women, not equivalent to social isolation.

In Western societies, women are socialized to a gender-specific role characterized by nurturing, compassion, caring, concern, and empathy. Given these skills and values, women of all ages are consistently found to have more close friends, to be on more intimate terms with close friends, and to have a wider and more complex network of friends compared to men (Grambs, 1989; Lewittes, 1988). In a study of elderly widows (Arling, 1976), contact with adult children was unrelated to psychological well-being whereas maintaining closeness with friends and neighbors was associated with fewer feelings of loneliness and greater self-esteem. Even when limited by institutionalization, elderly women continued to develop and maintain balanced and active social networks consisting of other residents, staff, kin and outside friends (Powers, 1996). Interestingly, more is not always better. Reeves and Darville (1994) studied the extent of and satisfaction with social networks in retired women. Whereas frequency of social contact and variety of contact did not influence life satisfaction, the *disparity* between preferred and actual social contact did affect satisfaction – both more and less social activity than that desired were associated with low satisfaction.

A balance between giving and receiving in social relationships is referred to as reciprocity. Most comfort and pleasure is gained in social relationships that are characterized by a more or less equal exchange of giving and receiving. Unfortunately, elderly persons are often in the situation of being the recipient of help; because of illness or disability or frailty, they may be unable to return instrumental, financial, or emotional aid. Being either the donor or the receiver in an unbalanced relationship has been found to be associated with poor mental health, less satisfaction with the relationship, and negative affect (Albert and Cattell, 1994). This may explain the lack of psychological benefits from closeness with adult children: 'old women may feel that their families give them support out of a sense of duty'(Unger and Crawford, 1992: 526), whereas, with friends, there can be the expectation and realization of reciprocity.

The absence of a particular vulnerability for depression associated with biological loss of fertility suggests that most middle-and old-age women do not view themselves as reproductive robots but as persons with multiple roles and accumulated, valuable wisdom. The scholarly research has consistently noted that employed women fare better – both physically and psychologically – than do unemployed women (Haertel et al., 1992; Hibbard and Pope, 1992). This has been interpreted to mean that multiple roles are beneficial, perhaps because of the expanded reinforcement potential – if a woman has a good partner and a good job and loses one of these, the rewards from the remaining role will 'see her through' the crisis. Men whose lives are limited to work roles are particularly vulnerable to the 'stress of retirement' as they are losing their only role. Further psychological benefits may accrue from skills learned from managing the complexities of juggling time and tasks, switching focus in response to needs of others, and prioritizing demands – skills that may serve women well as they age.

There is considerable evidence documenting a strong influence of socioeconomic status (SES) on physical and psychological well-being, disability, and mortality (e.g. Hemingway et al., 1997; Marmot et al., 1997):

The relationship of low socioeconomic status and poor health rises to the top of the findings over and over again, across different disease outcomes, in different age groups, and in different areas of the world. The strength and consistency of this relationship has been remarkable. (Guralik and Leveille, 1997: 728)

That poverty bestows a multitude of pathways to psychological distress is of particular importance to women.

The 'feminization of poverty' has been lamented by the women's movement for decades; this trend escalates with age with elderly women's income at 57 percent of elderly men's (Belgrave, 1993). While a greater percentage of women than men over 65 live in poverty in most countries of the world, the largest discrepancy is found in the U.S. (Hardy and Hazelrigg, 1993, 1995). These authors suggest that the differences are due to women's typical working conditions characterized by low wages, low job security, and lack of fringe benefits. Keith (1993) adds that women have numerous work interruptions due to family responsibilities, are more likely to experience gender discrimination, and have fewer benefits including retirement pensions. Lack of material resources precludes access to quality health care, nutritious food, and environments safe from pollution and violence, and increases vulnerability to disability, disease, and chronic illness. These, coupled with the prominent lack of control endemic to the poor and the oppressed, may culminate in psychological distress.

SUMMARY

In spite of sexist and agist cultural imperatives, women seem to fare well when progressing through middle and old age. The traditional gender roles accorded to women have facilitated habits and skills of considerable value in maintaining psychological well-being: flexibility and openness when adapting to multiple roles, complex demands, and fluctuating life circumstances; absence of a compelling need to control others; and highly developed social skills. Paradoxically, the same tradition that facilitates these qualities in women also places women at risk with regard to material resources through gender discrimination in education and employment. The best predictor of psychological well-being in the elderly is physical well-being; the best predictor of physical well-being is access to sufficient material resources. Consequently, the skills and knowledge women accumulate throughout their lives – ones which serve them well as they age – can only be fully expressed and beneficial when women have the material resources adequate for a life style characterized by knowledge of health risks and health strategies, environments free of violence and pollution, nutritious food, quality health care, and experiences of personal control and self-efficacy.

NOTES

1. Functional capacity refers to the ability to perform everyday activities such as bathing, obtaining and preparing food, and exercising
2. This interpretation applies primarily to women who have sufficient material resources and physical health to meet the challenge successfully; my intention is not to diminish the stress, trauma, and helplessness experienced by the many elderly women who live with poverty and poor health

REFERENCES

Albert, S.J. and Cattell, M.G. (1994) *Old Age in Global Perspective: Cross-Cultural and Cross-National Views.* New York: G.K. Hall

Arling, B. (1976) The elderly widow and her family, neighbors, and friends. *Journal of Marriage and the Family,* 38, 757–768

Belgrave, L.L. (1993) Discrimination against older women in health care. *Journal of Women and Aging,* 5, 181–189

Davis, M.A., Moritz, D.J., Neuhaus, J.M., Barclay, J.D. and Gee, L. (1997) Living arrangements, changes in living arrangements, and survival among community dwelling older adults. *American Journal of Public Health,* 87, 371–37

Gannon, L. (1999) *Women and Aging: Transcending the Myths.* London: Routledge

Gergen, M. (1989) Loss of control among the aging? A critical reconstruction. In P.S. Fry (Ed.)

Psychological Perspectives of Helplessness and Control in the Elderly (pp. 261–290). New York: North-Holland

Grambs, J.D. (1989) *Women over Forty: Visions and Realities*. New York: Springer

Guralik, J.M. and Leveille, S.G. (1997) Annotation: Race, ethnicity, and health outcomes: unraveling the mediating role of socioeconomic status. *American Journal of Public Health*, 87, 728–729

Haertel, U., Heiss, G., Filipiak, B. and Doering, A. (1992) Cross-sectional and longitudinal associations between high density lipoprotein cholesterol and women's employment. *American Journal of Epidemiology*, 135:,68–78

Hardy, M.A. and Hazelrigg, L.E. (1995) Gender, race/ethnicity, and poverty in later life. *Research on Aging*, 15: 243–278

Hekhausen, J. and Schultz, R. (1993) A life-span theory of control. *Psychological Review*, 102, 284–304

Hemingway, H., Nicholson, A., Stafford, M., Roberts, R. and Marmot, M. (1997) The impact of socioeconomic status on health functioning as assessed by the SF-36 questionnaire: The Whitehall II study. *American Journal of Public Health*, 87, 1484–1491

Hibbard, J.H. and Pope, C.R. (1992) Women's employment, social support, and mortality. *Women and Health*, 18 119–133

Howie, L. (1992–1993) Old women and widowhood: A dying status passage. *Omega*, 26 223–233

Keith, V. (1993) Gender, financial strain, and psychological distress among older adults. *Research on Aging*, 15, 123–147

Koenig, H.G. and Blazer, D.G. (1992) Epidemiology of geriatric affective disorders. *Clinics in Geriatric Medicine*, 8, 235–251

Lachman, M.E. and Weaver, S.L. (1998) Sociodemographic variations in the sense of control by domain: Findings from the MacArthur Studies of Midlife. *Psychology and Aging*, 13, 553–562

Lewittes, H.J. (1988) Just being friendly means a lot: Women, friendship, and aging. *Women and Health*, 14, 139–159

Logue, B.J. (1991) Taking charge: Death control as an emergent women's issue. *Women and Health*, 17: 97–121

Marmot, M., Ryff, C.D., Bumpass, L.L., Shipley, M. and Marks, N.F. (1997) Social inequalities in health: Next questions and converging evidence. *Social Science and Medicine*, 44, 901–910

Nolen-Hoeksema, S., Parker, L.E. and Larson, J. (1994) Ruminative coping with depressed mood following loss. *Journal of Personality and Social Psychology*, 67, 92–104

Pearlin, L. (1975) Sex roles and depression. In N. Datan (Ed.) *Life-Span Developmental Psychology: Normative Life Crises*. New York: Academic Press

Powers, B.A. (1996) Relationships among older women living in a nursing home. *Journal of Women and Aging*, 8, 179–198

Radloff, I. (1975) Sex differences in depression: the effects of occupation and marital status. *Sex Roles*, 1, 249–265

Reeves, J.B. and Darville, R.L. (1994) Social contact pattern and satisfaction with retirement of women in dual-career earner families. *International Journal of Aging and Human Development*, 39, 163–175

Rodin, J. (1989) Sense of control: Potentials for intervention. *Annals of the American Academy of Political and Social Sciences*, 503, 29–42

Schlossberg, N.K. (1980) A model for analyzing human adaptation to transition. *The Counseling Psychologist*, 9, 2–18

Seligman, M.E.P. (1975) *Helplessness*. San Francisco: Freeman

Simon, G., Gater, R., Kisely, S. and Piccinelli, M. (1996) Somatic symptoms of distress: An international primary care study. *Psychosomatic Medicine*, 58, 481–488

Thompson, L.W., Gallagher-Thompson, D., Futterman, A., Gilewski, M.J. and Peterson, J. (1991) The effects of late-life spousal bereavement over a 30-month interval. *Psychology and Aging*, 6, 434–441

Unger, R. and Crawford, M. (1992) *Women and Gender*. New York: McGraw-Hill

CHAPTER 57

THE PARADOX OF OLDER WOMEN'S HEALTH

Rosemary Leonard and Ailsa Burns

INTRODUCTION

The paradox of older women's health is that, although statistics show that older women are prone to the problems of menopause, osteoporosis, arthritis and a myriad of other conditions, most older women report to national surveys that their health is very good or at least satisfactory. Although there is no doubt that health problems do increase with age, the number of people affected and the degree to which they are handicapped by their conditions often seems to be exaggerated (see Gannon, and Baty, in this volume). In Australia, for example, the most common long-term health conditions among people aged 45 and over are eyesight disorders (70 percent of women) followed by arthritis (37 percent of women) and hypertension (30 percent of women) (ABS, 1994, Cat. No. 6344). Disability also increases with age. The Social Policy Directorate (1995) reports that 65 percent of people aged 75 years and over reporting a disability, compared with 43 percent of people aged 60 to 74 years. Disability was proportionally lower for women (38 percent) than men (48 percent) in the 60 to 74 age group, but the same (65 percent) in the 75+ age group. However, the majority of people with a disability feel that it does not interfere with their lives; in fact, over half reported no, or only a mild handicap, that is, one requiring minimal aid. Although the severity of handicap increased with age, only 20 percent of people over 75 years report a profound handicap.

Self-reported indicators of health status show that although the proportion of men and women reporting poor health increases with age, that proportion never exceeds 15 percent. Up to the age of 74, 60 percent of women report good or excellent health (ABS, 1994, Cat. No. 4366, 4365). Nor is Australia unique in this. In the U.S., 74 percent of non-institutionalized persons aged 65 to 74 consider their health to be good, very good or excellent compared with others their age, as do 67 percent of persons aged 75 and over (Hobbs and Damon, 1996). In Canada, in 1994, about 75 percent of those living at home rated their health as good, very good or excellent (Statistics Canada, 1997).

The overall picture of good health among older women needs to be highlighted. It is invariably and inappropriately overshadowed by the detailed reporting of disability, disease and death among the aged, thus giving a very misleading picture of disease and decay instead of the more realistic picture of high energy and good health, until 'the terminal drop' (Onyx, 1999).

This gap between health, or I should say illness statistics and women's lived experience reflects fundamental differences in assumptions. The illness statistics are part of a medical model which assumes a 'rise and fall' model of the life span. The women's reports are more consistent with a life-course approach.

Rise and fall models assume a steady increase in almost all physical and cognitive abilities throughout childhood, adolescence, and young adulthood, followed by stability though middle age and then a gradual decline in all functioning. The model is also well represented in the writings of both economists and health service professionals (Clare and Tulpule, 1994; McCallum and Geselhart, 1996). Further, the extent to which this model is the dominant model of aging in society is reflected in everyday discourses (e.g. we speak of older people as 'over the hill' or 'past it') and the acquisition of any condition associated with aging may be treated as a sign that all mental and physical functions are deteriorating. The rise and fall model fits our everyday experience that those at the bottom, young children and older people, are less valued than those at midlife who are 'at their peak'; those 'on the way up' are more valued than those 'on the way down.'

An easy outcome of the assumption of a rise and fall model of the life-course is that aging itself becomes seen as undesirable and therefore open to medical intervention. In our present society more and more issues are becoming medicalized, as the medical profession takes up a powerful role in determining normality (Russell and Schofield, 1986). One result of medicalization is that when health issues associated with aging are studied the emphasis is often on the delaying of the 'downward slide' of aging by artificially maintaining youth. For example the menopause industry encourages women to avoid, at considerable expense, a normal aspect of aging. Further, McCallum and Geselhart (1996) highlight the way in which expensive, and often inappropriate, publicly funded interventions for older people lead them to be seen as greedy burdens on the taxpayer. In contrast, little attention is given to those conditions which older women most need help with in order to live full lives. When aging itself becomes viewed as a medical condition in need of treatment there is no room for the possibility of new opportunities or personal growth.

Life-course models, consistent with personological and feminist approaches, value the integrity of the whole person with a past, present and future (see Greene, in this volume). Research from a life-course perspective emphasizes the path through life of people within their social and historical context. That is, it considers both the intra-personal factors such as people's interests and anxieties and also the external factors such as social expectations or access to resources which shape a life path that maintains some coherence and yet is open to change. The story line is a concept borrowed from narrative theory which is used by a number of researchers for understanding coherence through the life-course (e.g.

Gergen, 1990; McAdams, 1985; Helson and Picano, 1990). We choose, create and at times revise our life stories and it is these stories which both direct our future choices and goals and makes sense of past experiences. Out of the stream of everyday life, certain events are labelled as important because they contribute to the plot; others are seen as trivial. However life-story writing is not a purely individual activity. The social environment, as set by the cultural-historical context, defines what constitutes a normal story. In each society there will be a dominant plot, which most women will approximate, and a few alternative plots. For example, the dominant plot in many Western countries is for women to finish their education, work, marry, have children, and return to the workforce part time and then later full time. As Gergen (1990) points out, the story line after midlife is usually depicted as one of loss as children leave home; then follow the losses of fertility, work, husband, health and finally death. Yet many of these so-called losses can be a source of new-found freedom and energy. Even in health, many problems may be minor inconveniences rather than tragic losses. Of course not all women follow the dominant story-line. They may follow one of the alternative plots on offer, such as 'career woman' or 'single mother on pension'. Even those who choose totally idiosyncratic life-courses may nevertheless use the dominant stories as reference points against which decisions are made.

Unlike most health studies which focus on a particular disease or condition which health researchers identify as needing to be cured or managed, life-course models do not make assumptions about what is important but elicit from the participants which events are of significance for them. Life-course approaches allow people to be active in the construction of their identities while taking into account the opportunities and constraints of the particular historical time and social context. A woman's health status, then, is seen as just one factor in the web of opportunities and constraints within which she makes her life. What are relevant are the conditions that may enhance or diminish potential for personal growth and fulfilment. Some of these conditions (e.g. 'lived experience') increase with age, others may decrease. Many may be simply irrelevant. Further, unlike most health research, a life-course approach would consider how the cure or management of a condition fits in with the way a women lives her life. In short, a life-course approach puts health issues in context and, therefore, in perspective.

Our recent study illustrates one way health is contextualized in a life-course approach. The study explored the turning points in their lives reported by 60 midlife and older women from three cohorts (born 1931–36, 1941–46 and 1951–56). All the women were married or previously married and had low incomes. The life-review section of the women's interview covered seven topics including health and fitness. For each of these topics the interviewee was asked to go through her life describing her 'career'. For the topic of health there was an additional question asking women to rate their current level of health (excellent, good, fair, poor). Following the life-review interview, respondents were asked to nominate the turning points in their lives which allowed respondents to select and prioritize their own significant life events. The analysis considered the importance of both age at which the turning point occurred and cohort effects (Leonard and Burns, 1999).

In keeping with the national survey (ABS, 1994, Cat. No. 4366, 4365) the women in our study were generally positive about their health despite numerous problems, with the oldest cohort being more positive than the younger ones. The proportion who rated their health as 'good' or 'excellent' (as opposed to 'fair' or 'poor') was 72 percent for the women in their forties or fifties but 89 percent for those in their sixties. Interview material, however, showed that a wide range of health statuses could be encompassed by one rating. For example, women who rated their health as 'good' ranged from a woman who ran a nine kilometre fun-run each year to those with severe migraines, rheumatoid arthritis, and blood pressure, back and knee problems.

The turning points that were identified were classified as involving predominantly a role transition, an adversity or an experience of personal growth. The most frequently reported turning points were not marriage or motherhood, as might be expected, but personal growth experiences involving psychological 'self-work', such as deciding to become more independent, or to change one's lifestyle. The next most common was the adversity of the death of a relative or friend, which acted as a turning point in diverse emotional and philosophical ways.

Despite the specific attention given to health in the life review, very few turning points related to health problems. Of the 604 turning points identified by the 60 women in the study only 23 (3.8 percent) related to physical health and nine (1.5 percent) related to mental health problems. Further, examining the age at which these problems arose we found that the identification of physical health problems as turning points did not increase with age. The majority (16/23) of these problems occurred when the women were aged 20 to 40 years and only four of the 23 were reported for when the women were over 40. Menopause was identified as a turning point by only two women and both were positive about the experience. One felt that she had managed the change very well. The other worked in a menopause clinic and felt that the experience gave her greater credibility in her work. Rather than health problems, it was personal development experiences such as improving self-confidence, travel or education which increased after midlife.

Overall the picture was not one of decline after mid-life but one of improvement with age (see Lyon and Griffin, in this volume). Those in their fifties or sixties identified less illness, fewer adversities and more personal growth than those in their forties. We intend to contact the women every five years to see how their lives continue. Hopefully they will continue to improve for some years to come.

Illness and disability can cause distress and handicap at any age and all groups need their concerns addressed so we can create enjoyable and socially contributive lives at any age. The paradox of older women's health is resolved when health is seen pragmatically. It is good, even if a minor aid such as glasses or walking stick is necessary, as long as it does not interfere with the important things in life.

REFERENCES

Australian Bureau of Statistics (1990) *National Health Survey: Lifestyle and Health* Australia. Cat. No. 4366, Canberra

Australian Bureau of Statistics (1994) *Women's Health*. Cat. No. 4365, Canberra

Clare, R. and Tulpule, A. (1994) *Australia's Ageing Society*. EPAC Background Paper No 37, Economic Planning and Advisory Council, Canberra

Gergen, M. (1990) Finished at 40, Women's development within the patriarchy. *Psychology of Women Quarterly,* 14, 471–493

Helson, R. and Picano, J. (1990) Is the traditional role bad for women? *Journal of Personality and Social Psychology,* 59, 311–320

Hobbs, F. and Damon, B. (1996) *65+ in the United States*. Washington, D.C.:Bureau of Census, U.S. Department of Commerce

Leonard, R. and Burns, A. (1999, in press) Turning points in the lives of mid-life and older women. *Australian Psychologist*

McAdams, D. P. (1985) *Power, Intimacy, and the Life Story*. Homewood, IL: Dorsey Press

McCallum, J. and Geselhart, K. (1996) *Australia's New Aged*. Sydney: Allen and Unwin

Onyx, J. (1999) The facts. In J. L. Onyx and R. Reed (Eds.) *Revisioning Aging: The Empowerment of Older Women*. New York: Peter Lang

Russell, C. and Schofield, T. (1986) *Where It Hurts: A Sociology of Health for Health Workers*. Sydney: Allen & Unwin

Social Policy Directorate (1995) *Older People in NSW*. Canberra: ABS

Statistics Canada (1997) A Portrait of Seniors in Canada. 89–519–XPE. Statistics Canada

CHAPTER 58

WORKING WITH OLDER WOMEN: DEVELOPMENTS IN CLINICAL PSYCHOLOGY

Frances J. Baty

INTRODUCTION

Although most older people – those aged 65 years and above – consider that their general health is good (see Leonard and Burns, in this volume; Sidell, 1995), over 30 percent will, in any one year, experience significant mental health problems such as anxiety and depression (e.g. Goudie and Richards, 1993). Such problems leave older people vulnerable to physical illness (e.g. Blaum, 1999) and loss of independence (e.g. Fifer *et al.*, 1994). The great majority of older people experiencing mental health problems will be women. One reason is demographics – the feminization of old age (Aitken and Griffin, 1996; Arber and Ginn, 1991) – but other influences include the economic, social and cultural disadvantages which are experienced by older women in Western society (Peace, 1996; Arber and Ginn, 1995; Myers, 1992) and which are known to affect health.

This chapter is based on my own experience in the National Health Service (NHS) and is about what clinical psychologists can offer older women with mental health problems, such as anxiety and depression. Specifically, it is about how clinical psychology services are influenced by the health care system within which they are provided and about how the interventions initiated by the clinician must take account not only of psychological factors, but also of the context within which an individual lives her life.

SERVICE ISSUES

In the United Kingdom, the NHS provides almost all health services. A patient with a mental health problem will first contact the Primary Care services, e.g. her general practitioner (GP) and may then be referred to the Secondary Care services for assessment and treatment by hospital-based specialists, e.g. psychiatrists or clinical psychologists. As all NHS services are free to the individual patient, there are no financial barriers to older women obtaining access to the full range of mental health services. However, other potential barriers exist. Only a small proportion – probably well under 10 percent – of older women with significant anxiety and depression are even referred to Secondary Care. Of those who are, referral often occurs only after their difficulties have become severe and more intransigent, leading to the breakdown of their life in the community. Hospital-based services are often located some distance from residential areas and, having less access to private transport and with public transport links often complex and/or poor, older women frequently have difficulty in attending hospital appointments. Any physical disabilities and/or poor health can make the journey even more daunting.

When they do attend Secondary Services, older women do not have equal access to all treatments. Thus, although medication is less acceptable than psychological approaches to older women (Moffat *et al.*, 1995), they are the group least likely to receive talk-based therapies (Wallen *et al.*, 1987). They are the group most likely to have psychotropic medication prescribed (Catalan *et al.*, 1988), with significant risk of side-effects (Grohmann, *et al.*, 1989).

Psychological treatments, when they are provided, are less effective within Secondary Care settings than when delivered in an individual's own environment (Church, 1986). Hospital-based community services, such as psychogeriatric outreach teams, have been shown to be unsuccessful in improving mental health (Jenkins and MacDonald, 1994). One consequence of this inequity is that older women are more likely than older men to be admitted into residential care (Peace *et al.*, 1997), with resultant high levels of persisting psychological distress (Neville *et al.*, 1995; Stirling, 1993).

Although the Secondary Care services deal with only a small proportion of older people with mental health problems, they receive by far the bigger proportion of the funding, so that the mental health needs of the great majority of older women remain unaddressed.

However, changes are being introduced into the NHS, influenced by the World Health Organisation Strategy for Health for All in Europe by 2000 AD. One consequence will be that many clinical services, which currently are provided only in hospital settings, will increasingly be the responsibility of Primary Care, with specialists working as members of Primary Care Teams. For some three years, I have been providing specialist clinical psychology services for older people in Primary Care settings (Baty, 1998). The next section illustrates some of the advantages, for older women, of such services and some of the changes in therapeutic approach which this development has encouraged.

THERAPEUTIC ISSUES

The biomedical approach to mental health, which has developed within Secondary Care, has resulted in a neglect of other factors – a neglect which has also been apparent in the intrapsychic stance of much clinical psychology theory (Ussher, 1992; Smail, 1991; Pilgrim, 1991). Primary Care services, on the other hand, tend to adopt a more psychosocial approach, considering an individual's mental and physical health within the context of her life and community. The shift to Primary Care of services which have hitherto been provided in a Secondary Care context is thus likely to increase awareness that psychological processes are significantly affected by economic, social and cultural inequalities. Although individual therapeutic contact cannot, of course, eliminate these inequalities, it can have a mediating effect on their impact, e.g. Titley (1993), Smail (1993), Holland (1992) and Watson and Williams (1992). This is illustrated in the following account of work with an 81-year-old woman, Mrs. Bennett. (Mrs. Bennett (not her real name) has given permission for the use of this clinical material.)

Mrs. Bennett had fallen and fractured her shoulder some 15 months earlier. She lost confidence and was unable to go out alone for a time. She lived alone but, following the fall, had stayed with her daughter for two months, as she had been unable to care for herself. She was referred by her GP because she had felt increasingly anxious in recent weeks and had experienced a panic attack. Mrs. Bennett was also having difficulty sleeping and was eating less. Her GP wondered whether she would be happier in residential accommodation.

Mrs. Bennett's husband and other close family had all died before she was 30, leaving her to support her two children. She had thus had to be very independent throughout her adult life and was finding her increased reliance on her daughter frustrating; the recent deaths of friends had left her feeling more isolated. Although still involved in community activities, she was finding previously enjoyed activities more demanding.

There were clear psychological factors and processes relevant to Mrs.

Bennett's distress – intrusive memories, cognitive and behavioral avoid-ance, negative thoughts about her capabilities and fears for her future. As all were significant in lowering her self-esteem and making her more vul-nerable to low mood and anxiety, standard cognitive-behavioral interven-tions were undertaken to address them.

However, Mrs. Bennett's distress had occurred in the context of the social supports and power available to her (Orford, 1992). Employing the concept of 'power maps' (Hagan and Smail, 1997), it was possible to map Mrs. Bennett's 'assets' (good material resources; no financial worries; active social life; family support) and 'liabilities' (loss of friends; loss of confidence; uncertainty over life and future; negative evaluation of phys-ical self). It appeared that many of the 'liabilities' – primarily Mrs. Bennett's assessment of herself – had been influenced by the negative evaluations and unequal position of older women in society (Aitken and Griffin, 1996; Blytheway, 1995; Vincent, 1995; Macdonald and Rich, 1984). An understanding of this required the addition of an historical perspec-tive to the 'map', to allow the experiences of different cohorts of women to be considered in terms of relative power and powerlessness and its impact on views and expectations (Giles, 1995; Hughes and Mtezuka, 1992).

For example, Mrs. Bennett's experience of work in the 1950s and its meaning for her had clearly been influenced by the changes occurring at that time – the return to cultural idealism about traditional roles, a resur-gence of the cult of domesticity and a redefinition of the work of men and women, reinforced by policies supporting women's retreat from the labor force (Holdsworth, 1988; Zones et al., 1987). Following from this, our ses-sions encompassed a wide-ranging consideration of the impact of current and past social factors upon her life. This was not 'imposed', nor present-ed in any formal, structured way, but developed because of the responses that I made to Mrs. Bennett's description of her life.

Many of these responses were shaped by the concepts of structured dependency and life-course (see Leonard and Burns, in this volume), familiar in the field of critical gerontology (Estes et al., 1992). Structured dependency describes the social processes by which unequal power rela-tionships are imposed on some people by others, e.g. the social processes of patriarchy creating structured dependence of women upon men. There are psychological and cultural aspects of dependency, as well as material and exploitative aspects and the effects of structured dependency change throughout the course of someone's life. Because they incorporate an his-torical component – a date – as well as the age and chronological sequence of a 'life cycle', life-courses provide one way of linking historical trends with everyday personal experience. Such perspectives have led to inno-vative developments in research (e.g. Leonard and Burns, in this volume), but I have found them to be useful also in therapy. They make possible the drawing of connections between 'key social processes; historical develop-ment and change; the patterns of cohort and generation; and the experi-ences and choices of individuals; and their personal development'

(Vincent,1995: 6) in a way that allows discussion of the impact of inequalities upon the events which an individual is describing.

Thinking in these terms allowed Mrs. Bennett to recognize the role
which external forces had played in shaping her life. She was not merely
an 81-year-old-woman, who was physically dependent and suffering
from anxiety; she was the sum of all of her experiences, including: the
goals achieved; the exploitation suffered; the choices available to her; and
the constraints imposed throughout her life. Instead of focussing solely
upon the present, Mrs. Bennett recognized and valued herself in the context of her whole life. She no longer evaluated herself solely in terms of
personal characteristics, such as being physically strong and independent,
and so found it acceptable to change the terms upon which she participated in activities rather than withdrawing from them because she was
'past my sell-by date'. Mrs. Bennett also started to challenge some of society's negative evaluation of older women and, perceiving herself as having a place in the continuity of history, began to feel less disconnected
from the people that she met socially, all of whom were younger than her.
This reduced her feelings of isolation and that she was 'the last of my generation'. That she was one of the few who could recall tramcars in the
High Street became something to commemorate and share, rather than to
mourn.

The Primary Care setting was relevant in a number of other ways. As
the surgery was within walking distance, it was physically easier for Mrs.
Bennett to attend. It was also familiar to her: she reported that she would
not have gone to see a psychologist in a hospital, fearing the stigma and
the unknown. Indeed, she was more familiar with the surroundings than
I was, which was useful in altering the power imbalance in our relationship. That the service was located in the heart of her community made it
easier for Mrs. Bennett to introduce topics which were important to her.

Of course, prejudice can exist in Primary Care as much as in the
Secondary Care services and Mrs. Bennett's GP had some stereotyped
views about older women. However, because he knew her well, it was
possible for me to encourage him to question and later modify some of his
assumptions – something that would have been much harder to achieve if
Mrs. Bennett had been only one of many people passing briefly through
the service.

SUMMARY

This relatively limited intervention – attending her GP's surgery to see me
on five occasions, over a three-month period – resulted in major improvements in Mrs. Bennett's well-being which were still being maintained two
years later. The cognitive-behavioral interventions were necessary to
allow Mrs Bennett to overcome the more acute signs of anxiety. This
symptom reduction is the main outcome of psychological treatment within traditional mental health settings. However, being seen in a Primary
Care setting and the use of the concepts of structured dependency and life

course by the clinician, enabled Mrs. Bennett to discuss and understand the impact of social factors and power relations upon her life and her feelings about herself. This allowed her to reject some of those feelings and other people's views, to believe more in her own judgment, to recognize her self-worth and so to maintain the life which she valued. This work illustrates one way in which clinical psychology can start to move towards the goals of community clinical psychology (Orford, 1998) and so better address the impact of disadvantage.

REFERENCES

Aitken, L. and Griffin, G. (1996) *Gender Issues in Elder Abuse*. London: Sage

Arber, S. and Ginn, J. (1995) *Connecting Gender and Ageing*. Buckingham: Open University Press

Arber, S. and Ginn, J. (1991) *Gender and Later Life. A Sociological Analysis of Resources and Constraints*. London: Sage Publications

Baty, F.J. (1998) A clinical psychology service for older adults: the integrated primary care model. *PSIGE Newsletter*, 67, 3–6

Blaum, C.S. (1999) Depressive symptoms in older Americans as great a risk factor as smoking for developing new diseases. Paper presented to annual meeting of the Gerontological Society of America, San Francisco, 22 November

Blytheway, B. (1995) *Ageism*. Buckingham: Open University Press

Catalan, J., Gath, D.H., Bond, M., Edmonds, G. *et al.* (1988) General Practice Patients on long term psychotropic drugs: A controlled investigation. *British Journal of Psychiatry*, 152. (cited in J. Williams, Mental Health Services that Empower Women: The Challenge to Clinical Psychology. Paper presented to the British Psychological Society, Division of Clinical Psychology, Conference 1993)

Church, M. (1986) Issues in psychological therapy. In I. Hanley and M. Gilhooley, *Psychological Therapies for the Elderly*. London: Croom Helm

Estes, C., Binney, E.A. and Culbertson, R.A. (1992) The gerontological imagination: Social influences on the development of gerontology, 1945–present. *International Journal of Ageing and Human Development*, 35 (1), 49–65

Fifer, S.K., Mathias, S.D., Patrick, D.L., Mazonson, P.E., Lubeck, D.P. and Buesching, D.P. (1994) Untreated anxiety among adult primary care patients in a health maintenance organization. *Archives of General Psychiatry*, 51, 740–750

Giles, J. (1995) *Women, Identity and Private Life in Britain, 1900–50*. London: Macmillan

Goudie, F. and Richards, G. (1993) The psychological needs of older adults and their carers in primary care settings. Unpublished report, Community Health, Sheffield, April

Grohmann, R., Schmidt, L.G., Spiess, K.C. and Ruther, E. (1989) Agranulocytosis and significant leucopenia with neuroleptic drugs: Results from the AMUP program. Scientific update meeting: Clozapine (Leponex/Clozaril) *Psychopharmacology*, 99 (Suppl.), 109–112. (cited in J. Williams, Mental Health Services that Empower Women: The Challenge to Clinical Psychology. Paper presented to the British Psychological Society, Division of Clinical Psychology, Conference 1993)

Hagan, T. and Smail, D. (1997) Power-mapping I. Background and basic methodology. *Journal of Community and Applied Social Psychology*, 4, 257–269

Holdsworth, A. (1988) *Out of the Doll's House. The Story of Women in the Twentieth Century*. London: BBC Books

Holland, S. (1992) From social abuse to social action: a neighbourhood psychotherapy and social action project for women. In J.M. Ussher and P. Nicolson (Eds.) *Gender Issues in Clinical Psychology* (pp. 68–77). London: Routledge

Hughes, B. and Mtezuka, E.M. (1992) Social work and older women. In M. Langan and L. Day (Eds.) *Women, Oppression and Social Work* (pp. 220–241). London: Routledge and Kegan Paul

Jenkins, D. and McDonald, A. (1994) Should general practitioners refer more of their elderly depressed patients to psychiatric services? *International Journal of Geriatric Psychiatry*, 9, 461–465

Macdonald, B. and Rich, C. (1984) *Look Me in the Eye: Old Women, Ageing and Ageism*. London. Women's Press

Moffat, F. Mohr, C. and Ames, D. (1995) A group therapy programme for depressed and anxious elderly inpatients. *International Journal of Geriatric Psychiatry*, 10, 37– 40

Myers, J.E. (1992) Mature women: confronting the social stereotypes. In J.A. Lewis, B.A. Hayes, L.J. Bradley (Eds.) *Counselling Women over the Life Span* (pp. 211–240). Denver: Love Publishing

Neville, P.G., Boyle, A., Brooke, S., Baillon, S., Scothern, G. and Broome, C. (1995) Time for change: psychiatric morbidity in residential homes for elderly people. *International Journal of Geriatric Psychiatry*, 10, 561 -567

Orford, J. (1998) Have we a theory of community clinical psychology? *Clinical Psychology Forum*, 122, 6–10

Orford, J. (1992) *Community Psychology: Theory and Practice*. Chichester: Wiley

Peace, S.M. (1996) The forgotten female: social policy and older women. In C. Phillipson and A. Walker (Eds.) *Ageing and Social Policy: A Critical Assessment*. Aldershot: Gower

Peace, S.M., Kellaher, L.A. and Willocks, D.M. (1997) *Re-evaluating Residential Care*. Buckingham: Open University Pres

Pilgrim, D. (1991) Psychotherapy and social blinkers. *Psychologist*, 4 (2), 52–55

Sidell, M. (1995) *Health in Old Age. Myth, Mystery and Management*. Buckingham: Open University Press

Smail, D. (1991) Towards a radical environmentalist psychology of help. *Psychologist*, 14 (2), 61–64

Smail, D. (1993) *The Origins of Unhappiness*. London: HarperCollins

Stirling, E. (1993) Refuge or rescue: relocation of elderly people in residential care. Paper presented to Annual Conference of British Psychological Society, Division of Clinical Psychology, Special Interest Group in Elderly People (PSIGE), University of Kent

Titley, M. (1993) Working with Older Adults. In *The Gender Resource Pack: A Training and Practice Resource for Clinical Psychology*. Exeter: Department of Clinical and Community Psychology, Exeter Community Health Services Trust

Ussher, J.M. (1992) Science sexing psychology: positivistic science and gender bias in clinical psychology. In J.M.Ussher and P. Nicolson (Eds.) *Gender Issues in Clinical Psychology* (pp. 39–67). London: Routledge

Vincent, J.A. (1995) *Inequality and Old Age*. London: UCL Press Limited

Wallen, J., Pincus, H.A., Goldman, H.H. and Marcus, S.E. (1987) Psychiatric consultations in short term general hospitals. Archives of General Psychiatry, 44 (2) 163–168. (cited in J. Williams, Mental Health Services that Empower Women: The Challenge to Clinical Psychology. Paper presented to the British Psychological Society, Division of Clinical Psychology Conference 1993)

Watson, G. and Williams, J. (1992) Feminist practice in therapy. In J.M.Ussher and P. Nicolson (Eds.) *Gender Issues in Clinical Psychology* (pp. 212–236). London: Routledge

Zones, J.S., Estes, C.L. and Binneys, E.A. (1987) Gender, public policy and the oldest old. *Ageing and Society*, 7, 275–302

INDEX